Frommer's

POSTCARDS

FROM

PARIS

A perfect introduction to Paris is a stroll along the banks of the Seine.
See chapter 6. © Robert Holmes Photography.

Paris's flower markets are a feast for the eyes and the nose. The biggest one is on Ile de la Cité, along the Seine—see chapter 8. © Robert Holmes Photography.

The Seine by night and by boat. See chapter 6 for details on taking a bateau-mouche cruise down the river. Above © Malcolm/Image Bank; opposite © Dave G. Houser Photography.

Cliché or not, the Jardin des Tuileries has long been a favorite spot for lovers. See chapter 7 for a walking tour that will take you through the gardens. © Bryan F. Peterson/The Stock Market.

The ever-controversial, inside-out Centre Pompidou (known locally as Beaubourg) has finally reopened. See chapter 6 for a description of this museum of modern art. © Matthew Weinreb/Image Bank.

The Hôtel de Ville is not a hotel at all but Paris's City Hall. See chapter 6 for the gruesome history of the building's site. © Catherine Karnow Photography.

If Paris had nothing else to offer, many would still flock here for the food. See chapter 5 for our favorite bakeries and chapter 8 for our favorite places to buy fresh produce, chocolate, and other foodstuffs. Top © Steven Rothfeld/Tony Stone Images; bottom © Bill Gallery/ Viesti Associates, Inc.; opposite © Robert Holmes Photography.

Notre-Dame is at the very center of Paris, geographically and historically. See chapter 6 for the story of the city's most famous church. Opposite © Kevin Galvin Photography. Left © Harald Sund/Image Bank; below © Herbert Hartmann/Image Bank.

Even subway stations can be works of art in Paris. This art nouveau one is at Porte Dauphine. © Stephen Studd/Tony Stone Images.

Even if you don't buy anything, Galeries Lafayette department store is worth visiting for its grandiose early-1900s architecture. See chapter 8. © Romilly Lockyer/Image Bank.

The Louvre, with its controversial glass pyramid in the middle, lives up to its reputation as one of the world's greatest museums. See chapter 6. Opposite © Kevin Galvin Photography; above © Dave Bartruff Photography.

The Musée Picasso offers a more intimate museum experience. See chapter 6. © Catherine Karnow Photography.

The Château de Versailles is a tribute to the folly and opulence of France's grand century. Its Hall of Mirrors (bottom photo) was the setting for the treaty that ended World War I. See chapter 10. Both photos © Robert Holmes Photography.

Giverny, home of impressionist painter Claude Monet, makes for a lovely and inspiring getaway from the city. See chapter 10. Above © Robert Holmes Photography; left © James Martin/Tony Stone Images.

Les Deux Magots café, in St-Germain-des-Prés, is one of Paris's great literary landmarks. See chapters 5 & 6. © Bob Krist Photography.

When should I travel to get the best airfare?
Where do I go for answers to my travel questions?
What's the best and easiest way to plan and book my trip?

frommers.travelocity.com

Frommer's, the travel guide leader, has teamed up with **Travelocity.com**, the leader in online travel, to bring you an in-depth, easy-to-use resource designed to help you plan and book your trip online.

At **frommers.travelocity.com**, you'll find free online updates about your destination from the experts at Frommer's plus the outstanding travel planning and purchasing features of Travelocity.com. Travelocity.com provides reservations capabilities for 95 percent of all airline seats sold, more than 47,000 hotels, and over 50 car rental companies. In addition, Travelocity.com offers more than 2,000 exciting vacation and cruise packages. Travelocity.com puts you in complete control of your travel planning with these and other great features:

Expert travel guidance from Frommer's - over 150 writers reporting from around the world!

Best Fare Finder - an interactive calendar tells you when to travel to get the best airfare

Fare Watcher - we'll track airfare changes to your favorite destinations

Dream Maps - a mapping feature that suggests travel opportunities based on your budget

Shop Safe Guarantee - 24 hours a day / 7 days a week live customer service, and more!

Whether traveling on a tight budget, looking for a quick weekend getaway, or planning the trip of a lifetime, Frommer's guides and Travelocity.com will make your travel dreams a reality. You've bought the book, now book the trip!

Here's what the critics say about Frommer's:

"Amazingly easy to use. Very portable, very complete."
—*Booklist*

♦

"The only mainstream guide to list specific prices. The Walter Cronkite of guidebooks—with all that implies."
—*Travel & Leisure*

♦

"Complete, concise, and filled with useful information."
—*New York Daily News*

♦

"Hotel information is close to encyclopedic."
—*Des Moines Sunday Register*

♦

"Detailed, accurate and easy-to-read information for all price ranges."
—*Glamour Magazine*

Other Great Guides for Your Trip:

Frommer's®

Paris
2001

by Darwin Porter & Danforth Prince

HUNGRY MINDS, INC.

New York, NY • Cleveland, OH • Indianapolis, IN

ABOUT THE AUTHORS

Veteran travel writers **Darwin Porter** and **Danford Prince** have written numerous best-selling Frommer's guides, notably to France, Italy, England, and Germany. Porter, who was bureau chief for the *Miami Herald* when he was 21, has lived in Paris periodically and written about the city for many years. For several years, Prince lived in the city as a member of the Paris bureau of the *New York Times*.

HUNGRY MINDS, INC.

909 Third Avenue
New York, NY 10022
www.frommers.com

ISBN 0-7645-6133-2
ISSN 0899-3203

Editor: Ron Boudreau
Production Editor: Jenaffer Brandt, M. Faunette Johnston
Photo Editor: Richard Fox
Design by Michele Laseau
Staff Cartographers: John Decamillis, Roberta Stockwell, Elizabeth Puhl
Production by Hungry Minds Indianapolis Production Services

Front cover photo: The City of Light's signature symbol rising above the surrounding streets

SPECIAL SALES

For general information on Hungry Minds' products and services please contact our Consumer Care department; within the U.S. at 800-762-2974, outside the U.S. at 317-572-3993 or fax 317-572-4002. For sales inquiries and reseller information, including discounts, bulk sales, customized editions, and premium sales, please contact our Customer Care department at 800-434-3422.

Manufactured in the United States of America.

5 4 3 2

Contents

List of Maps   vii

1   The Best of Paris   1

1 Frommer's Favorite Paris
Experiences   2

2 Best Hotel Bets   4

3 Best Dining Bets   6

2   Planning Your Trip: The Basics   10

1 Visitor Information   10

2 Entry Requirements & Customs
Regulations   11

3 Money   13

*The French Franc, the U.S. Dollar,
the British Pound & the Euro*   13

The Euro & You   14

4 When to Go   15

Paris Calendar of Events   16

5 Health & Insurance   20

6 Tips for Travelers with Special
Needs   21

7 Getting There   25

*Flying for Less: Tips for Getting the
Best Airfares*   26

Planning Your Trip: An Online Directory   34

1 Top Travel-Planning Web
Sites   34

*What You'll Find at the Frommer's
Site*   35

Airline Web Sites   38

2 Top Web Sites for Paris   42

*Checking E-mail at Internet
Cafes*   43

Paris, Je t'Adore   45

3   Getting to Know the City of Light   48

1 Essentials   48

The Arrondissements in Brief   49

2 Getting Around   56

Fast Facts: Paris   59

4   Where to Stay   64

1 On the Right Bank   65

Family-Friendly Accommodations
75

2 On the Left Bank   83

3 Near the Airports   97

4 Gay-Friendly Hotels   97

5 Where to Dine 99

1 Food for Thought 99
2 Restaurants by Cuisine 101
3 On the Right Bank 104
La Gastronomie 101 109
Le Grand Fromage 122
Family-Friendly Restaurants 129

4 On the Left Bank 133
In Pursuit of the Perfect Parisian Pastry 146
5 The Top Cafes 148
6 Gay-Friendly Restaurants 153

6 Exploring Paris 154

1 Attractions by Arrondissement 156
2 The Top Attractions: From the Arc de Triomphe to the Tour Eiffel 167
Some Louvre Tips 174
3 The Major Museums 177
4 The Important Churches 183
5 Architectural & Historic Highlights 186
A Passage to the Passages 190
6 Neighborhood Highlights 190

The Mother of the Lost Generation 197
7 Specialty Museums 198
8 Parks & Gardens 204
9 Cemeteries 207
10 Especially for Kids 211
11 Literary Landmarks 213
12 Paris Underground 215
13 Organized Tours 216
14 A Day at the Races 217

7 Strolling Around Paris 218

Walking Tour 1: Montmartre 218
Walking Tour 2: The Latin Quarter 222

Walking Tour 3: The Marais 224

8 Shopping 231

1 The Shopping Scene 231
2 Shopping A to Z 234

The Scent of a Parisian 250

9 Paris After Dark 252

1 The Performing Arts 252
2 The Club & Music Scene 254
A Bar Crawl in Trendy Ménilmontant 261
More After-Dark Diversions 262

3 Bars, Pubs & Clubs 264
4 Gay & Lesbian Bars & Clubs 267
5 Literary Haunts 269

10 Side Trips from Paris 271

1 Versailles: Louis XIV's Pleasure Palace 271
A Weekend in London 273

Food Fit for a King 277
2 The Forest & Château of Rambouillet 278

3 The Cathedral at Chartres   280
   To Taste a Madeleine   282
4 Giverny: In the Footsteps of
   Claude Monet   284

5 Disneyland Paris: Come Meet
   Monsieur Mickey   285
6 Fontainebleau: House of the
   Centuries   291

Appendix A: Paris in Depth   294

1 History 101   294
   Dateline   294
2 City of the Arts   303

3 Architecture Through the
   Ages   306

Appendix B: Useful Terms & Phrases   309

1 Glossary of French-Language
   Terms   309

2 Glossary of Basic Menu
   Terms   316

Index   321

General Index   331
Accommodations Index   324

Restaurant Index   325

List of Maps

Paris Arrondissements   50

Hotels in the Heart of the Right Bank   66

Hotels Near Place Charles de Gaulle   77

Hotels in the Heart of the Left Bank   84

Hotels Near the Eiffel Tower &
Invalides   93

Restaurants in the Heart of the Right
Bank   106

Restaurants Near Place Charles de
Gaulle   119

Restaurants in the Heart of the Left
Bank   134

Restaurants Near the Eiffel Tower &
Invalides   143

The Major Attractions   158

The Louvre, Tuileries &
Les Halles (1er & 4e)   160

The Opéra, Bourse & Grands
Boulevards (2e, 9e & 10e)   161

The Marais, Beaubourg & Bastille
(3e, 4e & 11e)   162

The Latin Quarter & St-Germain-des-
Prés (5e, 6e & 7e)   163

The Eiffel Tower & Invalides (7e)   164

The Champs-Elysées (8e & 17e)   165

Trocadéro & the 16e   166

Notre-Dame de Paris   169

The Louvre   173

Ile de la Cité & Ile St-Louis   193

Montmartre   195

The Bois de Boulogne   206

The Père-Lachaise Cemetery   208

Walking Tour 1: Montmartre   219

Walking Tour 2: The Latin
Quarter   223

Walking Tour 3: The Marais   225

The Ile de France   272

Versailles   275

Notre-Dame de Chartres   281

Disneyland Paris   286

Fontainebleau   292

An Invitation to the Reader

In researching this book, we discovered many wonderful places—hotels, restaurants, shops, and more. We're sure you'll find others. Please tell us about them, so we can share the information with your fellow travelers in upcoming editions. If you were disappointed with a recommendation, we'd love to know that too. Please write to:

Frommer's Paris 2001
Hungry Minds, Inc.
909 Third Avenue
New York, NY 10022

An Additional Note

Please be advised that travel information is subject to change at any time—and this is especially true of prices. We therefore suggest that you write or call ahead for confirmation when making your travel plans. The authors, editors, and publisher cannot be held responsible for the experiences of readers while traveling. Your safety is important to us, however, so we encourage you to stay alert and be aware of your surroundings. Keep a close eye on cameras, purses, and wallets, all favorite targets of thieves and pickpockets.

What the Symbols Mean

✪ **Frommer's Favorites**

Our favorite places and experiences—outstanding for quality, value, or both.

The following abbreviations are used for credit cards:

AE	American Express	DISC	Discover
CB	Carte Blanche	MC	MasterCard
DC	Diners Club	V	Visa

Find Frommer's Online

www.frommers.com offers up-to-the-minute listings on almost 200 cities around the globe—including the latest bargains and candid, personal articles updated daily by Arthur Frommer himself. No other Web site offers such comprehensive and timely coverage of the world of travel.

The Best of Paris

According to polls in 2000, the French people, even the traditionally cynical Parisians, are putting aside their 1990s economic woes and becoming more optimistic. And Paris is facing the 21st century with a bright face, looking better than it has in years after the completion of such monumental projects as the cleaning of the Louvre, Opéra, and Notre-Dame and the sprucing up of much of its riverfront. (Even the ferocious windstorm that tore at the city in December 1999 didn't keep it down for long, though it'll be years before the replacement trees reach the lush maturity of the ones that were felled.) Always the City of Light, Paris will be even more dazzling in 2001, with greater illuminations than ever before.

Paris may not be Europe's most happening city—London still retains that position. But Paris remains queen of the continent, with more museums, hotter nighttime diversions, better hotels (many also rejuvenated for the millennium), finer and more varied shops, and the most talented stable of chefs in the world.

The discovery of the City of Light and the experience of making it your own is and always has been the most compelling reason to visit. If you're a first-timer, everything in Paris, of course, will be new to you. If you've been away for a while, expect changes: Taxi drivers may no longer correct your fractured French but address you in English—and that's tantamount to a revolution. More Parisians have a rudimentary knowledge of English, and the country, at least at first glance, seems less hysterically xenophobic than in past years—spending your much-needed francs, you likely won't be looked at as an "ugly American" anymore. Part of this derives from Parisians' interest in music, videos, and films from foreign countries, and part is caused by France's growing awareness of its role within a united Europe.

Yet France has never been more concerned about the loss of its identity, as it continues to attract an increasing number of immigrants from its former colonies. Many have expressed concern that the country will lose the battle to keep its language strong, distinct, and unadulterated by foreign (particularly American) slang or catchwords (*le weekend,* for example). In fact, the rancor of France's collective xenophobia has been increasingly redirected toward the many immigrants seeking better lives in Paris, where the infrastructure has nearly been stretched to its limits.

Though Paris is in flux culturally and socially, it lures travelers for the same reasons it always has. You'll still find grand old sights like the

Tour Eiffel, Notre-Dame, the Arc de Triomphe, Sacré-Coeur, and all those atmos-
pheric cafes, as well as trendy new projects like the Grand Arche de La Défense, the
Cité des Sciences et de l'Industrie, the Cité de la Musique, and the Bibliothéque
François-Mitterrand. And don't forget the parks, gardens, and squares; the Champs-
Elysées and other grand boulevards; and the river Seine and its quays. Paris's beauty is
still overwhelming, especially in the illumination of night, when it certainly is the City
of Light.

1 Frommer's Favorite Paris Experiences

- **Whiling Away an Afternoon in a Parisian Cafe.** The cafe is where passionate
  meetings of writers, artists, philosophers, thinkers, and revolutionaries once took
  place (perhaps still do). Parisians stop by their favorite cafes to meet current
  lovers and friends, to make new ones, or to sit in solitude with a newspaper or
  book. Whether you order a small coffee or the most expensive cognac in the
  house, nobody will hurry you from your invaluable viewpoint on Paris life. For
  our recommendations, see "The Top Cafes," in chapter 5.
- **Strolling Along the Seine.** Such painters as Sisley, Turner, and Monet have
  fallen under the Seine's spell. On its banks, lovers still walk hand in hand, anglers
  still cast their lines, and *bouquinistes* still peddle their mix of postcards, 100-
  year-old pornography, and tattered histories of Indochina. Clochards still seek a
  home for the night under its bridges, and the Bateaux-Mouches still ply its
  waters. For a spectacular view of the Louvre, cross the city's first iron bridge, the
  pont des Arts, one of only four pedestrian bridges. Paris's oldest and most famous
  bridge is the ironically named pont-Neuf (New Bridge), from where you have an
  excellent view of the Palais de Justice and Sainte-Chapelle on Ile de la Cité.
- **Window-Shopping in the Faubourg St-Honoré.** In the 1700s, the wealthiest
  of Parisians resided in the faubourg St-Honoré; today the quarter is home to
  stores catering to the rich, particularly on rue du faubourg St-Honoré and avenue
  Montaigne. Even if you don't buy anything, it's great to window-shop big names
  like Hermès, Dior, Laroche, Courrèges, Cardin, and Saint-Laurent. If you want
  to browse in the stores, be sure to dress the part. See chapter 8 for the lowdown
  on these boutiques.
- **Taking Afternoon Tea à la Française.** Drinking tea in London has its charm,
  but the Parisian *salon de thé* is unique. Skip over those cucumber-and-watercress
  sandwiches and delve into a luscious dessert like the Mont Blanc, a creamy purée
  of sweetened chestnuts and meringue once beloved by the Aga Khan. The grandest Parisian tea salon is **Angélina,** but you might also want to stop by **Berthillon,**
  especially if you want to try one of its scrumptious ice creams, or the **Café/
  Restaurant/Salon de Thé Bernardaud,** especially if you want your tea served on
  gorgeous Bernardaud porcelain. See chapter 5 for details on all three.
- **Attending a Ballet or an Opera.** In 1989, the **Opéra Bastille** was inaugurated
  to compete with the grande dame of the music scene, the **Opéra Garnier,** which
  then was reserved for dance only and soon closed for renovations. The Garnier
  reopened a few years ago, and opera has joined dance in the rococo splendor
  created by Charles Garnier, beneath a controversial ceiling by Chagall. The modern Bastille, France's largest opera house, with curtains by designer Issey Miyake,
  features opera and symphony performances in four concert halls (its main hall
  seats 2,700). Whether for a performance of Bizet or Tharp, dress with pomp and
  circumstance. See chapter 9 for details on both houses.

- **Spending a Day at the Races.** Paris boasts eight tracks for horse racing. The most famous and the classiest is **Longchamp,** in the Bois de Boulogne, the site of the Prix de l'Arc de Triomphe and Grand Prix (see chapter 6). These and other top races are major social events, so you'll have to dress up (buy your outfit on rue du Faubourg St-Honoré—see entry above). Take the Métro to Porte d'Auteuil, then a special bus from there to the track. The racing newspaper *Paris Turf* and weekly entertainment magazines have details about race times.

- **Exploring Ile de la Cité's Flower Market.** A fine finish to any Monday to Saturday spent meandering along the Seine is a stroll through the **Marché aux Fleurs,** place Louis-Lépine (see chapter 8). Here you can buy rare flowers, the gems of the French Riviera, bouquets that have inspired artists throughout the centuries. Even the most basic hotel room will feel like a luxury suite once you fill it with bunches of carnations, lavender, roses, tulips, and the like. On Sunday, the area is transformed into the famed **Marché aux Oiseaux,** where you can admire rare birds from around the world.

- **Watching the Show at the Folies-Bergère.** Often denounced, the showcase at the **Folies-Bergère** has been pleasing audiences since 1868, even though classic acts like Maurice Chevalier, Mistinguett, and Josephine Baker (who performed her famous banana dance here) vanished long ago. True, the Tour Eiffel cancan is a bit corny and the show has become less daring, but those ladies in their sequins, feathers, and pom-poms still evoke an older Paris, immortalized on a Manet canvas. The show, tacky or not, seems to go on forever. See chapter 9 for details.

- **Discovering Hidden Montmartre.** This is Paris's most touristy area. However, far removed from the area's top draw, Sacré-Coeur, awaits the neighborhood of the true Montmartrois. Wander the back streets away from the souvenir shops. Arm yourself with a good map and seek out such streets as rue Lepic (refresh yourself at the Lux Bar at no. 12), rue Constance, rue Tholozé (with its view over the Paris rooftops), rue des Abbesses, and rue Germain-Pilón. None of these is famous, but each boasts buildings whose detailing shows the pride and care permeating Paris's architecture. Flank out from these and discover dozens of other streets on your own. At dusk, sit on Sacré-Coeur's top steps and watch as Paris turns into the City of Light.

- **Checking Out the Marchés.** A daily Parisian ritual is ambling through one of the open-air markets to buy fresh food—perhaps a properly creamy Camembert or a pumpkin-gold cantaloupe—to be eaten before sundown. You can take part in this time-honored tradition by purchasing the makings for a picnic in a park or even in your room. Like artists, the vendors arrange their wares into a mosaic of vibrant colors: Sanguine, an Italian citrus with juice the color of a brilliant orange sunset; ruby-red peppers; golden-yellow bananas from Martinique—all dazzle the eye. Our favorite market is on rue Montorgueil, beginning at rue Rambuteau, 1er (Métro: Les Halles). On mornings at this grubby little cluster of food stalls, we've spotted some of France's finest chefs stocking up for the day.

- **Sipping Cocktails at Willi's.** Back in the early 1970s, the first-timer to Paris might arrive with a copy of Hemingway's *A Moveable Feast* and, taking the author's endorsement to heart, head for Harry's Bar at "Sank roo doe Noo." Harry's is still around but now draws an older, conservative clientele. Today's chic younger expats head for **Willi's Wine Bar** (see chapter 9), where the long-haired young bartenders are mostly English, as are the waitresses, dressed in Laura

Ashley garb. The place is like an informal club for Brits, Australians, and Yanks, especially in the afternoon. Some 300 wines await your selection.

- **Calling on the Dead.** You don't have to be a ghoul to be thrilled by a visit to Europe's most famous cemetery: **Père-Lachaise.** You can pay your respects to the likes of Jim Morrison, Gertrude Stein and Alice B. Toklas, Oscar Wilde, Yves Montand and Simone Signoret, Edith Piaf, Isadora Duncan, Abélard and Héloïse, Frédéric Chopin, Marcel Proust, Eugène Delacroix, and more. And the residents aren't the only fascination—the tomb designs are intriguing and often eerie. Laid out in 1803 on a hill in Ménilmontant, the cemetery offers a surprise a minute with its bizarre monuments, unexpected views, and ornate sculpture. See chapter 6 for details.

- **Going Gourmet at Fauchon.** An exotic world of food, **Fauchon** (see chapter 8) offers more than 20,000 products from around the globe. Everything you never knew you were missing is in aisle after aisle of coffees, spices, pastries, fruits, vegetables, rare Armagnacs, and much more. Take your pick: Toganese mangoes, Scottish smoked salmon, preserved cocks' combs, Romanian rose-petal jelly, blue-red Indian pomegranates, golden Tunisian dates (only from the most famous oasis), larks stuffed with foie gras, dark morels from France's rich soil, Finnish reindeer's tongue, century-old eggs from China, and a Creole punch from Martinique reputed to be the best anywhere.

- **Attending a Free Concert.** Summer brings one of the joys of Paris: free concerts in parks and churches all over the city. Pick up an entertainment weekly for details. Some of the best concerts are held at the **American Church in Paris,** 65 quai d'Orsay, 7e (☎ **01-40-62-05-00;** Métro: Alma-Marceau; RER: Pont de l'Alma). **Sainte-Chapelle** is known for its splendid concerts several times a week; call the box office at 4 bd. du Palais, 1er (☎ **01-53-73-78-50;** Metro: Cité).

- **Sneaking Away from It All.** When the glory and pomp of Paris overcome us, we take the A1 RER train to **St-Germain-en-Laye,** 21 kilometers (13 miles) northwest. This suburb was once the residence of the French kings, from François I to Louis XIV (the "Sun King"), who was born here. Visitors often overlook this area, but Parisians adore it and often come here to escape the summer heat. You can visit the Château Vieux, where Louis XIV lived, but mostly you'll want to wander around the streets, parks, and gardens. A meal at the Pavillon Henri IV, a hotel/restaurant named for the king who in the 1500s built a home on this site for his illegitimate children, will bring your day to perfection. The Sun King romped here with his mistress, Mme de Montespan, and in 1843 Dumas wrote *The Three Musketeers* at the pavilion. Whatever your main dish, order it with béarnaise sauce, said to have been invented here.

2 Best Hotel Bets

For full details on the following hotels, turn to chapter 4.

- **Best Newcomer:** Opened in 1998, the **Hôtel de Vendôme,** 1 place Vendôme, 1er (☎ **01-42-60-32-84**), enjoys one of the world's most prestigious addresses. In the former Embassy of Texas (yes, there was one when that state was a nation), the hotel has been vastly restored and redesigned for opulent living. Media darlings check in for a touch of Right Bank elegance and glamour—and so can you.

- **Best for Business Travelers:** Corporate types from all over the world converge at the **Hôtel Balzac,** 6 rue Balzac, 8e (☎ **01-44-35-18-00**), a belle-époque town house with a good business center 2 blocks from many of the business offices along the Champs-Elysées. Its restaurant serves some of the best food in town and is suitable for entertaining clients.

- **Best for Families:** An affordable Left Bank choice is the **Hôtel de Fleurie,** 32–34 rue Grègoire-de-Tours, 6e (☎ **01-53-73-70-00**), in the heart of St-Germain-des-Prés. The accommodations are thoughtfully appointed, and many connecting rooms with two large beds are perfect for families. Children under 12 stay free with their parents.

- **Best Value:** Not far from the Champs-Elysées, the **Résidence Lord Byron,** 5 rue de Chateaubriand, 8e (☎ **01-43-59-89-98**), is a classy little getaway that's far from opulent but is clean and comfortable and worth every franc. Another good choice is the **Hôtel de Lutèce,** 65 rue St-Louis-en-l'Ile, 4e (☎ **01-43-26-23-52**). The hotel resembles a Breton country house and has flourished despite forever refusing to raise its rates. Its rooms, with antiques and fine reproductions, provide an affordable elegance.

- **Best Location:** The chic **Pavillon de la Reine,** 28 place des Vosges, 3e (☎ **01-40-29-19-19**), occupies an elegant cream-colored 17th-century mansion. It not only has a garden courtyard but also opens onto Paris's most harmonious and beautiful square—and its oldest—place des Vosges of Victor Hugo fame.

- **Best View:** Of the 32 rooms at the **Hôtel du Quai-Voltaire,** 19 quai Voltaire, 7e (☎ **01-42-61-50-91**), 28 open onto views of the Seine. If you stay here, you'll be following in the footsteps of Wilde, Baudelaire, and Wagner. This 17th-century abbey was transformed into a hotel back in 1856 and ever since has been welcoming guests who appreciate its tattered charms.

- **Best for Nostalgia:** If you yearn for a Left Bank "literary" address, make it the **Odéon-Hôtel,** 3 rue de l'Odéon, 6e (☎ **01-43-25-90-67**), in heart of the 6th arrondissement, filled with the ghosts of Gide, Hemingway, Fitzgerald, Joyce, and Stein and Toklas. Evoking a Norman country inn, this hotel of considerable charm lures with its high, crooked ceilings, exposed beams, and memories of yesterday.

- **Best for Stargazing:** The tycoons, hot stars, and hotter mistresses of yesterday—Douglas Fairbanks and Mary Pickford, William Randolph Hearst and Marion Davies—knew where to stay back then. Tom Cruise and his ilk know *the* address in Paris is still the **Hôtel de Crillon,** 10 place de la Concorde, 8e (☎ **01-44-71-15-00**), once the palace of the duc de Crillon. If you want its grandest suite and have a discriminating taste for the macabre, ask for the Marie AntoinetteApartment—it exhibits Antoinette-style elegance, and its namesake was beheaded practically at the doorstep of this deluxe citadel.

- **Best for Opulence:** Now owned my Mohammed al-Fayed, the **Hôtel Ritz,** 15 place Vendôme, 1er (☎ **01-43-16-30-30**), has dripped with wealth, luxury, and decadence since César Ritz opened it in 1898. Barbara Hutton, Coco Chanel, and Marcel Proust are just a few names inscribed in its glorious guest book; if you're into romantic tragedy, remember this was where Princess Diana and Dodi al-Fayed had their last meal. By staying here you can join the parade of Saudi oil princes, Milanese divas, and movie legends—if you have big bucks.

- **Best-Kept Secret:** Built in 1913 and long in a seedy state, the fully restored **Terrass Hôtel,** 12–14 rue Joseph-de-Maistre, 18e (☎ **01-46-06-72-85**), is now the only four-star choice in Montmartre, an area not known for luxury accommodations. Its rooms take in far-ranging views of the Tour Eiffel, Arc de Triomphe, and Opéra Garnier.

- **Best Historic Hotel:** Inaugurated by Napoléon III in 1855, the **Hôtel du Louvre,** place André-Malraux, 1e (☎ **01-44-58-38-38**), was once described by a French journalist as "a palace of the people, rising adjacent to the palace of kings." Today, the hotel offers luxurious accommodations and panoramic views down avenue de l'Opéra.

- **Best for Romance:** Until the 1970s, **L'Hôtel,** 13 rue des Beaux-Arts, 6e (☎ **01-44-41-99-00**), was a fleabag filled with drunks and addicts (in 1900 Oscar Wilde died here penniless). Millions of francs of renovations later, the rooms that were once cramped and claustrophobic are now ravishingly romantic, wrought like small jewel boxes.

- **Best Trendy Hotel:** A converted town house, the **Hôtel Costes,** 239 rue St-Honoré, 1er (☎ **01-42-44-50-50**), evokes the imperial heyday of Napoléon III. Fashion headliners especially like it—Costes is the choice of many a lanky model, as the Paris offices of *Harper's Bazaar* are close at hand. If you're into heavy swags, patterned fabrics, jewel-tone colors, and lavish accessories, this can be your gilded-age address.

- **Best Service:** Though you can't fault the flawless decor of the **Hôtel Plaza Athénée,** 25 av. Montaigne, 8e (☎ **01-53-67-66-65**), the billionaires check in because they get the royal treatment from the jaded but indulgent and ever-so-polite staff. In an upscale neighborhood between the Seine and the Champs-Elysées, the Plaza Athénée offers service that's impeccable.

3 Best Dining Bets

For full details on the following restaurants, turn to chapter 5.

- **Best Chef:** Can there be any doubt? Proud owner of six Michelin stars, **Alain Ducasse,** 59 av. Raymond-Poincaré, 16e (☎ **01-47-27-12-27**), has taken Paris by storm, assuming the throne of semiretired Joël Robuchon now that he splits his time between his restaurant here and his one in Monte Carlo. He artfully combines produce from every French region in a cuisine that's contemporary but not quite new, embracing the Mediterranean without abandoning France.

- **Best All-Around Restaurant:** Named for a 14th-century chef who wrote one of the oldest known books on French cookery, **Taillevent,** 15 rue Lamennais, 8e (☎ **01-44-95-15-01**), occupies a grand 19th-century town house off the Champs-Elysées. Though its owner likes to keep about 60% of the crowd French, we suggest you try for a reservation at Paris's most outstanding all-around restaurant.

- **Best Newcomer:** Though every escaped kitchen scullion claims to be the "new Robuchon," you're likely to find his dead ringer at **L'Astor,** in the Hôtel Astor, 11 rue d'Astorg, 8e (☎ **01-53-05-05-20**), where Eric Lecerf reigns. As a kind of Richelieu to Lecerf's Louis XIII, Robuchon still drops in two to three times a week, and though some of his dishes are served, the menu has become Lecerf's.

- **Best Old-Fashioned Bistro:** Established back in 1931 and bouncing back from a period of decline, **Allard,** 41 rue St-André-des-Arts, 6e (☎ **01-43-26-48-23**), is better than ever from its zinc bar to its repertoire of the classics we associate with traditional French cuisine—escargots, frogs' legs, foie gras, *boeuf à la mode,* and cassoulet. This is a good bet for a real Left Bank bistro ambience.

- **Best Underappreciated Restaurant:** Henri Faugeron may no longer be the media darling he once was, but his **Faugeron,** 52 rue de Longchamp, 16e (☎ **01-47-04-24-53**), is just as stunning as ever, though the dishes may not be as "revolutionary" as he proclaims. The food is outstanding and uses only the freshest of ingredients, handled with skill by a stellar kitchen staff.

- **Best Decor:** Declared a French national treasure, the belle-époque **Le Train Bleu** in the Gare de Lyon, 12e (☎ **01-43-43-09-06**), evokes the heyday of the gilded age. Completely restored, the restaurant boasts heavy purple velvet hangings, boxes sprinkled with green plants, Napoléon III antiques, gleaming brass, and lighting fixtures made of bronze and Bohemia opaline-shaped glass cups.
- **Best View:** A penthouse restaurant, **La Tour d'Argent,** 15–17 quai de la Tournelle, 5e (☎ **01-43-54-23-31**), is owned by shrewd ex-playboy Claude Terrail, who pays part of Notre-Dame's electric bill to illuminate the cathedral at night for his diners' pleasure. Dining here is a theatrical event.
- **Best for Stargazing:** No, it's not Taillevent or even Alain Ducasse. On the see-and-be-seen circuit, the star is the **Buddha Bar,** 8 rue Boissy d'Anglas, 8e (☎ **01-53-05-90-00**). The crowd doesn't actually come for the cuisine, though its fusion of French and Pacific Rim is exceedingly well executed. If you don't want to dine, stop by the hip lacquered bar across from the dining room.
- **Best Unkept Secret:** In the heart of the Latin Quarter, **Perraudin,** 157 rue St-Jacques, 5e (☎ **01-46-33-15-75**), duplicates the allure of an early-1900s bistro. You get the feeling Emile Zola could walk in the door at any minute. It offers great food and great value, with old-fashioned dining that's too rapidly disappearing from the city.
- **Best Brasserie:** Head for the Left Bank and the **Brasserie Balzar,** 49 rue des Ecoles, 5e (☎ **01-43-54-13-67**), opened in 1898. If you dine on the familiar French food here, you'll be following in the footsteps of Sartre and Camus and countless others. You can even have a complete dinner in the middle of the afternoon.
- **Best Baby Bistro:** A few years ago, several great French chefs realized the average visitor can't afford the haute cuisine served at their restaurants, so they created "baby bistros" to serve superb food at affordable prices. The best of these is a sideshow created by one of the grandest chefs, Jacques Cagna: **La Rôtisserie d'Armaillé,** 6 rue d'Armaillé, 17e (☎ **01-42-27-19-20**), near place de l'Etoile.
- **Best Seafood:** The fattest lobsters and prawns in the Rungis market emerge on platters at **Goumard,** 9 rue Duphot, 1er (☎ **01-42-60-36-07**), so chic that even the toilets are classified as historic monuments. Nothing is allowed to interfere with the taste of the sea: You'll have to fly to the Riviera to find a better bouillabaisse.
- **Best *Cuisine Bourgeoise* (Comfort Food):** If today Joyce, Verlaine, Valéry, and Hemingway rose from the grave and strode into the **Crémerie-Restaurant Polidor,** 41 rue Monsieur-le-Prince, 6e (☎ **01-43-26-95-34**), they wouldn't notice any difference, not even on the menu, but would calmly ask for their napkins locked in a cabinet in back with their names on them.
- **Best Atmosphere:** A favorite of Colette and Cocteau, the world-famous **Le Grand Véfour,** 17 rue de Beaujolais, 1er (☎ **01-42-96-56-27**), at the Palais-Royal, has an interior classified as a historic monument. Incidentally, it serves some of the most refined cuisine in Paris.
- **Best for Opulence:** Although "Pierre Cardin's place," as it's called, has an ever-growing list of detractors, **Maxim's,** 3 rue Royale, 8e (☎ **01-42-65-27-94**), is still the ultimate choice for art nouveau grandeur, just as it was decades ago when Leslie Caron dined here with Louis Jourdan in *Gigi*.
- **Best Lyonnais Cuisine:** Lyon is hailed as France's gastronomic capital, and the best place in Paris to introduce yourself to this regional cuisine is at **Aux Lyonnais**, 32 rue St-Marc, 2e (☎ **01-42-96-65-04**). This fin-de-siècle bistro turns out all the dishes for which Lyon is famous, from perfectly prepared

pike dumplings to large Lyonnais sausages—all washed down, of course, with Beaujolais.

- **Best Kosher Food:** If corned beef, pastrami, herring, and dill pickles thrill you, head to **rue des Rosiers** in the 4th arrondissement (Métro: St-Paul). John Russel wrote that rue des Rosiers is the "last sanctuary of certain ways of life; what you see there in miniature is Warsaw before the ghetto was razed." North African overtones reflect the long-ago arrival of Jews from Morocco, Tunisia, and Algeria. The best time to go is Sunday morning: You can wander the streets eating as you go— apple strudel, Jewish rye bread, pickled lemons, smoked salmon, and *merguez,* a spicy smoked sausage from Algeria. Many spots offer sit-down meals, like **Chez Jo Goldenberg,** 7 rue des Rosiers, 4e (☎ 01-48-87-20-16), where the *carpe farcie* (stuffed carp) is outstanding and the beef goulash a fine runner-up.

- **Best American Cuisine:** A Yankee outpost in Les Halles, **Joe Allen,** 30 rue Pierre-Lescot, 1er (☎ 01-42-36-70-13), serves the finest burgers in the city. Desserts include real New York cheesecake, pecan pie with fresh pecans imported from the United States, and the inspired cultural fusion of American brownies made with French chocolate.

- **Best Pizza:** The **Chicago Pizza Pie Factory,** 5 rue de Berri, 8e (☎ 01-45-62-50-23), is devoted to the almighty pizza pie, with the chef creating endless delicious variations on eight themes.

- **Best Vegetarian Cuisine:** One of the best-known veggie restaurants in the Marais is **Aquarius,** 54 rue Ste-Croix-de-la-Bretonnerie, 4e (☎ 01-48-87-48-71). Choose from the array of soups and salads or have a mushroom tart or a galette of wheat with raw vegetables. In this rustic 17th-century setting you can expect flavorful, wholesome, and generous meals.

- **Best Wine Cellar:** At the elegant **Lasserre,** 17 av. Franklin-D.-Roosevelt, 8e (☎ 01-43-59-53-43), you'll find not only wonderful food but also one of the great wine cellars of France, with some 180,000 bottles.

- **Best for Cheese:** Cheese is king at **Androuët,** 6 rue Arsène-Houssaye, 8e (☎ 01-42-89-95-00). Many cheese lovers opt for a bottle of wine, a green salad, and all-you-can-eat choices from the most sophisticated *dégustation de fromages* in the world.

- **Best on the Champs-Elysées:** The specialties of Denmark are served with flair at the **Copenhague/Flora Danica,** 142 av. des Champs-Elysées, 8e (☎ 01-44-13-86-26). In summer you can dine on the terrace of this "Maison du Danemark."

- **Best Late-Night Dining:** Nowhere else in Paris can you be more assured of getting a good meal at 3am than at **Au Pied de Cochon,** 6 rue Coquillière, 1er (☎ 01-40-13-77-00). Though everyone lauds its grilled pig's feet with béarnaise sauce, few have noticed you can also find some of the freshest oysters in town here.

- **Best Wine Bar:** Named after owner Mark Williamson, **Willi's Wine Bar,** 13 rue des Petit-Champs, 1er (☎ 01-42-61-05-09), is as close as Paris gets to a typical London wine bar. Excellent-quality wines are available by the glass. You can meet that strange creature here, the tweedy Frenchman. For details, see chapter 9.

- **Best for Breakfast:** At **Les Ambassadeurs,** 10 place de la Concorde, 8e (☎ 01-44-71-15-00), you can enjoy breakfast along with the diplomatic elite amid the marble and crystal of the Hôtel de Crillon.

- **Best for Tea:** Try **Angélina,** 226 rue de Rivoli, 1er (☎ 01-42-60-82-00), for a view of haute couture's lionesses having their tea. The house specialty is the Mont Blanc, a combination of chestnut cream and meringue. If you're looking for luscious ice cream along with your tea, try **Berthillon,** 31 rue St-Louis-en-l'Ile, 4e (☎ **01-43-54-31-61**).

- **Best for Picnic Fare:** For the most elegant picnic fixings in town, go to **Fauchon,** 26 place de la Madeleine, 8e (☎ **01-47-42-60-11**), where you'll find a complete charcuterie and famous pastry shop. It's said to offer 20,000 kinds of imported fruits, vegetables, and other exotic delicacies, snacks, salads, and canapés, all packed to take out. For details, see chapter 8.
- **Best Champagne Julep:** While you wait for a table at **Closerie des Lilas,** 171 bd. du Montparnasse, 6e (☎ **01-40-51-34-50**), savor the best champagne julep in the world at the bar.
- **Best People Watching:** Spend an afternoon on the terrace of the **Café de la Paix,** place de l'Opéra, 9e (☎ **01-40-07-30-20**), and watch the world go by. See and be seen or settle into anonymity while enjoying the vast variety of faces in this international mingling joint.

2 Planning Your Trip: The Basics

This chapter provides the nuts-and-bolts details you'll need before setting off for Paris—everything from information sources to money matters to the major airlines and how to save money on your flight. For resources on the Web, see **"Planning Your Trip: An Online Directory,"** following this chapter.

1 Visitor Information

TOURIST OFFICES

Your best source of information is the **French Government Tourist Office,** which you can reach at the following addresses:

IN THE UNITED STATES   444 Madison Ave., 16th Floor, New York, NY 10022 (☎ **212/838-7800**); 676 N. Michigan Ave., Suite 3360, Chicago, IL 60611 (☎ **312/751-7800**); 9454 Wilshire Blvd., Suite 715, Beverly Hills, CA 90212 (☎ **310/271-6665;** fax 310/276-2835). To request information at any of these offices, call the **France on Call** hot line at ☎ **410/286-8310.**

IN CANADA   Maison de la France/French Government Tourist Office, 1981 av. McGill College, Suite 490, Montréal, PQ H3A 2W9 (☎ **514/288-4264;** fax 514/845-4868); 30 St. Patrick St., Suite 700, Toronto, ON M5T 3A3 (☎ **416/491-7622;** fax 416/979-7587).

IN THE UNITED KINGDOM   Maison de la France/French Government Tourist Office, 178 Piccadilly, London, W1V 0AL (☎ **0891/244-123;** fax 020/7943-6594).

IN IRELAND   Maison de la France/French Government Tourist Office, 10 Suffolk St., Dublin 2, Ireland (☎ **01/679-0813;** fax 01/880-7772).

IN AUSTRALIA   French Tourist Bureau, 25 Bligh St., Sydney, NSW 2000 (☎ **02/9231-5244;** fax 02/9221-8682).

E-MAIL & WEB SITES

You can e-mail the French Government Tourist Office at **info@ francetourism.com** or **fgto@mcs.net.** The office's Web site is at **www.francetourism.com.**

Major Internet sites like Yahoo! (**www.yahoo.com**), Excite (**www. excite.com**), Lycos (**www.lycos.com**), and Infoseek (**www.infoseek.com**) contain subcategories on travel, country/regional information, and culture—search these for links to Web sites specializing in Paris. For specifics on Paris-related Web sites, see **"Planning Your Trip: An Online Directory,"** following this chapter.

2 Entry Requirements & Customs Regulations

PASSPORT & VISAS

All non-French nationals need a **valid passport** to enter France (check its expiration date). The French government no longer requires visas for **U.S. citizens,** providing they're staying less than 90 days. For longer stays, they must apply for a long-term visa, residence card, or temporary-stay visa. Each requires proof of income or a viable means of support in France and a legitimate purpose for remaining in the country. Applications are available from the **Consulate Section of the French Embassy,** 4101 Reservoir Rd. NW, Washington, DC 20007 (☎ **202/944-6000**), or from the **Visa Section of the French Consulate,** 10 E. 74th St., New York, NY 10021 (☎ **212/606-3689**). Visas are required for students planning to study in France even if the stay is less than 90 days.

At the moment, citizens of **Australia, Canada, New Zealand, Switzerland, Japan,** and **European Union countries** do not need visas.

If your passport is lost or stolen, head to your consulate as soon as possible for a replacement.

Passport applications are downloadable from the Internet at the following sites: http://travel.state.gov (U.S.); www.dfait-maeci.gc.ca/passport (Canada); www. open.gov. uk/ukpass/ukpass.htm (U.K.); www.irlgov.ie/iveagh/foreignaffairs/services (Ireland); www.dfat.gov.au/passports (Australia).

CUSTOMS REGULATIONS

WHAT YOU CAN BRING INTO FRANCE   Customs restrictions differ for citizens of European Union (EU) countries and citizens of non-EU countries.

For Non-EU Nationals   You can bring in duty-free 200 cigarettes, 100 cigarillos, 50 cigars, or 250 grams of smoking tobacco. This amount is doubled if you live outside Europe. You can also bring in 2 liters of wine and either 1 liter of alcohol over 22 proof or 2 liters of wine under 22 proof. In addition, you can bring in 50 grams (1.75 ounces) of perfume, a quarter liter (250ml) of eau de toilette, 500 grams (1 pound) of coffee, and 200 grams (half pound) of tea. Visitors 15 and over may also bring in other goods totaling 1,200F ($192); the allowance for those 14 and under is 600F ($96). (Customs officials tend to be lenient about general merchandise, realizing the limits are unrealistically low.)

For EU Citizens   Visitors from fellow European Union countries can bring into France any amount of goods as long as it's intended for their personal use—not for resale.

WHAT YOU CAN BRING HOME FROM FRANCE   **For U.S. Citizens** If you've been out of the country for 48 hours or more, you can bring back into the States $400 worth of goods (per person) without paying a duty. On the first $1,000 worth of goods over $400 you pay a flat 10%. Beyond that, it works on an item-by-item basis. There are a few restrictions on amount: 1 liter of alcohol (you must be over 21), 200 cigarettes, and 100 cigars. Antiques over 100 years old and works of art are exempt from the $400 limit, as is anything you mail home. Once per day, you can mail yourself $200 worth of goods duty-free; mark the package "For Personal Use." You can also mail to other people up to $100 worth of goods per person per day; label each package

"Unsolicited Gift." Any package must state on the exterior a description of the contents and their values. You can't mail alcohol, perfume (it contains alcohol), or tobacco products.

For more details on regulations, check out the **U.S. Customs Service** Web site at www.customs.ustreas.gov or contact the office at P.O. Box 7407, Washington, DC 20044 (☎ **202/927-6724**) to request the free "Know Before You Go" pamphlet.

To prevent the spread of diseases, you can't bring in any plants, fruits, vegetables, meats, or other foodstuffs. This includes even cured meats like salami. You may bring in the following: bakery goods, all but the softest cheeses (the rule is vague, but if the cheese is at all spreadable, don't risk confiscation), candies, roasted coffee beans and dried tea, fish (packaged salmon is OK), seeds for veggies and flowers (but not for trees), and mushrooms. Check out the USDA's Web site at www.aphis.usda.gov/ oa/travel.html for more details.

For Canadian Citizens   For a clear summary of Canadian rules, write for the booklet "I Declare," issued by **Revenue Canada,** 2265 St. Laurent Blvd., Ottawa K1G 4KE (☎ **800/461-9999** or 613/993-0534), or check out the Web site www.ccra-adrc.gc.ca. Canada allows its citizens a $750 exemption if you're gone for 7 days of longer (only $200 if you're gone between 48 hours and 7 days), and you're allowed to bring back duty-free 200 cigarettes, 50 cigars, 1.5 liters of wine *or* 1.14 liters of liquor *or* 8.5 liters of beer or ale. In addition, you're allowed to mail gifts to Canada at the rate of $60 a day, provided they're unsolicited and aren't alcohol or tobacco (write on the package "Unsolicited Gift, Under $60 Value").

For U.K. Citizens   You'll go through a separate Customs exit (the "Blue Exit") especially for EU travelers. You can bring home almost as much as you like of any goods from any EU country (theoretical limits run along the lines of "90 litres of wine"). If you're returning home from a non-EU country, you're allowed to bring home 200 cigarettes, 2 liters of table wine plus 1 liter of spirits or 2 liters of fortified or sparkling wine, 60 ml/cc of perfume, 250 ml/cc of toilet water, and a total of £145 in other goods. For more information, get in touch with **Her Majesty's Customs and Excise Office,** Berkeley House, 304 Regents Park Rd., Finchley, London N3 2JY (☎ **020/7865-4400** in central London; call 020/7202-4227 for other locations), or check out its Web site at www.hmce.gov.uk/public/travel.

For Australian Citizens   The duty-free allowance in Australia is A$400 or, for those under 18, A$200. Upon returning to Australia, citizens can bring in 250 cigarettes or 250 grams of loose tobacco and 1.125 liters of alcohol. A helpful brochure, available from Australian consulates or Customs offices, is "Know Before You Go." For more information, contact **Australian Customs Services,** GPO Box 8, Sydney NSW 2001 (☎ **1300-363-263** within Australia; 02/6275-6666 from overseas).

For New Zealand Citizens   The duty-free allowance for New Zealand is NZ$700. Citizens over 17 can bring back 200 cigarettes or 50 cigars or 250 grams of tobacco (or a mix of all three if their combined weight does not exceed 250 grams); plus 4.5 liters of wine *or* beer, plus 1.125 liters of liquor. Most questions are answered in the free "Advice to Travellers" pamphlet available at New Zealand consulates and Customs offices. For more information, contact the **New Zealand Customshouse,** 17–21 Whitmore St., Box 2218, Wellington (☎ **800/428-786** or 04-473-6099), or check out its Web site at www.customs.govt.nz.

3 Money

CURRENCY

French currency is based on the **franc (F),** which consists of 100 **centimes (c).** Coins come in units of 5c, 10c, 20c, and 50c and 1F, 2F, 5F, and 10F. Notes come in denominations of 20F, 50F, 100F, 200F, 500F, and 1,000F. The front of the 200F note honors Gustave Eiffel, creator of the Eiffel Tower, father of experimental aerodynamics, and part-designer of New York's Statue of Liberty.

Note: The franc will remain France's currency only until July 1, 2002. Then the **euro,** which has already been introduced, will take over completely. See "The Euro & You," below.

All banks are equipped for foreign exchange, and you'll find exchange offices at the airports and airline terminals. Banks are open Monday to Friday, 9am to noon and 2 to 4pm. Major bank branches also open their exchange departments on Saturday, 9am to noon.

When converting your home currency into French francs, be aware that rates vary. Your hotel will probably offer the worst exchange rate. In general, banks offer the best rate, but even banks charge a commission for the service,

The French Franc, the U.S. Dollar, the British Pound & the Euro

Because exchange rates fluctuate, this table should be used only as a general guide.

At this writing, **$1 U.S. = about 6.30F (or 1F = 16¢);** this was the rate of exchange used to calculate the dollar values given in this book. At this writing, **£1 = about 10.10F (or 1F = 10 pence);** this was the rate of exchange used to calculate the pound values in the table below. As a rough guideline, subject to multiple revisions as the currency increases in viability and visibility, **1€ = about $1 U.S., 6.6 French francs, or 63 U.K. pence.**

FF	U.S.$	U.K.£	Euro
1	0.16	0.10	0.15
2	0.32	0.20	0.30
3	0.48	0.30	0.45
4	0.64	0.40	0.60
5	0.80	0.50	0.75
6	0.96	0.60	0.90
7	1.12	0.70	1.05
8	1.28	0.80	1.20
9	1.44	0.90	1.35
10	1.60	1.00	1.50
15	2.40	1.50	2.25
20	3.20	2.00	3.00
25	4.00	2.50	3.75
50	8.00	5.00	7.50
75	12.00	7.50	11.25
100	16.00	10.00	15.00

The Euro & You

The **euro** (**€ or EUR),** the new single European currency, became the official currency of France and 10 other countries on January 1, 1999. You'll likely see prices in restaurants, shops, and so on listed in both French francs and euros. However, the franc will remain the only currency for cash transactions until December 21, 2001 (you can use it in noncash transactions, as with checks and credit cards). At that time, euro banknotes and coins will be introduced, and franc banknotes and coins will be withdrawn from circulation during a maximum 6-month transition period.

For more details on the euro, check out the Web site **www.europa. eu.int/euro.**

often $5, depending on the transaction. Whenever you can, stick to the big Paris banks, like Crédit Lyonnais, which usually offer the best exchange rates and charge the least commission. Always make sure you have enough francs for "le weekend."

ATMS

Using ATMs is the fastest, easiest, and least expensive way to change money. You take advantage of the bank's bulk exchange rate (better than anything you'll get on your own exchanging cash or traveler's checks) and, unless your home bank charges you for using a nonproprietary ATM, you won't have to pay a commission.

Both the **Cirrus** (☎ 800/424-7787; www.mastercard.com/atm) and the **Plus** (☎ 800/843-7587; www.visa.com/atms) networks have automated ATM locators listing the banks in Paris that will accept your card. Or just search out any machine with your network's symbol emblazoned on it. Be sure to check the daily withdrawal limit before you depart and ask whether you need a new PIN (see "A PIN Alert" below).

CREDIT CARDS

Credit cards are invaluable when traveling. They're a safe way to carry money, and they provide a convenient record of all your expenses, and you can withdraw cash advances from your credit cards at any bank (though you'll start paying hefty interest on the advance the moment you receive the cash and won't receive frequent-flyer miles on an airline credit card). At most banks, you don't even need to go to a teller; you can get a cash advance at the ATM with your PIN (see "A PIN Alert" above).

Almost every credit-card company has an emergency toll-free number you can call if your wallet or purse is stolen. The company may be able to wire you a cash advance off your credit card immediately and, in many

A PIN Alert

Make sure the PINs on your bank cards and credit cards will work in Paris. You usually need a four-digit code (six digits often won't work). Also keep in mind that you're usually able to access only your checking account, not savings, from ATMs abroad.

places, can deliver an emergency card in a day or two. The issuing bank's toll-free number is usually on the back of the credit card—though that doesn't help you if the card was stolen. Citicorp Visa's U.S. emergency number is ☎ **800/ 336-0472** or 410/581-3836 (collect). American Express cardholders and traveler's check holders should call ☎ **800/ 221-7282** for all money emergencies. MasterCard holders should call ☎ **800/307-7309.**

TRAVELER'S CHECKS

These days, traveler's checks seem less necessary than they used to because most cities have 24-hour ATMs allowing you to withdraw small amounts of cash as needed. Many banks, however, impose a fee every time a card is used at an ATM in a different city or bank. If you're withdrawing money every day, you might be better off with traveler's checks—provided you don't mind showing ID every time you want to cash a check.

American Express (☎ **800/221-7282;** www.americanexpress.com) is one of the largest issuers, and its checks are the most commonly accepted. It'll also sell checks to holders of certain types of American Express cards at no commission. **Thomas Cook** (☎ **800/223-7373** in the U.S. and Canada, 0800/622-101 in the U.K., or 44-1733/294-451 collect from other parts of the world; www.thomascook.com) issues MasterCard traveler's checks. **Citicorp** (☎ **800/645-6556** in the U.S. and Canada, or 813/623-1709 collect from anywhere else in the world; www.citicorp.com) and many other banks issue checks under their own name or under MasterCard or Visa.

4 When to Go

In August, Parisians traditionally leave town for their annual holiday and put the city on a skeleton staff to serve visitors. July has also become a popular vacation month, with many a restaurateur shuttering up for a month-long respite.

Hotels, especially first-class and deluxe, are easy to come by in July and August. Budget hotels, on the other hand, are likely to be full during these months of student invasion. You might also try to avoid the first 2 weeks in October, when the annual auto show attracts thousands of enthusiasts.

THE WEATHER: APRIL IN PARIS?

Balmy weather in Paris has prompted more popular songs and love ballads than weather conditions in any other city. But the weather here is actually quite fickle. Rain is much more common than snow throughout the winter, prompting many longtime residents to complain about the occasional bone-chilling dampness.

In recent years, Paris has had only about 15 snow days a year, and there are only a few oppressively hot days (over 86°F) in midsummer. What will most likely chill a Parisian heart, however, are blasts of rapidly moving air—wind tunnels sweep along the city's long boulevards, channeled by bordering buildings of uniform height. Other than the occasional winds and rain (which add an undeniable drama to many of the city's panoramas), Paris offers some of the most pleasant weather of any capital in Europe, with a highly tolerable average temperature of 53°F.

HOLIDAYS

Holidays in France are known as *jours feriés.* Shops and banks are closed, as well as many (but not all) restaurants and museums. Major holidays include January 1, Easter, Ascension Day (40 days after Easter), Pentecost (seventh

Sunday after Easter), May 1, May 8 (VE Day), July 14 (Bastille Day), August 15 (Assumption of the Virgin Mary), November 1 (All Saints' Day), November 11 (Armistice Day), and December 25 (Christmas).

Paris Calendar of Events

Check the Paris Tourist Office Web site at www.paris-touristoffice.com and other Web sites above or in **"Planning Your Trip: An Online Directory,"** for up-to-the-minute details on these and other events.

January

- **International Ready-to-Wear Fashion Shows (Salon International de Prêt-à-Porter),** Parc des Expositions, 15e. Hundreds of designers, from the giants to the virtually unknown, unveil their visions (hallucinations?) about what you should be wearing 6 months down the road. The event in the massive Porte de Versailles convention facilities is geared to wholesalers, retailers, buyers, journalists, and industry professionals, but for the 130F ($20.80) entrance fee, the rules are usually bent for the merely fashion conscious. Much more exclusive are the *défilés* (fashion shows) held around the same time at the headquarters of individual houses like Lagerfeld, Lanvin, Courrèges, and Valentino. For details, call ☎ **01-44-94-70-00.** Mid-January to mid-February.

February

- **Special Exhibitions, Special Concerts:** During Paris's grayest month, look for a splash of temporary expositions and concerts designed to perk up the city. Concerts and theaters spring up at such diverse sites as the **Salle Pleyel,** 252 rue du faubourg St-Honoré, 8e (☎ **01-45-61-53-00;** Métro: Ternes); the **Théâtre des Champs-Elysées,** 15 av. Montaigne, 8e (☎ **01-49-52-50-50;** Métro: Alma-Marceau); and the **Maison Radio-France,** 116 av. du Président-Kennedy, 16e (☎ **01-42-30-15-16;** Métro: Passy-Ranelagh). Also look for openings of new operas at the **Opéra Bastille,** 2 place de la Bastille, 4e (☎ **01-43-43-96-96;** Métro: Bastille), and operas and dance at the **Opéra Garnier,** place de l'Opéra, 9e (☎ **01-40-01-17-89);** concerts beneath Europe's most famous glass pyramid, the **Pyramide du Louvre,** 1er (☎ **01-40-20-52-29;** Métro: Musée du Louvre); and the **Salle Cortot,** 78 rue Cardinet, 17e (☎ **01-47-63-85-72;** Métro: Malesherbes). A copy of *Pariscope* or *L'Officiel des Spectacles* is the best info source.

March

- **Foire du Trône,** Bois de Vincennes, 12e. A mammoth amusement park its fans promote as France's largest country fair, the Foire du Trône boasts origins dating from the year 957, when merchants met with farmers on a nearby site to exchange grain and wine. This high-tech continuation of that tradition, held on the lawns of the Pelouse de Reuilly, incorporates a Ferris wheel, carousels, acrobats, jugglers, fire eaters, and amusements and diversions that seem like a Gallic Coney Island. It's open Sunday to Thursday 2pm to midnight and Friday and Saturday 2pm to 1am. For details, call ☎ **01-46-27-52-29.** Late March to late May.

April

- **International Marathon of Paris.** Beginning on the Champs-Elysées at 9am, runners take over many of Paris's boulevards in a televised race that draws competitors from around the world. Depending on their speed and endurance, participants arrive at the finishing point on avenue Foch, 16e, beginning about 2¹/₂ hours later. If you haven't felt like jogging lately, this event might inspire you. For details, call ☎ **01-41-33-15-68.** First weekend in April.

- **Les Grandes Eaux Musicales,** Versailles. These musical events are intended to re-create the atmosphere of the ancient regime. On these rare occasions, the fountains of the parks around the palace are turned on, with special emphasis on the Neptune Fountain, which sits squarely in front of the best view of the château. You can promenade in the garden and listen to the drifting music of French composers (Couperin, Charpentier, Lully) and others (Mozart, Haydn) whose careers thrived during the years of the palace's construction. The music is generally recorded, but concerts take place every Sunday 11:15am to 3:30pm. For details, call ☎ **01-39-24-88-88.** April to early October.

May

- **VE Day,** citywide. The celebration commemorating the capitulation of the Nazis on May 7, 1945, lasts 4 days in Paris, with a parade along the Champs-Elysées and additional ceremonies in Reims. Pro-American sentiments are probably higher during this festival than at any other time of the Parisian calendar. May 5 to 8.
- **Grand Steeplechase de Paris,** Auteuil and Longchamp racetracks, Bois de Boulogne. This is a counterpoint to the horse races conducted at Chantilly (below). For details, call ☎ **01-49-10-20-30.** May 28.
- **French Open Tennis Championship,** Stade Roland-Garros, 16e. The Open features 10 days of Grand Slam men's and women's tennis, with European and South American players traditionally dominating on the hot, dusty red courts. For details, call ☎ **01-47-43-48-00.** Late May to mid-June.

June

- **Prix du Jockey Club** (June 6 at 2pm) **& Prix Diane-Hermès** (June 8 at 2pm), Hippodrome de Chantilly. Thoroughbreds from as far away as Kentucky and Brunei, as well as mounts sponsored by Europe's old and new fortunes, compete in a very civil format broadcast around France and talked about in horsey circles around the world. On race days, as many as 30 trains depart from Paris's Gare du Nord for Chantilly, where they're met by free shuttle buses to the track. Alternatively, buses depart on race days from place de la République and Porte de St-Cloud, on a schedule that coincides with the beginning and end of the races. For details on this and all other equine events in this calendar, call ☎ **01-49-10-20-30.**
- **Fête de St-Denis,** St-Denis. This series presents 4 days of artfully contrived music in the burial place of the French kings, a grim early Gothic monument in this industrialized northern suburb. For details, call ☎ **01-48-13-06-07.** June 13 to July 3.
- **Paris Air Show,** Le Bourget. This is where France's military-industrial complex shows off enough high-tech hardware to make anyone think twice about invading La Patrie. Fans, competitors, and industrial spies mob the airport's exhibition halls for a taste of what Gallic technocrats have wrought. For details, call ☎ **01-53-23-33-33.** June 14 to 18 (in odd-numbered years only).
- **Fête Chopin,** Orangerie du Parc de Bagatelle, Versailles. Hear all you ever wanted to hear from the Polish exile who lived most of his life in Paris

at these piano recitals. For details, call ☎ **01-45-00-22-19.** June 19 to July 14.

- **Festival du Marais,** the Marais. A major event for the arts, this festival offers the finest in classical music, traditional and modern dance, and plays in the historic *hôtels* (mansions) and churches of this district in the 4th arrondissement. For details, call ☎ **01-48-87-60-08.** Mid-June to mid-July.

- **Fête de la Musique,** citywide. This celebration at the summer solstice is the one day noise laws don't apply in Paris. Musicians and wannabes pour out into the streets, where you can make music with anything, even if it means banging two garbage cans together or driving around blowing your car horn (illegal otherwise). You might hear anything from newly arrived Russians on the balalaikas to Cubans playing salsa rhythms. There are musical parties in virtually all the open spaces, with more organized concerts at place de la Bastille and place de la République and in La Villette and the Latin Quarter. For details, call ☎ **01-40- 03-94-70.** June 21.

- **Gay Pride Parade,** place de l'Odéon to place de la Bastille. A week of expositions and parties climaxes in a massive parade patterned after those in New York and San Francisco. It's followed by a dance at the Palais de Bercy, a major convention hall/sports arena. For details, contact the **Centre Gai et Lesbien,** 3 rue Keller, 75011 Paris (☎ **01-43-57-21-47**). June 24.

- **La Course des Garçons de Café,** throughout the city. There's no more amusing race in Paris. Balancing heavily loaded trays, the *garçons* (both waiters and waitresses) line up in front of the Hôtel de Ville in the 4th arrondissement and then race for 5 miles through the streets, ending back at the Hôtel de Ville. Some obviously don't make it. A Sunday in the last week of June or the first week of July.

- **La Villette Jazz Festival,** La Villette. This dynamic homage to the art of jazz incorporates 50 concerts in churches, auditoriums, and concert halls in all neighborhoods of this Paris suburb. Past festivals have included Herbie Hancock, Shirley Horn, Michel Portal, and other artists from around the world. For details, call ☎ **08-03-30-63-06.** Late June to the first week in July.

July

- **Tour de France.** This is Europe's most visible, most highly contested, and most overabundantly televised bicycle race. Crews of wind-tunnel-tested athletes speed along an itinerary tracing the six sides of the French "hexagon" and detouring deep into the Massif Central and across the Swiss Alps. The race is decided at a finish line drawn across the Champs-Elysées. For details, call ☎ **01-41-33-15-00.** July 3 to 21.

- ✪ **Bastille Day,** citywide. This celebration of the 1789 storming of the Bastille is the accepted birth date of modern France, and festivities reach their peak in Paris with street fairs, pageants, fireworks, and feasts. The day begins with a parade down the Champs-Elysées and ends with fireworks in Montmartre. Wherever you are, before the end of the day you'll hear Piaf warbling "La Foule" ("The Crowd"), the song that celebrated her passion for the stranger she met and later lost in a crowd on Bastille Day, and lots of people singing "La Marseillaise." July 14.

- **Paris Quartier d'Eté,** Latin Quarter. For 4 weeks, the Arènes de Lutèce or the Sorbonne's Cour d'Honneur host pop orchestral concerts. The dozen or so concerts are usually grander than the outdoor setting would imply and include performances by the Orchestre de Paris, Orchestre National de France, and Baroque Orchestra of the European Union. On the fringes you can find plays, jazz concerts, and parades in the Tuileries. For details, call ☎ **01-44-94-98-00** or fax 01-44-94-98-01. July 15 to August 15.

September

- **Fête Musique en l'Ile,** 4th, 5th, and 6th arrondissements. A series of concerts, most dignified masses composed from the 17th to the late 19th century, are given in various medieval churches. Sites include St-Louis-en-l'Ile, St-Severin, and St-Germain-des-Prés. For details, call ☎ **01-43-55-47-09.** September 5 to October 17.

- **Biennale des Antiquaires,** Cour Carrée at the Louvre or the Grand Palais. Antiques dealers and lovers from all over the world gather at this gilded event in even-numbered years. Precious furnishings and objets d'art are displayed in the underground exhibit halls linked to the Louvre or perhaps in the Grand Palais once it's restored. For details, call ☎ **08-36-68-31-12** or 01-49-52-53-54. Usually first week in September.

- **Festival d'Automne (Autumn Festival),** citywide. Paris welcomes the return of its residents from their August holidays with an ongoing and eclectic festival of modern music, ballet, theater, and modern art. Venues include art galleries, churches, concert halls, auditoriums, and parks throughout Paris. There's a great emphasis on experimental works, which the festival's promoters scatter judiciously between more traditional productions. Depending on the event, tickets cost from 100 to 300F ($16 to $48). For details, contact the **Festival d'Automne,** 156 rue de Rivoli, 75001 Paris (☎ **01-53-45-17-00;** fax 01-53-45-17-01). Late September to mid-December.

- **International Ready-to-Wear Fashion Shows (Salon International de Prêt-à-Porter),** Parc des Expositions, 15e. More of what took place at the fashion shows in January (above), with a stress on what le beau monde will be wearing next spring. Early September.

October

- ✪ **Paris Auto Show,** Parc des Expositions, 15e. Glitzy attendees and lots of hype attend this showcase for European car design. The auto show takes place near the Porte de Versailles in western Paris. In addition, a permanent exhibit on French auto design at the Cité des Sciences et de l'Industrie is upgraded and enriched during October. For details, call ☎ **01-56-88-22-40.** Fifteen days in early October in even-numbered years.

- **Prix de l'Arc de Triomphe,** Hippodrome de Longchamp, 16e. France's answer to England's Ascot is the country's most prestigious horse race, culminating the equine season in Europe. For details, call ☎ **01-49-10-20-30.** Early October.

- **Fête de Jazz de Paris,** citywide. Some of the world's best-known jazz artists descend on Paris for this 14-day jazz fest, followed by their aficionados. Clubs both high- and lowbrow throw open their doors. The atmosphere is dark and smoky, the crowds hip. For details, call ☎ **01-47-83-33-58.** Mid-October to early November.

November

- **Armistice Day,** citywide. The signing of the controversial document that ended World War I is celebrated with a military parade from the Arc de Triomphe to the Hôtel des Invalides. November 11.

- **Fête d'Art Sacré (Festival of Sacred Art).** A dignified series of classical concerts is held in five of the oldest and most recognizable churches of Paris. For details, call ☎ **01-44-70-64-10.** Mid-November to mid-December.
- **Release of the Beaujolais Nouveau,** citywide. Parisians eagerly await the yearly release of the first of the new Beaujolais, that fruity wine from Burgundy. Signs are posted in bistros, wine bars, and cafes—these places report their heaviest patronage of the year during this celebration from the vineyards. Third Thursday in November.

December

- **Paris Boat Show (Salon International de la Navigation de Plaisance),** Parc des Expositions, 15e. This is Europe's most visible exposition of what's afloat and of interest to wholesalers, retailers, individual boat owners (or wannabes), and anyone involved in the business of waterborne holidaymaking. For details, call ☎ **01-41-90-47-10,** fax 01-41-90-47-00, or check on the Web at www.parisboatshow.rggd-olp.fr. Eight days in early December.
- **Fête de St-Sylvestre (New Year's Eve),** citywide. It's most boisterously celebrated in the Latin Quarter around the Sorbonne. At midnight, the city explodes. Strangers kiss strangers, and boulevard St-Michel and the Champs-Elysées become virtual pedestrian malls. December 31.

5 Health & Insurance

STAYING HEALTHY

If you're worried about getting sick away from home, you may want to consider **medical travel insurance** (see below). In most cases, however, your existing health plan will provide all the coverage you need. Be sure to carry your ID card in your wallet. If you suffer from a chronic illness, consult your doctor before your departure. For conditions like epilepsy, diabetes, or heart problems, wear a **Medic Alert Identification Tag** (☎ **800/825-3785;** www.medicalert.org), which will immediately alert doctors to your condition and give them access to your records through Medic Alert's 24-hour hot line. Membership is $35, plus a $15 annual fee.

Pack prescription medications in your carry-on luggage. Carry written prescriptions in generic, not brand-name, form, and dispense all prescription medications from their original labeled vials. Also bring along copies of your prescriptions in case you lose your pills or run out.

The **International Association for Medical Assistance to Travelers (IAMAT)** (☎ **716/754-4883** or 416/652-0137; www.sentedx.net/~iamat), offers tips on travel and health concerns in Europe and lists many local English-speaking doctors.

INSURANCE

There are three kinds of travel insurance: trip cancellation, medical, and stolen/lost luggage. **Trip-cancellation insurance** is a good idea if you've paid a large portion of your vacation expenses up front. The other two types, however, don't make sense for most travelers. *Note*: Check your existing policies before you buy any additional coverage.

Your existing health insurance should cover you if you get sick while on vacation (though if you belong to an HMO, you should check to see whether you're fully covered when away from home). If you need hospital treatment, most health insurance plans and HMOs will cover out-of-country hospital visits and procedures, at least to some extent. However, most make you pay the bills up front at the time of care, and you'll get a refund after you've returned and filed all the paperwork. Members of **Blue Cross/Blue Shield** can now use their cards at select hospitals in most major cities worldwide (☎ **800/810-BLUE;** www.bluecares.com). For independent travel health-insurance providers, see below.

Your homeowner's insurance should cover **stolen luggage.** Most airlines are responsible for up to $2,500 on domestic flights if they lose your luggage and for around $635 per piece of checked baggage on international flights. If you plan to carry anything more valuable than that, keep it in your carry-on bag if possible.

The differences between travel assistance and insurance are often blurred, but in general the former offers on-the-spot assistance and 24-hour hot lines (mostly oriented toward medical problems), while the latter reimburses you for travel problems (medical, travel, or otherwise) after you've filed the paperwork. The coverage you should consider will depend on how much protection is already contained in your existing health insurance or other policies. Some credit-card companies may insure you against travel accidents if you buy plane, train, or bus tickets with their cards. Before buying additional insurance, read your policies and agreements carefully. Some credit cards offer automatic flight insurance against death or dismemberment in case of an airplane crash. Call your insurers or credit-card companies if you have any questions.

If you do require extra insurance, try one of these reputable issuers: **Access America,** 6600 W. Broad St., Richmond, VA 23230 (☎ **800/284-8300;** www.accessamerica.com); **Travel Guard International,** 1145 Clark St., Stevens Point, WI 54481 (☎ **800/ 826-1300;** www.travel-guard.com); **Travel Insured International, Inc.,** P.O. Box 280568, East Hartford, CT 06128 (☎ **800/2 43-3174;** www.travelinsured.com); **Columbus Travel Insurance,** 279 High St., Croydon CR0 1QH (☎ **020/7375-0011** in London; www2.columbusdirect.com); **Travelex Insurance Services,** P.O. Box 9408, Garden City, NY 11530-9408 (☎ **800/228-9792;** www.travelex-insurance.com).

Companies specializing in accident and medical care include **MEDEX International,** P.O. Box 5375, Timonium, MD 21094-5375 (☎ **888/ MEDEX-00** or 410/453-6300; fax 410/453-6301; www.medexassist.com), and **Travel Assistance International,** 1133 15th St. NW, Suite 400, Washington, DC 20005 (☎ **800/ 821-2828** or 202/828-5894; fax 202/828-5896; www.worldwideassistance.com).

6 Tips for Travelers with Special Needs

FOR TRAVELERS WITH DISABILITIES

A disability shouldn't stop anyone from traveling, and there are more resources than ever before. Facilities in Paris for travelers with disabilities are certainly better than you'll find in most cities. Every year the French government does more and more to help ease life for individuals with disabilities. Nearly all modern hotels in France now have rooms designed especially for persons with disabilities. Older hotels, unless renovated, may not provide important features like elevators, special toilet facilities, or ramps for wheelchair accessibility. Depending on how specialized your needs are, it's best to contact each hotel directly and make your special needs known before you arrive.

Most high-speed trains in France can deal with wheelchairs, and guide dogs ride free. Older trains have special compartments built for wheelchair boarding. On the Paris Métro, persons with disabilities can sit in wider seats provided for their comfort. Some stations don't have escalators or elevators, however, and this may present problems.

A World of Options, a 658-page book of resources for the persons with disabilities, covers everything from biking trips to scuba outfitters. It costs $35 ($30 for members) and is available from **Mobility International USA,** P.O. Box 10767, Eugene, OR 97440 (☎ **541/343-1284,** voice/TDD; www.miusa.org). Annual membership is $35, which includes the quarterly newsletter *Over the Rainbow.* In addition, **Twin Peaks Press,** P.O. Box 129, Vancouver, WA 98666 (☎ **360/694-2462**), publishes travel-related books for people with disabilities.

The **Moss Rehab Hospital** in Philadelphia has been providing friendly and helpful phone advice and referrals to travelers with disabilities for years through its **Travel Information Service** at ☎ **215/456-9603** or 215/456-9602 TTY (www. mossresourcenet.org).

To gain access to its vast network of connections in the travel industry, you can join the **Society for the Advancement of Travel for the Handicapped (SATH),** 347 Fifth Ave., Suite 610, New York, NY 10016 (☎ **212/447-7284;** fax 212/725-8253; www.sath.org), for $45 annually, $30 for seniors/students. It provides info sheets on destinations and referrals to tour operators specializing in traveling with individuals with disabilities. Its quarterly magazine, *Open World for Disability and Mature Travel,* is full of good information and resources; a year's subscription is $13 ($21 outside the U.S.).

You can obtain a copy of *Air Transportation of Handicapped Persons* by writing to Free Advisory Circular No. AC12032, Distribution Unit, U.S. Department of Transportation, Publications Division, M-4332, Washington, DC 20590.

Travelers with vision impairments should contact the **American Foundation for the Blind,** 11 Penn Plaza, Suite 300, New York, NY 10001 (☎ **800/232-5463** or 212/502-7600; www.afb.org), for information on traveling with Seeing Eye dogs.

A nonprofit French organization equipped to answer your questions is the **APF Evasion (Association des Paralysés de France),** 17 bd. Auguste-Blanqui, 75013 Paris (☎ **01-40-78-69-00**). Occasionally, it organizes tours through France (sometimes farther afield) for small groups; if you show an interest in participating, it'll make special efforts to hire English-speaking guides and monitors. If you don't want to travel as part of a group, it'll try to put you in contact with a fully enabled paid escort.

FOR GAYS & LESBIANS

France is one of the world's most tolerant countries toward gays and lesbians, and no special laws discriminate against them. "Gay Paree" boasts a large gay population, with dozens of gay clubs, restaurants, organizations, and services. Before leaving home, you might want to pick up a copy of *Frommer's Gay & Lesbian Europe,* with fabulous chapters on Paris and Nice and the Côte d'Azur.

The **International Gay & Lesbian Travel Association (IGLTA),** 4331 N. Federal Hwy., Suite 304, Ft. Lauderdale, FL 33308 (☎ **800/448-8550;** fax 954/776-3303; www.iglta.com), is a great general resource. Members ($100 to join, plus $150 a year) get a newsletter and membership directory, but even nonmembers can get advice on specialist travel agencies (or search for local ones on the Web site). General gay/lesbian travel agencies include **Our Family Abroad,** 40 W. 57th St., Suite 430, New York, NY 10019 (☎ **800/999-5500;** www.familyabroad.com), and **Islanders/Kennedy Travels,** 314 Jericho Turnpike, Floral Park, NY 11001 (☎ **800/988-1181;** www. kennedytravel.com).

Out & About, 8 W. 19th St., Suite 401, New York, NY 10011 (☎ **800/ 929-2268** or 212/645-6922), is a newsletter packed with good info on the global gay scene. A 1-year/10-issue subscription is $49. *Our World,* P.O. Box 685195, Austin, TX 78768 (☎ **800/850-5951;** www.gayweb.com/208/ ourworld.html), is a slicker monthly magazine promoting and highlighting travel bargains and opportunities. Annual subscription rates are $35 in the U.S. and $45 overseas.

One of the best sources for gay/lesbian activities is the **Centre Gai et Lesbien,** 3 rue Keller, 11e (☎ **01-43-57-21-47;** Métro: Bastille), open daily 2 to 6pm. On Sunday, **Le Café Positif** at the center features music, cabaret, and details about AIDS and sexually transmitted diseases. **SOS Ecoute Gay** at ☎ **01-44-93-01-02** is a gay hot line designed to creatively counsel persons with gay-related problems. The phone is answered by volunteers, some of whom aren't as skilled and helpful as others. A phone counselor responds to calls Monday and Wednesday 8 to 10pm and Tuesday, Thursday, and Friday 6 to 8pm. Also helpful is **La Maison des Femmes,** 163 rue de Charenton, 12e (☎ **01-43-43-41-13;** Métro: Reuilly-Diderot), offering information about Paris for lesbians and bisexual women and sometimes sponsoring informal dinners and get-togethers. Call any Wednesday 4 to 7pm for details.

Gai Pied's publication ***Guide Gai*** (revised annually) is the best source of information on gay and lesbian clubs, hotels, restaurants, organizations, and services in the capital. Lesbian or bisexual women might also like to pick up a copy of ***Lesbia,*** if only to check out the ads. These and other publications are available at Paris's largest gay bookstore, **Les Mots à la Bouche,** 6 rue Ste-Croix-de-la-Bretonnerie, 4e (☎ **01-42-78-88-30**). Hours are Monday to Saturday 11am to 11pm and Sunday 2 to 8pm. Both French- and English-language publications are available.

FOR SENIORS

Don't be shy about asking for discounts, but always carry some kind of ID, like a driver's license, showing your date of birth. And mention the fact you're a senior when you first make your travel reservations. For example, many hotels offer senior discounts. In most cities, people over 60 qualify for reduced admission to theaters, museums, and other attractions and discounted fares on public transportation.

Members of the **American Association of Retired Persons (AARP),** 601 E St. NW, Washington, DC 20049 (☎ **800/424-3410** or 202434-2277; www.aarp.org), get discounts not only on hotels but also on airfares and car rentals. AARP offers members a wide range of special benefits, including *Modern Maturity* magazine and a monthly newsletter.

The nonprofit **National Council of Senior Citizens,** 8403 Colesville Rd., Suite 1200, Silver Spring, MD 20910 (☎ **301/578-8800**), offers a newsletter six times a year (partly devoted to travel tips) and discounts on hotel and auto rentals; annual dues are $13 per person or couple. **Golden Companions,** P.O. Box 5249, Reno, NV 89513 (☎ **800/392-1256** or 631/454-0880), helps travelers 45-plus find compatible companions through a personal voice-mail service. Contact them for details.

Mature Traveler, a monthly 12-page newsletter on senior travel, is a valuable resource, available by subscription ($30 a year) from GEM Publishing Group, Box 50400, Reno, NV 89513-0400. Another helpful publication is *101 Tips for the Mature Traveler,* available from Grand Circle Travel, 347 Congress St., Suite 3A, Boston, MA 02210 (☎ **800/221-2610** or 617/350-7500; fax 617/346-6700).

Grand Circle Travel, 347 Congress St., Suite 3A, Boston, MA 02210 (☎ **800/ 221-2610** or 617/350-7500; www.gct.com), is also one of the hundreds of travel agencies specializing in vacations for seniors. Many of these packages, however, are of the tour-bus variety, with free trips thrown in for those who organize groups of 10 or more. Seniors seeking more independent travel should probably consult a regular travel agent. **SAGA International Holidays,** 222 Berkeley St., Boston, MA 02116 (☎ **800/343-0273;** www.sagaholidays.com), offers inclusive tours and cruises for those 50 and older. SAGA also sponsors the more substantial **Road Scholar Tours** (☎ **800/621-2151**).

Variations on the same theme, **Elderhostel** and the University of New Hampshire's **Interhostel** provide educational travel for seniors. On these escorted tours, the days are packed with seminars, lectures, and field trips, and the sightseeing is led by academic experts. **Elderhostel,** 75 Federal St., Boston, MA 02110-1941 (☎ **877/426-8056;** www.elderhostel.org), arranges study programs for those 55 and over (and a spouse or companion of any age) in the United States and in 77 countries around the world, including France. Most courses last about 3 weeks and many include airfare, accommodations in student dorms or modest inns, meals, and tuition. Write or call for a free catalog that lists upcoming courses and destinations. **Interhostel** (☎ **800/733-9753;** www.learn.unh.edu) takes travelers 50 and over (with companions over 40) and offers 2- and 3-week trips, mostly international. The courses in both programs are ungraded, involve no homework, and often focus on the liberal arts. They're not luxury vacations but are fun and fulfilling.

FOR STUDENTS

Paris offers student discounts on nearly everything, from museums to movies. The best resource for students is the **Council on International Educational Exchange (CIEE).** It can set you up with an ID card (see below), and its travel branch, **Council Travel Service** (☎ **800/226-8624;** www.ciee.com), is the biggest student travel agency operation in the world. It can get you discounts on plane tickets, rail passes, and the like.

From CIEE you can obtain the student traveler's best friend, the $18 **International Student Identity Card (ISIC).** It's the only officially acceptable form of student ID, good for cut rates on rail passes, plane tickets, and other discounts. It also provides you with basic health and life insurance and a 24-hour help line. If you're no longer a student but are still under 26, you can get from the same people a **GO 25 card,** which will get you the insurance and some of the discounts.

In Canada, **Travel CUTS,** 200 Ronson St., Ste. 320, Toronto, ONT M9W 5Z9 (☎ **800/667-2887** or 416/614-2887; www.travelcuts.com), offers similar services. **Campus Travel,** 52 Grosvenor Gardens, London SW1W 0AG (☎ **020/7730-3402;** www.campustravel.co.uk), opposite Victoria Station, is Britain's leading specialist in student and youth travel.

Planning Basics

BY PLANE
THE MAJOR AIRLINES

FROM NORTH AMERICA One of the best choices for travelers in the southeastern United States and the Midwest is **Delta Airlines** (☎ 800/241-4141; www.delta-air.com). From cities like New Orleans, Phoenix, Columbia (South Carolina), and Nashville, Delta flies to Atlanta, connecting every evening with a nonstop flight to Paris. Delta also operates daily nonstop flights to Paris from Cincinnati and New York. All these flights depart late enough in the day to permit easy transfers from much of Delta's vast North American network.

Another excellent choice is **United Airlines** (☎ 800/538-2929; www.ual.com), with nonstop flights from Chicago, Washington, D.C., and San Francisco to Paris. United also offers discounted fares in the low and shoulder seasons to London from five major North American hubs. From London, it's an easy train and Hovercraft or Chunnel connection to Paris, a fact that tempts many passengers to spend a weekend in London either before or after their visit to Paris.

Another good option is **Continental Airlines** (☎ 800/231-0856; www.flycontinental.com), serving the Northeast and much of the Southwest through its busy hubs in Newark and Houston. From both of those cities, Continental provides nonstop flights to Paris. Flights from Newark depart daily, while flights from Houston depart between four and seven times a week, depending on the season.

TWA (☎ 800/221-2000; www.twa.com), operates daily nonstop service to Paris from New York and in summer several flights a week from Boston and Washington, D.C. In summer, TWA also flies to Paris from St. Louis several times a week nonstop and from Los Angeles three times a week, with connections in St. Louis or New York. In winter, flights from Los Angeles and Washington, D.C., are suspended and flights from St. Louis are routed with brief touchdowns en route to Paris in New York or Boston.

The French flag carrier, **Air France** (☎ 800/237-2747; www.airfrance.com), offers daily or several-times-a-week flights to Paris from Newark; Washington, D.C.; Miami; Chicago; New York; Houston; San Francisco; Los Angeles; Boston; Cincinnati; Atlanta; Montréal; Toronto; and Mexico City.

American Airlines (☎ 800/433-7300; www.aa.com), provides daily nonstop flights to Paris from Dallas/Fort Worth, Chicago, Miami, Boston, and New York. And **USAirways** (☎ 800/428-4322; www.usairways.com), offers daily nonstop service from Philadelphia to Paris.

If you'd like to see London before traveling on to Paris, there are dozens of **British Airways** (☎ 800/247-9297; www.british-airways.com) flights from North America and Canadian cities like Toronto and Montréal to London.

Sample Flying Times

The flying time to Paris from New York is about 7 hours; from Chicago, 9 hours; from Los Angeles, 11 hours; from Atlanta, about 8 hours; from Washington, D.C., about $7\frac{1}{2}$ hours; from London, about 1 hour; from Edinburgh, 2 hours; from Dublin, 2 hours; from Sydney, $21\frac{1}{2}$ hours; from Auckland, $23\frac{1}{4}$ hours.

Flying for Less: Tips for Getting the Best Airfares

Passengers in the same airplane cabin rarely pay the same fare for their seats. Business travelers who need to buy tickets at the last minute, change their itinerary at a moment's notice, or get home before the weekend pay the full fare. Passengers who can book their tickets long in advance, who don't mind staying over Saturday night, or who are willing to travel on a Tuesday, Wednesday, or Thursday after 7pm will pay a fraction of that fare.

Here are some great ways to save money so you can splurge on that gourmet meal at Taillevent or that classic suit at Chanel:

- **Take advantage of APEX fares.** Advance-purchase booking or APEX fares are often the key to getting the lowest fare. You generally must be willing to make your plans and buy your tickets as far ahead as possible: The **21-day APEX** is seconded only by the **14-day APEX.** Since the number of seats allocated to APEX fares is sometimes less than 25% of plane capacity, the early bird gets the low-cost seat. There's often a surcharge for flying on a weekend, and cancellation and refund policies can be strict.

- **Watch for sales.** You'll almost never see them during July and August or the Thanksgiving or Christmas seasons, but at other times you can get great deals. If you already hold a ticket when a sale breaks, it may even pay to exchange it, which usually incurs a $50 to $75 charge. If your schedule is flexible, ask if you can secure a cheaper fare by **staying an extra day** or by **flying midweek.** (Many airlines won't volunteer this information.)

- **Find a low fare with a consolidator (aka bucket shop).** A consolidator buys seats in bulk from airlines and sells them to the public at prices below even the airlines' discounted rates. Their small boxed ads usually run in the Sunday travel section. **Council Travel** (☎ **800/226-8624;** www.counciltravel.com) and **STA Travel** (☎ **800/781-4040;** www.sta.travel.com) cater especially to young travelers, but their bargain prices are available to all ages. **Travel Bargains** (☎ **800/AIR-FARE;** www.1800airfare.com) was once owned by TWA but now offers the deepest discounts on many other airlines, with a 4-day advance purchase. Other consolidators are **1-800-FLY-CHEAP**

You can fly first from, say, New York to London, then take the BA shuttle flight to Paris following a holiday in England.

Canadians usually choose **Air Canada** (☎ **800/776-3000** from the U.S. and Canada; www.aircanada.ca) for flights to Paris from Toronto and Montréal. Nonstop flights from Montréal and Toronto depart every evening. Two of the nonstop flights from Toronto are shared with Air France and feature Air France aircraft.

FROM THE UNITED KINGDOM   From London, **Air France** (☎ **0845/084-5111;** www.airfrance.com) and **British Airways** (☎ **0345/222-111** in the U.K.; www.british-airways.com) fly frequently to Paris, offering up to 17 flights daily from Heathrow. **Aer Lingus** (☎ **800/223-6537** in the U.S., or 01-886-31-54; www.aerlingus.ie) has frequent direct flights from Dublin to Paris throughout the day. Many commercial travelers also use regular flights from the London City Airport in the Docklands. There are also direct flights to (www. 1800flycheap. com); **TFI Tours International** (☎ **800/ 745-8000** or 212/736-1140), a clearinghouse for unused seats; and "rebators" like **Travel Avenue** (☎ **800/333-3335** or 312/876-1116) and the **Smart Traveller** (☎ **800/448-3338** in the U.S. or 305/448-3338; www. smarttraveller.com), which rebate part of their commissions to you.

- **Book a seat on a charter flight.** Most charter operators advertise and sell their seats through travel agents. Before deciding to take a charter, however, check the ticket restrictions: You may be asked to buy a tour package, pay in advance, be amenable if the departure day is changed, pay a service charge, fly on an airline you're not familiar with (un-usual), and pay harsh penalties if you cancel—but be understanding if the charter doesn't fill up and is canceled up to 10 days before departure. Summer charters fill up more quickly than others and are almost sure to fly, but if you decide on a charter, seriously consider cancellation and baggage insurance.

- **Look into courier flights.** Companies that hire couriers use your luggage allowance for their business baggage; in return, you get a deeply discounted ticket. Flights are often offered at the last minute, and you may have to arrange a pretrip interview to make sure you're right for the job. One reliable courier service is **Now Voyager** (☎ **212/ 431-1616**), open Monday to Friday 10am to 5:30pm and Saturday noon to 4:30pm. It also offers noncourier discounted fares, so call the company even if you don't want to fly as a courier.

- **Join a travel club.** Both **Moment's Notice** (☎ **718/234-6295**) and **Sears Discount Travel Club** (☎ **800/433-9383,** or 800/255-1487 to join) supply unsold tickets at discounted prices. You pay an annual membership fee to get the club's hot line number. Of course, you're limited to what's availableand have to be flexible.

- **Search for deals on the Web.** It's possible to get some great deals on airfare, hotels, and car rentals via the Internet. For details on getting the most from the Web, see "Planning Your Trip: An Online Directory" following this chapter.

Paris from major cities like Manchester, Edinburgh, and Southampton. For more information, contact Air France, British Airways, or British Midland (☎ **0870/607-0555;** www.flybritishmidland.com).

There are no hard-and-fast rules about getting the best deals for European flights. Daily papers often carry ads for companies offering cheap flights; highly recommended companies include **Trailfinders** (☎ **020/ 7987-5400**), which sells discounted fares, and **Avro Tours** (☎ **020/ 8715-0000**), which operates charters. In London, you'll find many ticket consolidators (who buy inventories of tickets from airlines and then resell them cheaply) in the neighborhood of Earl's Court and Victoria Station. For your own protection, make sure the company is a member of the IATA, ABTA, or ATOL. **CEEFAX,** a British TV information service received by many private homes and hotels, presents details of package holidays and flights to Europe and beyond.

FROM AUSTRALIA   Getting to Paris from Australia is rather difficult, as Air France has discontinued all its flights to/from the country. However, the French-based airline **A.O.M.** (☎ **01/4979-1000;** triel.info.unicaen.fr/aom) flies twice weekly from Sydney to Paris. **British Airways** (☎ **02/8904-8844;** www.british-airways.com) flies daily from both Sydney and Melbourne to London for a connecting flight to Paris. **Qantas** (☎ **13-12-11;** www. qantas.com) doesn't fly to Paris but goes to London, where plentiful connections exist for the hop across the Channel. Qantas also flies from Auckland to Sydney, where you catch a flight to London.

PARIS AIRPORTS

Paris has two major international airports: **Orly** (☎ **01-49-75-15-15**), 14 kilometers (8^1/$_2$ miles) south of the city, and **Charles de Gaulle,** or **Roissy** (☎ **01-48-62-22-80**), 23 kilometers (14^1/$_4$ miles) northeast. A 106F ($16.95) Air France shuttle operates between the two airports about every 30 minutes, taking 50 to 75 minutes.

CHARLES DE GAULLE AIRPORT (ROISSY)   At Charles de Gaulle, foreign carriers use Aérogare 1 and Air France uses Aérogare 2. From Aérogare 1, you take a moving walkway to the passport checkpoint and the Customs area. The two terminals are linked by a shuttle bus (*navette*).

The free shuttle bus connecting Aérogare 1 with Aérogare 2 also transports passengers to the Roissy rail station, from which fast **RER trains** leave every 15 minutes for such Métro stations as Gare du Nord, Châtelet, Luxembourg, Port Royal, and Denfert-Rochereau. The train fare from Roissy to any point in central Paris is 69F ($11.05) in first class or 49F ($7.85) in second. You can also take an **Air France shuttle bus** to central Paris for 75F ($12). It stops at the Palais des Congrès (Porte Maillot), then continues on to place Charles de Gaulle–Etoile, where underground lines can carry you farther along to any other point. Depending on traffic, the ride takes between 45 and 55 minutes. The shuttle departs about every 12 minutes between 5:40am and 11pm.

Another option, the **Roissybus** (☎ **01-48-04-18-24**), departs from a point near the corner of the rue Scribe and place de l'Opéra every 15 minutes 5:45am to 11pm. The cost for the 45- to 50-minute ride is 48F ($7.70).

Taxis from Roissy into the city will run about 220F ($35.20) on the meter. At night (8pm to 7am), fares are about 40% higher. Long queues of both taxis

---

The New Airport Shuttle

Cheaper than a taxi for one or two people but more expensive than airport buses and trains, the new **Airport Shuttle,** 2 av. Général-Leclerc, 14e (☎ **01-43-21-06-78;** fax 01-43-21-35-67; www.paris-anglo.com/clients/ashuttle.html; e-mail ashuttle@club-internet.fr), will pick you up in a minivan at Charles de Gaulle or Orly and take you to your hotel for 120F ($19) for one person or 89F ($14) per person for parties of two or more. It'll take you out to the airports from your hotel for the same price. The **Paris Airport Service,** BP 41, CEDEX 94431 Chennevières (☎ **01-49-62-78-78;** fax 01-49-62-78-79; e-mail pas@magic.fr), offers a similar service costing 145F ($23) for one person or 180F ($29) for two or more persons from Charles de Gaulle and 115F ($18) for one person or 135F ($22) for two or more persons from Orly. Both companies accept Visa and MasterCard, with 1-day advance reservations required.

and passengers form outside each of the airport's terminals in a surprisingly orderly fashion.

ORLY AIRPORT   Orly has two terminals: Orly Sud (south) for international flights and Orly Ouest (west) for domestic flights. A free shuttle bus links them together.

Air France buses leave exit E of Orly Ouest and from exit F, Platform 5 of Orly Sud every 12 minutes 5:45am to 11pm, heading for Gare des Invalides in central Paris at a cost of 45F ($7.20) one-way. Other buses depart for place Denfert-Rochereau in the south of Paris at a cost of 35F ($5.60).

An alternative method for reaching central Paris involves taking a free shuttle bus that leaves both of Orly's terminals at intervals of about every 15 minutes for the nearby **RER train station** (Pont de Rungis/Aéroport d'Orly), from which RER trains take 30 minutes to reach the city center. A trip to Les Invalides, for example, costs 47F ($7.50).

A **taxi** from Orly to the center of Paris costs about 155F ($24.80) and is higher at night and on weekends. Returning to the airport, **buses** to Orly leave from the Invalides terminal to either Orly Sud or Orly Ouest every 15 minutes, taking about 30 minutes.

Caution: Don't take a meterless taxi from Orly Sud or Orly Ouest—it's much safer (and usually cheaper) to hire a metered cab from the taxi queues, which are under the scrutiny of a police officer.

BY TRAIN

If you're already in Europe, you might decide to travel to Paris by train, especially if you have a Eurailpass. Even if you don't, the cost is relatively low. For example, a round-trip first-class fare between Paris and London is $438 ($298 in second), but you can cut costs to $218 with a second-class 14-day advance purchase (nonrefundable) round-trip fare. Rail passes or individual rail tickets within Europe are available at most travel agencies, at any office of **Rail Europe** (☎ **800/4-EURAIL** in the U.S.; www.raileurope.com) or **Eurostar** (☎ **800/EUROSTAR** in the U.S., 0990/300-003 in London, 01-44-51-06-02 in Paris; www.eurostar.com).

In London, an especially convenient place to buy rail tickets to virtually anywhere is **Wasteels, Ltd.** (☎ **020/7834-6744**), opposite Platform 2 in Victoria Station, London SW1V 1JZ. Occasionally, Wasteels charges a £5 ($8.50) fee for its services, but its info warrants the fee and the company's staff spends a generous amount of time planning itineraries with each client. Some of the most popular passes, including Inter-Rail and EuroYouth, are available only to those under 26 for unlimited second-class travel in 26 European countries.

PARIS TRAIN STATIONS

There are six major train stations in Paris: **Gare d'Austerlitz,** 55 quai d'Austerlitz, 13e (serving the southwest, with trains from the Loire Valley, the Bordeaux country, and the Pyrénées); **Gare de l'Est,** place du 11 Novembre 1918, 10e (serving the east, with trains from Strasbourg, Nancy, Reims, and beyond to Zurich, Basel, Luxembourg, and Austria); **Gare de Lyon,** 20 bd. Diderot, 12e (serving the southeast with trains from the Côte d'Azur, Provence, and beyond to Geneva, Lausanne, and Italy); **Gare Montparnasse,** 17 bd. Vaugirard, 15e (serving the west, with trains from Brittany); **Gare du Nord,** 18 rue de Dunkerque, 15e (serving the north, with trains from Holland, Denmark, Belgium, and northern Germany); and **Gare St-Lazare,** 13 rue d'Amsterdam, 8e (serving the northwest, with trains from Normandy).

For general train information and to make reservations, call ☎ 08-36-35-35-35 daily 7am to 8pm. Buses operate between rail stations. Each of these stations has a Métro stop, making the whole city easily accessible. Taxis are also available at designated stands at every station. Look for the sign that says TÊTE DE STATION. Be alert in train stations, especially at night.

BY BUS

Bus travel to Paris is available from London and many other cities on the Continent. In the early 1990s, the French government established strong incentives for long-haul buses not to drive into the center of Paris, so the arrival/departure point for Europe's largest bus operators, **Eurolines France,** is a 35-minute Métro ride from central Paris, at the terminus of Métro line 3 (Gallieni), in the eastern suburb of Bagnolet. Despite this inconvenience, many people prefer bus travel. Eurolines France is at 28 av. du Général-de-Gaulle, 93541 Bagnolet (☎ 08-36-69-52-52).

Long-haul buses are equipped with toilets and stop at mealtimes for rest and refreshment. The price of a round-trip ticket between Paris and London (a 7-hour trip) is 480F ($76.80) for passengers 26 or over and 430F ($68.80) for passengers under 26.

Because Eurolines doesn't have a U.S.-based sales agent, most people wait until they reach Europe to buy their tickets. Any European travel agent can arrange these purchases. If you're traveling to Paris from London, contact **Eurolines (U.K.) Ltd.,** 52 Grosvenor Gardens, Victoria, London SW1 (☎ 0990/143219), for information or credit-card sales.

BY CAR

Driving in Paris is definitely not recommended. Parking is difficult, traffic is dense, and networks of one-way streets make navigation, even with the best of maps, a problem. If you do drive, remember that Paris is encircled by a ring road called the *périphérique.* Always obtain detailed directions to your destination, including the name of the exit on the périphérique you're looking for (exits aren't numbered). Avoid rush hours. Few hotels, except the luxury ones, have garages, but the staff will usually be able to direct you to one nearby.

The **major highways** into Paris are A1 from the north (Great Britain and Benelux); A13 from Rouen, Normandy, and other points of northwest France; A10 from Bordeaux, the Pyrénées, France's southwest, and Spain; A6 from Lyon, the French Alps, the Riviera, and Italy; and A4 from Metz, Nancy, and Strasbourg in eastern France.

BY FERRY FROM ENGLAND

Despite competition from the Chunnel, services aboard ferries and hydrofoils operate day and night in all seasons, with the exception of last-minute cancellations during fierce storms. Many channel crossings are carefully timed to coincide with the arrival/departure of major trains (especially those between London and Paris); trains let you off a short walk from the piers. Most ferries carry cars, trucks, and massive amounts of freight, but some hydrofoils take passengers only. The major routes include at least 12 trips a day between Dover or Folkestone and Calais or Boulogne. Hovercraft and hydrofoils make the trip from Dover to Calais, the shortest distance across the Channel, in just 40 minutes during good weather; the slower-moving ferries might take several hours, depending on weather conditions and tides. If you're bringing a car, it's important to make reservations, as space below decks is usually crowded. Timetables can vary depending on weather conditions and many other factors.

The leading operator of ferries across the Channel is **P&O Stena Lines** (call BritRail for reservations at ☎ **800/677-8585** in North America or 087/0600-0611 in England). It operates car and passenger ferries between Portsmouth, England, and Cherbourg, France (three departures a day; 4^1/$_4$ hours each way during daylight hours, 7 hours each way at night); between Portsmouth and Le Havre, France (three a day; 5^1/$_2$ hours each way). Most popular are the routes it operates between Dover and Calais, France (25 sailings a day; 75 minutes each way), costing £25 ($42.50) one-way adults or £12 ($20.40) children.

The shortest and by far the most popular route is between Calais and Dover. **Hoverspeed** operates at least 12 hovercraft crossings daily; the trip takes 35 minutes. It also runs a SeaCat (a catamaran propelled by jet engines) that takes slightly longer to make the crossing between Boulogne and Folkestone; the SeaCats depart about four times a day on the 55-minute voyage. For reservations and information, call Hoverspeed (☎ **800/677-8585** for reservations in North America or 0870/5240241 in England). Typical one-way fares are £25 ($42.50) per person.

If you plan to transport a rental car between England and France, check in advance with the rental company about license and insurance requirements and additional drop-off charges. And be aware that many car-rental companies, for insurance reasons, forbid transport of one of their vehicles over the water between England and France. Transport of a car each way begins at 75F ($12).

UNDER THE CHANNEL

One of the great engineering feats of our time, the $15-billion Channel Tunnel (Chunnel) opened in 1994, and the **Eurostar Express** now has daily service from London to both Paris and Brussels. The 31-mile journey takes 35 minutes, though the actual time spent in the Chunnel is only 19 minutes. Stores selling duty-free goods, restaurants, service stations, and bilingual staffs are available to travelers on both sides of the Channel.

Eurostar tickets are available through **Rail Europe** (☎ **800/4-EURAIL;** www.raileurope.com). A one-way first-class nonrefundable ticket costs $179 ($219 if refundable); in second class, a nonrefundable one-way ticket goes for $109 ($149 if refundable). In Great Britain, make reservations for Eurostar at ☎ **0345/484950;** in the United States, call ☎ **800/EUROSTAR.** Chunnel train traffic is roughly competitive with air travel, if you calculate door-to-door travel time. Trains leave from London's Waterloo Station and arrive in Paris at the Gare du Nord.

The tunnel also accommodates passenger cars, charter buses, taxis, and motorcycles, transporting them under the Channel from Folkestone, England, to Calais, France. It operates 24 hours a day, running every 15 minutes during peak travel times and at least once an hour at night. You can buy tickets at the tollbooth at the tunnel's entrance. With **Le Shuttle,** gone are the days of weather-related delays, seasickness, and advance reservations.

Before boarding Le Shuttle, motorists stop at a tollbooth and pass through British and French immigration services at the same time. They then drive onto a half-mile-long train and travel through the tunnel. During the ride, motorists stay in bright air-conditioned carriages, remaining inside their cars or stepping outside to stretch their legs. When the trip is completed, they simply drive off. Total travel time is about an hour. Once on French soil, British drivers must remember to drive on the right-hand side of the road.

For a look at package deals with the Chunnel, turn to "A Weekend in London," in chapter 10.

BY PACKAGE TOUR

Package tours aren't the same thing as escorted tours. They're simply a way to buy airfare and accommodations at the same time. For popular destinations like Paris, they're a smart way to go because they save you a lot of money. In many cases, a package that includes airfare, hotel, and transportation to/from the airport will cost you less than just the hotel alone would have, had you booked it yourself. That's because packages are sold in bulk to tour operators, who resell them to the public at a cost that drastically undercuts standard rates.

Packages, however, vary widely. Some offer a better class of hotels than others. Some offer the same hotels for lower prices. Some offer flights on scheduled airlines, while others book charters. In some packages, your choice of accommodations and travel days may be limited. Some packages let you choose between escorted vacations and independent vacations; others will allow you to add on just a few excursions or escorted day trips (also at lower prices than you could locate on your own) without booking an entirely escorted tour. Each destination usually has one or two packagers that are cheaper than the rest because they buy in even greater bulk. If you spend the time to shop around, you'll save in the long run.

FINDING A PACKAGE DEAL   The best place to start your search is the travel section of your local Sunday newspaper. Also check the ads in the back of national travel magazines like *Travel & Leisure, National Geographic Traveler,* and *Condé Nast Traveler.*

Liberty Travel (☎ **888/271-1584** to be connected with the agent closest to you; www.libertytravel.com), one of the biggest packagers in the Northeast, often runs a full-page ad in the Sunday papers. You won't get much in the way of service, but you will get a good deal. **American Express Vacations** (☎ **800/241-1700;** www.americanexpress.com) is another option. Check out its **Last Minute Travel Bargains** site, offered in conjunction with **Continental Airlines** (www6.americanexpress.com/travel/lastminutetravel/default.asp), with deeply discounted vacation packages and reduced airline fares that differ from the E-savers bargains Continental e-mails weekly to subscribers. **Northwest Airlines** (www.nwa.com) offers a similar service. Posted on Northwest's Web site every Wednesday, its **Cyber Saver Bargain Alerts** offer special hotel rates, package deals, and discounted airline fares.

Another good resource is the airlines themselves, which often package their flights together with accommodations. Fly-by-night packagers are uncommon but do exist; when you buy your package through the airline, however, you can be pretty sure the company will still be in business when your departure date arrives. Among the airline packagers, your options are **American Airlines FlyAway Vacations** (☎ **800/321-2121;** www.aa.com), **Delta Dream Vacations** (☎ **800/872-7786;** www.delta-air.com), and **US Airways Vacations** (☎ **800/455-0123;** www.usairways.com). Delta Dream Vacations offers a full package called Jolie France, lasting 10 nights and costing $3,718 to $4,178 for two, taking in not only Paris but also some of France's regional highlights, like Tours, Bordeaux, Carcassonne, Nice, Nìmes, and Dijon. All hotels, tours, and breakfasts are included, plus four dinners.

The **French Experience,** 370 Lexington Ave., Room 812, New York, NY 10017 (☎ **212/986-1115;** fax 212/986-3808; www.frenchexperience.com; e-mail info@frenchexperience.com), offers inexpensive tickets to Paris on most scheduled airlines and arranges tours and stays in various types and categories of country inns, hotels, private château, and B&Bs. In addition, it takes reservations for about 30 small hotels in Paris and arranges short-term apartment rentals in the city or farmhouse rentals in the countryside and offers all-inclusive packages in Paris as well as prearranged package tours of various regions of France. Any tour can be adapted to suit individual needs.

Planning Your Trip: An Online Directory

by Lynne Bairstow

Lynne Bairstow is the coauthor of *Frommer's Mexico* and the editorial director of *e-com* magazine.

Day by day, the Internet becomes more integrated into our lives—including the way we plan and book our travel. By early 2000, one in every ten trips was being booked online, a trend that's sure to accelerate.

The Internet not only provides a wealth of destination information but also gives you the chance to compare experiences with fellow travelers, ask experts for pretrip advice, seek out discounted fares once accessible only to travel industry insiders, and stay in touch via e-mail while you're away. The instant communication and storehouse of information have revolutionized the way travel is researched, reserved, and realized.

This Online Directory will help you take better advantage of the travel planning information available online, and it's best used in conjunction with this book. Part 1 lists general Internet resources that can make any trip easier, such as sites for obtaining the best possible prices on airline tickets. In Part 2 you'll find some top online guides for Paris, organized by category.

Keep in mind this isn't a comprehensive list but a discriminating selection to get you started. Recognition is given to sites based on their content value and ease of use and aren't paid for—unlike some Web-site rankings, which are based on payment. Finally, remember this is a press-time snapshot of leading Web sites—some undoubtedly will have evolved, changed, or moved by the time you read this.

1 Top Travel-Planning Web Sites

While the Internet was once a conglomerate of sites for researching places to visit, several key companies have emerged that offer comprehensive travel planning and booking. In addition to the Frommer's Online (see box, above), we list the other top online travel agencies below, along with some more specialized services.

WHY BOOK ONLINE?

Online agencies have come a long way over the past few years, now providing tips for finding the best fare and giving suggested dates or times to travel that yield the lowest price if your plans are flexible. Other sites even allow you to establish the price you're willing to pay,

What You'll Find at the Frommer's Site

We highly recommend **Arthur Frommer's Budget Travel Online**
(**www.frommers.com**) as an excellent travel planning resource. Of
course, we're a little biased, but you'll find indispensable travel tips,
reviews, monthly vacation giveaways, and online booking. Among the
site's most popular features is the regular "Ask the Expert" bulletin
boards, which feature one of the Frommer's authors answering your questions via online postings.

Subscribe to Arthur Frommer's Daily Newsletter (**www.frommers.com/
newsletters**) to receive the latest travel bargains and inside travel secrets in
your e-mailbox every day. You'll read daily headlines and articles from the
dean of travel himself, highlighting last-minute deals on airfares, accommodations, cruises, and package vacations. You'll also find great travel
advice by checking our Tip of the Day or Hot Spot of the Month.

Search our Destinations archive (**www.frommers.com/destinations**) of
more than 200 domestic and international destinations for great places to
stay, tips for traveling there, and what to do while you're there. Once you've
researched your trip, the online reservation system (**www.frommers.
com/booktravelnow**) takes you to Frommer's favorite sites for booking
your vacation at affordable prices.

and they check the airlines' willingness to accept it. However, in some cases,
these sites may not always yield the best price. Unlike a travel agent, for example, they may not have access to charter flights offered by wholesalers.

Online booking sites aren't the only places to reserve airline tickets—all
major airlines have their own Web sites and often offer incentives—bonus
frequent-flyer miles or net-only discounts, for example—when you buy online
or buy an e-ticket.

The new trend is toward conglomerated booking sites. By mid-2000, a con-
sortium of U.S. and European airlines are planning to launch an as-yet
unnamed Web site that will offer fares lower than those available through
travel agents. United, Delta, Northwest, and Continental have initiated this
effort, based on their success at selling airline seats at their own online sites.

The best of the travel planning sites are now highly personalized; they store
your seating preferences, meal preferences, tentative itineraries, and credit card
information, allowing you to plan trips or check agendas quickly.

In many cases, booking your trip online can be better than working with a
travel agent. It gives you the widest variety of choices, control, and the 24-hour
convenience of planning your trip when you choose. All you need is some
time—and often a little patience—and you're likely to find the fun of online
travel research will greatly enhance your trip.

WHO SHOULD BOOK ONLINE?

Online booking is best for travelers who want to know as much as possible
about their options, those who have flexibility in their travel dates and are
looking for the best price, and bargain hunters driven by a good value who are
open-minded about where they travel.

One of the biggest successes in online travel for both passengers and airlines
is the offer of last-minute specials, such as American Airlines' weekend deals or

More people still look online than book online, partly due to fear of putting their credit card numbers out on the Net. Secure encryption and increasing experience buying online have removed this fear for most travelers. In some cases, however, it's simply easier to buy from a local travel agent who can deliver your tickets to your door (especially if your travel is last minute or you have special requests). You can find a flight online and then book it by calling a toll-free number or contacting your travel agent, though this is somewhat less efficient. To be sure you're in secure mode when you book online, look for a little icon of a key (in Netscape) or a padlock (in Internet Explorer) at the bottom of your Web browser.

other Internet-only fares you must purchase online. Another advantage is that you can cash in on incentives for booking online, such as rebates or bonus frequent-flyer miles.

Business and other frequent travelers also have found numerous benefits in online booking, as the advances in mobile technology provide them with the ability to check flight status, change plans, or get specific directions from handheld computing devices, mobile phones, and pagers. Some sites will even e-mail or page passengers if their flights are delayed.

Online booking is increasingly able to accommodate complex itineraries, even for international travel. The pace of evolution on the Net is rapid, so you'll probably find additional features and advancements by the time you visit these sites. What the future holds for online travelers is ever-increasing personalization, customization, and reaching out to you.

TRAVEL PLANNING & BOOKING SITES

Below are listings for sites for planning and booking travel. The sites offer domestic and international flight, hotel, and rental-car bookings, plus news, destination information, and deals on cruises and vacation packages. Free (one-time) registration is required for booking.

✪ Travelocity (incorporates Preview Travel). **www.travelocity.com; www.previewtravel.com; www.frommers.travelocity.com**

Travelocity is Frommer's online travel planning/booking partner. Travelocity uses the SABRE system to offer reservations and tickets for more than 400 airlines, plus reservations and purchase capabilities for more than 45,000 hotels and 50 car-rental companies. An exclusive feature of the SABRE system is its **Low Fare Search Engine,** which automatically searches for the three lowest-priced itineraries based on a traveler's criteria. Last-minute deals and consolidator fares are included in the search. If you book with Travelocity, you can select specific seats for your flights with online seat maps and also view diagrams of the most popular commercial aircraft. Its hotel finder provides street-level location maps and photos of selected hotels. With the **Fare Watcher** e-mail feature, you can select up to five routes and receive e-mail notices when the fare changes by $25 or more.

Travelocity's **Destination Guide** includes updated information on some 260 destinations worldwide—supplied by Frommer's.

Note to AOL Users: You can book flights, hotels, rental cars, and cruises on AOL at keyword: Travel. The booking software is provided by Travelocity/ Preview Travel and is similar to the Internet site. Use the AOL "Travelers Advantage" program to earn a 5% rebate on flights, hotel rooms, and car rentals.

Expedia. expedia.com

Expedia is Travelocity's major competitor. It offers several ways of obtaining the best possible fares: **Flight Price Matcher** service allows your preferred airline to match an available fare with a competitor; a comprehensive **Fare Compare** area shows the differences in fare categories and airlines; and **Fare Calendar** helps you plan your trip around the best possible fares. Its main limitation is that like many online databases, Expedia focuses on the major airlines and hotel chains, so don't expect to find too many budget airlines or one-of-a-kind B&Bs here.

TRIP.com. www.trip.com

TRIP.com began as a site geared toward business travelers, but its innovative features and highly personalized approach have broadened its appeal to leisure travelers as well. It is the leading travel site for those using mobile devices to access Internet travel information.

TRIP.com includes a trip-planning function that provides the average and lowest fare for the route requested, in addition to the current available fare. An on-site "newsstand" features breaking news on airfare sales and other travel specials. Among its most popular features are Flight TRACKER and intelliTRIP. **Flight TRACKER** allows users to track any commercial flight en route to its destination anywhere in the United States., while accessing real-time FAA-based flight monitoring data. **intelliTRIP** is a travel search tool that allows users to identify the best airline, hotel, and rental-car rates in less than 90 seconds.

In addition, the site offers e-mail notification of flight delays, plus city resource guides, currency converters, and a weekly e-mail newsletter of fare updates, travel tips, and traveler forums.

Yahoo! Travel. www.travel.yahoo.com

Yahoo! is currently the most popular of the Internet information portals, and its travel site is a comprehensive mix of online booking, daily travel news, and destination information. The **Best Fares** area offers what it promises, plus provides feedback on refining your search if you have flexibility in travel dates or times. There is also an active section of Message Boards for discussions on travel in general and specific destinations.

SPECIALTY TRAVEL SITES

Although the sites listed above provide the most comprehensive services, some travelers have specialized needs that are best met by a site catering specifically to them.

For adventure travelers, **iExplore** (**www.iexplore.com**) is a great source for information and booking adventure and experiential travel, as well as related services and products. The site combines the secure Internet booking functions with hands-on expertise and 24-hour live customer support by seasoned adventure travelers, for those interested in trips off the beaten path. The company is a supporting member of the Ecotourism Society and is committed to environmentally responsible travel worldwide.

Another excellent site for adventure travelers is **Away.com** (**www.away. com**), which features unique vacations for challenging the body, mind, and spirit. Trips may include cycling in the Loire Valley, taking an African safari, or assisting in the excavation of a Mayan ruin. For those without the time for such an extended exotic trip, offbeat weekend getaways are also available. Services include a customer service center staffed with experts to answer calls and e-mails, plus a network of over 1,000 prescreened tour operators. Trips are categorized by cultural, adventure, and green travel. Away.com also offers a Daily Escape e-mail newsletter.

Airline Web Sites

Below are the Web sites for the major airlines serving Paris. These sites offer schedules and flight booking, and most have pages where you can sign up for e-mail alerts for weekend deals and other late-breaking bargains.

Aer Lingus. www.aerlingus.ie

Air Canada. www.aircanada.ca

Air France. www.airfrance.com

American Airlines. www.aa.com

British Airways. www.british-airways.com

Continental Airlines. www.flycontinental.com

Delta. www.delta-air.com

Qantas. www.qantas.com

TWA. www.twa.com

United Airlines. www.ual.com

US Airways. www.usairways.com

GORP (Great Outdoor Recreation Pages; **www.gorp.com**) has been a standard for adventure travelers since its founding in 1995 by outdoor enthusiasts Diane and Bill Greer. Tapping their own experiences, they created this Web site that offers the unique travel destinations and encourages active participation by fellow GORP visitors through the sophisticated menu of online forums, contests, and discussions.

For travelers who prefer more unique accommodations, **InnSite** (**www.innsite.com**) offers listings for inns and B&Bs in all U.S. states and dozens of countries around the globe. Find an inn at your destination, have a look at images of the rooms, check prices and availability, and then send e-mail to the innkeeper if you have further questions. This is an extensive directory of bed-and-breakfast inns but includes listings only if the proprietors submitted one (*Note:* It's free to get an inn listed). The descriptions are written by the innkeepers, and many listings link to the inn's own Web sites, where you can find more information and images.

Another good resource for mostly one-of-a-kind places in the United Sates and abroad is **Places to Stay** (**www.placestostay.com**), which focuses on resort accommodations.

"Have Kids, Still Travel!" is the motto of the **Family Travel Forum** (FTF; **www.familytravelforum.com**), a site dedicated to the ideals, promotion, and support of travel with children. FTF is supported by memberships, which are available in flexible prices from a $2.95 monthly fee to a heftier annual fee for more comprehensive services. Since no advertising is accepted, FTF provides its members with honest, unbiased information, informed advice, and practical tips designed to make traveling with children a healthier, safer, hassle-free experience, not to mention a better value.

TOP VACATION PACKAGE SITES

Both **Expedia** and **Travelocity** (see above) offer excellent selections and searches for complete vacation packages. Travelers can search by destination and desired dates coupled with how much they're willing to spend. Travelocity has a valuable

"Cruise Critic" function, to help would-be cruisers obtain first-hand accounts of the quality and details of a cruise from recent passengers.

Travel wholesalers, like **Apple Vacations** (**www.applevacations.com**) and **Funjet** (**www.funjet.com**) are also good starting points, but they still require that the final booking be handled through a travel agent.

As travel agents tend to be more expert at sorting through the values in vacation packages, you might find **Vacation.com** (**www.vacation.com**) helpful in previewing packages and finding an appropriate agent to help you book the deal. This site represents a nationwide network of 9,800 local travel agencies that specialize in finding the best values in cruises, vacation packages, tours, and other leisure travel services. To find a Vacation.com member agency, enter your Zip code and the Vacation.com Agency Finder will locate a nearby office.

LAST-MINUTE DEALS & OTHER ONLINE BARGAINS

There's nothing airlines hate more than flying with lots of empty seats. The Net has enabled airlines to offer last-minute bargains to entice travelers to fill those seats. Most of these are announced on Tuesday or Wednesday and are valid for travel the following weekend, but some can be booked weeks or months in advance. You can sign up for weekly e-mail alerts at airlines' sites (for their Web sites, see "Airline Web Sites," above) or check sites that compile lists of these bargains, such as **Smarter Living** or **WebFlyer** (see below). To make it easier, visit a site that'll round up all the deals and send them in one convenient weekly e-mail. But last-minute deals aren't the only online bargains; other sites can help you find value even if you haven't waited until the eleventh hour. Increasingly popular are services that let you name the price you're willing to pay for an air seat or vacation package and travel auction sites.

❂ 1travel.com. www.1travel.com
Here you'll find deals on domestic and international flights, cruises, hotels, and all-inclusive resorts like Club Med. 1travel.com's **Saving Alert** compiles last-minute air deals so you don't have to scroll through multiple e-mail alerts. A feature called "Drive a little using low-fare airlines" helps map out strategies for using alternate airports to find lower fares. And **Farebeater** searches a database that includes published fares, consolidator bargains, and special deals exclusive to 1travel.com. *Note:* The travel agencies listed by 1travel.com have paid for placement.

Cheap Tickets. www.cheaptickets.com
Cheap Tickets has exclusive deals that aren't available through more mainstream channels. One caveat about the Cheap Tickets site is that it'll offer fare quotes for a route and later show this fare isn't valid for your dates of travel— most other Web sites, such as Expedia, consider your dates of travel before showing what fares are available. Despite its problems, Cheap Tickets can be worth the effort because its fares can be lower than those offered by its competitors.

Bid for Travel. www.bidfortravel.com
Bid for Travel is another of the travel auction sites, similar to Priceline (see below), which are growing in popularity. In addition to airfares, Internet users can place a bid for vacation packages and hotels.

Go4less.com. www.go4less.com
Specializing in last-minute cruise and package deals, Go4less has some excellent offers. The **Hot Deals** section gives an alphabetical listing by destination of super discounted packages.

While most people learn about last-minute weekend deals from e-mail dispatches, it can be best to find out precisely when these deals become available. Because the deals are limited, they can vanish within hours—sometimes even minutes—so it pays to log on as soon as they're available. Check the pages devoted to these deals on airlines' Web pages to get the info. An example: Southwest's specials are posted at 12:01am Tuesdays (Central time). So if you're looking for a cheap flight, stay up late and check Southwest's site to grab the best new deals.

LastMinuteTravel.com. www.lastminutetravel.com
Suppliers with excess inventory come to this online agency to distribute unsold airline seats, hotel rooms, cruises, and vacation packages. It's got great deals, but you have to put up with an excess of advertisements and slow-loading graphics.

Moment's Notice. www.moments-notice.com
As the name suggests, Moment's Notice specializes in last-minute vacation and cruise deals. You can browse for free, but if you want to purchase a trip you have to join Moment's Notice, which costs $25. Go to **World Wide Hot Deals** for a complete list of special deals in international destinations.

✪ **Priceline.com. travel.priceline.com**
Even people who aren't familiar with many Web sites have heard about Priceline.com. Launched in 1998 with a $10-million ad campaign featuring William Shatner, Priceline lets you "name your price" for domestic and international airline tickets and hotel rooms. In other words, you select a route and dates, guarantee with a credit card, and make a bid for what you're willing to pay. If one of the airlines in Priceline's database has a fare lower than your bid, your credit card will automatically be charged for a ticket.

But you can't say when you want to fly—you have to accept any flight leaving between 6am and 10pm on the dates you selected, and you may have to make a stopover. No frequent-flyer miles are awarded, and tickets are nonrefundable and can't be exchanged for another flight. So if your plans change, you're out of luck. Priceline can be good for travelers who have to take off on short notice (and thus unable to qualify for advance-purchase discounts). But be sure to shop around first, because if you overbid, you'll be required to purchase the ticket—and Priceline will pocket the difference between what it paid for the ticket and what you bid.

Priceline says that over 35% of all reasonable offers for domestic flights are being filled on the first try, with much higher fill rates on popular routes (New York to San Francisco, for example). They define "reasonable" as not more than 30% below the lowest generally available advance-purchase fare for the same route.

Smarter Living. www.smarterliving.com
Best known for its e-mail dispatch of weekend deals on 20 airlines, Smarter Living also keeps you posted about last-minute bargains on everything from Windjammer Cruises to flights to Iceland.

SkyAuction.com. www.skyauction.com
This auction site has categories for airfare, travel deals, hotels, and much more.

Travelzoo.com. www.travelzoo.com
At this Internet portal, over 150 travel companies post special deals. It features a Top 20 list of the best deals on the site, selected by its editorial staff each

Online Directory

Wednesday night. This list is also available via an e-mailing list, free to those who sign up.

WebFlyer. www.webflyer.com
WebFlyer is a comprehensive online resource for frequent flyers and also has an excellent listing of last-minute air deals. Click on **Deal Watch** for a round-up of weekend deals on flights, hotels, and rental cars from domestic and international suppliers.

ONLINE TRAVELER'S TOOLBOX

Veteran travelers usually carry some essential items to make their trips easier. The following is a selection of online tools to smooth your journey.

ATM Locator: Visa. www.visa.com/pd/atm/
ATM Locator: MasterCard. www.mastercard.com/atm
Use these sites to find ATMs in hundreds of cities in the United States and around the world. Both include maps for some locations and both list airport ATM locations, some with maps. *Tip:* You'll usually get a better exchange rate using ATMs than exchanging traveler's checks at banks, but check in advance to see what kind of fees your bank will assess for using an overseas ATM.

CDC Travel Information. www.cdc.gov/travel/index.htm
Health advisories and recommendations for inoculations from the U.S. Centers for Disease Control and Prevention. The CDC site is good for an overview, but it's best to consult your personal physician to get the latest information on required vaccinations or other health precautions.

✪ Foreign Languages for Travelers. www.travlang.com
Here you can learn basic terms in more than 70 languages and click on any underlined phrase to hear what it sounds like. (*Note:* Free audio software and speakers are required.) It also offers hotel and airline finders with excellent prices and a simple system to get the listings you're looking for.

Intellicast. www.intellicast.com
Here you'll find weather forecasts for all 50 states and cities around the world. Note that temperatures are in Celsius for many international destinations, so don't think you'll need that winter coat for your next trip to Athens.

✪ Mapquest. www.mapquest.com
The best of the mapping sites lets you choose a specific address or destination, and in seconds it'll return a map and detailed directions. It really is easier

Online Directory

Travel Discussion Sites

One of the best sources of travel information is word-of-mouth from someone who has just been there. Internet discussion groups are offering an unprecedented way for travelers around the globe to connect and share experiences. The **Frommer's Online** site (**www.frommers.com**) offers these message boards and also areas where you can pose questions to the guidebook writers themselves in the section "Ask the Expert." **Yahoo! Travel, Expedia,** and **Travelocity** are other good sources of online travel discussion groups.

The granddaddy of specialized discussions on particular topics, is **Usenet,** a collection of over 50,000 newsgroups. You'll find a comprehensive listing at **Deja News (www.dejanews.com/usenet/)** or at **www.liszt.com.**

than calling, asking, and writing down directions. The site also links to special travel deals and helpful sites.

Net Cafe Guide. www.netcafeguide.com/mapindex.htm
Stop here to locate Internet cafes at hundreds of locations around the globe. Catch up on your e-mail, log on to the Web, and stay in touch with the home front, usually for just a few dollars per hour.

Tourism Offices Worldwide Directory. www.towd.com
This is an extensive listing of tourism offices, some with links to these offices' Web sites.

Travelers' Tales. www.travelerstales.com
Considered the best in compilations of travel literature, Travelers' Tales are an award-winning series of books grouped by destination (Mexico, Italy, France, China.) or by theme (Love & Romance, The Ultimate Journey, Women in the Wild, The Adventure of Food). It's a new kind of travel book that offers a description of a place or type of journey through the experiences of many travelers. It makes for a perfect traveling companion.

The Travelite FAQ. www.travelite.org
Here you'll find tips on packing light, choosing luggage, and selecting appropriate travel wear—helpful if you always tend to pack too much or are a compulsive list maker.

Universal Currency Converter. www.xe.net/currency
Come here to see what your dollar or pound is worth in more than a hundred other countries.

U.S. Customs Service Traveler Information. www.customs.ustreas.gov/travel/index.htm
Wondering what you're allowed to bring in to the United States? Check at this thorough site, which includes maximum allowance and duty fees.

U.S. State Department Travel Warnings. travel.state.gov/travel_warnings.html
You'll find reports on places where health concerns or unrest might threaten U.S. travelers. Keep in mind that these warnings can be somewhat dated and conservative. You can also sign up to receive State Department briefings via e-mail.

Web Travel Secrets. www.web-travel-secrets.com
If this list leaves you yearning for more travel-oriented sites, Web Travel Secrets offers one of the best compilations around. One section offers advice and tips on how to find the lowest prices for airlines, hotels, and cruises. The other section provides a comprehensive listing of Web travel links for airfare deals, airlines, booking engines, cars, cruise lines, discount travel and best deals, general travel resources, hotels and hotel discounters, search engines, and travel magazines and newsletters.

2 Top Web Sites for Paris

Information updated by Cheryl Pientka

Cheryl Pientka is the coauthor of *Frommer's Paris from $70 a Day* and *France For Dummies* and the author of *Paris For Dummies*.

Most of the following sites give you the option of using English or French. Though many first come up in French, follow the icons for English versions. If it's not evident at first, scroll down to find an American or a British flag.

Checking E-mail at Internet Cafes

Until a few years ago, most travelers who checked their e-mail while traveling carried a laptop—an expensive and often technologically problematic option. Thankfully, Web-based free e-mail programs have made it much easier to check your mail.

Just open an account at any one of the numerous "freemail" providers—the original leaders continue to be **Hotmail** (hotmail.com), **Excite** (www.excite.com), and **Yahoo! Mail** (mail.yahoo.com), though many are available. AOL users should check out **AOL Netmail,** and USA.NET (**www.usa.net**) comes highly recommended for functionality and security. You can find hints, tips, and a mile-long list of freemail providers at **www.emailaddresses.com**. Then all you'll need to check your mail is a Web connection, easily available at Net cafes and copy shops around the world. After logging on, just point the browser to your freemail's Internet address, enter your username and password, and you'll have access to your mail. From these sites, you can download all your e-mail—even from office accounts—or your local or national Internet Service Provider address. There'll be a section generally called "check other mail" that allows you to add the names of other e-mail servers.

The downside is that most Web-based e-mail sites allow a maximum of only 3MB capacity per mail account, which can fill up quickly. Also, message sending and receiving isn't immediate; some messages may be delayed by several hours or even days.

Internet cafes have become ubiquitous, so for a few dollars an hour you'll be able to check your mail and send messages from virtually anywhere in the world. Interestingly, these cafes tend to be more common in very remote areas, where they may offer the best form of access for an entire community, especially if phone lines are difficult to obtain.

The following Paris Web bars, listed by arrondissement, charge modest fees (also see "Internet Access" under "Fast Facts: Paris" in chapter 3): **Cristal Palace,** 43 bd. de Sébastopol, 1er (☎ **01-42-36-22-22;** Métro: Châtelet); **Cybercafé de Paris,** 11 and 15 rue des Halles, 1er (☎ **01-42-21-11-11;** Métro: Châtelet); **Cyberia,** in the Centre Pompidou, Place Georges-Pompidou, 4e (☎ **01-44-54-53-49;** Métro: Rambuteau or Hôtel de Ville); **Clickside,** 14 rue Domat, 5e (☎ **01-56-81-03-00;** Métro: St-Michel or Maubert Mutualité); **Village Web,** 18 rue de la Bucherie, 5e (☎ **01-44-07-20-15;.** Métro: St-Michel); **Café Orbital,** 13 rue de Médicis, 6e (☎ **01-43-25-76-77;** Métro: Odéon); **Cyber Cube,** 5 rue Mignon, 6e (☎ **01-53-10-30-50;** Métro: Odéon or St-Michel); **Station Internet Rive Gauche,** 37 rue du Cherche Midi, 6e (☎ **01-40-51-17-57;** Métro: Rennes or Vanneau); **Virgin Megastore,** 52 av. des Champs-Elysées, 8e (☎ **01-49-53-50-00;** Métro: Palais Royal–Musée du Louvre); **The Cyberzen @ Café,** 85 rue Amelot, 11e (☎ **01-53-36-76-13;** Métro: St-Sébastien Froissart); **Cyber Cube,** 12 rue Daval, 11e (☎ **01-49-29-67-67;** Métro: Bastille); **High Tech Café,** 66 bd. de Montparnasse, 14e (☎ **01-45-38-67-61;** Métro: Vavin).

CITY GUIDES

Champs Elysees. www.champselysees.org
Click around the neighborhood map for shops, restaurants, and movies in the neighborhood. If you prefer to skip the crowds, check out the 360-degree views of the area on the site. Poor English, heavy on advertising.

✪ **Jack's Inimitable Guide to Paris. www. i_am/jack.travel/htmArticlesParis/ ParisHtml/**
Jack has put together dozens of walking tours, organized by arrondissement, where he combines history with opinions and vivid descriptions of the streets. Print out some of the pages and walk with Jack into museums and attractions, around the Latin Quarter, and through other neighborhoods. His Secret and Unexpected Paris section leads you to places he claims are tough to find. Though his English isn't the best, his knowledge of the subject is.

Paris.Com. www.paris.com
You'll find no surprises here, just the usual tourist sites. The restaurants are those listed in *Le Gourmet Parisien,* a guide distributed free in the restaurants that pay to advertise. The lodging section, consisting of uncritical reviews accompanying photos of the rooms, is this site's strength.

Paris Digest. www.parisdigest.com
This independent site contains articles that link you to restaurants, some hotels, museums, monuments, parks, and activities. It includes history about the city and tips for getting around. Surprisingly few restaurants are listed, and they're categorized by their decor or good views.

Paris France Guide. www.parisfranceguide.com
Brought to you by the publisher of such magazines as *Living in France, Study in France,* and *What's On in France,* this site has lots of useful information about Paris, such as current articles and listings on nightlife, restaurants, events, theater, and music.

Paris Free Voice/thinkparis.com. parisvoice.com or thinkparis.com
The online version of the monthly *Paris Voice* is hip and opinionated for "English-speaking Parisians." The calendar of events includes music, movies, and performance art listings. There are also restaurant reviews and guides like "Where to Kiss in Paris."

✪ **Paris Pages. www.paris.org**
There's so much information on this site it sometimes takes a while to download. The lodging reviews are organized by area and the monuments that stand nearby. The city guide includes an event calendar, shop listings, a map of attractions with details about each, and photo tours. Some sections—like French Classes Around the World—won't help you prepare for your trip but assure how widespread is this site's audience.

Paris Tourist Office. www.paris-touristoffice.com
Here you'll find information on city events arranged by week, month, favorites, and year, plus the closest Métro stops for museums, lodging, restaurants, and nightlife. Rent a scooter through their list of transportation services. Tour parks and gardens and discover Paris's trendy arrondissements.

Smartweb: Paris. www.smartweb.fr/paris
This city guide shows the big attractions, such as the Louvre and Eiffel Tower, and includes history, photos, admission fees, and hours. Navigate the shopping and gallery listings organized by district and preview the airports' terminals. Click on maps to get the weather and subway information. You can even see

Paris, Je t'Adore

✪ **Bonjour Paris** (www.bparis.com; AOL Keyword: Bonjour; CompuServe: Go: Paris) is one of the most comprehensive and fun sites about life in Paris, written from an American expatriate point of view. Nowhere else will you find reviews of new restaurants, a plea for contributions to help repair the Maison de Balzac (badly damaged in the 1999 Christmas storm), and articles on bicycle fever, the French love affair, and inline skating on places des Vosges coexisting happily with guides to French cheese and wine and reviews of recent French films. The French news of the week is analyzed by a Pulitzer Prize–nominated writer. Hotel recommendations and travel tips abound. Message boards debate cultural differences and offer readers restaurant, food, and wine picks. In the numerous chat sessions you can learn to speak French better, get recipes, or talk about French literature, among other subjects. Suzy Gershman, author of Frommer's "Born to Shop" series, relates the latest trends in fashion and travel and her favorite finds.

In 1996, some American expat journalists living in Paris decided to start a unique online guide to the city that had captured their hearts by writing articles on topics that concerned or amused them; they launched Bonjour Paris on America Online and drew an excellent response. Two years later, Karen Fawcett, one of the journalists, bought it and commissioned her son, Miles, the founder of a company developing Web sites for nonprofit organizations, to create a user-friendly interface. Bonjour Paris launched on the Web in January 1999. Karen is now the site's president, monitoring it and managing to answer almost all the hundreds of reader e-mails she receives each day. She's slowly broadening Bonjour Paris with more reportage from outside the capital.

photos of the graffiti dedicated to Princess Diana on the torch and wall surrounding place de l'Alma, above the underpass where Diana was killed in a car accident August 31, 1997.

MAJOR ATTRACTIONS

Catacombs of Paris. www.multimania.com/houze
Here you can read the fascinating history of Paris's underground cemetery and even look at creepy photos.

Château de Versailles. www.chateauversailles.com
This handy site is full of information on Louis XIV, the Sun King, and his humble abode. Read the history and see pictures of the grounds and the works of art that hang from the palace walls. *Note:* This site is visited often; you may get a "server too busy" message.

Disneyland Paris. www.disneylandparis.com
You can reserve your hotel online or get an idea of the Disneyland Paris travel package that fits your needs. It includes videos that let you preview attractions in the park's sections: Fantasyland, Frontierland, Discoveryland, Adventureland, and Main Street USA. (Download the free QuickTime software to see them.) The dining and lodging guides describe each establishment with photos and more QuickTime videos. There's also a section where kids can "meet" Disney characters and print out games.

Eiffel Tower. www.tour-eiffel.fr
Here you can read the history of the tower and download a free version of QuickTime VR software to get simulated views from the top.

✪ **Giverny & Vernon. giverny.org**
If you plan to visit the region forever associated with Claude Monet, you'll find loads of useful travel and transportation information here. Run down details on the area's castles, museums, and places of archaeological interest, as well as the artist's famous gardens.

Louvre Museum Official Website. www.louvre.fr
After checking out their descriptions of the guided tours, permanent collections, and temporary exhibits, download the free QuickTime VR software to take a virtual stroll through the museum. *Mona Lisa* awaits your visit. The site also links you to two sites where you can buy tickets online.

Musée de la Musique. www.cite-musique.fr
The museum exhibits over 4,500 musical instruments from the Renaissance to the present. Hours, admission, and contact information make up only part of the site. You can also peruse photos of the Cité de la Musique, in which the museum is located, as well as of pianos, harps, and other instruments in the museum's collections, get a schedule of performances in the concert hall, and buy tickets online.

Musée d'Orsay. www.musee-orsay.fr
Come here to see some of the sculpture, architecture, painting, and photography collections accompanied by history and descriptions of the pieces and artists. Get practical information about events, guided tours, hours, admission, and directions. Also described is the history of the museum itself, a former train station.

Musée National de la Legion d'Honneur. www.musee-legion-honneur.com
The Legion of Honor Museum depicts the history of France's highest honor from the Crusades to the present. Accompanied by brief descriptions, a virtual photo tour shows you around Hôtel de Salm, where the collections are housed, and the museum's collections. Though it's tough to find, look for the Useful Information section that outlines hours, admission, and directions.

Musée Rodin. www.musee-rodin.fr
Here you can preview the grounds and collections of Rodin's sculptures, paintings, engravings, photos, and sketches. Read a bio of the artist, history of the museum, and details of the garden. The operating hours, admission, directions, and address will help get you there. Print out maps of the displays, so you know where you're going once you arrive.

Paris Museum Pass. www.intermusees.com
Don't care about the temporary exhibits and just want to see classic art? This budget pass gets you into permanent collections around the city. Find out where it's accepted and how to get it.

Pompidou Centre. www.cnac-gp.fr
A huge amount of information and pictures of the Pompidou's collections are posted here. You might have to look hard for the English-language icon. Art buffs will have a field day searching through the museum's catalog of artwork in the Documentation section. Also presented are new media exhibits in the Works On-Line section.

DINING GUIDES

Pubs and Bars in Paris. www.net-europa.com/gap
About 200 Parisian bars are organized by and given points for best ambience, worst ambience, cheapest, most expensive, and best for late-night drinks. The editors have been describing and reviewing pubs and bars since 1996.

Paris Inside Out. www.parisanglo.com/guide/entertainment/ eatdrink/resto_value.html
This guide for Americans and British living abroad by a book publisher offers an excellent dining section with reviews of restaurants and bars.

Paris Zagat. www.zagat.com
You must register (it's free) to access this site. Choose Paris from the pull-down menu and see what other travelers have to say about the local cuisine and service. At press time, Zagat announced it would be receiving $31 million in equity financing from investors to help it expand on the Internet.

TRANSPORTATION

Aéroports de Paris. www.paris-airports.com
Click on the small American flag on the home page for an English version of this site. For the Charles de Gaulle and Orly airports, find listings of terminal maps, parking, airlines, boutiques, hotels, restaurants, and car-rental agencies. The accessibility information for travelers with disabilities might help out on landing.

RATP. www.ratp.fr/index.eng.html
Métro, RER, and bus maps as well as street maps to the city will help get you around. Also helpful is the information on the lines, timetables, and journeys of Noctambus, the bus that runs in the hours the Métro is closed, between 1am and 5:30am. RATP links to Subway Navigator, which shows you how to use the Métro from one point to another.

✪ **Subway Navigator. metro.ratp.fr:10001/bin/cities/english**
This amazing site provides detailed subway route maps for Paris and other French cities, as well as more than 60 cities around the world. Select a city and enter your departure and arrival points. Subway Navigator maps out your route and tells you how long the trip should take. It'll even show your route on a subway map.

3 Getting to Know the City of Light

Ernest Hemingway called the many splendors of Paris a "moveable feast" and wrote, "There is never any ending to Paris, and the memory of each person who has lived in it differs from that of any other." It's this aura of personal discovery that has always been the most compelling reason to come to Paris. And perhaps that's why France has been called *le deuxième pays de tout le monde*—"everybody's second country."

The Seine not only divides Paris into the Right Bank and the Left Bank but also seems to split the city into two vastly different sections and ways of life. Depending on your time, interest, and budget, you may quickly decide which section of Paris suits you best.

1 Essentials

VISITOR INFORMATION

At the airports are small **info offices** where for a fee their staffs will help you make a hotel reservation. But the prime source is the **Office de Tourisme de Paris,** 127 av. des Champs-Elysées, 8e (☎ **08-36-68-31-12** or 01-49-52-53-54; fax 01-49-52-53-00; www.paris-touristoffice.com; Métro: Charles de Gaulle–Etoile or George V), where you can obtain info about both Paris and the provinces. It's open daily April to October 9am to 8pm and November to March 11am to 6pm (closed May 1 and December 25). The staff will make an accommodations reservation for you on the same day you want a room: 8F ($1.30) for hostels and *foyers* ("homes"), 20F ($3.25) one-star hotels, 25F ($4) two-star hotels, and 40F ($6) three-star hotels. It's often very busy in summer, so you'll probably have to wait in line.

There are **other branches** in the base of the Eiffel Tower (open May to October, Monday to Saturday 8am to 8pm) and in the arrivals hall of the Gare de Lyon (open year-round Monday to Saturday 8am to 8pm). All these offices will give you free copies of the English-language *Time Out* and *Paris User's Guide.*

CITY LAYOUT

Paris is surprisingly compact. Occupying 1,119 sq. kilometers (432 sq. miles), it's home to more than 10 million people. The city is divided into 20 municipal wards called ***arrondissements,*** each with its own mayor, city hall, police station, and central post office. Some even have remnants of market squares.

If you are lucky enough to have lived in Paris as a young man, then wherever you go for the rest of your life, it stays with you, for Paris is a moveable feast.
　　　　　　　　　　　　　　　—Ernest Hemingway, *A Moveable Feast* (1964)

The river Seine divides Paris into the **Right Bank** (Rive Droite) to the north and the **Left Bank** (Rive Gauche) to the south. These designations make sense when you stand on a bridge and face downstream; watching the water flow out toward the sea, to your right is the north bank, to your left the south. Thirty-two bridges link the banks of the Seine, some providing access to the two small islands at the heart of the city, **Ile de la Cité,** the city's birthplace and site of Notre-Dame, and **Ile St-Louis,** a moat-guarded oasis of sober 17th-century mansions. These islands can cause some confusion to walkers who think they've just crossed a bridge from one bank to the other, only to find themselves caught up in an almost medieval maze of narrow streets and old buildings.

MAIN ARTERIES & STREETS　As part of Napoléon III's massive urban redevelopment project, Baron Georges-Eugène Haussmann forever changed the look of Paris between 1860 and 1870 by creating the legendary boulevards: St-Michel, St-Germain, Haussmann, Malesherbes, Sébastopol, Magenta, Voltaire, and Strasbourg.

The "main street" on the Right Bank is, of course, the **Champs-Elysées,** beginning at the Arc de Triomphe and running to place de la Concorde. Haussmann also created avenue de l'Opéra (as well as the Opéra), and the 12 avenues that radiate starlike from the Arc de Triomphe, giving it its original name, place de l'Etoile (*étoile* means "star"); it was renamed place Charles de Gaulle following the general's death and is often referred to as **place Charles de Gaulle–Etoile.**

Haussmann also cleared Ile de la Cité of its medieval buildings, transforming it into a showcase for Notre-Dame. Finally, he laid out the two elegant parks on the western and southeastern fringes of the city: the **Bois de Boulogne** and the **Bois de Vincennes.**

STREET MAPS　If you're staying more than 2 or 3 days, buy an inexpensive pocket-size book that includes the *plan de Paris* by arrondissement, available at all major newsstands and bookshops. If you can find it, the little forest-green *Paris Classique l'Indispensable* is a thorough, well-indexed, and accurate guide to the city and its suburbs. Most map guides provide you with a Métro map, a foldout map of the city, and indexed maps of each arrondissement, with all streets listed and keyed. We've given you a head start by including a **free full-color foldout map** at the back of this guide.

The Arrondissements in Brief

Each of Paris's 20 arrondissements possesses a unique style and flavor. You'll want to decide which district appeals most to you and then try to find accommodations there. Later on, try to visit as many areas as you can so you can get the full taste of Paris.

1ST ARR. (MUSÉE DU LOUVRE/LES HALLES)　"I never knew what a palace was until I had a glimpse of the Louvre," wrote Nathaniel Hawthorne. Perhaps the world's greatest art museum, the **Louvre,** a former royal residence, still lures all visitors to Paris to the 1st arrondissement. Walk through the **Jardin des Tuileries,** Paris's most formal garden (originally laid out by Le Nôtre, gardener to Louis XIV). Pause to take in the classic beauty of **place Vendôme,** the opulent home of the Hôtel Ritz.

Paris Arrondissements

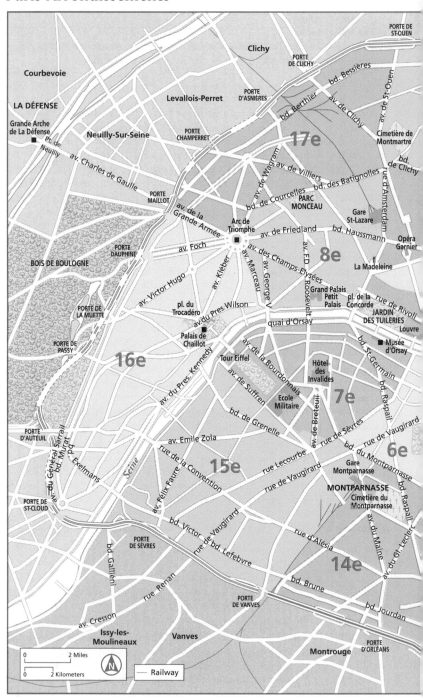

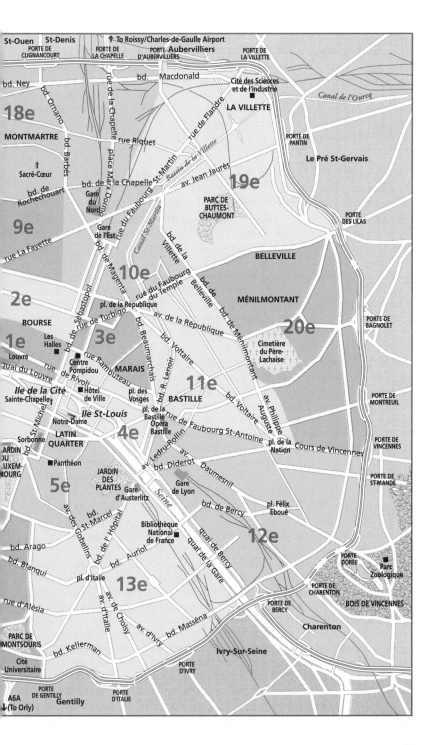

St-Ouen St-Denis
PORTE DE
CLIGNANCOURT

To Roissy/Charles-de-Gaulle Airport
PORTE DE
LA CHAPELLE

PORTE
D'AUBERVILLIERS

PORTE Aubervilliers

PORTE DE
LA VILLETTE

bd. Ney

bd. Macdonald

Cité des Sciences
et de l'Industrie

Canal de l'Ourcq

18e

LA VILLETTE

MONTMARTRE

rue de la Chapelle

rue Riquet

rue de Flandre

PORTE DE
PANTIN

Sacré-Cœur

bd. Ornano

bd. Barbès

place Marx Dormoy

bd. de la Chapelle

Bassin de la Villette

St-Martin

av. Jean Jaurès

Le Pré St-Gervais

19e

bd. de
Rochechouart

Gare
du
Nord

rue du Faubourg

PARC DE
BUTTES-
CHAUMONT

9e

Gare
de l'Est

Canal St-Martin

bd. de Magenta

bd. de la
Villette

PORTE
DES LILAS

rue La Fayette

BELLEVILLE

PORTE
DES LILAS

2e

10e

rue du Faubourg
du Temple

bd. de Belleville

MÉNILMONTANT

BOURSE

bd. de Sébastopol

pl. de la République

av. de la République

bd. de Ménilmontant

20e

PORTE DE
BAGNOLET

1e
Louvre

Les
Halles

rue de Turbigo

3e

bd. Beaumarchais

bd. Voltaire

Cimetière
du Père-
Lachaise

quai du Louvre

Centre
Pompidou

rue Rambuteau

rue de Rivoli

MARAIS

bd. R. Lenoir

11e

PORTE DE
MONTREUIL

Île de la Cité
Sainte-Chapelle

Hôtel
de Ville

pl. des
Vosges

BASTILLE

bd. Voltaire

av. Philippe
Auguste

Notre-Dame

Île St-Louis

pl. de la
Bastille
Opéra
Bastille

rue de Faubourg St-Antoine

PORTE DE
VINCENNES

rue St-Michel

LATIN
QUARTER

4e

av. Ledru-Rollin

pl. de la
Nation

Cours de Vincennes

Sorbonne

Panthéon

av. Daumesnil

PORTE DE
ST-MANDÉ

JARDIN
DU
LUXEM-
BOURG

bd. Diderot

JARDIN
DES
PLANTES

5e

Gare
d'Austerlitz

Gare
de Lyon

Seine

bd.
St-Marcel

av. des Gobelins

rue de l'Hôpital

Bibliothèque
National
de France

bd. de Bercy

pl. Félix
Eboué

bd. Arago

quai de Bercy

12e

bd. Blanqui

bd. Auriol

quai de la Gare

PORTE
DORÉE

Parc
Zoologique

pl. d'Italie

13e

av. de Choisy

av. d'Italie

PORTE DE
CHARENTON

BOIS DE VINCENNES

rue d'Alésia

bd. Masséna

Charenton

PARC DE
MONTSOURIS

bd. Kellerman

PORTE DE
BERCY

Ivry-Sur-Seine

Cité
Universitaire

PORTE
D'IVRY

A6A
(To Orly)

PORTE
DE GENTILLY
Gentilly

PORTE
D'ITALIE

Finding an Address

The key to finding any address in Paris is looking for the arrondissement number, rendered either as a number followed by "e" or "er" (1er, 2e, and so on) or more formally as part of the postal code (the last two digits indicate the arrondissement—75007 indicates the 7th arrondissement, 75017 the 17th). Numbers on buildings running parallel to the Seine usually follow the course of the river—east to west. On north-south streets, numbering begins at the river.

Zola's "belly of Paris" (Les Halles) is no longer the food-and-meat market of Paris (traders moved to the new, more accessible suburb of Rungis); today, the **Forum des Halles** is a center of shopping, entertainment, and culture.

2ND ARR. (LA BOURSE) Home to the **Bourse** (stock exchange), this Right Bank district lies mainly between the Grands Boulevards and rue Etienne-Marcel. From Monday to Friday, the shouts of brokers—*"J'ai!"* (I have it!) or *"Je prends!"* (I'll take it!)—echo across place de la Bourse until it's time to break for lunch, when the movers and shakers of French capitalism channel their hysteria into the area restaurants. Much of the eastern end of the arrondissement (**Le Sentier**) is devoted to wholesale outlets of the Paris garment district, where thousands of garments are sold (usually in bulk) to buyers from clothing stores throughout Europe. "Everything that exists elsewhere exists in Paris," wrote Victor Hugo in *Les Misérables,* and this district provides ample evidence of that.

3RD ARR. (LE MARAIS) This district embraces much of Le Marais (the swamp), one of the best loved of the old Right Bank neighborhoods. (It extends into the 4th as well.) After decades of seedy decay, Le Marais recently made a comeback, though it may never again enjoy the prosperity of its 17th-century aristocratic heyday; today it contains Paris's **gay neighborhood,** with lots of gay/lesbian restaurants, bars, and stores, as well as the remains of the old Jewish quarter, centered on **rue des Rosiers.** Two of the district's chief attractions are the **Musée Picasso,** a kind of pirate's ransom of painting and sculpture the Picasso estate had to turn over to the French government in lieu of the artist's astronomical death duties, and the **Musée Carnavalet,** which brings to life the history of Paris from prehistoric times to the present.

4TH ARR. (ILE DE LA CITÉ/ILE ST-LOUIS & BEAUBOURG) At times it seems as if the 4th has it all: not only Notre-Dame on Ile de la Cité, but Ile St-Louis and its aristocratic town houses, courtyards, and antiques shops. **Ile St-Louis,** a former cow pasture and dueling ground, is home to dozens of 17th-century mansions and 6,000 lucky louisiens, its permanent residents. Seek out **Ile de la Cité**'s two glorious Gothic churches, **Sainte-Chapelle** and **Notre-Dame,** a majestic structure that, according to poet e.e. cummings, doesn't budge an inch for all the idiocies of this world. You'll find France's finest bird and flower markets along with the nation's law courts, which Balzac described as a "cathedral of chicanery." It was here that Marie Antoinette was sentenced to death in 1793. The 4th is also home to the freshly renovated **Centre Pompidou,** one of the top three attractions in France. After all this pomp and glory, you can retreat to **place des Vosges,** a square of perfect harmony and beauty where Victor Hugo lived from 1832 to 1848 and penned many of his famous masterpieces. (His house is now a museum—see chapter 6.)

5TH ARR. (LATIN QUARTER) The Quartier Latin is the intellectual heart and soul of Paris. Bookstores, schools, churches, smoky jazz clubs, student dives, Roman ruins, publishing houses, and expensive and chic boutiques characterize the district.

Discussions of Artaud or Molière over long cups of coffee may be rarer than in the past, but they aren't at all out of place here. Beginning with the founding of the **Sorbonne** in 1253, the quarter was called Latin because all students and professors spoke the scholarly language. You'll follow in the footsteps of Descartes, Verlaine, Camus, Sartre, James Thurber, Elliot Paul, and Hemingway as you explore this historic area. Changing times have brought Greek, Moroccan, and Vietnamese immigrants, among others, hustling everything from couscous to fiery-hot spring rolls and souvlaki. The 5th borders the Seine, and you'll want to stroll along quai de Montebello, inspecting the inventories of the *bouquinistes,* who sell everything from antique Daumier prints to yellowing copies of Balzac's *Père Goriot* in the shadow of Notre-Dame. The 5th also has the **Panthéon,** built by a grateful Louis XV after he'd recovered from the gout and wanted to do something nice for Ste-Geneviève, Paris's patron saint. It's the resting place of Rousseau, Gambetta, Zola, Braille, Hugo, Voltaire, and Jean Moulin, the World War II Resistance leader whom the Gestapo tortured to death.

6TH ARR. (ST-GERMAIN/LUXEMBOURG)   This is the heartland of Paris publishing and, for some, the most colorful Left Bank quarter, where waves of earnest young artists still emerge from the famous Ecole des Beaux-Arts. The secret of the district lies in discovering its narrow streets, hidden squares, and magnificent gardens. To be really authentic, stroll with an unwrapped loaf of sourdough bread from the wood-fired ovens of **Poilâne** at 8 rue du Cherche-Midi. Everywhere you turn in the area, you'll encounter famous historic and literary associations, none more so than on **rue Jacob.** At no. 7, Racine lived with his uncle as a teenager; Richard Wagner resided at no. 14 from 1841 to 1842; Ingres once lived at no. 27 (now it's the offices of the French publishing house Editions du Seuil); and Hemingway once occupied a tiny upstairs room at no. 44. The 6th takes in the **Jardin du Luxembourg,** a 60-acre playground where Isadora Duncan went dancing in the predawn hours and a destitute Ernest Hemingway went looking for pigeons for lunch, carrying them in a baby carriage back to his humble flat for cooking.

7TH ARR. (EIFFEL TOWER/MUSÉE D'ORSAY)   Paris's most famous symbol, the **Tour Eiffel,** dominates Paris and especially the 7th, a Left Bank district of respectable residences and government offices. The tower is now one of the most recognizable landmarks in the world, despite the fact that many Parisians (especially its nearest neighbors) hated it when it was unveiled in 1889. Many of Paris's most imposing monuments are in the 7th, like the **Hôtel des Invalides,** which contains Napoléon's Tomb and the Musée de l'Armée, and the **Musée d'Orsay,** the world's premier showcase of 19th-century French art and culture, housed in the old Gare d'Orsay. But there's much hidden charm here as well. **Rue du Bac** was home to the swashbuckling heroes of Dumas's *The Three Musketeers* and to James McNeill Whistler, who moved to no. 110 after selling his *Mother*. Auguste Rodin lived at what's now the **Musée Rodin,** 77 rue de Varenne, until his death in 1917.

8TH ARR. (CHAMPS-ELYSÉES/MADELEINE)   The prime showcase of the 8th is the **Champs-Elysées,** stretching grandly from the **Arc de Triomphe** to the purloined Egyptian obelisk on **place de la Concorde.** By the 1980s, the Champs-Elysées had become a garish strip, with too much traffic, too many fast-food joints, and too many panhandlers. In the 1990s, Jacques Chirac, then the Gaullist mayor, launched a massive cleanup, broadening the sidewalks and planting new rows of trees. Now you'll find fashion houses, elegant hotels, and expensive restaurants and shops. Everything in the 8th is the city's "best, grandest, and most impressive": It has the best restaurant (**Taillevent**); the sexiest strip joint (**Crazy Horse Saloon**); the most splendid square (**place de la Concorde**); the best rooftop cafe (**La Samaritaine**); the grandest hotel (the **Crillon**); the most impressive triumphal arch (**Arc de Triomphe**); the most expensive residential street (**avenue Montaigne**); the world's oldest subway station (**Franklin D. Roosevelt**); and the most ancient monument (the 3,300-year-old **Obelisk of Luxor**).

9TH ARR. (OPÉRA GARNIER/PIGALLE)   From the Quartier de l'Opéra to the strip joints of Pigalle (the infamous "Pig Alley" for World War II GIs), the 9th endures, even if fickle fashion prefers other addresses. Over the decades, the 9th has been celebrated in literature and song for the music halls that brought gaiety to the city. No. 17 bd. de la Madeleine was the death site of Marie Duplessis, who gained fame as the heroine Marguerite Gautier in Alexandre Dumas the younger's *La Dame aux camélias*. (Greta Garbo later redoubled Marie's legend by playing her in the film *Camille*.) At **place Pigalle,** gone is the cafe La Nouvelle Athènes, where Degas, Pissarro, and Manet used to meet. Today, you're more likely to encounter nightclubs in the area. Other major attractions include the **Folies Bergère,** where cancan dancers have been high-kicking it since 1868. More than anything, it was the rococo **Opéra Garnier** (home of the notorious Phantom) that made the 9th the last hurrah of Second Empire opulence. Renoir hated it, but several generations later, Chagall did the ceilings. Pavlova danced *Swan Lake* here, and Nijinsky took the night off to go cruising.

10TH ARR. (GARE DU NORD/GARE DE L'EST)   The **Gare du Nord** and **Gare de l'Est,** along with porno houses and dreary commercial zones, make the 10th one of the least desirable arrondissements for living, dining, or sightseeing. We always try to avoid it, except for two longtime favorite restaurants (see chapter 5): **Brasserie Flo,** 7 cour des Petites-Ecuries, best known for its formidable choucroute, a heap of sauerkraut garnished with everything; and **Julien,** 16 rue du faubourg St-Denis, called the poor man's Maxim's for its belle-époque interiors and moderate prices.

11TH ARR. (OPÉRA BASTILLE)   For many years, this quarter seemed to sink lower and lower into poverty and decay, overcrowded by working-class immigrants from the far reaches of the former Empire. The opening of the **Opéra Bastille,** however, has given the 11th new hope and new life. The facility, called the "people's opera house," stands on the landmark place de la Bastille, where on July 14, 1789, 633 Parisians stormed the fortress and seized the ammunition depot, as the French Revolution swept across the city. Over the years, the prison held Voltaire, the Marquis de Sade, and the mysterious "Man in the Iron Mask." The 11th has its charms, but they exist only for those who seek them out. **Le Marché** at place d'Aligre, for example, is surrounded by a Middle Eastern food market and is a good place to hunt for secondhand bargains: Everything is cheap, and though you must search hard for treasures, they often appear.

12TH ARR. (BOIS DE VINCENNES/GARE DE LYON)   Very few out-of-towners came here until a French chef opened a restaurant called **Au Trou Gascon** (see chapter 5). The 12th's major attraction remains the **Bois de Vincennes,** sprawling on the eastern periphery of Paris. This park has been a longtime favorite of French families, who enjoy its zoos and museums, its royal château and boating lakes, and most definitely its **Parc Floral de Paris,** a celebrated flower garden boasting springtime rhododendrons and autumn dahlias. Venture into the dreary **Gare de Lyon** for **Le Train Bleu,** a restaurant whose ceiling frescoes and art nouveau decor are classified as national artistic treasures; the food's good too (see chapter 5). The 12th, once a depressing urban wasteland, has been singled out for budgetary resuscitation and is beginning to sport new housing, shops, gardens, and restaurants. Many of these will occupy the site of the former Reuilly rail tracks.

Impressions

In Paris they simply stared when I spoke to them in French; I never did succeed in making those idiots understand their language.
—Mark Twain, *Wisdom and Ignorance* (1869)

13TH ARR. (GARE D'AUSTERLITZ)   Centered around the grimy **Gare d'Austerlitz,** the 13th might have its devotees, but we've yet to meet one. British snobs who flitted in and out of the train station were among the first of the district's foreign visitors and in essence wrote the 13th off as a dreary working-class counterpart of London's East End. The 13th is also home to Paris's **Chinatown,** stretching for 13 square blocks around the Tolbiac Métro stop. It emerged out of the refugee crisis at the end of the Vietnam War, taking over a neighborhood that had been mostly Arab-speaking peoples. Today, recognizing the overcrowding that's now endemic in the district, the Paris civic authorities are imposing new, not particularly welcome, restrictions on population densities.

14TH ARR. (MONTPARNASSE)   The northern end of this large arrondissement is devoted to **Montparnasse,** home of the "lost generation" and former stamping ground of Stein, Toklas, Hemingway, and other American expats of the 1920s. After World War II, it ceased to be the center of intellectual life, but the memory lingers in its cafes. One of the monuments that sets the tone of the neighborhood is **Rodin's statue of Balzac** at the junction of boulevard Montparnasse and boulevard Raspail. At this corner are some of the world's most famous **literary cafes,** including La Rotonde, Le Select, La Dôme, and La Coupole. Though Gertrude Stein avoided them (she loathed cafes), all the other American expatriates, including Hemingway and Fitzgerald, had no qualms about enjoying a drink here (or quite a few of them, for that matter). Stein stayed at home (27 rue de Fleurus) with Alice B. Toklas, collecting paintings, including those of Picasso, and entertaining the likes of Max Jacob, Apollinaire, T. S. Eliot, and Matisse.

15TH ARR. (GARE MONTPARNASSE/INSTITUT PASTEUR)   A mostly residential district beginning at **Gare Montparnasse,** the 15th stretches all the way to the Seine. In size and population, it's the largest quarter of Paris but attracts few tourists and has few attractions, except for the **Parc des Expositions,** the **Cimetière du Montparnasse,** and the **Institut Pasteur.** In the early 20th century, many artists—like Chagall, Léger, and Modigliani—lived in this arrondissement in a shared atelier known as "The Beehive."

16TH ARR. (TROCADÉRO/BOIS DE BOULOGNE)   Originally the village of Passy, where Benjamin Franklin lived during most of his time in Paris, this district is still reminiscent of Proust's world. Highlights include the **Bois de Boulogne;** the **Jardin du Trocadéro;** the **Maison de Balzac;** the **Musée Guimet** (famous for its Asian collections); and the **Cimetière de Passy,** resting place of Manet, Talleyrand, Giraudoux, and Debussy. One of the largest of the city's arrondissements, it's known today for its well-heeled bourgeoisie, its upscale rents, and some rather posh (and, according to its critics, rather smug) residential boulevards. The arrondissement also has the best vantage of the Eiffel Tower, **place du Trocadéro.**

17TH ARR. (PARC MONCEAU/PLACE CLICHY)   Flanking the northern periphery of Paris, the 17th incorporates neighborhoods of conservative bourgeois respectability (in its western end) and less affluent neighborhoods in its eastern end. It boasts two of the greatest restaurants of Paris, **Guy Savoy** and **Michel Rostang** (see chapter 5).

18TH ARR. (MONTMARTRE)　The 18th is the most famous outer quartier of Paris, containing **Montmartre,** the **Moulin Rouge, Sacré-Coeur,** and ultratouristy **place du Tertre.** Utrillo was its native son, Renoir lived here, and Toulouse-Lautrec adopted the area as his own. The most famous enclave of artists in Paris's history, the **Bateau-Lavoir,** of Picasso fame, gathered here. Max Jacob, Matisse, and Braque were all frequent visitors. Today, place Blanche is known for its prostitutes, and Montmartre is filled with honky-tonks, too many souvenir shops, and terrible restaurants. You can still find pockets of quiet beauty, though. The city's most famous flea market, the **Marché aux Puces de Clignancourt,** is another landmark.

19TH ARR. (LA VILLETTE)　Today, visitors come to what was once the village of La Villette to see the much-publicized angular **Cité des Sciences et de l'Industrie,** a spectacular science museum and park built on a site that for years was devoted to the city's slaughterhouses. Mostly residential, and not at all upscale, the district is one of the most ethnically diverse in Paris, the home of people from all parts of the former Empire. A highlight is **Les Buttes Chaumont,** a park where kids can enjoy puppet shows and donkey rides.

20TH ARR. (PÈRE-LACHAISE CEMETERY)　The 20th's greatest landmark is **Père-Lachaise Cemetery,** the resting place of Jim Morrison, Edith Piaf, Marcel Proust, Oscar Wilde, Isadora Duncan, Sarah Bernhardt, Gertrude Stein and Alice B. Toklas, Colette, and many, many others. Otherwise, the 20th arrondissement is a dreary and sometimes volatile melting pot comprising residents from France's former colonies. Though nostalgia buffs sometimes head here to visit Piaf's former neighborhood, **Ménilmontant-Belleville,** it has been almost totally bulldozed and rebuilt since the bad old days when she grew up here.

2　Getting Around

Paris is a city for strollers whose greatest joy in life is rambling through unexpected alleyways and squares. Only when you're dead tired and can't walk another step or have to go all the way across town in a hurry, should you consider using the swift and dull means of urban transport.

For information on the city's public transportation, call ☎ **08-36-68-77-14.**

BY MÉTRO & RER

The **Métro** (☎ **08-36-68-77-14**) is the easiest and most efficient way to get around Paris. Most stations display a map of the system at the entrance. Within Paris, you can transfer between the subway and the RER regional trains for no additional cost. To make sure you catch the right train, find your destination, then visually follow the line it's on to the end of the route and note its name. This is the sign you look for in the stations and the name you'll see on the train. Transfer stations are known as *correspondances.* (Note that some require long walks—Châtelet–Les Halles is the most notorious.)

Few trips will require more than one transfer. Some stations have maps with push-button indicators that'll help you plot your route by lighting up when you press the button for your destination. A ride on the urban lines costs 8F ($1.30) to any point within the 20 arrondissements of Paris, as well as to many of its near suburbs. A bulk

A Métro Map Note

See the inside front cover of this guide for a full-color Paris Métro map.

Discount Passes

You can buy a **Paris Visite pass,** valid for 1 to 5 days on the public transport system, including the Métro, the city buses, the RER (regional express) trains within Paris city limits, and even the funicular to the top of Montmartre. (The RER has both first- and second-class compartments, and the pass lets you travel in first class.) The cost is 55F ($8.80) for 1 day, 90F ($14.40) for 2 days, 120F ($19.20) for 3 days, or 175F ($28) for 5 days. The card is available at the **Services Touristiques de la RATP (Régie Autonome des Transports Parisiens)**, with offices at place de la Madeleine, 8e (☎ **08-36-68-77-14** or 01-44-68-20-20; Métro: Madeleine; www.ratp.fr), and 54 quai de la Rapée, 12e (☎ **01-44-68-20-20** or 08-36-68-77-14; Métro: Gare de Lyon); the tourist offices (see above); or the main Métro stations.

Another pass available to visitors is **Carte Mobilis,** allowing unlimited travel on all bus, Métro, and RER lines in Paris during a 1-day period for 32F to 72F ($5.10 to $11.50), depending on the zone. You will need to provide a passport-size photo of yourself. You can buy the pass at any Métro station.

purchase of 10 tickets (which are bound together into what the French refer to as a *carnet*) costs 55F ($8.80). Métro fares to outlying suburbs on the Sceaux, the Noissy–St-Léger, and St-Germain-en-Laye lines cost more and are sold on an individual basis depending on the distance you travel.At the entrance to the Métro station, insert your ticket into the turnstile and pass through. Take the ticket back, since it may be checked by uniformed police officers when you leave the subway. There are also occasional ticket checks on the trains, platforms, and passageways. If you're changing trains, get out and determine which direction (final destination) on the next line you want, then follow the bright orange CORRESPONDANCE signs until you reach the proper platform. Don't follow a SORTIE sign, which means "exit." If you exit, you'll have to pay another fare to resume your journey.

The Paris Métro runs daily 5:30am to around 1:15am, at which time all underground trains reach their final terminus at the end of each of their respective lines. Be alert that the last train may pass through central Paris as much as an hour before that time. The subways are reasonably safe at any hour, but beware of pickpockets.

BY BUS

Bus travel is much slower than the subway. Most buses run 7am to 8:30pm (a few operate to 12:30am, and 10 operate during the early-morning hours). Service is limited on Sunday and holidays. Bus and Métro fares are the same and you can use the same *carnet* tickets on both. At certain stops, signs list the destinations and numbers of the buses serving that point. Destinations are usually listed north to south and east to west. Most stops along the way are also posted on the sides of the buses. To catch a bus, wait in line at the bus stop. Signal the driver to stop the bus and board.

Most bus rides (including any that begin and end within Paris's 20 arrondissements) require one ticket, but there are some destinations in the suburbs that require up to, but never more than, two. If you intend to use the buses a lot, pick up an **RATP bus map** at its offices on place de la Madeleine and quai de la Rapée (see "Discount Passes," above) or at any tourist office. For details on bus and Métro routes, call ☎ **08-36-68-41-14.**

The same entity that maintains Paris's network of Métros and buses, the **RATP** (☎ **08-36-68-77-14**), has initiated a motorized mode of transport designed exclusively as a means of appreciating the city's visual grandeur. Known as the **Balabus,** it's a fleet of big-windowed orange-and-white motor coaches whose most visible drawback is their limited hours—they run only on Sunday and national holidays noon to 9pm, April 15 to September 30. The coaches journey in both directions between the Gare de Lyon and the Grande Arche de La Défense, encompassing some of the city's most monumental vistas and making regular stops. Presentation of two Métro tickets (16F/$2.55), a valid Carte Mobilis (see above), or a valid Paris Visite pass (see above) will carry you along the entire route. You'll recognize the bus and the route it follows by the "Bb" symbol emblazoned on each bus's side and on signs posted beside the route it follows.

BY CAR

Again, don't even think about driving in Paris. The streets are narrow, with confusing one-way designations, and parking is next to impossible. Besides, most visitors don't have the ruthlessness required to survive in Parisian traffic. Think about renting a car only if you plan to explore the Ile de France and beyond.

You can rent cars from locally based agencies like **Autorent,** 18 rue de la Convention, 15e (tel. 01-45-54-22-45; Métro: Boucicaut), or from competitors like **Rent-a-Car,** 79 rue de Bercy, 12e (☎ 01-43-45-15-15; Métro: Gare de Lyon), and **Inter Touring Service**, 117 bd. Auguste-Blanqui, 13e (☎ 01-45-88-52-37; Metro: Glacière). **Budget** (☎ 800/472-3325 in the U.S. and Canada; www.budgetrentacar. com) maintains about 30 locations in Paris, with its largest branch at 81 av. Kléber, 16e (☎ 01-47-55-61-00; Métro: Trocadéro). **Hertz** (☎ 800/654-3001 in the U.S. and Canada; www.hertz.com) maintains about 15 locations in Paris, including offices at the airports and the main office at 27 rue St-Ferdinand, 17e (☎ 01-45-74-97-39; Métro: Argentine). Be sure to ask about any promotional discounts. **Avis** (☎ 800/331-2112 in the U.S. and Canada; www.avis.com) has offices at both airports, as well as a headquarters at 5 rue Bixio, 7e (☎ 01-44-18-10-50; Métro: Ecole Militaire), near the Eiffel Tower. **National** (☎ 800/227-3876 in the U.S. and Canada; www.nationalcar.com) is represented in Paris by **Europcar,** whose largest office is at 165 bis rue de Vaugirard (☎ 01-44-38-61-61; Métro: St-Sulpice). It has offices at both airports as well.

BY TAXI

Taxi drivers are organized into an effective lobby to keep their number limited to 15,000, and it's nearly impossible to get one at rush hour. You can hail regular cabs on the street when their signs read *libre*. Taxis are easier to find at the many stands near Métro stations.

The flag drops at 14F ($2.25), and you pay 3.58F (55¢) per kilometer. At night, expect to pay 5.94F (95¢) per kilometer. On airport trips you're not required to pay for the driver's empty return ride. You're allowed several small pieces of luggage free if they're transported inside and don't weigh more than 5kg (11 pounds). Heavier suitcases carried in the trunk cost 6F to 10F (95¢ to $1.60) apiece, depending on their size. Tip 12% to 15%—the latter usually elicits a *merci*. To radio cabs, call

---

A Taxi Warning

Always check the taxi's meter to make sure you're not paying the previous passenger's fare. Beware of cabs without meters, which often try to snare tipsy patrons outside nightclubs—always settle the tab in advance.

☎ **01-45-85-85-85,** 01-49-36-10-10, or 01-42-70-00-42 (you'll be charged from the point where the taxi begins the drive to pick you up).

BY BICYCLE

To bike through the streets and parks of Paris, perhaps with a baguette tucked under your arm, might've been a fantasy of yours since you saw your first Maurice Chevalier film. In recent years, the city has added many miles of right-hand lanes designated for cyclists as well as hundreds of bike racks. (When these aren't available, many Parisians simply chain their bikes to fences or lampposts.) Cycling is especially popular in the larger parks and gardens.

Paris-Vélos, 2 rue du Fer-à-Moulin, 5e (☎ **01-43-37-59-22;** Métro: Censier-Daubenton), rents by the day, weekend, or week, charging 90F to 160F ($14.40 to $25.60) per weekday, 160F to 220F ($25.60 to $35.20) Saturday and Sunday, and 450F to 600F ($72 to $96) per week. You must leave a 2,000F ($320) deposit. It's open Monday to Saturday 10am to 12:30pm and 2 to 7pm.

BY BOAT

April and mid-October, the **Batobus** (☎ **01-44-11-33-44**), a series of 150-passenger ferries with big windows for viewing the riverfronts, operates at 15-minute intervals daily 10am to 7pm. Boats chug along between the quays at the base of the Eiffel Tower and the quays at the base of the Louvre, stopping at the Musée d'Orsay, St-Germain-des-Prés, Notre-Dame, and the Hôtel de Ville. Transit between each stop is 20F ($3.20), though most passengers opt to pay a flat rate (good all day) of 60F ($9.60) per adult or 30F ($4.80) for children under 12, then settle back and watch the monuments. Photo ops are countless aboard this leisurely but intensely panoramic "floating observation platform."

Fast Facts: Paris

American Express From its administrative headquarters in the Paris suburb of Reuil-Malmaison, at 4 rue de Louis-Blériot, 92561, Rueil-Malmaison CEDEX, the largest travel service in the world, operates a 24-hour hot line at ☎ **01-47-77-70-00.** Day-to-day services, like tours and money exchange, are available at 11 rue Scribe, 9e, 75009 Paris (☎ **01-47-77-77-07;** Métro: Opéra), or the smaller branch at 38 av. Wagram, 8e, 75008 Paris (☎ **01-42-27-58-80;** Métro: Ternes). Both are open Monday to Friday 9am to 6:30pm, with money-changing services ending at 4:45pm. The rue Scribe office is open Saturday 9am to 5:30pm (no mail pickup).

Banks American Express may be able to meet most of your banking needs. If not, banks in Paris are open Monday to Friday 9am to 4:30pm. A few are open on Saturday. Ask at your hotel for the location of the bank nearest you. Shops and most hotels will cash your traveler's checks, but not at the advantageous rate a bank or foreign-exchange office will give you, so make sure you've allowed enough funds for "le weekend."

Business Hours Opening hours in France are erratic, as befits a nation of individualists. Most museums close 1 day a week (often Tuesday) and national holidays; hours tend to be 9:30am to 5pm. Some museums, particularly the smaller ones, close for lunch noon to 2pm. Most French museums are open Saturday, but many close Sunday morning and reopen in the afternoon. (See chapter 6 for specific times.) Generally, **offices** are open Monday to Friday 9am to 5pm, but don't count on it. Always call first. **Large stores** and **chain stores** are open 9 or 9:30am (often 10am) to 6 or 7pm without a break for lunch. Some **shops,** particularly those operated by foreigners, open at 8am and close at 8 or 9pm. In some **small stores,** the lunch break can last 3 hours, beginning at 1pm.

Dentists For emergency dental service, call **S.O.S. Dentaire** at ☎ **01-43-37-51-00**) Monday to Friday 8pm to midnight and Saturday and Sunday 9:30am to midnight. You can also call or visit the **American Hospital,** 63 bd. Victor-Hugo, Neuilly (☎ **01-46-41-25-43;** Métro: Pont de Levallois or Pont de Neuilly; Bus: 82). A 24-hour English/French dental clinic is on the premises.

Doctors See "Hospitals," below.

Drugstores After regular hours, ask at your hotel where the nearest 24-hour *pharmacie* is. You'll also find the address posted on the doors or windows of other drugstores in the neighborhood. One all-night drugstore is the **Pharmacy les Champs,** in La Galerie Les Champs, 84 av. des Champs-Elysées, 8e (☎ **01-45-62-02-41;** Métro: George V).

Electricity In general, expect 200 volts AC (60 cycles), though you'll encounter 110 and 115 volts in some older establishments. Adapters are needed to fit sockets. Many hotels have two-pin (in some cases, three-pin) sockets for electric razors. It's best to ask at your hotel before plugging in any electrical appliance.

Embassies/Consulates If you have a passport, immigration, legal, or other problem, contact your consulate. Call before you go, as they often keep strange hours and observe both French and home-country holidays.

The Embassy of the **United States,** at 2 av. Gabriel, 8e (☎ **01-43-12-22-22;** Métro: Concorde), is open Monday to Friday 9am to 6pm. Passports are issued at its consulate at 2 rue St-Florentin (☎ **01-43-12-22-22;** Métro: Concorde). Getting a passport replaced costs $55. The Embassy of **Canada** is at 35 av. Montaigne, 8e (☎ **01-44-43-29-00;** Métro: F. D. Roosevelt or Alma-Marceau), open Monday to Friday 9am to noon and 2 to 4pm. The Canadian consulate is at the embassy. The Embassy of the **United Kingdom** is at 35 rue du faubourg St-Honoré, 8e (☎ **01-44-51-31-00;** Métro: Concorde or Madeleine), open Monday to Friday 9:30am to 12:30pm and 2:30 to 5pm. The consulate is at 16 rue d'Anjou, 8e (☎ **01-44-66-29-79;** Métro: Consulate), open Monday to Friday 9:30am to 12:30pm and 2:30 to 5pm. The Embassy of **Australia** is at 4 rue Jean-Rey, 15e (☎ **01-40-59-33-00;** Métro: Bir Hakeim), open Monday to Friday 9:15am to noon and 2:30 to 4:30pm. The Embassy of **New Zealand** is at 7 ter rue Léonard-de-Vinci, 16e (☎ **01-45-00-24-11;** Métro: Victor Hugo), open Monday to Friday 9am to 1pm and 2:30 to 6pm. The Embassy of **Ireland** is at 12 av. Foch, 16e (☎ **01-44-17-67-00;** Métro: Argentine), open Monday to Friday 9:30am to noon.

Emergencies For the police, call ☎ **17;** to report a fire, call ☎ **18.** For an ambulance, call the fire department at ☎ **01-45-78-74-52;** a fire vehicle rushes patients to the nearest emergency room. For **S.A.M.U.,** an independently operated, privately owned ambulance company, call ☎ **15.** For less urgent matters, you can reach the police at 9 bd. du Palais, 4e (☎ **01-53-71-53-71** or 01-53-73-53-73; Métro: Cité).

Hospitals Open Monday to Saturday 8am to 7pm, **Central Médical Europe,** 44 rue d'Amsterdam, 9e (☎ **01-42-81-93-33;** Métro: Liège), maintains contacts with medical and dental practitioners in all fields. Appointments are recommended. Another choice is the **American Hospital of Paris,** 63 bd. Victor-Hugo, Neuilly (☎ **01-46-41-25-43;** Métro: Pont de Levallois or Pont de Neuilly; Bus: 82), which operates 24-hour medical and dental service. An additional clinic is the **Centre Figuier,** 2 rue du Figuier (☎ **01-42-78-55-53;** Métro: St-Paul). Call before visiting.

Internet Access   To surf the Net or check your e-mail, try the **Cybercafé Latino,** 13 rue de l'Ecole Polytechnique, 5e (☎ **01-40-51-86-94;** www.cybercafelatino.com; Métro: Maubert-Mutualité), open Monday to Saturday 10am to midnight, or **Le Rendez-vous Toyota,** 79 av. des Champs-Elysées (☎ **01-56-89-29-79;** www.lrv.toyota.fr; Métro: George V), open Monday to Thursday 10:30am to 9pm and Friday and Saturday 10:30am to midnight. See also **Le Web Bar** in chapter 9.

Liquor Laws   You'll find it easier to buy wine, beer, or spirits in France than in England or other countries. Supermarkets, smaller grocery stores, and cafes all sell alcoholic beverages. The legal drinking age is 16, but persons under that age can be served an alcoholic drink in a bar or restaurant if accompanied by a parent or legal guardian. Wine and liquor are sold every day of the week, year-round. Hours of cafes vary. Some open at 6am, serving drinks to 3am; others are open 24 hours. Bars and nightclubs may stay open as late as they wish.

The Breathalyzer test is in use in France, and a motorist is considered "legally intoxicated" with 0.5 grams of alcohol per liter of blood (the more liberal U.S. law is 1 gram per liter). If convicted, a motorist faces a stiff fine and a possible prison term of 2 months to 2 years. If bodily injury results, sentences can range from 2 years to life.

Mail/Post Offices   Most post offices in Paris are open Monday to Friday 8am to 7pm and Saturday 8am to noon. The **main post office** (**PTT**) for Paris is at 52 rue du Louvre, 75001 Paris (☎ **01-40-28-20-00;** Métro: Louvre). It's open 24 hours a day for the sale of stamps, phone calls, and sending faxes and telegrams, with limited hours (Monday to Friday 8am to 5pm and Saturday 8am to noon) for more esoteric financial services like the sale of money orders. Stamps can also usually be purchased at your hotel reception desk and at cafes with red TABAC signs. You can send faxes at the main post office in each arrondissement.

Airmail letters within Europe cost 3F (50¢); to the United States and Canada, 4.40F (70¢); and to Australia and New Zealand, 5.10F (80¢). You can have mail sent to you *poste restante* (general delivery) at the main post office for a small fee. Take an ID, such as a passport, if you plan to pick up mail. American Express (see above) also offers a *poste restante* service, but you may be asked to show an American Express card or traveler's checks.

Newspapers/Magazines   English-language newspapers are available at nearly every kiosk. Published Monday to Saturday, the *International Herald-Tribune* is the most popular paper with visiting Americans and Canadians; the *Guardian* provides a British point of view. For those who read in French, the leading domestic newspapers are *Le Monde, Le Figaro,* and *Libération;* the top magazines are *L'Express, Le Point,* and *Le Nouvel Observateur.* Kiosks are generally open daily 8am to 9pm.

Pets   If you have certificates from a vet and proof of rabies vaccination, you can bring most house pets into France.

Police   Call ☎ 17 for emergencies. The principal Préfecture is at 9 bd. du Palais, 4e (☎ **01-53-71-53-71;** Métro: Cité).

Rest Rooms   If you're in dire need, duck into a cafe or brasserie to use the lavatory. It's customary to make some small purchase if you do so. In the street, the domed self-cleaning lavatories are a decent option if you have small change; Métro stations and underground garages usually have public lavatories, but the degree of cleanliness varies.

Safety   In Paris, be especially aware of child pickpockets. They roam the capital, preying on tourists around attractions like the Louvre, Eiffel Tower, and Notre-Dame, and they also often strike in the Métro, sometimes blocking a victim from the escalator. A band of these young thieves can clean your pockets even while you try to fend them off. Their method is to get very close to a target, ask for a handout (sometimes), and deftly help themselves to your money or passport.

Although public safety is not as much a problem in Paris as it is in large American cities, concerns are growing. Robbery at gun or knifepoint is uncommon here, but not unknown. Be careful.

Taxes   See chapter 8 for an explanation of the value-added tax refund.

Telephone   Public phones are found in cafes, restaurants, Métro stations, post offices, airports, and train stations and occasionally on the streets. Finding a coin-operated telephone in France is an arduous task. A simpler and more widely accepted method of payment is the *télécarte,* a prepaid calling card available at kiosks, post offices, and Métro stations and costing 49F to 97.50F ($7.85 to $15.60) for 50 and 120 units, respectively. A local call costs 1 unit, which provides you with 6 to 18 minutes of conversation, depending on the rate. Avoid making calls from your hotel, which might double or triple the charges.

To call **long distance within France,** dial the 10-digit number (9-digit in some cases outside Paris) of the person or place you're calling. To make a **direct international call,** first dial 00, listen for the tone, then slowly dial the country code, the area code, and the local number. The country code for the **USA** and **Canada** is 1; **Great Britain**, 44; **Ireland**, 353; **Australia**, 61; **New Zealand**, 64; **South Africa**, 27.

An easy and relatively inexpensive way to call home is **USA Direct/AT&T WorldConnect.** From within France, dial any of the following numbers: ☎ **0800/99-0011,** -1011, -1111, -1211. Then follow the prompt, which will ask you to punch in the number of either your AT&T credit card or a MasterCard or Visa. Along with the United States, the countries participating in the system—referred to as WorldConnect—include **Canada,** the **United Kingdom, Ireland, Australia,** and **New Zealand.** By punching in the number of the party you want in any of these countries, you'll avoid the surcharges imposed by the hotel operator. An AT&T operator will be available to help you with complications arising during the process.

Time   France is usually 6 hours ahead of eastern standard time in the United States. French daylight saving time lasts from around April to September, when clocks are set 1 hour ahead of the standard time.

Country & City Codes

The **country code** for France is **33.** The **city code** for Paris (as well as for all cities in the Ile de France region) is **1;** use this code if you're calling from outside France. If you're calling Paris from within Paris or from anywhere else in France, use **01,** which is now built into all phone numbers in the Ile de France, making them 10 digits long.

Tipping   By law, all bills show *service compris,* which means the tip is included; additional gratuities are customarily given as follows: For **hotel staff,** tip the porter 6F to 10F (95¢ to $1.60) per item of baggage and 10F ($1.60) per day for the chambermaid. You're not obligated to tip the concierge, doorman, or anyone else unless you use his or her services. In **cafes** and **restaurants,** waiter service is usually included, though you can leave a couple of francs. Tip **taxi drivers** 12% to 15% of the amount on the meter. In **theaters** and **restaurants,** give cloakroom attendants at least 5F (80¢) per item. Give **rest room attendants** in nightclubs and such places about 2F (30¢). Give **cinema** and **theater ushers** about 2F (30¢). Tip the **hairdresser** about 15%, and don't forget to tip the person who gives you a shampoo or a manicure 10F ($1.60). For **guides** for group visits to museums and monuments, 5F to 10F (80¢ to $1.60) is a reasonable tip.

Water   Drinking water is generally safe, though it has been known to cause diarrhea in some unaccustomed stomachs. If you ask for water in a restaurant, it'll be bottled water (for which you'll pay), unless you specifically request tap water (*l'eau du robinet*).

4 Where to Stay

Paris boasts some 2,000 hotels—with about 80,000 rooms—spread across its 20 arrondissements. They range from the Ritz and the Crillon to dives so repellent even George Orwell, author of *Down and Out in Paris and London*, wouldn't have considered checking in. (Of course, you won't find any of those in this guide!) We've included deluxe places for those who can afford to live like the Sultan of Brunei as well as a wide range of moderate and inexpensive choices for the rest of us.

Most visitors, at least those from North America, come to Paris in July and August. Many French are on vacation then and trade fairs and conventions come to a halt, so there are usually plenty of rooms, even though these months have traditionally been the peak season for European travel. In most hotels, February is just as busy as April or September because of the volume of business travelers and the increasing number of tourists who've learned to take advantage of off-season discount airfares.

Since hot weather rarely lasts long in Paris, few hotels, except the deluxe ones, provide air-conditioning. If you're trapped in a garret on a hot summer night, you'll have to sweat it out. You can open your window to get some cooler air, but open windows admit the nuisance of noise pollution. To avoid this, you can request a room in back when reserving.

WHICH BANK IS FOR YOU?

The river dividing Paris geographically and culturally demands you make a choice. Are you more **Left Bank,** wanting a room in the heart of St-Germain, perhaps where Jean-Paul Sartre and Simone de Beauvoir once spent the night? Or are you more **Right Bank,** preferring sumptuous quarters like those at the Crillon, perhaps where Tom Cruise and Nicole Kidman once slept? Would you rather look for that special old curio in a dusty shop on the Left Bank's rue Jacob or inspect the latest Lagerfeld or Dior couture on the Right Bank's avenue Montaigne? Each of Paris's neighborhoods has its own flavor, and your experiences and memory of Paris will likely be formed by where you choose to stay.

If you desire chic surroundings, choose a Right Bank hotel That puts you near the most elegant shops and within walking distance of major sights like the Arc de Triomphe, place de la Concorde, the Jardin des Tuileries, the Opéra Garnier, and the Louvre. The best

Reading the Government Ratings

The French government grades hotels with a star system, ranging from one star for a simple inn to four stars for a deluxe hotel. Moderately priced hotels usually get two or three stars. This system is based on a complicated formula of room sizes, facilities, plumbing, elevators, dining options, renovations, and so on. In one-star hotels, the bathrooms are often shared and the facilities extremely limited (such as no elevator), and the rooms may not have phones or TVs; breakfast is often the only meal served. In two- or three-star hotels, there are usually elevators, and rooms will likely have baths, phones, and TVs. In four-star hotels, you'll get the works, with all the amenities plus facilities and services like room service, 24-hour concierges, elevators, and perhaps even health clubs.

However, the system is a bit misleading. For tax reasons, a four-star hotel might deliberately elect to have a three-star rating, which, with the hotel's permission, is granted by the government. The government won't add a star where it's not merited, but with the hotel's request will remove a star.

Right Bank hotels are near the Arc de Triomphe in the 8th arrondissement, though many first-class lodgings cluster near the Trocadéro and Bois du Boulogne in the 16th or near the Palais des Congrès in the 17th. If you'd like to be near place Vendôme, try for a hotel in the 1st. Also popular are the increasingly fashionable Marais and Bastille areas in the 3rd and 4th arrondissements and Les Halles/Beaubourg, home of the Centre Pompidou and Les Halles shopping mall, in the 3rd.

If you want less formality and tiny bohemian streets, head for the Left Bank, where prices are traditionally lower. Hotels that cater to students are found in the 5th and 6th arrondissements, the 5th known as the Latin Quarter. These areas, with their literary overtones, boast the Sorbonne, the Panthéon, the Jardin du Luxembourg, cafe life, bookstores, and publishing houses. The 7th arrondissement provides a touch of avant-garde St-Germain.

1 On the Right Bank

We'll begin with the most centrally located arrondissements on the Right Bank, then work our way through the more outlying neighborhoods.

1ST ARRONDISSEMENT (LOUVRE/LES HALLES)
VERY EXPENSIVE

✪ **Hôtel Costes.** 239 rue St-Honoré, 75001 Paris. ☎ **01-42-44-50-50.** Fax 01-42-44-50-01. 83 units. A/C MINIBAR TV TEL. 2,250–3,500F ($360–$560) double; 5,250–5,500F ($840–$880) suite. AE, DC, MC, V. Métro: Tuileries or Concorde.

Grand style and a location close to the headquarters of some of Paris's most upscale shops as well as the offices of *Harper's Bazaar* attract lots of high-style fashion types. The town house–style premises was a *maison bourgeoise* for many generations, presenting a severely dignified facade. In 1996, it was richly adorned with jewel-toned colors, heavy swagged curtains, and lavish Napoléon III accessories. Today, everything about it evokes the rich days of the Gilded Age, especially the guest rooms. Though small, they're cozy and ornate, with one or two large beds, CD players, and fax machines.

Dining: Four dining rooms, each with a different decorative theme and all overlooking the Italianate-style inner courtyard, are chock-a-block with chinoiserie, dried

Hotels in the Heart of the Right Bank

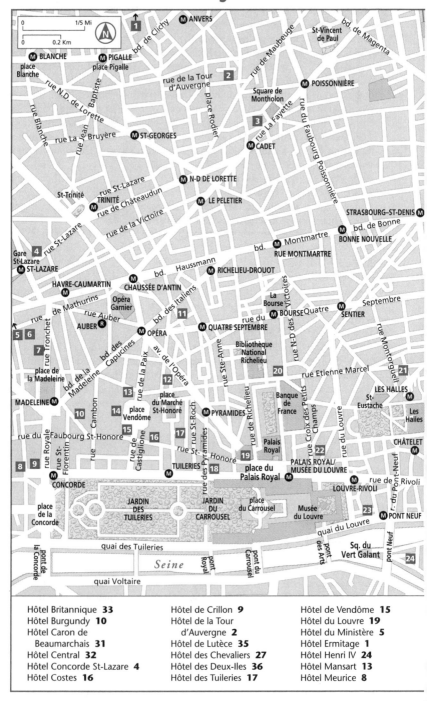

Hôtel Britannique **33**

Hôtel Burgundy **10**

Hôtel Caron de
    Beaumarchais **31**

Hôtel Central **32**

Hôtel Concorde St-Lazare **4**

Hôtel Costes **16**

Hôtel de Crillon **9**

Hôtel de la Tour
    d'Auvergne **2**

Hôtel de Lutèce **35**

Hôtel des Chevaliers **27**

Hôtel des Deux-Iles **36**

Hôtel des Tuileries **17**

Hôtel de Vendôme **15**

Hôtel du Louvre **19**

Hôtel du Ministère **5**

Hôtel Ermitage **1**

Hôtel Henri IV **24**

Hôtel Mansart **13**

Hôtel Meurice **8**

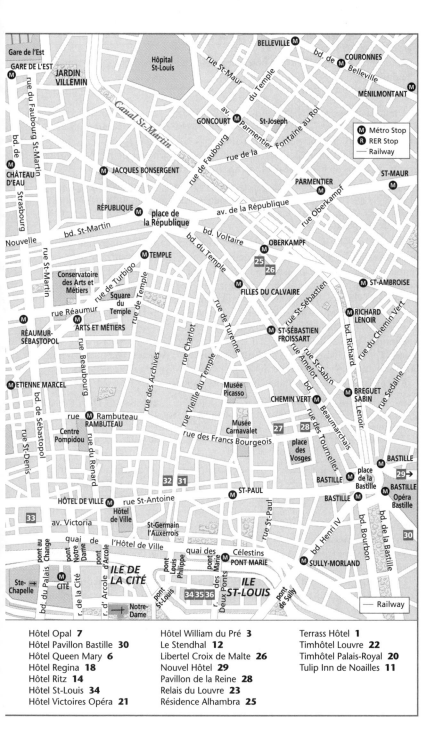

Hôtel Opal **7**
Hôtel Pavillon Bastille **30**
Hôtel Queen Mary **6**
Hôtel Regina **18**
Hôtel Ritz **14**
Hôtel St-Louis **34**
Hôtel Victoires Opéra **21**

Hôtel William du Pré **3**
Le Stendhal **12**
Libertel Croix de Malte **26**
Nouvel Hôtel **29**
Pavillon de la Reine **28**
Relais du Louvre **23**
Résidence Alhambra **25**

Terrass Hôtel **1**
Timhôtel Louvre **22**
Timhôtel Palais-Royal **20**
Tulip Inn de Noailles **11**

Best Hotel Bets

See chapter 1 for a list of our hotel favorites—the best newcomer, the best view, and more.

and framed flowers, and 19th-century art. Open daily noon to 1am, they feature delectable dishes like grilled scallops and a grilled version of steak tartare with all the spicy ingredients of its original (raw) version.

Amenities: Concierge, 24-hour room service, dry cleaning/laundry, baby-sitting, gym with steam room, indoor pool, massage, car-rental desk.

🟊 **Hôtel de Vendôme.** 1 place Vendôme, 75001 Paris. ☎ **01-42-60-32-84.** Fax 01-49-27-97-89. E-mail: reservations@hoteldevendome.com. 29 units. A/C MINIBAR TV TEL. 2,800–3,200F ($448–$512) double; 4,500–5,500F ($720–$880) suite. AE, DC, MC, V. Métro: Concorde or Opéra.

The Embassy of Texas when that state was a nation, this jewel box opened in 1998 at one of the world's most prestigious addresses. Though the guest rooms are only moderate in size, you live in opulent comfort. Most of the rooms are in classic Second Empire style with luxurious beds, tasteful fabrics, and well-upholstered hand-carved furnishings. The security is fantastic, with TV intercoms. This new version of the hotel replaces a lackluster one that stood here for a century, and its facade and roof are classified as historic monuments by the French government.

Dining: The Café de Vendôme is directed by Gérard Sallé, who has worked at some of Paris's premier addresses, like the Bristol and the Plaza Athénée. The cuisine is imaginative, the setting rather austere but elegant.

Amenities: Concierge, 24-hour room service, laundry.

Hôtel du Louvre. Place André-Malraux, 75001 Paris. ☎ **800/888-4747** in the U.S. and Canada, or 01-44-58-38-38. Fax 01-44-58-38-01. www.hoteldulouvre.com. E-mail: hoteldulouvre@hoteldulouvre.com. 195 units. A/C MINIBAR TV TEL. 2,050–4,000F ($328–$640) double; from 4,500F ($720) suite. Ask about midwinter discounts. AE, DC, MC, V. Parking 100F ($16). Métro: Palais Royal.

When Napoléon III inaugurated the hotel in 1855, French journalists described it as "a palace of the people, rising adjacent to the palace of kings." In 1897, Camille Pissarro moved into a room with a view that inspired many of his landscapes. Between the Louvre and the Palais Royal, the hotel has a decor of marble, bronze, and gilt. The guest rooms are quintessentially Parisian, filled with souvenirs of the belle époque. Most were renovated between 1996 and 1998. Some are small, but most are medium-size—with elegant fabrics and upholstery, excellent carpeting, double-glazed windows, comfortable beds, and traditional wood furniture.

Dining/Diversions: Le Bar "Defender" is a cozy hideaway, with mahogany trim, Scottish overtones, and a collection of single-malt whiskeys; a pianist plays after dusk. There's also the French Empire Brasserie du Louvre, whose tables extend to the terrace in fine weather.

Amenities: Concierge, 24-hour room service, laundry/dry cleaning, valet, baby-sitting, business center.

Hôtel Meurice. 228 rue de Rivoli, 75001 Paris. ☎ **01-44-58-10-10.** Fax 01-44-58-10-15. 160 units. A/C MINIBAR TV TEL. 3,500–4,000F ($560–$640) double; from 6,500F ($1,040) suite. Métro: Tuileries or Concorde.

After a spectacular 2-year renovation, the landmark Meurice reopened in mid-2000 better than ever. Since the early 1800s it has been welcoming the royal and the rich and even the radical: The deposed king of Spain, Alfonso XIII, once occupied suite

108; the mad genius Salvador Dalí made the Meurice his headquarters, as did General von Cholritz, the Nazi who ruled Paris during the occupation. The mosaic floors, elaborate plaster ceilings, hand-carved moldings, and art nouveau glass roof atop the Winter Garden look like new. Each guest room is individually decorated with period pieces, fine carpets, Italian and French fabrics, rare marbles, and modern features like fax and Internet access. Louis XVI and Empire styles predominate. Our favorites and the least expensive are the sixth-floor dormer rooms. Some rooms have painted ceilings of puffy clouds and blue skies along with canopied beds.

Dining/Diversions: Le Meurice remains a citadel of haute cuisine, though many of its dishes are lighter (yet still exquisitely flavored) than before. The Fontainebleau Bar is one of the new chic rendezvous places, and the Winter Garden is the most elegant place in Paris for drinks or high tea.

Amenities: Concierge, 24-hour room service, laundry/dry cleaning, secretarial service, new spa with state-of-the-art facilities, fitness area, massage, beauty treatments.

Hôtel Regina. 2 place des Pyramides, 75001 Paris. ☎ **01-42-60-31-10.** Fax 01-40-15-95-16. www.regina-hotel.com. E-mail: reservation@regina-hotel.com. 120 units. A/C MINIBAR TV TEL. 1,550–2,250F ($248–$360) double; from 2,250F ($360) suite. AE, DC, MC, V. Free parking. Métro: Pyramides or Tuileries.

Until a radical renovation upgraded its old-fashioned grandeur in 1995, this hotel slumbered adjacent to rue de Rivoli's equestrian statue of Joan of Arc. The management has poured millions into the renovation, retaining the patina of the art nouveau interior and making historically appropriate improvements. The guest rooms are richly decorated; those overlooking the Tuileries enjoy panoramic views as far away as the Eiffel Tower. The public areas contain every period of Louis furniture imaginable, Oriental carpets, 18th-century paintings, and bowls of flowers. Fountains play in a flagstone-covered courtyard, site of alfresco cafe tables and an extension of the hotel's restaurant.

Dining: In Le Pluvinel, conservative French cuisine is served in an art deco atmosphere. Pluvinel is closed on weekends, when there's only a less appealing but more affordable bistro-style snack bar.

Amenities: Concierge, 24-hour room service, twice-daily maid service, laundry/dry cleaning, valet, baby-sitting, secretarial service, in-room massage, conference room; visits to nearby health club arranged on request.

✪ **Hôtel Ritz.** 15 place Vendôme, 75001 Paris. ☎ **800/223-6800** in the U.S. and Canada, or 01-43-16-30-30. Fax 01-43-16-31-78. www.ritzparis.com. E-mail: resa@ritzparis.com. 175 units. A/C MINIBAR TV TEL. 3,600–4,500F ($576–$720) double; from 6,200F ($992) suite. AE, DC, MC, V. Parking 230F ($36.80). Métro: Opéra.

The Ritz is Europe's greatest hotel, an enduring symbol of elegance on one of Paris's most beautiful and historic squares. César Ritz, the "little shepherd boy from Niederwald," converted the private Hôtel de Lazun into a luxury hotel that he opened in

---

Café & a Croissant?

Hotel breakfasts are fairly uniform and include your choice of coffee, tea, or hot chocolate; a freshly baked croissant and roll; and limited quantities of butter and jam or jelly. It can be at your door moments after you call for it and is served at almost any hour. (When we mention breakfast charges in our listings, we refer to continental breakfasts only.) Breakfasts with eggs, bacon, ham, or other items must be ordered from the à la carte menu. For a charge, larger hotels serve the full or "English" breakfast, but smaller hotels typically serve only the continental variety.

A Hotel Tale

During Paris's occupation, on August 25, 1944, Ernest Hemingway "liberated" the Ritz. Armed with machine guns, "Papa" and a group of Allied soldiers pulled up to the hotel in a Jeep, intent on capturing Nazis and freeing, if only symbolically, the landmark. After a sweep from the cellars to the roof, the group discovered the Nazis had already fled. Hemingway led his team to the Ritz bar to order a round of dry martinis. In commemoration of the 50th anniversary of the liberation, the renovated Bar Hemingway reopened on August 25, 1994.

1898. With the help of the culinary master Escoffier, he made the Ritz a miracle of luxury living.

In 1979, the Ritz family sold the hotel to Egyptian businessman Mohammed al Fayed, who refurbished it and added a cooking school. (You may remember that his son, Dodi al Fayed, and Princess Diana dined here before they set out on their fateful drive.) Two town houses were annexed, joined by a long arcade lined with miniature display cases representing 125 of Paris's leading boutiques. The public salons are furnished with museum-caliber antiques. Each guest room is uniquely decorated, most often with Louis XIV or XV reproductions; all have fine rugs, marble fireplaces, tapestries, brass beds, and more. The spacious marble bathrooms are among the city's most luxurious, filled with deluxe toiletries, scales, private phones, cords to summon maids and valets, robes, full-length and makeup mirrors, and dual basins. Ever since Edward VII got stuck in a too-narrow bathtub with his lover of the evening, the tubs at the Ritz have been deep and big. The hotel has its own workshop to repair and reproduce the plumbing.

Dining/Diversions: The Espadon grill room is one of the finest in Paris. The Ritz Supper Club includes a bar, a salon with a fireplace, a restaurant, and a dance floor. You can order drinks in either the Bar Vendôme or the Bar Hemingway.

Amenities: Concierge, 24-hour room service, laundry, valet, health club with pool and massage parlor, florist, shops, squash court.

EXPENSIVE

Hôtel des Tuileries. 10 rue St-Hyacinthe, 75001 Paris. ☎ **01-42-61-04-17.** Fax 01-49-27-91-56. www.members.aol.com/htuileri/. E-mail: htuileri@aol.com. 26 units. A/C MINIBAR TV TEL. 890–1,400F ($142.40–$224) double. AE, DC, MC, V. Parking 110F ($17.60). Métro: Tuileries or Pyramides.

On a quiet narrow street, this hotel occupies a 17th-century town house Marie Antoinette used when she left Versailles for unofficial Paris visits. Don't expect mementos of the queen, as all the frippery of her era was long ago stripped away. But in honor of its royal antecedents, the hotel's public areas and guest rooms are filled with copies of Louis XV furniture—a bit dowdy but still comfortable.

Amenities: Room service (daily 7am to 11pm), newspaper delivery on request.

MODERATE

Hôtel Britannique. 20 av. Victoria, 75001 Paris. ☎ **01-42-33-74-59.** Fax 01-42-33-82-65. www.hotel-britannic.com. E-mail: mailbox@hotel-britannique.fr. 40 units. MINIBAR TV TEL. 790–1,080F ($126.40–$172.80) double. AE, DC, MC, V. Parking 100F ($16). Métro: Châtelet.

Conservatively modern and plush, this much-renovated 19th-century hotel near Les Halles, the Pompidou, and Notre-Dame, was re-rated with three stars after a complete renovation in the mid-1980s. The place not only is British in name but also seems to have cultivated an English style of graciousness. The guest rooms may be small, but they're immaculate and soundproof, with comfortable beds and safe-deposit boxes. A satellite receiver gets U.S. and U.K. TV shows. The reading room is a cozy retreat. Room service from a limited menu is available (daily 12:30 to 9pm).

✪ **Hôtel Burgundy.** 8 rue Duphot, 75001 Paris. ☎ **01-42-60-34-12.** Fax 01-47-03-95-20. www.perso.wanadoo.fr/hotel.burgundy. E-mail: hotel.burgundy@iname.com. 89 units. MINIBAR TV TEL. 980F ($156.80) double; 1,600F ($256) suite. AE, DC, MC, V. Métro: Madeleine or Concorde.

The Burgundy is one of this outrageously expensive area's best values. The frequently renovated building began as two adjacent town houses in the 1830s, one a pension where Baudelaire wrote some of his eerie poetry in the 1860s and the other a bordello. They were linked by British-born managers, who insisted on using the English name. Radically renovated in 1992, the hotel hosts many North and South Americans and features conservatively decorated rooms and comfortable beds. The Charles Baudelaire restaurant is open for lunch and dinner Monday to Friday. There's no bar, but drinks are served in the lobby during meal hours. Amenities include limited concierge service, room service (daily 6:30am to 9:30pm), laundry/dry cleaning, and a conference room.

Hôtel Mansart. 5 rue des Capucines, 75001 Paris. ☎ **01-42-61-50-28.** Fax 01-49-27-97-44. www.hotel.esprit.de.france.com. E-mail: hotel.mansart@wanadoo.fr. 57 units. MINIBAR TV TEL. 600–900F ($96–$144) double; 1,600F ($256) suite. AE, DC, MC, V. Métro: Opéra or Madeleine.

After operating as a glorious wreck for many decades, this hotel—designed by its namesake—was fully renovated in 1991 and offers some of the lowest rates in this pricey area. The public rooms contain Louis reproductions and startling floor-to-ceiling geometric designs inspired by the inlaid marble floors (or formal gardens) of the French Renaissance. The small- to medium-size guest rooms are subtly formal and comfortable, though only half a dozen of the suites and most expensive rooms actually overlook the famous square. Twenty rooms are air-conditioned. Breakfast is the only meal served.

Relais du Louvre. 19 rue des Prêtres, 75001 Paris. ☎ **01-40-41-96-42.** Fax 01-40-41-96-44. 20 units. MINIBAR TV TEL. 900–1,000F ($144–$160) double; 1,300–2,200F ($208–$352) suite. AE, DC, MC, V. Parking 80F ($12.80). Métro: Louvre or Pont Neuf.

One of the neighborhood's most up-to-date hotels opened in 1991, midway between the wings at the eastern end of the Louvre. Between 1800 and 1941, its upper floors contained the printing presses that recorded the goings-on in Paris's House of Representatives. Its street level held the Café Momus, favored by Voltaire, Hugo, and intellectuals of the day and where Puccini set one of the pivotal scenes of *La Bohème*. The guest rooms are boldly colored, with modern conveniences, soundproof windows, reproduction furniture, and grace notes like French doors opening in some cases onto tiny balconies. Many rooms are a bit small, but others contain roomy sitting areas. Breakfast can be served in the rooms from 6:30 to 11:30am.

INEXPENSIVE

Hôtel Henri IV. 25 place Dauphine, 75001 Paris. ☎ **01-43-54-44-53.** 21 units, 3 with shower only. 190–210F ($30.40–$33.60) double without shower; 250–270F ($40–$43.20) double with shower. Rates include breakfast. No credit cards. Métro: Pont Neuf.

Four hundred years ago, this decrepit narrow building housed the printing presses used for the edicts of Henri IV. Today one of the most famous and most consistently crowded budget hotels in Europe sits in a dramatic location at the westernmost tip of Ile de la Cité, beside a formal park. The crowd is mostly bargain-conscious academics, journalists, and francophiles, many of whom reserve rooms as much as 2 months in advance. The low-ceilinged lobby, a flight above street level, is cramped and bleak; the

Splish, Splash . . . Taking a Bath

Throughout the hotels in this chapter, expect the bathrooms in very expensive and expensive hotels to be a bit larger than normal, with fine toiletries and plush towels and perhaps bathrobes. The bathrooms in moderate and inexpensive hotels tend to be cramped but still acceptable, with towels that are perhaps a bit less plush than those at expensive places.

In the listings, we haven't discussed bathrooms unless they vary from this norm—if they're especially opulent or especially bare-bones. Be aware that some hotels offer tub/shower combinations, some offer shower stalls, and some offer a mix. If this is important to you, request your preference when reserving. Also be aware that almost all hotels, except the inexpensive ones, include hair dryers in the bathrooms.

---

creaky stairway leading to the guest rooms is almost impossibly narrow. The rooms are considered romantically threadbare by many and run-down and substandard by others. Each contains a sink, but not even the trio of rooms with showers have toilets.

Timhôtel Louvre. 4 rue Croix des Petits-Champs, 75001 Paris. ☎ **01-42-60-34-86.** Fax 01-42-60-10-39. 56 units. TV TEL. 680–700F ($108.80–$112) double. AE, DC, MC, V. Métro: Palais Royal.

This hotel and its sibling, the Timhôtel Palais-Royal, are mirror images of each other, at least inside; they're part of a new breed of two-star business hotels cropping up around France. These Timhôtels share the same manager and the same temperament, and though the rooms at the Palais-Royal branch are a bit larger than the ones here, this branch is so close to the Louvre as to be almost irresistible. The ambience is standardized modern, with monochromatic guest rooms and wall-to-wall carpeting that was upgraded in 1998. Breakfast is served rather anonymously from a self-service cafeteria. The **Timhôtel Palais-Royal** is at 3 rue de la Banque, 75002 Paris (☎ **01-42-61-53-90;** fax 01-42-60-05-39; Métro: Bourse).

2ND ARRONDISSEMENT (LA BOURSE)
EXPENSIVE

Hôtel Victoires Opéra. 56 rue Montorgueil, 75002 Paris. ☎ **01-42-36-41-08.** Fax 01-45-08-08-79. E-mail: hakimb@club-internet.fr. 26 units. A/C MINIBAR TV TEL. 1,400F ($224) double, 1,800F ($288) junior suite. Métro: Les Halles.

Head to this little charmer if you want a reasonably priced place convenient to Les Halles and the Pompidou as well as to the Marais, with its shops and gay and straight restaurants. It's a classically decorated hotel, evoking the era of Louis Philippe. Recent renovations include the addition of a private bathroom for every room. Since a junior suite is priced about the same as a double, request a suite—you'll enjoy the extra space. Most of the rooms are alike, comfortable but a bit tiny. They're reached by elevator from the second floor. Skip the hotel breakfast (which costs extra) and cross the street to Stohrer at no. 51, one of Paris's most historic pâtissèries, founded in 1730 by the pâtissier to Louis XV.

Le Stendhal. 22 rue Danielle-Casanova, 75002 Paris. ☎ **01-44-58-52-52.** Fax 01-44-58-52-00. www.small-hotel.com. 20 units. A/C MINIBAR TV TEL. 1,470–1,660F ($235.20–$265.60) double; from 1,800F ($288) suite. AE, DC, MC, V. Parking 100F ($16). Métro: Opéra.

Opened in 1992, this hotel mixes a young hip style with a sense of tradition. Its location, close to the glamorous place Vendôme jewelry stores, couldn't be grander. Overall, the effect is that of a boutique-style *hôtel de luxe* that seems like a Parisian version of an upscale English B&B. The rooms, accessible via a tiny elevator, have vivid color schemes. Most are small but not without their charm. The red-and-black Stendhal Suite pays homage to the author, who made this his private home for many years and died here in 1842.

Dining: Breakfast is served in a stone cellar with a vaulted ceiling. A small bar adjoins the lobby but offers little allure. Simple meals can be ordered and are served in the rooms or at the bar anytime.

Amenities: Receptionist/concierge to arrange baby-sitting, dry cleaning, secretarial services, car rentals.

MODERATE

Tulip Inn de Noailles. 9 rue de la Michodière, 75002 Paris. ☎ **800/344-1212** in the U.S., or 01-47-42-92-90. Fax 01-49-24-92-71. www.hoteldenoailles.com. E-mail: Tulip.Inn.de. Noailles@wanadoo.fr. 61 units. TV TEL. 750–980F ($120–$156.80) double; 1,200F ($192) suite. Rates include breakfast if you book directly with hotel. AE, DC, MC, V. Métro: 4 Septembre or Opéra.

If you're looking for a postmodern hotel in the style of Putman and Starck, book in here. Proprietor Martine Falck has turned this old-fashioned place in a great location into a refined art deco choice with bold colors and cutting-edge style. Yet the prices remain reasonable. The guest rooms come in various shapes and sizes but all are comfortable; half are air-conditioned. A favorite is no. 601 with its own terrace. Amenities include room service (daily 7:30am to 10pm for breakfast service and drinks only), laundry service, a private safe in the office, and a small gym and sauna.

3RD ARRONDISSEMENT (LE MARAIS)
VERY EXPENSIVE

✪ **Pavillon de la Reine.** 28 place des Vosges, 75003 Paris. ☎ **01-40-29-19-19.** Fax 01-40-29-19-20. www.pavillon-de-la-Reine.com. E-mail: pavillon@club-internet.fr. 55 units. A/C MINIBAR TV TEL. 1,950–2,150F ($312–$344) double; 2,150–2,500F ($344–$400) duplex; 2,600–3,900F ($416–$624) suite. AE, DC, MC, V. Free parking. Métro: Bastille.

Built in 1986, this cream-colored neoclassical villa blends in seamlessly with the rest of place des Vosges—you enter through an arcade opening onto a small formal garden. The Louis XIII decor evokes the square's heyday, and wing chairs with flame-stitched upholstery combine with iron-banded Spanish antiques to create a rustic feel. Each guest room is unique but all have a warm decor of weathered beams and reproductions of famous oil paintings. Most rooms are of good size; some come with private safes and some are duplexes with sleeping lofts above cozy salons. The preferred rooms are on the upper floors opening onto the romantic square.

Dining: The hotel has an "honesty bar" and a limited 24-hour room-service menu.

Amenities: Receptionist/concierge to arrange massage; dry cleaning; car rentals; show, concert, and theater tickets.

MODERATE

Hôtel des Chevaliers. 30 rue de Turenne, 75003 Paris. ☎ **01-42-72-73-47.** Fax 01-42-72-54-10. 24 units. MINIBAR TV TEL. 660–700F ($105.60–$112) double; 874F ($139.85) triple. Métro: Chemin Vert or St-Paul.

Half a block from the northwestern edge of place des Vosges, this renovated hotel occupies a dramatic corner building whose 17th-century vestiges have been elevated into high art. These include the remnants of a stone-sided well in the cellar, a sweeping stone barrel vault covering the breakfast area, half-timbering artfully exposed in the stairwell, and Louis XIII accessories that'll remind you of the hotel's origins. Each guest room is comfortable and well maintained.

4TH ARRONDISSEMENT (ILE DE LA CITÉ/ILE ST-LOUIS & BEAUBOURG)
MODERATE

✪ **Hôtel Caron de Beaumarchais.** 12 rue Vieille-du-Temple, 75004 Paris. ☎ **01-42-72-34-12.** Fax 01-42-72-34-63. www.carondebeaumarchais.com. 19 units. A/C MINIBAR TV TEL. 730–810F ($116.80–$129.60) double. AE, DC, MC, V. Métro: St-Paul or Hôtel de Ville.

Built in the 18th century and gracefully upgraded in 1998, this good-value choice features floors of artfully worn gray stone, antique reproductions, and elaborate fabrics based on antique patterns. Hotelier Alain Bigeard likes his primrose-colored guest rooms to evoke the taste of the French gentry in the 18th century, when the Marais was the scene of high-society dances or even duels, and most retain their original ceiling beams. The smallest units overlook the interior courtyard, and the top-floor rooms are tiny but have panoramic balcony views across the Right Bank.

✪ **Hôtel de Lutèce.** 65 rue St-Louis-en-l'Ile, 75004 Paris. ☎ **01-43-26-23-52.** Fax 01-43-29-60-25. www.france-hotel-guide.com/h75004lutece.htm. 23 units. A/C TV TEL. 900F ($144) double; 1,100F ($176) triple. AE, MC, V. Métro: Pont Marie or Cité.

This hotel feels like a country house in Brittany. The lounge, with its old fireplace, is graciously furnished with antiques and contemporary paintings. Ranging in size from small to medium, each of the individualized guest rooms boasts antiques, adding to a refined atmosphere that attracts celebrities like the duke and duchess of Bedford. Many were renovated in 1998. The hotel is comparable in style and amenities to the Deux-Iles (see below), under the same ownership.

Hôtel des Deux-Iles. 59 rue St-Louis-en-l'Ile, 75004 Paris. ☎ **01-43-26-13-35.** Fax 01-43-29-60-25. 17 units. A/C TEL. 890F ($142.40) double. AE, MC, V. Métro: Pont Marie.

This much-restored 17th-century town house was an inexpensive hotel until 1976, when an elaborate decor with lots of bamboo and reed furniture and French provincial touches was added. The result is an unpretentious but charming hotel with a great location. The guest rooms are on the small side, however. A garden of plants and flowers off the lobby leads to a basement breakfast room with a fireplace. Amenities include room service (daily 7:30am to 8pm) and laundry/dry cleaning.

✪ **Hôtel St-Louis.** 75 rue St-Louis-en-l'Ile, 75004 Paris. ☎ **01-46-34-04-80.** Fax 01-46-34-02-13. www.paris-hotel.tm.fr/saint-louis-marais. 21 units. TEL. 775–875F ($124–$140) double. MC, V. Métro: Pont Marie.

Proprietors Guy and Andrée Record maintain a charming family atmosphere at this antique-filled small hotel in a 17th-century town house. Despite a full renovation completed in 1998, it represents an incredible value considering its prime location on Ile St-Louis. Expect cozy, slightly cramped rooms. With mansard roofs and old-fashioned moldings, the top-floor rooms sport tiny balconies with sweeping rooftop views. The breakfast room is in the cellar, with 17th-century stone vaulting.

8TH ARRONDISSEMENT (CHAMPS-ELYSÉES/MADELEINE)
VERY EXPENSIVE

✪ **Hôtel Balzac.** 6 rue Balzac, 75008 Paris. ☎ **800/457-4000** in the U.S. and Canada, or 01-44-35-18-00. Fax 01-44-35-18-05. E-mail: hotelbalzac@wanadoo.fr. 70 units. A/C MINIBAR TV TEL. 2,200F ($352) double; from 3,300F ($528) suite. AE, DC, MC, V. Parking 150F ($24). Métro: George V.

If the Crillon and the Ritz are Rolls-Royces, then the Balzac is a Bentley, boasting a well-trained formal staff. Elegant and discreet, it opened in 1986 in a belle-époque

---

ⓘ Family-Friendly Accommodations

Hôtel de Fleurie *(see p. 87)*   In the heart of St-Germain-des-Prés, this has long been a Left Bank family favorite. The hotel is known for its *chambres familiales*— two connecting rooms with a pair of large beds in each room. Children under 12 stay free with their parents.

Hôtel du Ministère *(see p. 78)*   For the family on a budget that doesn't mind cramped quarters, the Ministère is one of the best bets in this expensive area near the Champs-Elysées.

Hôtel St-Louis *(see p. 74)*   The family atmosphere cultivated by proprietors Guy and Andreé Record is a precious commodity in Paris these days. This 17th-century town house is set on historic Ile St-Louis and priced with families in mind.

Résidence Lord Byron *(see p. 78)*   The Byron is not only a good value and an unusually family-oriented place for the swanky 8th arrondissement but also is only a 10-minute walk from many of the city's major monuments.

Timhôtel Louvre *(see p. 75)*   This is an especially convenient choice because it offers some rooms with four beds for the price of a double. And the location near the Louvre is irresistible.

---

mansion, then was redecorated in 1994 by English designer Nina Campbell. Most of the guest rooms are medium to spacious in size, with modern furniture, double glazing, private safes, mirrored closets, and king-size beds.

Dining: In a prominent spot near the elegant lobby is Pierre Gagnaire's eponymous restaurant (see chapter 5). Its namesake is a promising culinary newcomer to Paris whose three-star cuisine has impressed critics throughout France.

Amenities: Concierge, 24-hour room service, dry cleaning/laundry.

Hôtel Bristol. 112 rue du faubourg St-Honoré, 75008 Paris. ☎ **01-53-43-43-00.** Fax 01-53-43-43-26. www.hotel-bristol.com. E-mail: resa@hotel-bristol.com. 156 units. A/C MINI-BAR TV TEL. 3,400–3,800F ($544–$608) double; 6,600F ($1,056) suite. AE, DC, MC, V. Free parking. Métro: Miromesnil.

This palace is near the Palais d'Elysée (home of the French president), on the shopping street running parallel to the Champs-Elysées. The classic 18th-century Parisian facade has a glass-and-wrought-iron entryway, where you're greeted by uniformed English-speaking attendants. Hippolyte Jammet founded the Bristol in 1924, installing many valuable antiques and Louis XV and XVI furnishings. The guest rooms are opulent, with either antiques or well-made reproductions, inlaid wood, bronze, crystal, Oriental carpets, and original oil paintings. Each room is freshened every 3 years. Personalized old-world service is rigidly maintained here—some guests find it forbidding, others absolutely adore it.

Dining/Diversions: In a greenhouse-style room overlooking the garden, the Restaurant d'Eté (Summer Restaurant) is open April to October, and the richly paneled Restaurant d'Hiver (Winter Restaurant) is open the rest of the year. Tea and drinks are served at the sometimes irritatingly reverent Bristol Bar or in the garden.

Amenities: Concierge, 24-hour room service, business center with translation services, hairdresser, massage parlor, sauna, conference rooms, heated indoor pool, rooftop solarium with view of Sacré-Coeur (open daily 6:30am to 10:30pm).

✪ **Hôtel de Crillon.** 10 place de la Concorde, 75008 Paris. ☎ **800/241-3333** in the U.S. and Canada, or 01-44-71-15-00. Fax 01-44-71-15-04. www.crillon.com. E-mail: crillon@crillon.com. 163 units. A/C MINIBAR TV TEL. 3,500–4,300F ($560–$688) double; from 4,950F ($792) suite. AE, DC, MC, V. Parking 150F ($24). Métro: Concorde.

One of Europe's grand hotels, the Crillon sits across from the U.S. Embassy. The 200-plus-year-old building, once the palace of the duc de Crillon, has been a hotel since the early 1900s and is now owned by Jean Taittinger of the champagne family. The public salons boast 17th- and 18th-century tapestries, gilt-and-brocade furniture, chandeliers, fine sculpture, and Louis XVI chests and chairs. The guest rooms are large and luxurious. Some are spectacular, like the Leonard Bernstein Suite, which has one of the maestro's pianos and one of the grandest views of any hotel room in Paris. The marble bathrooms are sumptuous as well, with deluxe toiletries, dual sinks, robes, and (in some) thermal taps.

Dining: The elegant Les Ambassadeurs serves a *menu dégustation* at lunch on weekends and every evening and offers a businessperson's lunch Monday to Friday. We've ranked its breakfast menu a Best Bet (see chapter 1). In the more informal L'Obélisque, the menu choices are less experimental.

Amenities: Concierge, 24-hour room service, laundry, valet, secretarial/translation service, meeting and conference rooms, garden-style courtyard with restaurant service, shops.

Hôtel Plaza Athénée. 25 av. Montaigne, 75008 Paris. ☎ **800/223-6800** in the U.S. and Canada, or 01-53-67-66-65. Fax 01-53-67-66-66. E-mail: email@hotel-plaza-athenee-fr. 188 units. A/C MINIBAR TV TEL. 3,700–4,200F ($592–$672) double; from 5,800F ($928) suite. AE, MC, V. Parking 150F ($24). Métro: F. D. Roosevelt or Alma-Marceau.

The Plaza Athénée, an 1889 art nouveau marvel, is a landmark of discretion and style. About half the celebrities visiting Paris have been pampered here; in the old days, Mata Hari used to frequent the place. The finest public room is the Montaigne Salon, paneled in grained wood and dominated by a marble fireplace. The quietest guest rooms overlook a courtyard with awnings and parasol-shaded tables; they have ample closet space, and their large tiled bathrooms contain double basins. Some rooms overlooking avenue Montaigne have views of the Eiffel Tower. In 1999, the hotel completed a radical overhaul, creating larger rooms out of some of the smaller, less desirable ones.

Dining/Diversions: Le Régence offers superb food—try the lobster soufflé. For lunch, the Grill Relais Plaza is the meeting place of dress designers and personalities from the worlds of publishing, cinema, and art. The Bar du Plaza is a favorite spot for a late-night drink.

Amenities: Concierge, 24-hour room service, laundry, conference rooms, beauty salon, massage, fitness club.

EXPENSIVE

Hôtel Concorde St-Lazare. 108 rue St-Lazare, 75008 Paris. ☎ **800/888-4747** in the U.S. outside New York State and Canada, 212/752-3900 in New York State, 0171/630-1704 in London, or 01-40-08-44-44. Fax 01-42-93-01-20. www.concordestlazare-paris.com. E-mail: stlazare@concordestlazare-paris.com. 300 units. A/C MINIBAR TV TEL. 1,450–2,500F ($232–$400) double; 2,800–6,000F ($448–$960) suite. AE, DC, MC, V. Parking 150F ($24). Métro: St-Lazare.

Across from the St-Lazare rail station, this hotel—the area's best—was built in 1889 for the visitors flocking to the Universal Exposition. During the late 1990s, each of the guest rooms was elevated to modern standards of comfort and redecorated. Many rooms (medium-size to quite large) have high ceilings, especially those on the lower

Hotels Near Place Charles de Gaulle

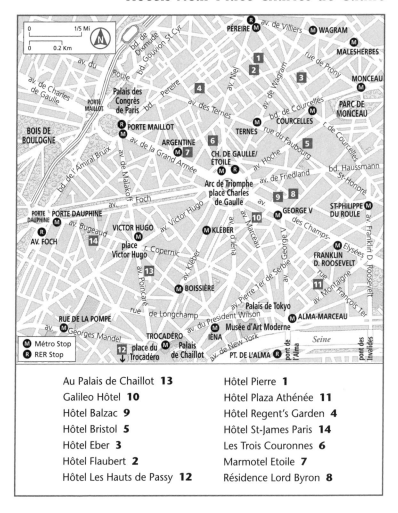

Au Palais de Chaillot **13**	Hôtel Pierre **1**
Galileo Hôtel **10**	Hôtel Plaza Athénée **11**
Hôtel Balzac **9**	Hôtel Regent's Garden **4**
Hôtel Bristol **5**	Hôtel St-James Paris **14**
Hôtel Eber **3**	Les Trois Couronnes **6**
Hôtel Flaubert **2**	Marmotel Etoile **7**
Hôtel Les Hauts de Passy **12**	Résidence Lord Byron **8**

floors, which also have double-glazed windows to cut down on the noise. The beds are plush and comfortable.

Dining/Diversions: Le Golden Black is an American bar; the Café Terminus offers daily brasserie service noon to 11pm; and the Bistrot 108 serves provincial dishes and great vintages by the glass. There's a room devoted to French billiards—the only room of its kind in any Paris hotel.

Amenities: Concierge, 24-hour room service, laundry, valet, baby-sitting.

MODERATE

Galileo Hôtel. 54 rue Galilée, 75008 Paris. ☎ **01-47-20-66-06.** Fax 01-47-20-67-17. 27 units. A/C MINIBAR TV TEL. 950F ($152) double. AE, DC, MC, V. Métro: Charles de Gaulle–Etoile or George V.

For years, *Frommer's Paris* has been recommending the Hôtel des Deux-Iles and Hôtel de Lutèce on St-Louis-en-l'Ile. Now the owners of those hotels, Roland and Elisabeth

Buffat, have invaded the 8th arrondissement with this boutique-style hotel. A short walk from the Champ-Elysées, the town-house hotel is the epitome of French elegance and charm. The guest rooms are medium in size for the most part and a study in understated taste, decorated in various shades of cocoa and beige. The most spacious are nos. 501 or 502, with a glass-covered veranda you can use even in winter. For such a tony neighborhood, the prices are moderate. Breakfast is the only meal served.

Hôtel Queen Mary. 9 rue Greffulhe, 75008 Paris. ☎ **01-42-66-40-50.** Fax 01-42-66-94-92. www.hotelqueenmary.com. E-mail: hotelqueenmary@wanadoo.fr. 36 units. A/C MINIBAR TV TEL. 780–995F ($124.80–$159.20) double; 1,400F ($224) suite. AE, DC, MC, V. Parking 80F ($12.80). Métro: Madeleine or Havre-Caumartin.

Meticulously renovated inside and out, this early-1900s hotel is graced with an iron-and-glass canopy, ornate wrought iron, and the kind of detailing normally reserved for more expensive hotels. The public rooms have touches of greenery and reproductions of mid-19th-century antiques; each guest room has an upholstered headboard, comfortable beds, and mahogany furnishings, plus a carafe of sherry. All the rooms, ranging from small to medium, were fully renovated in 1998.

✪ Résidence Lord Byron. 5 rue de Chateaubriand, 75008 Paris. ☎ **01-43-59-89-98.** Fax 01-42-89-46-04. www.escapade-paris.com. E-mail: lord.byron@escapade-paris.com. 31 units. MINIBAR TV TEL. 890–990F ($142.40–$158.40) double; from 1,390F ($222.40) suite. AE, DC, MC, V. Parking 75F ($12). Métro: George V. RER: Etoile.

Off the Champs-Elysées on a curving street of handsome buildings, the Lord Byron may not be as grand as other hotels in the neighborhood, but it's more affordable. Unassuming and a bit staid, it's exactly what repeat guests want: a sense of luxury, solitude, and understatement, a fine choice for families. The guest rooms are small to medium. You can eat breakfast in the dining room or in a shaded inner garden.

INEXPENSIVE

Hôtel du Ministère. 31 rue de Surène, 75008 Paris. ☎ **01-42-66-21-43.** Fax 01-42-66-96-04. www.argia.fr/hotel-ministere. E-mail: hotel-ministere@argia.fr. 28 units. A/C MINIBAR TV TEL. 690–840F ($110.40–$134.40) double; from 890F ($142.40) junior suite. AE, MC, V. Métro: Madeleine or Miromesnil.

The Ministère is a winning choice near the Champs-Elysées and the American Embassy, though it's far from Paris's cheapest budget hotel. Long a family hotel, it received new owners in 1999 who began a program of refurbishing, making the hotel better than ever. The guest rooms are on the small side, but each is comfortably appointed and well maintained; many have oak beams and furnishings that, though worn, are still serviceable. Try to avoid a room on the very top floor, as you'll be too cramped. Breakfast is the only meal served.

Hôtel Opal. 19 rue Tronchet, 75008 Paris. ☎ **01-42-65-77-97.** Fax 01-49-24-06-58. www.hotels.fr/opal. E-mail: h_opal@club-internet.fr. 36 units. A/C MINIBAR TV TEL. 590–730F ($94.40–$116.80) double. Extra bed 100F ($16). AE, DC, V. Parking 130F ($20.80) nearby. Métro: Madeleine.

This rejuvenated hotel is a real find behind La Madeleine church and near the Opéra Garnier. The guest rooms are somewhat tight but very clean and comfortable, and many of them are air-conditioned. Those on the top floor are reached by a narrow staircase; some have skylights. Most rooms have twin brass beds. Reception will make arrangements for parking at a nearby garage.

9TH & 10TH ARRONDISSEMENTS (OPÉRA GARNIER/ GARE DU NORD)

INEXPENSIVE

Hôtel de la Tour d'Auvergne. 10 rue de la Tour d'Auvergne, 75009 Paris. ☎ **01-48-78-61-60.** Fax 01-49-95-99-00. 24 units. TV TEL. 550–750F ($88–$120) double. AE, DC, MC, V. Métro: Cadet or Anvers.

This building was erected before Baron Haussmann reconfigured Paris's avenues around 1870. Later, Modigliani rented a room here for 6 months, and the staff will tell you Victor Hugo and Auguste Rodin briefly lived on this street. The interior was long ago modernized into a glossy internationalism. The guest rooms are meticulously coordinated, yet the small decorative canopies over the headboards make them feel cluttered. Though the views over the back courtyard are uninspired, even gloomy, some guests request rear rooms for their relative quiet. Every year, five rooms are renovated, so the comfort level is kept at a high standard.

Hôtel William du Pré. 3 rue Mayran, 75009 Paris. ☎ **01-48-78-68-35.** Fax 01-45-26-08-70. 30 units. TV TEL. 490–515F ($78.40–$82.40) double. AE, MC, V. Parking 60F ($9.60). Métro: Cadet.

Boasting a dignified facade, this 19th-century building was bought by a chain of unpretentious hotels and renovated in 1992. The guest rooms are clean and uncomplicated, though the decor is a bit cold. Each is soundproof thanks to double-glazing and has a safe. The front rooms overlook one of the area's largest public gardens, a verdant oasis in an otherwise congested commercial neighborhood; fifth- and second-floor rooms offer small wrought-iron balconies. The hotel serves breakfast in a cellar room showing vestiges of the original masonry.

11TH & 12TH ARRONDISSEMENTS (OPÉRA BASTILLE/ BOIS DE VINCENNES)

MODERATE

Hôtel Pavillon Bastille. 65 rue de Lyon, 75012 Paris. ☎ **01-43-43-65-65.** Fax 01-43-43-96-52. www.france-paris.com. E-mail: hotel-pavillon@akamail.com. 25 units. A/C MINIBAR TV TEL. 840–955F ($134.40–$152.80) double; 1,375F ($220) suite. AE, DC, MC, V. Parking 85F ($13.60). Métro: Bastille.

Hardly your cozy little backstreet digs, this is a bold, brassy, innovative hotel in a 1991 town house across from the Opéra Bastille and a block south of place de la Bastille. A 17th-century fountain graces the courtyard between the hotel and the street. The guest rooms have twin or double beds, partially mirrored walls, and contemporary built-in furniture. If you're looking for a bargain, note that the cheapest rooms have the same size and configuration as the more expensive *chambres privilegées* (the extra cost gets you amenities like slippers, better cosmetics, fruit baskets, and a complimentary bottle of wine—not worth it). The English-speaking staff is friendly and efficient, offering room service, baby-sitting, and laundry/valet service. Breakfast is served below the ceiling vaults of the cellar.

INEXPENSIVE

Libertel Croix de Malte. 5 rue de Malte, 75011 Paris. ☎ **01-48-05-09-36.** Fax 01-43-57-02-54. www.libertel.com. 29 units. TV TEL. 610F ($97.60) double. AE, MC, V. Métro: Oberkampf.

A member of a nationwide chain of mostly two-star hotels, this is a well-maintained choice whose business has been increasing thanks to a radical 1992 overhaul and its proximity to the Opéra Bastille and the Marais. The hotel consists of buildings of two and three floors, one of which is accessible through a shared breakfast room. There's a landscaped courtyard in back with access to a lobby bar. The cozy guest rooms contain brightly painted modern furniture accented with vivid green, blue, and pink patterns that flash back to the 1960s.

Nouvel Hôtel. 24 av. du Bel-Air, 75012 Paris. ☎ **01-43-43-01-81.** Fax 01-43-44-64-13. 28 units. TV TEL. 480–650F ($76.80–$104) double. AE, DC, MC, V. Métro: Nation.

This hotel evokes the French provinces far more than urban Paris. Surrounded by greenery in a neighborhood rarely visited by tourists, the Nouvel conjures a calmer day, when parts of Paris still seemed like small country towns. The beauty of the place is most visible from the inside courtyard, site of warm-weather breakfasts, the only meal served. Winding halls lead to small guest rooms overlooking either the courtyard or, less appealingly, the street. Each contains flowered fabrics and old-fashioned furniture.

Résidence Alhambra. 13 rue de Malte, 75011 Paris. ☎ **01-47-00-35-52.** Fax 01-43-57-98-75. www.hotelalhambra.fr. E-mail: serviceclient@hotelalhambra.fr. 58 units. TV TEL. 340–370F ($54.40–$59.20) double; 450–500F ($72–$80) triple. AE, DC, MC, V. Parking 100F ($16). Métro: Oberkampf.

Named for the famous cabaret/vaudeville theater that once stood nearby, the Alhambra was built in the 1800s. A radical renovation in 1989 plus upgrades in the late 1990s gave the hotel its fine contemporary format. In the rear garden, its two-story chalet offers eight additional guest rooms. The rather small accommodations are bland but comfortable, each in a monochromatic pastel scheme that differs from floor to floor. Breakfast is the only meal served, but a wide array of restaurants is nearby around place de la République and place de la Bastille.

16TH ARRONDISSEMENT (TROCADÉRO/BOIS DE BOULOGNE)
VERY EXPENSIVE

Hôtel Saint-James Paris. 43 av. Bugeaud, 75016 Paris. ☎ **800/525-4800** in the U.S. and Canada, or 01-44-05-81-81. Fax 01-44-05-81-82. www.saint-james_paris.com. 48 units. A/C MINIBAR TV TEL. 2,100F ($336) double; from 2,750F ($440) suite. AE, DC, MC, V. Métro: Porte Dauphine. RER: Av. Foch.

In an 1892 stone building inspired by a château in the French countryside, the Saint-James is as grand as any of the very expensive hotels in the more visible (and central) neighborhoods of Paris. It's set among the staid yet luxurious residences of the 16th arrondissement, and staying here gives you access to the private restaurant, bar, and fitness center reserved for aristocratic Parisian members. You'll find it intimate and warm, even if exclusivity and snobbery are part of its image. The guest rooms are spacious, the older ones featuring art deco detailing, the more newly renovated ones with sleek contemporary styling. All have private safes.

Dining: The hotel has a restaurant open daily for lunch, serving classic French cuisine. The bar contains a polished-oak library with some 10,000 leather-bound books.

Amenities: Concierge, 24-hour room service, health club with Jacuzzi and sauna, billiard room.

INEXPENSIVE

Au Palais de Chaillot Hôtel. 35 av. Raymond-Poincaré, 75016 Paris. ☎ **01-53-70-09-09.** Fax 01-53-70-09-08. www.auchaillothotel.com. E-mail: hapc@club-internet.fr. 28 units. TV TEL. 570F ($91.20) double; 680F ($108.80) triple; 640F ($102.40) junior suite. Métro: Victor Hugo or Trocadéro.

When Thierry and Cyrille Pien, brothers trained in the States, opened this excellent hotel in 1997, budgeteers came running. Between the Champ-Elysées and Trocadéro, the town house was restored from top to bottom and the result is a contemporary yet

Finding Your Way

To locate 16th- and 17th-arrondissement hotels, turn to the "Hotels Near Place Charles de Gaulle" map on page 77.

informal style of Parisian chic. The guest rooms come in various shapes and sizes and are furnished with a light touch, with bright colors and wicker; half are air-conditioned, and nos. 61, 62, and 63 afford partial views of the Eiffel Tower. Room service for breakfast (daily 7am to noon) and drinks are offered (24 hours); breakfast is served on a small terrace in fair weather.

✪ **Hôtel Les Hauts de Passy.** 37 rue de l'Annonciation, 75016 Paris. ☎ **01-42-88-47-28.** Fax 01-42-88-99-09. 31 units. TV TEL. 450F ($72) double; 490F ($78.40) double with two beds. MC, V. Parking 95F ($15.20). Métro: La Muette or Passy.

Across the river from the Eiffel Tower in a chic residential neighborhood, this terrific hotel sits on a pedestrian-only street where an outdoor market takes place every day except Monday. All the rooms were recently renovated and are inviting, with new mattresses, large pillows, and double-glazed windows. The baths, though small, are squeaky clean. Breakfast is served in a bright room opening onto a patio in summer. However, just outside the front door is a wonderful *boulangerie* where you can have breakfast while watching the market bustle. Be patient with the hotel staff, as their English is minimal.

17TH ARRONDISSEMENT (PARC MONCEAU)
MODERATE

Hôtel Eber. 18 rue Léon-Jost, 75017 Paris. ☎ **01-46-22-60-70.** Fax 01-47-63-01-01. 18 units. A/C TV TEL. 690–830F ($110.40–$132.80) double; 1,250–1,500F ($200–$240) suite. AE, DC, MC, V. Parking 100F ($16). Métro: Courcelles.

Hidden on a quiet side street, this early-1900s three-star hotel is comfortably rustic, with exposed stone and wood paneling, paneled ceilings, and a Renaissance-style fireplace. The guest rooms are quite pleasant, and most have armchairs for reading. The courtyard provides a quiet oasis for breakfast and afternoon tea.

Hôtel Regent's Garden. 6 rue Pierre-Demours, 75017 Paris. ☎ **01-45-74-07-30.** Fax 01-40-55-01-42. TEL. www.bestwestern.com. E-mail: hotel.regents.garden@wanadoo.fr. 39 units. A/C MINIBAR TV TEL. 810–1,600F ($129.60–$256) double. AE, DC, MC, V. Parking 55F ($8.80). Métro: Ternes or Charles de Gaulle–Etoile.

Near the convention center and the Arc de Triomphe, the Regent's Garden has a proud heritage: Napoléon III built this stately château for his physician. The interior resembles a classically decorated country house. Fluted columns mark the entryway, which leads to a casual mix of furniture in the lobby. The guest rooms have flower prints on the walls, traditional French furniture, and tall soundproof windows. There are two gardens, one with ivy-covered walls and umbrella-shaded tables—a perfect place to meet other guests.

INEXPENSIVE

Hôtel Flaubert. 19 rue Rennequin, 75017 Paris. ☎ **01-46-22-44-35.** Fax 01-43-80-32-34. 36 units. MINIBAR TV TEL. 550–580F ($88–$92.80) double. AE, DC, MC, V. Métro: Ternes or Charles de Gaulle–Etoile.

The staff here long ago became accustomed to handling all the problems their international guests might have. Terra-cotta tiles and bentwood furniture in the public areas make for an efficient if not lushly comfortable setting for breakfast. Though the lush climbing plants in the courtyard overshadow the guest rooms, they're nonetheless appealing and (particularly those beneath the mansard's eaves) cozy, small to medium in size.

Les Trois Couronnes. 30 rue de l'Arc-de-Triomphe, 75017 Paris. ☎ **01-43-80-46-81.** Fax 01-46-22-53-96. www.easynet.fr/hotel3s/hotel.htm. E-mail: hotel3s@easynet.fr. 20 units. MINIBAR TV TEL. 455–695F ($72.80–$111.20) double. AE, DC, MC, V. Parking 100F ($16). Métro: Charles de Gaulle–Etoile.

This prestigious older hotel in Paris's business hub is within easy access of the Métro and many of the city's attractions. With its blend of art deco and art nouveau, it was radically redecorated and upgraded in 1995 and is under an enthusiastic new management. The cheerful guest rooms, small and old-fashioned but pleasant, take in the surrounding area. There's a small bar and a restaurant adjacent to the lobby. Laundry service is available.

Marmotel Etoile. 34 av. de la Grande Armée, 75017 Paris. ☎ **01-47-63-57-26.** Fax 01-45-74-25-27. 23 units. MINIBAR TV TEL. 470–490F ($75.20–$78.40) double. AE, MC, V. Métro: Argentine.

This hotel is on an inconvenient side of place Charles de Gaulle–Etoile, and you have to ford a roaring river of traffic to get to the nearby Champs-Elysées. The guest rooms are simple and small but comfortable. The ones overlooking the carefully landscaped flagstone-covered courtyard benefit from an unexpected oasis of calm; those fronting the avenue's traffic are less peaceful.

18TH ARRONDISSEMENT (MONTMARTRE)
VERY EXPENSIVE

✪ **Terrass Hôtel.** 12–14 rue Joseph-de-Maistre, 75018 Paris. ☎ **01-46-06-72-85.** Fax 01-42-52-29-11. www.terrass-hotel.com. E-mail: terrass@francenet.fr. 101 units. MINIBAR TV TEL. 1,390–1,540F ($222.40–$246.40) double; 1,860F ($297.60) suite. Rates include breakfast. AE, DC, MC, V. Métro: Place de Clichy or Blanche.

Built in 1913 and richly renovated into a plush but traditional style in 1991, this is the only four-star hotel on the Butte Montmartre. In an area filled with some of Paris's seediest hotels, this place is easily in a class of its own. Its main advantage is its location amid Montmartre's bohemian atmosphere (or what's left of it). Staffed by English-speaking employees, it has a large marble-floored lobby ringed with blond oak paneling and accented with 18th-century antiques and even older tapestries. The guest rooms are high-ceilinged and well upholstered, often featuring views.

Dining/Diversions: The Terrass offers an elegant street-level restaurant and a seventh-floor summer garden terrace with bar/food service and sweeping views. In colder weather, the Lobby Bar offers live piano music and a working fireplace.

Amenities: Concierge, room service (daily 7am to 2pm and 7 to 10:15pm), laundry/dry cleaning, currency exchange, car rentals, tour desk, conference facilities.

INEXPENSIVE

Hôtel Ermitage. 24 rue Lamarck, 75018 Paris. ☎ **01-42-64-79-22.** Fax 01-42-64-10-33. 12 units. TEL. 530F ($84.80) double. No credit cards. Parking 60F ($9.60). Métro: Lamarck-Caulaincourt.

Built in 1870 of chiseled limestone in the Napoléon III style, this hotel's facade might remind you of a perfectly proportioned small villa. It's set in a calm area, a brief uphill stroll from Sacré-Coeur. Views extend out over Paris, and there's a verdant garden in the back courtyard. The small guest rooms evoke a countryside auberge with exposed ceiling beams, flowered wallpaper, and casement windows opening onto the garden or a street seemingly airlifted from the provinces. Breakfast is the only meal served.

2 On the Left Bank

We'll begin with the most centrally located arrondissements on the Left Bank, then work our way through the more outlying neighborhoods.

5TH ARRONDISSEMENT (LATIN QUARTER)
MODERATE

Grand Hôtel St-Michel. 19 rue Cujas, 75005 Paris. ☎ **01-46-33-33-02.** Fax 01-40-46-96-33. www.123france.com. E-mail: grand.hotel.st.michel@wanadoo.fr. 46 units. MINIBAR TV TEL. 890F ($142.40) double; 1,400F ($224) suite. AE, DC, MC, V. Métro: Cluny–La Sorbonne. RER: Luxembourg or St-Michel.

Built in the 19th century, this hotel is larger and more businesslike than many of the town house–style inns nearby. It basks in the reflected glow of Brazilian dissident Georges Amado, whose memoirs (released in 1996) recorded his 2-year literary sojourn in one of the rooms. The public rooms are tasteful, with oil portraits and rich upholsteries. In 1997, the hotel completed a renovation and moved from two- to three-star status. The changes enlarged some rooms, lowering their ceilings and adding modern amenities like minibars, but retained old-fashioned touches like wrought-iron balconies (fifth floor only). Sixth-floor rooms offer interesting views over the rooftops.

Hôtel Abbatial St-Germain. 46 bd. St-Germain, 75005 Paris. ☎ **01-46-34-02-12.** Fax 01-43-25-47-73. www.abbatial.com. E-mail: abbatial@hotellerie.net. 43 units. A/C MINIBAR TV TEL. 750–850F ($120–$136) double. AE, MC, V. Parking 110F ($17.60). Métro: Maubert-Mutualité.

The origins of this hotel run deep: Interior renovations have revealed such 17th-century touches as dovecotes and massive oak beams. In the early 1990s, a radical restoration made the public areas especially appealing and brought the small rooms, furnished in faux Louis XVI, up to modern standards. All windows are double-glazed, and the fifth- and sixth-floor rooms enjoy views over Notre-Dame. Breakfast is served under the vaulted ceiling of the stone-sided cellar.

Hôtel Agora St-Germain. 42 rue des Bernardins, 75005 Paris. ☎ **01-46-34-13-00.** Fax 01-46-34-75-05. E-mail: agorastg@hotellerie.net 39 units. A/C MINIBAR TV TEL. 760–860F ($121.60–$137.60) double; 980F ($156.80) triple. AE, DC, MC, V. Parking 130F ($20.80). Métro: Maubert-Mutualité.

One of the best of the neighborhood's moderately priced choices, this hotel occupies a building constructed in the early 1600s, probably to house a group of guardsmen protecting the brother of the king at his lodgings nearby. It's in the heart of the artistic/historic Paris and offers compact soundproof guest rooms, each not particularly fashionably furnished. Room service is offered (daily 7:30 to 10:30am).

Hôtel des Arènes. 51 rue Monge, 75005 Paris. ☎ **01-43-25-09-26.** Fax 01-43-25-79-56. 52 units. MINIBAR TV TEL. 695F ($111.20) double. AE, MC, V. Parking 100F ($16). Métro: Monge or Cardinal Lemoine.

In a 19th-century building whose chiseled stone facade evokes fine old traditions, this hotel offers well-maintained modern guest rooms. Many in back overlook the tree-dotted ruins of Paris's ancient Roman arena, unearthed in 1865. The staff is over-worked and somewhat distracted and the place a bit anonymous, but the location is appealing. Breakfast is served in a simple windowless room in the hotel's cellar.

Hôtel des Grands Hommes. 17 place du Panthéon, 75005 Paris. ☎ **01-46-34-19-60.** Fax 01-43-26-67-32. 32 units. A/C MINIBAR TV TEL. 800F ($128) double; 900–1,200F ($144–$192) suite. AE, DC, MC, V. Parking 90F ($14.40). Métro: Cardinal Lemoine or Luxembourg.

Hotels in the Heart of the Left Bank

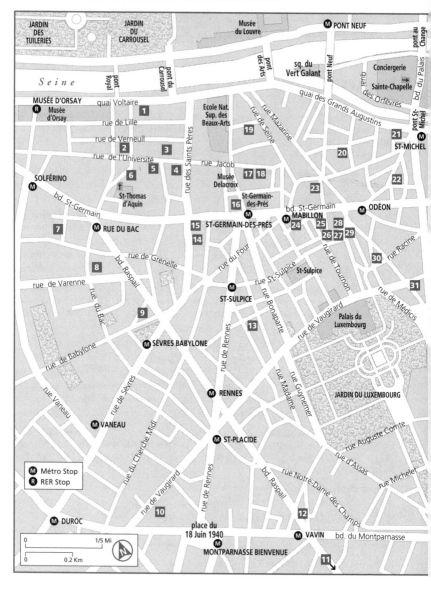

Built in the 18th century and renovated in the early 1990s, this hotel offers direct pro-file views (from many rooms) of the Panthéon. All but a handful of the accommodations have exposed ceiling beams and pleasantly old-fashioned furnishings that sometimes include brass beds. Second- and fifth-floor rooms have small balconies; fifth- and sixth-floor rooms have the best views; and those with the most space are on the ground floor. The welcome is charming from the English-speaking staff.

Hôtel des Jardins du Luxembourg. 5 impasse Royer-Collard, 75005 Paris. ☎ **01-40-46-08-88.** Fax 01-40-46-02-28. www.france-hotel-guie.com. 26 units. A/C MINIBAR TV TEL.

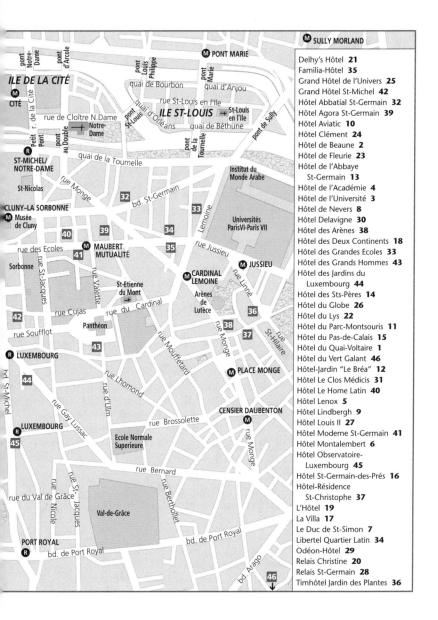

Delhy's Hôtel **21**
Familia-Hôtel **35**
Grand Hôtel de l'Univers **25**
Grand Hôtel St-Michel **42**
Hôtel Abbatial St-Germain **32**
Hôtel Agora St-Germain **39**
Hôtel Aviatic **10**
Hôtel Clément **24**
Hôtel de Beaune **2**
Hôtel de Fleurie **23**
Hôtel de l'Abbaye
  St-Germain **13**
Hôtel de l'Académie **4**
Hôtel de l'Université **3**
Hôtel de Nevers **8**
Hôtel Delavigne **30**
Hôtel des Arènes **38**
Hôtel des Deux Continents **18**
Hôtel des Grandes Ecoles **33**
Hôtel des Grands Hommes **43**
Hôtel des Jardins du
  Luxembourg **44**
Hôtel des Sts-Pères **14**
Hôtel du Globe **26**
Hôtel du Lys **22**
Hôtel du Parc-Montsouris **11**
Hôtel du Pas-de-Calais **15**
Hôtel du Quai-Voltaire **1**
Hôtel du Vert Galant **46**
Hôtel-Jardin "Le Bréa" **12**
Hôtel Le Clos Médicis **31**
Hôtel Le Home Latin **40**
Hôtel Lenox **5**
Hôtel Lindbergh **9**
Hôtel Louis II **27**
Hôtel Moderne St-Germain **41**
Hôtel Montalembert **6**
Hôtel Observatoire-
  Luxembourg **45**
Hôtel St-Germain-des-Prés **16**
Hôtel-Résidence
  St-Christophe **37**
L'Hôtel **19**
La Villa **17**
Le Duc de St-Simon **7**
Libertel Quartier Latin **34**
Odéon-Hôtel **29**
Relais Christine **20**
Relais St-Germain **28**
Timhôtel Jardin des Plantes **36**

810–860F ($129.60–$137.60) double. AE, DC, MC, V. Parking 95F ($15.20). Métro: Cluny–La Sorbonne. RER: Luxembourg.

Built during Baron Haussmann's 19th-century overhaul of Paris, this hotel boasts an imposing facade of honey-colored stone accented with ornate iron balconies. The interior is outfitted in strong, clean lines, often with groupings of art deco furnishings. The high-ceilinged guest rooms, some with Provençal tiles and ornate moldings, are well maintained, the size ranging from small to medium. Best of all, they overlook a quiet dead-end alley, ensuring relatively peaceful nights. Some have balconies overlooking the rooftops.

Hôtel Moderne St-Germain. 33 rue des Ecoles, 75005 Paris. ☎ **01-43-54-37-78.** Fax 01-43-29-91-31. www.tulipinn.com. E-mail: hotel@tulipinn.com. 45 units. TV TEL. 590–840F ($94.40–$134.40) double; 750–1,050F ($120–$168) triple. AE, DC, MC, V. Parking 170F ($27.20). Métro: Maubert-Mutualité.

In the heart of the Latin Quarter, the Grand Hôtel Moderne was completely reno-vated in 1998. Its charming owner, Mme Gibon, welcomes guests warmly to her spotless rooms. In the rooms fronting rue des Ecoles, double-glazed aluminum windows hush the traffic. Though the rooms are small, this is still one of the neighborhood's better three-star hotels. Guests enjoy access to the sauna and Jacuzzi at the Hôtel Sully next door.

Hôtel Observatoire-Luxembourg. 107 bd. St-Michel, 75005 Paris. ☎ **01-46-34-10-12.** Fax 01-46-33-73-86. E-mail: fa.sol@wanadoo.fr. 37 units. TV TEL. 780–935F ($124.80–$149.60) double. AE, DC, MC, V. Métro: Cluny–La Sorbonne. RER: Luxembourg.

The hotel's simple art nouveau facade is something of an architectural oddity in this neighborhood. Many of its rooms, especially those on the fifth and sixth floors, over-look either the Jardin du Luxembourg across the street or the nearby St-Jacques church. (Room 507, though not the largest, boasts the best view, encompassing both trees and medieval architecture.) The mattresses are a bit older than you might hope for but nonetheless comfortable. A successful 1992 renovation upgraded the public areas; they're streamlined and angular but softened by bright colors. Breakfast is served in the cellar dining room.

Hôtel-Résidence St-Christophe. 17 rue Lacépède, 75005 Paris. ☎ **01-43-31-81-54.** Fax 01-43-31-12-54. E-mail: hotelstchristophe@compuserve.com. 31 units. MINIBAR TV TEL. 680F ($108.80) double. AE, DC, MC, V. Parking 100F ($16). Métro: Place Monge.

This hotel, in one of the Latin Quarter's undiscovered but charming areas, has a gra-cious English-speaking staff. It was created in 1987 when a derelict hotel was con-nected to a butcher shop. All the small- to medium-size rooms were successfully renovated in 1998, with Louis XV–style furniture, wall-to-wall carpeting, and firm mattresses. Breakfast is the only meal served, but the staff offers advice about neigh-borhood bistros.

INEXPENSIVE

✪ **Familia-Hôtel.** 11 rue des Ecoles, 75005 Paris. ☎ **01-43-54-55-27.** Fax 01-43-29-61-77. 30 units. MINIBAR TV TEL. 390–595F ($62.40–$95.20) double. AE, DC, MC, V. Métro: Jussieu or Maubert-Mutualité.

As the name implies, this is a hotel that has been family run for decades. Many per-sonal touches make the place unique, and it was lavishly renovated in 1998. The walls of 14 rooms are graced with finely executed sepia-colored frescoes of Parisian scenes. Eight rooms have restored stone walls and seven have balconies with delightful views over the Latin Quarter.

Hôtel des Grandes Ecoles. 75 rue de Cardinal-Lemoine, 75005 Paris. ☎ **01-43-26-79-23.** Fax 01-43-25-28-15. www.hotel-grandes-ecoles.com. E-mail: ecoles@wanadoo.fr. 51 units. TEL. 530–630F ($84.80–$100.80) double. MC, V. Parking 100F ($16). Métro: Cardinal Lemoine or Monge.

Few other hotels in the neighborhood offer so much low-key charm at such reasonable prices. It's composed of a trio of high-ceilinged buildings, interconnected via a sheltered courtyard where in warm weather singing birds provide a worthy substitute for the TVs deliberately missing from the rooms. The guest rooms are artfully old-fashioned, with feminine touches like Laura Ashley–inspired flowered upholsteries and ruffles. Many offer views of a garden whose trellises and flower beds evoke the countryside. Thanks to dozens of restaurants in the neighborhood, no one seems to mind the hotel's lack of a restaurant, and breakfast is served in the garden when possible.

○ **Hôtel Le Home Latin.** 15–17 rue du Sommerard, 75005 Paris. ☎ **01-43-26-25-21.** Fax 01-43-29-87-04. 54 units. TV TEL. 595–650F ($95.20–$104) double. AE, V. Parking 85F ($13.60). Métro: St-Michel or Maubert-Mutualité.

This is one of Paris's most famous budget hotels, known since the 1970s for its simple lodgings. The blandly functional rooms were renovated in 1999; some have small balconies overlooking the street. Those facing the courtyard are quieter than those fronting the street. The elevator doesn't reach beyond the fifth floor, but to make up for the stair climb, the sixth floor's *chambres mansardées* offer a romantic location under the eaves and panoramic rooftop views.

Timhôtel Jardin des Plantes. 5 rue Linné, 75005 Paris. ☎ **01-47-07-06-20.** Fax 01-47-07-62-74. www.hotels.fr/opal. E-mail: h_opal@club-internet.fr. 33 units. TV TEL. 700–780F ($112–$124.80) double. AE, DC, MC, V. Parking 80F ($12.80). Métro: Jussieu. Bus: 67 or 89.

Opened in 1986 and renovated in 1997, this two-star Timhôtel lies across from the Jardin des Plantes, the botanical gardens created by order of Louis XIII's doctors in 1626 (there are still some 15,000 medicinal herbs in the gardens). Some of the small but well-equipped guest rooms open onto flowered terraces. The hotel has a small roof terrace, a vaulted basement lounge, a sauna, and a brasserie/snack bar where breakfast is served.

6TH ARRONDISSEMENT (ST-GERMAIN/LUXEMBOURG)
VERY EXPENSIVE

Relais Christine. 3 rue Christine, 75006 Paris. ☎ **01-40-51-60-80.** Fax 01-40-51-60-81. www.relais-christine.com. E-mail: relaisch@club-internet.fr. 51 units. A/C MINIBAR TV TEL. 1,850–2,200F ($296–$352) double; 2,500—4,300F ($400–$688) duplex or suite. AE, DC, MC, V. Free parking. Métro: Odéon.

The Relais Christine welcomes you into what was a 16th-century Augustinian cloister. You enter from a narrow cobblestone street into first a symmetrical courtyard and then an elegant reception area with baroque sculpture and Renaissance antiques. Each guest room is uniquely decorated with wooden beams and Louis XIII–style furnishings; the rooms come in a wide range of styles and shapes, and some are among the Left Bank's largest, with extras like mirrored closets, plush carpets, thermostats, and even sometimes balconies facing the outer courtyard. The least attractive, smallest, and dimmest rooms are those in the interior.

Dining/Diversions: Off the reception area is a paneled sitting room/bar area ringed with 19th-century portraits and comfortable leather chairs. The breakfast room is in a vaulted cellar; the ancient well and massive central stone column are part of the cloister's former kitchen.

Amenities: Concierge, 24-hour room service, laundry, baby-sitting.

EXPENSIVE

○ **Hôtel de Fleurie.** 32–34 rue Grégoire-de-Tours, 75006 Paris. ☎ **01-53-73-70-00.** Fax 01-53-73-70-20. www.hotel-de-fleurie.tm.fr. E-mail: bonjour@hotel-de-fleurie.tm.fr. 29 units. A/C MINIBAR TV TEL. 1,000–1,350F ($160–$216) double; 1,700–1,800F ($272–$288) family room. Children 12 and under stay free in parents' room. AE, DC, MC, V. Métro: Odéon or St-Germain-des-Prés.

Off boulevard St-Germain on a colorful little street, the Fleurie is one of the best of the "new" old hotels, its statuary-studded façade recapturing a 17th-century elegance. The stone walls have been exposed in the reception salon, where you check in at a refectory desk. About half the guest rooms and bathrooms were renovated in 1999, and many have elaborate curtains and antique reproductions. This hotel has long been a family favorite—interconnecting doors in certain pairs of rooms create safe havens the hotel refers to as *chambres familiales.*

Dining: Breakfast is the only meal served, though there's a small bar.

Amenities: Concierge, room service (daily 7 to 11am), laundry/dry cleaning, car rentals arranged.

✪ **Hôtel de l'Abbaye St-Germain.** 10 rue Cassette, 75006 Paris. ☎ **01-45-44-38-11.** Fax 01-45-48-07-86. www.hotel-abbaye.com. E-mail: hotel.abbaye@wanadoo.fr. 46 units. A/C TV TEL. 1,160–1,650F ($185.60–$264) double; 2,150–2,300F ($344–$368) suite. Rates include breakfast. AE, MC, V. Métro: St-Sulpice.

Built in the early 1700s as a convent for the Eglise St-Germain, this place later became a youth hostel and has since been transformed into a charming boutique hotel. Its brightly colored rooms have traditional furniture like you'd find in a private club, plus touches of sophisticated flair. In front is a small garden and in back a verdant court-yard with a fountain, raised flower beds, and masses of ivy and climbing vines. If you don't mind the expense, one of the most charming rooms has a terrace overlooking the upper floors of neighboring buildings.

Dining/Diversions: Breakfast is the only meal served, but the public areas include a trio of salons and a bar.

Amenities: Concierge, 24-hour room service, laundry/dry cleaning, car rentals arranged.

La Villa. 29 rue Jacob, 75006 Paris. ☎ **01-43-26-60-00.** Fax 01-46-34-63-63. www.villa-saintgermain.com. E-mail: hotel@villa-saintgermain.com. 32 units. A/C MINIBAR TV TEL. 1,250–1,800F ($200–$288) double; from 2,000F ($320) suite. AE, MC, V. Métro: St-Germain-des-Prés.

This hotel's facade resembles those of many of the other buildings in the neighbor-hood. Inside, however, the decor is a minimalist ultramodern creation thoroughly rejecting all traditional French aesthetics. The public areas and guest rooms contain Bauhaus-like furniture; the lobby's angular lines are somewhat softened with bouquets of leaves and flowers. Most unusual are the baths, whose shimmering stainless steel; pink, black, or beige marble; and chrome surfaces are either post-Sputnik or post-modern, depending on your frame of reference.

Amenities: Concierge, 24-hour room service, laundry/dry cleaning.

✪ **L'Hôtel.** 13 rue des Beaux-Arts, 75006 Paris. ☎ **01-44-41-99-00.** Fax 01-43-25-64-81. www.l-hotel.com. E-mail: reservation@l-hotel.com. 27 units. A/C MINIBAR TV TEL. 600–3,000F ($96–$480) double; from 1,700F ($272) suite. AE, DC, MC, V. Métro: St-Germain-des-Prés.

This boutique hotel was once a 19th-century fleabag called the Alsace, whose major distinction was that Oscar Wilde died there, broke and in despair. But today's guests aren't anywhere near poverty row: This was the sophisticated creation of late French actor Guy-Louis Duboucheron, and show-business and fashion celebrities love it. The guest rooms vary in size, style, and price, from quite small to deluxe, but all have non-working fireplaces, safes, and fabric-covered walls. An eclectic collection of antiques pops up here and there: The spacious 2,800F ($448) room contains the original fur-nishings and memorabilia of stage star Mistinguette, a frequent performer with Mau-rice Chevalier and his on-again/off-again lover. Her pedestal bed is set in the middle of the room, surrounded by mirrors, as she liked to see how she looked or "performed" at all times.

Dining: Breakfast and afternoon tea are served in a greenhouse-style room.

Amenities: Concierge, room service (daily 6:30am to 11pm), baby-sitting, laundry, valet.

Odéon-Hôtel. 3 rue de l'Odéon, 75006 Paris. ☎ **01-43-25-90-67.** Fax 01-43-25-55-98. www.odeonhotel.fr. E-mail: odeon@odeonhotel.fr. 33 units. A/C TV TEL. 912–1,512F ($145.90–$241.90) double. AE, DC, MC, V. Parking 100F ($16). Métro: Odéon.

Reminiscent of a modernized Norman country inn, the Odéon offers charming rustic touches like exposed beams, rough stone walls, high crooked ceilings, and tapestries mixed with contemporary fabrics, mirrored ceilings, and black leather furnishings. Conveniently located near both the Théâtre de l'Odéon and boulevard St-Germain, the Odéon stands on the first street in Paris to have pavements (1779) and gutters. By the turn of the 20th century, this area, which had drawn the original Shakespeare & Co. bookshop to no. 12 rue de l'Odéon, began attracting such writers as Gertrude Stein and her coterie. The guest rooms are small to medium in size but charming.

Relais St-Germain. 9 carrefour de l'Odéon, 75006 Paris. ☎ **01-43-29-12-05.** Fax 01-46-33-45-30. 22 units. A/C MINIBAR TV TEL. 1,600–1,850F ($256–$296) double; 2,100F ($336) suite. Rates include breakfast. AE, DC, MC, V. Métro: Odéon.

Adapted from a 17th-century building, the St-Germain is an oasis of charm and comfort. It's comparable to the Relais Christine, its nearest competitor, but with a more accommodating staff. The decor is a medley of traditional and modern, evoking a charming provincial house. All the necessary amenities have been tucked in under the beams, including safes and soundproofing. Four rooms feature kitchenettes, and two of the suites come with terraces.

Dining: The Comptoir du Relais, a bistro/wine bar, is a cozy retreat where you can order such dishes as potted goose pâté, pork-and-pistachio sausage, and any number of sandwiches with traditional French bread.

Amenities: Limited concierge services, room service (daily 7am to 10pm), dry cleaning/laundry, newspaper delivery on request, twice-daily maid service.

MODERATE

Grand Hôtel de l'Univers. 6 rue Grégoire-de-Tours, 75006 Paris. ☎ **01-43-29-37-00.** Fax 01-40-51-06-45. E-mail: grandhotelunivers@wanadoo.fr. 34 units. A/C MINIBAR TV TEL. 880–950F ($140.80–$152) double. AE, DC, MC, V. Métro: Odéon.

In the 1400s, this was home to a family of the emergent bourgeoisie, and the hotel exudes charm and tranquillity. The pleasantly renovated guest rooms are cramped but well maintained and have safes; some provide panoramic views over the crooked rooftops. La Bonbonnière (The Candy Box) is a red-and-white confection of a bedroom. Amenities include room service (daily 7 to 11am) and newspaper delivery on request. Breakfast is served in the cellar beneath the 500-year-old stone vaults. The small bar serves guests only.

Hôtel Aviatic. 105 rue de Vaugirard, 75006 Paris. ☎ **01-53-63-25-50.** Fax 01-53-63-25-55. www.www.aviatic.fr. E-mail: welcome@aviatic.fr. 43 units. A/C MINIBAR TV TEL. 680–1,180F ($108.80–$188.80) double. AE, DC, MC, V. Parking 120F ($19.20). Métro: Montparnasse-Bienvenue.

Completely remodeled, this is a bit of old Paris in an interesting section of Montparnasse, with a modest inner courtyard and a vine-covered wall lattice, surrounded by cafes popular with artists, writers, and jazz musicians. It has been a family-run hotel for a century and has an English-speaking staff. The reception lounge boasts marble columns, brass chandeliers, antiques, and a petit salon. The guest rooms were renovated in stages throughout the 1990s, and each has a safe.

Hôtel des Deux Continents. 25 rue Jacob, 75006 Paris. ☎ **01-43-26-72-46.** Fax 01-43-25-67-80. www.france-hotel-guide.com. 41 units. TV TEL. 795–895F ($127.20–$143.20) double; 1,080F ($172.80) triple. MC, V. Métro: St-Germain-des-Prés.

Built from three interconnected antique buildings, each between three and six stories high, this hotel is a reliable choice with a sense of Latin Quarter style. The carefully coordinated guest rooms, renovated between 1992 and 1998, range from small to medium and include reproductions of antique furnishings and soundproof upholstered walls.

Hôtel des Sts-Pères. 65 rue des Sts-Pères, 75006 Paris. ☎ **01-45-44-50-00.** Fax 01-45-44-90-83. E-mail: hotelsts.peres@wanadoo.fr. 39 units. MINIBAR TV TEL. 800–1,150F ($128–$184) double; 1,700F ($272) suite. AE, MC, V. Métro: St-Germain-des-Prés or Sèvres-Babylone.

This hotel off boulevard St-Germain is comparable to the Odéon, and there's no better recommendation than the long list of guests who return again and again (the late Edna St. Vincent Millay loved the camellia-trimmed garden). The hotel, designed by Louis XIV's architect, Jacques-Ange Gabriel, is decorated in part with antique paintings, tapestries, and mirrors. Many of the guest rooms face a quiet courtyard. Most sought after is the *chambre à la fresque*, with a 17th-century painted ceiling. The hotel has installed new plumbing and replastered and repainted the rooms. When weather permits, breakfast is served in the courtyard.

Hôtel du Pas-de-Calais. 59 rue des Sts-Pères, 75006 Paris. ☎ **01-45-48-78-74.** Fax 01-45-44-94-57. E-mail: lepasdecalais@horeca.tm.fr. 41 units. A/C TV TEL. 850–920F ($136–$147.20) double. AE, DC, MC, V. Parking 200F ($32). Métro: St-Germain-des-Prés or Sèvres-Babylone.

The Pas-de-Calais was built in the 17th century for the Lavalette family, and its elegant facade, with massive wooden doors, has been retained. Romantic novelist Chateaubriand lived here from 1811 to 1814, but its most famous guest was Jean-Paul Sartre, who struggled with the play *Les Mains Sales* (The Red Gloves) in room 41. The hotel is a bit weak on style, but as one longtime guest confided, despite the updates, "we still stay here for the memories." The modern guest rooms have been renovated in the past few years; inner rooms surround a modest courtyard with two garden tables and several trellises. Off the lobby is a pleasant sitting room.

Hôtel-Jardin "Le Bréa." 14 rue Bréa, 75006 Paris. ☎ **01-43-25-44-41.** Fax 01-44-07-19-25. 23 units. TV TEL. 770–900F ($123.20–$144) double; 900F ($144) triple. AE, DC, MC, V. Métro: Vavin.

Though the building containing this hotel originally had a garden in back, it was long ago covered with a roof and assimilated into the floor plan. Today, bright colors deck the public rooms, which lead to efficiently decorated small guest rooms that were partially renovated in 1997. To balance the lack of space, you can expect a polite welcome, and the neighborhood is convenient to Montparnasse's shops, cinemas, and razzle-dazzle.

Hôtel Le Clos Médicis. 56 rue Monsieur-le-Prince, 75006 Paris. ☎ **01-43-29-10-80.** Fax 01-43-54-26-90. E-mail: clos_medicis@compuserve.com. 38 units. A/C MINIBAR TV TEL. 790–1,200F ($126.40–$192) double. AE, DC, MC, V. Parking 150F ($24). Métro: Odéon. RER: Luxembourg.

The location of this relatively new hotel, across from the Jardin du Luxembourg, is a major advantage. You'll find a verdant garden with lattices and exposed stone walls, a lobby with modern spotlights and simple furniture, and a multilingual staff. The warmly colored guest rooms, small to medium in size, are comfortable. Breakfast is the only meal served.

Hôtel Louis II. 2 rue St-Sulpice, 75006 Paris. ☎ **01-46-33-13-80.** Fax 01-46-33-17-29. www.france-hotel-guide.com. E-mail: louis2@club-internet.fr. 22 units. A/C MINIBAR TEL. 620–920F ($99.20–$147.20) double; 1,100F ($176) triple. AE, DC, MC, V. Métro: Odéon.

In an 18th-century building, this hotel offers guest rooms decorated in rustic French tones. Afternoon drinks and morning coffee are served in the reception salon, where gilt-framed mirrors, fresh flowers, and antiques radiate a provincial aura, like something out of Proust. The generally small soundproof rooms with exposed beams and lace bedding complete the impression. Many visitors ask for the romantic attic rooms. TVs are available on request.

Hôtel St-Germain-des-Prés. 36 rue Bonaparte, 75006 Paris. ☎ **01-43-26-00-19.** Fax 01-40-46-83-63. www.hotel-st-ger.com. E-mail: hotelsaintgermain@wanadoo.fr. 30 units. MINIBAR TV TEL. 1,020–1,350F ($163.20–$216) double; from 1,750F ($280) suite. Rates include breakfast. AE, V. Métro: St-Germain-des-Prés.

Most of this hotel's attraction comes from its enviable location in the Latin Quarter, behind a well-known Left Bank street. Janet Flanner, the legendary 1920s *New Yorker* correspondent, lived here for a while. Renovated within the past few years, the guest rooms are small but charming, with antique ceiling beams and safes; air-conditioning is available in most. The public areas are severely elegant.

Libertel Quartier Latin. 9 rue des Ecoles, 75006 Paris. ☎ **800/949-7562** in the U.S., or 01-44-27-06-45. Fax 01-43-25-36-70. www.libertel-hotels.com. 29 units. MINIBAR TV TEL. 1,082F ($173.10) double; 1,213F ($194.10) suite. AE, DC, MC, V. Parking 100F ($16) nearby. Métro: Jussieu.

This century-old hotel in a neighborhood crowded with Latin Quarter color was radically upgraded in 1997, with each guest room transformed into a temple to French literature. Expect a hardworking articulate staff, book-lined public rooms, and small guest rooms where the comfortable furniture is offset with framed portraits of authors like Colette, Gide, and Prévert. Breakfast is the only meal served.

INEXPENSIVE

Delhy's Hôtel. 22 rue de l'Hirondelle, 75006 Paris. ☎ **01-43-26-58-25.** Fax 01-43-26-51-06. 21 units, 7 with bathroom. TV TEL. 356F ($56.95) double without bathroom, 446F ($71.35) double with bathroom; 586F ($93.75) triple with bathroom. Rates include breakfast. AE, DC, MC, V. Métro: St-Michel.

On a narrow crooked alley in the Latin Quarter's densest part, this circa-1400 building was acquired by François I as a home for one of his mistresses. Don't expect luxury, but look for charming touches that help compensate for the lack of an elevator. The staircase is listed as a national relic, and most of the compact guest rooms still have the original, almost fossilized, timbers and beams. The rooms were for the most part renovated in the late 1990s. If you get a room without a bath, you'll have to go down to the ground floor for access to the public facilities.

Hôtel Clément. 6 rue Clément, 75006 Paris. ☎ **01-43-26-53-60.** Fax 01-44-07-06-83. E-mail: hotelment@worldnet.fr. 31 units. A/C TV TEL. 560–680F ($89.60–$108.80) double; 780F ($124.80) suite. AE, DC, V. Métro: Mabillon.

This hotel sits on a quiet narrow street, within sight of the twin towers of St-Sulpice church. From the 1700s, the building was renovated several years ago into a bright, uncomplicated design. The guest rooms are simple and small, in some cases not much bigger than the beds they contain. On the premises is a simple bistro with specialties from the Auvergne.

Hôtel Delavigne. 1 rue Casimir-Delavigne, 75006 Paris. ☎ **01-43-29-31-50.** Fax 01-43-29-78-56. www.hoteldelavigne.com. E-mail: resa@hoteldelavigne.com. 34 units. TV TEL. 640–720F ($102.40–$115.20) double. MC, V. Métro: Odéon.

Despite radical modernization, you can still get a sense of the building's 18th-century origins. The public areas feature an attractively rustic use of chiseled stone, some of which is original. The high-ceilinged guest rooms are tasteful, sometimes with wooden furniture, often with upholstered headboards, and sometimes with Spanish-style wrought iron. Breakfast is the only meal served.

Hôtel du Globe. 15 rue des Quatre-Vents, 75006 Paris. ☎ **01-46-33-62-69.** Fax 01-46-33-62-69. E-mail: hotelglobe@post.club-internet.fr. 15 units, 14 with bathroom. TV TEL. 495–595F ($79.20–$95.20) double. MC, V. Closed 3 weeks in Aug. Métro: Mabillon, Odéon, or St-Sulpice.

This 17th-century building occupies an evocative street, and inside you'll find most of the original stonework and dozens of original timbers and beams. There's no elevator (you have to lug your suitcases up a very narrow antique staircase) and no breakfast area (trays are brought to your room). Each guest room is decorated with individual old-fashioned flair. *A tip*: The rooms with tubs are almost twice as large as those with shower stalls. The largest and most desirable rooms are nos. 1, 12 (with a baldaquin-style bed), 14, 15, and 16. The room without a bathroom is a single at 270F ($43.20).

Hôtel du Lys. 23 rue Serpente, 75006 Paris. ☎ **01-43-26-97-57.** Fax 01-44-07-34-90. 22 units. TV TEL. 550F ($88) double; 680F ($108.80) triple. Rates include breakfast. MC, V. Métro: Cluny–La Sorbonne or St-Michel.

With tall casement windows and high ceilings from the 17th century, this cozy place has functioned as a hotel since the turn of the 20th century. There's no elevator, a fact that guarantees you'll make frequent use of the historic staircase. The guest rooms have different patterns of curtains and wallpaper, and about a quarter were renovated in 1998. Don't expect attentive service; the Lys is like an upscale dorm, with guests pursuing an array of interests and activities in the area. Breakfast can be served in your room.

7TH ARRONDISSEMENT (EIFFEL TOWER/MUSÉE D'ORSAY)
VERY EXPENSIVE

✪ **Hôtel Montalembert.** 3 rue de Montalembert, 75007 Paris. ☎ **800/447-7462** in the U.S. and Canada, or 01-45-49-68-68. Fax 01-45-49-69-49. www.montalembert.com. E-mail: welcome@hotel-montalembert.fr. 56 units. A/C MINIBAR TV TEL. 1,800–2,400F ($288–$384) double; 2,950F ($472) junior suite; 4,400F ($704) suite. AE, DC, MC, V. Parking 120F ($19.20). Métro: Rue du Bac.

Unusually elegant for the Left Bank, the Montalembert was built in 1926 in beaux arts style. It was restored between 1989 and 1992 and hailed as a smashing success, borrowing sophisticated elements of Bauhaus and postmodern design in honey beiges, creams, and golds. The guest rooms are spacious, except for some standard doubles, which are quite small unless you're a very thin model. All have safes.

Dining/Diversions: Favored by area artists, writers, publishers, and antiques dealers, the stylish Le Montalembert provides excellent service and exceptionally good food based on market-fresh ingredients. Dishes include traditional veal chops with wild mushrooms, along with more inventive fare. Expect crowds for weekday lunches. In summer, dining is offered on the terrace. The hotel also has a full-fledged bar.

Amenities: Concierge who can arrange for practically anything, 24-hour room service, privileges at nearby health club.

Hotels Near the Eiffel Tower & Invalides

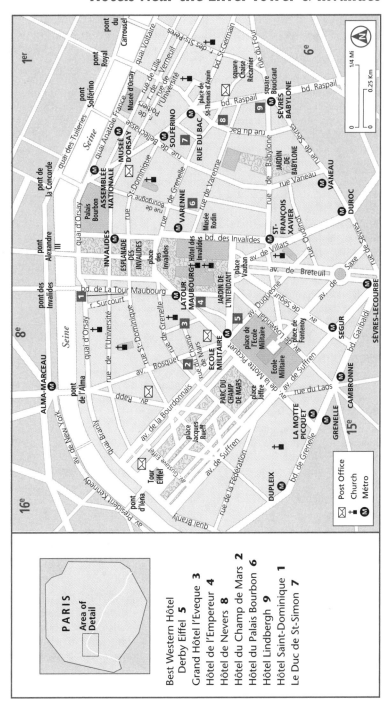

Best Western Hôtel
Derby Eiffel **5**
Grand Hôtel l'Eveque **3**
Hôtel de l'Empereur **4**
Hôtel de Nevers **8**
Hôtel du Champ de Mars **2**
Hôtel du Palais Bourbon **6**
Hôtel Lindbergh **9**
Hôtel Saint-Dominique **1**
Le Duc de St-Simon **7**

EXPENSIVE

Hôtel de l'Université. 22 rue de l'Université, 75007 Paris. ☎ **01-42-61-09-39.** Fax 01-42-60-40-84. www.hoteluniversite.com. 27 units. A/C TV TEL. 850–1,300F ($136–$208) double. AE, MC, V. Métro: St-Germain-des-Prés.

Long favored by well-heeled parents of North American students studying in Paris, this 300-year-old town house filled with antiques enjoys a location in a discreetly upscale neighborhood. Number 54 is a favorite room, containing a rattan bed and period pieces. Another charmer is no. 35 with a fireplace, opening onto a courtyard with a fountain. The most expensive accommodation, at 1,300F ($208), has a small terrace overlooking the surrounding rooftops. The bistro-style breakfast room opens onto the courtyard.

Le Duc de St-Simon. 14 rue de St-Simon, 75007 Paris. ☎ **01-44-39-20-20.** Fax 01-45-48-68-25. 34 units. TEL. 1,375–1,500F ($220–$240) double; from 1,925F ($308) suite. AE, MC, V. Métro: Rue du Bac.

On a quiet residential street, this is the only hotel in the area to pose a serious challenge to the Montalembert. Two immortal cafes, Les Deux Magots and Le Flore, are a few steps away. The small villa has a tiny front garden and an 1830s decor with trompe-l'oeil panels, a frescoed elevator, and climbing wisteria gracing the courtyard. Each guest room is unique and sure to include at least one antique; a few are ridiculously small, but most offer adequate space. The service reflects the owner's extensive training in the art of pampering guests. TVs are available on request.

   Amenities: Concierge who can arrange for just about anything, room service (daily 7:30am to 10:30pm).

MODERATE

Best Western Hôtel Derby Eiffel. 5 av. Duquesne, 75007 Paris. ☎ **800/528-1234** in the U.S. and Canada, or 01-47-05-12-05. Fax 01-47-05-43-43. www.derbyeiffelhotel.com. E-mail: info@derbyeiffelhotel.com. 43 units. A/C MINIBAR TV TEL. 750–900F ($120–$144) double; 900F ($144) suite. AE, DC, MC, V. Métro: Ecole Militaire.

Converted to three-star status in the early 1990s, this hotel facing the Ecole Militaire contains airy public areas. Our favorite is a glass-roofed conservatory in back, filled year-round with plants and used as a breakfast area. The soundproof and conservatively modern guest rooms employ thick fabrics and soothing neutral colors. Most front-facing rooms offer views of the Eiffel Tower. In 1998, enormous sums were spent upgrading the rooms and bathrooms and generally improving the hotel's interior aesthetics.

Hôtel de l'Académie. 32 rue des Sts-Pères, 75007 Paris. ☎ **800/246-0041** in the U.S. and Canada, or 01-45-49-80-00. Fax 01-45-49-80-10. www.academiehotel.aol.com. E-mail: aaacademie@aol.com. 34 units. A/C MINIBAR TV TEL. 690–990F ($110.40–$158.40) double; 1,290–1,590F ($206.40–$254.40) suite. AE, DC, MC, V. Parking 150F ($24). Métro: St-Germain-des-Prés.

The exterior walls and old ceiling beams are all that remain of this 17th-century residence of the duc de Rohan's private guards. In 1999, the hotel was completely renovated to include an elegant reception area. The up-to-date guest rooms have an Ile-de-France decor and views over the neighborhood's 18th- and 19th-century buildings. By American standards the rooms are small, but they're average for Paris. The staff speaks English.

✪ **Hôtel du Quai-Voltaire.** 19 quai Voltaire, 75007 Paris. ☎ **01-42-61-50-91.** Fax 01-42-61-62-26. 33 units. TV TEL. 670–720F ($107.20–$115.20) double; 870F ($139.20) triple. AE, DC, MC, V. Parking 110F ($17.60) nearby. Métro: Musée d'Orsay or Palais Royal.

Built in the 1600s as an abbey, then transformed into a hotel in 1856, the Quai-Voltaire is best known for its illustrious guests, like Wilde, Wagner, and Baudelaire, who occupied rooms 47, 55, and 56, respectively. Camille Pissarro painted Le Pont Royal from the window of his fourth-floor room. Many guest rooms in this modest inn have been renovated, most overlooking the bookstalls and boats of the Seine. You can have drinks in the bar or small salon, and simple meals (like omelets and salads) can be prepared for those who prefer to eat in.

Hôtel Lenox. 9 rue de l'Université, 75007 Paris. ☎ **01-42-96-10-95.** Fax 01-42-61-52-83. www.lenoxsaintgermain.com. 34 units. TV TEL. 700–1,150F ($112–$184) double; 1,600F ($256) duplex suite. AE, DC, MC, V. Métro: Rue du Bac.

The Lenox is a favorite for those seeking reasonably priced accommodations in St-Germain-des-Prés. In 1910, T. S. Eliot spent a summer here "on the old man's money" when it was just a basic pension. Today this much-improved place offers a helpful staff and cramped but comfortable guest rooms radically and expensively upgraded in 1996; they evoke the chintzes and furniture of an English country house. Many returning guests request the attic duplex with its tiny balcony and skylight.

INEXPENSIVE

Grand Hôtel L'Eveque. 29 rue Cler, 75007 Paris. ☎ **01-47-05-49-15.** Fax 01-45-50-49-36. www.hotel-leveque.com. E-mail: info@hotelleveque.com. 50 units. TV TEL. 380–400F ($60.80–$64) double. AE, MC, V. Métro: Ecole Militaire.

Built in the 1930s, this hotel draws lots of English-speaking guests, many of whom appreciate its proximity to the Eiffel Tower. In 1998, the interior was completely renovated and repainted. The pastel-colored guest rooms retain an art deco inspiration, with small lockboxes for valuables, just enough space to be comfortable, and double-insulated windows overlooking a courtyard in back or the street in front.

Hôtel de Beaune. 29 rue de Beaune, 75007 Paris. ☎ **01-42-61-24-89.** Fax 01-49-27-02-12. 19 units. MINIBAR TV TEL. 510–550F ($81.60–$88) double. AE, DC, MC, V. Métro: Rue du Bac.

This 19th-century white hotel is a stone's throw from some upscale antiques stores and near the Musée d'Orsay. A renovation was completed in 1998. The guest rooms are small and efficiently furnished but lack imagination, though you should get a good night's sleep.

Hôtel de l'Empereur. 2 rue Chevert, 75007 Paris. ☎ **01-45-55-88-02.** Fax 01-45-51-88-54. www.franc.hotel.guide.com/h75007empereur.htm. E-mail: globeman@easynet.fr. 38 units. MINIBAR TV TEL. 470–530F ($75.20–$84.80) double. AE, DC, MC, V. Parking 110–150F ($17.60–$24) across the street. Métro: Latour-Maubourg.

This convenient hotel was built in the early 1700s and enjoys a loyal group of repeat visitors. There's an elevator to haul you and your luggage to one of the smallish but attractively decorated guest rooms. In 1998, the two top floors were renovated. There's no restaurant or bar, but a nearby restaurant will send up platters of food on request.

Hôtel de Nevers. 83 rue du Bac, 75007 Paris. ☎ **01-45-44-61-30.** Fax 01-42-22-29-47. www.l-gf.com/hotel-de-nevers. 11 units. MINIBAR TV TEL. 415–520F ($66.40–$83.20) double. No credit cards. Métro: Rue du Bac.

This is one of the neighborhood's most historic choices—it was a convent from 1627 to 1790, when it was disbanded by the Revolution. The building is *classé*, meaning any restoration must respect the original architecture. That precludes an elevator, so you'll have to use the beautiful white staircase. The cozy and pleasant guest rooms contain a mix of antique and reproduced furniture. Rooms 10 and 11 are especially sought after for their terraces overlooking a corner of rue du Bac or a rear courtyard.

Hôtel du Champ de Mars. 7 rue du Champ de Mars, 75007 Paris. ☎ **01-45-51-52-30.** Fax 01-45-51-64-36. www.hotel-du-champ-de-mars.com. 25 units. TV TEL. 425–460F ($68–$73.60) double. MC, V. Parking 100–150F ($16–$24) in nearby public parking lot. Métro: Ecole Militaire.

Favored by families, this hotel sits close to the park flanking the base of the Eiffel Tower. It offers clean and simple guest rooms that are frilly and pretty enough to be referred to as "coquettish" by the manager. In 1998, most of the rooms were renovated and redecorated, retaining their charm and rather cramped dimensions. The most memorable of the public areas is a stone-sided breakfast room, which serves the hotel's only meal.

Hôtel du Palais Bourbon. 49 rue de Bourgogne, 75007 Paris. ☎ **01-44-11-30-70.** Fax 01-45-55-20-21. www.globe-market.com/h75007palaisbourbon.htm. E-mail: htlbourbon@aol.com. 32 units. MINIBAR TV TEL. 610F ($97.60) double; 710F ($113.60) triple. MC, V. Métro: Varenne.

The solid stone walls of this 18th-century building aren't nearly as grand as those of the embassies and stately private homes nearby. But don't be put off by the tight entrance hall and rather dark halls: Though the guest rooms on the upper floors are larger, all the rooms are pleasantly decorated, with carefully crafted built-in furniture. The staff is well informed and can direct you to all the nearby monuments and attractions.

Hôtel Lindbergh. 5 rue Chomel, 75007 Paris. ☎ **01-45-48-35-53.** Fax 01-45-49-31-48. www.hotellindbergh.com. E-mail: linhotel@club-internet.fr. 26 units. TV TEL. 510–670F ($81.60–$107.20) double; 760–860F ($121.60–$137.60) triple or quad. AE, DC, MC, V. Parking 70F ($11.20). Métro: Sèvres-Babylone or St-Sulpice.

About a 3-minute walk from St-Germain-des-Prés, this hotel has streamlined and simple medium-size guest rooms. Breakfast is the only meal served, but the staff will point out worthy restaurants nearby—an inexpensive bistro, Le Cigale, is a few buildings away. Room service is available (daily 7am to 7pm).

Hôtel Saint-Dominique. 62 rue St-Dominique, 75007 Paris. ☎ **01-47-05-51-44.** Fax 01-47-05-81-28. 34 units. MINIBAR TV TEL. 540–580F ($86.40–$92.80) double. AE, DC, MC, V. Métro: Latour-Maubourg or Invalides.

Part of this place's charm derives from its division into three buildings connected through an open-air courtyard. The most visible of these was an 18th-century convent—you can still see its battered ceiling beams and structural timbers in the reception area. The guest rooms aren't large, but each is warm and simply decorated; many have wallpaper in nostalgic patterns.

13TH & 14TH ARRONDISSEMENTS (GARE D'AUSTERLITZ/ MONTPARNASSE)
INEXPENSIVE

Hôtel du Parc-Montsouris. 4 rue du Parc de Montsouris, 75014 Paris. ☎ **01-45-89-09-72.** Fax 01-45-80-92-72. www.hotelduparcmontsouris.com. E-mail: hotelduparcmontsouris@wanadoo.fr. 35 units. TV TEL. 350–460F ($56–$73.60) double; 550F ($88) suite. AE, MC, V. Métro: Porte d'Orléans. RER: Cité-Universitaire.

The residential neighborhood is far removed from central Paris's bustle, the staff is a bit absentminded, and the decor doesn't pretend to be stylish, but the prices are reasonable enough that this two-star hotel (a simple structure built in the 1930s) attracts loyal repeat guests; they might be parents of students studying at the nearby Cité Universitaire or provincial clothiers attending fashion shows at the nearby Porte de Versailles. The guest rooms are low-key and quiet, each renovated in the late 1990s.

Hôtel du Vert Galant. 41 rue Croulebarbe, 75013 Paris. ☎ **01-44-08-83-50.** Fax 01-44-08-83-69. 15 units. MINIBAR TV TEL. 460–510F ($73.60–$81.60) double. Parking 35F ($5.60). AE, DC, MC, V. Métro: Corvisart or Gobelins.

Verdant climbing plants and shrubs make this hotel feel like an auberge deep in the French countryside. The smallish guest rooms have tiled or carpeted floors, nice unfussy furniture, and (in most cases) views of the garden or the public park across the street. One of the place's best aspects is the Basque inn next door, the Auberge Etchegorry, sharing the same management; hotel guests receive a discount, enjoying set-price menus for 100F ($16).

3 Near the Airports

EXPENSIVE

Hilton Paris Orly Airport. Aéroport Orly, 267 Orly Sud, 94544 Val-de-Marne. ☎ **800/445-8667** in the U.S. and Canada, or 01-45-12-45-12. Fax 01-45-12-45-00. www.hilton.com. 359 units. A/C MINIBAR TV TEL. 930F ($148.80) double; 1,200–1,400F ($192–$224) suite. AE, DC, MC, V. Parking 90F ($14.40). Free shuttle bus between hotel and both Orly terminals; 40-minute taxi ride from central Paris, except during rush hours.

Boxy and bland, the Hilton at Orly remains a solid and well-maintained hotel business travelers appreciate for its convenience. Incoming planes can't penetrate the guest rooms' sound barriers, guaranteeing you a decent shot at a night's sleep. (And unlike the 24-hour Charles de Gaulle Airport, Orly is closed to arriving flights midnight to 6am.) The rooms are standard for a chain hotel.

Dining: The hotel has the upscale Gastronomique open Monday to Friday for lunch and dinner and a less expensive bistro serving lunch and dinner daily.

Amenities: Concierge, 24-hour room service, laundry, exercise room, sauna, nearby tennis courts.

Hôtel Sofitel Paris Aéroport CDG. Aéroport Charles de Gaulle, Zone Central, B.P. 20248, 95713 Roissy. ☎ **800/221-4542** in the U.S. and Canada, or 01-49-19-29-29. Fax 01-49-19-29-00. www.accor.com. 352 units. A/C MINIBAR TV TEL. 980–1,500F ($156.80–$240) double; from 2,250F ($360) suite. AE, DC, MC, V. Parking 164F ($26.25). Free shuttle bus service to/from airport.

Many travelers shuttle happily through this bustling but somewhat anonymous member of the nationwide French chain. It employs a multilingual staff that's accustomed to accommodating constantly arriving and departing international business travelers. Renovated in 1998, the conservative monochromatic guest rooms are soundproof havens against the all-night roar of jets.

Dining: International food with a French slant is served at a ground-floor restaurant and a bar.

Amenities: Concierge, 24-hour room service, business center, video movies in several languages, pool, sauna.

4 Gay-Friendly Hotels

Though any hotel recommended in this guide is considered at least tolerant of same-sex couples, these two hotels are especially welcoming of gay guests. For the location of the Pierre, see the "Hotels Near Place Charles de Gaulle" map on page 77; for the location of the Central, see the "Hotels in the Heart of the Right Bank" map on pages 66–67. For full coverage of Paris's gay/gay-friendly hotels and restaurants, see *Frommer's Gay & Lesbian Europe.*

EXPENSIVE

Hôtel Pierre. 25 rue Théodore-de-Banville, 75017 Paris. ☎ **01-47-63-76-69.** Fax 01-43-80-63-96. 50 units. MINIBAR TV TEL. 890–2,200F ($142.40–$352) double. AE, DC, MC, V. Parking 100F ($16). Métro: Péreire.

At the end of a residential street a short walk from the Arc de Triomphe, the gay-friendly Pierre was named as a facetious comparison to a favorite New York hotel when the owners combined three 19th-century buildings into a modern hotel with art deco styling. The stylish guest rooms, renovated in 1999, have Empire-style furnishings and safes with combination locks. There's no restaurant or bar, but room service is available Monday to Friday 7am to 10:30pm.

INEXPENSIVE

Hôtel Central. 33 rue Vieille-du-Temple, 75004 Paris. ☎ **01-48-87-99-33.** Fax 01-42-77-06-27. 7 units, 1 with bathroom. TEL. 535F ($85.60) double without bathroom, 650F ($104) double with bathroom. MC, V. Métro: Hôtel de Ville.

This is Paris's most famous all-out gay hotel, with rooms on the second, third, and fourth floors of an 18th-century building. If you arrive from 8:30am to 5pm, you'll find a registration staff one floor above street level; otherwise, you'll have to retrieve your room keys and register at the street-level bar, Le Central (see chapter 9). Frankly, many visitors prefer the bar over the guest rooms, but if you want a hotel that'll put you in the middle of the gay scene, this is it. The guest rooms are simple and serviceable but show wear and tear. With a single exception, one private bathroom is shared for each two rooms. Women are welcome but rare.

Where to Dine 5

Welcome to the city that prides itself on being the world's culinary capital. Only in Paris can you turn onto the nearest little crooked side street, enter the first nondescript bistro you see, sit down at a bare wobbly table, order from an illegibly hand-scrawled menu, and get a truly memorable meal.

1 Food for Thought

THE RESTAURANT SCENE

THE SIX-STAR CHEF If Paris today boasts a king chef—the equivalent of yesteryear's Escoffier—it's none other than Alain Ducasse, who has become the first chef to garner six Michelin stars in a single year. Three were awarded to his eponymous **Alain Ducasse** in Paris and three to his swanky Louis XV in Monte Carlo's Hôtel de Paris. Monsieur Ducasse commutes regularly between Paris and Monaco. If food critics have any lament about this master chef, it's that he spends far too much time serving classical French dishes, which many chefs do well, and too little time creating new ones from his vast storehouse of culinary creativity. Ducasse also runs **Spoon, Food & Wine,** a new bistro serving everything but the exquisite cuisine that earned him his galaxy of stars. Here he offers the likes of macaroni and cheese with gravy (you heard that right), barbecued ribs, and blackened chicken breast. And, yes, that's Philadelphia Cream Cheese on the cheese tray.

THE ASIAN INVASION The exciting news in 2001 is that Paris is buzzing with excitement over not French cuisine but **Asian cuisine**—one headline proclaimed, "The Asian tiger sleeps with the French lamb." A Franco-Asian alliance binds many of the most fashionable restaurants, where the dishes are often from former French colonies, like Cambodian ginger fish wrapped in a banana leaf. There are many dizzying menu items in Paris today—Japanese, Vietnamese, Thai, Philippine, and the inevitable Chinese. Sake and sushi aren't quite as commonplace as *coq au vin* and *pommes frites*, but Asian delicacies abound.

PARIS'S RANGE OF RESTAURANTS Paris boasts a surplus of restaurants and cafes. Ultraexpensive temples of gastronomy include Alain Ducasse, L'Astor, Alain Senderens, Taillevent, Pierre Gagnaire, Lasserre, Jacques Cagna, Le Grand Véfour, and La Tour d'Argent.

Belle-époque Maxim's, the world's most famous restaurant, is still going strong, as overrated and overpriced as ever.

Savvy diners confine their trips to luxe places for special occasions. An array of other choices awaits, including simpler restaurants dispensing cuisines from every province of France and from former colonies like Morocco and Algeria. Paris has hundreds of restaurants serving exotic **international fare,** reflecting the changing complexion of Paris itself and the city's increasing appreciation for food from other cultures. Your most memorable meal in Paris may turn out to be Vietnamese or West African.

You'll also find hundreds of **bistros, brasseries,** and **cafes** to choose from. Many bistros can be chic and elegant, sometimes heavily Mediterranean in style, but others dispense gutsy fare, including the *pot-au-feu* the chef's grandmother prepared for him as a kid. Brasseries are often open 24 hours, including Alsatian establishments that serve sauerkraut with an array of pork products. Cafes too are not just places for an aperitif, a *café au lait*, or a croissant; many serve rib-sticking fare as well, certainly entrecôte with french fries but often classics like *blanquette de veau* (veal in white sauce).

More attention in the late 1990s focused on the **wine bar,** a host of which we recommend in chapter 9. Originally, wine bars concentrated on their lists of wines, featuring many esoteric choices and ignoring the food except for some *charcuterie* (cold cuts) and cheeses. Today, you're likely to be offered various daily specials, from homemade *foie gras* to *boeuf à la mode* (marinated beef braised with red wine and served with vegetables).

Paris prices may seem extravagant to visitors from other parts of the world, particularly those who don't live in big cities, but there has been an emergence of moderately priced **informal restaurants** here, and we recommend several. Although they're not as fashionable as they once were, still on the scene are **baby bistros,** reasonably priced spin-offs from deluxe restaurants where you can get a taste of a famous chef's cuisine without breaking the bank. We've covered the best of them.

DINING SAVOIR-FAIRE

- Three-star dining remains extremely expensive, with appetizers sometimes priced at $50 and dinners easily costing $200 per person in the top Michelin-starred dining rooms of celebrated chefs. But you can get around that high price tag in many places by **dining at lunch** (when prices are always cheaper) and ordering a **prix-fixe (fixed-price) menu** at lunch or dinner.
- In France, **lunch** (as well as dinner) tends to be a full-course meal with meat, vegetables, salad, bread, cheese, dessert, wine, and coffee. It may be difficult to find a restaurant that serves the type of light lunch North Americans usually eat. Cafes, however, offer sandwiches, soup, and salads in a relaxed setting.
- Average visitors head for the old-fashioned family-run **bistro,** and we've ferreted out the best ones. In today's Paris, tradition and nostalgia, along with affordable prices, make these bistros busier than ever, especially since so many are being forced out of existence because of rising rents.
- **Coffee** in France is served after the meal and carries an extra charge. The French consider it barbaric to drink coffee during the meal, and, unless you specifically order it with milk (*au lait*), it'll be served black. In more conscientious places, it's prepared as the traditional *café filtre*, a slow but rewarding java draw.

Best Restaurant Bets

See chapter 1 for a list of our restaurant favorites—the best chef, the best view, the best baby bistro, and more.

Mystifying Menu?

If you need help distinguishing a *blanquette de veau* from a *crème brûlée,* turn to the glossary of French-language menu terms in Appendix B.

- In years gone by, no man would consider dining out, even at the neighborhood bistro, without a suit and tie and no woman would be seen without a smart dress or suit. That **dress code** is more relaxed now, except in first-class and luxe establishments. Relaxed doesn't mean sloppy jeans and jogging attire, however. Parisians still value style, even when dressing informally.
- In terms of **tips,** in simple bistros, leave the small change on the table; in luxe or first-class places, add another 5% to the bill.

2 Restaurants by Cuisine

ALGERIAN
Au Clair de Lune (p. 112)
Wally Le Saharien (p. 124)

ALSATIAN
Bofinger (p. 114)
Brasserie de l'Ile St-Louis (p. 115)
Brasserie Flo (p. 125)

AMERICAN
Chicago Pizza Pie Factory (p. 122)
Hard Rock Cafe (p. 123)
Joe Allen (p. 109)

ASIAN
Café Indochine (p. 122)
Kambodia (p. 130)

AUVERGNAT
L'Ambassade d'Auvergne (p. 113)
Restaurant Bleu (p. 148)

BASQUE
Auberge Etchegorry (p. 144)
Chez l'Ami Jean (p. 144)

BRETON
✪ Chez Michel (p. 126)

BURGUNDIAN
Chez Pauline (p. 105)

CAFES
Brasserie Lipp (p. 149)
Café Beaubourg (p. 149)
Café Cosmos (p. 149)
Café de Flore (p. 149)

Café de la Musique (p. 149)
✪ Café de la Paix (p. 150)
Café de l'Industrie (p. 150)
Café des Hauteurs (p. 150)
Café Marly (p. 150)
Café/Restaurant/Salon de Thé
    Bernardaud (p. 151)
Fouquet's (p. 151)
La Coupole (p. 151)
La Rotonde (p. 151)
Le Café Zephyr (p. 152)
Le Gutenberg (p. 152)
Le Procope (p. 152)
Le Rouquet (p. 152)
Les Deux Magots (p. 152)

CAMBODIAN
Kambodia (p. 130)

CANTONESE
Chez Vong (p. 108)
China Club (p. 127)

CENTRAL EUROPEAN
✪ Chez Jo Goldenberg (p. 116)
La Cagouille (p. 145)

CHINESE
China Club (p. 127)
Le Canton (p. 141)

CREOLE
Babylone (p. 112)

DANISH
Copenhague/Flora Danica (p. 120)

FRENCH (MODERN)

- ✪ Alain Ducasse (p. 128)
- Alcazar Bar & Restaurant (p. 138)
- Bofinger (p. 114)
- ✪ Buddha Bar (p. 119)
- Café la Parisienne (p. 115)
- Carré des Feuillants (p. 104)
- ✪ Chez Diane (p. 140)
- Chez Jean (p. 123)
- ✪ Jacques Cagna (p. 137)
- Julien (p. 126)
- L'Amazonial (p. 153)
- L'Ambroisie (p. 113)
- L'Arpège (p. 141)
- ✪ Lasserre (p. 116)
- ✪ L'Astor (p. 117)
- Le Bistro d'á Côté Flaubert (p. 132)
- ✪ Le Violon d'Ingres (p. 141)
- Lucas-Carton (Alain Senderens) (p. 117)
- Marc-Annibal de Coconnas (p. 114)
- ✪ Michel Rostang (p. 132)
- ✪ Pierre Gagnaire (p. 118)
- Restaurant Opéra (p. 124)
- Shozan (p. 120)
- ✪ Taillevent (p. 118)

FRENCH (TRADITIONAL)

- ✪ Alain Ducasse (p. 128)
- ✪ Allard (p. 138)
- Astier (p. 127)
- Au Clair de Lune (p. 112)
- Au Gourmet de l'Ile (p. 115)
- ✪ Au Pied de Cochon (p. 105)
- Au Pied de Fouet (p. 114)
- Aux Charpentiers (p. 139)
- ✪ Aux Lyonnais (p. 112)
- Bistro de la Grille (p. 139)
- Bofinger (p. 114)
- Brasserie Balzar (p. 136)
- Brasserie de l'Ile St-Louis (p. 115)
- Chartier (p. 125)
- Chez André (p. 121)
- ✪ Chez Diane (p. 140)
- Chez Edgard (p. 121)
- Chez Georges (p. 111)
- Chez Georges (p. 132)
- Chez Gramond (p. 138)
- Chez Jean (p. 123)
- Chez Pauline (p. 105)
- Chez René (p. 136)

- Closerie des Lilas (p. 138)
- ✪ Crémerie-Restaurant Polidor (p. 140)
- Dame Tartine (p. 116)
- Eclache & Cie (p. 153)
- ✪ Faugeron (p. 130)
- ✪ Guy Savoy (p. 131)
- ✪ Jacques Cagna (p. 137)
- ✪ Jamin (p. 130)
- Julien (p. 126)
- La Butte Chaillot (p. 131)
- La Cagouille (p. 145)
- La Clementine (p. 112)
- La Grille (p. 125)
- L'Ambassade d'Auvergne (p. 113)
- L'Ambroisie (p. 113)
- L'Ami Louis (p. 113)
- La Petite Chaise (p. 142)
- La Petite Hostellerie (p. 136)
- La Poule au Pot (p. 110)
- La Rose de France (p. 110)
- ✪ La Rôtisserie d'Armaillé (p. 132)
- La Rôtisserie d'en Face (p. 139)
- ✪ Lasserre (p. 116)
- ✪ La Tour d'Argent (p. 133)
- La Tour de Monthléry (Chez Denise) (p. 110)
- Laudurée (p. 121)
- L'Ebauchoir (p. 128)
- Le Berry's (p. 123)
- Le Bistro d'á Côté Flaubert (p. 132)
- Le Bistro de l'Etoile (p. 131)
- Le Café du Commerce (p. 147)
- Le Grand Véfour (p. 105)
- ✪ Le Grand Zinc (p. 125)
- ✪ Lescure (p. 111)
- Les Gourmets des Ternes (p. 123)
- Le 30 (Chez Fauchon) (p. 120)
- ✪ Le Train Bleu (p. 127)
- Le Vaudeville (p. 111)
- Le Vieux Bistro (p. 114)
- ✪ Le Violon d'Ingres (p. 141)
- Marc-Annibal de Coconnas (p. 114)
- Marie-Louise (p. 133)
- Maxim's (p. 118)
- Michel Rostang (p. 132)
- Perraudin (p. 137)
- Restaurant des Beaux-Arts (p. 141)
- Restaurant Opéra (p. 124)
- ✪ Taillevent (p. 118)
- Trumilou (p. 116)

GASCONY
✪ Au Trou Gascon (p. 126)

INDIAN
Yugaraj (p. 139)

INDOCHINESE
Café Indochine (p. 122)

INTERNATIONAL
L'Amazonial (p. 153)
Le Fumoir (p. 108)
Spoon, Food & Wine (p. 120)

ITALIAN
Il Cortile (p. 108)

JAPANESE
Isama (p. 114)
Shozan (p. 120)

JEWISH
✪ Chez Jo Goldenberg (p. 116)

KOREAN
Shing-Jung (p. 123)

LANDES
Restaurant du Marché (p. 146)

LATE NIGHT
✪ Au Pied de Cochon (p. 105)
Babylone (p. 112)
La Poule au Pot (p. 110)
La Tour de Monthléry (Chez Denise)
    (p. 110)
Le Vaudeville (p. 111)

LEBANESE
Al Dar (p. 136)

LIGHT FARE
✪ Angélina (p. 108)

LOIRE VALLEY (ANJOU)
Au Petit Riche (p. 124)

LYONNAIS
✪ Aux Lyonnais (p. 112)

MEDITERRANEAN
Il Cortile (p. 108)

MOROCCAN
Mansouria (p. 128)

NORTHERN FRENCH
Le Bambouche (p. 142)

ORGANIC
Le Grain de Folie (p. 133)

PACIFIC RIM
✪ Buddha Bar (p. 119)

PIZZA
Chicago Pizza Pie Factory (p. 122)

PROVENÇAL
Campagne et Provence (p. 136)
Chez Janou (p. 113)
La Bastide Odéon (p. 140)

PYRENÉE
La Fontaine de Mars (p. 144)

SEAFOOD
Goumard (p. 104)
Keryado (p. 145)
La Grille (p. 125)
Paul Minchelli (p. 142)

SENEGALESE
Le Manguier (p. 128)
Paris-Dakar (p. 126)

SOUTHWESTERN FRENCH
Chez l'Ami Jean (p. 144)
Chez Lulu (p. 145)
La Fermette du Sud-Ouest (p. 110)
La Fontaine de Mars (p. 144)
La Régalade (p. 146)

TEA
✪ Angélina (p. 108)
Café/Restaurant/Salon de Thé
    Bernardaud (p. 151)

THAI
Blue Elephant (p. 127)

VEGETARIAN
✪ Aquarius (p. 115)
Le Grain de Folie (p. 133)

VIETNAMESE
Le Canton (p. 141)

Ducasse Lite

If you're traveling on a lean budget, you can still get a peek into the celestial world of **Alain Ducasse** by dropping into the bar at his avenue Raymond-Poincaré restaurant and ordering one of the best arrays of tapas in town. Of course, you'll have to put up with a lot of fashionable cigar smoke.

---

3 On the Right Bank

We'll begin with the most centrally located arrondissements on the Right Bank, then work our way through the more outlying neighborhoods.

1ST ARRONDISSEMENT (MUSÉE DU LOUVRE/LES HALLES)
VERY EXPENSIVE

Carré des Feuillants. 14 rue de Castiglione (near place Vendôme and the Tuileries), 1er. ☎ **01-42-86-82-82.** Fax 01–42–86–07–71. Reservations required far in advance. Main courses 240–280F ($38.40–$44.80); fixed-price menu 340F ($54.40) at lunch, 880F ($140.80) at dinner. AE, DC, MC, V. Mon–Fri noon–2:30pm; Mon–Sat 7:30–10:30pm. Closed first 3 weeks in Aug. Métro: Tuileries, Concorde, Opéra, or Madeleine. FRENCH (MODERN).

When leading chef Alain Dutournier turned this 17th-century convent into a restaurant, it was an overnight success. The interior is like an early-1900s bourgeois house with several small salons opening onto a skylit courtyard, across from which is a glass-enclosed kitchen. You'll find a sophisticated reinterpretation of cuisine from France's southwest, using seasonally fresh ingredients and lots of know-how. Examples are roasted veal kidneys cooked in their own fat; grilled wood pigeon served with chutney and polenta; rabbit filet in bitter-chocolate sauce with quince; and roasted leg of suckling lamb from the Pyrénées with autumn vegetables. Lighter dishes are scallops wrapped in parsley-infused puff pastry served with cabbage and truffles and mullet-studded risotto with lettuce. For dessert, try a slice of pistachio cream cake with candied tangerines.

Goumard. 9 rue Duphot, 1er. ☎ **01-42-60-36-07.** Fax 01–42–60–04–54. Reservations required far in advance. Main courses 190–380F ($30.40–$60.80); fixed-price lunch 390F ($62.40); *ménu gastronomique* (tasting menu) 780F ($124.80). AE, DC, MC, V. Tues–Sat 12:30–2:30pm and 7:30–10:30pm. Closed 2 weeks in Aug. Métro: Madeleine or Concorde. SEAFOOD.

Opened in 1872, this landmark is one of Paris's leading seafood restaurants. It's so devoted to the fine art of preparing fish that other food is strictly banned from the menu (if you happen to dislike fish, the staff will orally present a limited roster of meat dishes). The decor consists of an unusual collection of Lalique crystal fish displayed in artificial aquariums. Even more unusual are the men's and women's rest rooms, now classified as historic monuments; the commodes were designed by the art nouveau master cabinetmaker Majorelle in the early 1900s. Much of the seafood is flown in directly from Brittany daily. Examples are a *craquant* (crispy) of crayfish in its own herb salad, lobster soup with coconut, grilled seawolf filet with a fricassée of artichokes and Provençal pistou, a grilled turbot salad on a bed of artichokes with tarragon, and poached turbot with hollandaise sauce, served with leeks in vinaigrette. In all these dishes nothing (no excess butter, spices, or salt) is allowed to interfere with the natural flavor of the sea. Be prepared for some unusual food—the staff will help translate the menu items for you.

⚫ **Le Grand Véfour.** 17 rue de Beaujolais, 1er. ☎ **01-42-96-56-27.** Fax 01–42–86–80–71. Reservations required far in advance. Main courses 230–380F ($36.80–$60.80); fixed-price menu 360–790F ($57.60–$126.40) at lunch, 790F ($126.40) at dinner. AE, CB, DC, MC, V. Mon–Fri 12:30–2pm and 7:30–10:15pm. Métro: Louvre. FRENCH (TRADITIONAL).

This restaurant has been around since the reign of Louis XV, though not under the same name. Napoléon, Danton, Hugo, Colette, and Cocteau have dined here—as the brass plaques on the tables testify—and it's still a great gastronomic experience. Guy Martin, chef here for the past decade, bases many dishes on recipes from the French Alps. His best dish is roast lamb in a juice of herbs. Other specialties are noisettes of lamb with star anise and Breton lobster and the unusual cabbage sorbet in dark-chocolate sauce. The desserts are often grand, like the *gourmandises au chocolat*, a richness of chocolate served with chocolate sorbet.

MODERATE

⚫ **Au Pied de Cochon.** 6 rue Coquillière, 1er. ☎ **01-40-13-77-00.** Reservations recommended for lunch and dinner hours. Main courses 86–148F ($13.75–$23.70). AE, DC, MC, V. Daily 24 hours. Métro: Les Halles. FRENCH (TRADITIONAL)/LATE NIGHT.

Au Pied de Cochon's famous onion soup and namesake house specialty (grilled pig's feet with béarnaise sauce) still lure visitors, and where else in Paris can you be assured of getting a good meal at 3am? Two other specialties are the *tentation* (temptation) platter, including grilled pig's tail, pig's snout, and half a pig's foot with béarnaise and *frites*, and *andouillette* (chitterling sausages) with béarnaise. Two particularly flavorful but less unusual dishes are a *jarret* (shin) of pork, caramelized in honey and served on a bed of sauerkraut, and grilled pork ribs with sage sauce. On the street outside, you can buy some of the freshest oysters in town. The attendants will give you slices of lemon to accompany them, and you can down them on the spot.

Chez Pauline. 5 rue Villedo, 1er. ☎ **01-42-96-20-70.** Reservations recommended. Main courses 190–400F ($30.40–$64); fixed-price menu 220F ($35.20). AE, CB, DC, V. Mon–Fri 12:15–2:30pm and 7:30–10:30pm, Sat 7:30–10:30pm. Closed Sat–Sun May–early Sept. Métro: Palais Royal. BURGUNDIAN/FRENCH (TRADITIONAL).

Fans say this "bistrot de luxe" is a less expensive, less majestic version of Le Grand Véfour. The early–1900s setting is grand enough to impress a business client and lighthearted enough to attract an impressive roster of VIPs. You'll be ushered to a table on one of two levels, amid polished mirrors, red leather banquettes, and memorabilia of long-ago Paris. The emphasis is on the cuisine of central France, especially Burgundy, as shown by the liberal use of wines in favorites like cassoulet of Burgundian snails with bacon and tomatoes, *boeuf bourguignonne* (braised beef in red-wine sauce) with tagliatelle, terrine of parslied ham, wild duckling filet with seasonal berries, salmon steak with green peppercorns, and ragout of wild hare in Pouilly aspic. Also wonderful is the roasted Bresse chicken with dauphinois potatoes. Dessert may

---

Don't Leave Home Without Them

No matter how long your stay in Paris, we suggest you save up and indulge in at least one break-the-bank French meal at a fabulous restaurant. The meal will be a memory you'll likely treasure long after you've recovered from paying the tab. However, to get a table at one of these places, *you must reserve far in advance*—at least a day or two ahead, sometimes even a few weeks or a few months ahead! We suggest you look over our listings at home and then call for reservations before you leave on your trip or at least call the minute you get into town.

Restaurants in the Heart of the Right Bank

Angélina **32**
Aquarius **57**
Astier **51**
Au Clair de Lune **39**
Au Gourmet de l'Ile **66**
Au Petit Riche **9**
Au Pied de Cochon **41**
Au Trou Gascon **67**
Aux Lyonnais **17**

Babylone **38**
Berthillon **67**
Blue Elephant **72**
Bofinger **76**
Brasserie de
  l'Ile St-Louis **64**
Brasserie Flo **14**
Buddha Bar **24**
Café Beaubourg **56**

Café Bernardaud **23**
Café de la Musique **48**
Café de la Paix **19**
Café de l'Industrie **73**
Café la Parisienne **59**
Café Marly **45**
Café Zephyr **12**
Carré des Feuillants **31**
Chartier **10**

Chez Georges **36**
Chez Janou **71**
Chez Jean **5**
Chez Jo Goldenberg **68**
Chez Michel **1**
Chez Pauline **33**
Chez Vong **53**
China Club **75**
Dalloyau **30**

Dame Tartine **60**
Eclache & Cie **58**
Fauchon (Le 30) **21**
Goumard **28**
Hard Rock Café **11**
Il Cortile **29**
Isama **65**
Joe Allen **54**
Julien **15**

L'Amazonial **61**

L'Ambassade
  d'Auvergne **55**

L'Ambroisie **69**

L'Ami Louis **52**

L'Astor **8**

La Clementine **16**

La Fermette du
  Sud-Ouest **42**

La Grille **4**

La Poule au Pot **43**

La Rose de France **47**

La Samaritaine **41**

La Tour de Monthléry
  (Chez Denise) **44**

Laudurée Royale **26**

Le 30 (Chez Fauchon) **21**

L'Ebauchoir **74**

Le Berry's **6**

Le Fumoir **46**

Le Grain de Folie **2**

Le Grand Véfour **35**

Le Grand Zinc **13**

Le Gutenberg **40**

Le Manguier **50**

Lerch **78**

Le Train Bleu **77**

Le Vaudeville **18**

Le Vieux Bistro **62**

Lescure **27**

Lucas-Carton
  (Alain Senderens) **22**

Mansouria **66**

Marc-Annibal de
  Coconnas **70**

Marie-Louise **6**

Maxim's **25**

Paris-Dakar **49**

Restaurant Opéra **20**

Shing-Jung **7**

Stohrer **37**

Trumilou **63**

Wally Le Saharien **3**

Willi's Wine Bar **34**

include a *clafoutis* (pastry) of apricots and raspberries lightly sautéed in sugar as well as caramelized rice pudding. Owner/chef André Genin is an author of children's books, some on the value and techniques of French cuisine.

Il Cortile. In the Hôtel Castille, 37 rue Cambon, 1er. ☎ **01-44-58-45-67.** Reservations recommended. Main courses 100–150F ($16–$24). AE, DC, DISC, MC, V. Mon–Fri noon–2:30pm and 7:30–10:30pm. Métro: Concorde or Madeleine. ITALIAN/MEDITERRANEAN.

Flanking the verdant courtyard of a discreet small hotel, this much-talked-about restaurant serves the best Italian food in Paris. During warm weather, tables are set up in an enclosed patio—a welcome luxury in this congested neighborhood. The cuisine is fresh, inventive, and seasonal. Dishes are from throughout Italy, with emphasis on the north, as shown by a special promotion of wines of Tuscany and the Piedmont. Look for items like *farfalle* pasta with squid ink and fresh shellfish, fettuccine with *pistou* (pasta in a soup made from various vegetables), and an award-winning version of guinea fowl (spit-roasted and served with artfully shaped slices of the bird's gizzard, heart, and liver, it comes with polenta). The service is virtually flawless: The Italian-speaking staff is diplomatic and good humored. If you want to see what's cooking, ask for a seat with a view of the open rotisserie, where spit-roasted hens and guinea fowl slowly spin.

Le Fumoir. 6 rue de l'Amiral-Coligny, 1er. ☎ **01-42-92-00-24.** Reservations recommended. Main courses 105–120F ($16.80–$19.20). Salads, pastries, and snacks daily 11am–1am; complete menu daily noon–3pm and 7–11:30pm. AE, CB, V. Métro: Louvre. INTERNATIONAL.

Stylish and breezy, this upscale brasserie is set in an antique building a few steps from the Louvre. Currently, it's one of the most fashionable places in Paris to be seen eating or drinking. In a high-ceilinged room of warm but somber browns and indirect lighting, you can order salads, pastries, and drinks at off-hours and platters of more substantial food at conventional mealtimes. Examples are codfish filet with onions and herbs, sliced rack of veal simmered in its own juices with tarragon, calf's liver with onions, lamb chops with grilled tuna steak, and herring in mustard-flavored cream sauce.

INEXPENSIVE

✪ **Angélina.** 226 rue de Rivoli, 1er. ☎ **01-42-60-82-00.** Reservations accepted for lunch, not for teatime. Pot of tea for 1 35–36F ($5.60–$5.75); sandwiches and salads 58–98F ($9.30–$15.70); main courses 68–135F ($10.90–$21.60). AE, V. Mon–Fri 9am–7pm, Sat–Sun 9am–7:30pm (lunch 11:45am–3pm). Métro: Tuileries. TEA/LIGHT FARE.

In the high-rent area near the Inter-Continental (though on a section of rue de Rivoli that's getting scuzzy), this *salon de thé* combines fashion-industry glitter and bourgeois respectability. The carpets are plush, the ceilings are high, and the gilded accessories have the right amount of patina. This place has no equal when it comes to viewing the lionesses of haute couture over tea and delicate sandwiches. The overwrought and slightly snooty waitresses bear silver trays with light platters, pastries, drinks, and tea or coffee to tiny marble-topped tables. Lunch usually offers a salad and a *plat du jour* like chicken salad, steak tartare, sole meunière, or poached salmon. The house specialty, designed to go well with tea, is a Mont Blanc, a combination of chestnut cream and meringue.

Chez Vong. 10 rue de la Grande-Truanderie, 1er. ☎ **01-40-26-09-36.** Reservations recommended. Main courses 100–145F ($16–$23.20); fixed-price lunch 150F ($24). AE, DC, MC, V. Mon–Sat noon–2:30pm and 7pm–midnight. Métro: Etienne-Marcel. CANTONESE.

This is the kind of Les Halles restaurant you head for when you've had your fill of grand French cuisine and grander culinary pretensions. The decor is a soothing mix of

La Gastronomie 101

In a nation devoted to the pursuit of gastronomic excellence, you'll find a wide array of chefs (skilled and otherwise) eager to impart a few of their culinary insights—for a fee. A knowledge of at least rudimentary French is a good idea before you enroll, though a visual demonstration of any technique is often more valuable than reading or hearing about it. The cooking schools below will send you information in English or French if you contact them in advance; their courses might be attended by professional chefs and serious or competitive connoisseurs.

Based at the Hôtel Ritz, where Escoffier helped César Ritz make his hotel legendary, is the **Ritz-Escoffier Ecole de Gastronomie Française,** 15 place Vendôme, 75001 Paris (☎ **888/801-1126** in the U.S. or 01-43-16-30-50; fax 01-43-16-31-50; www.ritzparis.com). Famed for his titanic rages in the kitchens of the French and English aristocrats who engaged him to prepare their banquets and also for his well-publicized culinary codifications, Georges-Auguste Escoffier (1846–1935) taught the Edwardian Age how to eat. Ritz-Escoffier demonstrations are held Monday and Thursday 3 to 5:30pm at 275F ($44). Classes (taught in French or English) in specific techniques, like baking, working with pastry, and fish preparation, cost 5,700F to 6,000F ($912 to $960) for 1 week. The 12-week Ritz-Escoffier course, at 74,000F ($11,840), presents an overview of most aspects of the repertoire of French cuisine and is popular with passionate amateurs and ambitious professional chefs.

Opened in 1895, **Le Cordon Bleu,** 8 rue Léon-Delhomme, 75015 Paris (☎ **800/457-CHEF** in the U.S. or 01-53-68-22-50; fax 914/426-0104; www.cordonbleu.net), is France's most famous cooking school. Cordon Bleu's most prestigious and popular offering is the 9-month course that exposes you to every aspect of the French culinary process. At graduation, you're issued a certificate of competence—highly prized in the restaurant world. Many gourmets prefer a less intense immersion and opt for either a 4-day workshop or a 3-hour demonstration class. Enrollment in either of these is on a first-come, first-served basis; it's 220F ($35.20) for a demonstration of every aspect of preparing at least one (and sometimes two or three) complicated culinary specialty from start to finish, and it's 5,070F ($811.20) for a 4-day culinary workshop covering most of the major categories of food preparation (soup, terrines, meats, fish, desserts). Also of interest to professional chefs (or wannabes) is the 4-week course in catering at 27,800F ($4,448).

green and browns, steeped in a Chinese colonial ambience that evokes early-1900s Shanghai. Menu items feature shrimp and scallops served as spicy as you like, including a super-hot version with garlic and red peppers; "joyous beef" that mingles sliced filet with pepper sauce; chicken in puff pastry with ginger; and a tempting array of fresh fish dishes. The whims of fashion have decreed this one of the restaurants of the moment, so it's full of folk from the worlds of entertainment and the arts.

Joe Allen. 30 rue Pierre-Lescot, 1er. ☎ **01-42-36-70-13.** Reservations recommended for dinner. Main courses 75–140F ($12–$22.40); fixed-price menu 112–140F ($17.90–$22.40). AE, MC, V. Daily noon–1am. Métro: Etienne-Marcel. AMERICAN.

Joe Allen long ago invaded Les Halles with his hamburger. Though the New York restaurateur admits "it's a silly idea," it works, and it's easily Paris's best burger. While listening to the jukebox, you can order savory black-bean soup, spicy chili, juicy sirloin steak, barbecued spareribs, or apple pie. Joe Allen is getting more sophisticated, however, catering to modern tastes with dishes like grilled salmon with coconut rice and sun-dried tomatoes. His saloon is the only place in Paris serving authentic New York cheesecake and real pecan pie, and thanks to French chocolate, he feels his brownies are better than those in the States. Giving the brownies tough competition are the California chocolate-mousse pie, strawberries Romanoff, and coconut-cream pie. On a regular night, if you haven't made a reservation for dinner, expect to wait at the New York bar for at least 30 minutes.

La Fermette du Sud-Ouest. 31 rue Coquillière, 1er. ☎ **01-42-36-73-55.** Reservations recommended. Main courses 70–105F ($11.20–$16.80); fixed-price menu (at lunch and before 9pm at dinner) 90–145F ($14.40–$23.20). MC, V. Mon–Sat noon–2:30pm and 7:30–10:30pm. Métro: Les Halles. SOUTHWESTERN FRENCH.

In the heart of one of Paris's most ancient neighborhoods, a stone's throw from Ste-Eustache church, this restaurant occupies the site of a 1500s convent. After the Revolution, the convent was converted into a coaching inn that preserved the original stonework and massive beams. La Fermette prepares rich, savory stews and confits celebrating agrarian France, serving them on the ground floor and on a mezzanine resembling a medieval choir loft. Menu items include an age-old but ever-popular magret of duckling with flap mushrooms, *andouillette* (chitterling sausages), and a sometimes startling array of *cochonailles* (pork products and by-products) you probably need to be French to appreciate. Cassoulet is an enduring specialty.

La Poule au Pot. 9 rue Vauvilliers, 1er. ☎ **01-42-36-32-96.** Reservations recommended. Main courses 100–150F ($16–$24); fixed-price menu 160F ($25.60). MC, V. Tues–Sun 7pm–5am. Métro: Louvre or Les Halles. FRENCH (TRADITIONAL)/LATE NIGHT.

This bistro welcomes late-night carousers and show-biz personalities looking for a meal after a performance. (Past aficionados have included the Rolling Stones, Prince, and Johnny Hallyday.) The decor is authentically art deco, the ambience nurturing. The time-tested and savory menu items include a salad of warm goat cheese on toast, pan-fried stingray with capers, burgundy-style snails, country pâté on a bed of onion marmalade, and a succulent version of the restaurant's namesake, chicken in a pot with slices of pâté and fresh vegetables (in summer, it can be served cold, on a bed of lettuce, with vinaigrette sauce).

La Rose de France. 24 place Dauphine, 1er. ☎ **01-43-54-10-12.** Reservations recommended. Main courses 80–100F ($12.80–$16); menu du jour 140F ($22.40). AE, V. Mon–Fri noon–2pm and 7–10pm. Closed last 3 weeks in Aug and 15 days at end of Dec. Métro: Cité or Pont Neuf. FRENCH (TRADITIONAL).

At this restaurant on Ile de la Cité near Notre-Dame, around the corner from the Pont Neuf, you'll dine with a crowd of young Parisians who know they can expect a good meal at reasonable prices. Founded more than 30 years ago by its present owner, M. Cointepas, it can be relied on for fresh food served in a friendly atmosphere. In warm weather the sidewalk tables overlooking the Palais de Justice are most popular. Main dishes include sweetbreads, veal chop flambéed with Calvados and served with apples, beef filet en crôte, and lamb chops seasoned with Provençal herbs and served with gratin of potatoes. For dessert, try the fruit tart of the day or the sorbet of the month.

La Tour de Monthléry (Chez Denise). 5 rue des Prouvaires, 1er. ☎ **01-42-36-21-82.** Main courses 65–130F ($10.40–$20.80). V. Open continuously Mon 7am–Sat 7am. Métro: Louvre or Les Halles. FRENCH (TRADITIONAL)/LATE NIGHT.

This restaurant is both workaday and stylish—no small feat considering its gregarious owner, Denise Bénariac, has maintained her reign here for more than 30 years. Amid a decor that has changed little since 1900 (note the long nickel-plated bar near the entrance), you can order hearty, unfussy cuisine. The food tastes best late after a long night of carousing. Menu items include grilled pig's trotters, mutton stew, steak with peppercorns, stuffed cabbage, and a golden-velvety pâté of chicken livers. Wine goes with this kind of food beautifully, and the restaurant complies by recommending several worthy but unpretentious vintages.

♻ **Lescure.** 7 rue de Mondovi, 1er. ☎ **01-42-60-18-91.** Main courses 26–84F ($4.15–$13.45); 4-course fixed-price menu 110F ($17.60). MC, V. Mon–Fri noon–2:15pm and 7–11pm. Closed 3 weeks in Aug. Métro: Concorde. FRENCH (TRADITIONAL).

This minibistro is a major find—one of the few reasonably priced restaurants near place de la Concorde, animated and appealing. You'll get a lot for your franc. The tables on the sidewalk are tiny, and there isn't much room inside, but what this place does have is rustic charm. The kitchen is wide open, and the aroma of drying bay leaves, salami, and garlic pigtails hanging from the ceiling fills the room. Expect *cuisine bourgeoise*—nothing innovative, just substantial hearty fare. Perhaps begin with *pâté en croûte* (pâté in pastry). Main-course house specialties include *confit de canard* (duckling) and cabbage stuffed with salmon. The chef's fruit tarts are a favorite dessert. In autumn and winter, expect a savory repertoire of game dishes like venison and pheasant.

2ND ARRONDISSEMENT (LA BOURSE)
MODERATE

Chez Georges. 1 rue du Mail, 2e. ☎ **01-42-60-07-11.** Reservations required. Main courses 125–165F ($20–$26.40). AE, MC, V. Mon–Sat noon–2:15pm and 7–9:45pm. Closed 3 weeks in Aug. Métro: Bourse. FRENCH (TRADITIONAL).

This bistro is something of a local landmark, opened in 1964 near La Bourse (stock exchange) and run by three generations of the same family. Naturally, at lunch it's packed with stock-exchange members. The owners serve what they call *la cuisine bourgeoise* (comfort food). Waiters bring around bowls of appetizers, like celery rémoulade, to get you started. You can follow with sweetbreads with morels, duck breast with cèpe mushrooms, classic cassoulet, or *pot-au-feu* (beef simmered with vegetables). A delight is sole filet with a sauce made from Pouilly wine and crème fraîche. Beaujolais goes great with this hearty food.

Le Vaudeville. 29 rue Vivienne, 2e. ☎ **01-40-20-04-62.** Reservations recommended in the evenings. Main courses 80–140F ($12.80–$22.40); fixed-price menu 138F ($22.10) at lunch, 138–189F ($22.10–$30.25) at dinner. AE, DC, MC, V. Daily noon–3:30pm and 7pm–1am. Métro: Bourse. FRENCH (TRADITIONAL)/LATE NIGHT.

Adjacent to La Bourse (stock exchange), this bistro has retained its marble walls and art deco carvings from 1918. In summer, tables dot a terrace amid banks of geraniums. The place is boisterous and informal, often welcoming groups of six or eight

Taking an Ice Cream Break at Berthillon

A landmark on Ile St-Louis after three dozen years in business, the *salon de thé* **Berthillon,** 31 rue St-Louis-en-l'Ile, 4e (☎ **01-43-54-31-61;** Métro: Pont Marie), offers the world's best selection of delectable ice creams. Try gingerbread, bitter-chocolate mousse, rhubarb, melon, kumquat, black currant, or any exotic fresh fruit in season—more than 50 flavors to choose from and nothing artificial. Parisians have flocked to this place in such numbers that gendarmes have been called out to direct the traffic of ice cream aficionados. It's open Wednesday to Sunday 10am to 8pm.

diners at a time. A bar near the entrance provides a perch if your reservation is delayed. The bountiful roster of platters includes snails in garlic butter, shellfish, smoked salmon, sauerkraut, and grilled meats. Three dishes reign as enduring favorites: fresh codfish with mashed potatoes and truffle juice, fresh escalope of warm foie gras with grapes, and *tête du veaux* (veal's head). The main value is the fixed-price menu.

INEXPENSIVE

Au Clair de Lune. 13 rue Française, 2e. ☎ **01-42-33-59-10.** Main courses 54–72F ($8.65–$11.50); fixed-price menu 68F ($10.90). DC, MC, V. Daily noon–2:30pm and 7:30–11pm. Métro: Etienne-Marcel or Sentier. ALGERIAN/FRENCH (TRADITIONAL).

This neighborhood staple has flourished in the heart of Paris's wholesale garment district since the 1930s, when Algeria was a distinct part of the French-speaking world. Today you'll dine in a long narrow room whose walls are hung with colorful Berber carpets and whose patrons are likely to include shop workers from the nearby wholesale clothiers. On the menu is always the Algerian staple of couscous, as well as an array of oft-changing daily specials such as veal stew, shoulder or rack of lamb, grilled fish, and roast chicken. The portions are so large you should take along a ravenous appetite. The wines are from throughout France and North Africa.

✪ **Aux Lyonnais.** 32 rue St-Marc, 2e. ☎ **01-42-96-65-04.** Reservations required. Main courses 70–90F ($11.20–$14.40). AE, DC, MC, V. Mon–Sat 11:30am–3pm and 6:30–11:30pm. Métro: Bourse or Richelieu-Drouot. LYONNAIS/FRENCH (TRADITIONAL).

A LYON LE COCHON ES ROI! proclaims the sign. Pig may be king at this fin-de-siècle bistro (with walls molded with roses and garlands, brass globe lamps, potted palms, and etched glass), just behind La Bourse, but the competent kitchen staff does everything well. After a meal here, you'll know why Lyon is called the gastronomic capital of France. Everything is washed down with Beaujolais. Launch your repast with one of the large Lyonnais sausages, though a favorite opener remains a chicory salad with bacon and slices of hot sausages. Poached eggs in red-wine sauce and grilled pig's feet still appear on the menu. Pike dumplings are always prepared to perfection and served classically in white-butter sauce. The upside-down apple pie with crème fraîche is the dessert of choice.

Babylone. 34 rue Tiquetonne, 2e. ☎ **01-42-33-48-35.** Main courses 70–120F ($11.20–$19.20). V. Daily 8pm–8am. Métro: Etienne-Marcel or Sentier. CREOLE/LATE NIGHT.

This place honors the French Caribbean island of Guadeloupe with culinary specialties like *accras* (fritters) of codfish and Creole *boudin* (blood sausage), which usually preface main courses like fricassée of shrimp or chicken and *colombo* (stew) of baby goat. Look for African masks, touches of zebra skin, and photos of the divas and celebs (Diana Ross, Stevie Wonder, Jesse Jackson, French sports stars, fashion models) who've dined here. Don't think of coming before dark. After 2am or so, the focus shifts away from the hearty Caribbean soul food toward reggae, jazz, and cocktails.

La Clementine. 5 rue St-Marc, 2e. ☎ **01-40-41-05-65.** Reservations required. Main courses 85F ($13.60); fixed-price menu 145F ($23.20). AE, MC, V. Mon–Fri noon–2:30pm and 8–10:30pm. Métro: Bourse or Grands Boulevards. FRENCH (TRADITIONAL).

In an antique building adjacent to the Musée Grévin, this well-managed bistro serves time-honored food with an occasional individualistic flair. Among early-1900s panels, polished brass, and mirrors, you can order pepper steak, codfish steak studded with lard, oven-braised veal served in its own juices, and an unusual preparation of chicken breast with goat cheese. The *fondant au chocolat* (chocolate candy) seems to be an assiduously guarded, long-cherished family recipe. There's room for barely 25 diners, so advance reservations are important.

3RD ARRONDISSEMENT (LE MARAIS)
EXPENSIVE

L'Ami Louis. 32 rue du Vertbois, 3e. ☎ **01-48-87-77-48.** Reservations required far in advance. Main courses 195–320F ($31.20–$51.20). AE, DC, MC, V. Wed–Sun noon–2pm and 8–11pm. Closed July 19–Aug 25. Métro: Temple. FRENCH (TRADITIONAL).

L'Ami Louis is in one of central Paris's least fashionable neighborhoods, far removed from the part of the Marais that has become chic, and its facade has seen better days. It was one of Paris's most famous brasseries in the 1930s, thanks to its excellent food served in copious portions and its old-fashioned decor. Its traditions are fervently maintained today. Amid a "brown gravy" decor (the walls retain a smoky patina), dishes like roasted suckling lamb, pheasant, venison, confit of duckling, and endless slices of foie gras may commune on your marble-topped table. Though some whisper that the ingredients aren't as select as they were in the restaurant's heyday, its sauces are as thick as they were between the wars. Don't save room for dessert, which isn't very good.

INEXPENSIVE

Chez Janou. 2 rue Roger-Verlomme, 3e. ☎ **01-42-72-28-41.** Reservations recommended. Main courses 68–98F ($10.90–$15.70). No credit cards. Daily noon–3pm and 7:30pm–midnight. Métro: Chemin-Vert. PROVENÇAL.

On one of the narrow 17th-century streets behind place des Vosges, this unpretentious bistro operates from a pair of cramped but cozy dining rooms filled with memorabilia from Provence. The service is brusque and sometimes hectic. The menu items include dishes like large shrimp with pastis sauce, *brouillade des pleurotes* (baked eggs with oyster mushrooms), velouté of frogs' legs, fondue of ratatouille, gratin of mussels, and a simple but savory *daube provençale*, sometimes compared to pot roast. There's a covered terrace.

L'Ambassade d'Auvergne. 22 rue de Grenier St-Lazare, 3e. ☎ **01-42-72-31-22.** Reservations recommended. Main courses 88–120F ($14.10–$19.20); fixed-price menu 170F ($27.20). AE, MC, V. Daily noon–2pm and 7:30–11pm. Closed 2 weeks in Aug. Métro: Rambuteau. AUVERGNAT/FRENCH (TRADITIONAL).

You enter this rustic tavern through a busy bar with heavy oak beams, hanging hams, and ceramic plates. This favorite showcases the culinary generosity of France's most isolated region, the Auvergne, whose pork products are widely celebrated. Examples are a chicory salad with apples and pieces of country ham; pork braised with cabbage, turnips, and white beans; grilled tripe sausages with mashed potatoes and cantal cheese with garlic; and pork jowls with green lentils. Nonpork specialties are pan-fried duck liver with gingerbread, perch filets steamed in verbena tea, and roasted rack of lamb with wild mushrooms. Dessert might be a poached pear with crispy almonds and caramel sauce or a wine-flavored sorbet.

4TH ARRONDISSEMENT (ILE DE LA CITÉ/ILE ST-LOUIS & BEAUBOURG)
VERY EXPENSIVE

✪ **L'Ambroisie.** 9 place des Vosges, 4e. ☎ **01-42-78-51-45.** Reservations required far in advance. Main courses 320–530F ($51.20–$84.80). AE, MC, V. Tues–Sat noon–1:30pm and 8–9:30pm. Métro: St-Paul. FRENCH (TRADITIONAL & MODERN).

One of Paris's most talented chefs, Bernard Pacaud has drawn world attention with his vivid flavors and expert culinary skill. He trained at Le Vivarois before striking out on his own, first on the Left Bank and now at this early-17th-century town house in Le Marais, with two high-ceilinged salons whose decor vaguely recalls an Italian palazzo. In summer, there's outdoor seating as well. Pacaud's tables are nearly always filled with satisfied diners who come back again and again to see where his imagination will take him next. The dishes change seasonally and may include fricassée of Breton lobster with a civet/red-wine sauce, served with a purée of peas; turbot filet braised with celery, served with a julienne of black truffles; or one of our favorite dishes in all Paris, *poulard de Bresse demi-deuil hommage à la Mère Brazier* (chicken roasted with black truffles and truffled vegetables in a style invented by a Lyonnais matron after World War II). An award-winning dessert is the *tarte fine sablée* served with bitter chocolate and vanilla-flavored ice cream.

MODERATE

Bofinger. 5–7 rue de la Bastille, 4e. ☎ **01-42-72-87-82.** Reservations recommended. Main courses 75–196F ($12–$31.35); fixed-price menu 189F ($30.25). AE, DC, MC, V. Mon–Fri noon–3pm and 6:30pm–1am, Sat–Sun noon–1am. Métro: Bastille. ALSATIAN/FRENCH (TRADITIONAL & FRENCH).

Opened in the 1860s, Bofinger is the oldest Alsatian brasserie in town and certainly one of the best. It's a belle-époque dining palace, resplendent with shiny brass and stained glass. Weather permitting, you can dine on an outdoor terrace. Affiliated today with La Coupole, Julien, and Brasserie Flo, the restaurant has updated its menu, retaining only the most popular of its traditional dishes, like sauerkraut and a well-prepared sole meunière. Recent additions have included roasted leg of lamb with a fondant of artichoke hearts and a purée of parsley, grilled turbot with a *brandade* of fennel, and stingray filet with chives and burnt-butter sauce. Shellfish, including an abundance of fresh oysters and lobster, is almost always available in season.

Isama. 4 quai d'Orléans, 4e. ☎ **01-40-46-06-97.** Reservations recommended. Sushi and sashimi 10–35F ($1.60–$5.60) per piece; meals 75–225F ($12–$36), depending on the fish and how many pieces ordered. Tues–Sat noon–2pm and 7:30–10pm. Métro: Pont Marie. JAPANESE.

Dining here is guaranteed to evoke a sense of cultural dislocation—the staff is mostly from Japan and few speak very much French or English. That, however, is part of the place's allure for its loyal customers, many of whom work in the arts. The staff is quick to tell you that only authentic Japanese versions of sushi and sashimi are served, with absolutely none of what they call California/Japanese cuisine. Begin a meal with miso soup or some pickled vegetables, as a prelude for the wide array of fish (tuna, salmon, whitefish, fluke, snapper, bluefish, oysters, clams, shrimp, and more) that forms this restaurant's backbone. Lingering isn't encouraged.

Le Vieux Bistro. 14 rue du Cloître-Notre-Dame, 4e. ☎ **01-43-54-18-95.** Main courses 90–140F ($14.40–$22.40). MC, V. Daily noon–2pm and 7:30–11pm. Métro: Cité. FRENCH (TRADITIONAL).

Few other restaurants offer so close-up, and so forbidding, a view of the massive walls of Paris's largest cathedral, visible through lacy curtains from the windows of the front dining room. To reach it, you'll bypass a dozen souvenir stands, then settle into one of the two old-time dining rooms for a flavorful meal of French staples. You can order snails with garlic butter, filet mignon roasted in a bag and served with marrow sauce, veal filets, and a classic dessert, *tarte tatin* (studded with apples and sugar, drenched with Calvados, and capped with fresh cream).

Marc-Annibal de Coconnas. 2 bis place des Vosges, 4e. ☎ **01-42-78-58-16.** Reservations required. Main dishes 90–140F ($14.40–$22.40); fixed-price menu 135F ($21.60). AE, DC, MC, V. Wed–Sun noon–2:30pm and 7:30–10:30pm. Métro: Bastille or St-Paul. FRENCH (TRADITIONAL & MODERN).

Chef Claude Terrail (owner of La Tour d'Argent) serves superb cuisine in this restaurant named after the legendary rake whose peccadillos scandalized place des Vosges.

The restaurant features a Louis XIII decor of high-backed chairs and elegantly rustic accessories. Menu items change frequently but present a cost-conscious alternative to the grand cuisine served by other restaurants in the chain. Look for foie gras maison, baked goat's cheese dunked in white wine, roasted half-duckling with mashed potatoes, coq au vin, and desserts like *crème brûlée* with honey. None of these items sets off fireworks, but the ingredients are fresh and harmonious and the prices fair for the quality.

INEXPENSIVE

✪ **Aquarius.** 54 rue Ste-Croix-de-la-Bretonnerie, 4e. ☎ **01-48-87-48-71.** Main courses 45–64F ($7.20–$10.25); fixed-price menu 95F ($15.20). MC, V. Mon–Sat noon–10:15pm. Métro: Hôtel de Ville. RER: Châtelet–Les Halles. VEGETARIAN.

In a 17th-century building whose original stonework forms part of the earthy decor, this is one of the best-known vegetarian restaurants in Le Marais. The owners serve only a limited array of (strictly organic) wine, and smoking is expressly forbidden. Their flavorful meals are healthfully prepared and come in generous portions. Choose from an array of soups and salads; a galette of wheat served with crudités and mushroom tarts; or a country plate composed of fried mushrooms and potatoes, garlic, and goat cheese, served with a salad.

Au Gourmet de l'Ile. 42 rue St-Louis-en-l'Ile, 4e. ☎ **01-43-26-79-27.** Reservations required. Main courses 70–95F ($11.20–$15.20); fixed-price menu 150–185F ($24–$29.60). AE, MC, V. Wed–Sun noon–2pm and 7–10:30pm. Métro: Pont Marie. FRENCH (TRADITIONAL).

Locals swear by the cuisine at Au Gourmet de l'Ile, whose fixed-price meals are among Paris's best bargains. The setting is beautiful, with a beamed ceiling, walls from the 1400s, and candlelit tables. In the window is a sign emblazoned with AAAAA, which, roughly translated, stands for the Amiable Association of Amateurs of the Authentic Andouillette. These chitterling sausages are soul food to the French. Popular and tasty too are *la charbonnée de l'Ile*, a savory pork with onions, and stuffed mussels in shallot butter. The fixed-price menu includes a choice of 15 appetizers, 15 main courses, salad or cheese, and 15 desserts.

Brasserie de l'Ile St-Louis. 55 quai de Bourbon, 4e. ☎ **01-43-54-02-59.** Main courses 85–130F ($13.60–$20.80). MC, V. Thurs–Tues noon–midnight. Closed Aug. Métro: Pont Marie or Cité. ALSATIAN/FRENCH (TRADITIONAL).

This is the kind of retro-chic brasserie where the likes of Brigitte Bardot, Elizabeth Taylor, Grace Jones, and John Frankenheimer have scheduled informal meals and rendezvous. Little about the place's patina and paneled decor has changed since the 1880s, giving it an aura modern competitors can only try to imitate. The menu is conservative and well prepared, including an always-popular version of Alsatian sauerkraut, cassoulet in the old-fashioned style of Toulouse, calf's liver, and a succulent *jarret* of pork with warm apple marmalade.

Café la Parisienne. 10 rue Brise-Miche, 4e. ☎ **01-42-78-44-11.** Reservations recommended. Main courses 55–85F ($8.80–$13.60). AE, DC, MC, V. Apr–Sept daily 8am–midnight (last order); Oct–Mar daily 10am–11pm (last order). Métro: Rambuteau, Hôtel de Ville, or Châtelet–Les Halles. FRENCH (MODERN).

Whimsical and often chaotic, this appealing restaurant shares something of the avant-garde aesthetic of its neighbor, the Centre Pompidou, and was renovated in mid-1999. It was named after the bread rations that were issued here during World War II and has an enviable location beside the medieval St-Merri church and a charming fountain by Jean Tingueley and Niki de Saint-Phalle, spinning, spitting, and bobbing animatedly; in fair weather, tables and chairs overlook it. You might begin with beef (or shark!) carpaccio with green salad, then follow with noisette of lamb flavored with whiskey and fresh thyme or fricassée of poultry with morels. Finish with *glace Berthillon*, Paris's best ice cream. There's also a beautiful terrace where you can enjoy a breathtaking view.

✪ **Chez Jo Goldenberg.** 7 rue des Rosiers, 4e. ☎ **01-48-87-20-16.** Reservations required. Main courses 75–110F ($12–$17.60). AE, DC, MC, V. Daily noon–1am. Métro: St-Paul. JEW-ISH/CENTRAL EUROPEAN.

This is the best-known restaurant on the "Street of the Rose Bushes." Albert Goldenberg, the doyen of Jewish restaurateurs in Paris, long ago moved to choicer surroundings (69 av. de Wagram, 17e), but his brother, Joseph, has remained here. Dining is on two levels, one for nonsmokers. Look for the collection of samovars, the white fantail pigeon in a wicker cage, and the interesting paintings. The *carpe farcie* (stuffed carp) is a preferred selection, but the beef goulash is also good. We like the eggplant moussaka and the pastrami. The menu also offers Israeli wines, but M. Goldenberg admits they're not as good as French wine. Live Yiddish music is presented every night beginning at 9pm, and special menus are presented during Jewish holidays—reservations are a must.

Dame Tartine. 2 rue Brise-Miche, 4e. ☎ **01-42-77-32-22.** Platters 32–45F ($5.10–$7.20). MC, V. Daily noon–midnight. Métro: Rambuteau. FRENCH (TRADITIONAL).

Don't expect intimacy or haute gastronomy here: It's hectic, with streams of diners on their way to and from the nearby Centre Pompidou and students counting their francs. You can expect simple but generous platters like salads, chicken with curry or cinnamon sauce, salmon with coconut-and-curry sauce, ham steak, and fried fish filet with tartar sauce. Most are served with bread, so you can create your own open-faced sandwich. Most of the artwork on the wall is for sale.

Trumilou. 84 quai de l'Hôtel-de-Ville, 4e. ☎ **01-42-77-63-98.** Reservations recommended Sat–Sun. Main courses 75–100F ($12–$16); fixed-price menu 80–98F ($12.80–$15.70). MC, V. Daily noon–3pm and 7–11pm. Métro: Hôtel de Ville. FRENCH (TRADITIONAL).

This is one of the most popular of the restaurants surrounding Paris's Hôtel de Ville and has welcomed most of France's politicians, including George Pompidou, who came here frequently before he was elected president. ("As soon as they become president, they opt for grander restaurants," say the good-natured owners, the Drumonds.) The countrified decor includes a collection of farm implements and family memorabilia, amid a clutch of tables. Most diners remain on the street level, though additional seating is in the cellar. The menu rarely changes and doesn't need to, with chicken Provençal, sweetbreads "in the style of our grandmother," duckling with plums, stuffed cabbage, and *blanquette de veau* (veal in white sauce).

8TH ARRONDISSEMENT (CHAMPS-ELYSÉES/MADELEINE)

If you're a homesick Yank and just can't resist the lure of fajitas, a thousand types of burgers, high-octane libations like the Indecent Proposal, and endless American souvenirs, head to **Planet Hollywood,** 78 av. des Champs-Elysées, 8e (☎ **01-53-83-78-21;** Métro: George V or F. D. Roosevelt), open daily 11:30am to 1am.

VERY EXPENSIVE

✪ **Lasserre.** 17 av. Franklin-D.-Roosevelt, 8e. ☎ **01-43-59-53-43.** Fax 01-45-63-72-23. Reservations required far in advance. Main courses 170–280F ($27.20–$44.80); fixed-price menu 340F ($54.40) at lunch, 800F ($128) at dinner. AE, MC, V. Tues–Sat 12:30–2:30pm; Mon–Sat 7:30–10:30pm. Closed Aug. Métro: F. D. Roosevelt. FRENCH (TRADITIONAL & MODERN).

A Parisian *Pique-nique*

One of the best ways to save money and also to participate in Parisian life is to picnic. Go to a *fromagerie* for some cheese; to a *boulangerie* for a baguette or two; to a *charcuterie* for some pâté, sausage, or salad; and to a *pâtisserie* for some luscious pastries. Add a friendly bottle of Côtes du Rhone—it usually goes well with picnics—and you'll have the makings of a delightful and typically French meal you can take to the nearest park or along the banks of the Seine. Pretend you're in Manet's *Déjeuner sur l'herbe* and enjoy! (Don't forget the corkscrew!)

This elegant restaurant was a simple bistro before World War II, but it has since become a legend attracting world gourmands. The main salon stretches two stories high, with a mezzanine on each side. Tall silk-draped arched windows frame tables set with fine porcelain, gold-edged crystal glasses, and silver candelabras. The ceiling is painted with white clouds and a cerulean sky, but in good weather the staff slides back the roof to reveal the real sky. The food is a mix of classicism and originality; count on high drama in the presentation. The appetizers are among Paris's finest, including truffle salad, three-meat terrine, and Chablis-flavored Belon oysters. The signature main course is poached sole filets *Club de la Casserole*, in puff pastry with asparagus tips and asparagus-flavored cream sauce, but also wonderful are the veal kidneys flambé and pigeon André Malraux. Among the spectacular desserts are soufflé Grand Marnier and three fresh sorbets of the season. The wine cellar, with some 180,000 bottles, is among the city's most remarkable.

✪ **L'Astor.** In the Hôtel Astor, 11 rue d'Astorg, 8e. ☎ **01-53-05-05-20.** Fax 01-53-05-05-30. Reservations required far in advance. Main courses 110–240F ($17.60–$38.40); fixed-price menu 298–580F ($47.70–$92.80). AE, DC, MC, V. Mon–Fri noon–2pm and 7:30–10pm. Closed Aug. Métro: St-Augustin. FRENCH (MODERN).

What happens to a great French chef when he retires? If he's lucky enough and respected enough, he takes on the title of "culinary consultant" and attaches himself to a restaurant where he can drop in several times a week to keep an eye on things. That's what happened when guru Joël Robuchon retired from his avenue Raymond-Poincaré citadel in favor of a quieter life (his replacement there was Alain Ducasse). The chef here is respected Eric Lecerf, who knows better than anyone else how to match his master's tours-de-force. The setting is a gray-and-white enclave beneath an etched-glass art deco ceiling, with luxurious touches inspired by the 1930s and 1940s. Expect an almost religious devotion to Robuchon's specialties and less emphasis on newer dishes created by Lecerf. Examples of "classic Robuchon" are caramelized sea urchins in aspic with fennel-flavored cream sauce, eggplant-stuffed cannelloni with tuna filets and olive oil, and spit-roasted Bresse chicken with flap mushrooms. Items created by Lecerf include carpaccio of Breton lobster with olive oil and tomato confit, roasted and braised rack of lamb, and pigeon supreme with cabbage and foie gras.

Lucas-Carton (Alain Senderens). 9 place de la Madeleine, 8e. ☎ **01-42-65-22-90.** Fax 01-42-65-06-23. Reservations required several days ahead for lunch and several weeks ahead for dinner. Main courses 240–700F ($38.40–$112); fixed-price lunch 395F ($63.20); fixed-price dinner 1,300F ($208). AE, DC, MC, V. Tues–Fri noon–2:30pm; Mon–Sat 8–10:15pm. Closed 3 weeks in Aug. Métro: Madeleine. FRENCH (MODERN).

When Alain Senderens took over this landmark belle-époque restaurant, he added some welcome modern touches and a brilliant culinary repertoire. The dining rooms downstairs and private rooms upstairs boast mirrors, fragrant bouquets of flowers, and wood paneling that has been polished every week since its installation in 1900. Every dish is influenced by Senderens's creative flair. Menu items, which change seasonally, include polenta with black truffles, duckling Apicius (roasted with honey and spices), pastillade of rabbit, and sweetbreads with acidified carrot juice. The chestnuts purée is a perfect way to end a meal. Senderens is constantly experimenting—his latest sensations are lobster roasted with vanilla and *poularde demi-deuil*, a Bresse hen whose flesh has been scored with black truffles (the resulting black-and-white flesh is supposed to be "in partial mourning"); it's accompanied by saffron-flavored rice.

Maxim's. 3 rue Royale, 8e. ☎ **01-42-65-27-94.** Fax 01-40-17-02-91. Reservations required far in advance. Main courses 225–330F ($36–$52.80) at lunch, 300–470F ($48–$75.20) at dinner. AE, DC, MC, V. Mon–Sat 12:30–2:30pm and 7:30–10:30pm. Métro: Concorde. FRENCH (TRADITIONAL).

Maxim's is the world's most legendary restaurant. Michelin no longer bothers to recommend it, much less give it stars, but Maxim's carries on in its overpriced way. And with the almost shameless exploitation by its present owners (clothing-industry giant Pierre Cardin took over in 1981), branches with replicas of the belle-époque decor have popped up in New York, Beijing, Tokyo, Moscow, and Shanghai. The place was a favorite of Edward VII, prince of Wales, and Louis Jourdan—at that time considered "the handsomest man in the world"—took Leslie Caron to dine here in *Gigi*. Today, rich tourists from around the world occupy fabled tables where Onassis wooed Callas. Though not always available, billiby soup—made with mussels, white wine, cream, celery, onions, parsley, and coarsely ground pepper—is a classic opener. Another favorite, sole Albert (named after the late maître d'), is flavored with chopped herbs, bread crumbs, and a large glass of vermouth. Other specialties are beef filet cooked with truffles, noisettes of lamb with foie gras, and Bresse chicken with tarragon sauce. For dessert, try the *tarte tatin*.

✪ **Pierre Gagnaire.** 6 rue Balzac, 8e. ☎ **01-44-35-18-25.** Fax 01-44-35-18-37. Reservations are imperative and difficult to make. Main courses 310–460F ($49.60–$73.60); fixed-price menu 520–950F ($83.20–$152) at lunch, 950F ($152) at dinner. AE, DC, MC, V. Mon–Fri 12:30–2:15pm; Sun–Fri 7–10pm. Métro: George V. FRENCH (MODERN).

Though the PR here may be the worst in Paris, if you're able to make a reservation, it's worth the effort. The menus are seasonally adjusted to take advantage of France's rich bounty; Pierre Gagnaire, the famous owner, demands perfection, and the chef has a dazzling way of blending flavors and textures. One critic wrote, "Picasso stretched the limits of painting; Gagnaire does it with cooking." Try anything from a menu that changes every 2 months: Examples are freshwater crayfish cooked tempura style with thin-sliced flash-seared vegetables and sweet-and-sour sauce as well as turbot cooked in a bag and served with fennel and Provençal lemons. Chicken with truffles is part of a two-tiered service—first the breast in a wine-based aspic, second the thighs chopped into roughly textured pieces. For dessert, try the chocolate soufflé served with a frozen parfait and Sicilian pistachios.

✪ **Taillevent.** 15 rue Lamennais, 8e. ☎ **01-44-95-15-01.** Fax 01-42-25-95-18. Reservations required weeks, even months, in advance for lunch and dinner. Main courses 295–500F ($47.20–$80). AE, DC, MC, V. Mon–Fri noon–2:30pm and 7–10pm. Closed Aug. Métro: George V. FRENCH (MODERN & TRADITIONAL).

Taillevent opened in 1946 and has climbed steadily in excellence until today it ranks as Paris's most outstanding all-around restaurant, challenged only by Lucas-Carton, Pierre Gagnaire, and Lasserre in this highly competitive area. The restaurant, named after famous 14th-century chef Guillaume Tirel Taillevent, who wrote one of the oldest known books on French cookery, is set in a grand 19th-century town house off the Champs-Elysées, with paneled rooms and crystal chandeliers. The place is small, as the

Restaurants Near Place Charles de Gaulle

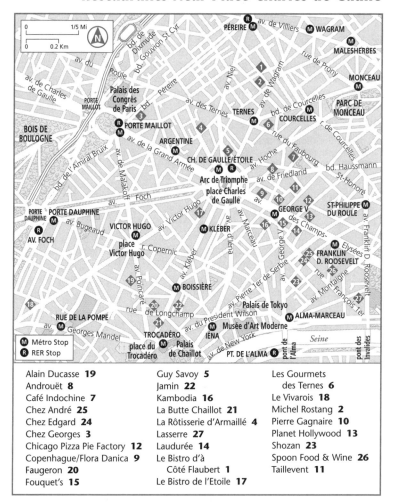

Alain Ducasse **19**	Guy Savoy **5**	Les Gourmets
Androuët **8**	Jamin **22**	des Ternes **6**
Café Indochine **7**	Kambodia **16**	Le Vivarois **18**
Chez André **25**	La Butte Chaillot **21**	Michel Rostang **2**
Chez Edgard **24**	La Rôtisserie d'Armaillé **4**	Pierre Gagnaire **10**
Chez Georges **3**	Lasserre **27**	Planet Hollywood **13**
Chicago Pizza Pie Factory **12**	Laudurée **14**	Shozan **23**
Copenhague/Flora Danica **9**	Le Bistro d'à	Spoon Food & Wine **26**
Faugeron **20**	Côté Flaubert **1**	Taillevent **11**
Fouquet's **15**	Le Bistro de l'Etoile **17**	

owner wishes, since it permits him to give personal attention to every facet of the operation and maintain a discreet club atmosphere. You might begin with a *boudin* (sausage) of Breton lobster à la Nage, cream of watercress soup with Sevruga caviar, or duck liver with spice bread and ginger. Main courses include red snapper with black olives, Scottish salmon cooked in sea salt with a sauce of olive oil and lemons, and cassolette of crayfish from Brittany. Dessert might be a *nougatine glacé* with pears. The wine list is among the best in Paris. Though owner M. Vrinat likes Americans, it isn't always easy for visitors from the States and other countries to book a table, since he prefers about 60% of his guests to be French.

EXPENSIVE

✪ **Buddha Bar.** 8 rue Boissy d'Anglas, 8e. ☎ **01-53-05-90-00.** Reservations required far in advance. Main courses 115–260F ($18.40–$41.60). AE, MC, V. Mon–Fri noon–3pm; daily 7pm–12:30am. Métro: Concorde. FRENCH (MODERN)/PACIFIC RIM.

This place is hot, hot, hot—and still remains Paris's restaurant of the moment. A location on a chic street near the Champs-Elysées and place de la Concorde and an allegiance to a fusion of French, Asian, and Californian cuisines guarantees trendy diners devoted to the whims of fashion. The vast dining room is presided over by a giant Buddha, and the cutting-edge culinary theme combines Japanese sashimi, Vietnamese spring rolls, lacquered duck, sautéed shrimp with black-bean sauce, grilled chicken skewers with orange sauce, sweet-and-sour spareribs, and crackling squab à l'orange. There are two sittings for dinner: 7 to 9pm and 10:30pm to 12:30am. Many come here just for a drink in the carefully lacquered hip bar, upstairs from the street-level dining room.

Copenhague/Flora Danica. 142 av. des Champs-Elysées, 8e. ☎ **01-44-13-86-26.** Reservations recommended far in advance. Main courses 70–180F ($11.20–$28.80); fixed-price menu 175–260F ($28–$41.60). AE, DC, MC, V. Daily noon–2:30pm and 7:15–11pm. Restaurant Copenhague closed Aug and Jan 1–7. Métro: George V. DANISH.

Danish specialties are served with flair at the "Maison du Danemark," in many ways the best restaurant on the Champs-Elysées, with a terrace for midsummer dining. There are two dining areas: the street-level Flora Danica and the somewhat more formal Restaurant Copenhague upstairs. To be thoroughly Danish, order an aperitif of aquavit and ignore the wine list in favor of Carlsberg. Menu items include reindeer terrine, foie gras, smoked salmon, fresh shrimp, and elegant open-faced sandwiches. The house specialty is a platter of Scandinavian delicacies drawn from the many seafood and dairy specialties the Danes prepare exceptionally well. Our preferred dish is grilled Norwegian salmon cooked on one side only.

Le 30 (Chez Fauchon). 30 place de la Madeleine, 8e. ☎ **01-47-42-56-58.** Reservations recommended far in advance, especially for lunch. Main courses 150–310F ($24–$49.60); fixed-price lunch 390F ($62.40). AE, DC, MC, V. Mon–Sat 12:15–2:30pm and 7:30–10:30pm. Métro: Madeleine. FRENCH (TRADITIONAL).

In 1990, Fauchon, one of Europe's most legendary delicatessens (see chapter 8), transformed one of its upper rooms into an airy pastel-colored showplace that caught on immediately as a lunch spot for local bankers, stockbrokers, and merchants. Menu selections employ the freshest ingredients available downstairs and may include crayfish tails roasted with sweet spices; foie gras with pepper-and-champagne sauce; warm oysters with a cauliflower-and-parsley purée; crayfish roasted with fennel, smoke-flavored salt, and saffron-flavored vinegar; and sole strips poached in vanilla-flavored coffee sauce.

Shozan. 11 rue de la Trmoille, 8e. ☎ **01-47-23-37-32.** Reservations recommended far in advance. Main courses 140–180F ($22.40–$28.80); fixed-price menu 230F ($36.80) at lunch, 400F ($64) at dinner. AE, DC, MC, V. Mon–Fri noon–2:30pm; Mon–Sat 7–10:30pm. Closed 15 days in Aug. Métro: Alma-Marceau. FRENCH (MODERN)/JAPANESE.

East and West form a perfect synthesis in this Franco-Japanese alliance. It's not for the traditionalist, but trendy young Paris enjoys the new flavors. For example, the classic foie gras appears as foie gras sushi with sansho pepper and the roast lamb comes with a green-tea crust. The roast tuna with buckwheat seed and the scampi concoction are delectable. A chef's specialty is lobster with white-sesame sauce spiked with sweet sake. Famous interior designer Christian Liaigre created the stunning setting, dominated by wood and leather; you sit at wooden tables without cloths.

Spoon, Food & Wine. In the Hôtel Marignan-Elysée, 14 rue Marignan, 8e. ☎ **01-40-76-34-44.** Reservations recommended far in advance. Appetizers, main courses, vegetable side dishes 65–180F ($10.40–$28.80). Mon–Fri noon–2:30pm and 7–11:30pm. AE, DC, V. Métro: F. D. Roosevelt. INTERNATIONAL.

This hypermodern venture of *wunderkind* chef Alain Ducasse has been hailed as a "restaurant for the millennium" and condemned by some Parisian food critics as

You Paid What?

47,000 hotels, 700 airlines, 50 rental car companies. And a few million ways to save money.

Travelocity.com
A Sabre Company

Go Virtually Anywhere.

AOL Keyword: Travel

Will you have enough stories to tell your grandchildren?

Yahoo! Travel

surreal and a bit absurd. The claustrophobic dining room evokes stylish Paris and California, and the cuisine roams the world for inspiration, with such middlebrow offerings as American macaroni and cheese, a BLT, barbecued ribs, chicken wings, and pastrami. Other dishes evoke Italy, Latin America, Asia, and India. The steamed lobster with mango chutney is a winner. For a "vegetable garden," you can mix and match among 15 ingredients, including iceberg lettuce. Pasta comes with a selection of five sauces.

MODERATE

Chez André. 12 rue Marbeuf (at rue Clement-Marot), 8e. ☎ **01-47-20-59-57.** Reservations recommended. Main courses 89–150F ($14.25–$24); fixed-price menu 180F ($28.80). AE, DC, MC, V. Daily noon–1am. Métro: F. D. Roosevelt. FRENCH (TRADITIONAL).

Chez André is one of the neighborhood's favorite bistros. Its major drawback is you'll feel a bit left out in the cold if you're not a regular. Outside, a discreet red awning stretches over an array of shellfish on ice; inside, an art nouveau decor includes etched glass and masses of flowers. This has been on a landmark on rue Marbeuf since 3 years before the invasion of France in 1940. It remains the same as it was when it was founded (an agreement was made with the original owners). The old-style cuisine on the menu includes pâté of thrush, Roquefort in puff pastry, grilled veal kidneys, roast rack of lamb, and bouillabaisse, several kinds of omelets, calves' head vinaigrette, a potage du jour, and fresh shellfish, along with several reasonably priced wines. For variety, some locals opt for the *plat du jour*. The dessert choices may be rum baba, chocolate cake, or a daily pastry.

Chez Edgard. 4 rue Marbeuf, 8e. ☎ **01-47-20-51-15.** Main courses 90–175F ($14.40–$28). AE, DC, MC, V. Mon–Sat noon–3pm and 7pm–12:30am. Métro: F. D. Roosevelt. FRENCH (TRADITIONAL).

A chic crowd of locals regard this belle-époque restaurant as their favorite spot, and ebullient owner Paul Enmussa makes a special point of welcoming them as if they were members of his family. This fashionable bistro serves the same kind of food and attracts the same type of clients as Chez André (above). The noise level sometimes reaches quite a din. Specialties include duckling breast, red mullet with basil in puff pastry, and several terrines, including one made from scallops. Also offered is a range of well-prepared meat dishes. In winter, seafood and oysters are shipped in from Brittany. The ice-cream sundaes (listed with other desserts on a special menu) are yummy, and this is one of the few places in Paris serving a banana split. There's a small terrace, but most guests prefer to eat inside on one of the semiprivate banquettes.

Ladurée. 75 av. des Champs-Elysées, 8e. ☎ **01-40-75-08-75.** Reservations required for the restaurant, not for the cafe. Main courses 150–250F ($24–$40); pastries from 25F ($4). AE, DC, MC, V. Daily 7:30am–1am. FRENCH (TRADITIONAL).

Ladurée, acclaimed since 1862 as one of Paris's grand cafes (located near La Madeleine), has invaded the Champs-Elysées, adding a touch of class to this neighborhood of fast-food places. This offshoot expanded in 1999 and caters to an international set wearing everything from Givenchy to GAP. The belle-époque setting is ideal for sampling Ladurée's celebrated macaroons—not the sticky coconut version familiar to Americans but two almond meringue cookies, flavored with vanilla, coffee, strawberry, pistachio, or other flavor, stuck together with butter cream. The menu of talented young chef Pierre Hermé is constantly adjusted to take advantage of the freshest daily ingredients and may include a crisp and tender pork filet with potato-and-parsley purée and marinated red mullet filets on a salad of cold ratatouille. If you're looking for a midafternoon pick-me-up to accompany your tea and macaroons, consider a dish of ice cream scented with rose petals and fresh raspberries. The service isn't always efficient.

Le Grand Fromage

Cheese is king at ✪ **Androuët,** 6 rue Arsène-Houssaye, 8e (☎ **01-42-89-95-00;** Métro: Charles de Gaulle–Etoile). True, it's a novelty restaurant, but if you're devoted to cheese, there's nothing like it in Europe. Opened in 1909 by M. Androuët, who frequently asked friends over to sample cheese and wine, the place is now an institution. To accommodate continued and growing popularity, it moved to new headquarters in 1997. Most of the dishes are concocted with a cheese base. An impressive array of wines, well-prepared green salads, and ultra-fresh bread is available to accompany whatever you order. Examples are a fondue of three cheeses, beef filet with Roquefort sauce flambéed with Calvados, and *magret de canard* (duckling). Many cheese lovers, however, opt for just a bottle of wine, a green salad, and all-you-can-eat choices from the most sophisticated *dégustation des fromages* (cheese tasting) in the world. Six platters, each loaded with a different category of cheese (one with goat cheeses, another with triple crèmes, and so on), are brought to your table, allowing you to select random samples. Reservations are required. Main courses are 110F to 280F ($17.60 to $44.80), fixed-price meals are 250F to 300F ($40 to $48), and the *dégustation des fromages* is 300F ($48). Androuët is open Monday to Friday noon to 2:30pm and Monday to Saturday 7:30 to 11pm.

INEXPENSIVE

Café Indochine. 195 rue du faubourg St-Honoré, 8e. ☎ **01-53-75-15-63.** Reservations recommended. Main courses 80–118F ($12.80–$18.90); fixed-price menu 175F ($28). AE, MC, V. Mon–Fri noon–2:30pm; Mon–Sat 7–11:30pm. Métro: Etoile or Ternes. INDOCHINESE/ASIAN.

The setting evokes the French colonial empire at its peak and includes art objects from Laos, Cambodia, and Thailand. In any of the street-level dining rooms, you can enjoy a mix of the cuisines of at least four nations. Caramelized pork or chicken, cooked with coconut milk, accents an array of shrimp, scallops, and beef dishes prepared with red or green curry as well as fiery-hot soups. For a novelty, try the shrimp and scallops with calamari and pepper-flavored basil sauce, steamed fish wrapped in a banana leaf, or a Thai version of bouillabaisse. Equally appealing are the grilled meats, served with a spicy sauce that goes especially well with wine or any of the medley of international beers. Recently the chefs have made the food lighter by using less oil and steaming many items.

Chicago Pizza Pie Factory. 5 rue de Berri, 8e. ☎ **01-45-62-50-23.** Reservations accepted only on weekdays for groups of 8 or more. Pizza for 2 88–149F ($14.10–$23.85); pizza for 4 129–195F ($20.65–$31.20); fixed-price lunch 51–71F ($8.15–$11.35). AE, DC, MC, V. Sun–Thurs 11:30am–1am, Fri–Sat 11:30am–5am. Métro: George V. AMERICAN/PIZZA.

Off the Champs-Elysées, you'll find a busy tribute to the city of Chicago in a former garage. The bar is outfitted with anything and everything to do with Chicago: photos, sports banners, and all manner of kitsch. The dining room is as large and raucous as the Windy City itself. It serves the best pizza in Paris, prepared in endless variations on eight basic themes, as well as mud pie, cheesecake, and marvelous high-fat brownies. The management proudly refuses, except under dire circumstances, to serve burgers of any kind. No one will mind if you bypass the food in favor of a drink at the bar (happy hour in the restaurant is 4 to 7pm and at the bar 6 to 8pm); during these times some drinks (but not beer) are reduced in price.

Le Berry's. 46 rue de Naples, 8e. ☎ **01-40-75-01-56.** Reservations recommended. Main courses 56–85F ($8.95–$13.60); fixed-price menu 100F ($16). MC, V. Mon–Fri noon–2:30pm; Mon–Sat 7pm–1am. Métro: Villiers. FRENCH (TRADITIONAL).

This inexpensive bistro, with a setting celebrating rugby, complements one of the area's grandest restaurants, Le Grenadin. Its platters emerge from the same kitchen and are infused with the same kind of zeal as those presented next door for three times the price. Don't expect cutting-edge fare, but do look for honest dishes from France's agrarian heartland and a refreshing lack of pretension. The dishes listed on a chalkboard include fricassée of chicken with olives and mashed potatoes, thin-sliced smoked ham from Sancerre, veal filet with red-wine sauce, raw pike with cabbage, and a traditional Berry pear tart.

Les Gourmets des Ternes. 87 bd. de Courcelles, 8e. ☎ **01-42-27-43-04.** Main courses 85–135F ($13.60–$21.60). AE, MC, V. Mon–Fri noon–2:30pm and 7–10pm. Métro: Ternes. FRENCH (TRADITIONAL).

Les Gourmets des Ternes caters to hordes who appreciate its affordable prices and lack of pretension. Despite the brusque service, satisfied diners have included the mayor of Atlanta, who wrote the bistro a thank-you letter, as well as hundreds of ordinary folks from this neighborhood. Thriving in this spot since 1892, the place retains an early-1900s paneled decor, with some additions from the 1950s, including bordeaux-colored banquettes, mirrors, wooden panels, touches of brass, and paper tablecloths. The finely grilled signature dishes include rib steak with marrow sauce and fries; country pâtés and sausages; sole, turbot, and monkfish; and satisfying desserts like peach Melba and *baba au Rhum* (rum cake with raisins).

Shing-Jung. 7 rue Clapeyron, 8e. ☎ **01-45-22-21-06.** Reservations recommended for dinner. Main courses 80–110F ($12.80–$17.60); fixed-price menu 65–75F ($10.40–$12) at lunch, 100–200F ($16–$32) at dinner. Mon–Fri noon–2:30pm and 7–10:30pm, Sat–Sun 7–10:30pm. Métro: Rome. KOREAN.

Of the 30 or so Korean restaurants in Paris, Shing-Jung is the best, known for low prices. Its sashimi is comparable to Japanese versions, though the portions of the fresh tuna, salmon, or daurade tend to be more generous. A specialty is the Korean barbecue called *bulgoogi*, which seems more authentic thanks to a clever decor juxtaposing Korean chests and paintings.

9TH ARRONDISSEMENT (OPÉRA GARNIER/PIGALLE)

Like its counterparts from Hong Kong to Reykjavík, the **Hard Rock Cafe,** 14 bd. Montmartre, 9e (☎ **01-53-24-60-00;** Métro: Grand Boulevards or Richelieu-Drouot), offers musical memorabilia as well as musical selections from 35 years of rock. The crowd appreciates the juicy steaks, hamburgers, veggie burgers, salads, and heaping platters of informal French-inspired food. It's open daily 11:30am to 2am.

EXPENSIVE

Chez Jean. 8 rue St-Lazare, 9e. ☎ **01-48-78-62-73.** Reservations recommended far in advance. Main courses 130–210F ($20.80–$33.60); fixed-price menu 195F ($31.20). MC, V. Mon–Fri noon–2:30pm and 7–11pm, Sat–Sun 7–11pm. Métro: Notre-Dame de Lorette, Opéra, or Cadet. FRENCH (TRADITIONAL & MODERN).

There's been a brasserie of some sort on this site since around 1900. Amid well-oiled pinewood panels and carefully polished copper, you can choose from some of grandmother's favorites as well as more modern dishes like risotto with lobster and squid ink, scallops with endive fricassée, lamb roasted with basil, "nougat" of oxtails with balsamic vinaigrette, and pavé of duckling with honey sauce and exotic mushroom fricassée. The changing menu attracts fans who consider the food a lot more sophisticated than that served at other brasseries (the chefs gained their experience in upscale restaurants).

Restaurant Opéra. In the Grand Hôtel Inter-Continental, place de l'Opéra, 9e. ☎ **01-40-07-30-10.** Reservations recommended far in advance. Main courses 189–320F ($30.25–$51.20); fixed-price menu 240–585F ($38.40–$93.60). AE, DC, MC, V. Mon–Fri noon–2pm and 7:30–10:30pm. Closed July 15–Aug and Dec 18–Jan 2. Métro: Opéra. FRENCH (TRADITIONAL & MODERN).

This elegant restaurant is set in a hotel that has played an important role in Parisian history since 1860. If you dine here, you'll join the roll of patrons like Salvador Dalí, Josephine Baker, Marlene Dietrich, Maurice Chevalier, Maria Callas, and Marc Chagall, who often came here while working on the famous ceiling of the nearby Opéra. One of the best things is the way the staff doesn't take itself too seriously. You can enjoy an apéritif in the ornate bar before heading for the jewel box of a dining room. The menu isn't a prisoner of the past but is seasonal and fairly inventive. You can start with a sautéed veal head and foot ravioli if you're adventurous or maybe a medley of foie gras or a lobster salad. Follow with the perfect filet of John Dory (a delicately fleshed fish not unlike turbot or sole) with celery or sweetbreads fried with pistachios, lemon, and licorice. *Tout chocolat* is *the* dessert for chocoholics.

MODERATE

Au Petit Riche. 25 rue Le Peletier, 9e. ☎ **01-47-70-68-68.** Reservations recommended. Main courses 94–135F ($15.05–$21.60); fixed-price menu 165F ($26.40) at lunch, 140–180F ($22.40–$28.80) at dinner. AE, DC, MC, V. Mon–Sat noon–2:15pm and 7pm–midnight. Métro: Le Peletier or Richelieu-Drouot. LOIRE VALLEY (ANJOU).

When it opened in 1865, this bistro was the food outlet for the Café Riche next door; today it offers yesterday's grandeur and simple well-prepared food. You'll be ushered to one of five areas crafted for maximum intimacy, with red velour banquettes, ceilings painted with allegorical themes, and accents of brass and frosted glass. The wine list favors Loire Valley vintages that go well with such dishes as *rillettes* and *rillons* (potted fish or meat, especially pork) in Vouvray wine aspic, poached fish with buttery white-wine sauce, old-fashioned blanquette of chicken, and seasonal game dishes like civet of rabbit.

Wally Le Saharien. 36 rue Rodier, 9e. ☎ **01-42-85-51-90.** Reservations recommended. Main courses 150F ($24); fixed-price dinner 240F ($38.40). MC, V. Tues–Sat noon–2pm, Mon–Sat 7–10pm. Métro: Anvers. ALGERIAN.

Head to this dining room—lined with desert photos and tribal artifacts crafted from ceramics, wood, and weavings—for an insight into the spicy, slow-cooked cuisine that fueled the colonial expansion of France into North Africa. The set-price dinner menu begins with a trio of starters: a spicy soup, stuffed and grilled sardines, and a savory *pastilla* of pigeon in puff pastry. This can be followed by any of several kinds of couscous or a *méchouia* (slow-cooked tart) of lamb dusted with an optional coating of sugar, according to your taste. *Merguez*, the cumin-laden spicy sausage of the North African world, factors importantly into any meal, as does homemade (usually honey-infused) pastries. End your meal with traditional mint-flavored tea.

INEXPENSIVE

Chartier. 7 rue de faubourg Montmartre, 9e. ☎ **01-47-70-86-29.** Main courses 38–54F ($6.10–$8.65). MC, V. Daily 11:30am–3pm and 6–10pm. Métro: Grands Boulevards. FRENCH (TRADITIONAL).

Opened in 1896, this unpretentious fin-de-siècle restaurant, long a budget favorite, is now an official monument featuring a whimsical mural with trees, a flowering stair-case, and an early depiction of an airplane; it was painted in 1929 by a penniless artist who executed his work in exchange for food. The menu follows brasserie-style traditions, including items you might not dare to eat—boiled veal's head, tripe, tongue, sweetbreads, lamb's brains, chitterling sausages—as well as some old-time tempters. The waiter will steer you through dishes like *boeuf bourguignonne, pot-au-feu* (a best-seller, combining beef, turnips, cabbage, and carrots), pavé of rump steak, and at least five kinds of fish. The prices are low, even for a three-course meal, a fact that as many as 320 diners appreciate at a time.

✪ **Le Grand Zinc.** 5 rue de faubourg Montmartre, 9e. ☎ **01-47-70-88-64.** Main courses 57–110F ($9.10–$17.60); fixed-price menu 100F ($16). AE, DC, MC, V. Mon–Sat noon–midnight. Métro: Grands Boulevards. FRENCH (TRADITIONAL).

The Paris of the 1880s lives on here. You make your way into the restaurant past baskets of *bélons* (brown-fleshed oysters) from Brittany, a year-round favorite. The specialties of the house are *coq au vin* (chicken in white wine) and old-fashioned savory staples like rack of lamb, rump steak, veal chops with morels, and even a simple form of Provençal bouillabaisse. Nothing ever changes—certainly not the time-tested recipes.

10TH ARRONDISSEMENT (GARE DU NORD/GARE DE L'EST)
MODERATE

Brasserie Flo. 7 cour des Petites-Ecuries, 10e. ☎ **01-47-70-13-59.** Reservations recommended. Main courses 90–168F ($14.40–$26.90); fixed-price menu 138F ($22.10) at lunch, 189F ($30.25) at dinner; fixed-price late-night supper (after 10pm) 142F ($22.70). AE, DC, MC, V. Daily noon–3pm and 7pm–1:30am. Métro: Château d'Eau or Strasbourg–St-Denis. ALSATIAN.

This remote restaurant is a bit hard to find, but once you arrive (after walking through passageway after passageway), you'll see that fin-de-siècle Paris lives on. The restaurant opened in 1860 and has changed its decor very little since. The house specialty is *la formidable choucroute* (a heaping mound of sauerkraut with boiled ham, bacon, and sausage) for two. The onion soup and sole meunière are always good, as is the warm foie gras and guinea hen with lentils. Look for the *plats du jour,* ranging from roast pigeon to veal fricassée with sorrel.

La Grille. 80 rue du Faubourg-Poissonière, 10e. ☎ **01-47-70-89-73.** Reservations required. Main courses 100–170F ($16–$27.20). AE, DC, MC, V. Mon–Fri noon–2:30pm and 7:15–10pm. Métro: Poissonière. FRENCH (TRADITIONAL)/SEAFOOD.

Few other moderate restaurants are as hotly pursued by Parisians as this nine-table holdover from another age. For at least a century after the French Revolution, fishermen from coastal Dieppe used this place as a springboard for carousing and cabaret-watching after delivering their fish to Les Halles market. The holy grail at La Grille is an entire turbot prepared tableside with an emulsified white-butter sauce. If the turbot doesn't appeal, consider the seafood terrine, *boeuf bourguignonne,* or marinated sardine filets; the high-calorie, high-satisfaction desserts include chocolate mousse and vanilla custard. (Incidentally, the restaurant name derives not from a grill used for cooking but from the 200-year-old wrought-iron grills in front, classified as national treasures and among the best examples of their kind in Paris.)

INEXPENSIVE

✪ **Chez Michel.** 10 rue de Belzunce, 10e. ☎ **01-44-53-06-20.** Reservations recommended. Fixed-price menu 180F ($28.80); *menu dégustation* 280F ($44.80). MC, V. Tues–Sat noon–2pm and 7pm–midnight. Métro: Gare du Nord. BRETON.

Adapting to the tastes and income level of its loyal crowd, this restaurant near the Gare du Nord serves generous portions of well-prepared Breton dishes. At least part of this food derives from the northwestern origins of owner/chef Thierry Breton. In a pair of dining rooms accented with exposed wood, you'll enjoy the fruits of the fields and sea-coast, densely flavored and traditional; they include veal chops fried in butter and served with gratin of potatoes enriched with bits of calf's foot gelatin and codfish filets served on beds of tomatoes and onions and a tapenade of black olives. The appropriate conclusion to a meal is a snifter of Calvados, the apple-based brandy of the northern French coast.

Julien. 16 rue du faubourg St-Denis, 10e. ☎ **01-47-70-12-06.** Reservations required. Main courses 90–150F ($14.40–$24); fixed-price menu 189F ($30.25). AE, DC, MC, V. Daily noon–3pm and 7pm–1:30am. Métro: Strasbourg–St-Denis. FRENCH (TRADITIONAL & MODERN).

"The poor man's Maxim's," Julien offers an opportunity to dine in one of the most sumptuous belle-époque interiors in Paris. Of special interest are the murals representing the four seasons and the sometimes very fashionable crowd. The food served is in the style of *cuisine bourgeoise,* but without the heavy sauces. The sumptuous starter courses include eggplant caviar and wild mushroom salad. Among the main courses are Gascony cassoulet, sliced foie gras with lentils, fresh salmon with sorrel, and chateaubriand béarnaise. The wine list is extensive and reasonably priced.

Paris-Dakar. 95 rue du faubourg St-Martin, 10e. ☎ **01-42-08-16-64.** Reservations recommended. Main courses 73–99F ($11.70–$15.85); fixed-price menu 59–179F ($9.45–$28.65) at lunch, 129–179F ($20.65–$28.65) at dinner. AE, MC, V. Sat–Sun and Mon–Thurs noon–3pm; Tues–Sun 7pm–2am. Métro: Gare de l'Est. SENEGALESE.

Named after the famous rally that carries vehicles across the world's toughest terrain, this restaurant celebrates the culinary traditions of France's former colonies in West Africa. After receiving a genuine welcome, you'll have the option of sampling such Senegalese dishes as *yassa* (chicken braised with limes and onions); *maffé* (beef fried with peanuts, onions, and spice); and the national dish, *thiepbkoudiene* (fish sautéed with rice, fresh vegetables, and fiery chiles). The lunch menu is attractively priced. If you're adventurous, ask for a glass of the palm wine, fermented from coconuts in a style common in West Africa.

11TH & 12TH ARRONDISSEMENTS (OPÉRA BASTILLE/BOIS DE VINCENNES)
EXPENSIVE

✪ **Au Trou Gascon.** 40 rue Taine, 12e. ☎ **01-43-44-34-26.** Reservations required far in advance. Main courses 145–165F ($23.20–$26.40); fixed-price menu 200F ($32) at lunch, 320F ($51.20) at dinner. AE, DC, MC, V. Mon–Fri noon–2pm; Mon–Sat 7:30–10pm. Closed Aug. Métro: Daumesnil. GASCONY.

One of Paris's most acclaimed chefs, Alain Dutournier launched his cooking career in southwest France's Gascony region. His parents mortgaged their own inn to allow Dutournier to open an early-1900s bistro in an unfashionable part of the 12th arrondissement. At first he got little business, but word eventually spread of a savant in the kitchen who practiced authentic *cuisine moderne.* His wife, Nicole, is the welcoming hostess, and the wine steward has distinguished himself for his exciting cave containing several little-known wines along with a fabulous collection of Armagnacs. It's estimated the wine cellar has some 800 varieties. Start with fresh duck foie gras cooked in a terrine or Gascony cured ham cut from the bone. Main courses include fresh tuna with braised cabbage, the best cassoulet in town, and chicken from the Chalosse region of Landes, which Dutournier roasts and serves in its own drippings.

Blue Elephant. 43 rue de la Roquette, 11e. ☎ **01-47-00-42-00.** Reservations recommended far in advance. Main courses 85–160F ($13.60–$25.60); fixed-price dinner 275F ($44). AE, DC, MC, V. Mon–Fri noon–2:30pm and 7pm–midnight, Sun noon–2:30pm and 7–11pm. Métro: Bastille. THAI.

At this Paris branch of an international chain of stylish Thai restaurants, the decor artfully evokes the jungles of Southeast Asia, interspersed with Thai sculptures and paintings. The menu items are succulent, infused with lemongrass, curries, and the aromas that make Thai cuisine so distinctive. Examples are a salad made with *pomelo*, a Thai fruit that's larger and tarter than a grapefruit, studded with shrimp and herbs; salmon soufflé served in banana leaves; chicken in green-curry sauce; and grilled fish with passion fruit.

MODERATE

Astier. 44 rue Jean-Pierre-Timbaud, 11e. ☎ **01-43-57-16-35.** Reservations recommended. Fixed-price menu 120–145F ($19.20–$23.20). V. Mon–Fri noon–2pm and 8–11pm. Métro: Oberkampf. FRENCH (TRADITIONAL).

Nobody could accuse this place of being glamorous, understanding that well-prepared hearty food has its own allure. The mandatory set menu is a good value, with at least 10 choices for each of four courses. Examples include roasted rabbit with mustard sauce, *racasse* (scorpionfish) with fresh spinach, grilled steaks and chops of all kinds, and duckling breast with foie-gras cream sauce. There's also a superbly varied cheese platter and desserts like crème caramel and chocolate mousse.

China Club. 50 rue de Charenton, 12e. ☎ **01-43-43-82-02.** Main courses 70–190F ($11.20–$30.40); fixed-price dinner 155F ($24.80); fixed-price Sun dinner 100F ($16). AE, MC, V. Sun–Thurs 7pm–2am, Fri–Sat 7pm–3am. Closed Aug. Métro: Bastille or Ledru-Rollin. CHINESE/CANTONESE.

Evoking 1930s Hong Kong, this favorite existed long before a bunch of trendy new Asian restaurants opened to challenge its supremacy. China Club is still going strong, still laughing at the upstarts, and still offering one of the best meals in the Bastille quarter. The food is mainly Cantonese, prepared with flair and taste. Before dinner, you might want to enjoy a drink in the upstairs smoking lounge. Nearly everything is good, especially the sautéed shrimp and calamari, Shanghai chicken, and red rice sautéed with vegetables. The menu is vast so you'll have plenty of choices. Downstairs, the Sing Song club has live music, including something called Sino-French jazz, but only on Friday and Saturday.

✪ **Le Train Bleu.** In the Gare de Lyon, 12e. ☎ **01-43-43-09-06.** Reservations recommended. Main courses 100–185F ($16–$29.60); fixed-price menu 255F ($40.80), including wine. AE, DC, MC, V. Daily 11:30am–3pm and 7–11pm. Métro: Gare de Lyon. FRENCH (TRADITIONAL).

To reach this restaurant, climb the ornate double staircase facing the Gare de Lyon's grimy platforms. The restaurant and station were built along with the Grand Palais, Petit Palais, and pont Alexandre-III for the 1900 World Exhibition. Inaugurated by the French president in 1901 and renovated and cleaned at great expense in 1992, Le Train Bleu boasts a decor classified as a national artistic treasure, with a lavishly frescoed ceiling, bronze statues, mosaics, mirrors, banquettes, and 41 belle-époque murals (each celebrating the distant corners of the French-speaking world, which join Paris via its rail network). The formally dressed staff is fast and efficient, in case you're about to catch a train. You can choose from well-prepared soufflé of brill, escargots in Chablis sauce, steak tartare, loin of lamb Provençal, veal kidneys in mustard sauce, rib of beef for two, and rum cake with raisins.

INEXPENSIVE

L'Ebauchoir. 43 rue de Cîteaux, 12e. ☎ **01-43-42-49-31.** Reservations recommended for dinner. Main courses 75–100F ($12–$16); fixed-price lunch 68F ($10.90). MC, V. Mon–Sat noon–2:30pm and 8–10:30pm. Métro: Faidherbe-Chaligny. FRENCH (TRADITIONAL).

Tucked into a neighborhood rarely visited by foreigners and featuring a 1950s decor that has become fashionable again, this bistro attracts neighborhood carpenters, plumbers, and electricians, as well as an occasional journalist and screenwriter. With buffed aluminum trim and plaster-and-stucco walls tinted dark orange-yellow and blue, the place might remind you of a canteen in an auto factory. You can order surprisingly generous and well-prepared stuffed sardines, snapper filet with olive oil and garlic, crabmeat soup, fried calf's liver with coriander and honey, and rack of lamb combined with saddle of lamb.

Le Manguier. 67 av. Parmentier, 11e. ☎ **01-48-07-03-27.** Reservations recommended. Main courses 70–95F ($11.20–$15.20). AE, MC, V. Mon–Fri noon–3pm, Mon–Sat 7pm–2am. Métro: Parmentier. SENEGALESE.

Many of the patrons who dine here don't know much about Senegalese cuisine, but thanks to a charming welcome and live music presenting African jazz at its most compelling, they tend to come back. The decor evokes a West African fishing village. You can order zesty fare like roast chicken marinated with lime and served with onions, smoked shark meat, and the national dish, *thiebkoudiene* (a delectable blend of fish, rice, and fresh vegetables). The medley is perked up with a selection of fiery sauces you apply yourself. The drinks of choice are beer, a rum-based cocktail (*Le Dakar*), and wine.

Mansouria. 11 rue Faidherbe, 11e. ☎ **01-43-71-00-16.** Reservations recommended. Main courses 98–158F ($15.70–$25.30); fixed-price menu 135F ($21.60) at lunch, 182–280F ($29.10–$44.80) at dinner. MC, V. Tues–Sat noon–2pm and 7:30–11pm, Mon 7:30–11pm. Métro: Faidherbe-Chaligny. MOROCCAN.

One of Paris's most charming Moroccan restaurants occupies a much-restored building midway between place de la Bastille and place de la Nation. The minimalist decor combines futuristic architecture with bare white walls accented only with sets of antique doors and portals from the sub-Sahara. The menu items are artfully prepared. Look for six kinds of couscous, including versions with chicken, beef brochettes, or lamb, onions, and almonds. *Tagines* are succulent chicken or fish, prepared with aromatic herbs and slow cooked in clay pots that are carried to your table.

16TH ARRONDISSEMENT (TROCADÉRO/BOIS DE BOULOGNE)
VERY EXPENSIVE

✪ **Alain Ducasse.** In the Le Parc Hôtel, 59 av. Raymond-Poincaré, 16e. ☎ **01-47-27-12-27.** Fax 01-47-27-31-22. Reservations required 8 weeks in advance. Main courses 385–510F ($61.60–$81.60); fixed-price menu 480F ($76.80) at lunch, 950–1,490F ($152–$238.40) at dinner. AE, DC, MC, V. Mon–Fri noon–2pm and 7:45–10pm. Closed mid-July to mid-Aug. Métro: Trocadéro. FRENCH (MODERN & TRADITIONAL).

The celebrated Monte Carlo chef has won over Paris since taking over the reins from the great Joël Robuchon (now semiretired—see the entry for L'Astor). This six-star Michelin chef divides his time between Paris and Monaco, though he insists he doesn't repeat himself in the Paris restaurant. In this restored mansion he seeds his

ⓘ Family-Friendly Restaurants

Meals at Paris's grand restaurants are rarely suitable for young children. Nevertheless, many parents drag their kids along, often to the annoyance of other diners. You may have to make some compromises, such as dining earlier than most Parisians. **Hotel dining rooms** can be another good choice for family dining. They usually have children's menus or at least one or two *plats du jour* cooked for children, like spaghetti with meat sauce.

If you take your child to a **moderate** or an **inexpensive restaurant,** ask if the restaurant will serve a child's plate. If not, order a *plat du jour* or *plat garni*, which will be suitable for most children, particularly if a dessert is to follow. Most **cafes** welcome children throughout the day and early evening. At a cafe, children always seem to like the sandwiches (try a *croque monsieur*), the omelets, and the *pommes frites* (crispy french fries). Though this chapter lists a number of cafes (see "The Top Cafes," below), one that particularly appeals to children is **La Samaritaine,** 75 rue de Rivoli (☎ **01-40-41-20-20;** Métro: Pont Neuf). The snack bar down below doesn't have a panoramic view, but the fifth-floor restaurant does. You can take children to the top and order ice cream for them at teatime daily 3:30 to 6pm. The snack bar is open daily 9:30am to 7pm.

Les Drug Stores, 149 bd. St-Germain-des-Prés, 6e, and at Publicis Champs-Elysées, 133 av. des Champs-Elysées, 8e—like American drug stores but with sections for upscale gift items and food service—also welcome children, especially in the early evening, as do most **tearooms,** and you can tide the kids over with pastries and ice cream if dinner will be late. You could also try a **picnic** in the park or one the many fast-food chains, like **Pizza Hut** and **McDonald's,** all over the city.

- **Androuët** *(see p. 122)*   If your kids love cheese, they'll get the fill of a lifetime here, where cheese enters all the dishes. Especially delectable is the ravioli stuffed with goat cheese.
- **Café la Parisienne** *(see p. 115)*   This is the ideal choice when visiting the Beaubourg, with a captivating view of the most playful fountain in Paris from its terrace.
- **Chicago Pizza Pie Factory** *(see p. 122)*   There are no frogs' legs or snails to gross out little minds and stomachs at the Chicago Pizza Pie Factory, just the City of Light's best pizza followed by a kid-pleasing cheesecake.
- **Crémerie-Restaurant Polidor** *(see p. 140)*   One of the most popular restaurants on the Left Bank, this reasonably priced dining room is so family friendly it calls its food *cuisine familiale.* This might be the best place to introduce your child to bistro food.
- **Hard Rock Cafe** *(see p. 123)*   At the Paris branch of this chain, good old American burgers and more are served against a background of rock memorabilia and loud rock music.
- **Joe Allen** *(see p. 109)*   This American restaurant in Les Halles delivers everything from chili to chocolate mousse pie to the best hamburgers in Paris.
- **Planet Hollywood** *(see p. 116)*   On the Champs-Elysées, you and your kids can find everything American, from fajitas to countless types of burgers.

dishes with produce from every corner of France—rare local vegetables, fish from the coasts, and dishes incorporating cardoons, turnips, celery, turbot, cuttlefish, and Bresse fowl. His French cuisine is contemporary and Mediterranean yet not new.

Finding Your Way

To locate 16th- and 17th-arrondissement restaurants, turn to the "Restaurants Near Place Charles de Gaulle" map on page 119.

Though many dishes are light, Ducasse isn't afraid of lard, as he proves by his thick, oozing slabs of pork grilled to a crisp. He's kept a single Robuchon dish on the menu as a tribute: the famed caviar in aspic with cauliflower cream. The wine list is based on the fine cellar left by Robuchon. Ducasse has added many new acquisitions from France's vineyards but has also opened his cellar to young wine growers of his generation, including those from Germany, Switzerland, Spain, and Italy.

✪ **Faugeron.** 52 rue de Longchamp, 16e. ☎ **01-47-04-24-53.** Fax 01-47-55-62-90. Reservations required far in advance. Main courses 250–360F ($40–$57.60); fixed-price menu 320–700F ($51.20–$112) at lunch, 550–700F ($88–$112) at dinner. AE, MC, V. Mon–Fri noon–2pm and 7–10pm (Oct–Apr dinner only, Sat 7–10pm). Closed Aug. Métro: Trocadéro. FRENCH (TRADITIONAL).

Henri Faugeron is an inspired chef who many years ago opened this restaurant as an elegant yet unobtrusive backdrop for his superb cuisine, which he calls "revolutionary." The interior of this early-1900s building now glitters with discreet touches of gilt and has a sun motif emblazoned on the ceiling. Even so, the food outshines its surroundings. Much of the zesty cuisine depends on the season and market, since Faugeron chooses only the freshest ingredients. In winter your taste for truffles can be indulged by one of the many dishes expertly prepared, like the brunoise of truffles with asparagus and olive oil and the ravioli stuffed with truffles and foie gras. Roasted leg of milk-fed veal and lamb and crispy-skinned quail are also great choices. If you want something really esoteric, consider the *vol-au-vent* of lobster, sweetbreads, and morels.

✪ **Jamin.** 32 rue de Longchamp, 16e. ☎ **01-45-53-00-07.** Fax 01-45-53-00-15. Reservations required far in advance. Main courses 185–230F ($29.60–$36.80); fixed-price menu 280–410F ($44.80–$65.60) at lunch, 410F ($65.60) at dinner. AE, DC, MC, V. Mon–Fri 12:30–2pm and 7:30–10pm. Métro: Trocadéro. FRENCH (TRADITIONAL).

In the 1980s, the great chef Joël Robuchon became a sensation at this very spot. Now in charge is Robuchon's longtime second in command, Benoit Guichard, who is clearly inspired by his master but is an imaginative chef in his own right. Guichard has chosen pale green panels and pink banquettes (referred to as "ItaloNew Yorkaise") for a soothing backdrop to his brief but well-chosen menu. Lunches can be relatively simple, though each dish, like a beautifully seasoned salmon tartare, is done to perfection. Classic technique and a homage to tradition characterize the cuisine—John Dory with celery and fresh ginger; pigeon sausage with foie gras, pistachios, and mâche lettuce; and beef shoulder so tender it had obviously been braising for hours. A particularly earthy dish celebrates various parts of the sow that are usually rejected, blending the tail and cheeks on a platter with walnuts and fresh herbs. Finish with a *tarte tatin.*

MODERATE

Kambodia. 15 rue de Bassano, 16e. ☎ **01-47-23-31-80.** Reservations required. Main courses 90–110F ($14.40–$17.60); fixed-price lunch 118–148F ($18.90–$23.70). AE, DC, MC, V. Mon–Fri noon–2:30pm, Mon–Sat 7:30–11pm. Métro: George V. CAMBODIAN/ASIAN.

The waiters, all dressed in black cotton tunics, will welcome you to this excellent eatery that serves some of the best and most flavor-filled Asian dishes in Paris. The basement atmosphere has been called "Zen-like," but the service is welcoming and it's a good choice for a romantic dinner not far from the Champs-Elysées. Fresh ingredients are used, the best from the Asian markets. Our favorite dish is a superb seafood *pot-au-feu*. One Cambodian dish that's a delight is ginger fish wrapped in a banana leaf.

La Butte Chaillot. 110 bis av. Kléber, 16e. ☎ **01-47-27-88-88.** Reservations recommended. Main courses 98–118F ($15.70–$18.90); fixed-price menu 150–195F ($24–$31.20). AE, DC, MC, V. Daily noon–2:30pm and 7pm–midnight. Métro: Trocadéro. FRENCH (TRADITIONAL).

This baby bistro showcases culinary high priest Guy Savoy and draws a busy crowd from the affluent neighborhood's many corporate headquarters. Diners congregate in posh but congested areas tinted in salmon and dark yellow. Menu items change weekly (sometimes daily) and betray a strange sense of mass production not unlike that found in a luxury cruise line's dining room. Examples are a sophisticated medley of terrines; a "low-fat" version of chunky mushroom soup; a salad of snails and herbed potatoes; succulent rack of lamb; and roasted rabbit with sage and a compote of onions, bacon, and mushrooms. A starkly contemporary stainless-steel staircase leads to extra seating in the cellar.

INEXPENSIVE

Le Bistro de l'Etoile. 19 rue Lauriston, 16e. ☎ **01-40-67-11-16.** Reservations recommended. Main courses 96–115F ($15.35–$18.40); fixed-price lunch 135–165F ($21.60–$26.40). AE, DC, MC, V. Mon–Fri noon–2:30pm, Mon–Sat 7:30pm–midnight. Métro: Charles de Gaulle–Etoile. FRENCH (TRADITIONAL).

This is the most interesting of three baby bistros, each with the same name, clustered around place Charles de Gaulle–Etoile. They serve affordable versions of the grand cuisine featured in superstar Guy Savoy's nearby two-star restaurant (see below). The setting is a warmly contemporary dining room in shades of butterscotch and caramel. Menu items include a *mijotée* (pork and sage cooked over low heat for hours, coming out extremely tender, almost mushy), codfish studded with lard and prepared with a coconut-lime sauce, and red snapper filets with caramelized endive and exotic mushrooms. A particularly interesting sampler combines three of Savoy's creations on a platter—a cup of lentil cream soup, a fondant of celery, and a pan-fried slice of foie gras. Expect some odd terms on the dessert menu, which only a professional chef can fully describe: An example is spice bread baked in the fashion of *pain perdu* (lost bread) garnished with banana sorbet and pineapple sauce.

17TH & 18TH ARRONDISSEMENTS (PARC MONCEAU/ MONTMARTRE)
VERY EXPENSIVE

✪ **Guy Savoy.** 18 rue Troyon, 17e. ☎ **01-43-80-40-61.** Fax 01-46-22-43-09. Reservations required 1 week in advance. Main courses 250–700F ($40–$112); *menu dégustation* (tasting menu) 980F ($156.80). AE, DC, MC, V. Mon–Fri noon–2pm, Mon–Sat 7:30–10:30pm. Métro: Charles de Gaulle–Etoile or Ternes. FRENCH (TRADITIONAL).

Consistently named one of the five or six hottest chefs in Europe, Guy Savoy serves the kind of food he likes to eat, prepared with consummate skill. We think he has a slight edge over his nearest rival, Michel Rostang (below), though Ducasse surpasses them both. Though the food is superb and meals comprise as many as nine courses, the portions are small; you won't necessarily be satiated at the end. The menu changes with the seasons but may include a light cream soup of lentils and crayfish, duckling foie gras with aspic and gray salt, and red snapper with a liver-and-spinach sauce served with crusty potatoes. If you come in the right season, you may have a chance to order masterfully prepared game like mallard and venison. Savoy is fascinated with mushrooms and has been known to serve a dozen types, especially in autumn.

✪ **Michel Rostang.** 20 rue Rennequin, 17e. ☎ **01-47-63-40-77.** Fax 01-47-63-82-75. Reservations required far in advance. Main courses 198–385F ($31.70–$61.60); fixed-price menu 365–660F ($58.40–$105.60) at lunch, 660–860F ($105.60–$137.60) at dinner. AE, DC, MC, V. Tues–Fri 12:30–2:30pm, Mon–Sat 8–10:30pm. Closed 2 weeks in Aug. Métro: Ternes. FRENCH (TRADITIONAL & MODERN).

Michel Rostang is one of Paris's most creative chefs, the fifth generation of a distinguished French "cooking family." His restaurant contains four dining rooms paneled in mahogany, cherry, or pearwood; some have frosted Lalique crystal panels. Changing every 2 months, the menu offers modern improvements on *cuisine bourgeoise.* Truffles are the dish of choice in midwinter, and you'll find racks of suckling lamb from the salt marshes of France's western seacoasts in spring; in game season, look for sophisticated preparations of pheasant and venison. Three year-round staples are quail eggs with a coque of sea urchins, fricassée of sole, and young Bresse chicken with crusty mushroom purée and a salad composed of the chicken's thighs.

EXPENSIVE

Le Bistro d'á Côté Flaubert. 10 rue Flaubert, 17e. ☎ **01-42-67-05-81.** Reservations recommended far in advance. Main courses 98–145F ($15.70–$23.20); fixed-price lunch 150F ($24). AE, DC, MC, V. Daily 12:30–2pm and 7:30–11pm. Métro: Ternes. FRENCH (TRADITIONAL & MODERN).

This is one of the four branches of Michel Rostang's baby bistro, each of which features a pared-down version of his *haute gastronomie* (see above). We feel this branch is the most interesting because it's just next door to the source. You'll enter a nostalgically decorated dining area ringed with unusual porcelain and antique copies of Michelin guides, some from around 1900. The venue is breezy, stylishly informal, and chic, with a simple menu enhanced by daily specials written on a chalkboard. Tantalizing items include ravioli stuffed with pulverized lobster, an upscale version of macaroni laced with Serrano ham, and *rable de lievre* (rabbit stew) *en cocotte.*

MODERATE

Chez Georges. 273 bd. Pereire, 17e. ☎ **01-45-74-31-00.** Reservations recommended. Main courses 98–190F ($15.70–$30.40). V. Daily noon–2:30pm and 7pm–midnight. Métro: Porte Maillot. FRENCH (TRADITIONAL).

Not to be confused with a bistro of the same name in the 2nd arrondissement, this worthy choice has flourished since 1926, despite an obscure location. The setting has changed little—cheerfully harassed waiters barge through a dining room sheathed with old-fashioned paneling and etched glass, and savory odors emerge from the hysterically busy kitchen. Two enduring specialties are leg of lamb with white kidney beans and standing rib roast with herbs (especially thyme) in its own juices and a gratin of potatoes. Preceding these might be Baltic herring in cream sauce, cheese ravioli, cabbage soup, or a wide selection of sausages and pork products that taste best when eaten with bread, butter, and sour pickles. The adventurous French love the calf's head and the braised veal trotters, both served cold in vinaigrette.

✪ **La Rôtisserie d'Armaillé.** 6 rue d'Armaillé, 17e. ☎ **01-42-27-19-20.** Reservations recommended. Fixed-price menu 165F ($26.40) at lunch, 230F ($36.80) at dinner. AE, DC, MC, V. Mon–Fri noon–2:30pm, Mon–Sat 7:30–11pm. Métro: Charles de Gaulle–Etoile. FRENCH (TRADITIONAL).

The impresario behind this attractive baby bistro is Jacques Cagna, who established his role as a gastronomic star long ago from his headquarters in the Latin Quarter (see below). The chic place is popular for business lunches and dinners, also drawing residents and shoppers from the grand neighborhood. It's ringed with light-colored wood paneling and banquettes with patterns of pink and green. At lunch, the menu includes

| **Can You Dine Badly in Paris?** |

The answer is an emphatic yes. Our mailbox fills with complaints from readers who've encountered haughty service and paid outrageous prices for what turned out to be swill. Often these complaints are about restaurants catering to tourists. Avoid them by following our suggestions or looking in nontouristy areas for new discoveries. If you ask Parisians for recommendations, be sure to specify that you're looking for restaurants where *they'd* dine, not where they think you as a tourist would dine.

---

a main course and a starter or dessert; the pricier dinner meal includes a starter, main course, and dessert. Either way, you'll have many choices in each category. Examples are wild mushroom flan with red-wine sauce, a salad of sweetbreads and crayfish, and rack of lamb with parsley and sage, with apple beignets and champagne-drenched pineapple-and-mango soup for dessert. The artwork features bucolic cows, pigs, and lambs that are likely to figure among the grilled steaks and chops featured on the menu.

INEXPENSIVE

Le Grain de Folie. 24 rue de la Vieuville, 18e. ☎ **01-42-58-15-57.** Reservations recommended. Main courses 50–70F ($8–$11.20); fixed-price menu 55–100F ($8.80–$16). No credit cards. Daily 12:30–2:30pm and 7:30–10:30pm. Métro: Abbesses. VEGETARIAN/ORGANIC.

Simple and wholesome, the cuisine at this vegetarian restaurant has been inspired by France, Greece, California, and India. The menu includes an array of salads, cereals, tarts, terrines, and casseroles. Dessert selections might include an old-fashioned tart or a fruit salad. The decor includes potted plants, exposed stone, and a gathering of masks from around the world. You can choose one of an array of wines or a frothy glass of vegetable juice to accompany your meal.

Marie-Louise. 52 rue Championnet, 18e. ☎ **01-46-06-86-55.** Reservations recommended. Main courses 80–125F ($12.80–$20); fixed-price menu 130F ($20.80). V. Tues–Sat noon–2pm and 7:30–10pm. Closed Aug. Métro: Simplon or Porte de Clignancourt. FRENCH (TRADITIONAL).

Opened in a decidedly unfashionable neighborhood in 1957 and named after the matriarch who first owned it, this bistro offers Paris views rarely seen by visitors who gravitate toward the Seine. The decor evokes old-time France with allusions to the establishment's birth in the age of Sputnik. Opt for a table on the busy main floor or on the quieter floor above. Again and again, longtime fans order *boeuf à la ficelle* (poached beef filet tied with string and served in its natural juices). Also popular are the sautéed monkfish with pasta, *coq au vin,* chicken Marie-Louise (with rice and paprika cream sauce), and grilled sirloin steak with pepper or béarnaise sauce.

4 On the Left Bank

We'll begin with the most centrally located arrondissements on the Left Bank and then survey the outlying neighborhoods.

5TH ARRONDISSEMENT (LATIN QUARTER)
VERY EXPENSIVE

✪ **La Tour d'Argent.** 15–17 quai de la Tournelle, 5e. ☎ **01-43-54-23-31.** Fax 01-44-07-12-04. Reservations required far in advance. Main courses 270–515F ($43.20–$82.40); fixed-price lunch 400F ($64). AE, DC, MC, V. Tues–Sun noon–2:30pm and 7:30–10:30pm. Métro: Maubert-Mutualité or Pont Marie. FRENCH (TRADITIONAL).

Restaurants in the Heart of the Left Bank

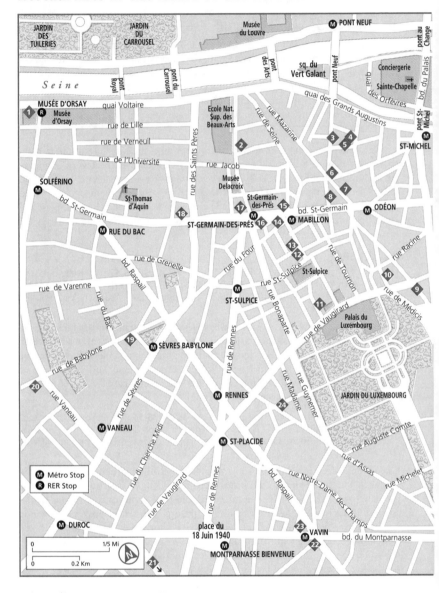

This penthouse restaurant, a national institution, serves up an amazing view over the Seine and the apse of Notre-Dame. Although La Tour d'Argent's long-established reputation as "the best" in Paris has been eclipsed, dining here remains an unsurpassed theatrical event. A restaurant of some sort has stood on this site since at least 1582: Mme de Sévigné refers to a cafe here in her celebrated letters, and Dumas used it as a setting for one of his novels. The fame of La Tour d'Argent spread during its ownership by Frédéric Delair, who started the practice of issuing certificates to diners who

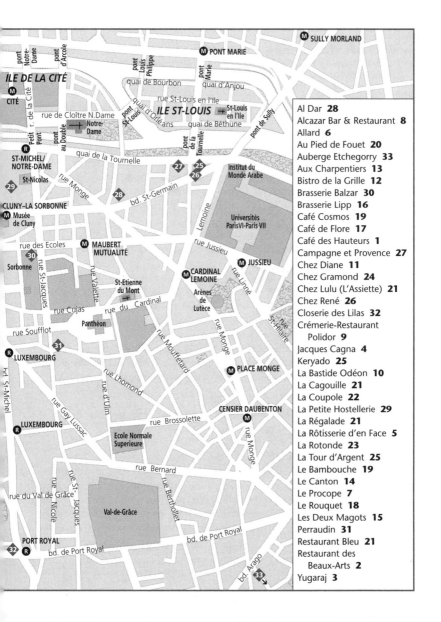

Map labels:

PONT MARIE · SULLY MORLAND

ÎLE DE LA CITÉ · CITÉ

pont Notre-Dame · pont d'Arcole · pont Louis Philippe · pont Marie

quai de Bourbon · quai d'Anjou

rue St-Louis en l'île · ÎLE ST-LOUIS · St-Louis en l'Île · quai de Béthune

r. de la Cité · rue de Cloître N.Dame · quai d'Orléans · pont St-Louis

Petit Pont · pont au Double · Notre-Dame · pont de la Tournelle · pont de Sully

ST-MICHEL/NOTRE-DAME · St-Nicolas · quai de la Tournelle · Institut du Monde Arabe

rue Monge · bd. St-Germain · Lemoine

CLUNY–LA SORBONNE · Musée de Cluny

Universités ParisVI-Paris VII

rue des Écoles · MAUBERT MUTUALITÉ · rue Jussieu · JUSSIEU

Sorbonne · rue St-Jacques · rue Valette · CARDINAL LEMOINE · rue Linné · rue St-Hilaire

rue Cujas · rue du Cardinal · St-Étienne du Mont · Arènes de Lutèce

rue Soufflot · Panthéon · rue Mouffetard · rue Monge

LUXEMBOURG · PLACE MONGE

bd. St-Michel · rue Lhomond · rue d'Ulm

rue Gay Lussac · CENSIER DAUBENTON

LUXEMBOURG · École Normale Supérieure · rue Brossolette · rue Monge

rue Bernard

rue du Val de Grâce · rue St-Jacques · rue Nicole · Val-de-Grâce · rue Berthollet

PORT ROYAL · bd. de Port Royal · bd. de Port Royal · bd. Arago

Restaurant list:

Al Dar **28**
Alcazar Bar & Restaurant **8**
Allard **6**
Au Pied de Fouet **20**
Auberge Etchegorry **33**
Aux Charpentiers **13**
Bistro de la Grille **12**
Brasserie Balzar **30**
Brasserie Lipp **16**
Café Cosmos **19**
Café de Flore **17**
Café des Hauteurs **1**
Campagne et Provence **27**
Chez Diane **11**
Chez Gramond **24**
Chez Lulu (L'Assiette) **21**
Chez René **26**
Closerie des Lilas **32**
Crémerie-Restaurant
  Polidor **9**
Jacques Cagna **4**
Keryado **25**
La Bastide Odéon **10**
La Cagouille **21**
La Coupole **22**
La Petite Hostellerie **29**
La Régalade **21**
La Rôtisserie d'en Face **5**
La Rotonde **23**
La Tour d'Argent **25**
Le Bambouche **19**
Le Canton **14**
Le Procope **7**
Le Rouquet **18**
Les Deux Magots **15**
Perraudin **31**
Restaurant Bleu **21**
Restaurant des
  Beaux-Arts **2**
Yugaraj **3**

ordered the house specialty—*caneton* (pressed duckling). The birds are numbered: The first was served to Edward VII in 1890, and now they're up over 1 million! Under the sharp eye of current owner Claude Terrail, the cooking is superb and the service impeccable. A good part of the menu is devoted to duck, but the kitchen does know how to prepare other dishes. We especially recommend you start with the pheasant consommé or the pike-perch quenelles André Terrail and follow with the ravioli with foie gras or the salmon and turbot *à la Sully*.

MODERATE

Brasserie Balzar. 49 rue des Ecoles, 5e. ☎ **01-43-54-13-67.** Reservations strongly recommended. Main courses 75–125F ($12–$20). AE, MC, V. Daily noon–midnight. Métro: Odéon or Cluny–La Sorbonne. FRENCH (TRADITIONAL).

Opened in 1898, Brasserie Balzar is battered but cheerful, with some of Paris's friendliest waiters. The menu makes almost no concessions to nouvelle cuisine and includes pepper steak, sole meunière, sauerkraut with ham and sausage, pig's feet, and fried calf's liver served without garnish. Be warned that if you want just coffee or a drink, you probably won't get a table at meal hours. But the staff will be happy to serve you if you want to have a full dinner in the midafternoon, accustomed as they are to the odd hours of their many patrons. Former patrons have included both Sartre and Camus (who often got in arguments), James Thurber, countless professors from the nearby Sorbonne, and bevys of English and American journalists.

Chez René. 14 bd. St-Germain, 5e. ☎ **01-43-54-30-23.** Reservations recommended. Main courses 80–170F ($12.80–$27.20); fixed-price lunch 170F ($27.20). V. Tues–Sat 12:15–2:15pm and 7:45–11pm. Closed Aug and 15 days in Dec. Métro: Maubert-Mutualité. FRENCH (TRADITIONAL).

Restaurants like this used to be widespread, particularly on the Left Bank, but many became pizzerias. Opened in 1957, Chez René maintains its allegiance to the tenets of French cuisine. The staff is often overwhelmed and the seating cramped as only a bistro can be. The dining room isn't fancy, but its patrons return loyally for the steady and reliable stream of food and the frequently changing *plats du jour*. For an appetizer, try the wild mushrooms laced with butter and garlic or the platter of country-style sausages. You'll find such reliable old-time fare as *boeuf bourguignonne* and *blanquette de veau* (veal in white sauce). Enjoy it all with a bottle of Beaujolais.

INEXPENSIVE

Al Dar. 8 rue Frédéric-Sauton, 5e. ☎ **01-43-25-17-15.** Reservations recommended. Main courses 85–92F ($13.60–$14.70). AE, DC, MC, V. Daily noon–midnight. Métro: Maubert-Mutualité. LEBANESE.

This well-respected restaurant works hard to popularize the savory cuisine of Lebanon. You'll dine on dishes like *taboulé*, a refreshing combination of finely chopped parsley, mint, milk, tomatoes, onions, lemon juice, olive oil, and salt; *baba ganoush*, pulverized and seasoned eggplant; and *hummus*, pulverized chickpeas with herbs. These can be followed with savory roasted chicken; tender minced lamb prepared with mint, cumin, and Mediterranean herbs; and any of several kinds of delectable tangines and couscous.

Campagne et Provence. 25 quai de la Tournelle, 5e. ☎ **01-43-54-05-17.** Reservations recommended. Fixed-price lunch 120F ($19.20); 2-course fixed-price dinner 195F ($31.20); 3-course fixed-price dinner 230F ($36.80). V. Tues–Fri noon–2pm, Mon–Sat 7:30–11pm. Métro: Maubert-Mutualité. PROVENÇAL.

This restaurant is across from Ile de la Cité beside a quay. Bouquets of dried flowers garnish the pale blue walls, and the upholstery hints of Provence's blue sky. The waiters are likely to speak with the modulated accents of southern France. The savory food served includes a salad of wild Provençal mesclun garnished with Parmesan, *compôte d'oignons* (Provençal tart) flavored with onions or a combination of sardines and red mullet, and grilled fish with risotto. A particularly tasty dessert is the anise-flavored crème brûlée.

La Petite Hostellerie. 35 rue de la Harpe (just east of bd. St-Michel), 5e. ☎ **01-43-54-47-12.** Fixed-price menu 65–89F ($10.40–$14.25). Tues–Sat noon–2pm, Mon–Sat 6:30–11pm. Closed 2 weeks in Feb and 3 weeks in Aug. AE, DC, MC, V. Métro: St-Michel or Cluny–La Sorbonne. FRENCH (TRADITIONAL).

This 1902 restaurant has a ground-floor dining room that's usually crowded and a larger upstairs one (seating 100) with attractive 18th-century woodwork. People come for the cozy ambience and decor, decent French country cooking, polite service, and excellent prices. The fixed-price dinner menu might feature favorites like *coq au vin*, duckling *á l'orange*, and steak with mustard sauce. Start with onion soup or stuffed mussels and finish with cheese or salad and peach Melba or apple tart. Rue de la Harpe is a side street north of boulevard St-Germain.

✪ **Perraudin.** 157 rue St-Jacques, 5e. ☎ **01-46-33-15-75.** Main courses 59F ($9.45); fixed-price menu 63F ($10.10) at lunch, 150F ($24) at dinner. No credit cards. Tues–Fri noon–2:15pm, Mon–Sat 7:30–10:15pm. Closed 2 weeks in Aug. Métro: Cluny–La Sorbonne. RER: Luxembourg. FRENCH (TRADITIONAL).

Everything about this place—decor, cuisine, price, and service—attempts to duplicate an early-1900s bistro. This one was built in 1870 as an outlet for coal and wine (sold as remedies against the cold). Eventually, it evolved into the wood-paneled bistro you see today, where little has changed since Zola was buried nearby in the Pantheon. The walls look like they've been marinated in tea; the marble-topped tables, old mirrors, and Parisian vaudeville posters have likely been here forever. Reservations aren't made in advance: Instead, diners usually drink a glass of kir at the zinc-topped bar as they wait. (Tables turn over quickly.) The menu includes roast leg of lamb with dauphinois potatoes, navarin of lamb, *boeuf bourguignonne*, and grilled salmon with sage sauce. An onion tart, pumpkin soup, or a terrine can precede the main course.

6TH ARRONDISSEMENT (ST-GERMAIN/LUXEMBOURG)
VERY EXPENSIVE

✪ **Jacques Cagna.** 14 rue des Grands-Augustins, 6e. ☎ **01-43-26-49-39.** Fax 01-43-54-54-48. Reservations required far in advance. Main courses 180–350F ($28.80–$56); fixed-price menu 260–490F ($41.60–$78.40) at lunch, 490F ($78.40) at dinner. AE, DC, MC, V. Tues–Fri noon–2pm, Mon–Sat 7:30–10:30pm. Closed 3 weeks in Aug. Métro: St-Michel. FRENCH (TRADITIONAL & MODERN).

St-Germain knows no finer dining than at Jacques Cagna, a sophisticated restaurant in a 17th-century town house with massive timbers, burnished paneling, and 17th-century Dutch paintings. Jacques Cagna is one of the best classically trained chefs in Paris, though he's become a half-apostle to *cuisine moderne*. This is evident in his delectable carpaccio of pearly sea bream with caviar-lavished *céleri rémoulade* (celery root in mayonnaise with capers, parsley, gherkins, spring onions, chervil, chopped tarragon, and anchovy essence). Also sublime are the rack of suckling veal with ginger-and-lime sauce, Challons duckling in burgundy sauce, and fried scallops with celery and potatoes in truffle sauce. The menu is forever changing, according to the season and Cagna's inspirations, but if you're lucky it will include his line-caught sea bass served with caviar in a potato shell.

Street Eats ————————————————————————————————

You can find a large variety of street food sold everywhere from the Latin Quarter to outside the *grands magasins* on the Right Bank. Tasty sandwiches, crêpes, *frites,* and (in cold weather) delicious roasted chestnuts are just a few of the items available. The crêpes are especially good—freshly made and filled with your choice of ingredients: cheese, ham, egg (or a combination of these); chocolate and nuts; apricot jam; or some other treat.

EXPENSIVE

Closerie des Lilas. 171 bd. du Montparnasse, 6e. ☎ **01-40-51-34-50.** Reservations recommended far in advance (restaurant only). Main courses 120–220F ($19.20–$35.20); brasserie main courses 90–180F ($14.40–$28.80). AE, DC, V. Restaurant daily noon–3pm and 7:30–11pm. Brasserie daily 11:30am–1am. Métro: Port Royal or Vavin. FRENCH (TRADITIONAL).

Opened in 1847, the Closerie was long a social and culinary magnet for the avant-garde. The famous people who have sat in the "Pleasure Garden of the Lilacs" are almost countless: Gertrude Stein and Alice B. Toklas, Ingres, Henry James, Chateaubriand, Picasso, Hemingway, Apollinaire, Lenin and Trotsky (at the chess board), Whistler, and more. Today the crowd is likely to include a sprinkling of stars and the starstruck. The place resounds with the sometimes rather loud sounds of a jazz pianist, making the interior seem even more claustrophobic than it already is. It's sometimes tough to get a seat in what's called the *bateau* (boat) section, but you can make the wait a lot more enjoyable by ordering the world's best champagne julep at the bar. It's possible to have just coffee or a drink at the bar, though the food is better than ever. Try the veal kidneys with mustard, veal ribs in cider sauce, steak tartare, or pike-perch quenelles.

MODERATE

Alcazar Bar & Restaurant. 62 rue Mazarine, 6e. ☎ **01-53-10-19-99.** Reservations recommended. Main courses 95–160F ($15.20–$25.60); fixed-price lunch 140–160F ($22.40–$25.60). AE, DC, MC, V. Daily noon–5:30pm and 7pm–1am. Métro: Odéon. FRENCH (MODERN).

Paris's most high-profile *brasserie de luxe* is this artfully high-tech place funded by British restaurateur/*wunderkind* Sir Terence Conran. (His chain of restaurants in London has succeeded in captivating a tough audience of jaded European foodies.) It features an all-white futuristic decor in a large street-level dining room and a busy bar a floor above. Menu examples are grilled entrecôte with béarnaise sauce and fried potatoes, Charolais duckling with honey and spices, sashimi and sushi with lime, monkfish filet with saffron in puff pastry, and a collection of shellfish and oysters from the waters of Brittany. The wines are as stylish and diverse as you'd expect, and the trendy crowd tends to wear a lot of black.

✪ **Allard.** 41 rue St-André-des-Arts, 6e. ☎ **01-43-26-48-23.** Reservations required. Main courses 120–135F ($19.20–$21.60); fixed-price menu 150F ($24) at lunch, 150–200F ($24–$32) at dinner. AE, DC, MC, V. Mon–Fri 12:30–2:30pm and 7:30–11:30pm. Métro: St-Michel or Odéon. FRENCH (TRADITIONAL).

Long missing from this guide, this old-time bistro, opened in 1931, is back and as good as ever following a long decline. Once it was the leading bistro, although today the competition is too great to reclaim that reputation. In the front room is a zinc bar, a haven preferred by many celebrities over the years, including Mme Pompidou and movie actor Alain Delon. All the old Allard specialties are still offered, with quality ingredients deftly handled by the kitchen. Try the snails, foie gras, veal stew, or frogs' legs. We head here on Mondays for the *boeuf à la mode* (beef braised in red wine with carrots) and on Wednesdays for the *coq au vin*. The *cassoulet Toulousain* (casserole of white beans and goose and other meats) remains one of the Left Bank's best. For dessert, we vote for the *tarte tatin*.

Chez Gramond. 5 rue de Fleurs, 6e. ☎ **01-42-22-28-89.** Reservations recommended. Main courses 130–219F ($20.80–$35.05). MC, V. Mon–Sat noon–2:30pm and 7–10pm. Closed in Aug. Métro: Notre-Dame des Champs. FRENCH (TRADITIONAL).

Aficionados of the way France used to be seek out this place, and if you're looking for the kind of cuisine that used to satisfy the *grands intellectuels* of the Latin Quarter in the 1960s, you might find it appealing. It seats only 20 people, each of whom is treated to the savoir-faire of Auvergne-born Jean-Claude Gramond and his charming wife, Jeannine. Listed in purple ink that's duplicated on an old-time mimeograph machine in back, the menu items may include roasted partridge in wine sauce, suckling lamb with sorrel sauce, terrines of foie gras, seared scallops with butter sauce on a bed of leeks, and succulent lamb stew with white beans. Try the *soufflé Grand Marnier* for dessert. The wine list is carefully balanced and fairly priced.

La Rôtisserie d'en Face. 2 rue Christine, 6e. ☎ **01-43-26-40-98.** Reservations recommended. Fixed-price menu 100–159F ($16–$25.45) at lunch, 230F ($36.80) at dinner. AE, MC, V. Mon–Fri noon–2:30pm, Mon–Sat 7–11:30pm. Métro: St-Michel. FRENCH (TRADITIONAL).

This is Paris's most frequented baby bistro, operated by Jacques Cagna, whose vastly expensive restaurant (above) is across the street. The informal place features a postmodern decor with high-tech lighting and black lacquer chairs, and the simply prepared food is very good and uses high-quality ingredients. It includes several types of ravioli, pâté of duckling *en croûte* with foie gras, *friture d'éperlans* (tiny fried freshwater fish), and smoked Scottish salmon with spinach. Monsieur Cagna has added pork cheeks, based on an old family recipe. His Barbary duckling in red-wine sauce is incomparable.

Yugaraj. 14 rue Dauphine, 6e. ☎ **01-43-26-44-91.** Reservations recommended. Main courses 105–118F ($16.80–$18.90); fixed-price menu 110–290F ($17.60–$46.40) at lunch, 180–290F ($28.80–$46.40) at dinner. AE, DC, MC, V. Tues–Sun noon–2:15pm, daily 7–11pm. Métro: Odéon. INDIAN.

On two floors of an old Latin Quarter building, Yugaraj serves flavorful food based on the recipes of northern and (to a lesser degree) southern India. In rooms done in vivid shades of "Indian pink," with a formally dressed staff and lots of intricately carved Kashmiri panels and statues, you can sample the spicy, aromatic tandoori dishes that are all the rage in France. Seafood specialties are usually made with warm-water fish imported from the Seychelles, including thiof, capitaine, and bourgeois, prepared as they would be in Calcutta, with tomatoes, onions, cumin, coriander, ginger, and garlic. Curried lamb with coriander is a particular favorite.

INEXPENSIVE

Aux Charpentiers. 10 rue Mabillon, 6e. ☎ **01-43-26-30-05.** Reservations required. Main courses 90–125F ($14.40–$20); fixed-price menu 120F ($19.20) at lunch, 158F ($25.30) at dinner. AE, DC, MC, V. Daily noon–3pm and 7:30–11:30pm. Métro: Mabillon. FRENCH (TRADITIONAL).

This bistro, opened more than 130 years ago, was once the rendezvous of the master carpenters, whose guild was next door. Nowadays it's where young men take their dates. Though the food isn't especially imaginative, it's well prepared in the best tradition of *cuisine bourgeoise*—hearty but not refined. Appetizers include pâté of duck and rabbit terrine. Especially recommended as a main course is the roast duck with olives. The *plats du jour* recall French home cooking: salt pork with lentils, *pot-au-feu,* and stuffed cabbage. The wine list has a large selection of Bordeaux, including Château Gaussens.

Bistro de la Grille. 14 rue Mabillon, 6e. ☎ **01-43-54-16-87.** Reservations recommended. Main courses 70–110F ($11.20–$17.60); fixed-price menu 105F ($16.80) at lunch, 155F ($24.80) at dinner. MC, V. Daily noon–midnight. Limited menu available 3:30–7pm. Métro: Mabillon. FRENCH (TRADITIONAL).

Many of your fellow diners at this arts-conscious bistro are likely to own or work in nearby boutiques. If you're alone, you might opt to dine at the bar near the entrance, surrounded by photos of film stars from the early years of the French Pathé cinema. The tables upstairs are moderately more sedate than those on the bustling street level. Menu items arrive in generous portions but are rarely daring—platters of fresh shellfish, traditional bone marrow spread over roughly textured bread, sautéed salmon with wild mushrooms, and the ever-popular (at least in France) veal's head with capers and mayonnaise and mustard sauce. Desserts include traditional favorites like *tarte tatin, mousse au chocolat,* and *gratin de fruit de saison.*

✪ **Chez Diane.** 25 rue Servandoni, 6e. ☎ **01-46-33-12-06.** Reservations recommended for groups of 4 or more. Main courses 100–140F ($16–$22.40); fixed-price menu 160F ($25.60). V. Mon–Fri noon–2pm, Mon–Sat 8–11:30pm. Métro: St-Sulpice. FRENCH (TRADITIONAL & MODERN).

Come here for fashionable restaurant food at simple bistro prices. Designed to accommodate only 40 diners, this place is illuminated with Venetian glass chandeliers and paved with old-fashioned floor tiles. The deep ochres and terra-cottas are redolent of Provence's landscapes and villas. Chez Diane's offerings change with the seasons and the owners' inspirations. Recently we enjoyed sweetbreads in flap mushroom sauce, nuggets of wild boar in honey sauce, minced salmon terrine with green peppercorns, and a light-textured modern adaptation of *hachis Parmentier,* an elegant meat loaf lightened with parsley, chopped onions, and herbs. To finish with a sweet touch we recommend the *charlotte au fromage blanc,* a tasty cheesecake with blueberry sauce.

✪ **Crémerie-Restaurant Polidor.** 41 rue Monsieur-le-Prince, 6e. ☎ **01-43-26-95-34.** Main courses 40–76F ($6.40–$12.15); fixed-price menu (Mon–Fri) 55F ($8.80) at lunch, 100F ($16) at dinner. No credit cards. Daily noon–2:30pm, Mon–Sat 7pm–12:30am, Sun 7–11pm. Métro: Odéon. FRENCH (TRADITIONAL).

Crémerie Polidor is the most traditional bistro in the Odéon area, serving *cuisine familiale.* Its name dates from the early 1900s, when it specialized in frosted cream desserts, but the restaurant itself can trace its history back to 1845. The Crémerie was André Gide's favorite, and Joyce, Hemingway, Valéry, Artaud, and Kerouac also dined here. The place is still frequented largely by students and artists, who head for the rear. Peer beyond the lace curtains and brass hat racks to see drawers where repeat customers lock up their cloth napkins. Overworked but smiling waitresses with frilly aprons and T-shirts bearing the likeness of old mère Polidor serve the 19th-century cuisine. Try the pumpkin soup followed by *boeuf bourguignonne,* Basque-style chicken, or *blanquette de veau.* For dessert, get a chocolate, raspberry, or lemon tart— the best in all Paris.

La Bastide Odéon. 7 rue Corneille, 6e. ☎ **01-43-26-03-65.** Reservations recommended. Fixed-price menu 152–192F ($24.30–$30.70). MC, V. Tues–Sat 12:30–2pm and 7:30–11pm. Métro: Odéon. RER: Luxembourg. PROVENÇAL.

The sunny climes of Provence come through in the pale yellow walls, heavy oaken tables, and artfully arranged bouquets of wheat and dried roses. Chef Gilles Ajuelos, formerly employed in some grand restaurants, prepares a market-based cuisine. His simplest first courses are the most satisfying, like sardines and seared sweet peppers with olive oil and pine nuts, grilled eggplant with herbs and oil, and eggplant-stuffed roasted rabbit with olive toast and balsamic vinegar. Main courses include wild duckling with pepper sauce and exotica like lamb's feet and giblets. A winning dessert is the warm almond pie with prune and Armagnac ice cream.

Le Canton. 5 rue Gozlin, 6e. ☎ **01-43-26-51-86.** Reservations recommended. Main cours-es 40–59F ($6.40–$9.45); fixed-price menu 55–69F ($8.80–$11.05) at lunch, 75–90F ($12–$14.40) at dinner. MC, V. Mon–Sat noon–2:30pm and 7–11pm. Métro: St-Germain-des-Prés. CHINESE/VIETNAMESE.

The cuisine is exotic, especially the Vietnamese dishes, and the setting relaxing and evocative of Asia. Best of all, the food is affordable and more savory than at the near-by fast-food joints. Begin with any of the versions of *nem* (Vietnamese ravioli) stuffed with shrimp and vegetables. Delicate dim sum are available, as well as main courses like salt-and-pepper shrimp, Szechuan-style chicken, and the best-selling Yorkson shrimp quick-fried with garlic, peppers, and onions. The soups are wonderful. The chefs amply use basil, the smell of which permeates the two dining rooms.

Restaurant des Beaux-Arts. 11 rue Bonaparte, 6e. ☎ **01-43-26-92-64.** Reservations rec-ommended. Main courses 65–115F ($10.40–$18.40); fixed-price menu 105F ($16.80). MC, V. Daily noon–2:15pm and 7–10:45pm. Métro: St-Germain-des-Prés. FRENCH (TRADITIONAL).

Does the city's most famous budget restaurant please everyone? Hardly. Have there been complaints about bad food and service? Some. Is it packed daily? Inevitably. That means it must please thousands every year, drawn to its cheap prices, large portions, and stick-to-the-ribs dishes. The best tables are upstairs, but on the main floor you can see the steaming pots in the open kitchen. This is what a provincial family might cook at home—*bourguignon navarin d'agneau* (lamb chops with carrots, onions, and toma-toes), trout with saffron sauce, rabbit leg with mustard sauce, and codfish filet with garlic sauce.

7TH ARRONDISSEMENT (EIFFEL TOWER/MUSÉE D'ORSAY)
VERY EXPENSIVE

L'Arpège. 84 rue de Varenne, 7e. ☎ **01-47-05-09-06.** Fax. 01-44-18-98-39. Reservations required far in advance. Main courses 340–560F ($54.40–$89.60); fixed-price lunch 490F ($78.40); *menu dégustation* (tasting menu) 1,400F ($224). AE, DC, MC, V. Mon–Fri 12:30–2pm and 7:30–10pm. Métro: Varenne. FRENCH (MODERN).

L'Arpège is best known for Alain Passard's adventurous specialties—no restaurant in the 7th serves better food. Across from the Musée Rodin in a prosperous residential neighborhood, L'Arpège has claimed the site of what for years was the world-famous L'Archestrate, where Passard worked in the kitchens. Amid a modern decor of etched glass, burnished steel, monochromatic oil paintings, and pearwood paneling, you can enjoy innovative specialties like Breton lobster in sweet-and-sour rosemary sauce, scal-lops prepared with cauliflower and lime-flavored grape sauce, and pan-fried duck with juniper and lime sauce. The signature dessert is a candied tomato stuffed with 12 kinds of dried and fresh fruit and served with anise-flavored ice cream.

EXPENSIVE

✪ **Le Violon d'Ingres.** 135 rue St-Dominique, 7e. ☎ **01-45-55-15-05.** Fax 01-45-55-48-42. Reservations required at least 3 to 4 days in advance. Main courses 180–210F ($28.80–$33.60); fixed-price menu 240F ($38.40) lunch, 490F ($78.40) at dinner. AE, MC, V. Tues–Sat noon–2:30pm and 7–10:30pm. Closed 2 weeks in Aug. Métro: Ecole Militaire. FRENCH (TRADITIONAL & MODERN).

This restaurant is quickly becoming Paris's pièce de résistance. There's talk that chef/owner Christian Constant will be "the new Robuchon," though many Parisian chefs are vying for that lofty position. Those who are fortunate enough to dine in the Violon's warm atmosphere of rose-colored wood, soft cream walls, and elegant chintz fabrics patterned with old English tea roses always rave about the cleverly artistic dish-es. They range from a starter of pan-fried foie gras with gingerbread and spinach salad to more elegant main courses like lobster ravioli with crushed vine-ripened tomatoes, roasted veal in a light and creamy milk sauce served with tender spring vegetables, and even a selection from the rotisserie, like spit-roasted leg of lamb rubbed with fresh garlic and thyme. Chef Constant keeps a well-chosen selection of wine to accompany his meals. The service is charming and discreet.

Paul Minchelli. 54 bd. de la Tour-Maubourg, 7e. ☎ **01-47-05-89-86.** Reservations required far in advance. Main courses 160–490F ($25.60–$78.40). MC, V. Tues–Sat noon–3pm and 8–11pm. Closed Aug. Métro: La Tour Maubourg. SEAFOOD.

This restaurant had a powerful impact on the dining scene when it opened in 1994. Much of the appeal comes from its deliberate earthiness and refusal to indulge in gratuitous rituals. The cuisine of Marseille-born Paul Minchelli is described even by his financial backers as "marginal," rejecting Paris's culinary conventions in favor of an old-fashioned Provençal technique. He's said to have reinvented fish (or at least the way we cook it) by stripping away extra sauces and conflicting flavors to reveal the true "taste of the sea." In a dining room boasting Norwegian birchwood stained to a distinctive yellow, modern furniture, and round seascapes evocative of the portholes on a ship, you can order dishes like raw saltwater fish with only olive oil, salt, and pepper; old-fashioned merlan Colbert; grilled John Dory; sea bass filet steamed in seaweed, lobster cooked with honey and spices, and one of the best herring salads in Paris. *Be warned*: There aren't many alternatives for those who dislike fish.

MODERATE

La Petite Chaise. 36–38 rue de Grenelle, 7e. ☎ **01-42-22-13-35.** Reservations required. Fixed-price menu 125–195F ($20–$31.20). AE, V. Daily noon–2pm and 7–11pm. Métro: Sèvres-Babylone or St-German-des-Prés. FRENCH (TRADITIONAL).

This is Paris's oldest restaurant, opened as an inn in 1680 by the baron de la Chaise at the edge of what was a large hunting preserve. (According to popular lore, the baron used the upstairs bedrooms for afternoon dalliances, between fox and pheasant hunts.) Very Parisian, the "Little Chair" invites you into a world of cramped but attractive tables, very old wood paneling, and ornate wall sconces. A vigorous chef has brought renewed taste and flavor to this longtime favorite, and the four-course set menu offers a large choice of dishes in each category. Examples are a salad with duck breast strips on a bed of fresh lettuce, seafood-and-scallop ragout with saffron, beef filet with green peppercorns, and poached fish with steamed vegetables served in a sauce of fish and vegetable stock and cream.

Le Bambouche. 15 rue de Babylone, 7e. ☎ **01-45-49-14-40.** Reservations recommended. Main courses 110–190F ($17.60–$30.40); fixed-price menu 190F ($30.40). AE, MC, V. Mon–Fri noon–2:30pm and 8–11pm. Métro: Sèvres-Babylone. NORTHERN FRENCH.

Still struggling to gain a niche, Le Bambouche charges prices that are more reasonable than you'd expect for cuisine with this degree of finesse. Meals are served in a pair of dining rooms painted in the colors of ancient Pompeii or Renaissance Tuscany (dark ochre and burnt orange), depending on your point of view. Menu items change with the season but are likely to include roasted foie gras wrapped in glazed Parma ham, served with fresh asparagus; cream of cauliflower soup with truffles and essence of lobster; sea bass braised with fresh vegetables and anise; and caramelized Corrèze veal chops with tea sauce. The desserts might include chocolate mousse served with dried fruit and herb-flavored ice cream.

Restaurants Near the Eiffel Tower & Invalides

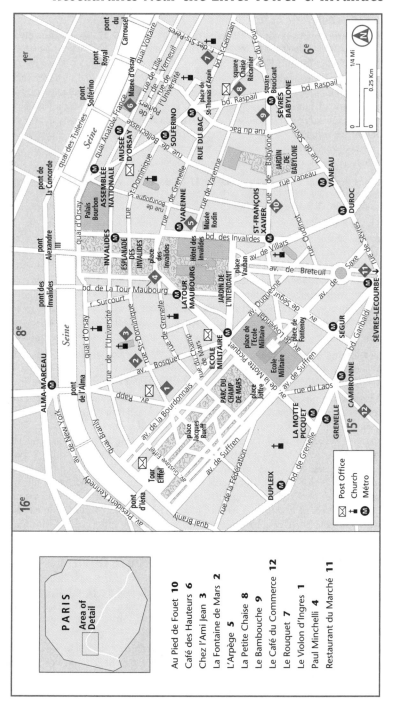

PARIS
Area of Detail

Au Pied de Fouet **10**
Café des Hauteurs **6**
Chez l'Ami Jean **3**
La Fontaine de Mars **2**
L'Arpège **5**
La Petite Chaise **8**
Le Bambouche **9**
Le Café du Commerce **12**
Le Rouquet **7**
Le Violon d'Ingres **1**
Paul Minchelli **4**
Restaurant du Marché **11**

Post Office
Church
Métro

INEXPENSIVE

Au Pied de Fouet. 45 rue de Babylone, 7e. ☎ **01-47-05-12-27.** Main courses 50–70F ($8–$11.20). No credit cards. Mon–Sat noon–2:30pm, Mon–Fri 7–9:30pm. Closed Aug. Métro: Vaneau. FRENCH (TRADITIONAL).

Au Pied de Fouet is one of the neighborhood's smallest, oldest, and most reasonably priced restaurants. In the 1700s, it was a stopover for carriages en route to Paris from other parts of Europe, offering wine, food, and stables. Don't expect a leisurely or attentive meal: Food and drink will disappear quickly from your table, under the gaze of others waiting their turn. The dishes are solid and unpretentious and include *blanquette de veau, petit salé* (a savory stew made from pork and vegetables), and *sole meunière*, a warhorse of French cuisine but always good.

Chez l'Ami Jean. 27 rue Malar, 7e. ☎ **01-47-05-86-89.** Reservations recommended. Main courses 80–100F ($12.80–$16). MC, V. Mon–Sat noon–3pm and 7–10:30pm. Métro: Invalides. BASQUE/SOUTHWESTERN FRENCH.

This restaurant was opened by a Basque nationalist in 1931, and ardent fans claim its Basque cuisine and setting are the most authentic on the Left Bank. Decorative details include wood panels, memorabilia from *pelote* (a Basque game like jai alai) and soccer, and red-and-white woven tablecloths like the ones sold in Bayonne. Menu items include cured Bayonne ham; herb-laden Béarn-influenced vegetable soups; a succulent omelet with peppers, tomatoes, and onions; squid stewed in its own ink and served with tomatoes and herbs; and *poulet basquaise*, cooked with spicy sausage, onions, peppers, and very strong red wine. In springtime, look for a truly esoteric specialty rarely available elsewhere: *saumon de l'Adour* (Adour salmon) with béarnaise sauce.

La Fontaine de Mars. 129 rue St-Dominique, 7e. ☎ **01-47-05-46-44.** Reservations recommended. Main courses 70–150F ($11.20–$24). AE, MC, V. Daily noon–2:30pm and 7:30–11pm. Métro: Ecole Militaire. PYRENÉE/SOUTHWESTERN FRENCH.

The restaurant name derives not from its location near the Champ de Mars but from the historic stone fountain on its tree-lined terrace. You'll find a sometimes boisterous dining room on the street level, plus two cozier and calmer upstairs rooms whose round tables and wooden floors make you feel like you're in a private home. An additional 70 or so seats become available by the fountain whenever weather permits. Much of the cuisine derives from the Pyrénées and southwestern France, bearing rich, heady flavors that go well with robust red wines. Examples are duckling confit with parsley potatoes, a Toulouse-inspired cassoulet, veal chops with morels, and red mullet or monkfish filets with herb-flavored butter. Our favorite dessert is a thin tart filled with a sugared purée of apples, capped with more apples, and garnished with Calvados and prunes.

13TH ARRONDISSEMENT (GOBELINS/PORTE D'IVRY)
MODERATE

Auberge Etchegorry. 41 rue Croulebarbe, 13e. ☎ **01-44-08-83-51.** Reservations recommended. Main courses 90–100F ($14.40–$16); fixed-price menu 145–180F ($23.20–$28.80). AE, DC, V. Mon–Sat noon–2:30pm and 7:30–10:30pm. Métro: Gobelins or Corvisart. BASQUE.

Its windows overlook a verdant patch of lawn that's so green you might for a moment imagine you've entered a rustic countryside inn. Dark paneling, deep colors, hanging hams and pigtails of garlic, and lacy curtains emulate the Basque country, the corner of southwestern France adjacent to Spain. Victor Hugo and Chateaubriand ate here in centuries past. The cramped tables are a drawback, but not much of one in this rich atmosphere. The menu includes a roster of specialties like cassoulet, magret of duckling, beef filet with peppercorns, a peppery omelet known as *piperades*, cocottes of mussels, and terrines or pan-fried slices of foie gras. The comfortable three-star Hôtel du Vert Galant is associated with the restaurant (see chapter 4).

INEXPENSIVE

Keryado. 32 rue de Regnault, 13e. ☎ **01-45-83-87-58.** Reservations recommended. Main courses 80–145F ($12.80–$23.20); fixed-price menu 110–150F ($17.60–$24). MC, V. Mon–Sat noon–2:30pm, Tues–Sat 7:30–10:30pm. Métro: Porte d'Ivry. SEAFOOD.

Since it was taken over by a sophisticated management in 1992, this blue-and-white seafood bistro has specialized in a dish only the most dedicated or arrogant chef would try at home: bouillabaisse. This fish stew has led to more lost reputations, crack-ups, and suicides than any other dish in the history of French cuisine. Fortunately, Keryado's version is as rich, savory, and satisfying as what you'd get in some of the best restaurants of Provence. And it's a relatively modest 145F ($23.20) per person. If bouillabaisse isn't your cup of soup, consider other fish dishes like *chaudrée de poissons aïoli*, a stew pot of filets from six types of fish, laced with a rich garlicky broth. Slightly more experimental is a stingray with green cabbage and curry.

14TH & 15TH ARRONDISSEMENTS (GARE MONTPARNASSE/DENFERT-ROCHEREAU)
MODERATE

Chez Lulu (L'Assiette). 181 rue du Château, 14e. ☎ **01-43-22-64-86.** Reservations recommended. Main courses 150–200F ($24–$32); fixed-price menu 200F ($32). AE, MC, V. Wed–Sun noon–2:30pm and 8–10:30pm. Closed Aug. Métro: Gaîté. SOUTHWESTERN FRENCH.

Everything about this place appeals to a nostalgic crowd seeking down-to-earth prices and flavorful food. You'll recognize it by the bordeaux-colored facade and potted plants in the windows. The place was a *charcuterie* (pork butcher's shop) in the 1930s and today maintains some of its old accessories. Mitterrand used to drop in with his cronies for oysters, crayfish, sea urchins, and clams. The food is unashamedly inspired by Paris's long tradition of bistro cuisine, with a few twists. Examples are chanterelle mushroom salad; *rillettes* (a roughly textured pâté) of mackerel; roasted guinea fowl; and desserts made on the premises, including a crumbly version of apple cake with fresh North African figs. Particularly delicious is a *petit salé* (stew with vegetables) of duckling with wine from the Poitou region of west-central France.

La Cagouille. 10–12 place Constantine-Brancusi, 14e. ☎ **01-43-22-09-01.** Reservations recommended. Main courses 120–180F ($19.20–$28.80); fixed-price menu 150–250F ($24–$40). AE, V. Daily noon–2pm and 5:30–10:30pm. Métro: Gaîté. FRENCH (TRADITIONAL)/CENTRAL EUROPEAN.

Don't expect to find meat at this temple of seafood—burly and genteel owner Gérard Allamandou refuses to feature it on his menu. Everything about La Cagouille is a testimonial to a modern version of the culinary arts of La Charente, the flat sandy district hugging the Atlantic south of Bordeaux. In a trio of simple oak-sheathed dining rooms with marble-topped tables, you'll sample seafood prepared as simply and naturally as possible, with no fancy sauces or elaborate cooking techniques. Allamandou's preferred fish is red mullet, which might appear sautéed in a bland oil or baked in rock salt. The name of the place derives from the regional symbol of La Charnte: the sea snail, whose preparation is elevated to a fine culinary art here. Look for a vast assemblage of all-French, mostly white wines and at least 150 cognacs.

In Pursuit of the Perfect Parisian Pastry

Could it be true, as rumor has it, that more eggs, sugar, cream, and butter per capita are consumed in Paris than in any other city, with the possible exception of Vienna? From a modern-day Proust sampling a buttery madeleine to a child munching a *pain au chocolat* (chocolate-filled croissant), everyone in Paris seems to be looking for two things: the perfect lover and the perfect pastry, not necessarily in that order. As a Parisian food critic once said, "A day without a pastry is a day in hell!"

Who'd think of beginning a morning in Paris without a *croissant* or two—not prepackaged ones made with leadlike dough but freshly baked treats, flaky and light and made with real butter, preferably from Norman cows. The Greeks may have invented pastry making, but the French perfected it. Some French pastries have made a greater impact than others. The croissant and the *brioche*, a yeasty sweet breakfast bread, are baked around the world today, as is the fabled *éclair au chocolat* (chocolate éclair), a choux pastry filled with whipped cream or pastry cream and topped with chocolate. Another pastry you should sample on its home turf (you'll never get it quite right in your own kitchen) is the *Napolitain*—layers of cake flour and almonds alternating with fruit purée. (Don't confuse this term with *Neapolitan*, meaning sweets and cakes made with layers of two or more colors, each layer flavored differently.) Very much in vogue is the *millefeuille* ("thousand leaves"), made by arranging thin layers of flaky pastry one on top of the other, along with layers of cream or thick fruit purée or jam; the American version of this is the napoleon.

Here are some of our favorite pâtisseries. **Stohrer,** 51 rue Montorgueil, 2e (☎ **01-42-33-38-20;** Métro: Les Halles), has been going strong ever since it was opened by Louis XV's pastry chef in 1730. With a day's notice, you can order an 18th-century specialty, *un pithivier,* a.k.a. *une galette des rois* (puff pastry made with almond paste). Available at any time is one of the most luscious desserts in Paris, *baba au rhum,* or its even richer cousin, *un Ali Baba,* which also incorporates cream-based rum-and-raisin filling. Stohrer boasts an interior decor classified as a national historic treasure, with

---

La Régalade. 49 av. Jean-Moulin, 14e. ☎ **01-45-45-68-58.** Reservations recommended. Fixed-price menu 185F ($29.60). V. Tues–Fri noon–2:15pm and 7pm–midnight, Sat 7pm–midnight. Closed mid-July to mid-Aug. Métro: Alésia. SOUTHWESTERN FRENCH.

The setting is a convivial bistro with banquettes the color of aged Bordeaux wine, congenially harassed service, and unexpectedly good food. The set menu presents a choice of at least 10 starters, 10 main courses, and about a dozen freshly made desserts or selections from a cheese tray. The inspiration is Yves Camdeborde's, known for his training at the posh Hôtel de Crillon. The menu changes with the seasons but is likely to include wild boar filet with red-wine sauce, a savory mix of potatoes with blood sausage, and an always-popular platter of fried goose liver served on toasted slices of spice bread.

Restaurant du Marché. 57–59 rue de Dantzig, 15e. ☎ **01-48-28-31-55.** Reservations recommended. Main courses 140–170F ($22.40–$27.20); fixed-price menu 168F ($26.90). AE, DC, MC, V. Mon–Fri noon–2:30pm, Mon–Sat 7–11pm. Métro: Porte de Versailles. LANDES.

Though little about the decor of this place has changed since the 1930s, its wood panels are waxed constantly and the bouquets of fresh flowers frequently replenished.

frescoes of damsels in 18th-century costume bearing flowers and (what else?) pastries.

Opened in 1862, a few steps from La Madeleine, **Ladurée Royale,** 16 rue Royale, 8e (☎ **01-42-60-21-79;** Métro: Madeleine), is Paris's dowager tearoom. A hot young pastry chef, Pierre Hermé, is the new "star of the *macaron,*" a pastry for which this place is celebrated. Karl Lagerfeld comes here and raves about them, as did the late ambassador Pamela Harriman. This macaroon isn't the sticky coconut version known to many, but two almond meringue cookies, flavored with chocolate, vanilla, pistachio, coffee, or other flavor, stuck together with buttercream. You may also want to try one of Hermé's latest creations—the *Coeur du Faubourg,* a lusciously dense chocolate cake with layers of caramel and apricots.

In business since Napoléon was in power, **Dalloyau,** 101 rue du faubourg St-Honoré, 8e (☎ **01-42-99-90-00;** Métro: St-Philippe du Roule), has a name instantly recognizable throughout Paris; it supplies pastries to the Elysée Palace (the French White House) and many Rothschild mansions nearby. Its specialties are *Le Dalloyau,* praline cake filled with almond meringue that's marvelously light textured, and the famous *Mogador* (chocolate cake, chocolate mousse, and a fine layer of raspberry jam). Unlike Stohrer, Dalloyau has a tearoom (open daily 8am to 7:30pm) one floor above street level, where ladies who lunch can drop in for a slice of pastry that Dalloyau warns is "too fragile to transport, or to mail, over long distances."

The best way to end your pastry tour of Paris is to follow Proust's lead and sample a *madeleine,* a buttery tea cake shaped like a tiny scallop shell. We head for **Lerch,** 4 rue Cardinal-Lemoine, 5e (☎ **01-43-26-15-80;** Métro: Cardinal Lemoine), founded in 1971 by the Alsatian-born Lerch family. It sells goods to luminaries like Martha Stewart as well as to the Proust fans who come hoping the madeleine will "invade the[ir] senses with exquisite pleasure," as it did for the narrator of *A la recherce du temps perdu.* Ideally, the madeleine is dipped into tea, preferably the slightly lime-flavored *tilleul.*

Menu items derive from dishes popular in and around Bordeaux and include an impressive roster of that region's wines to accompany the platters of traditional foie gras, deboned hare stuffed with foie gras and braised in red wine and brandy, and hen stewed with vegetables and Armagnac. The restaurant's name derives from the fact that many of its fresh, unusual ingredients are supplied directly by producers in the Landes district, near Bordeaux.

INEXPENSIVE

Le Café du Commerce. 51 rue du Commerce, 15e. ☎ **01-45-75-03-27.** Reservations recommended. Main courses 61–73F ($9.75–$11.70); fixed-price menu 87–113F ($13.90–$18.10). AE, DC, MC, V. Daily noon–midnight. Métro: Emile Zola, Commerce, or La Motte–Picquet. FRENCH (TRADITIONAL).

Le Café is one of this area's best dining bargains. Opened in 1921, the trilevel brasserie was renovated in the late 1980s, its decor designed to hearken back to the glory days of the 1920s, with dozens of verdant plants and photos of the various writers who scribbled manuscripts on its premises. The tables are illuminated by an overhead atrium. The menu choices are old-fashioned, with no attempt at modernity or high style;

examples are warm goat cheese on a bed of lettuce, *poulet sauce estragon* (chicken tarragon), duck breast with green-pepper sauce, *sole meunière, croustillant de porc au miel* (crispy baked pork with honey sauce), and escalope of salmon with sage sauce. Crème caramel or chocolate mousse makes for a satisfying dessert.

Restaurant Bleu. 46 rue Didot, 14e. ☎ **01-45-43-70-56.** Reservations required. Fixed-price menu 110–170F ($17.60–$27.20) at lunch, 130–170F ($20.80–$27.20) at dinner. MC, V. Tues–Sat noon–2:30pm and 7:30–10:15pm. Closed Aug. Métro: Alésia. AUVERGNAT.

Why is this restaurant named blue? The answer is no secret—it's in honor of the eyes of chef/owner Simon Christian, who has been entertaining Paris diners for the last 6 years. The decor evokes a market town's inn, with dark paneling, farm implements, paintings of barnyard animals (especially sheep), and souvenirs of long ago. The English-speaking hostess recommends a house specialty (*truffade des bergers*) to anyone who doesn't know a *saucisson* from a *saucisse*. Made with potatoes, goose fat, Auvergnat cheese, and parsley, it's a worthy opener for main courses like grilled Charolais beefsteak with a sauce made from heady Cahors red wine, grilled blood sausage, braised pork shoulder, and cassoulet of fish. Prune tarts make a flavorful ending. There are only about 40 seats, so reservations are important.

5 The Top Cafes

As surely everyone knows, the cafe is a Parisian institution. Parisians use them as combination club/tavern/snack bars, almost as extensions of their living rooms. They're spots where you can sit alone reading your newspaper, doing your homework, or writing your memoirs; meet a friend or lover; nibble at a hard-boiled egg; or drink yourself into oblivion. At cafes you meet your dates to go on to a show or to stay and talk. Above all, cafes are for people watching.

Their single common denominator is the encouragement of leisurely sitting. Regardless of whether you have one small coffee or the house's most expensive cognac, nobody will badger, pressure, or hurry you. If you wish to sit there until the place closes, that's your affair. Cafes keep flexible hours, depending on the season, the traffic, and the part of town they're in. Nearly all stay open until 1 or 2am, and a few are open all night.

Coffee, of course, is the chief drink. It comes black in a small cup, unless you specifically order it *au lait* (with milk). Tea (*thé*, pronounced tay) is also fairly popular but is generally not of a high quality. If you prefer beer, we advise you to pay a bit more for the imported German, Dutch, or Danish brands, which are much better than the local brew. If you insist on a French beer, at least order it *à pression* (draft), which is superior. There's also a vast variety of fruit drinks, as well as Coca-Cola, which can be rather expensive. French chocolate drinks—either hot or iced—are absolutely superb and on par with the finest Dutch brands. They're made from ground chocolate, not a chemical compound.

Now just a few words on cafe etiquette. You don't pay when you get your order—only when you intend to leave. Payment indicates you've had all you want. *Service compris* means the tip is included in your bill, so it isn't necessary to tip extra; still, most people leave an extra franc or so. You'll hear the locals call for the "*garçon*," but as a foreigner it would be more polite to say "*monsieur*." All waitresses, on the other hand, are addressed as "*mademoiselle*," regardless of age or marital status. In the smaller cafes, you may have to share your table. In that case, even if you haven't exchanged a word with your table companion, when you leave it's customary to bid him or her *au revoir*.

Brasserie Lipp. 151 bd. St-Germain, 6e. ☎ **01-45-48-53-91.** Full meals average 280F ($44.80); *café au lait* 18F ($2.90). Daily 9am–2am; restaurant service 11am–1am. AE, DC, MC, V. Métro: St-Germain-des-Prés.

On the day of Paris's liberation in 1944, late owner Roger Cazes welcomed Hemingway as the first man to drop in for a drink. Then as now, famous people often drop by for beer, wine, and conversation. Cazes's nephew, Michel-Jacques Perrochon, now runs this quintessential Parisian brasserie, where the food is secondary, yet quite good, providing you can get a seat (an hour and a half waiting time is customary if the management doesn't know you). The specialty is *choucroute garni*, Paris's best—you get not only sauerkraut but also a thick layer of ham and braised pork, which you can down with the house Riesling (a white wine) or beer. Even if you don't go inside for a drink, you can sit at a sidewalk table to enjoy a cognac and people watch.

Café Beaubourg. 100 rue St-Martin, 4e. ☎ **01-48-87-63-96.** Glass of wine 23–40F ($3.70–$6.40); beer 27–40F ($4.30–$6.40); American breakfast 110F ($17.60); sandwiches and platters 30–120F ($4.80–$19.20). AE, DC, MC, V. Sun–Thurs 8–1am, Fri–Sat 8–2am. Métro: Rambuteau or Hôtel de Ville.

Located next to the all-pedestrian plaza of the Centre Pompidou, this is a trendy avant-garde cafe with soaring concrete columns and a minimalist decor. Many of the regulars work in the neighborhood's eclectic shops and galleries. You can order salads, omelets, grilled steak, chicken Cordon Bleu, pastries, and daily platters. In warm weather, tables are set up on the sprawling outdoor terrace, providing a great place to watch the young and the restless go by.

Café Cosmos. 101 bd. du Montparnasse, 6e. ☎ **01-43-26-74-36.** *Café espresso* 25F ($4); platters 42–85F ($6.70–$13.60); fixed-price lunch 69F ($11.05). AE, DC, MC, V. Daily 7–2am. Métro: Vavin.

Does today's generation have a cafe to equal the Lost Generation's Select or Coupole? Perhaps it's the ultramodern Cosmos, where you might rub elbows with a French film star or an executive ("no one writes novels anymore"). The cafe features wooden tables, black leather chairs, and black clothing in winter—the perfect backdrop for smoked salmon with toast, rumpsteak with roquefort sauce, or grilled tuna steak.

Café de Flore. 172 bd. St-Germain, 6e. ☎ **01-45-48-55-26.** *Café espresso* 24F ($3.85); glass of beer 42F ($6.70). Daily 7–1:30am. Métro: St-Germain-des-Prés.

Sartre—the granddaddy of existentialism, a key figure in the Resistance movement, and a renowned cafe-sitter—often came here during World War II. Wearing a leather jacket and beret, he sat at his table and wrote his trilogy, *Les Chemins de la Liberté* (The Roads to Freedom). Camus, Picasso, and Apollinaire also frequented the Flore. The cafe is still going strong, though the famous patrons have moved on and tourists have taken up all the tables. The menu offers omelets, salads, pavé of beef with pepper sauce, sole meunière, and more.

Café de la Musique. In the Cité de la Musique, 212 av. Jean-Jaurès, 19e. ☎ **01-48-03-15-91.** *Plats du jour* 70F ($11.20). AE, DC, MC, V. Daily 7–2am (full menu daily 11am–midnight). Métro: Porte de Pantin.

This cafe's location in one of the grandest of Mitterrand's *grands travaux* guarantees a crowd passionately devoted to music; the recorded sounds that play in the background are likely to be more diverse and more eclectic than those in any other cafe in Paris. The red-and-green velour setting might remind you of a modern opera house, with windows overlooking nearby place de la Fontaine. On the menu you'll find pasta with shellfish, roast pork in cider sauce, and braised stingray in black butter sauce.

Wednesdays 10pm to 1am brings a program of live jazz and Fridays 10pm to 1am bring live music; Saturdays a DJ entertains with disco music.

✪ **Café de la Paix.** Place de l'Opéra, 9e. ☎ **01-40-07-30-20.** *Café espresso* 19F ($3.05); fixed-price menu 138F ($22.10) for 2 courses, 178F ($28.50) for 3 courses. Daily noon–midnight. Métro: Opéra.

This hub of the tourist world rules place de l'Opéra, and the legend goes that if you sit here long enough, you'll see someone you know passing by. Huge, grandiose, frighteningly fashionable, and sometimes brusque and anonymous, it harbors not only Parisians but also, at one time or another, nearly every visiting American—a tradition dating from the end of World War I. Once Emile Zola sat on the terrace; later, Hemingway and Fitzgerald frequented it. The best news for tourists who stop in for a bite is that prices have recently been lowered because of stiff competition in the area. Menu items may include escalope of veal with mushrooms and cream sauce, seafood *bourride* (stew) in the style of Provence, and beef filet with red-wine/mushroom sauce.

Café de l'Industrie. 16 rue St-Sabin, 11e. ☎ **01-47-00-13-53.** Glass of wine 19–26F ($3.05–$4.15); main courses 50–80F ($8–$12.80). MC, V. Sun–Fri 10–2am. Métro: Bastille or Breguier-Sabin.

Founded just before the outbreak of World War II, this cafe received a vital new lease on life after the opening of the nearby Opéra Bastille. Today, its three dining rooms boast a decor evoking aspects of both the tropics and faux-baroque Europe, with green plants and lots of original oil paintings by long-term patrons. Known for decanting obscure vintages from the Touraine and the region around Beaujolais, it appeals to photographers and lesser-known characters in French-speaking show biz. If you're hungry, consider any of the generous *plats du jour*. Examples are leeks steeped in vinaigrette, *boeuf bourguignonne*, fried haddock, and tagliatelle with salmon, chives, and cream sauce.

Café des Hauteurs. In the Musée d'Orsay, 1 rue de Bellechasse, 7e. ☎ **01-42-84-12-16.** Salads 38–66F ($6.10–$10.55). AE, MC, V. Tues–Wed and Fri–Sun 10am–5pm, Thurs 10am–9pm. Métro: Solférino. RER: Musée d'Orsay. FRENCH.

The designers of the Musée d'Orsay recognized the fatigue that can sometimes come with a museum visit. That's why this fifth-floor cafe is midway between a bar and a short-term rest home, where you can recuperate in front of a sweeping view stretching as far as Notre-Dame and Sacré-Coeur and looking over the glass-encased mechanism of a huge clock. In addition to the usual doses of caffeine and alcohol, you can order platters more substantial than a snack but less filling than the main course of a conventional meal. Examples are smoked salmon with shrimp salad and rye bread and a platter of assorted cheeses.

Café Marly. In the Cour Napoléon du Louvre, 93 rue de Rivoli, 1er. ☎ **01-49-26-06-60.** Reservations recommended. Main courses 110–150F ($17.60–$24). AE, DC, MC, V. Daily 8–2am (meals 11:30am–1am). Métro: Palais Royal or Musée du Louvre.

In 1994, the French government gave the green light for a cafe and restaurant to open in one of the Louvre's most historic courtyards, accessible only from a point close to the famous glass pyramid that rises above the Cour Marly. It has become a favorite refuge of Parisians trying to escape the traffic roar on rue de Rivoli. Anyone is welcome to sit

---

Did You Know?

You'll pay substantially less in a cafe if you stand at the counter rather than sit at a table, since there's no service charge.

down for a *café au lait* daily 8am to 2am. But more substantial fare is the norm here, served in one of three dining rooms done in tones of burgundy, black, and gilt. Menu items include club sandwiches, fresh fish, pepper steak, and an array of upscale bistro-inspired food. In summer, outdoor tables overlook the celebrated courtyard.

Café/Restaurant/Salon de Thé Bernardaud. 11 rue Royale, 8e. ☎ **01-42-66-22-55.** Reservations recommended at lunch. Continental breakfast 55F ($8.80); lunch main courses 90–130F ($14.40–$20.80); afternoon tea with pastry 75F ($12). MC, V. Mon–Sat 8am–7pm. Métro: Concorde. FRENCH.

Few other Paris cafes/tearooms mingle salesmanship with culinary pizzazz as effectively as this one. It was opened in 1995 by the venerable Limoges-based manufacturer of porcelain Bernardaud, and the staggeringly beautiful stuff is on display everywhere. Occupying some of Europe's most expensive commercial real estate, the medium-green space is upscale art deco in style. Lunchtime is flooded with employees of the nearby offices, and you can opt for just a salad or something more substantial, like a medley of fresh fish in herb sauce with vegetables. Afternoon tea adds a new twist: A staff member will present a choice of five porcelain patterns in which your tea will be served, and if you finish your Earl Grey with a fixation on the pattern you've chosen, you'll be directed into the adjacent showroom to place your order.

Fouquet's. 99 av. des Champs-Elysées, 8e. ☎ **01-47-23-70-60.** Glass of wine from 36F ($5.75); sandwiches 55F ($8.80); main courses 160–380F ($25.60–$60.80); fixed-price menu 285F ($45.60). AE, MC, V. Daily 8–2am. Restaurant noon–3pm and 7pm–12:30am; bar 9–2am. Métro: George V.

Fouquet's has been collecting anecdotes and a patina since it was founded in 1901. A celebrity favorite, it has attracted Chaplin, Chevalier, Dietrich, Churchill, Roosevelt, and Jackie O. The premier cafe on the Champs-Elysées sits behind a barricade of potted flowers at the edge of the sidewalk. You can choose a table in the sunshine or retreat to the glassed-in elegance of the leather banquettes and rattan furniture of the grill room. Though this is a full-fledged restaurant, with a beautiful formal dining room on the second floor, most visitors come by just for a glass of wine, coffee, or sandwich.

La Coupole. 102 bd. du Montparnasse, 14e. ☎ **01-43-20-14-20.** Breakfast buffet 89F ($14.25); main courses 89–188F ($14.25–$30.10) at lunch, 109–188F ($17.45–$30.10) at dinner; fixed-price menu 138–189F ($22.10–$30.25) at lunch, 189F ($30.25) at dinner before 10:30pm, 138–189F ($22.10–$30.25) after 10:30pm. AE, DC, MC, V. Daily 8:30–1am (breakfast buffet Mon–Fri 7:30–10:30am). Métro: Vavin.

Born in 1927 and once a leading center of artistic life, La Coupole is now the epitome of the grand Paris brasserie in Montparnasse. Former patrons included Josephine Baker, Henry Miller, Dalí, Calder, Hemingway, Fitzgerald, and Picasso. The sweeping outdoor terrace is among the finest in Paris. At one of its sidewalk tables, you can sit and watch the passing scene and order a coffee or a cognac VSOP. The food is quite good, despite the fact that the dining room resembles an enormous rail station waiting room. Try main dishes like *sole meunière*, cassoulet, fresh oysters, shellfish, and some of the best pepper steak in Paris. The waiters are as rude and inattentive as ever, and aficionados of the place wouldn't have it any other way.

La Rotonde. 105 bd. du Montparnasse, 6e. ☎ **01-43-26-68-84.** Glass of wine 23F ($3.70); fixed-price menu 75F ($12) at lunch, 190F ($30.40) at dinner. AE, MC, V. Cafe daily 7–1am; food service daily noon–2am. Métro: Vavin.

Once patronized by Hemingway, the original Rotonde faded into history but is immortalized in the pages of *The Sun Also Rises*, in which Papa wrote, "No matter what cafe in Montparnasse you ask a taxi driver to bring you to from the right bank of the river, they always take you to the Rotonde." Lavishly upgraded, its reincarnation has a paneled art deco elegance and shares the once-hallowed site with a motion-picture theater. The menu includes hearty fare like pepper steak with *pommes frites,* shellfish in season, and sea bass filets with herb-flavored lemon sauce.

Le Café Zephyr. 12 bd. Montmartre, 9e. ☎ **01-47-70-80-14.** *Café au lait* 29F ($4.65); *plats du jour* 65–92F ($10.40–$14.70). MC, V. Mon–Sat 8–2am, Sun 8am–10pm. Métro: Rue Montmartre.

The patrons of this cafe like it for the quiet refuge it provides in the midst of a heavily commercialized bustling neighborhood. Understated and sedate, it holds firmly to its roots in an increasingly modern and international area of Paris. Stop by for a leisurely *café au lait* or a light snack, but don't expect any culinary masterpieces—you're more likely to enjoy the atmosphere than the food.

Le Gutenberg. 64 rue Jean-Jacques Rousseau, 1er. ☎ **01-42-36-14-90.** *Café au lait* 11F ($1.75); *sandwiches* 15F ($2.40); *plats du jour* 49F ($7.85). No credit cards. Mon–Fri 8am–7pm, Sat noon–3:30pm. Métro: Louvre-Rivoli.

Behind the largest post office in France and named in honor of the printing presses that used to operate nearby, this is the most evocative and authentic of the cafes close to the Louvre. There's a zinc-top bar and two inner rooms loaded with antique mirrors and uniformed staff members. No one can agree on whether the place is 150 or 225 years old. The food runs the gamut from light broths and simple salads to roasted duck breast with orange sauce and pork tenderloin with red wine and apples.

Le Procope. 13 rue de l'Ancienne-Comédie, 6e. ☎ **01-40-46-79-00.** Reservations recommended. Main courses 100–150F ($16–$24). AE, MC, V. Daily noon-midnight. Métro: Odéon FRENCH.

To ardent fans of French history, this is the holy grail of Parisian cafes. Opened in 1686, it occupies a three-story townhouse whose architectural details are categorized as a historic monument. Inside, nine salons and dining rooms, each of whose 300-year-old walls have been carefully preserved and painted a deep red, are available for langourous afternoon coffee breaks or well-presented meals. Menu items include platters of shellfish, onion soup *au gratin, coq au vin,* duck breast in honey sauce; and grilled versions of various meats and fish. Every day between 3 and 7pm, the place makes itself available to sightseers who come to look but not necessarily eat and drink at the site that welcomed such movers and shakers as Diderot, Voltaire, Georges Sand, Victor Hugo, and Oscar Wilde. Of special charm is the ground-floor room outfitted like an antique library.

Le Rouquet. 188 bd. St-Germain, 7e. ☎ **01-45-48-06-93.** *Café au lait* 13–23F ($2.10–$3.70); *plats du jour* 60F ($9.60). MC, V. Mon–Sat 7am–9pm. Métro: St-Germain-des-Prés.

Despite its conventional food and high prices, Le Rouquet enjoys an enviable cachet and sense of chic, partly because it competes on a less flamboyant scale with the nearby Café de Flore and Les Deux Magots and partly because the decor hasn't changed since a 1954 remodeling. Less than 60 yards from St-Germain church, you can sit for as long as you want, watching a crowd of stylish Italians and Americans performing shopping and people-watching rituals barely altered since Le Roquet's founding in 1922.

Les Deux Magots. 6 place St-Germain-des-Prés, 6e. ☎ **01-45-48-55-25.** *Café au lait* 25F ($4); *whiskey soda* 70F ($11.20); *plats du jour* 90–140F ($14.40–$22.40). AE, DC, V. Daily 7:30–1:30am. Métro: St-Germain-des-Prés.

This legendary hangout for the sophisticated residents of St-Germain-des-Prés becomes a tourist favorite in summer. Visitors monopolize the few sidewalk tables as the waiters rush about, seemingly oblivious to anyone's needs. Regulars from around

AT&T Direct® Service

AT&T Access Numbers

Aruba	800-8000	Czech Rep. ▲	00-42-000-101
Australia	1-800-551-155	Egypt●(Cairo)†	510-0200
Austria●	0800-200-288	France	0-800-99-0011
Bahamas	1-800-872-2881	Germany	0800-2255-288
Barbados+	1-800-872-2881	Greece●	00-800-1311
Belgium●	0-800-100-10	Guam	1-800-2255-288
Bermuda+	1-800-872-2881	Hong Kong	800-96-1111
Cayman Isl.+	1-800-872-2881	Hungary	06-800-01111
China, PRC▲	10811	India ✱.➤	000-117
Costa Rica	0-800-0-114-114	Ireland ✓	1-800-550-000

AT&T Direct® Service

AT&T Access Numbers

Aruba	800-8000	Czech Rep. ▲	00-42-000-101
Australia	1-800-551-155	Egypt●(Cairo)†	510-0200
Austria●	0800-200-288	France	0-800-99-0011
Bahamas	1-800-872-2881	Germany	0800-2255-288
Barbados+	1-800-872-2881	Greece●	00-800-1311
Belgium●	0-800-100-10	Guam	1-800-2255-288
Bermuda+	1-800-872-2881	Hong Kong	800-96-1111
Cayman Isl.+	1-800-872-2881	Hungary	06-800-01111
China, PRC▲	10811	India ✱.➤	000-117
Costa Rica	0-800-0-114-114	Ireland ✓	1-800-550-000

Israel	1-800-94-949		Philippines●	105-11
Italy●	172-1011		Portugal▲	0800-800-128
Jamaica●	1-800-872-2881		Singapore	800-0111-111
Japan●▲	005-39-111		Spain	900-99-00-11
Malaysia●	1800-80-0011		Switzerland●	0-800-89-0011
Mexico●▽	001-800-288-2872		Thailand✔	001-999-111-11
Neth. Ant.○	001-800-872-2881		Turkey●	00-800-12277
Netherlands●	0800-022-9111		U.K.	0800-89-0011
New Zealand●	000-911		U.K.	0800-013-0011
Panama	800-001-0109		Venezuela	800-11-120

FOR EASY CALLING WORLDWIDE

1. Just dial the AT&T Access Number for the country you are calling from.
2. Dial the phone number you're calling.   *3.* Dial your card number.

For access numbers not listed ask any operator for **AT&T Direct®** Service.
In the U.S. call 1-800-331-1140 for a wallet guide listing all worldwide AT&T Access Numbers.

Visit our Web site at: **www.att.com/traveler**
Bold-faced countries permit country-to-country calling outside the U.S.

● Public phones may require coin or card deposit to place call.
✦ Outside of Cairo, dial "02" first.
✚ May not be available from every phone/payphone.
✦ Public phones and select hotels.
✔ Use U.K. access number in N. Ireland.
✦ When calling from public phones, use phones marked "Lenso."
✱ When calling from public phones, use phones marked "Ladatel."
▼ Not available from public phones.
✖ Available from phones with international calling capabilities or from most Public Calling Centers.
○ From St. Maarten or phones at Bobby's Marina, use 1-800-872-2881.

When placing an international call *from* the U.S., dial 1 800 CALL ATT.

© 1/2000

TIMBUKTU   KALAMAZOO

AT&T Direct® Service

The easy way to call home from anywhere.

Global
connection
with the AT&T
Network

AT&T
direct
service

For the easy way to call home, take the attached wallet guide.

Make Learning Fun & Easy

With IDG Books Worldwide

Frommer's

FOR DUMMIES

WEBSTER'S NEW WORLD

Betty Crocker's

the Unofficial Guide

CliffsNotes™
www.cliffsnotes.com

BURPEE

ARCO

HOWELL BOOK HOUSE™

the neighborhood reclaim it in the off-season. Les Deux Magots was once a gathering place of the intellectual elite, like Sartre and de Beauvoir and Giraudoux. Inside are the two large statues of Confucian wise men (*magots*) that give the cafe its name. The crystal chandeliers are too brightly lit, but the regulars seem to be accustomed to the glare. After all, some of them even read their daily newspapers here. You can order salads, pastries, ice cream, or one of the daily specials; the fresh fish is usually a good bet.

6 Gay-Friendly Restaurants

Though any restaurant recommended in this guide is at least tolerant of same-sex couples, these two restaurants are especially welcoming of gay diners. For their locations, see the "Restaurants in the Heart of the Right Bank" map on page 106. For full coverage of Paris's gay/gay-friendly hotels and restaurants, see *Frommer's Gay & Lesbian Europe.*

INEXPENSIVE

Eclache & Cie. 10 rue St-Merri, 4e. ☎ **01-42-74-62-62.** Reservations recommended. Main courses 70–90F ($11.20–$14.40); fixed-price menus 100–120F ($16–$19.20). AE, DC, MC, V. Daily noon–1am. Metro: Hôtel de Ville. FRENCH (TRADITIONAL).

The setting is warm and cozy, with antique lamps flickering from the rough stone walls, and everything is richly steeped in a sense of admiration for French country inns. Dining on the terrace is lovely, thanks to the restaurant's position on a quiet dead-end street. Menu items are what you'd expect from a cuisine-conscious *grand-mère,* with heaping platters of *blanquette de veau,* grilled steak with béarnaise or pepper sauce, salmon with sage sauce, and roasted rack of lamb with rosemary and thyme. About 80% of the crowd is gay male.

L'Amazonial. 3 rue Ste-Opportune, 1er. ☎ **01-42-33-53-13.** Reservations recommended. Main courses 65–120F ($10.40–$19.20); fixed-price menus 85–129F ($13.60–$20.65). AE, MC, V. Daily noon–3pm and 7pm–1:30am. Métro: Châtelet. FRENCH (MODERN)/ INTERNATIONAL.

One of Paris's most popular gay restaurants is in the heart of the Marais, occupying a 19th-century building with a flowered terrace extending onto the pavement The dining room incorporates decorative elements from ancient Greece and Egypt and the Amazon basin. The menu is sometimes startling, featuring items like ostrich steak with exotic mushrooms; more conservative dishes include Barbados-style grilled prawns, *feijoada* (a Brazilian stew with beans and meat, usually pork); and *plats de jour* like flank steak with béarnaise sauce. Beware the standoffish waiters.

6 Exploring Paris

Paris is a city where taking in the street life—shopping, strolling, and hanging out—should claim as much of your time as sightseeing in churches or museums. Having a gourmet picnic in the Bois de Boulogne, taking a sunrise amble along the Seine, spending an afternoon bartering at a flea market—Paris bewitches you with these kinds of experiences. For all the Louvre's beauty, you'll probably remember the Latin Quarter's crooked alleyways better than the 370th oil painting of your visit.

SIGHTSEEING SUGGESTIONS FOR THE FIRST-TIMER

IF YOU HAVE 1 DAY   Get up early and begin your day with some live theater by walking the streets around your hotel. Find a little cafe and order a typical Parisian breakfast of coffee and croissants. If you're a museum and monument junkie and don't dare return home without seeing the "must" sights, know that the two top museums are the **Musée du Louvre** and **Musée d'Orsay** and the three top monuments are the **Tour Eiffel, Arc de Triomphe,** and **Notre-Dame** (which you can see later in the day). If it's a toss-up between the Louvre and the d'Orsay, we'd make it the Louvre because it holds a greater variety of works. If you need to choose among the monuments, we'd make it the Tour Eiffel just for the panoramic view of the city.

If your day is too short to visit museums or wait in line for the tower, we suggest you spend most of your time strolling the streets. The most impressive neighborhood is on **Ile St-Louis,** the most elegant place for a walk. After exploring this island and its mansions, wander at will through such Left Bank districts as **St-Germain-des-Prés** and the area around **place St-Michel,** the heart of the student quarter. As the sun sets, head for **Notre-Dame,** standing majestically along the banks of the Seine. This is a good place to watch the shadows fall over Paris as the lights come on for the night. Afterward, walk along the Seine, where vendors sell books and souvenir prints. Promise yourself a return visit and have dinner in the Left Bank bistro of your choice.

IF YOU HAVE 2 DAYS   Follow the above for day 1, except now you can fit in on day 2 more of the top five sights we mention above. Day 1 covered a lot of the Left Bank, so if you want to explore the Right Bank, begin at the **Arc de Triomphe** and stroll down the **Champs-Elysées,** Paris's main boulevard, until you reach the Egyptian obelisk at **place de la Concorde,** where some of France's most notable figures lost their heads on the guillotine. Place de la Concorde affords terrific views of **La Madeleine,** the **Palais Bourbon,** the **Arc de Triomphe,** and the **Musée du Louvre.** Nearby **place Vendôme** is well worth a visit, as it represents the Right Bank at its most elegant, with the Hôtel Ritz and Paris's top jewelry stores. Now we suggest a rest stop in the **Jardin de Tuileries,** directly west and adjacent to the Louvre. After a bistro lunch, go for a walk in the **Marais** to get a total contrast to monumental Paris. Our favorite stroll is along narrow **rue des Rosiers,** at the heart of the Jewish community. And don't miss **place des Vosges.** After a rest at your hotel, select one of the restaurants down in **Montparnasse,** following in Hemingway's footsteps. This area is far livelier at night.

IF YOU HAVE 3 DAYS Spend days 1 and 2 as above. As you've already gotten a look at the Left Bank and the Right Bank, this day should be about following your special interests. You might target the restored **Centre Pompidou** and the **Musée Carnavalet,** Paris's history museum. If you're a Monet fan, you might head for the **Musée Marmottan–Claude Monet.** Or perhaps you'd rather wander the sculpture garden of the **Musée Rodin.** If you select the **Musée Picasso,** you can use part of the morning to explore a few of the Marais's art galleries. After lunch, spend the afternoon on **Ile de la Cité,** where you'll get not only to see Notre-Dame again but also to visit the **Conciergerie,** where Marie Antoinette and others were held captive before they were beheaded. And you certainly can't miss the stunning stained glass of **Sainte-Chapelle** in the Palais de Justice. After dinner, if your energy holds, you can sample Paris's nightlife—whatever you fancy, the dancers at the **Lido** or the **Folies-Bergère** or a smoky Left Bank jazz club or a frenzied disco. If you'd like to just sit and have a drink, Paris has some of the most elegant hotel bars in the world—try the **Crillon** or the **Plaza Athénée.**

IF YOU HAVE 4 DAYS For your first 3 days, follow the above. On day 4, head to **Versailles,** 21 kilometers (13 miles) south of Paris, the greatest attraction in the Ile de France. When Louis XIV decided to move to the suburbs, he created a spectacle unlike anything the world had ever seen. The good news is that most of the palace remains intact, in all its opulence and glitter. A full day here almost feels like too little time. After you return to Paris for the night, take a good rest and spend the evening wandering around the Left Bank's **Latin Quarter,** enjoying the student cafes and bars and selecting your bistro of choice for the evening. Two of the livelier streets for wandering are rue de la Huchette and rue Monsieur-le-Prince.

IF YOU HAVE 5 DAYS Spend days 1 to 4 as above. On day 5, devote at least a morning to a neglected area: **Montmartre,** the community formerly known for its artists perched atop the highest of Paris's seven hills. Though the starving artists who made it the embodiment of *la vie de bohème* have long departed, there's much to enchant you, especially if you wander the back streets and avoid place du Tertre. Away from the tacky shops and sleazy clubs, you'll see the picture-postcard lanes and staircases known to Picasso, Toulouse-Lautrec, and Utrillo. Of course, it's virtually mandatory to visit **Sacré-Coeur,** for the view if nothing else. Since it's your last night in Paris, let your own interests take over. Lovers traditionally spend it clasping hands in a walk along the Seine; less goggle-eyed visitors can still find a full agenda. We suggest a final evening at **Willi's Wine Bar** (see chapter 9), with more than 250 vintages and good food to go along with it. For a nightcap, we always head for the **Hemingway Bar** at the Ritz, where Garbo, Coward, and Fitzgerald once lifted their glasses. If that's too elegant, head for **Closerie des Lilas** in the 6th arrondissement, where you can rub shoulders with the movers and shakers of the film and fashion industries.

1 Attractions by Arrondissement

For the locations of these sights, see the **overview map** on page 158 and the individual **neighborhood maps** on pages 160–166.

THE RIGHT BANK
1ST ARR. (MUSÉE DU LOUVRE/LES HALLES)

Arc de Triomphe du Carrousel (p. 204)
Forum des Halles (p. 194)
Galerie Nationale du Jeu de Paume (p. 178)
✪ Jardin des Tuileries (p. 204)
Jardin du Carrousel (p. 204)
Les Halles (p. 192)
Musée des Arts Décoratifs (p. 199)
✪ Musée du Louvre (p. 172)
Musée du Parfum (p. 204)
Palais Royal (p. 189)
Place Vendôme (p. 155)
✪ St-Eustache (p. 185)
St-Germain l'Auxerrois (p. 186)

3RD ARR. (LE MARAIS)

Hôtel de Rohan (p. 203)
Hôtel de Clisson (p. 202)
Hôtel le Pelletier de St-Fargeau (p. 179)
Musée Carnavalet (p. 179)
Musée Cognacq-Jay (p. 198)
Musée d'Art et d'Histoire du Judaïsm (p. 202)
Musée de la Chasse (p. 203)
Musée de l'Histoire de France (p. 202)
✪ Musée Picasso (p. 181)

4TH ARR. (ILE DE LA CITÉ/ILE ST-LOUIS/BEAUBOURG)

Atelier Brancusi (p. 178)
✪ Cathédrale de Notre-Dame (p. 168)
✪ Centre Pompidou (p. 177)
Conciergerie (p. 187)
Hôtel de Lauzun (p. 192)
Hôtel de Ville (p. 188)
Hôtel Dieu (p. 191)
Hôtel Lambert (p. 192)
Maison de Victor Hugo (p. 214)
No. 9 quai d'Anjou (p. 192)
Place des Vosges (p. 214)
Pont Neuf (p. 191)
Rue des Rosiers (p. 155)

✪ Sainte-Chapelle (p. 175)
Square du Vert Galant (p. 191)
St-Louis-en-l'Ile (p. 192)

8TH ARR. (CHAMPS-ELYSÉES/MADELEINE)

American Cathedral of the Holy Trinity (p. 183)
✪ Arc de Triomphe (p. 167)
Champs-Elysées (p. 154)
Grand Palais (p. 183)
La Madeleine (p. 184)
Musée Cernuschi (p. 198)
✪ Musée Jacquemart-André (p. 179)
Musée Nissim de Camondo (p. 200)
Parc Monceau (p. 207)
Petit Palais (p. 183)
Place de la Concorde (p. 154)

9TH ARR. (OPÉRA GARNIER/PIGALLE)

Musée Grévin (p. 212)
Paristoric (p. 203)

10TH ARR. (GARE DE NORD/GARE DE L'EST)

Musée de Baccarat (p. 201)

11TH ARR. (OPÉRA BASTILLE)

Musée Edith Piaf (p. 200)
Villa Calte (p. 200)

12TH ARR. (BOIS DE VINCENNES/GARE DE LYON)

Musée des Arts d'Afrique et d'Océanie (p. 199)
Parc Zoologique de Paris (p. 213)

16TH ARR. (TROCADÉRO/BOIS DE BOULOGNE)

Bois de Boulogne (p. 205)
Carrefour des Cascades (p. 206)
Cimetière de Passy (p. 210)
Grande Cascade (p. 206)
Hippodrome d'Auteuil (p. 206)
Hippodrome de Longchamp (p. 206)

Jardin d'Acclimatation (p. 213)
Maison de Balzac (p. 214)
Musée d'Art Moderne de la Ville de
    Paris (p. 199)
Musée de la Marine (p. 212)
Musée des Enfants (p. 199)
Musée du Vin (p. 204)
✪ Musée Marmottan–Claude Monet
    (p. 179)
Musée National des Arts
    Asiatiques–Guimet (p. 200)
Panthéon Bouddhique (p. 201)
Parc de Bagatelle (p. 206)

18TH ARR. (MONTMARTRE)
✪ Basilique du Sacré-Coeur (p. 167)
✪ Bateau-Lavoir (p. 194)
Cimetière de Montmartre (p. 211)
Cimetière St-Vincent (p. 210)
Espace Montmartre Dalí (p. 194)
Musée de l'Erotisme (p. 203)
Musée de Vieux Montmartre (p. 194)
St-Pierre (p. 194)

19TH ARR. (LA VILLETTE)
Cité des Sciences et de l'Industrie
    (p. 211)
La Géode (p. 212)
Musée de la Musique (p. 199)
Parc de La Villette (p. 212)

20TH ARR. (PÈRE-LACHAISE CEMETERY)
✪ Cimetière du Père-Lachaise (p. 207)

THE LEFT BANK
5TH ARR. (LATIN QUARTER)
Arènes de Lutèce (p. 186)
Hôtel du Vieux-Paris (p. 214)
Institut du Monde Arabe (p. 202)
Mosquée de Paris (p. 184)
Musée National d'Histoire Naturelle
    (p. 212)
Musée National du Moyen Age/
    Thermes de Cluny (p. 212)
Panthéon (p. 189)
Roman Baths (p. 181)
Rue de la Huchette (p. 213)
St-Etienne-du-Mont (p. 185)
Val-de-Grâce (p. 186)

6TH ARR. (ST-GERMAIN/ LUXEMBOURG)
Institut de France (p. 188)
Jardin du Luxembourg (p. 205)
Musée National Eugène Delacroix
    (p. 181)
Musée Zadkine (p. 200)
Palais du Luxembourg (p. 205)
Rue Monsieur-le-Prince (p. 214)
Rue Visconti (p. 196)
St-Germain-des-Prés (p. 184)
St-Sulpice (p. 185)
20 rue Jacob (p. 196)
27 rue de Fleurus (p. 196, 197)

7TH ARR. (EIFFEL TOWER/ MUSÉE D'ORSAY)
Champ de Mars (p. 176)
Eglise du Dôme/Napoléon's Tomb
    (p. 171)
Hôtel des Invalides (p. 170)
Les Egouts (p. 215)
Musée de l'Armée (p. 170)
Musée des Plans-Reliefs (p. 171)
✪ Musée d'Orsay (p. 174)
Musée Rodin (p. 182)
Palais Bourbon/Assemblée Nationale
    (p. 189)
✪ Tour Eiffel (p. 176)

13TH ARR. (GARE D'AUSTERLITZ)
Bibliothèque Nationale de France
    (p. 187)
Manufacture Nationale des Gobelins
    (p. 201)

14TH ARR. (MONTPARNASSE)
Cimetière du Montparnasse (p. 210)
Les Catacombs (p. 215)
Tour Montparnasse (p. 197)

15TH ARR. (GARE MONTPARNASSE/INSTITUT PASTEUR)
Musée Bourdelle (p. 198)
La Grande Arche de La Défense
    (p. 188)
Musée National de Céramique de
    Sèvres (p. 201)

The Major Attractions

American Cathedral of
  of the Holy Trinity **10**
Arc de Triomphe **2**
Arènes de Lutèce **44**
Basilique du Sacré-Coeur **22**
Basilique St-Denis **22**
Bibliothèque Nationale
  de France **42**
Cathédrale Notre-Dame **51**
Centre Pompidou **27**
Cimetière du Montmartre **22**
Cimetière de Passy **4**
Cimetière de St-Vincent **22**
Cimetière du
  Montparnasse **21**
Cimetière du Père-Lachaise **23**
Conciergerie **53**
Forum des Halles **26**
Galerie National du
  Jeu de Paume **14**

Grand Palais **11**
Grande Arche de
  La Défense **2**
Hôtel des Invalides
  (Napoléon's Tomb) **19**
Hôtel de Ville **31**
Institut de France **34**
Jardin des Plantes **43**
Jardin des Tuileries **15**
Jardin du Luxembourg **38**
Le Madeleine **13**
Les Catacombs **39**
Les Egouts **8**
Maison de Balzac **6**
Maison de Victor Hugo **30**
Mosquée de Paris **41**
Musée Carnavalet **29**
Musée de Cluny **48**
Musée de l'Orangerie **16**
Musée d'Orsay **17**

Musée du Louvre **33**
Musée Jacquemart-André **3**
Musée Marmottan–
  Claude Monet **5**
Musée National
  Eugène Delacroix **36**
Musée Picasso **28**
Musée Rodin **20**

Palais Bourbon/
Assemblée Nationale **18**
Palais Royal **24**
Panthéon **45**
Petit Palais **12**
Place de l'Alma **9**
Sorbonne **47**
Sainte-Chapelle **52**

St-Etienne-du-Mont **46**
St-Eustache **25**
St-Germain l'Auxerrois **32**
St-Germain-des-Prés **35**
St-Julien-le-Pauvre **50**
St-Séverin **49**
St-Sulpice **37**
Tour Eiffel **7**
Val-de-Grâce **40**

0   .28 Miles
0   .45 Kilometers

The Louvre, Tuileries & Les Halles (1er & 4e)

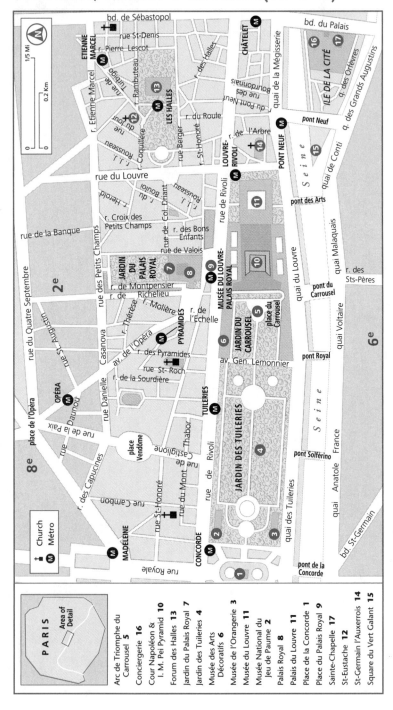

Arc de Triomphe du Carrousel 5
Conciergerie 16
Cour Napoléon & I. M. Pei Pyramid 10
Forum des Halles 13
Jardin du Palais Royal 7
Jardin des Tuileries 4
Musée des Arts Décoratifs 6
Musée de l'Orangerie 3
Musée du Louvre 11
Musée National du Jeu de Paume 2
Palais Royal 8
Palais du Louvre 11
Place de la Concorde 1
Place du Palais Royal 9
Sainte-Chapelle 17
St-Eustache 12
St-Germain l'Auxerrois 14
Square du Vert Galant 15

The Opéra, Bourse & Grands Boulevards (2e, 9e & 10e)

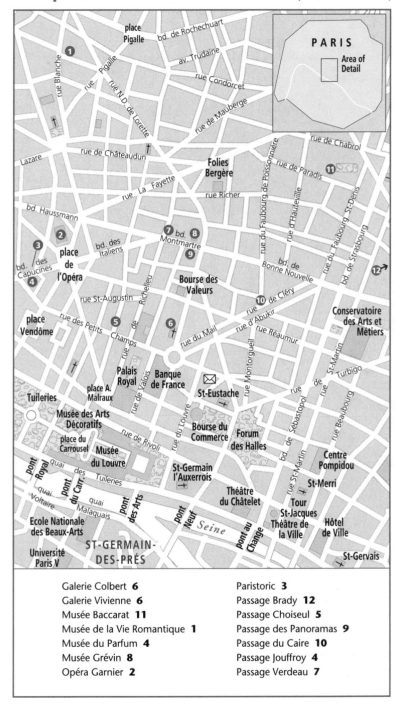

Galerie Colbert **6**
Galerie Vivienne **6**
Musée Baccarat **11**
Musée de la Vie Romantique **1**
Musée du Parfum **4**
Musée Grévin **8**
Opéra Garnier **2**

Paristoric **3**
Passage Brady **12**
Passage Choiseul **5**
Passage des Panoramas **9**
Passage du Caire **10**
Passage Jouffroy **4**
Passage Verdeau **7**

The Marais, Beaubourg & Bastille (3e, 4e & 11e)

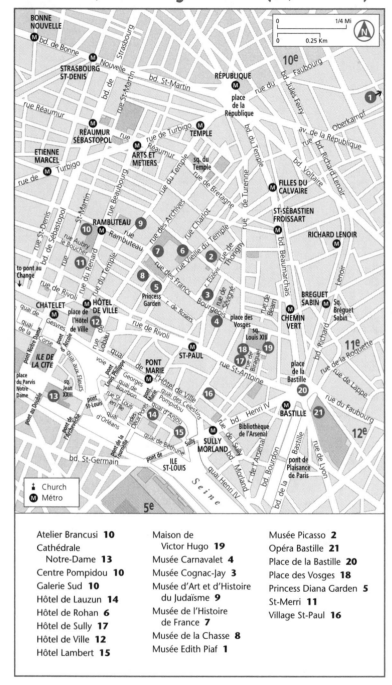

Atelier Brancusi **10**
Cathédrale
  Notre-Dame **13**
Centre Pompidou **10**
Galerie Sud **10**
Hôtel de Lauzun **14**
Hôtel de Rohan **6**
Hôtel de Sully **17**
Hôtel de Ville **12**
Hôtel Lambert **15**

Maison de
  Victor Hugo **19**
Musée Carnavalet **4**
Musée Cognac-Jay **3**
Musée d'Art et d'Histoire
  du Judaïsme **9**
Musée de l'Histoire
  de France **7**
Musée de la Chasse **8**
Musée Edith Piaf **1**

Musée Picasso **2**
Opéra Bastille **21**
Place de la Bastille **20**
Place des Vosges **18**
Princess Diana Garden **5**
St-Merri **11**
Village St-Paul **16**

The Latin Quarter & St-Germain-des-Prés (5e, 6e & 7e)

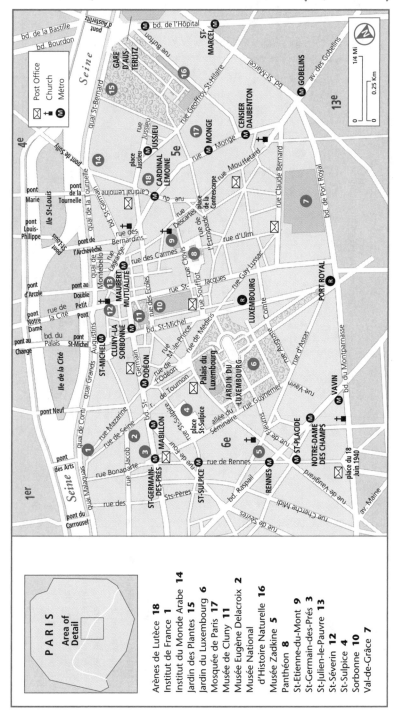

Arènes de Lutèce **18**
Institut de France **1**
Institut du Monde Arabe **14**
Jardin des Plantes **15**
Jardin du Luxembourg **6**
Mosquée de Paris **17**
Musée de Cluny **11**
Musée Eugène Delacroix **2**
Musée National
  d'Histoire Naturelle **16**
Musée Zadkine **5**
Panthéon **8**
St-Etienne-du-Mont **9**
St-Germain-des-Prés **3**
St-Julien-le-Pauvre **13**
St-Séverin **12**
St-Sulpice **4**
Sorbonne **10**
Val-de-Grâce **7**

163

The Eiffel Tower & Invalides (7e)

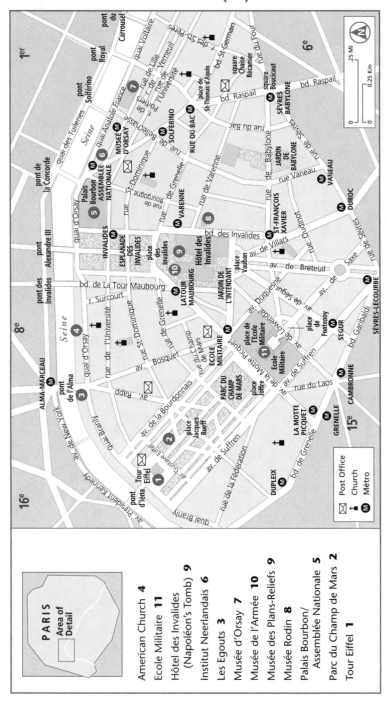

PARIS
Area of
Detail

American Church **4**

Ecole Militaire **11**

Hôtel des Invalides
(Napoléon's Tomb) **9**

Institut Neerlandais **6**

Les Egouts **3**

Musée d'Orsay **7**

Musée de l'Armée **10**

Musée des Plans-Reliefs **9**

Musée Rodin **8**

Palais Bourbon/
Assemblée Nationale **5**

Parc du Champ de Mars **2**

Tour Eiffel **1**

☒ Post Office

✝■ Church

Ⓜ Métro

The Champs-Elysées (8e & 17e)

Church ⛪
Métro Ⓜ
Railway —

0 — 1/4 Mi
0 — 0.25 Km

Area of Detail

PARIS

Arc de Triomphe **5**
American Cathedral
  of the Holy Trinity **7**
Grand Palais **11**
Jardins des Tuileries **16**
La Madeleine **14**
Musée Cernuschi **1**
Musée d'Art Moderne **8**
Musée Jacquemart-
  André **4**

Musée Nissim de
  Camondo **2**
Office de Tourisme **6**
Palais de l'Elysée **13**
Parc Monceau **3**
Petit Palais **12**
Place de la Concorde **15**
Place de l'Alma **9**
Théâtres des
  Champs-Elysées **10**

Trocadéro & the 16e

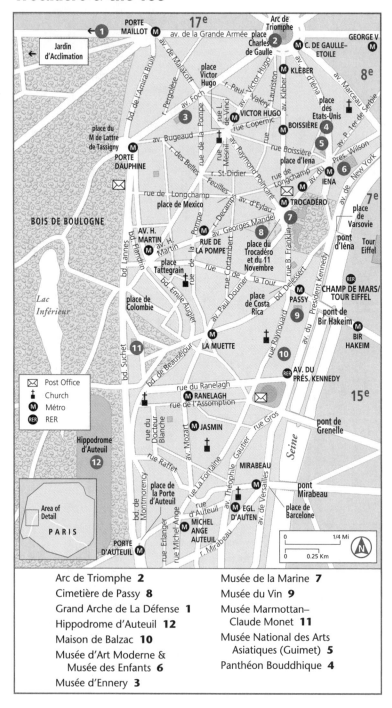

Arc de Triomphe **2**
Cimetière de Passy **8**
Grand Arche de La Défense **1**
Hippodrome d'Auteuil **12**
Maison de Balzac **10**
Musée d'Art Moderne & Musée des Enfants **6**
Musée d'Ennery **3**

Musée de la Marine **7**
Musée du Vin **9**
Musée Marmottan–Claude Monet **11**
Musée National des Arts Asiatiques (Guimet) **5**
Panthéon Bouddhique **4**

2 The Top Attractions: From the Arc de Triomphe to the Tour Eiffel

✪ **Arc de Triomphe.** Place Charles de Gaulle–Etoile, 8e. ☎ **01-55-37-73-77.** Admission 40F ($6.40) adults, 25F ($4) ages 12–25; children 11 and under free. Apr–Sept daily 9:30am–11pm; Oct–Mar daily 10am–10:30pm. Métro: Charles de Gaulle–Etoile.

At the western end of the Champs-Elysées, the Arc de Triomphe suggests one of those ancient Roman arches, only it's larger. Actually, it's the biggest triumphal arch in the world, about 163 feet high and 147 feet wide. To reach it, *don't try to cross the square,* Paris's busiest traffic hub. With a dozen streets radiating from the "Star," the round-about has been called by one writer "vehicular roulette with more balls than numbers" (death is certain!). Take the underground passage and live a little longer.

Commissioned by Napoléon in 1806 to commemorate the victories of his Grand Armée, the arch wasn't ready for the entrance of his new empress, Marie-Louise, in 1810 (he'd divorced Joséphine because she couldn't provide him an heir). It served its ceremonial purpose anyway but wasn't completed until 1836, under the reign of Louis-Philippe. Four years later, Napoléon's remains, brought from his grave on St. Helena, passed under the arch on their journey to his tomb at the Hôtel des Invalides. Since that time it has become the focal point for state funerals. It's also the site of the permanent tomb of the unknown soldier, in whose honor an eternal flame is kept burning.

The greatest state funeral was Victor Hugo's in 1885; his coffin was placed under the arch, and much of Paris turned out to pay tribute. Another notable funeral was in 1929 for Ferdinand Foch, supreme commander of the Allied forces in World War I. The arch has been the centerpiece of some of France's proudest moments and some of its most humiliating defeats, notably those of 1871 and 1940. The memory of German troops marching under the arch that had come to symbolize France's glory is still painful to the French. Who can forget the 1940 newsreel of the Frenchman standing on the Champs-Elysées weeping as the Nazi stormtroopers goose-stepped through Paris? The arch's happiest moment occurred in 1944, when the liberation of Paris parade passed beneath it. That same year, Eisenhower paid a visit to the tomb of the unknown soldier, a new tradition among leaders of state and important figures. After Charles de Gaulle's death, the French government (despite protests from anti-Gaullists) voted to change the name of this site from place de l'Etoile to place Charles de Gaulle. Nowadays it's often known as place Charles de Gaulle–Etoile.

Of the sculptures on the monument, the best known is Rude's *Marseillaise,* a.k.a. *The Departure of the Volunteers.* J. P. Cortot's *Triumph of Napoléon in 1810,* and Etex's *Resistance of 1814* and *Peace of 1815* also adorn the facade. The monument is engraved with the names of hundreds of generals (those underlined died in battle) who commanded French troops in Napoleonic victories.

You can take an elevator or climb the stairway to the top, where there's an exhibition hall with lithographs and photos depicting the arch throughout its history. From the observation deck, you have the finest view of the Champs-Elysées and landmarks like the Louvre, the Eiffel Tower, Sacré-Coeur, and La Défense.

✪ **Basilique du Sacré-Coeur.** Place St-Pierre, 18e. ☎ **01-53-41-89-00.** www. paris.org/Monuments/Sacre-Coeur. Admission free to basilica; joint ticket to dome and crypt 30F ($4.80) adults, 16F ($2.55) students/children. Apr–Sept daily 9am–7pm; Oct–Mar daily 9am–6pm. Métro: Abbesses; then take the elevator to the surface and follow the signs to the *funiculaire,* which goes up to the church for the price of a Métro ticket.

Sacré-Coeur is one of Paris's most characteristic landmarks and has been the subject of much controversy. One Parisian called it "a lunatic's confectionery dream." An offended

Zola declared it "the basilica of the ridiculous." Sacré-Coeur has had warm supporters as well, including poet Max Jacob and artist Maurice Utrillo. Utrillo never tired of drawing and painting it, and he and Jacob came here regularly to pray. Atop the *butte* (hill) in Montmartre, its multiple gleaming white domes and campanile (bell tower) tower over Paris like a 12th-century Byzantine church. But it's not that old. After France's 1870 defeat by the Prussians, the basilica was planned as a votive offering to cure France's misfortunes. Rich and poor alike contributed money to build it. Construction began in 1876, and though the church wasn't consecrated until 1919, perpetual prayers of adoration have been made here day and night since 1885. The interior is brilliantly decorated with mosaics: Look for the striking Christ on the ceiling and the mural of his Passion at the back of the altar. The stained-glass windows were shattered during the struggle for Paris in 1944 but have been well replaced. The crypt contains a relic of what some of the devout believe is Christ's sacred heart—hence, the name of the church.

On a clear day you can see for 35 miles from the dome. You can also walk around the church's inner dome, peering down like a pigeon (one is likely to be keeping you company).

✪ **Cathédrale de Notre-Dame.** 6 place du Parvis Notre-Dame, 4e. ☎ **01-42-34-56-10.** www.paris.org/Monuments/NDame. Admission free to cathedral; towers and crypt 35F ($5.60) adults, 23F ($3.70) ages 12–25/over 60, children under 12 free; museum and treasury 15F ($2.40) adults, 10F ($1.60) ages 12–25/over 60, children under 12 free. Cathedral daily 8am–6:45pm year-round. Towers and crypt Apr–Sept daily 9:30am–6pm, Oct–Mar daily 10am–5:15pm. Museum Wed and Sat–Sun 2:30–5pm. Treasury Mon–Sat 9:30–11:30am and 1–5:45pm. Métro: Cité or St-Michel. RER: St-Michel.

Notre-Dame is the heart of Paris and even of the country itself: Distances from the city to all parts of France are calculated from a spot at the far end of place du Parvis, in front of the cathedral, where a circular bronze plaque marks **Kilomètre Zéro.**

The cathedral's setting on the banks of the Seine has always been memorable. Founded in the 12th century by Maurice de Sully, bishop of Paris, Notre-Dame has grown and grown over the years, changing as Paris has changed, often falling victim to whims of decorative taste. Its famous flying buttresses (the external side supports, giving the massive interior a sense of weightlessness) were rebuilt in 1330. Though many disagree, we feel Notre-Dame is more interesting outside than in, and you'll want to walk all around it to fully appreciate this "vast symphony of stone." Better yet, cross over the pont au Double to the Left Bank and view it from the quay.

The histories of Paris and Notre-Dame are inseparable. Many prayed here before going off to fight in the Crusades. "Our Lady of Paris" wasn't spared by the revolutionaries, who destroyed the Galerie des Rois and converted the building into a secular temple. Later, Napoléon crowned himself emperor here, yanking the crown out of Pius VII's hands and placing it on his own head before crowning his Joséphine empress (see David's *Coronation of Napoléon* in the Louvre). But carelessness, vandalism, embellishments, and wars of religion had already demolished much of the previously existing structure.

Exploring Ile de la Cité

After visiting Notre-Dame, try to take some time to explore Ile de la Cité and its other main attractions, the infamous **Conciergerie** (see page 187) and the lovely **Sainte-Chapelle** (see page 175), best seen in radiant sunlight.

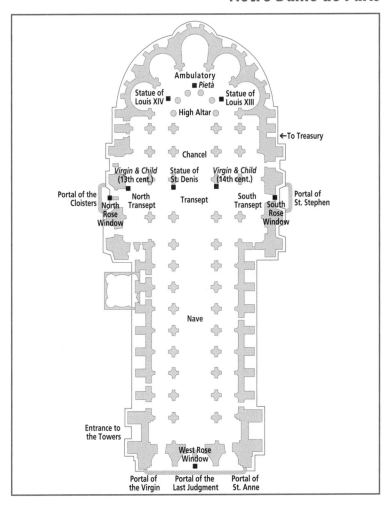

The cathedral was once scheduled for demolition, but, because of the popularity of Victor Hugo's *Hunchback of Notre-Dame* and the revival of interest in the Gothic period, a movement mushroomed to restore the cathedral to its original glory. The task was completed under Viollet-le-Duc, an architectural genius. The houses of old Paris used to crowd in on Notre-Dame, but during his redesigning of the city Baron Haussmann ordered them torn down to show the cathedral to its best advantage from the parvis. This is the best vantage for seeing the three sculpted 13th-century portals.

On the left, the **Portal of the Virgin** depicts the signs of the zodiac and the coronation of the Virgin, an association found in dozens of medieval churches. The restored central **Portal of the Last Judgment** depicts three levels: The first shows Vices and Virtues; the second, Christ and his Apostles; and above that, Christ in triumph after the Resurrection. The portal is a close illustration of the Gospel according to Matthew. Over it is the remarkable **west rose window,** 31 feet wide, forming a showcase for a statue of the Virgin and Child. On the far right is the **Portal of St. Anne,** depicting scenes like the Virgin enthroned with Child; it's Notre-Dame's best preserved and the most perfect piece of sculpture. Equally interesting (though often missed) is the **Portal of the Cloisters** (around on the left), with its dour-faced 13th-century Virgin, a survivor among the figures that originally adorned the facade. (Alas, the Child she's holding has been decapitated.) Finally, on the Seine side of Notre-Dame, the **Portal of St. Stephen** traces that saint's martyrdom.

If possible, come to see Notre-Dame at sunset. Inside, of the three giant medallions warming the austere cathedral, the **north rose window** in the transept, from the mid-13th century, is best. The main body of the church is typically Gothic, with slender, graceful columns. In the **choir,** a stone-carved screen from the early 14th century depicts such biblical scenes as the Last Supper. Near the altar stands the 14th-century *Virgin and Child,* highly venerated among Paris's faithful. In the **treasury** are displayed vestments and gold objects, including crowns. Exhibited are a cross presented to Haile Selassie, former emperor of Ethiopia, and a reliquary given by Napoléon. Notre-Dame is especially proud of its relic of the True Cross and the Crown of Thorns.

Finally, to visit those grimy **gargoyles** immortalized by Hugo, you have to scale steps leading to the twin square **towers** rising to a height of 225 feet. Once there, you can closely inspect the devils (some giving you the raspberry), hobgoblins, and birds of prey. Look carefully and you may see the hunchback Quasimodo with Esmerelda.

Approached through a garden behind Notre-Dame is the **Mémorial des Martyrs Français de la Déportation de 1945 (Deportation Memorial),** jutting out on the very tip of Ile de la Cité. Here birds chirp and the Seine flows gently by, but the memories are far from pleasant. The memorial commemorates the French citizens who were deported to concentration camps like Auschwitz and Buchenwald during World War II. Carved into stone are these blood-red words (in French): "Forgive, but don't forget." The memorial is open Monday to Friday 8:30am to 9:45pm and Saturday and Sunday 9am to 9:45pm. Admission is free.

Hôtel des Invalides (Napoléon's Tomb). Place des Invalides, 7e. ☎ **01-44-42-37-72.** Admission to Musée de l'Armée, Napoléon's Tomb, and Musée des Plans-Reliefs 38F ($6.10) adults, 28F ($4.50) ages 12–18; children 11 and under free. Oct–Mar daily 10am–5pm; Apr–May and Sept daily 10am–6pm; June–Aug daily 10am–7pm. Closed Jan 1, May 1, Nov 1, and Dec 25. Métro: Latour-Maubourg, Varenne, or Invalides.

In 1670, the Sun King decided to build this "hotel" to house disabled soldiers. It wasn't an entirely benevolent gesture, however, since the men had been injured, crippled, or blinded while fighting his battles. When the building was finally completed (Louis XIV had long been dead), a gilded dome by Jules Hardouin-Mansart crowned it and its corridors stretched for miles. The best way to approach the Invalides is by crossing over the Right Bank via the early-1900s pont Alexander-III and entering the cobblestone forecourt, where a display of massive cannons makes a formidable welcome.

Before rushing on to Napoléon's Tomb, you may want to visit the world's greatest military museum, the **Musée de l'Armée.** In 1794, a French inspector started collecting weapons, uniforms, and equipment, and with the accumulation of war material over the centuries, the museum has become a horrifying documentary of man's self-destruction. Viking swords, Burgundian battle axes, 14th-century blunderbusses, Balkan khandjars, American Browning machine guns, war pitchforks, salamander-engraved Renaissance serpentines, a 1528 Griffon, musketoons, grenadiers . . . if it can kill, it's enshrined here. As a sardonic touch, there's even the wooden leg of General Daumesnil, the governor of Vincennes who lost his leg in the battle of Wagram. Oblivious to the irony of the act, the Nazis looted the place in 1940.

Among the outstanding acquisitions are suits of armor worn by the kings and dignitaries of France, including Louis XIV, the best of which are in the new Arsenal. The

The Little Corporal's Little Corporal

Legends have abounded that some of Napoléon's body parts went missing when he was reburied at the Invalides, notably his penis and heart. According to scholars, the two doctors who dissected the emperor placed all his body parts in an urn positioned between his legs. However, one wealthy gentleman in Connecticut frequently exhibits a penis preserved in alcohol, claiming it was once attached to the emperor.

most famous one, the "armor suit of the lion," was made for François I. Henri II ordered his suit engraved with the monogram of his mistress, Diane de Poitiers, and (perhaps reluctantly) that of his wife, Catherine de Médicis. Particularly fine are the showcases of swords and the World War I mementos, including those of American and Canadian soldiers—seek out the Armistice Bugle, which sounded the cease-fire on November 7, 1918, before the general cease-fire on November 11, 1918. The west wing's Salle Orientale shows arms of the Eastern world, including Asia and the Mideast Muslim countries, from the 16th to the 19th century. Turkish armor (look for Bajazet's helmet) and weaponry and Chinese and Japanese armor and swords are on display.

And then there's that little Corsican who became France's greatest soldier. Here you can see the plaster death mask Antommarchi made of him, as well as an oil by Delaroche, painted at the time of Napoléon's first banishment (April 1814) and depicting him as he probably looked, paunch and all. The First Empire exhibit displays Napoléon's field bed with his tent; in the room devoted to the Restoration, the 100 Days, and Waterloo, you can see his bedroom as it was at the time of his death on St. Helena. On the more personal side, you can view stuffed Vizir, a horse he owned, as well as a saddle he used mainly for state ceremonies. The Turenne Salon contains other souvenirs, like the hat Napoléon wore at Eylau, the sword from his Austerlitz victory, and his "Flag of Farewell," which he kissed before departing for Elba.

You can gain access to the **Musée des Plans-Reliefs** through the west wing. This collection shows French towns and monuments done in scale models (the model of Strasbourg fills an entire room) as well as models of military fortifications since the days of the great Vauban.

A walk across the Cour d'Honneur (Court of Honor) delivers you to the **Eglise du Dôme,** designed by Hardouin-Mansart for Louis XIV. The great architect began work on the church in 1677, though he died before its completion. The dome is the second-tallest monument in Paris (the Tour Eiffel is the tallest, of course). The hearse used at the emperor's funeral on May 9, 1821, is in the Napoléon Chapel.

To accommodate **Napoléon's tomb,** the architect Visconti had to redesign the church's high altar in 1842. First buried on St. Helena, Napoléon's remains were exumed and brought to Paris in 1840 on the orders of Louis-Philippe, who demanded the English return the emperor to French soil. The triumphal funeral procession passed beneath the Arc de Triomphe, down the Champs-Elysées, and to the Invalides, as snow swirled through the air. The remains were locked inside six coffins in this tomb made of red Finnish porphyry, with a green granite base. Surrounding it are a dozen amazonlike figures representing Napoléon's victories. Almost lampooning the smallness of the man, everything is done on a gargantuan scale. In his coronation robes, the statue of Napoléon stands 8½ feet high. The grave of the "King of Rome," his son by second wife Marie-Louise, lies at his feet. Napoléon's Tomb is surrounded by those of his brother, Joseph Bonaparte; the great Vauban, who built many of France's fortifications; World War I Allied commander Foch; and the vicomte de Turenne, the republic's first grenadier (actually, only his heart is entombed here).

✪ **Musée du Louvre.** 34–36 quai du Louvre, 1er. Main entrance in the glass pyramid, Cour Napoléon. ☎ **01-40-20-53-17** (01-40-20-51-51 recorded message, 08-03-80-88-03 advance credit-card sales). www.louvre.fr. Admission 45F ($7.20) before 3pm, 26F ($4.15) after 3pm and on Sun; free for age 17 and under; free first Sun of every month. Mon and Wed 9am–9:45pm (Mon short tour only), Thurs–Sun 9am–6pm. (Parts of the museum begin to close at 5:30pm.) 1^1/$_2$-hour English-language tours leave Mon and Wed–Sat various times of the day for 17F ($2.70); children 12 and under free with museum ticket. Métro: Palais Royal–Musée du Louvre.

The Louvre is the world's largest palace and largest museum. As a palace, it leaves us cold, except for its old section, the **Cour Carrée.** As a museum, it's one of the greatest art collections ever. To enter, you pass through I. M. Pei's controversial 71-foot **glass pyramid**—a startling though effective contrast of ultramodern against the palace's classical lines. Commissioned by the late president François Mitterrand and completed in 1989, it allows sunlight to shine on an underground reception area with a complex of shops and restaurants. Automatic ticket machines help relieve the long lines of yesteryear.

People on one of those "Paris-in-a-day" tours try to break track records to get a glimpse of the Louvre's two most famous ladies: the beguiling **Mona Lisa** and the armless **Venus de Milo.** (The scene at the *Mona Lisa* is a circus—as the staff looks idly on, viewers push and shove in front of her bulletproof glass and forbidden flashbulbs pop all over. Yet still she smiles that smile, at peace among the fracas.) The herd then dashes on a 5-minute stampede in pursuit of **Winged Victory,** the headless statue discovered at Samothrace and dating from about 200 B.C. In defiance of the assembly-line theory of art, we head instead for David's **Coronation of Napoléon,** showing Napoléon poised with the crown aloft as Joséphine kneels before him, just across from his **Portrait of Madame Récamier,** depicting Napoléon's opponent at age 23; she reclines on her sofa agelessly in the style of classical antiquity.

Then a big question looms: Which of the rest of the 30,000 works on display would you like to see?

Between the Seine and rue de Rivoli, the Palais du Louvre suffers from an embarrassment of riches, stretching for almost half a mile. In the days of Charles V, it was a fortress, but François I, a patron of Leonardo da Vinci, had it torn down and rebuilt as a royal residence. Less than a month after Marie Antoinette's head and body parted company, the Revolutionary Committee decided the king's collection of paintings and sculpture should be opened to the public. At the lowest point in its history, in the 18th century, the Louvre was home for anybody who wanted to set up housekeeping there. Laundry hung out the windows, corners were literally pigpens, and families built fires to cook their meals during the long winters. Napoléon ended all that, chasing out the squatters and restoring the palace. In fact, he chose the Louvre as the site of his wedding to Marie-Louise.

So where did all these paintings come from? The kings of France, notably François I and Louis XIV, acquired many of them, and others were willed to or purchased by the state. Many contributed by Napoléon were taken from reluctant donors: The church was one especially heavy and unwilling giver. Much of Napoléon's plunder had to be returned, though France hasn't yet seen its way clear to giving back all the booty.

The collections are divided into seven departments: **Egyptian Antiquities; Oriental Antiquities; Greek, Etruscan, and Roman Antiquities; Sculpture; Painting; Decorative Arts;** and **Graphic Arts.** A number of galleries, devoted to Italian paintings, Roman glass and bronzes, Oriental antiquities, and Egyptian antiquities, were opened in 1997 and 1998. If you don't have to do Paris in a day, perhaps you can come here several times, concentrating on different collections or schools of painting. Those with little time should go on one of the **guided tours** in English.

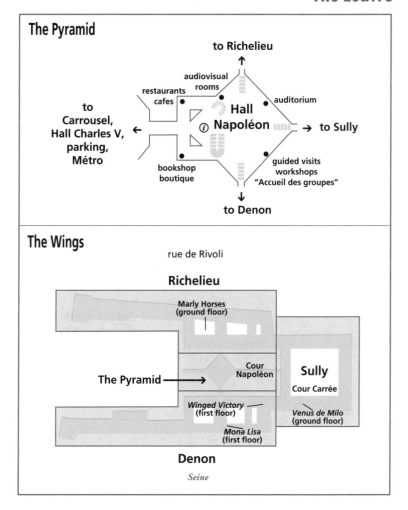

Acquired by François I to hang above his bathtub, Leonardo's much-traveled **La Gioconda** (**Mona Lisa**) has been the source of legend for centuries. Note the guard and bulletproof glass: The world's most famous painting was stolen in the summer of 1911 and found in Florence in the winter of 1913. At first, both the poet Guillaume Apollinaire and Picasso were suspected, but it was discovered in the possession of a former Louvre employee, who'd apparently carried it out under his overcoat. Less well known (but to us even more enchanting) are Leonardo's **Virgin and Child with St. Anne** and the **Virgin of the Rocks**.

After paying your respects to the "Smiling One," allow time to see some French works stretching from the Richelieu wing through the entire **Sully wing** and even overflowing into the **Denon wing.** It's all here: Watteau's **Gilles** with the mysterious boy in a clown suit staring at you; Fragonard's and Boucher's rococo renderings of the aristocracy; and the greatest masterpieces of David, including his stellar 1785 **The Oath of the Horatii** and the vast and vivid **Coronation of Napoléon.** Only Florence's Uffizi rivals the Denon wing for its Italian Renaissance collection—everything from

---

Some Louvre Tips

Long waiting lines outside the Louvre's pyramid entrance are notorious, but there are some tricks for avoiding them.

- Order tickets by phone at ☎ **08-03-80-88-03,** have them charged to your Visa or MasterCard, then pick them up at any FNAC store (see chapter 8). This gives you direct entry through the Passage Richelieu, 93 rue de Rivoli.
- Enter via the underground shopping mall, the Carrousel du Louvre, at 99 rue de Rivoli.
- Enter directly from the Palais Royal–Musée du Louvre Métro station.
- Buy Le Pass Musée et Monuments (Museum and Monuments Pass) allowing direct entry through the priority entrance at the Passage Richelieu, 93 rue de Rivoli. For details on the pass, see "The Major Museums," below.

Raphael's *Portrait of Balthazar Castiglione* to Titian's *Man with a Glove.* Veronese's gigantic *Wedding Feast at Cana,* a romp of Viennese high society in the 1500s, occupies an entire wall (that's Paolo himself playing the cello).

Of the Greek and Roman antiquities, the most notable collections, aside from the *Venus de Milo* and *Winged Victory,* are fragments of a **Parthenon frieze** (in the Denon wing). In Renaissance sculpture, you'll see Michelangelo's *Esclaves* (*Slaves*), originally intended for the tomb of Julius II but sold into other bondage. The Denon wing houses masterpieces like Ingres's *The Turkish Bath;* the **Botticelli frescoes** from the Villa Lemmi; Raphael's *La Belle Jardinière;* and Titian's *Open Air Concert.* The Sully wing is also filled with old masters, like Boucher's *Diana Resting After Her Bath* and Fragonard's *Bathers.*

The **Richelieu wing,** reopened in 1993 after decaying empty for years, was expanded to add some 230,000 square feet of exhibition space. It houses northern European and French paintings, along with decorative arts, French sculpture, Oriental antiquities (a rich collection of Islamic art), and the Napoléon III salons. One of its galleries displays 21 works Rubens painted in a space of only 2 years for Marie de Médicis's Palais de Luxembourg. The masterpieces here include Dürer's *Self-Portrait,* Van Dyck's *Portrait of Charles I of England,* and Holbein the Younger's *Portrait of Erasmus of Rotterdam.*

When you get tired, consider a pick-me-up at **Café Marly** in the Cour Napoléon (see chapter 5). This grandiose cafe overlooks the glass pyramid and offers coffees, pastries (by Paris's most legendary pastry-maker, Lenôtre), salads, sandwiches, and simple platters.

✪ **Musée d'Orsay.** 1 rue de Bellechasse or 62 rue de Lille, 7e. ☎ **01-40-49-48-14.** www.musee-orsay.fr. Admission 40F ($6.40) adults, 30F ($4.80) ages 18–24/seniors; children 17 and under free. Tues–Wed and Fri–Sat 10am–6pm, Thurs 10am–9:45pm, Sun 9am–6pm (June 20–Sept 20 opens 9am). Métro: Solférino. RER: Musée d'Orsay.

Architects created one of the world's greatest museums from a defunct rail station, the neoclassical Gare d'Orsay, across the Seine from the Louvre and the Tuileries. Don't skip the Louvre, of course, but come here even if you have to miss all the other art museums in town. The Orsay boasts an astounding collection devoted to the watershed years 1848 to 1914, with a treasure trove by the big names plus all the lesser known groups (the symbolists, pointillists, nabis, realists, and late romantics). The

80 galleries also include belle-époque furniture, photographs, objets d'art, and architectural models. There's even a cinema showing classic films.

A monument to the Industrial Revolution, the Orsay is covered by an arching glass roof allowing in floods of light. It displays works ranging from the creations of academic and historic painters like Ingres to Romanticists like Delacroix, to neo-realists like Courbet and Daumier. The impressionists and post-impressionists, including Manet, Monet, Cézanne, van Gogh, and Renoir, share space with the fauves, Matisse, the cubists, and the expressionists in a setting once used by Orson Welles to film a nightmarish scene in *The Trial,* based on Kafka's unfinished novel. You'll find Millet's sunny wheat fields, Barbizon landscapes, Corot's mists, and particolored Tahitian Gauguins all in the same hall.

But it's the impressionists who keep the crowds lining up. When the nose-in-the-air Louvre chose not to display their works, a great rival was born. Led by Manet, Renoir, and Monet, the impressionists shunned ecclesiastical and mythological set pieces for a light-bathed Seine, faint figures strolling in the Tuileries, pale-faced women in hazy bars, and even vulgar rail stations like the Gare St-Lazare. And the impressionists were the first to paint that most characteristic feature of Parisian life: the sidewalk cafe, especially in the artists' quarter of Montmartre.

The most famous painting from this era is Manet's 1863 *Déjeuner sur l'herbe* (**Picnic on the Grass**), whose forest setting with a nude woman and two fully clothed men sent shock waves through respectable society when it was first exhibited. Two years later, Manet's *Olympia* created another scandal by depicting a woman lounging on her bed and wearing nothing but a flower in her hair and high-heeled shoes; she's attended by an African maid in the background. Zola called Manet "a man among eunuchs."

One of Renoir's most joyous paintings is also here: the *Moulin de la Galette* (1876). Degas is represented by his paintings of racehorses and dancers; his 1876 cafe scene, *Absinthe,* remains one of his most reproduced works. Paris-born Monet was fascinated by the effect changing light had on Rouen Cathedral, and its stone bubbles to life in a series of five paintings—our favorite is *Rouen Cathedral: Full Sunlight.* Another celebrated work is by an American, Whistler's *Arrangement in Grey and Black: Portrait of the Painter's Mother,* better known as *Whistler's Mother.* It's said this painting heralded modern art, though many critics denounced it at the time as "Whistler's Dead Mother" because of its funereal overtones. Whistler was content to claim he'd made "Mummy just as nice as possible."

✪ **Sainte-Chapelle.** Palais de Justice, 4 bd. du Palais, 4e. ☎ **01-53-73-78-50.** Admission 35F ($5.60) adults, 23F ($3.70) students/ages 18–25; ages 17 and under free. Apr–Sept daily 9:30am–6:30pm; Oct–Mar daily 10am–5pm. Métro: Cité, St-Michel, or Châtelet–Les Halles. RER: St-Michel.

Countless writers have called this tiny chapel a jewel box. Yet that hardly suffices. Nor will it do to call it "a light show." Go when the sun is shining and you'll need no one else's words to describe the remarkable effects of natural light on Sainte-Chapelle. You approach the church through the Cour de la Sainte-Chapelle of the Palais de Justice. If it weren't for the chapel's 247-foot spire, the law courts here would almost swallow it up.

Begun in 1246, the bilevel chapel was built to house relics of the True Cross, including the Crown of Thorns acquired by St. Louis (the Crusader king, Louis IX) from the emperor of Constantinople. (In those days, cathedrals throughout Europe were busy acquiring relics for their treasuries, regardless of their authenticity. It was a seller's, perhaps a sucker's, market.) Louis IX is said to have paid heavily for his relics, raising the money through unscrupulous means. He died of the plague on a crusade and was canonized in 1297.

You enter through the *chapelle basse* (**lower chapel**), used by the palace servants; its supported by flying buttresses and ornamented with fleur-de-lis designs. The king and his courtiers used the *chapelle haute* (**upper chapel**), one of the greatest achievements of Gothic art; you reach it by ascending a narrow spiral staircase. Viewed on a bright day, the 15 stained-glass windows up there seem to glow with Chartres blue and with reds that have inspired the saying "wine the color of Sainte-Chapelle's windows." The walls consist almost entirely of the glass (612 square meters of it), which had to be removed for safekeeping during the Revolution and again during both world wars. In their Old and New Testament designs are embodied the hopes and dreams (and the pretensions) of the kings who ordered their construction. The 1,134 scenes depict the Christian story from the Garden of Eden through the Apocalypse, and you read them from bottom to top and from left to right. The great rose window depicts the Apocalypse.

Sainte-Chapelle stages **concerts** most nights in summer, with tickets at 120F to 150F ($19.20 to $24). Call ☎ **01-42-77-65-65** for more details (daily 11am to 6pm).

✪ **Tour Eiffel.** Champ de Mars, 7e. ☎ **01-44-11-23-23.** www.tour-eiffel.fr. Admission to first landing 22F ($3.50), second landing 44F ($7.05), third landing 62F ($9.90). Stairs to second floor 18F ($2.90). Sept–May daily 9:30am–11pm; June–Aug daily 9am–midnight. Fall and winter, stairs open only to 6:30pm. Métro: Trocadéro, Ecole Militaire, or Bir-Hakeim. RER: Champ de Mars–Tour Eiffel.

This is without doubt the single most recognizable structure in the world. Weighing 7,000 tons but exerting about the same pressure on the ground as an average-size person sitting in a chair, the wrought-iron tower wasn't meant to be permanent. It was built by Gustave-Alexandre Eiffel, the French engineer whose fame rested mainly on his iron bridges, to add flair to the 1889 Universal Exhibition. (Eiffel also designed the framework for the Statue of Liberty.) Praised by some and denounced by others (some called it a "giraffe," the "world's greatest lamppost," or the "iron monster"), the tower created as much controversy in the 1880s as I. M. Pei's glass pyramid at the Louvre did in the 1980s. What saved it from demolition in the early 1890s was the advent of radio—as the tallest structure in Europe at the time, it made a perfect spot to place a radio antenna (now a TV antenna).

The tower, including its 55-foot TV antenna, is 1,056 feet high. On a clear day you can see it from some 40 miles away. An open-framework construction, the tower unlocked the almost unlimited possibilities of steel construction, paving the way for the 20th century's skyscrapers. Skeptics said it couldn't be built, and Eiffel actually wanted to make it soar higher. For years it remained the tallest man-made structure on earth, until skyscrapers like the Empire State Building surpassed it.

We could fill an entire page with tower statistics. (Its plans spanned 6,000 square yards of paper, and it contains 2¹⁄₂ million rivets.) But forget the numbers. Just stand beneath the tower and look straight up. It's like a rocket of steel lacework shooting into the sky.

To see this landmark best, don't sprint—approach it gradually. We suggest taking the Métro to the Trocadéro stop and walking from the Palais de Chaillot to the Seine

---

Time Out at the Tower

When visiting the Eiffel Tower, try to leave some time for the **Champ de Mars,** 7e (Métro: Trocadéro, Ecole Militaire, or Bir-Hakeim), the gardens between the tower and the Military School. Laid out around 1770, these gardens were the world's fair grounds and the scene of many military parades.

Memorial to a Princess

Place de l'Alma (Métro: Alma-Marceau) has been turned into a tribute to the late Diana, princess of Wales, who was killed in an auto accident August 31, 1997, in the nearby underpass. The bronze flame in the center is a replication of the flame in the Statue of Liberty and was a 1987 gift by the *International Herald Tribune* to honor Franco-American friendship. Many bouquets and messages (and even grafitti) are still placed around the flame, which seems to have come to represent the princess.

Paris has also opened the **Center for Nature Discovery, Garden in Memory of Diana, Princess of Wales,** at 21 rue des Blancs-Manteaux in the Marais. The small park, which you can visit daily during daylight hours, is devoted to teaching children about nature and gardening and contains flowers, vegetables, and decorative plants.

---

to get the full effect of the tower and its surroundings; then cross the pont d'Iéna and head for the base, where you'll find elevators in two of the pillars—expect long lines. (When the tower is open, you can see the 1889 lift machinery in the eastern and western pillars.) You visit the tower in three stages: The **first landing** provides a view over the rooftops as well as a cinema museum showing films, restaurants, and a bar. The **second landing** offers a panoramic look at the city. The **third landing** gives the most spectacular view; Eiffel's office has been re-created on this level, with wax figures depicting the engineer receiving Thomas Edison.

Of course, it's the view most people come for, and this extends for 42 miles, theoretically (weather conditions tend to limit it). Nevertheless, it's fabulous, and the best time for visibility is about an hour before sunset.

3 The Major Museums

Turn to "The Top Attractions," above, for a comprehensive look at the **Musée du Louvre** and the **Musée d'Orsay.**

You can buy **Le Pass Musée et Monuments (Museum and Monuments Pass)** at any of the museums honoring it or at any branch of the Paris Tourist office (see chapter 3). It offers free entrance to the permanent collections of 65 monuments and museums in Paris and the Ile de France. A 1-day pass is 80F ($12.80), a 3-day pass 160F ($25.60), and a 5-day pass 240F ($38.40). See chapter 3 for details on the **Paris Visite** pass, valid for 1 to 5 days on the public transport system, including the Métro, the city buses, the RER (regional express) trains within Paris city limits, and even the funicular to the top of Montmartre.

✪ **Centre Pompidou.** Place Georges-Pompidou, 4e. ☎ **01-44-78-12-33.** www.cnac-gp.fr. Admission 30F ($4.80) adults, 20F ($3.20) students; under age 13 free. Special exhibits 40F ($6.40) adults, 30F ($4.80) students; under age 13 free. Wed–Mon 11am–9pm. Métro: Rambuteau, Hôtel de Ville, or Châtelet–Les Halles.

Reopened in January 2000 in what was called in the 1970s "the most avant-garde building in the world," the restored Centre Pompidou is packing in the art-loving crowds again. The dream of former president Georges Pompidou, this center for 20th- and 21st-century art, designed by Richard Rogers and Renzo Piano, opened in 1977 and quickly became the focus of controversy. Its bold exoskeletal architecture and the brightly painted pipes and ducts crisscrossing its transparent facade (green for water, red for heat, blue for air, yellow for electricity) were jarring in the old Beaubourg neighborhood. Perhaps the detractors were right all along—within 20 years the building began to deteriorate so badly a major restoration was called for. The renovation added 5,000 square feet of exhibit space and a rooftop restaurant, a cafe, and a boutique; in addition, a series of auditoriums were created for film screenings and dance, theater, and musical performances. Access for the visitors with disabilities has also been improved.

The Centre Pompidou encompasses five attractions:

The **Musée National d'Art Moderne (National Museum of Modern Art)** offers a large collection of 20th- and 21st-century art. With some 40,000 works, this is the big attraction, though only some 850 works can be displayed at one time. If you want to view some real charmers, seek out Calder's 1926 ***Josephine Baker,*** one of his earlier versions of the mobile, an art form he invented. You'll also find two examples of Duchamps' series of dada-style sculptures he invented in 1936: ***Boîte en Valise (1941)*** and ***Boîte en Valise (1968).*** And every time we visit we have to see Dalí's ***Hallucination partielle: Six images de Lénine sur un piano*** (1931), with Lenin dancing on a piano.

In the **Bibliothèque Information Publique (Public Information Library)** people have free access to a million French and foreign books, periodicals, films, records, slides, and microfilms in nearly every area of knowledge. The **Centre de Création Industriel (Center for Industrial Design)** emphasizes the contributions made in the fields of architecture, visual communications, publishing, and community planning; and the **Institut de Recherche et de Coordination Acoustique-Musique (Institute for Research and Coordination of Acoustics/Music)** brings together musicians and composers interested in furthering the cause of contemporary and traditional music. Finally, you can visit a re-creation of the jazz-age studio of Romanian sculptor Brancusi, the **Atelier Brancusi,** a minimuseum slightly separate from the rest of the action.

The museum's **forecourt** is a free "entertainment center" featuring mimes, fire eaters, would-be circus performers, and sometimes first-rate musicians. Don't miss the nearby **Stravinsky fountain,** containing mobile sculptures by Tinguely and Saint Phalle.

Galerie Nationale du Jeu de Paume. In the northeast corner of the Jardin des Tuileries/ 1 place de la Concorde, 1er. ☎ **01-42-60-69-69.** Admission 38F ($6.10) adults, 28F ($4.50) students; age 13 and under free. Tues noon–9:30pm, Wed–Fri noon–7pm, Sat–Sun 10am–7pm. Métro: Concorde.

For years, the Jeu de Paume was one of Paris's treasures, displaying some of the finest works of the impressionists. To the regret of many, that collection was hauled off to the Musée d'Orsay in 1986. After a $12.6-million face-lift, the Second Empire building was transformed into a state-of-the-art gallery with a video screening room. There's no permanent collection—a new show is mounted every 2 or 3 months. Sometimes the works of little-known contemporary artists are displayed; other times, exhibits feature unexplored aspects of established artists. Originally, Napoléon III built in this part of the gardens a ball court on which *jeu de paume,* an antecedent of tennis, was played— hence, the museum's name. The most infamous period in the gallery's history came during the Nazi occupation, when it served as an "evaluation center" for modern art- works: Paintings from all over France were shipped to the Jeu de Paume, and any condemned by the Nazis as "degenerate" was burned.

Museum Closing Days

Generally, all museums are closed on January 1, May 1, Bastille Day (July 14), and December 25.

Musée Carnavalet. 23 rue de Sévigné, 3e. ☎ **01-44-59-58-58.** Admission 35F ($5.60) adults, 18F ($2.90) ages 7–26; under 7 free. Tues–Sun 10am–5:40pm. Métro: St-Paul or Chemin-Vert.

If you enjoy history but history tomes bore you, spend an hour or two here for some insight into Paris's past, which comes alive in intimate detail, right down to the chessmen Louis XVI used to distract his mind while waiting to go to the guillotine. The comprehensive and lifelike exhibits are great for kids, too. The building, a renowned Renaissance palace, was built in 1544 by Pierre Lescot and Jean Goujon and later acquired by Mme de Carnavalet. The great François Mansart transformed it between 1655 and 1661.

The palace is best known because one of history's most famous letter writers, Mme de Sévigné, moved here in 1677. Fanatically devoted to her daughter (she ended up moving in with her because she couldn't bear their separation), she poured out nearly every detail of her life in her letters, virtually ignoring her son. A native of the Marais district, she died at her daughter's château in 1696. It wasn't until 1866 that the city of Paris acquired the mansion and turned it into a museum. Several salons cover the Revolution, with a bust of Marat, a portrait of Danton, and a model of the Bastille (one painting shows its demolition). Another salon tells the story of the captivity of the royal family at the Conciergerie, including the bed in which Mme Elisabeth (the sister of Louis XVI) slept and the exercise book of the dauphin.

Exhibits continue at the **Hôtel le Pelletier de St-Fargeau,** across the courtyard. On display is furniture from the Louis XIV period to the early 20th century, including a replica of Marcel Proust's cork-lined bedroom with his actual furniture, including his brass bed.

✪ **Musée Jacquemart-André.** 158 bd. Haussmann, 8e. ☎ **01-42-89-04-91.** Admission 49F ($7.85) adults, 37F ($5.90) ages 7–17; age 6 and under free. Daily 10am–6pm. Métro: Miromesnil or St-Philippe-du-Roule.

This is the finest museum of its type in Paris, the treasure trove of a couple devoted to 18th-century French paintings and furnishings, 17th-century Dutch and Flemish paintings, and Italian Renaissance works. Edouard André, the last scion of a family of Protestants who made a fortune in banking and industry in the 19th century, spent most of his life as an army officer stationed abroad; he eventually returned to marry a well-known portraitist of government figures and the aristocracy, Nélie Jacquemart, and they went on to compile a collection of rare decorative art and paintings in this 1850s town house.

In 1912, Mme Jacquemart willed the house and its contents to the Institut de France, which paid for an extensive renovation and enlargement. The salons drip with gilt and the ultimate in fin-de-siècle style. Works by Bellini, Carpaccio, Uccelo, Van Dyck, Rembrandt (*The Pilgrim of Emmaus*), Tiepolo, Rubens, Watteau, Boucher, Fragonard, and Mantegna are complemented by Houdon busts, Savonnerie carpets, Gobelin tapestries, della Robbia terra-cottas, and an awesome collection of antiques. Outstanding are the three 18th-century Tiepolo frescoes depicting spectators on balconies viewing Henri III's 1574 arrival in Venice.

Take a break from the gilded age with a cup of tea in Mme Jacquemart's high-ceilinged dining room, adorned with 18th-century tapestries. Salads, tarts, *tourtes* (round pastries filled with meat or fruit), and Viennese pastries are served during the museum's hours.

✪ **Musée Marmottan–Claude Monet.** 2 rue Louis-Boilly, 16e. ☎ **01-42-24-07-02.** Admission 40F ($6.40) adults, 25F ($4) ages 8–24; ages 7 and under free. Tues–Sun 10am–5pm. Métro: La Muette.

Want Even More of Monet?

Have you just been to the Musée Marmottan and found yourself entranced by Monet's spiritualism of light? We'd ordinarily suggest you head to the charming **Musée de l'Orangerie** in the Jardin des Tuileries, the home of the two oval rooms wrapped around with almost 360° of Monet's exquisite *Nymphéas,* the water lily series he painted especially for the museum. Alas, the Orangerie closed in October 1999 for an estimated 2-year restoration. An even better idea is traveling to his home and gardens at **Giverny,** where many of his paintings are displayed and where you can see the lily ponds in person. We've given a full account of the trip in chapter 10.

In the past, an art historian or two would sometimes venture here to the edge of the Bois de Boulogne to see what Paul Marmottan had donated to the Académie des Beaux-Arts. Hardly anyone else did until 1966, when Claude Monet's son, Michel, died in a car crash, leaving a then-$10-million bequest of his father's art to the little museum. The Académie suddenly found itself with 130-plus paintings, watercolors, pastels, and drawings . . . and a passel of Monet lovers, who can now trace the evolution of the great man's work in a single museum. The collection includes more than 30 paintings of Monet's house at Giverny and many of water lilies, his everlasting fancy, plus **Willow** (1918), **House of Parliament** (1905), and a **Renoir portrait** of the 32-year-old Monet. Ironically, the museum had always owned Monet's **Impression: Sunrise** (1872), from which the impressionist movement got its name. Paul Marmottan's original collection includes fig-leafed nudes, First Empire antiques, assorted objets d'art, Renaissance tapestries, bucolic paintings, and crystal chandeliers. You can also see countless miniatures donated by Daniel Waldenstein.

Musée National du Moyen Age/Thermes de Cluny (Musée de Cluny). In the Hôtel de Cluny, 6 place Paul-Painlevé, 5e. ☎ **01-53-73-78-00.** Admission 30F ($4.80) adults, 20F ($3.20) ages 18–25; age 17 and under free. Wed–Mon 9:15am–5:45pm. Métro: Cluny–La Sorbonne.

Along with the Hôtel de Sens in the Marais, the Hôtel de Cluny is all that remains of domestic medieval architecture in Paris. You enter through the cobblestoned Cour d'Honneur (Court of Honor), where you can admire the Flamboyant Gothic building with its clinging vines, turreted walls, gargoyles, and dormers with seashell motifs. First the Cluny was the mansion of a rich 15th-century abbot, built on top of/next to the ruins of a Roman bath (see below). By 1515, it was the residence of Mary Tudor, teenage widow of Louis XII and daughter of Henry VII and Elizabeth of York. Seized during the Revolution, the Cluny was rented in 1833 to Alexandre du Sommerard, who adorned it with his collection of medieval artworks; on his 1842 death, the building and the collection were bought back by the government.

This collection of medieval arts and crafts is superb. Most people come primarily to see the **Unicorn Tapestries,** the most acclaimed tapestries of their kind. A beautiful princess and her handmaiden, beasts of prey, and just plain pets—all the romance of the age of chivalry lives on in these remarkable yet mysterious tapestries discovered only a century ago in Limousin's Château de Boussac. Five seem to deal with the senses (one, for example, depicts a unicorn looking into a mirror held by a dour-faced maiden). The sixth shows a woman under an elaborate tent with jewels, her pet dog resting on an embroidered cushion beside her, with the lovable unicorn and his friendly companion, a lion, holding back the flaps. The background in red and green forms a rich carpet of spring flowers, fruit-laden trees, birds, rabbits, donkeys, dogs, goats, lambs, and monkeys.

The other exhibits range widely: Flemish retables; a 14th-century Sienese John the Baptist and other Italian sculptures; statues from Sainte-Chapelle (1243–48); gem-studded 12th- and 13th-century crosses; golden chalices, manuscripts, ivory carvings, vestments, leatherwork, jewelry, coins; a 13th-century Adam; and recently discovered heads and fragments of statues from Notre-Dame de Paris. In the fan-vaulted medieval chapel hang tapestries depicting scenes from the life of St. Stephen.

Downstairs are the ruins of the **Roman baths,** from around A.D. 200. Of these once-flourishing baths, the best-preserved section is seen in room X, the frigidarium (where one bathed in cold water). Once it measured 70 by 36 feet, rising to a height of 50 feet, with stone walls nearly 7 feet thick. The ribbed vaulting here rests on consoles evoking ships' prows. Credit for this unusual motif goes to the builders of the baths, Paris's boatmen. During Tiberius's reign, a column to Jupiter was found beneath Notre-Dame's chancel and is now on view in the court—called the "Column of the Boatmen," it's believed to be the oldest sculpture created in Paris.

Musée National Eugène Delacroix. 6 place de Furstenberg, 6e. ☎ **01-44-41-86-50.** Admission 30F ($4.80) adults, 23F ($3.70) ages 18–25/over 60; age 17 and under free. Wed–Mon 9:30am–5pm. Métro: St-Germain-des-Prés.

This museum is only for serious Delacroix groupies, among whom we include ourselves. If you admire this artist and want to see where he lived, worked, and died, this is worth at least an hour. Delacroix (1798–1863) is something of an enigma to art historians. Even his parentage is a mystery. Many believe Talleyrand had the privilege of fathering him. One biographer saw him "as an isolated and atypical individualist—one who respected traditional values, yet emerged as the embodiment of Romantic revolt." Baudelaire called him "a volcanic crater artistically concealed beneath bouquets of flowers." The museum is on one of the Left Bank's most charming squares, with a highly romantic garden. A large arch on a stone courtyard leads to Delacroix's studio—no poor artist's studio, but the tasteful creation of a solidly established man. Sketches, lithographs, watercolors, and oils are hung throughout, and a few mementos remain, like a lovely mahogany paint box. If you want to see more of Delacroix's work, head to the Chapelle des Anges in St-Sulpice (see "The Important Churches," later in this chapter).

✪ **Musée Picasso.** In the Hôtel Salé, 5 rue de Thorigny, 3e. ☎ **01-42-71-25-21.** www. paris.org/Musees/Picasso. Admission 30F ($4.80) adults, 20F ($3.20) ages 18–25/over 60; age 18 and under free. Apr–Sept Wed–Mon 9:30am–6pm; Oct–Mar Wed–Mon 9:30am–5:30pm. Métro: St-Paul, Filles du Calvaire, or Chemin Vert.

When it opened at the beautifully restored Hôtel Salé (Salt Mansion, built by a man who made his fortune by controlling the salt distribution in 17th-century France) in the Marais, the press hailed it as a "museum for Picasso's Picassos." And that's what it is. The state acquired the world's greatest Picasso collection in lieu of $50-million in inheritance taxes: 203 paintings, 158 sculptures, 16 collages, 19 bas-reliefs, 88 ceramics,

A Time-Saving Tip

Museums require you to check shopping bags and book bags, and sometimes lines for these can be longer than the ticket lines. If you value your time, leave your bags in your hotel room or don't go shopping before hitting the museums: Some lines can take 30 minutes. Ask if a museum has more than one check line, and, if so, go to the less frequented ones.

and more than 1,500 sketches and 1,600 engravings, along with 30 notebooks. These works span some 75 years of the artist's life and ever-changing style.

The range of paintings includes a remarkable 1901 self-portrait; *The Crucifixion* and *Nude in a Red Armchair;* and *Le Baiser (The Kiss), Reclining Nude,* and *Man with a Guitar,* all painted at Mougins on the Riviera in 1969 and 1970. Stroll through the handsome museum seeking your own favorite—perhaps a wicked one: *Jeune garçon à la langouste (Young Man with a Lobster),* painted in Paris in 1941. There are also several intriguing studies for *Les Demoiselles d'Avignon,* which shocked the establishment and launched cubism in 1907. Because the collection is so vast, temporary exhibits featuring items like his **studies of the Minotaur** are held twice per year. Also here is Picasso's own treasure trove of art, with works by Cézanne, Rousseau, Braque, Derain, and Miró. Picasso was fascinated with African masks, many of which are on view.

Musée Rodin. In the Hôtel Biron, 77 rue de Varenne, 7e. ☎ **01-44-18-61-10.** www. musee-rodin.fr. Admission 28F ($4.50) adults, 18F ($2.90) ages 18–25; age 17 and under free. Apr–Sept Tues–Sun 9:30am–5:45pm; Oct–Mar Tues–Sun 9:30am–4:45pm. Métro: Varenne.

Today, Rodin is acclaimed as the father of modern sculpture, but in a different era his work was labeled obscene. The world's artistic taste changed, and in due course the French government purchased Rodin's studio from 1910 until his death in 1917, this gray-stone 18th-century mansion in the faubourg St-Germain. The government restored the rose gardens to their 18th-century splendor, making them a perfect setting for Rodin's most memorable works.

In the courtyard are three world-famous creations. Rodin's first major public commission, *The Burghers of Calais* commemorated the heroism of six citizens of Calais who in 1347 offered themselves as a ransom to Edward III in return for ending his siege of their port. Perhaps the single best-known work, *The Thinker,* in Rodin's own words, "thinks with every muscle of his arms, back, and legs, with his clenched fist and gripping toes." Not completed when Rodin died, *The Gate of Hell,* as he put it, is "where I lived for a whole year in Dante's *Inferno.*"

Inside the building, the sculpture, plaster casts, reproductions, originals, and sketches reveal the freshness and vitality of a remarkable artist. You can practically see many of his works emerging from marble into life. Everybody is attracted to *Le Baiser (The Kiss),* of which one critic wrote, "the passion is timeless." Upstairs are two versions of the celebrated and condemned **nude of Balzac,** his bulky torso rising from a tree trunk (Albert E. Elsen commented on the "glorious bulging" stomach). Included are many versions of his *Monument to Balzac* (a large one stands in the garden), Rodin's last major work. Other significant sculptures are the soaring *Prodigal Son, The Crouching Woman* (the "embodiment of despair"), and *The Age of Bronze,* an 1876 study of a nude man modeled by a Belgian soldier. (Rodin was falsely accused of making a cast from a living model.) Generally overlooked is a room devoted to Rodin's mistress, Camille Claudel, a towering artist in her own right. She was his pupil, model, and lover, and created such works as *Maturity, Clotho,* and the recently donated *The Waltz* and *The Gossips.*

Looking for a Quick Escape?

The little alley behind the Musée Rodin winds its way down to a pond with fountains and flower beds and even sandpits for children. It's one of the most idyllic hidden spots in Paris.

Petit Palais. Av. Winston-Churchill, 8e. ☎ **01-42-65-12-73.** Admission 27F ($4.30) adults, 15F ($2.40) under age 25; free on Sun. Special exhibits 50F ($8) adults, 25F ($4) 26 and under. Tues–Sun 10am–5:40pm. Métro: Champs-Elysées.

Designed by Charles Girault, this small palace faces the **Grand Palais** (housing special exhibits; ☎ **01-44-13-17-30**); both were erected for the 1900 Universal Exhibition. The Petit Palais contains a hodgepodge of works for the serious art lover. Most people come for the temporary exhibits, not the permanent collections. Of the latter, the most prominent are the Dutuit and Tuck. In the **Dutuit Collection** are Egyptian, Greek, and Roman bronzes; rare ivory statues (the best of which is of a Roman actor); ancient Greek porcelains; enamels, sculpture, and hand-lettered and -painted manuscripts from the Middle Ages; and 17th-century Dutch and Flemish paintings, with works by Breughel the Younger (*The Wedding Pageant*), Rubens, Hobbema, Ruysdael, and more. The **Tuck Collection,** donated by Edward Tuck in 1930, is composed mainly of 18th-century decorative artwork, including tapestries, heavily gilded furniture, wood-paneled salons, and porcelains.

A number of rooms are dedicated to 19th-century French painting, with canvases by Manet, Courbet, Daumier, Corot, Delacroix, Sisley, Cassatt (*Le Bain*), Bonnard, Maurice Denis, and Edouard Vuillard. You'll also find works by David, Fragonard, and Greuze. The "academic school" is represented by the enormous compositions of Gustave Doré. The museum also has sculptures by Rodin, Bourdelle, Maillol, and Carpeaux and glassworks by Galle and Lalique.

4 The Important Churches

Turn to "The Top Attractions," above, for a full look at the **Cathédrale de Notre-Dame, Basilique du Sacré-Coeur,** and **Sainte-Chapelle.**

American Cathedral of the Holy Trinity. 23 av. George V, 8e. ☎ **01-53-23-84-00.** Admission free. Daily 9am–5pm. Sun Holy Eucharist 9am and 11am. Métro: Alma-Marceau or George V.

This cathedral is one of Europe's finest examples of Gothic Revival architecture and a growing center for music and art. Consecrated in 1886, it was created by George Edmund Street, best known for the London Law Courts. Aside from the great architecture, you'll find remarkable pre-Raphaelite stained-glass windows illustrating the *Te Deum,* an early-15th-century triptych by the Roussillon Master, an anonymous painter, probably a monk, a needlepoint collection including kneelers depicting the 50 state flowers, and the 50 state flags in the nave. A **Memorial Cloister** commemorates Americans who died in Europe in World War I and all the victims of World War II. Documentation in several languages explains these and other highlights. The cathedral is also a center of worship and community outreach, with a schedule of Sunday and weekday services in English. Les Arts George V, a cultural organization, presents reasonably priced choral concerts, lectures, and art shows.

Basilique St-Denis. Place de l'Hôtel-de-Ville, 2 rue de Strasbourg, St-Denis. ☎ **01-48-09-83-54.** Admission 32F ($5.10) adults, 21F ($3.35) seniors/students; age 11 and under free. Apr–Sept Mon–Sat 10am–7:30pm, Sun noon–6:30pm; Oct–Mar Mon–Sat 10am–5pm, Sun noon–5pm. Métro: St-Denis.

In the 12th century, Abbot Suger placed an inscription on the bronze doors here: "Marvel not at the gold and expense, but at the craftsmanship of the work." France's first Gothic building that can be dated precisely, St-Denis was the "spiritual defender of the State" during the reign of Louis VI ("The Fat"). The massive facade has a rose window and a crenellated parapet on the top similar to the fortifications of a castle.

The stained-glass windows—in stunning mauve, purple, blue, and rose—were restored in the 19th century.

The first bishop of Paris, St. Denis became the patron saint of the monarchy, and royal burials began here in the 6th century and continued until the Revolution. The sculpture designed for the **tombs**—some two stories high—span French artistic development from the Middle Ages to the Renaissance. (There are guided tours of the crypt, but in French only.) François I was entombed at St-Denis, and his funeral statue is nude, though he demurely covers himself with his hand. Other kings and queens here include Louis XII and Anne de Bretagne, as well as Henri II and Catherine de Médicis. Revolutionaries stormed through the basilica during the Terror, smashing many marble faces and dumping royal remains in a lime-filled ditch in the garden. (These remains were reburied under the main altar during the 19th century.) Free organ concerts are given Sundays at 11:15am.

La Madeleine. Place de la Madeleine, 8e. ☎ **01-44-51-69-00.** Admission free. Daily 7:30am–7pm. Métro: Madeleine.

La Madeleine is one of Paris's minor landmarks, dominating short rue Royale, which culminates in place de la Concorde. Though construction began in 1806, it wasn't consecrated as a church until 1842. Resembling a Roman temple, the building was intended as a monument to the glory of the Grande Armée (Napoléon's idea, of course). Later, several alternative uses were considered: the National Assembly, the Bourse, and the National Library. Climb the 28 steps to the facade and look back: You'll be able to see rue Royale, place de la Concorde and its obelisk, and (across the Seine) the dome of the Hôtel des Invalides. Don't miss Rude's *Le Baptême du Christ,* to the left as you enter.

Mosquée de Paris. Place du Puits-de-l'Ermite, 5e. ☎ **01-45-35-97-33.** Admission 15F ($2.40) adults, 10F ($1.60) students/children. Sat–Thurs 9:30am–5pm. Métro: Monge.

This beautiful pink marble mosque was built in 1922 to honor the North African countries that had given aid to France during World War I. Today, North Africans living in Paris gather on Friday, the Muslim holy day, and during Ramadan to pray to Allah. Short tours are given of the building, its central courtyard, and its Moorish garden; guides present a brief history of the Islamic faith. However, you may want just to wander around on your own, then join the students from nearby universities for couscous and sweet mint tea at the Muslim **Restaurant de la Mosquée de Paris** (☎ **01-43-31-18-14**), adjoining the grounds, open daily noon to 3pm and 7 to 10:30pm.

St-Germain-des-Prés. 3 place St-Germain-des-Prés, 6e. ☎ **01-43-25-41-71.** Admission free. Daily 8am–8pm. Métro: St-Germain-des-Prés.

Outside it's a handsome early-17th-century town house. Inside it's one of Paris's oldest churches, from the 6th century, when a Benedictine abbey was founded here by Childebert, son of Clovis. Alas, the marble columns in the triforium are all that remain from then. The Normans nearly destroyed the abbey at least four times. The

Gregorians Unplugged

St-Germain-des-Prés stages the most wonderful concerts on the Left Bank; it boasts fantastic acoustics and a marvelous medieval atmosphere. The church was built to accommodate an age without microphones, and the sound effects will thrill you. For more information, call ☎ **01-43-25-41-71.** Arrive about 45 minutes before the performance if you'd like a front-row seat. Ticket are 120F to 250F ($19.20 to $40).

present building has a Romanesque nave and a Gothic choir with fine capitals. At one time, the abbey was a pantheon for Merovingian kings. Restoration of the site of their tombs, **Chapelle de St-Symphorien,** began in 1981, and unknown Romanesque paintings were discovered on the triumphal arch. Among the others interred here are Descartes (his heart at least) and Jean-Casimir, the king of Poland who abdicated his throne. The Romanesque tower, topped by a 19th-century spire, is the most enduring landmark in St-Germain-des-Prés. Its church bells, however, are hardly noticed by the patrons of Les Deux Magots across the way.

When you leave the church, turn right on rue de l'Abbaye and have a look at the 17th-century pink **Palais Abbatial.**

St-Sulpice. Rue St-Sulpice, 6e. ☎ **01-46-33-21-78.** Admission free. Daily 7:30am–7:30pm. Métro: St-Sulpice.

Pause first outside St-Sulpice. The 1844 fountain by Visconti displays the sculpted likenesses of four bishops of the Louis XIV era: Fenelon, Massillon, Bossuet, and Flechier. Work on the church, at one time Paris's largest, began in 1646 as part of France's Catholic revival. Though laborers built the body by 1745, work on the bell towers continued until 1780, when one was finished and the other incomplete. One of the priceless treasures inside is Servandoni's rococo **Chapelle de la Madone (Chapel of the Madonna)**, with a Pigalle statue of the Virgin. The church has one of the world's largest organs, comprising 6,700 pipes; it has been played by musicians like Charles-Mari Widor and Marcel Dupré.

The real reason to come here is to see the Delacroix frescoes in the **Chapelle des Anges (Chapel of the Angels)**, the first on your right as you enter. Seek out his muscular Jacob wrestling (or dancing?) with an effete angel. On the ceiling, St. Michael is having some troubles with the Devil, and yet another mural depicts Heliodorus being driven from the temple. Painted in Delacroix's final years, the frescoes were a high point in his baffling career. If these impress you, pay the painter tribute by visiting the Musée Delacroix (see "The Major Museums").

St-Etienne-du-Mont. Place Ste-Geneviève, 5e. ☎ **01-43-54-11-79.** Admission free. Sept–June Mon–Sat 8:30am–noon and 2–7pm, Sun 8:30am–noon and 3–7:30pm; July–Aug Tues–Sun 10am–noon and 4–7pm. Métro: Cardinal Lemoine or Luxembourg.

Once there was an abbey here, founded by Clovis and later dedicated to St. Geneviève, the patroness of Paris. Such was the fame of this popular saint that the abbey proved too small to accommodate the pilgrimage crowds. Now part of the Lycée Henri IV, the Tour de Clovis (Tower of Clovis) is all that remains of the ancient abbey—you can see the tower from rue Clovis. Today the task of keeping St. Geneviève's cult alive has fallen on this church, practically adjoining the Panthéon. The interior is Gothic, an unusual style for a 16th-century church. Building began in 1492 and was plagued by delays until the church was finally finished in 1626.

Besides the patroness of Paris, such men as Pascal and Racine were entombed here. Though St. Geneviève's tomb was destroyed during the Revolution, the stone on which her coffin rested was discovered later, and her relics were gathered for a place of honor at St-Etienne. The church possesses a remarkable early-16th-century **rood screen:** Crossing the nave, it's unique in Paris—called spurious by some and a masterpiece by others. Another treasure is a wood-carved **pulpit,** held up by Samson, clutching a bone in one hand, with a slain lion at his feet. The fourth chapel on the right when you enter contains impressive 16th-century stained glass.

✪ **St-Eustache.** 2 rue du Jour, 1er. ☎ **01-42-36-31-05.** Admission free. Apr–Sept daily 8am–8pm; Oct–Mar daily 9am–7pm. Sun mass 9:30am, 11am, and 6pm; Sun organ recitals 5:30pm. Métro: Les Halles.

This mixed Gothic and Renaissance church completed in 1637 is rivaled only by Notre-Dame. Madame de Pompadour and Richelieu were baptized here, and Molière's funeral was held here in 1673. The church has been known for organ recitals ever since Liszt played here in 1866. Inside rests the **black-marble tomb** of Jean-Baptiste Colbert, the minister of state under Louis XIV; atop the tomb is his marble effigy flanked by statues of *Abundance* by Coysevox and *Fidelity* by Tuby. The church's most famous painting is Rembrandt's *The Pilgrimage to Emmaus.* There's a side entrance on rue Rambuteau.

St-Germain l'Auxerrois. 2 place du Louvre, 1er. ☎ **01-42-60-13-96.** Admission free. Daily 8am–8pm. Métro: Louvre.

Once it was the church for the Palais du Louvre, drawing an assortment of royalty, courtesans, men of art and law, and even local artisans. Sharing place du Louvre with Perrault's colonnade, the church contains only the foundation stones of its original 11th-century belfry. The primitive chapel that had stood here was greatly enlarged in the 14th century by the addition of side aisles and became a beautiful church, with 260 feet of stained glass, including some rose windows from the Renaissance. The intricately carved **church-wardens' pews** are outstanding, based on 17th-century Le Brun designs. Behind them is a **15th-century triptych** and **Flemish retable,** so badly lit you can hardly appreciate it. The organ was ordered by Louis XVI for Sainte-Chapelle. Many famous men were entombed here, including the sculptor Coysevox and the architect Le Vau. Around the chancel is an intricate **18th-century grille.**

   The saddest moment in the church's history was on August 24, 1572, the evening of the St. Bartholomew Massacre. The tower bells rang, signaling the supporters of Catherine de Médicis, Marguerite de Guise, Charles IX, and the future Henri III to launch a slaughter of thousands of Huguenots, who'd been invited to celebrate the marriage of Henri de Navarre to his cousin, Marguerite de Valois.

Val-de-Grâce. 1 place Alphonse-Laveran, 5e. ☎ **01-40-51-51-92.** Admission 30F ($4.80) adults; under 6 free. Tues–Wed noon–5pm, Sat 1–5pm, Sun 1–5pm (5pm is last entrance). Métro: Port Royal.

According to an old proverb, to understand the French you must like Camembert cheese, the pont Neuf, and the dome of Val-de-Grâce. Its origins go back to 1050, when a Benedictine monastery was built here. In 1619, Louis XIII appointed as abbess Marguerite Veni d'Arbouze, who asked Louis's wife, Anne of Austria, for a new monastery because the original was decaying. After 23 years of a childless marriage, Anne gave birth to a boy who went on to be known as the Sun King. To express his gratitude, Louis XIII approved the rebuilding of the church, and at the age of 7 on April 1, 1645, the future Louis XIV laid Val-de-Grâce's first stone. Mansart was the main architect, and to him we owe the facade in the Jesuit style. Le Duc, however, designed the dome, and Mignard added the frescoes. Le Mercier and Le Muet also had a hand in the church's fashioning. The church was turned into a military hospital in 1793 and an army school in 1850.

5 Architectural & Historic Highlights

Arènes de Lutèce. At rues Monge and Navarre, 5e. No phone. Admission free. May–Sept daily 10am–10pm; Oct–Apr daily 10am–5:30pm. Métro: Jussieu.

Discovered and partially destroyed in 1869, this amphitheater is Paris's second most important Roman ruin after the baths in the Musée de Cluny (see "The Major Museums," above). Today, the site is home to a small arena, not as grand as the original, and pleasant gardens. You may feel as if you've discovered a private spot in the heart of the city, but don't be fooled. Your solitude is sure to be interrupted, if not by groups of students playing soccer then at least by parents pushing strollers down the walking paths. This is an ideal spot for a picnic—bring a bottle of wine and fresh baguettes to enjoy in this vestige of the ancient city of Lutétia.

Bibliothèque Nationale de France, Site Tolbiac/François Mitterrand (French National Library). Quai François-Mauriac, 13e. ☎ **01-53-79-59-59.** Admission 20F ($3.20). No one under 16 admitted. Tues–Sat 10am–8pm, Sun noon–7pm. Métro: Bibliothèque François-Mitterrand.

Opened in 1996 with a dramatic futuristic design by Dominique Perrault (a quartet of 24-story towers evoking the look of open books), this is the last of the *grand projets* of the late François Mitterrand. It boasts the same grandiose scale as the Cité de la Musique (see "Specialty Museums," for its museum) and houses the nation's literary and historic archives; it's regarded as a repository of the French soul, replacing outmoded facilities on rue des Archives. The library incorporates space for 3,600 readers at a time, many of whom enjoy views over two levels of a garden-style courtyard that seems far removed from the urban congestion of Paris.

This is one of Europe's most user-friendly academic facilities, emphasizing computerized documentation and microfiche—a role model that'll set academic and literary priorities well into the future. The public has access to as many as 750,000 books and periodicals, with an additional 10 million historic (including medieval) documents shown only to qualified experts. Though the appeal of this place extends mainly to serious scholars researching French history and culture, there's a handful of special exhibits that might interest you, as well as concerts and lectures. Concert tickets rarely exceed 100F ($16) adults and 65F ($10.40) students, seniors, and children; a schedule is available at the library.

Conciergerie. 1 quai de l'Horloge, 4e. ☎ **01-53-73-78-50.** www.paris.org/ Monuments/Conciergerie. Admission 35F ($5.60) adults, 23F ($3.70) ages 18–25/over 60; children under 12 free. Apr–Sept daily 9:30am–6:30pm; Oct–Mar daily 10am–5pm. Métro: Cité, Châtelet, or St-Michel. RER: St-Michel.

London has its Bloody Tower and Paris its Conciergerie. Even though the Conciergerie had a long regal history before the Revolution, it was forever stained by the Reign of Terror and lives as an infamous symbol of the time when carts pulled up constantly to haul off fresh supplies of victims for Dr. Guillotin's wonderful little invention.

Much of the Conciergerie was built in the 14th century as an extension of the Capetian royal Palais de la Cité. You approach through its landmark twin towers, the **Tour d'Argent** (where the crown jewels were stored at one time) and **Tour de César,** but the vaulted **Salle des Gardes (Guard Room)** is the actual entrance. Even more interesting is the vast, dark, and foreboding Gothic **Salle des Gens d'Armes (Room of People at Arms)**, utterly changed from the days when the king used it as a banquet hall. However, architecture plays a secondary role to the list of prisoners who spent their last miserable days here. Few in its history endured tortures as severe as those imposed on Ravaillac, who assassinated Henry IV in 1610. In the Tour de César, he received pincers in the flesh and had hot lead and boiling oil poured on him like bath water before being executed (see the Hôtel de Ville entry below). During the Revolution, the Conciergerie became a symbol of terror to the nobility and enemies of the State. A short walk away, the Revolutionary Tribunal dispensed a skewed, hurried justice—if it's any consolation, the jurists didn't believe in torturing their victims, only in decapitating them.

After being seized by a crowd of peasants who stormed Versailles, Louis XVI and Marie Antoinette were brought here to await their trials. In failing health and shocked beyond grief, *l'Autrichienne* ("the Austrian," as she was called with malice) had only a small screen (sometimes not even that) to protect her modesty from the gaze of guards stationed in her cell. By accounts of the day, she was shy and stupid, though the evidence is that on her death she displayed the nobility of a true queen. (What's more, the famous "Let them eat cake" she supposedly uttered when told the peasants had no bread is probably apocryphal—besides, at the time cake flour was less expensive than bread flour, so even if she said this it wasn't meant coldbloodedly.) It was shortly before noon on the morning of October 16, 1793, when her executioners came for her, grabbing her and cutting her hair, as was the custom for victims marked for the guillotine.

Later, the Conciergerie housed other noted prisoners, including Mme Elisabeth; Mme du Barry, mistress of Louis XV; Mme Roland ("O Liberty! Liberty! What crimes are committed in thy name!"); and Charlotte Corday, who killed Marat with a kitchen knife while he was taking a sulphur bath. In time, the Revolution consumed its own leaders, such as Danton and Robespierre. Finally, even one of Paris's most hated men, public prosecutor Fouquier-Tinville, faced the guillotine to which he'd sent so many others. Among the few interned here who lived to tell the tale was America's Thomas Paine, who reminisced about his chats in English with Danton.

Hôtel de Ville. 29 rue de Rivoli, 4e. ☎ **01-42-76-43-43.** Admission free. Information center, Mon–Sat 9am–6:30pm. Métro: Hôtel de Ville.

On a large square with fountains and early-1900s lampposts, the 19th-century Hôtel de Ville isn't a hotel but Paris's grandiose City Hall. The medieval structure it replaced had witnessed countless municipally ordered executions. Henry IV's assassin, Ravaillac, was quartered alive on the square in 1610, his body tied to four horses that bolted in opposite directions. On May 24, 1871, the communards doused the City Hall with petrol, creating a blaze that lasted for 8 days. The Third Republic ordered the structure rebuilt, with many changes, even creating a Hall of Mirrors evocative of that at Versailles. For security reasons, the major splendor of this building is closed to the public. However, the information center sponsors exhibits on Paris in the main lobby.

Institut de France. 23 quai de Conti, 6e. ☎ **01-44-41-44-41.** Admission free (guests can walk into courtyard only). Métro: Pont Neuf or Odéon.

Designed by Louis Le Vau, this dramatic baroque building with an enormous cupola is the seat of all five Academies that dominate France's intellectual life—Française, Sciences, Inscriptions et Belles Lettres, Beaux-Arts, and Sciences Morales et Politiques. The members of the Academie Française (limited to 40), guardians of the French language referred to as "the immortals," gather here. Many are unfamiliar figures (though Jacques Cousteau and Marshall Pétain were members), and the Academy is remarkable for the great writers and philosophers who have *not* been invited to join— Balzac, Baudelaire, Diderot, Flaubert, Descartes, Proust, Molière, Pascal, Rousseau, and Zola, to name only a few. The cenotaph was designed by Coysevox for Mazarin.

La Grande Arche de La Défense. 1 place du parvis de La Défense, Puteaux, 15e. ☎ **01-49-07-27-57.** Admission 53F ($8.50) adults, 43F ($6.90) ages 6–18; ages 5 and under free. Daily 10am–6pm (last ascent). RER: La Défense.

Designed as the architectural centerpiece of the sprawling satellite suburb of La Défense, this massive steel-and-masonry arch rises 35 stories. It was built with the blessing of the late François Mitterrand and extends the magnificently engineered straight line linking the Louvre, Arc du Triomphe du Carrousel, Champs-Elysées, Arc de Triomphe, avenue de la Grande Armée, and place du Porte Maillot. The arch is ringed with a circular avenue patterned after the one winding around the Arc de Triomphe. The monument is tall enough to shelter Notre-Dame beneath its heavily trussed canopy. An elevator carries you up to an observation platform, where you get a view of the carefully planned geometry of the surrounding streets.

You'll notice nets rigged along the Grande Arche. When pieces of Mitterrand's *grand projet* started falling to the ground, a mesh was erected to catch fragments before they hit people on the head. Would this were true for all politicians' follies.

Palais Bourbon/Assemblée Nationale. 33 quai d'Orsay, 7e. ☎ **01-40-63-64-08.** Admission free. Hours vary, so call ahead. Métro: Assemblée Nationale.

The French parliament's lower house, the Chamber of Deputies, meets at this 1722 mansion built by the duchesse de Bourbon, a daughter of Louis XIV. You can make reservations for one of two types of visit as early as 6 months in advance. Tours on art, architecture, and basic French government processes are given Monday, Friday, and Saturday. They're in French (in English with advance booking). You may also observe sessions of the National Assembly, held Tuesday afternoon and all day Wednesday and Thursday beginning at 9:30am. Do remember this is a working government building and all visitors are subject to rigorous security checks.

Palais Royal. Rue St-Honoré, 1er. Admission free. Daily 8am–7pm. Métro: Palais Royal–Musée du Louvre.

The Palais Royal was originally known as the Palais Cardinal, for it was the residence of Cardinal Richelieu, Louis XIII's prime minister. Richelieu had it built, and after his death it was inherited by the king, who died soon after. Louis XIV spent part of his childhood here with his mother, Anne of Austria, but later resided at the Louvre and Versailles. The palace was later owned by the duc de Chartres et Orléans (see the entry for Parc Monceau under "Parks & Gardens"), who encouraged the opening of cafes, gambling dens, and other public entertainments. Though government offices occupy the Palais Royal and they're not open to the public, do visit the **Jardin du Palais Royal,** an enclosure bordered by arcades. Don't miss the main courtyard, with the controversial 1986 Buren sculpture—280 prison-striped columns, oddly placed.

Panthéon. Place du Panthéon, 5e. ☎ **01-44-32-18-00.** Admission 35F ($5.60) adults, 23F ($3.70) ages 12–25; age 11 and under free. Apr–Sept daily 9:30am–6:30pm; Oct–Mar daily 10am–6:15pm (last entrance 45 min. before closing). Métro: Cardinal Lemoine or Maubert-Mutualité.

Some of the most famous men in French history (Victor Hugo, for one) are buried here in austere grandeur, on the crest of the mount of St. Geneviève. In 1744, Louis XV vowed that if he recovered from a mysterious illness, he'd build a church to replace the decayed Abbaye de Ste-Geneviève. He recovered but took his time in fulfilling his promise. It wasn't until 1764 that Mme de Pompadour's brother hired Soufflot to design a church in the form of a Greek cross with a dome reminiscent of St. Paul's in London. When Soufflot died, his pupil Rondelet carried out the work, completing the structure 9 years after his master's death.

After the Revolution, the church was converted into a "Temple of Fame" and became a pantheon for the great men of France. Mirabeau was buried here, though his remains were later removed. Likewise, Marat was only a temporary tenant. Voltaire's body was exhumed and placed here—and allowed to remain. In the 19th century, the building changed roles so many times—a church, a pantheon, a church—that it was hard to keep its function straight. After Hugo was buried here, it became a pantheon once again. Other notable men entombed within are Rousseau, Soufflot, Zola, and Braille. Only one woman has so far been deemed worthy of placement here, Marie Curie, who joined her husband, Pierre. Most recently, the ashes of André Malraux were transferred to the Panthéon because, according to President Jacques Chirac, he "lived [his] dreams and made them live in us." As Charles de Gaulle's culture minister, Malraux decreed the arts should be part of the lives of all French people, not just Paris's elite.

A Passage to the Passages

Far from the crowds on the Grands Boulevards lie the iron-and-glass arcades that were the Western world's first malls, most built from the late 18th to the mid-19th century. At the time, merchants were looking for innovative ways to display their wares to the growing middle class. The unpaved streets were crowded, dirty, and badly lit, and glass-topped markets spared the stores' fashionable patrons the inconveniences of city life and launched a new pastime called window shopping. The remaining covered arcades are still havens for strolling and shopping, transporting you to an era when Paris set the standard for urban style.

The 2nd arrondissement has the greatest concentration of these charming galleries. The **Passage du Caire,** 2 place du Caire (Métro: Sentier), was built in 1798 to commemorate Napoléon's triumphal entry into Cairo; the facade reflects the Egyptomania of the time. The 1827 **Passage Choiseul,** 44 rue des Petits-Champs (Métro: Quatre-Septembre), is the longest and most animated arcade; discount shoes and clothing are piled outside the stores. The **Passage des Panoramas,** 11 bd. Montmartre and 10 rue St-Marc (Métro: Montmartre), opened in 1800 and was enlarged in 1834 with the addition of galleries Variétés, St-Marc, Montmartre, and Feydeau; this passage offers the largest choice of dining—Korean food, a cafeteria, tea salons, bistros—as well as outlets for stamps, clothes, and knickknacks. Across the street is the **Passage Jouffroy,** 10 bd. Montmartre and 9 rue de la Grange-Batelière (Métro: Montmartre), built between 1845 and 1846; the richness of its decoration—as well as the fact that it was the first heated gallery in Paris—made the Jouffroy an immediate hit.

The **Passage Verdeau,** 31 bis rue du faubourg Montmartre (Métro: Le Peletier), was built about the same time as the Jouffroy and has suffered in comparison to its more glamorous neighbor; not much appears to have changed since it opened, including the postcards and books that are the specialties. The 1823 ✪ **Galerie Vivienne,** 4 place des Petits-Champs, 5 rue de la Banque, and 6 rue Vivienne (Métro: Bourse), boasts by far the most sumptuous interior and has been designated a national monument; the arcade's neoclassical style has attracted upscale art galleries, hair salons, and fashionable boutiques. The classic friezes, mosaic floors, and graceful arches have been beautifully restored and linked to the adjoining **Galerie Colbert,** built in 1826 to capitalize on the Vivienne's success. For a complete change of pace, head north on rue St-Denis to the 1828 **Passage Brady,** 46 rue du faubourg St-Denis (Métro: Strasbourg–St-Denis), which has become an exotic bazaar, with Indian restaurants and spice shops scenting the air.

Before entering the crypt, note the striking frescoes: On the right wall are scenes from Geneviève's life and on the left are the saint with a white-draped head looking out over medieval Paris, the city whose patron she became, as well as Geneviève relieving victims of famine with supplies.

6 Neighborhood Highlights

Paris's neighborhoods often turn out to be attractions unto themselves. The 1st arrondissement, for example, probably has a higher concentration of attractions per block than anywhere else. Though all Paris's neighborhoods are worth wandering, some are more interesting than others. This is especially true of Montmartre, the Latin

Quarter, and the Marais, so we've featured them as walking tours in chapter 7. Our other favorites follow here.

For other strolls in the City of Light, see *Frommer's Memorable Walks in Paris.*

ISLANDS IN THE STREAM: ILE DE LA CITÉ & ILE ST-LOUIS

ILE DE LA CITÉ: WHERE PARIS WAS BORN   Medieval Paris, that blend of grotesquerie and Gothic beauty, bloomed on this island in the Seine (Métro: Cité). Ile de la Cité, which the Seine protects like a surrounding moat, has been known as "the cradle" of Paris ever since. As Sauval once observed, "The Island of the City is shaped like a great ship, sunk in the mud, lengthwise in the stream, in about the middle of the Seine."

Few have written more movingly about its heyday than Victor Hugo, who invited the reader "to observe the fantastic display of lights against the darkness of that gloomy labyrinth of buildings; cast upon it a ray of moonlight, showing the city in glimmering vagueness, with its towers lifting their great heads from that foggy sea." Medieval Paris was a city not only of legends and lovers but also of blood-curdling tortures and brutalities. No story illustrates this better than the affair of Abélard and his charge Héloïse, whose jealous and unsettled uncle hired ruffians to castrate her lover. (The attack predictably quelled their ardor, and he became a monk, she an abbess.) You can see their graves at Père-Lachaise (see "Cemeteries").

The island's undisputed stars are **Notre-Dame, Sainte-Chapelle,** and the **Conciergerie**—all described earlier in this chapter. Across from Notre-Dame is the **Hôtel Dieu,** built from 1866 to 1878 in neo-Florentine style. This is central Paris's main hospital, replacing the 12th-century hospital that ran the island's entire width. Go in the main entrance and take a break in the spacious neoclassical courtyard whose small garden and fountain make a quiet oasis.

Don't miss the ironically named **pont Neuf** ("New Bridge") at the tip of the island opposite from Notre-Dame. The span isn't new—it's actually Paris's oldest bridge, begun in 1578 and finished in 1604. In its day it had two unique features: It was paved and it wasn't flanked with houses and shops. Actually, with 12 arches, it's not one bridge but two (they don't quite line up)—one from the Right Bank to the island and the other from the Left Bank to the island. At the **Musée Carnavalet** (see "The Top Attractions"), a painting called *The Spectacle of Buffoons* shows what the bridge was like between 1665 and 1669. Duels were fought on it; the nobility's great coaches crossed it; peddlers sold their wares on it; and entertainers like Tabarin went there to seek a few coins from the gawkers. As public facilities were lacking, the bridge also served as a de facto outhouse.

Just past pont Neuf is the "prow" of the island, the **square du Vert Galant.** Pause to look at the equestrian statue of the beloved Henri IV, who was assassinated by Ravaillac (see the entry for the Conciergerie). A true king of his people, Henry was also (to judge from accounts) regal in the boudoir—hence the nickname "Vert Galant" (Old Spark). Gabrielle d'Estrées and Henriette d'Entragues were his best-known mistresses, but they had to share him with countless others, some of whom would casually catch his eye as he was riding along the streets. In fond memory of the king, the little triangular park continues to attract lovers. If at first it appears to be a sunken garden, that's because it remains at its natural level; the rest of the Cité has been built up during the centuries.

ILE ST-LOUIS   Cross pont St-Louis, the iron footbridge behind Notre-Dame, to Ile St-Louis and you'll find a world of tree-shaded quays, aristocratic town houses with courtyards, restaurants, and antiques shops. (You can also take the Métro to Sully-Morland or Pont Marie and cross the bridge.) The fraternal twin of Ile de la Cité, Ile

St-Louis is primarily residential; nearly all the houses were built from 1618 to 1660, lending the island a remarkable architectural unity. Plaques on the facades identify the former residences of the famous. **Marie Curie** lived at 36 quai de Béthune, near pont de la Tournelle, and sculptor **Camille Claudel** (Rodin's mistress) lived and worked in the Hôtel de Jassaud, 19 quai de Bourbon.

The most exciting mansion—though perhaps also the one with the saddest history—is the 1656–57 **Hôtel de Lauzun,** 17 quai d'Anjou, built for Charles Gruyn des Bordes. He married Geneviève de Mouy and had her initials engraved on much of the interior decor; their happiness was short-lived, however, because he was convicted of embezzlement and sent to prison in 1662. The next occupant was the duc de Lauzun, who resided there for only 3 years. He had been a favorite of Louis XIV until he asked for the hand of the king's first cousin, the duchesse de Montpensier. Louis refused and had Lauzun tossed into the Bastille. Eventually the duchesse pestered Louis into releasing her beloved, and they married secretly and moved here in 1682, but domestic bliss eluded them—they fought often and separated in 1684. Lauzun then sold the house to the grand-nephew of Cardinal Richelieu and his wife, the grand-niece of Cardinal Mazarin, who had such a grand time throwing parties they went bankrupt and separated. Baron Pichon bought it in 1842 and rented it out to a hashish club. Tenants Baudelaire and Gaultier regularly held hashish soirees in which Baudelaire did research for his *Les Paradis artificiels* and Gaultier for his *Le Club hes hachichins.* Now the mansion belongs to the city and is used to house official guests. The interior is sometimes open for temporary exhibits, so call the tourist office.

The **Hôtel Lambert,** 2 quai d'Anjou, was built in 1645 for Nicholas Lambert de Thorigny. The portal on rue St-Louis-en-l'Ile gives some idea of the splendor within, but the house's most startling element is the oval gallery extending into the garden. Designed to feature a library or an art collection, it's best viewed from the beginning of quai d'Anjou. Voltaire and his mistress, Emilie de Breteuil, lived here at one time—their raucous quarrels were legendary. The mansion also housed the Polish royal family, the Czartoryskis, for over a century, before becoming the residence of actress Michèle Morgan. It now belongs to the Rothschild family and isn't open to the public.

Numbers 9, 11, 13, and 15 quai d'Anjou also belonged to the Lambert family. At **no. 9** stands the house where painter/sculptor/lithographer Honoré Daumier lived from 1846 to 1863, producing hundreds of caricatures satirizing the bourgeoisie and attacking government corruption. He was imprisoned for 6 months because of his 1832 cartoon of Louis-Philippe swallowing bags of gold that had been extracted from the people.

Near the Hôtel de Lauzun is the church of **St-Louis-en-l'Ile,** no. 19 bis rue St-Louis-en-l'Ile. Despite a dour exterior, the ornate interior is one of the finest examples of Jesuit Baroque. Built between 1664 and 1726, this church has been and still is the site of many weddings—with all the white stone and gilt, you'll feel as if you're inside a wedding cake. Look for the 1926 plaque reading "In grateful memory of St. Louis in whose honor the city of St. Louis, Missouri, USA, is named." If you need a refreshment break, head for ice cream at **Berthillon,** 31 rue St-Louis-en-l'Ile.

RIGHT BANK HIGHLIGHTS

LES HALLES   For 8 centuries, **Les Halles** (Métro: Les Halles; RER: Châtelet–Les Halles) was the city's major wholesale fruit, meat, and vegetable market. In the 19th century, Zola called it "the underbelly of Paris." The smock-clad vendors, beef carcasses, and baskets of vegetables all belong to the past, for the original market, with zinc-roofed Second Empire "iron umbrellas," has been torn down. Today the action has moved to a steel-and-glass edifice at Rungis, a suburb near Orly. In 1979, the area

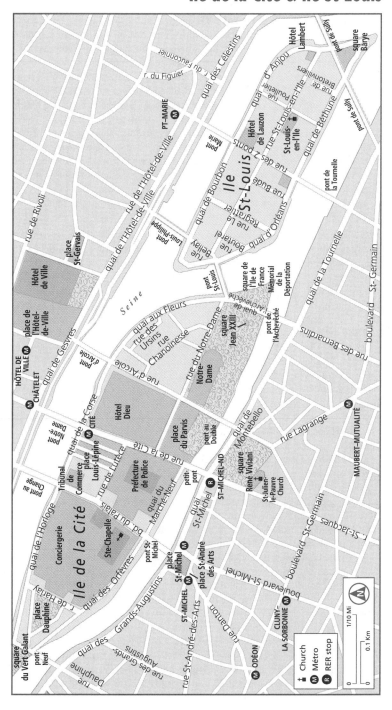

saw the opening of the **Forum des Halles,** 1–7 rue Pierre-Lescot, 1er. This large complex, much of it underground, contains shops, restaurants, and movie theaters. Many of the shops are unattractive, but others contain a wide display of merchandise that has made the mall popular with both residents and visitors.

For many visitors, a night on the town still ends in the wee hours with a bowl of onion soup at Les Halles, usually at **Au Pied de Cochon (The Pig's Foot),** 6 rue Coquillière, 1er (see chapter 5), or at **Au Chien Qui Fume (The Smoking Dog),** 33 rue du Pont-Neuf (☎ **01-42-36-07-42).** One of the most classic scenes of old Paris was elegantly dressed Parisians (many fresh from Maxim's) standing at a bar drinking cognac with blood-smeared butchers. Some writers have suggested that 19th-century poet Gérard de Nerval introduced the custom of frequenting Les Halles at such an unearthly hour. (His life was considered "irregular," and he hanged himself in 1855.)

A newspaper correspondent described today's scene this way: "Les Halles is trying to stay alive as one of the few places in Paris where one can eat at any hour of the night."

MONTMARTRE   Before its discovery and subsequent chic, Montmartre was a sleepy farming community, with windmills dotting the landscape. From the 1880s to just before World War I, the neighborhood enjoyed its golden age as the world's best-known art colony, where *la vie de bohème* reigned supreme. Following World War I, the pseudoartists flocked there in droves, with camera-snapping tourists hot on their heels. The real artists had long gone to such places as Montparnasse. For our **walking tour** of this neighborhood, see chapter 7.

Those who find the trek up to Paris's highest elevations too much of a climb may prefer to ride **Le Petit Train de Montmartre,** a miniature train that passes all the major landmarks; it seats 55 and offers English commentary. Board at place du Tertre (at St-Pierre) or place Blanche (near the Moulin Rouge). June to September, trains run daily 10am to 10pm (to 6pm the rest of the year); departures are every 30 to 40 minutes, and the round-trip fare is 32F ($5.10) adults and 18F ($2.90) children 3 to 12. For details, contact **Promotrain** at ☎ **01-42-62-24-00.** The simplest way to reach Montmartre is to take the **Métro** to Anvers, then walk up rue du Steinkerque to the **funicular,** which runs to the precincts of Sacré-Coeur daily 5:30am to 12:30am.

Besides **Sacré-Coeur** (see "The Top Attractions"), one of the most famous churches here is **St-Pierre,** rue du Mont-Cenis, originally a Benedictine abbey. It was consecrated in 1147; two of the columns in the choir stall are the remains of a Roman temple. Among the sculptured works, note the nun with the head of a pig, a symbol of sensual vice. At the entrance are three bronze doors sculpted by Gismondi in 1980: The middle door depicts the life of St. Peter; the left is dedicated to St. Denis, first bishop of Paris; and the right is dedicated to the Holy Virgin.

The **Espace Montmartre Dalí,** 11 rue Poulbot (☎ **01-42-64-40-10),** presents Dalí's phantasmagorical world with 330 original works, including his 1956 *Don Quixote* lithograph. It's open daily 10am to 6:30pm, charging 40F ($6.40) adults and 25F ($4) children 8 to 25; children under 8 are free. The **Musée de Vieux Montmartre,** 12 rue Cortot (☎ **01-46-06-61-11),** exhibits a wide collection of mementos of the area. This 17th-century house was once occupied by Dufy, van Gogh, Renoir, and Suzanne Valadon and her son, Utrillo. It's open Tuesday to Sunday 11am to 6pm. Admission is 25F ($4.25) adults and 20F ($3.40) children 10 and under.

Though gutted by fire in 1970, the **Bateau-Lavoir (Boat Warehouse),** place Emile-Goudeau, has been reconstructed. Picasso once lived in this cradle of cubism and, in the winter of 1905–06, painted one of the world's most famous portraits, *The Third Rose* (Gertrude Stein). Other residents were Kees van Dongen and Juan Gris;

Montmartre

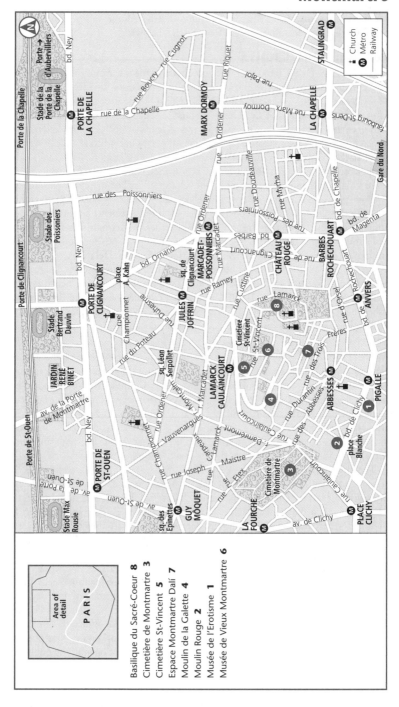

Basilique du Sacré-Coeur **8**
Cimetière de Montmartre **3**
Cimetière St-Vincent **5**
Espace Montmartre Dalí **7**
Moulin de la Galette **4**
Moulin Rouge **2**
Musée de l'Erotisme **1**
Musée de Vieux Montmartre **6**

Modigliani, Rousseau, and Braque had studios nearby. Also in this neighborhood is the **Cimetière de Montmartre** (see "Cemeteries," below).

LEFT BANK HIGHLIGHTS

ST-GERMAIN-DES-PRÉS   This neighborhood in the 6th arrondissement (Métro: St-Germain-des-Prés) was the postwar home of existentialism, associated with Sartre, de Beauvoir, Camus, and an intellectual bohemian crowd that gathered at **Café de Flore, Brasserie Lipp,** and **Les Deux Magots** (see chapter 5). Among them, black-clad poet and singer Juliette Greco was known as *la muse de St-Germain-des-Prés,* and to Sartre she was the woman who had "millions of poems in her throat." Her long hair, black slacks, black sweater, and black sandals launched a fashion trend adopted by young women everywhere. In the 1950s, new names appeared, like Françoise Sagan, Gore Vidal, and James Baldwin, but by the 1960s tourists became firmly entrenched.

St-Germain-des-Prés still retains an intellectually stimulating bohemian street life, full of many interesting bookshops, art galleries, *cave* (basement) clubs, bistros, and coffeehouses. But the stars of the area are two churches, **St-Germain-des-Prés,** 3 place St-Germain-des-Prés, 6e, and **St-Sulpice,** rue St-Sulpice, 6e (for both, see "The Important Churches"), and the **Musée National Eugène Delacroix,** 6 place de Furstemburg, 6e (see "The Major Museums"). Nearby, **rue Visconti** was designed for pushcarts and is worth visiting today. At **nos. 20–24** is the residence where dramatist Jean-Baptiste Racine died in 1699. And at **no. 17** is the house where Balzac established his printing press in 1825. (The venture ended in bankruptcy, forcing the author back to his writing desk.) Such celebrated actresses as Champmeslé and Clairon also lived here.

MONTPARNASSE   For the "lost generation," life centered around the literary cafes of Montparnasse, at the border of the 6th and 14th arrondissements (Métro: Montparnasse-Bienvenue). Hangouts like the **Dôme, Coupole, Rotonde,** and **Sélect** became legendary, as artists—especially American expatriates—turned their backs on Montmartre, dismissing it as too touristy. Picasso, Modigliani, and Man Ray came this way, and Hemingway was also a popular figure. So was Fitzgerald when he was poor (when he wasn't, you'd find him at the Ritz). Faulkner, MacLeish, Duncan, Miró, Joyce, Ford Madox Ford, and even Trotsky spent time here.

The most notable exception was Gertrude Stein, who never frequented the cafes. To see her, you had to wait for an invitation to her salon at **27 rue de Fleurus.** She bestowed this favor on Sherwood Anderson, Elliot Paul, Ezra Pound, and, for a time, Hemingway. When Pound launched himself into a beloved chair and broke it, he incurred Stein's wrath, and Hemingway decided there wasn't "much future in men being friends with great women" (for more on Gertrude, see the box "The Mother of the Lost Generation").

American expatriate writer Natalie Barney, who moved to Paris as a student in 1909 and stayed for over 60 years, held her grand salons at **20 rue Jacob** (actually in St-Germain-des-Prés)**.** Every Friday, her salon attracted the literati of her day, like Gertrude Stein, Djuna Barnes, Colette, Sherwood Anderson, T. S. Eliot, Janet Flanner, James Joyce, Sylvia Beach, Marcel Proust, and William Carlos Williams. The group met on and off for half a century, interrupted only by two world wars. Near place de Furstemburg, Barney's former residence is landmarked but not open to the public. In the garden you can see a small Doric temple bearing the inscription *A l'Amitié,* "to friendship."

Aside from the literary legends, one of the most notable characters of the sector was **Kiki de Montparnasse** (actually named Alice Prin, born illegitimate). She was raised

The Mother of the Lost Generation

"So Paris was the place that suited those of us that were to create the twentieth century art and literature, naturally enough." Gertrude Stein, who made this pronouncement, wasn't known for her modesty.

In the 1920s, she and her lover, Alice B. Toklas, became the most famous expats in Paris. To get an invitation to call on Lovey and Pussy (nicknames for Gertrude and Alice) at **27 rue de Fleurus,** in the heart of Montparnasse, was to be invited into the innermost circle of expatriate Paris. Though their former residence is in private hands and you can't go inside, literary fans flock to this fabled address to stare at the facade.

Though Gertrude didn't achieve popular success until the 1933 publication of her *Autobiography of Alice B. Toklas,* she was adored by many members of the Lost Generation—all except Ernest Hemingway, who tarred her in his posthumous memoir, *A Moveable Feast.* But to many sensitive young men (often gay) arriving from America in the 1920s, La Stein was "The Mother of Us All." These young fans hung onto her every word, while Alice baked her notorious hash brownies in the kitchen.

At rue de Fleurus, Gertrude and Alice surrounded themselves with modern paintings, including pieces by Vallotton, Toulouse-Lautrec, Picasso, Gauguin, and Matisse. Gertrude paid $1,000 for her first Matisse and $30 for her first Picasso. In fact, the two artists met here. The Saturday-night soirées became a Montparnasse legend, and one writer said her salon was engaged in an international conspiracy to promote modern art. Not all visitors came to worship, however. Gertrude was denounced by many, including avant-garde magazines of the time, which called her a "fraud, egomaniac, and publicity seeking." Braque called her claim to influence art in Paris "nonsense."

In spite of the attacks, jokes, and lurid speculation, Stein, at least in public, kept her ego intact. Bernard Fay once told her he'd met three people in his life who ranked as geniuses: Gide, Picasso, and herself. "Why include Gide?" Stein asked.

---

by her grandmother in Burgundy until her mother called her to Paris to work in a series of shops. When a sculptor discovered her, she became an artist's model and adopted her new name; soon she became a prostitute as well, and would bare her breasts to anyone who'd pay her 3F. She sang at **Le Jockey,** 127 bd. du Montparnasse, which no longer exists: In her black hose and garters, she captivated dozens of men, among them Frederick Kohner, who went so far as to entitle his memoirs *Kiki of Montparnasse.* Kiki later wrote her own memoirs, with an introduction by Hemingway. Papa called her "a Queen," noting that was "very different from being a lady."

Completed in 1973 and rising 688 feet above the skyline, the **Tour Montparnasse** (☎ **01-45-38-52-56**) was denounced by some critics as "bringing Manhattan to Paris." The city soon passed an ordinance outlawing any further structures of this size in the heart of Paris. Today, the modern tower houses a mammoth underground shopping mall as well as much of the infrastructure for the Gare de Montparnasse rail station. You can ride an elevator up to the 56th floor (where you'll find a bar and restaurant), then climb three flights to the roof terrace. The view includes virtually every important Paris monument, including Sacré-Coeur, Notre-Dame, and La Défense. Admission to the tower is 46F ($7.35) adults, 38F ($6.10) seniors, 35F

($5.60) students, and 30F ($4.80) children 5 to 14 (children 4 and under enter free). April to September, it's open daily 9:30am to 11:30pm; October to March, hours are Sunday to Friday 9:30am to 10:30pm.

The life of Montparnasse still centers around its cafes and exotic nightclubs, many only a shadow of what they used to be. Its heart is at the crossroads of **boulevard Raspail** and **boulevard du Montparnasse,** one of the settings of *The Sun Also Rises.* Hemingway wrote that "boulevard Raspail always made dull riding." Rodin's controversial statue of Balzac swathed in a large cape stands guard over the prostitutes who cluster around the pedestal. Balzac seems to be the only one in Montparnasse who doesn't feel the weight of time.

7 Specialty Museums

Be sure to turn to "The Top Attractions" and "The Major Museums" for the cream of the crop. "Especially for Kids" includes museums parents and kids will love. The museums reviewed below represent the curious, fascinating, and sometimes arcane balance of Paris's offerings.

ART & MUSIC MUSEUMS

Musée Bourdelle. 18 rue Antoine-Bourdelle, 15e. ☎ **01-49-54-73-73.** Admission 30F ($4.80) adults, 25F ($4) students, 15F ($2.40) children. Tues–Sun 10am–5:40pm. Métro: Falguière.

Here you can see works by the star pupil of Rodin, Antoine Bourdelle (1861–1929), who became a celebrated artist in his own right. Along with changed exhibits, the museum displays the artist's drawings, paintings, and sculptures and lets you wander through his studio, garden, and house. The original plaster casts of some of his greatest works are on display, but the most notable works are his 21 studies of Beethoven. Though some of the exhibits are badly captioned, you'll still feel the impact of Bourdelle's genius.

Musée Cernuschi. 7 av. Velázquez, 8e. ☎ **01-45-63-50-75.** Admission 35F ($5.60) adults, 25F ($4) students/seniors; age 17 and under free. Tues–Sun 10am–5:40pm. Métro: Monceau or Villiers. Bus: 30 or 94.

Bordering Parc Monceau, this small museum (another mansion whose owners stuffed it with art objects, then bequeathed everything to the city) is devoted to the arts of China. The bust of Henri Cernuschi (1820–96) is a self-perpetuating memorial to a man whose interest in the East was legendary. Though the collection is no match for the Guimet's (below), the museum has a number of treasures, like a 3-ton bronze Japanese Buddha, fine Neolithic potteries, and bronzes from the 14th century B.C., the most famous being a tiger-shaped vase. The jades, ceramics, and funeral figures are exceptional. Rounding out the exhibits are some ancient paintings, the best known of which is *Horses with Grooms,* attributed to Han Kan (A.D. 8th century). The museum also houses a good collection of contemporary Chinese paintings.

Musée Cognacq-Jay. In the Hôtel Donon, 8 rue Elzévir, 3e. ☎ **01-40-27-07-21.** Admission 22F ($3.50) adults, 15F ($2.40) ages 18–26; age 17 and under free. Tues–Sun 10am–5:40pm. Métro: St-Paul or Rambuteau.

The founders of La Samaritaine department store, Ernest Cognacq and his wife, Louise Jay, were fabled for their exquisite taste. To see what they accumulated from around the world, head for this museum in the 16th-century Hôtel Donon, with its Louis XV and Louis XVI paneled rooms. Some of the 18th century's most valuable decorative works are exhibited, ranging from ceramics and porcelain to delicate cabinets and paintings by Canaletto, Fragonard, Greuze, Chardin, Boucher, Watteau, and Tiepolo.

Musée d'Art Moderne de la Ville de Paris & Musée des Enfants. 11 av. du Président-Wilson, 16e. ☎ **01-53-67-40-00.** Admission 27F ($4.30) adults, 19F ($3.05) ages 18–24, 15F ($2.40) ages 7–17; age 6 and under free. Tues–Fri 10am–5:30pm, Sat–Sun 10am–7pm. Métro: Iéna or Alma-Marceau.

This museum bordering the Seine has a permanent collection of paintings and sculpture owned by the city, but come here only if visits to the d'Orsay and Louvre haven't satiated you. It presents ever-changing exhibits on individual artists from all over the world or on trends in international art. You'll find works by Chagall, Matisse, Léger, Rothko, Braque, Dufy, Picasso, Utrillo, and Modigliani. Seek out Pierre Tal Coat's *Portrait of Gertrude Stein* and keep Picasso's version of this difficult subject in mind. The **Musée des Enfants** has exhibits and shows for children.

Musée de la Musique. In the Cité de la Musique, 221 av. Jean-Jaurès, 19e. ☎ **01-44-84-44-84.** www.cite-musique.fr. Admission 35F ($5.60) adults, 25F ($4) students/age 60 and over, 10F ($1.60) age 17 and under. Visits with commentary, 60F ($9.60) adults, 45F ($7.20) students/age 60 and over, 20F ($3.20) age 17 and under. Tues–Thurs noon–6pm, Fri–Sat noon–7:30pm, Sun 10am–6pm. Métro: Porte de Pantin.

In the $120-million stone-and-glass Cité de la Musique, this museum serves as a tribute and testament to music. You can view 4,500 instruments from the 16th century to the present as well as paintings, engravings, and sculptures that relate to musical history. It's all here: cornets disguised as snakes, mandolins, lutes, zithers, antique music boxes, and even a postwar electric guitar. Models of the world's great concert halls and interactive display areas give you a chance to hear and better understand musical art and technology.

Musée des Arts d'Afrique et d'Océanie. 293 av. Daumesnil, 12e. ☎ **01-44-74-84-80.** Admission 30F ($4.80) adults; under age 18 free. Fri–Wed 10am–5:30pm. Métro: Porte Dorée.

In this art deco building constructed for the 1931 French Colonial exhibition, you'll find an extensive collection of central African art that's especially rich in carved masks, carved statues, and Aboriginal bark paintings, as well as some magnificent bronzes from Benin. There are also some art objects from the Pacific islands and a limited collection of woven carpets and gold jewelry from the Magreb region of Arab-speaking North Africa. In the cellars are aquariums and terrariums containing crocodiles, iguanas, and tortoises.

Musée des Arts Décoratifs. In the Palais du Louvre, 107 rue de Rivoli, 1er. ☎ **01-44-55-57-50.** Admission 35F ($5.60) adults, 25F ($4) ages 18–25; age 18 and under free. Tues and Thurs–Fri 11am–6pm, Wed 11am–9pm, Sat–Sun 10am–6pm. Métro: Palais Royal or Tuileries.

In the northwest wing of the Louvre's Pavillon de Marsan, this museum boasts furnishings, fabrics, wallpaper, and objets d'art from the Middle Ages to the present—but it's recommended only if you have an abiding interest in the subject. Notable on the first floor are the 1920s art deco boudoir, bath, and bedroom of couturier Jeanne Lanvin by designer Rateau. Decorative art from the Middle Ages to the Renaissance is on the second floor; rich collections from the 17th, 18th, and 19th centuries occupy

Museum Closing Days

Generally, all museums are closed on January 1, May 1, Bastille Day (July 14), and December 25.

the third and fourth floors. The fifth has centers on wallpaper and drawings and documentary centers detailing fashion, textiles, toys, crafts, and glass trends. The newest addition is a **Musée de la Publicité** (**Museum of Advertising**), with advertising posters from the 18th century and film, TV, and radio commercials from the 1930s to today. Architect Jean Nouvel designed a cutting-edge interior that also displays avant-garde video techniques.

Musée Edith Piaf. 5 rue Crespin-du-Gast, 11e. ☎ **01-43-55-52-72.** Admission free but donations appreciated. Mon–Thurs 1–6pm by appointment only. Métro: Ménilmontant.

This privately run museum is filled with Piaf memorabilia, like photos, costumes, and personal possessions. (If you don't phone in advance, you won't have the security code you'll need to buzz your way in.) The daughter of an acrobat, Giovanna Gassion grew up in this neighborhood and assumed the name of Piaf ("little sparrow"); her songs, like "La Vie en Rose" and "Non, je ne regrette rien," eventually were heard around the world. Nearby is the **Villa Calte,** a beautiful example of the fine architecture many locals are trying to save (ask for directions at the Piaf museum). Fronted by an intricate wrought-iron fence, the house has a pleasant garden where parts of Truffaut's *Jules et Jim* were filmed.

Musée National des Arts Asiatiques–Guimet. 6 place d'Iéna, 16e. ☎ **01-56-52-53-00.** Closed until mid-2001. Métro: Iéna or Alma-Marceau.

One of a trio of museums devoted to the art and archaeology of the Asian region from Afghanistan to Japan, this one was named for its founder, research chemist/industrialist Emile Guimet. The Guimet, opened in Lyon but transferred to Paris in 1889, received the Musée Indochinois du Trocadéro's collections in 1931 and the Louvre's Asian collections after World War II. The most interesting exhibits are Buddhas, serpentine monster heads, funereal figurines, and antiquities from the temple of Angkor Wat. Some galleries are devoted to Tibetan art, including fascinating scenes of the Grand Lamas entwined with serpents and demons. In 2000–2001, the main museum underwent renovations, adding several underground galleries; it hopes to open by summer 2001. The other two museums of the trio are the **Musée d'Ennery,** 59 av. Foch (closed indefinitely), and the **Panthéon Bouddhique** (below).

Musée Nissim de Camondo. 63 rue de Monceau, 8e. ☎ **01-53-89-06-50.** Admission 30F ($4.80) adults, 20F ($3.20) under age 18/over 60. Wed–Sun 10am–5pm. Closed Jan 1, May 1, Bastille Day (July 14), and Dec 25. Métro: Villiers.

Visit this museum for a keen insight into the decorative arts of the 18th-century. The pre–World War I town house was donated to the Musée des Arts Décoratif by Comte Moïse de Camondo in memory of his son, Nissim, a French aviator killed in combat during World War I. The museum is like the home of an aristocrat—rich with needlepoint chairs, tapestries (many from Beauvais or Aubusson), antiques, paintings, bas-reliefs, silver, Chinese vases, crystal chandeliers, Sèvres porcelain, Savonnerie carpets, and even a Houdon bust. The Blue Salon, overlooking Parc Monceau, is most impressive.

Musée Zadkine. 100 bis rue d'Assas, 6e. ☎ **01-43-26-91-90.** Admission 27F ($4.30) adults, 19F ($3.05) ages 7–26. Tues–Sun 10am–5:30pm. Métro: Notre-Dame des Champs.

This museum near the Jardin du Luxembourg was once the home of sculptor Ossip Zadkine (1890–1967), and his collection has been turned over to the city for public viewing. Included are some 300 pieces of sculpture, displayed in the museum and the garden. Some drawings and tapestries are also exhibited. At these headquarters where he worked from 1928 until his death, you can see how he moved from "left wing" cubism extremism to a renewed appreciation of the classic era. You can visit his garden for free even if you don't want to go into the museum—in fact, it's one of the finest places to relax in Paris on a sunny day, sitting on a bench taking in the two-faced *Woman with the Bird.*

Panthéon Bouddhique. 19 av. d'Iéna, 16e. ☎ **01-40-73-88-00.** Admission 16F ($2.55) adults, 12F ($1.90) students/under age 27; under age 7 free. Wed–Mon 9:45am–5:45pm. Métro: Iéna.

This museum retraces the religious pasts of China and Japan from the 4th to the 19th century. About 250 Japanese works of art represent Buddhist traditions and 33 Chinese masterpieces show the evolution of Buddhism as it passed from India to China and migrated to Japan, where it was embraced around A.D. 1000. Many pieces were acquired by Emile Guimet on his 1876 voyage to Japan. His booty included many sculptures from the Kamakura period (1192–1333) and the Muromachi-Momoyama period (14th to 16th centuries). The seasonally changing Japanese garden is an ideal place to meditate.

CRAFT & INDUSTRY MUSEUMS

Manufacture Nationale des Gobelins. 42 av. des Gobelins, 13e. ☎ **01-44-61-21-69.** Tours in French (with English pamphlets) 50F ($8) adults, 40F ($6.40) ages 7–24/65 or older; under 7 free. Tues–Thurs 2 and 2:45pm. Métro: Les Gobelins.

Did you know a single tapestry can take 4 years to complete, employing as many as three to five full-time weavers? The founder of this dynasty, Jehan Gobelin, came from a family of dyers and clothmakers and in the 15th century discovered a scarlet dye that made him famous. By 1601, Henry IV had become interested and imported from Flanders 200 weavers to make tapestries full-time. Oddly enough, until this endeavor the Gobelin family hadn't made any tapestries. Colbert, Louis XIV's minister, eventually bought the works, and under royal patronage the craftsmen set about executing designs by Le Brun. After the Revolution, the industry was reactivated by Napoléon. Les Gobelins is still going strong, and some of the antique high-warp looms are still in use. You can visit the studios (*ateliers*) of the weavers, who sit behind huge screens of thread, patiently inserting stitch after stitch.

Musée de Baccarat. 30 bis rue de Paradis, 10e. ☎ **01-47-70-64-30.** Admission 15F ($2.40) adults, 10F ($1.60) students, 7.50F ($1.20) under age 17/over 60. Mon–Sat 9am–6pm. Métro: Poissonnière or Château d'Eau.

In a Directoire building that houses Baccarat's headquarters, this museum resembles an ice palace filled with crystal of all shapes and sizes, with some of the most impressive pieces produced by the company through the years. Czars, royalty, and oil-rich sheiks have numbered among the best patrons of the prestigious company, established in 1764. At the museum entrance stands "Lady Baccarat," a chandelier in the form and size of a woman.

Musée National de Céramique de Sèvres. Grande Rue, Sèvres, 15e. ☎ **01-41-14-04-20.** Admission 30F ($4.80) adults, 23F ($3.70) ages 18–25; age 17 and under free. Wed–Mon 10am–5pm. Métro: Pont de Sèvres, then walk across the Seine to the Left Bank.

Next door to the Manufacture Nationale de Sèvres (see chapter 8), this museum boasts one of the world's finest collections of faïence and porcelain, some of which belonged to Mme du Barry, Mme de Pompadour's hand-picked successor as Louis XV's mistress (Mme de Pompadour *loved* Sèvres porcelain). On view is the Pompadour rose (which the English insisted on calling the rose du Barry), a style much in vogue in the 1750s and 1760s. The painter Boucher made some of the designs used by the factory, as did the sculptor Pajou (he created the bas-reliefs for the Opéra at Versailles). The factory pioneered what became known in porcelain as the Louis Seize (Louis XVI) style—it's all here, plus lots more, including works from Sèvres's arch rival, Meissen.

CULTURAL MUSEUMS

Institut du Monde Arabe (Institute of the Arab World). 1 rue des Fossés St-Bernard, 5e. ☎ **01-40-51-38-38.** Admission to permanent collections 25F ($4); to special exhibits 45F ($7.20); combined ticket 55F ($8.80). Tues–Sun 10am–6pm. Métro: Jussieu.

One of the finest modern structures in Paris, this glass-and-aluminum building was financed with funds from France and 20 Arab nations. It's much more than a museum, with a multimedia cultural center whose aim is to promote relations between France and the Arab world. The institute features art from three Arab regions, some from the 3rd century; a massive library with literary works and periodicals in Arabic, French, and English; and an auditorium where Arab movies and plays are presented. You can enjoy coffee or a light lunch at the 9th-floor restaurant/cafe while taking in the panoramic view from the terrace.

Musée d'Art et d'Histoire du Judaïsm (Museum of Jewish History and Art). 71 rue du Temple, 3e. ☎ **01-53-01-86-60.** Admission 40F ($6.40) adults; under age 18 free. Mon–Fri and Sun 10am–6pm. Métro: Rambuteau.

More Jews live in France than in any other European country except Russia, and as of 1998 this museum in the Marais, the old Jewish quarter, honors their history. Jacques Chirac, who inaugurated the museum, was the first French president to apologize for the pro-Nazi Vichy regime's role in persecuting Jews during World War II. Alas, the fate of the 78,000 French Jews deported during the war is hardly addressed. The museum provides an overview of European Jewish life since the Middle Ages, including religious objects and ancient manuscripts collected in the early 1800s by Isaac Strauss as well as the holdings of a small Jewish Art Museum founded in Paris in 1948. Rooms deal with themes like the role of Jews in the Italian Renaissance and the Dreyfus affair, the late-19th-century scandal over a Jewish army officer unjustly accused of treason. An entire room is dedicated to paintings and drawings by Marc Chagall, on loan from the Pompidou.

HISTORY MUSEUMS

Musée de l'Histoire de France. In the Hôtel de Soubise, 60 rue des Francs-Bourgeois, 3e. ☎ **01-40-27-61-78.** Admission 20F ($3.20) adults, 15F ($2.40) children/seniors. Wed–Mon 2–6pm. Métro: Hôtel de Ville or Rambuteau.

This palace has been steeped in French history since it was first built in 1371. The graceful baroque facade dates from 1705, when the building's exterior was redesigned by the much underrated architect Delamair for the prince and princesse de Soubise. In the early 1800s, Napoléon designated the building as the official repository for his archives, and it has served that function ever since. You enter through the colonnaded Cour d'Honneur (Court of Honor). But before going inside, walk around the corner to 58 rue des Archives to the medieval turreted gateway of the **Hôtel de Clisson.** (This mansion gave way to the palace of the ducs de Guise, who owned the property until it was bought by the Soubise family. The princesse de Soubise was once the mistress of Louis XIV, and apparently the Sun King was very generous, giving her the funds to remodel and redesign the palace.)

The archives contain documents that go back even further than Charlemagne. The letter collection is highly valued, exhibiting the penmanship of Marie Antoinette (a farewell letter), Louis XVI (his will), Danton, Robespierre, Napoléon I, and Joan of Arc (the museum has the only known living sketch of her). Even the jailer's keys to the old Bastille are here. One of the showcased rooms is the **Salon de la Princesse** (a.k.a the **Salon Ovale**), a richly decorated circular room one floor above street level. Sweeping expanses of gilt and crystal offset a series of ceiling frescoes by Van Loo, Boucher, and Natoire. Sometimes, the **Hôtel de Rohan,** around the corner on rue Vieille-du-Temple, contains some of the overflow from this place, but only in the form of temporary exhibits.

Paristoric. 11 bis rue Scribe, 9e. ☎ **01-42-66-62-06.** Admission 50F ($8) adults, 30F ($4.80) students/under age 18. Daily 9am–6pm (to 9pm Apr–Oct). Shows begin every hour on the hour. Métro: Opéra. RER: Auber.

This unique 45-minute multimedia show retraces the city's history in a state-of-the-art theater. The 2,000 years since Paris's birth unroll chronologically to the music of such varied musicians as Wagner and Piaf. Maps, portraits, and scenes from dramatic times are projected on the large screen as a running commentary (heard through headphones in one of 10 languages) gives details about art, architecture, and events. Many visitors come here first for a preview of what they want to see; others stop for a more in-depth look at what they've already visited.

THE OFFBEAT

Musée de la Chasse (Hunting Museum). In the Hôtel Guénégaud, 60 rue des Archives, 3e. ☎ **01-53-01-92-40.** Admission 30F ($4.80) adults, 15F ($2.40) students/seniors, 5F (80¢) ages 5–16; children 4 and under free. Tues–Sun 11am–6pm. Métro: Rambuteau or Hôtel de Ville.

Near the Musée Carnavalet, this mansion was also designed by Mansart, and its museum is for the specialist who likes to hunt, like Hemingway, for sport. Mounted heads are plentiful, from the antelope to the elephant, from the bushbuck to the waterbuck to the bush pig. You'll find a Rembrandt sketch of a lion, a number of Desportes wild-animal portraits, and rifles (many from the 17th century) inlaid with pearls or engraved with ivory. The outstanding hunt tapestries are often perversely amusing—one a cannibalistic romp, another showing a helmeted man standing eye to eye with a bear he's stabbing to death. The collection of paintings includes works by Rubens, Breughel, Oudry, Chardin, and Corot.

Musée de l'Erotisme. 72 bd. de Clichy, 18e. ☎ **01-42-58-28-73.** www.erotic-museum.com. Admission 40F ($6.40) adults; children under 17 not permitted. Daily 10am–2am. Métro: Blanche.

A tribute to the primal appeal of human sexuality, this art gallery/museum opened in 1997 in a 19th-century town house that had been a raunchy cabaret. It presents a tasteful but appealingly risqué collection of art and artifacts, with six floors boasting an oft-changing array of exhibits like erotic sculptures and drawings. The oldest object is a palm-sized ancient Roman *tintinabulum* (bell), a phallus-shaped animal with the likeness of a nude woman riding astride it. Modern objects include resin, wood, and plaster sculptures by French artist Alain Rose and works by American, Dutch, German, and French artists, including the free-form works of Robert Combas. Also look for everyday items with erotic themes from South America (terra-cotta pipes shaped like phalluses) and the States (a 1920s belt buckle that resembles a praying nun when it's fastened and a nude woman when it's open). The gift shop sells Asian amulets, African bronzes, and terra-cotta figurines from South America. There's also an art gallery where serious works of art are sold for 1,000F to 100,000F ($160 to $16,000).

Musée du Parfum (Perfume Museum). 39 bd. des Capucines, 1e. ☎ **01-42-60-37-14.** Admission free. Mon–Sat 9am–6pm. Métro: Opéra.

This museum is in an overhauled 19th-century theater on one of Paris's busiest thoroughfares. As you enter the lobby through a quiet courtyard, the lightly scented air will remind you why you're there—to appreciate perfume enough to buy a bottle in the ground-floor shop. But first, a short visit upstairs introduces you to the rudiments of perfume history. The copper containers with spouts and tubes were used in the distillation of perfume oils, and the exquisite collection of perfume bottles from the 17th to the 20th century is impressive. Even if perfume bores you, the air-conditioning is a welcome relief in summer, and the rest rooms are spotless and free.

Musée du Vin (Wine Museum). 5 rue des Eaux, 16e. ☎ **01-45-25-63-26.** Admission 35F ($5.60) adults, 29F ($4.65) students, 32F ($5.10) over age 60. Tues–Sun 10am–6pm. Métro: Passy.

This museum is in an ancient stone-and-clay quarry used by 15th-century monks as a wine cellar. It provides a good introduction to the art of wine making, displaying various tools, beakers, cauldrons, and bottles in a series of exhibits. The quarry is right below Balzac's house (see "Literary Landmarks," below), and the ceiling contains a trap door he used to escape from his creditors.

8 Parks & Gardens

JARDIN DES TUILERIES

The spectacular statue-studded ✪ **Jardin des Tuileries,** bordering place de la Concorde, 1er (☎ 01-44-50-75-01; Métro: Tuileries), are as much a part of Paris as the Seine. They were designed by Le Nôtre, Louis XIV's gardener and planner of the Versailles grounds. About 100 years before that, Catherine de Médicis ordered a palace built here, the **Palais des Tuileries,** connected to the Louvre; other occupants have included Louis XVI (after he left Versailles) and Napoléon. Twice attacked by enraged Parisians, it was finally burned to the ground in 1871 and never rebuilt. The gardens, however, remain. In orderly French manner, the trees are arranged according to designs and even the paths are arrow-straight. Breaking the sense of order and formality are bubbling fountains.

Seemingly half of Paris can be found in the Tuileries on a warm spring day, listening to the chirping birds and admiring the daffodils and tulips. As you walk toward the Louvre, you'll enter the **Jardin du Carrousel,** dominated by the **Arc de Triomphe du Carrousel,** at the Cour du Carrousel. Pierced with three walkways and supported by marble columns, the monument honors Napoléon's Grande Armée, celebrating its victory at Austerlitz on December 5, 1805. The arch is surmounted by statuary, a chariot, and four bronze horses.

JARDIN DU LUXEMBOURG

Hemingway once told a friend that the **Jardin du Luxembourg** (Métro: Odéon; RER: Luxembourg) "kept us from starvation." He related that in his poverty-stricken days in Paris, he wheeled a baby carriage (the vehicle was considered luxurious) through the gardens because it was known "for the classiness of its pigeons." When the gendarme went across the street for a glass of wine, the writer would eye his victim, preferably a plump one, then lure him with corn and "snatch him, wring his neck," and hide him under the blanket. "We got a little tired of pigeon that year," he confessed, "but they filled many a void."

Did You Know?

The odd name of the Jardins des Tuileries comes from the clay earth of the land here, once used to make roof tiles called *tuiles*.

Gone with the Wind

The most violent windstorm in France's history thundered through Paris on Christmas Day 1999, causing extensive damage to parks and gardens in the Ile de France. At Versailles, the wind toppled 10,000 trees and blew out some windows at the magnificent château. In Paris, Parc Monceau and the Tuileries were the hardest hit, with hundreds of trees uprooted or damaged. At the Père-Lachaise cemetery, the dense foliage protecting the gravesites has been destroyed. Minor damage also occurred to Notre-Dame and Sainte-Chapelle. All these places have now reopened for visits, and most of the visible structural damage has been fixed, but the difficult task of replanting the thousands of trees will take some time, and it'll be years before they return to their lush grandeur.

The Luxembourg has always been associated with artists, though children, Sorbonne students, and tourists predominate nowadays. Watteau came this way, as did Verlaine. Balzac, however, didn't like the gardens at all. In 1905, Gertrude Stein would cross them to catch the Batignolles/Clichy/Odéon omnibus, pulled by three gray mares, to meet Picasso in his studio at Montmartre, where he painted her portrait.

Marie de Médicis, the neglected wife of the roving Henri IV, ordered the **Palais du Luxembourg** built on this site in 1612, shortly after she was widowed. A Florentine by birth, the regent wanted to create another Pitti Palace, where she could live with her "witch" friend, Leonora Galigal. Architect Salomon de Brossee wasn't entirely successful, though the overall effect is Italianate. Alas, the queen didn't get to enjoy the palace, as she was forced into exile by her son, Louis XIII, when he discovered she was plotting to overthrow him. She died in poverty in Cologne. For her palace, she'd commissioned from Rubens 21 paintings that glorified her life, but they're now in the Louvre. You can visit the palace only the first Sunday of each month at 10:15am, for 50F ($8) adults or 40F ($6.40) 25 years or under. However, you must call ☎ 01-44-61-20-89 to make a reservation.

However, you don't come to the Luxembourg to visit the palace—not really. The gardens are the attraction. For the most part, they're in the classic French tradition: well groomed and formally laid out, the trees planted in patterns. A large central water basin is encircled by urns and statuary on pedestals, one honoring Paris's patroness, St. Geneviève, with pigtails reaching to her thighs. Another memorial is dedicated to Stendhal. It's a good place for kids: They can sail a toy boat, ride a pony, or attend an occasional Grand Guignol puppet show. And you can play *boules* with a group of elderly men who aren't ashamed to wear black berets and have Gauloises dangling from their mouths.

BOIS DE BOULOGNE

One of the most spectacular parks in Europe is the **Bois de Boulogne,** Porte Dauphine, 16e (☎ 01-40-67-90-82; Métro: Les Sablons, Porte Maillot, or Porte Dauphine), often called the "main lung" of Paris. Horse-drawn carriages traverse it, but you can also drive through. Its hidden pathways, however, can be discovered only by walking. You could spend days in the Bois de Boulogne and still not see everything.

Porte Dauphine is the main entrance, though you can take the Métro to Porte Maillot as well. West of Paris, the park was once a forest kept for royal hunts. It was in vogue in the late 19th century: Along avenue Foch, carriages with elegantly attired and coiffured Parisian damsels would rumble along with their foppish escorts. Nowadays,

The Bois de Boulogne

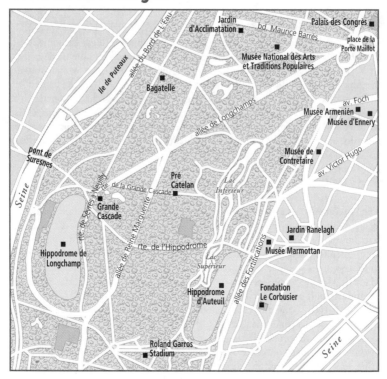

it's more likely to attract run-of-the-mill picnickers. (And at night, hookers and muggers are prominent, so be duly warned.)

When Napoléon III gave the grounds to the city in 1852, they were developed by Baron Haussmann. Separating Lac Inférieur from Lac Supérieur is the **Carrefour des Cascades** (you can stroll under its waterfall). The Lower Lake contains two islands connected by a footbridge. From the east bank, you can take a boat to these idyllically situated grounds, perhaps stopping off at the cafe/restaurant on one of them.

Restaurants in the bois are numerous, elegant, and expensive. The **Pré Catelan** contains a deluxe restaurant of the same name (☎ 01-44-14-41-14) occupying a gem of a Napoléon III–style château and a Shakespearean theater in a garden planted with trees mentioned in the bard's plays. Nearby is **La Grande Cascade** (☎ 01-45-27-33-51), once a hunting lodge for Napoléon III.

The **Jardin d'Acclimatation** at the northern edge of the park is for children, with a small zoo, an amusement park, and a narrow-gauge railway (see "Especially for Kids" for more details). Two racetracks, the **Hippodrome de Longchamp** and the **Hippodrome d'Auteuil,** are in the park (see "A Day at the Races"). The Grand Prix is run in June at Longchamp (the site of a medieval abbey). Fashionable Parisians always turn out for this, the women in their finest haute couture. To the north of Longchamp is the **Grand Cascade,** an artificial waterfall.

In the western section of the bois, the 60-acre **Parc de Bagatelle** owes it existence to a bet between the comte d'Artois (later Charles X) and Marie Antoinette, his sister-in-law. The comte wagered he could erect a small palace in less than 3 months, so he hired nearly 1,000 craftsmen (cabinetmakers, painters, Scottish landscape architect

Thomas Blaikie, more) and irritated the locals by requisitioning all shipments of stone and plaster arriving through Paris's west gates. He won his bet. If you're here in late April, it's worth visiting the Bagatelle just for the tulips. In late May, one of the finest rose collections in Europe is in full bloom. For some reason, as the head gardener confides to us, "This is the major rendezvous point in Paris for illicit couples." In September, the light is less harsh than in summer or even in February; when stripped of much of its greenery, the park's true shape can be seen.

PARC MONCEAU

Much of **Parc Monceau,** 8e (☎ **01-42-27-39-56;** Métro: Monceau or Villiers), is ringed with 18th- and 19th-century mansions, some evoking Proust's *Remembrance of Things Past.* Carmontelle designed it in 1778 for the duc d'Orléans (who came to be known as Philippe-Egalité), at the time the richest man in France. The duke was noted for his debauchery and pursuit of pleasure, so no ordinary park would do. It was opened to the public in the days of Napoléon III's Second Empire.

Monceau was laid out with an Egyptian-style obelisk, a medieval dungeon, a thatched farmhouse, a Chinese pagoda, a Roman temple, an enchanted grotto, various chinoiseries, and a waterfall. These fairy-tale touches have largely disappeared, except for a pyramid and an oval naumachia fringed by a colonnade. Now the park is filled with solid statuary and monuments, one honoring Chopin. In spring, the red tulips and magnolias are worth the air ticket to Paris.

9 Cemeteries

Sightseers often view Paris's cemeteries as being somewhat like parks, suitable places for strolling. The graves of celebrities past are also a major lure. Père-Lachaise, for example, is a major sightseeing goal; the other cemeteries are of lesser interest.

✪ **Cimetière du Père-Lachaise.** 16 rue du Repos, 20e. ☎ **01-43-70-70-33.** Admission free. Mon–Fri 8am–6pm, Sat 8:30am–6pm, Sun 9am–6pm (to 5:30pm early Nov–early Mar). Métro: Père-Lachaise.

When it comes to name dropping, this cemetery knows no peer; it has been called the "grandest address in Paris." A free map of Père-Lachaise is available at the newsstand across from the main entrance (also see the map on pages 208–209).

Everybody from **Sarah Bernhardt** to **Oscar Wilde** to **Richard Wright** is here, along with **Honoré de Balzac, Jacques-Louis David, Eugène Delacroix, Maria Callas, Max Ernst,** and **Georges Bizet. Colette** was taken here in 1954; her black granite slab always sports flowers, and legend has it that cats replenish the roses. In time the little sparrow, **Edith Piaf,** followed. The lover of George Sand, poet **Alfred de Musset,** was buried under a weeping willow. Napoléon's marshals, **Ney** and **Masséna,** lie here, as do **Frédéric Chopin** and **Molière. Marcel Proust's** black tombstone rarely lacks a tiny bunch of violets (he wanted to be buried beside his friend/lover, composer **Maurice Ravel,** but their families wouldn't allow it).

Impressions

Mrs. Allongby: They say, Lady Hunstanton, that when good Americans die they go to Paris.
Lady Hunstanton: Indeed? And when bad Americans die, where do they go?
Lord Illingworth: Oh, they go to America.
—Oscar Wilde, *A Woman of No Importance* (1893)

The Père-Lachaise Cemetery

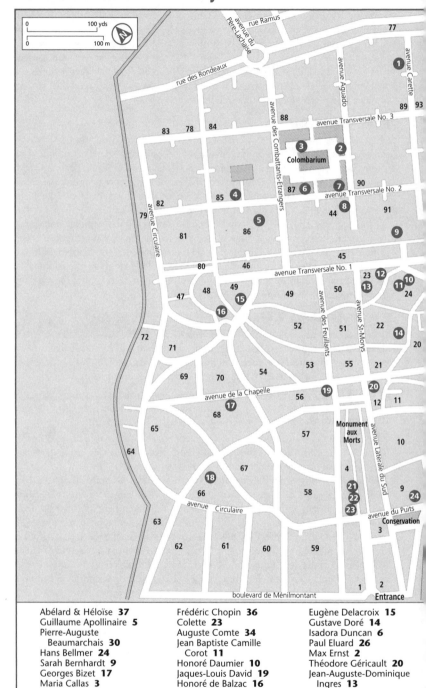

0   100 yds
0   100 m

rue Ramus
avenue du Père-Lachaise
rue des Rondeaux
avenue Ramus
avenue Aguado
avenue Carette
77
1
89   93
avenue Transversale No. 3
83   78   84   88
avenue des Combattants-Étrangers
3   2
Colombarium
4
85   87   6   7   90
avenue Transversale No. 2
82   79   avenue Circulaire   81   5   86   44   8   91
45   9
80   46   avenue Transversale No. 1
47   48   49   49   50   23   12
13   11   10   24
15   52   51   22   14
16   avenue des Feuillants   avenue St-Morys   20
72   71   53   55   21
69   70   54   56   19   20
avenue de la Chapelle   12   11
17   68   57   Monument   10
65   aux   Morts
64   4
18   67   21   9   24
66   58   22   23
avenue Circulaire   avenue du Puits   Conservation
63   avenue Latérale du Sud   3
62   61   60   59   1   2
boulevard de Ménilmontant   Entrance

Abélard & Héloïse **37**	Frédéric Chopin **36**	Eugène Delacroix **15**
Guillaume Apollinaire **5**	Colette **23**	Gustave Doré **14**
Pierre-Auguste	Auguste Comte **34**	Isadora Duncan **6**
Beaumarchais **30**	Jean Baptiste Camille	Paul Eluard **26**
Hans Bellmer **24**	Corot **11**	Max Ernst **2**
Sarah Bernhardt **9**	Honoré Daumier **10**	Théodore Géricault **20**
Georges Bizet **17**	Jaques-Louis David **19**	Jean-Auguste-Dominique
Maria Callas **3**	Honoré de Balzac **16**	Ingres **13**

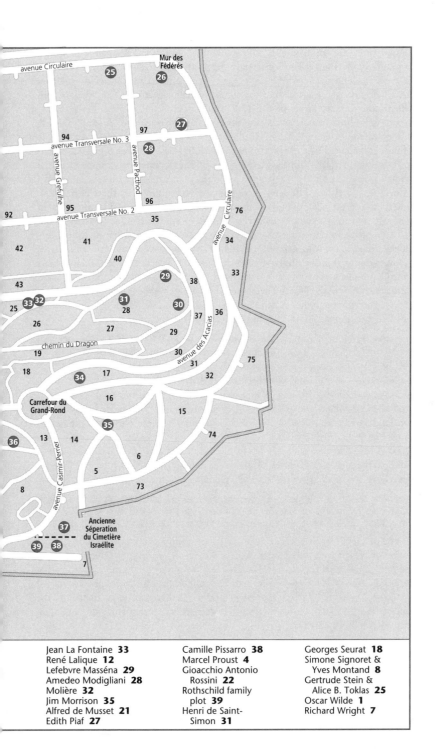

avenue Circulaire

Mur des
Fédérés

25 **26**

avenue Transversale No. 3

94 **97**

27

avenue Greffuhle

avenue Pacthod

28

avenue Transversale No. 2

95 **96**

92 **35** **76**

avenue Circulaire

41 **34**

42 **40** **33**

29 **38**

43 **31** **30** **37** **36**

25 **33 32** **28** **29**

26 **27** avenue des Acacias **75**

chemin du Dragon **30**

19 **31** **32**

18 **34** **17**

16 **15**

Carrefour du
Grand-Rond

35

13 **74**

36 **14**

avenue Casimir-Perrier

6

5

8 **73**

37

Ancienne
Séperation
du Cimetière
Israélite

39 **38**

7

Jean La Fontaine **33**
René Lalique **12**
Lefebvre Masséna **29**
Amedeo Modigliani **28**
Molière **32**
Jim Morrison **35**
Alfred de Musset **21**
Edith Piaf **27**

Camille Pissarro **38**
Marcel Proust **4**
Gioacchio Antonio
 Rossini **22**
Rothschild family
 plot **39**
Henri de Saint-
 Simon **31**

Georges Seurat **18**
Simone Signoret &
 Yves Montand **8**
Gertrude Stein &
 Alice B. Toklas **25**
Oscar Wilde **1**
Richard Wright **7**

Some tombs are sentimental favorites: Love-torn graffiti radiates half a mile from the tomb of Doors singer **Jim Morrison.** The great dancer **Isadora Duncan** came to rest in the Columbarium, where bodies have been cremated and "filed" away. If you search hard enough, you can find the tombs of that star-crossed pair **Abélard** and **Héloïse,** the ill-fated lovers of the 12th century—at Père-Lachaise, they've found peace at last. Other famous lovers also rest here: A stone is marked **"Alice B. Toklas"** on one side and **"Gertrude Stein"** on the other, and eventually France's First Couple of film were reunited when **Yves Montand** joined his wife, **Simone Signoret.** (Montand's gravesite attracted much attention in 1998: His corpse was exhumed in the middle of the night for DNA testing in a paternity lawsuit—he wasn't the father.)

Covering more than 110 acres, Père-Lachaise was acquired by the city in 1804. Nineteenth-century sculpture abounds, as each family tried to outdo the other in ornamentation and cherubic ostentation. Frenchmen who died in the Resistance or in Nazi concentration camps are also honored by monuments. Some French Socialists still pay tribute at the **Mur des Fédérés,** the anonymous gravesite of the Communards who were executed in the cemetery on May 28, 1871. When these last-ditch fighters of the Commune, the world's first anarchist republic, made their final desperate stand against the troops of the French government, they were overwhelmed, lined up against the wall, and shot in groups. A handful survived and lived hidden in the cemetery for years like wild animals, venturing into Paris at night to forage for food.

Cimetière du Montparnasse. 3 bd. Edgar-Quinet, 14e. ☎ **01-44-10-86-50.** Admission free. Mon–Fri 8am–6pm, Sat 8:30am–6pm, Sun 9am–6pm (to 5:15pm Nov–Mar). Métro: Edgar Quinet.

In the shadow of the Tour Montparnasse, this debris-littered cemetery is a burial ground of yesterday's celebrities. A map available to the left of the main gateway will direct you to the shared gravesite of its most famous couple, **Simone de Beauvoir** and **Jean-Paul Sartre.** Others resting here include **Samuel Beckett, Guy de Maupassant,** editor **Pierre Larousse** (famous for his dictionary), **Capt. Alfred Dreyfus,** auto tycoon **André Citroën,** sculptors **Ossip Zadkine** and **Constantin Brancusi,** actress **Jean Seberg,** composer **Camille Saint-Saëns,** photographer **Man Ray,** and **Charles Baudelaire,** who'd already written about "plunging into the abyss, Heaven or Hell."

Cimetière St-Vincent. 6 rue Lucien-Gaulard, 18e. ☎ **01-46-06-29-78.** Admission free. Mar 16–Nov 5 Mon–Fri 8am–6pm, Sat 8:30am–6pm, Sun 9am–6pm; Nov 6–Mar 15 Mon–Fri 8am–5:30pm, Sat 8:30am–5pm, Sun 9am–5pm. Métro: Lamarck-Caulaincourt.

Because of the artists and writers who have their resting place in the modest burial ground of St-Vincent, with a view of Sacré-Coeur on the hill, it's sometimes called "the most intellectual cemetery in Paris"—but that epithet seems more apt for other graveyards. Artists **Maurice Utrillo** and **Théopile-Alexandre Steinien** were buried here, as was musician **Arthur Honegger** and writer **Marcel Aymé.** In theory, the cemetery is open all day, but if you disturb the caretaker's lunch—any time from noon to 2pm—you'll regret it.

Cimetière de Passy. 2 rue du Comandant-Schloesing, 16e. ☎ **01-47-27-51-42.** Admission free. Mar–Nov daily 8:30am–5:45pm; Dec–Feb daily 8:30am–5:15pm. Métro: Trocadéro.

This cemetery runs along Paris's old northern walls, south and southwest of Trocadéro. It's a small graveyard, sheltered by chestnut trees, but it contains many gravesites of the famous—a concierge at the gate can guide you. Painters **Edouard Manet** and **Romaine Brooks** and composer **Claude Debussy** are tenants. Many great literary figures since 1850 were interred here, including **Tristan Bernard, Jean Giraudoux,** and **François de Croisset.** Also present are composer **Gabriel Fauré,** aviator **Henry**

Farman, actor **Fernandel,** and high priestess of the city's most famous literary salon, **Natalie Barney,** along with **Renée Vivien,** one of her many lovers.

Cimetière de Montmartre. 20 av. Rachel, 18e. ☎ **01-43-87-64-24.** Admission free. Mon–Fri 8am–6pm, Sat 8:30am–6pm, Sun 9am–6pm (to 5:30pm in winter). Métro: Blanche or Place Clichy.

This cemetery, from 1795, lies west of Montmartre and north of boulevard de Clichy. Russian dancer **Vaslav Nijinsky,** novelist **Alexandre Dumas** *fils,* impressionist **Edgar Degas,** and composers **Hector Berlioz** and **Jacques Offenbach** are interred here, along with **Stendhal** and lesser literary lights like **Edmond** and **Jules de Goncourt** and **Heinrich Heine.** A more recent tombstone honors **François Truffaut,** film director of the *nouvelle vague.* We like to pay our respects at the tomb of **Alphonsine Plessis,** heroine of *La Dame aux camélias,* and **Mme Récamier,** who taught the world how to lounge. **Emile Zola** was buried here, but his corpse was exhumed and promoted to the Panthéon in 1908. In tragic 1871, the cemetery was used for mass burials of victims of the Siege and the Commune.

10 Especially for Kids

If you're staying on the Right Bank, take the children for a stroll through the **Jardin des Tuileries** (see "Parks & Gardens"), where there are donkey rides, ice-cream stands, and a marionette show; at the circular pond, you can rent a toy sailboat. On the Left Bank, similar delights exist in the **Jardin du Luxembourg** (see "Parks & Gardens"). After a visit to the Eiffel Tower, you can take the kids for a donkey ride in the nearby **Champ de Mars** (see "The Top Attractions").

A great Paris tradition, **puppet shows** are worth seeing for their enthusiastic colorful productions—they're a genuine French child's experience. At the Jardin du Luxembourg, puppets reenact sinister plots set in Gothic castles and Oriental palaces; many young critics say the best puppet shows are held in the Champ de Mars.

On Sunday afternoon, French families head up to the **Butte Montmartre** to bask in the fiesta atmosphere. You can join in the fun: Take the Métro to Anvers and walk to the *funiculaire* (the silver cable car that carries you up to Sacré-Coeur). Once up top, follow the crowds to place du Tertre, where a Sergeant Pepper–style band will usually be blasting off-key and you can have the kids' pictures sketched by local artists. You can take in the views of Paris from the various vantage points and treat your children to ice cream. For a walking tour of Montmartre, see chapter 7.

Of course, your kids will likely want to check out the Gallic versions of Mickey Mouse and his pals, so see chapter 10 for details on **Disneyland Paris.**

MUSEUMS

Cité des Sciences et de l'Industrie. In the Parc de La Villette, 30 av. Corentine-Cariou, La Villette, 19e. ☎ **01-40-05-80-00.** Cité Pass (entrance to all exhibits) 50F ($8) adults, age 7 and under free; Géode 57F ($9.10). Tues–Sat 10am–6pm, Sun 10am–7pm. Métro: Porte de La Villette.

A city of science and industry has risen here from the most unlikely ashes. When a slaughterhouse was built on the site in the 1960s, it was touted as the most modern of its kind. It was abandoned as a failure in 1974, and the location on the city's northern edge presented the government with a problem. What could be built in such an unlikely place? In 1986, the converted premises opened as the world's most expensive ($642 million) science complex, designed to "modernize mentalities" in the service of modernizing society.

The place is so vast, with so many exhibits, that a single visit gives only an idea of the scope of the Cité. Busts of Plato, Hippocrates, and a double-faced Janus gaze silently at a tube-filled riot of high-tech girders, glass, and lights. The sheer dimensions pose a challenge to the curators of its constantly changing exhibits. Some exhibits are couched in Gallic humor—imagine using the comic-strip adventures of a jungle explorer to explain seismographic activity. **Explora,** a permanent exhibit, occupies the three upper levels of the building and examines four themes: the universe, life, matter, and communication. The Cité also has a **multimedia library,** a **planetarium,** and an **"inventorium"** for kids. The silver-skinned geodesic dome called **La Géode**—a 112-foot-high sphere with a 370-seat theater—projects the closest thing to a 3-D cinema in Europe and has several surprising additions, including a real submarine.

The Cité is in the **Parc de La Villette,** an ultramodern science park surrounding some of Paris's newest housing developments. This is Paris's largest park, with 136 acres of greenery—twice the size of the Tuileries. The playgrounds, fountains, and sculptures are all innovative creations. Here you'll find a belvedere, a video workshop for children, and information about exhibits and events, along with a cafe and restaurant.

Musée Grévin. 10 bd. Montmartre, 9e. ☎ **01-47-70-85-05.** Admission 58F ($9.30) adults, 38F ($6.10) children 14 and under. Apr–Aug daily 1–7pm; Sept–Mar daily 1–6:30pm; school holidays daily 10am–7pm. Ticket office closes 1 hour before museum. Métro: Grands Boulevards.

The Grévin is Paris's number-one waxworks. Comparisons to Madame Tussaud's are almost irresistible, but it isn't all blood and gore and doesn't shock as much as Tussaud's. It presents French history in a series of tableaux. Depicted are the 1429 consecration of Charles VII in the Cathédrale de Reims (armored Joan of Arc, carrying her standard, stands behind the king); Marguerite de Valois, first wife of Henri IV, meeting on a secret stairway with La Molle, who was soon to be decapitated; Catherine de Médicis with Florentine alchemist David Ruggieri; Louis XV and Mozart at the home of the marquise de Pompadour; and Napoléon on a rock at St. Helena, reviewing his victories and defeats. There are also displays of contemporary sports and political figures, as well as 50 of the world's best-loved film stars.

Two shows are staged frequently throughout the day. The first, called the **"Palais des Mirages,"** starts off as a sort of Temple of Brahma and through magically distorting mirrors changes into an enchanted forest, then a fête at the Alhambra in Granada. A magician is the star of the second show, **"Le Cabinet Fantastique;"** he entertains children of all ages.

Musée de la Marine. In the Palais de Chaillot, place du Trocadéro, 16e. ☎ **01-53-65-69-69.** Admission 38F ($6.10) adults, 25F ($4) ages 8–25/over 65; age 7 and under free. Wed–Mon 10am–5:30pm. Métro: Trocadéro.

If your children have saltwater in their veins, you may want to take them to this museum. Old ship models abound, like the big galley *La Réale,* the *Royal-Louis,* the rich ivory *Ville de Dieppe,* the gorgeous *Valmy,* and a **barge** built in 1811 for Napoléon I, which was used to carry Napoléon III and Empress Eugénie on their visit to Brest in 1858. You'll find some souvenirs of explorer Laperouse's wreck on Vanikoro Island in 1788 as well as many documents and artifacts concerning merchant fishing and pleasure fleets, oceanography, and hydrography, with films illustrating the subjects. Thematic exhibits explain ancient wooden shipbuilding and the development of scientific instruments.

Musée National d'Histoire Naturelle (Museum of Natural History). 57 rue Cuvier, 5e. ☎ **01-40-79-30-00.** Admission 10–40F ($1.60–$6.40) adults; age 3 and under free. Apr–Sept Wed–Mon 10am–6pm; Oct–Mar Wed–Mon 10am–5pm. Métro: Jussieu or Gare d'Austerlitz.

This museum in the Jardin des Plantes, founded in 1635 as a scientific research center by Guy de la Brosse, physician to Louis XIII, has a wide range of science and nature exhibits. The museum's **Grande Gallery of Evolution** recently received a $90-million restoration. At the entrance, an 85-foot skeleton of a whale greets you. One display containing the skeletons of dinosaurs and mastodons is dedicated to endangered and vanished species, and there are galleries specializing in the paleontology, anatomy, mineralogy, and botany. Within the museum's grounds are **tropical hothouses** containing thousands of species of unusual plant life and a **menagerie** with small animal life in simulated natural habitats.

AN AMUSEMENT PARK

Jardin d'Acclimatation. In the Bois de Boulogne, 16e. ☎ **01-40-67-90-82.** Admission 13F ($2.10); age 3 and under free. June–Sept daily 10am–7pm, Oct–May daily 10am–6pm. Métro: Sablons.

Paris's definitive children's park is the 25-acre Jardin d'Acclimation in the northern part of the Bois de Boulogne. This is the kind of place that satisfies tykes and adults alike but not teenagers. The visit starts with a ride on a green-and-yellow narrow-gauge train from Porte Maillot to the Jardin entrance, through a stretch of wooded park. (The train operates Wednesday, Saturday, and Sunday 1:30pm until the park closes; one-way fare is 6F/95¢.) En route you'll find a **house of mirrors,** an **archery range,** a **miniature-golf course, zoo animals,** a **bowling alley,** a **puppet theater** (performances Thursday, Saturday, Sunday, and holidays), a **playground,** a **hurdle-racing course, junior-scale rides, shooting galleries,** and **waffle stalls.** You can trot the kids off on a **pony** or join them in a **boat** on a mill-stirred lagoon. **La Prévention Routière** is a miniature roadway operated by the Paris police: Youngsters drive through in small cars equipped to start and stop and are required by two genuine Parisian gendarmes to obey all street signs and light changes. Inside the gate is an easy-to-follow map. The park is circular—follow the road in either direction, and it'll take you all the way around and bring you back to the train at the end.

A ZOO

Parc Zoologique de Paris. In the Bois de Vincennes, 53 av. de St-Maurice, 12e. ☎ **01-44-75-20-10.** Admission 40F ($6.40) adults, 30F ($4.80) children 4–15/students 16–25/over 60; age 3 and under free. Daily 9am–6pm (to 5pm Dec–Mar). Métro: Porte Dorée.

There's a modest zoo in the Jardin des Plantes, but without a doubt, the best zoo is here on the southeastern outskirts of Paris, quickly reachable by Métro. Many of this modern zoo's animals, who seem happy and are playful, live in settings similar to their natural habitat, hemmed in by rock barriers, not bars or cages. You'll never see an animal in a cage too small for it. The lion has an entire veldt to himself, and you can lock eyes comfortably across a deep protective moat. On a cement mountain like Disneyland's Matterhorn, exotic breeds of mountain goats and sheep leap from ledge to ledge or pose gracefully for hours watching the penguins in their pools at the mountain's foot. Keep well back from the bear pools or you might get wet.

11 Literary Landmarks

If there's a literary bone in your body, you'll feel a vicarious thrill on discovering the haunts of the famous writers and artists who've lived, worked, and played in Paris.

Take the Métro to place St-Michel to begin your tour. As you wander away from the Seine, you'll encounter **rue de la Huchette,** one of the Left Bank's most famous streets. Its inhabitants were immortalized in Eliot Paul's *The Last Time I Saw Paris.*

Continuing on, you'll enter the territory of the Beat Generation, home to the **Café Gentilhomme** (no longer there) described by Jack Kerouac in *Satori in Paris*. Allen Ginsberg's favorite, the **Hôtel du Vieux-Paris,** 9 rue Gît-le-Coeur, still attracts those in search of the Beats.

Stroll down **rue Monsieur-le-Prince,** the "Yankee alleyway," where Richard Wright, James McNeill Whistler, Henry Wadsworth Longfellow, and Oliver Wendell Holmes all lived at one time or another. During a famous visit in 1959, Martin Luther King Jr. came to call on Richard Wright, the Mississippi-born African-American novelist famous for *Native Son.* King climbed to the third-floor apartment at **no. 14,** only to find that Wright's opinions on the civil rights movement conflicted with his own. Whistler rented a studio at **no. 22,** and, in 1826, Longfellow lived for a short time at **no. 49.** Oliver Wendell Holmes Sr. lived at **no. 55.** After strolling along this street, you can dine at the former haunts of Kerouac and Hemingway. (See our recommendation of **Crémerie-Restaurant Polidor,** 41 rue Monsieur-le-Prince, 6e, in chapter 5.) Or cross back over to the Right Bank for a drink at the famed **Hôtel de Crillon,** 10 place de la Concorde, 8e (see chapter 4), where heroine Brett Ashley broke her promise to rendezvous with Jake Barnes in Hemingway's *The Sun Also Rises.* Zelda and F. Scott Fitzgerald lifted their glasses here as well.

For details on **Harry's New York Bar,** 5 rue Daunou, 2e, see "Literary Haunts" in chapter 9. For a description of **Les Deux Magots, Le Procope,** and **La Rotonde,** see "The Top Cafes" in chapter 5. And for coverage of the bookstore **Shakespeare and Company,** see chapter 8.

Here are two great museums for hardcore literary fans:

Maison de Balzac. 47 rue Raynouard, 16e. ☎ **01-55-74-41-80.** Admission 22F ($3.50) adults, 15F ($2.40) ages 26 and under/over age 60. Tues–Sun 10am–5:40pm. Métro: Passy or La Muette.

In the residential district of Passy, near the Bois de Boulogne, sits this modest house on the slope of a hill, with a small courtyard and garden. The great Honoré de Balzac fled to this house in 1840 after his possessions and furnishings were seized, and he lived here for 7 years (to see him you had to know a password). If a creditor knocked on the rue Raynouard door, Balzac was able to escape through the rue Berton exit. The museum's most notable memento is Balzac's "screech-owl" (his nickname for his tea kettle), which he kept hot throughout the night as he wrote *La Comédie humaine.* Also enshrined here are Balzac's writing desk and chair and a library of special interest to scholars. The little house is filled with reproduced caricatures of Balzac. A biographer once wrote: "With his bulky baboon silhouette, his blue suit with gold buttons, his famous cane like a golden crowbar, and his abundant, disheveled hair, Balzac was a sight for caricature." Though it should be completely repaired by the time you arrive, a tree or two crashed into the roof of this house during the fierce Christmas 1999 storm.

Maison de Victor Hugo. 6 place des Vosges, 4e. ☎ **01-42-72-10-16.** Admission 22F ($3.50) adults; age 26 and under free. Tues–Sun 10am–5:40pm. Closed national holidays. Métro: St-Paul, Bastille, or Chemin-Vert.

Today, theatergoers who've seen *Les Misérables,* even those who haven't read anything by Paris's great 19th-century novelist, come to place des Vosges to see where Victor Hugo lived and wrote. Some thought Hugo a genius, but Cocteau called him a madman, and an American composer discovered that in his old age he was carving furniture with his teeth! From 1832 to 1848, the novelist/poet lived on the second floor of the old Hôtel Rohan Guéménée, built in 1610 on what was then place Royale. The museum owns some of Hugo's furniture as well as pieces that once belonged to Juliette Drouet, the mistress with whom he lived in exile on Guernsey, one of the Channel Islands.

Worth the visit are Hugo's drawings, more than 450, illustrating scenes from his own works. Mementos of the great writer abound, including samples of his hand writing, his inkwell, and first editions of his works. A painting of Hugo's 1885 funeral procession at the Arc de Triomphe is on display, as are plentiful portraits and souvenirs of his family. Of the furnishings, a chinoiserie salon stands out. The collection even contains Daumier caricatures and a bust of Hugo by David d'Angers, which, compared to Rodin's, looks saccharine.

12 Paris Underground

Les Catacombs. 1 place Denfert-Rochereau, 14e. ☎ **01-43-22-47-63.** www.multimania. com/houze. Admission 33F ($5.30) adults, 22F ($3.50) seniors, 17F ($2.70) ages 7–25/ students; age 6 and under free. Tues–Fri 2–4pm, Sat–Sun 9–11am and 2–4pm. Métro: Denfert-Rochereau.

Every year an estimated 50,000 visitors explore some 1,000 yards of tunnel in these dank catacombs to look at 6 million ghoulishly arranged skull-and-crossbones skeletons. First opened to the public in 1810, this "empire of the dead" is now illuminated with overhead electric lights over its entire length. In the Middle Ages, the catacombs were quarries, but by the end of the 18th century, overcrowded cemeteries were becoming a menace to the public health. City officials decided to use the catacombs as a burial ground, and the bones of several million persons were transferred here. In 1830, the prefect of Paris closed the catacombs to the public, considering them obscene and indecent. During World War II, the catacombs were the headquarters of the French Resistance.

Les Egouts (Sewers of Paris). Pont de l'Alma, 7e. ☎ **01-53-68-27-81.** Admission 25F ($4) adults, 20F ($3.20) students/seniors/children 5–12; under 5 free. May–Oct Sat–Wed 11am–5pm; Nov–Apr Sat–Wed 11am–4pm. Closed 3 weeks in Jan. Métro: Alma-Marceau. RER: Pont de l'Alma.

Some sociologists assert that the sophistication of a society can be judged by the way it disposes of waste. If so, Paris receives good marks for its mostly invisible sewer network. Victor Hugo is credited with making them famous in *Les Misérables:* Jean Valjean takes flight through them, "all dripping with slime, his soul filled with a strange light." Hugo also wrote, "Paris has beneath it another Paris, a Paris of sewers, which has its own streets, squares, lanes, arteries, and circulation."

In the early Middle Ages, drinking water was taken directly from the Seine and wastewater poured onto fields or thrown onto the then-unpaved streets, transforming the urban landscape into a sea of rather smelly mud. Around 1200, the streets were paved with cobblestones, and open sewers ran down the center of each. These open sewers helped spread the Black Death, which devastated the city. In 1370, a vaulted sewer was built on rue Montmartre, draining effluents into a Seine tributary. During Louis XIV's reign, improvements were made, but the state of waste disposal in Paris remained deplorable.

During Napoléon's reign, $18^1/_2$ miles of sewer were constructed beneath the Parisian landscape. By 1850, as the Industrial Revolution made the manufacture of iron pipe and steam-digging equipment more practical, Baron Haussmann developed a system that used separate underground channels for drinking water and sewage. By 1878, it was 360 miles long. Beginning in 1894, the network was enlarged, and new laws required that discharge of all waste and storm-water runoff be funneled into the sewers. Between 1914 and 1977, an additional 600 miles were added beneath the pavements of a burgeoning Paris. Today, the network of sewers is 1,300 miles long. It contains freshwater mains, compressed air pipes, telephone cables, and pneumatic tubes. Every day, 1.2 million cubic meters of wastewater are collected and processed by a plant in the suburb of Achères. One of the largest in Europe, it's capable of treating more than 2 million cubic meters of sewage per day.

The city's *égouts* are constructed around four principal tunnels, one 18 feet wide and 15 feet high. As Hugo observed, it's like an underground city, with the street names clearly labeled. Further, each branch pipe bears the number of the building to which it's connected. These underground passages are truly mammoth. Sewer tours begin at pont de l'Alma on the Left Bank, where a stairway leads into the city's bowels. However, you often have to wait in line as much as half an hour. Visiting times might change during bad weather, as a storm can make the sewers dangerous. The tour consists of a film on sewer history, a small museum visit, and then a short trip through the maze. *Be warned:* The smell is pretty bad, especially in summer.

13 Organized Tours

BUS TOURS

Tours are offered by **Cityrama,** 147–149 rue St-Honoré, 1er (☎ **01-44-55-61-00;** Métro: Palais Royal or Musée du Louvre), which operates double-decker red-and-yellow buses with oversized windows and multilingual recorded commentaries giving an overview of Paris's history and monuments. The most popular is a 2-hour tour (150F/$24) departing from place des Pyramides, adjacent to rue de Rivoli, daily at 9:30 and 10:30am and 1:30 and 2:30pm, with additional tours Saturday and Sunday at 11:30am and March to October daily at 3:30 and 4:30pm. More detailed tours include the $1^1/_2$-hour morning tour (295F/$47.20) to the interiors of Notre-Dame and the Louvre on Monday, Wednesday, Friday, and Saturday and the $3^1/_2$-hour morning tours (320F/$51.20) to Versailles and $3^1/_2$-hour afternoon tours (275F/$44) to Chartres. And if you're interested in a night tour to see how the City of Light got its name, tours (150F/$24) depart daily at 10pm in summer and at 7pm in winter.

CRUISES ON THE SEINE

A Seine boat tour provides sweeping vistas of the riverbanks and some of the best views of Notre-Dame. Many of the boats have open sundecks, bars, and restaurants. **Bateaux-Mouche** cruises (☎ **01-42-25-96-10** for reservations, 01-40-76-99-99 for schedules; Métro: Alma-Marceau) depart from the Right Bank, next to pont de l'Alma, and last about 75 minutes, costing 40F ($6.40) adults and 20F ($3.20) children 5 to 15. May to October, tours leave daily at 20- to 30-minute intervals, beginning at 10am and ending at 11:30pm; November to April, there are at least nine departures daily 11am to 9pm, with a schedule that changes according to demand and the weather. Three-hour dinner cruises depart daily at 8:30pm and cost 500F to 800F ($80 to $128), depending on which fixed-price menu you order; jackets and ties are required for men.

Some people prefer longer excursions on the Seine and its network of canals. The 3-hour **Seine et le Canal St-Martin** tour, offered by **Paris Canal** (☎ **01-42-40-96-97**), requires advance reservations. The tour begins at 9:30am on the quays in front of the Musée d'Orsay (Métro: Solférino) and at 2:30pm in front of the Cité des Sciences et de l'Industrie at Parc de La Villette (Métro: Porte de La Villette). Excursions negotiate the waterways and canals of Paris, including the Seine, an underground tunnel below place de la Bastille, and the Canal St-Martin. Tours are offered twice daily mid-March to mid-November; the rest of the year, tours are only on Sunday.

The cost is 100F ($16) adults and children under 4 free. With the exception of trips on Sundays and holidays, prices are usually reduced to 75F ($12) for passengers 12 to 25 and over 60 and to 55F ($8.80) for children 4 to 11.

BIKE TOURS

The best are offered by **Bullfrog Bike Tours** (☎ 06-09-98-08-60), departing from avenue Gustave-Eiffel near the tower (look for a large green flag advertising the tours). May to September 15, tours leave daily at 11am and 3:30pm, costing 120F ($19.20). Night tours are at 9pm Monday and Thursday. You get an English-speaking look at Paris almost entirely on sidewalks, in parks, and along the Seine, taking in the most famous landmarks, like the Louvre and Notre-Dame.

14 A Day at the Races

Paris boasts an army of avid horse-racing fans who get to the city's eight racetracks whenever possible. Information on current races is available in newspapers and magazines like *Tierce, Paris-Turf, France-Soir,* and *L'Equipe,* all sold at kiosks throughout the city.

The epicenter of Paris horse racing is the **Hippodrome de Longchamp,** in the Bois de Boulogne (☎ 01-44-30-75-00; Métro: Auteuil, then a shuttle bus). Established in 1855, during the autocratic but pleasure-loving reign of Napoléon III, it's the most prestigious, boasts the greatest number of promising thoroughbreds, and awards the largest purse in France. The most important events at Longchamp are the **Grand Prix de Paris** in late June and the **Prix de l'Arc de Triomphe** in early October.

Another horse-racing venue is the **Hippodrome d'Auteuil,** also in the Bois de Boulogne (☎ 01-40-71-47-47; Métro: Auteuil, then a shuttle bus). Known for its steeplechases and obstacle courses, it sometimes attracts more than 50,000 Parisians at a time. Spectators appreciate the park's open-air promenades as much as they do the equestrian events. Opened in 1870, the racetrack is scattered over a sprawling 30 acres of parkland. It's designed to show to maximum advantage the skill and agility of both horses and riders. Races are conducted early March to late December.

7

Strolling Around Paris

The best way to discover Paris is on foot, using your own shoe leather. Our favorite walks are along the banks of the Seine and down the Champs-Elysées from the Arc de Triomphe to the Louvre, but in this chapter we highlight the attractions of Montmartre, the Latin Quarter, and the Marais.

For a greater selection of walking tours in the City of Light, see *Frommer's Memorable Walks in Paris.*

Walking Tour 1: Montmartre

Start: Place Pigalle (Métro: Pigalle).
Finish: Place Pigalle.
Time: 5 hours—more if you break for lunch. It's a 3-mile trek.
Best Time: Any day it isn't raining. Set out by 10am at the latest.
Worst Time: After dark.

Soft white three-story houses and slender barren trees sticking up from the ground like giant toothpicks—that's how Utrillo, befogged by absinthe, saw Montmartre. Toulouse-Lautrec brush-stroked it into a district of cabarets, circus freaks, and prostitutes. Today, Montmartre remains truer to the dwarfish Toulouse-Lautrec's conception than it does to Utrillo's.

Before all this, Montmartre was a sleepy farming community with windmills dotting the landscape. The name has always been the subject of disagreement, some maintaining it originated from the "mount of Mars," a Roman temple that crowned the hill, others asserting it means "mount of martyrs," a reference to the martyrdom of St. Denis, who was beheaded on the mountain along with fellow saints Rusticus and Eleutherius.

Turn right after leaving the Métro station and proceed down boulevard de Clichy, turn left at the Cirque Medrano, and begin the climb up rue des Martyrs. On reaching rue des Abbesses, turn left and walk along this street, crossing place des Abbesses. Go uphill along rue Ravignan, which leads directly to tree-studded place Emile-Goudeau, in the middle of rue Ravignan. At no. 13, across from the Timhôtel, is the:

1. **Bateau-Lavoir (Boat Washhouse),** called the cradle of cubism. Though gutted by fire in 1970, it has been reconstructed by the city. While Picasso lived here (1904–12), he painted one of the

Walking Tour 1: Montmartre

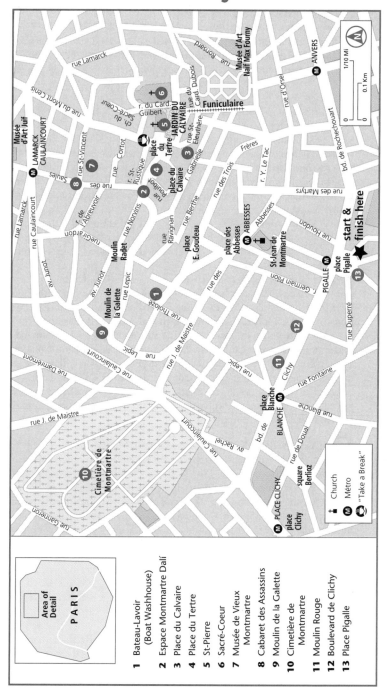

Area of Detail

PARIS

1 Bateau-Lavoir
   (Boat Washhouse)
2 Espace Montmartre Dalí
3 Place du Calvaire
4 Place du Tertre
5 St-Pierre
6 Sacré-Coeur
7 Musée de Vieux
   Montmartre
8 Cabaret des Assassins
9 Moulin de la Galette
10 Cimetière de
   Montmartre
11 Moulin Rouge
12 Boulevard de Clichy
13 Place Pigalle

Another Way to See Montmartre

Those finding the uphill climb to Paris's highest elevation too arduous can take the diesel-powered **Le Petit Train de Montmartre,** which rolls along the steep streets on a 35-minute guided tour (for details, see "Neighborhood Highlights," in chapter 6).

---

world's most famous portraits, *The Third Rose* (of Gertrude Stein), as well as *Les Demoiselles d'Avignon.* Other residents were van Dongen, Jacob, and Gris, and Modigliani, Rousseau, and Braque had studios nearby.

Rue Ravignan ends at place Jean-Baptiste-Clément. Go to the end of the street and cross onto rue Norvins (on your right). Here rues Norvins, St-Rustique, and des Saules collide a few steps from rue Poulbot, a scene captured in a famous Utrillo painting. Turn right and head down rue Poulbot. At no. 11, you'll come to the:

2. **Espace Montmartre Dalí,** 11 rue Poulbot (☎ **01-42-64-40-10**), a phantasmagorical world featuring 300 original Dalí works, including his famous 1956 lithograph of Don Quixote (see "Neighborhood Highlights," in chapter 6).

Rue Poulbot crosses tiny:

3. **Place du Calvaire,** which offers a panoramic view of Paris. On this square once lived artist/painter/lithographer Maurice Neumont (a plaque marks the house). From place du Calvaire, head east along rue Gabrielle, taking the first left north along the tiny street rue du Calvaire, which leads to Place du Tertre.

4. **Place du Tertre,** the old town square and now tourist central. All around the square run terrace restaurants with dance floors and colored lights while Sacré-Coeur gleams white through the trees. Here the cafes overflow with people, as do the indoor and outdoor art galleries. Some of the "artists" still wear berets (you'll be asked countless times if you want your portrait sketched in charcoal). So loaded with local color, applied as heavily as bad makeup, the square can seem somewhat gaudy and inauthentic.

☕ **TAKE A BREAK** Many restaurants in Montmartre, especially those around place du Tertre, are unabashed tourist traps. An exception is **La Crémaillère 1900,** 15 place du Tertre, 18e (☎ **01-46-06-58-59**). As its name suggests, this is a belle-époque dining room, retaining much of its original look, including Mucha paintings. You can sit on the terrace opening onto the square or retreat to the internal courtyard garden. A full menu is served throughout the day, including a standard array of French classics. Go any time daily noon to 12:30am.

Right off the square fronting rue du Mont-Cenis is:

5. **St-Pierre.** Originally a Benedictine abbey, it has played many roles—a Temple of Reason during the Revolution, a food depot, a clothing store, and even a munitions factory. These days, one of Paris's oldest churches is back to being a church (see "Neighborhood Highlights," in chapter 6).

Facing St-Pierre, turn right and follow rue Azaïs to:

6. **Sacré-Coeur,** overlooking square Willette. The basilica's Byzantine domes and bell tower loom above Paris and present a wide vista on sunny days (see "The Top Attractions," in chapter 6). Behind the church and clinging to the hillside are steep and crooked little streets that have survived the relentless march of progress. Facing the basilica, take the street on the left (rue du Cardinal-Guibert), then go left onto rue du Chevalier-de-la-Barre and right onto rue du Mont-Cenis. Continue on this street to rue Cortot, then turn left. At no. 12 is the:

7. Musée de Vieux Montmartre (☎ **01-46-06-61-11**), with a wide collection of mementos of the neighborhood (see "Neighborhood Highlights," in chapter 6). Luminaries like Dufy, van Gogh, Renoir, and Suzanne Valadon and her son, Utrillo, occupied this famous 17th-century house, and it was here that Renoir put the final touches on his *Moulin de la Galette* (see below).

From the museum, turn right, heading up rue des Saules past a winery, a reminder of the days when Montmartre was a farming village on the outskirts of Paris. A grape-harvesting festival is held here every October. The intersection of rue des Saules and rue St-Vincent is one of the most visited and photographed corners of the Butte. Here, on one corner, sits what was the famous old:

8. Cabaret des Assassins, long ago renamed **Au Lapin Agile** (see *"Chansonniers,"* in chapter 9). Picasso and Utrillo once frequented this little cottage, which numerous artists have patronized and painted. On any given afternoon, French folk tunes, love ballads, army songs, sea chanteys, and music-hall ditties will stream out of the cafe and onto the street.

Turn left on rue St-Vincent, passing the **Cimetière St-Vincent** on your right (see "Cemeteries," in chapter 6). Take a left onto rue Girardon and climb the stairs. In a minute or two, you'll spot on your right two of the windmills (*moulins*) that used to dot the Butte. One of these, at no. 75, is the:

9. Moulin de la Galette (entrance at 1 av. Junot), built in 1622 and immortalized in oil by Renoir (see the painting in the Musée d'Orsay). When the windmill was turned into a dance hall in the 1860s, it was named for the *galettes* (cakes made with flour ground inside the mills) it sold. Later, the dance hall was populated by Toulouse-Lautrec, van Gogh, and Utrillo. A few steps away at the angle of rec Lepic and rue Girardon is the second windmill, the **Moulin Radet,** now part of a restaurant.

Turn right onto rue Lepic and walk past **no. 54.** In 1886, van Gogh lived here with his brother Guillaumin. Take a right turn onto rue Joseph-de-Maistre, then left again on rue Caulaincourt until you reach the:

10. Cimetière de Montmartre, second in fame only to Père-Lachaise and haunt of Nijinsky, Dumas *fils,* Stendhal, Degas, and Truffaut, among others (see "Cemeteries," in chapter 6).

From the cemetery, take avenue Rachel, turn left onto boulevard de Clichy, and go to place Blanche, where stands a windmill even better known than the one in Renoir's painting, the:

11. Moulin Rouge, one of the world's most talked about nightclubs. It was immortalized by Toulouse-Lautrec. The windmill is still here and so is the cancan, but the rest has become an outrageously expensive, superslick variety show with a heavy emphasis on undraped females (see "Nightclubs & Cabarets," in chapter 9).

From place Blanche, you can begin a descent on:

12. Boulevard de Clichy, while fighting off the pornographers and hustlers trying to lure you into tawdry sex joints. With some rare exceptions, notably the citadels of the *chansonniers* (songwriters), boulevard de Clichy is one gigantic tourist trap. But everyone who comes to Paris invariably winds up here.

The boulevard strips and peels its way down to where you started:

13. Place Pigalle, center of nudity in Paris, named after a French sculptor, Pigalle, whose closest brush with nudity was a depiction of Voltaire in the buff. Toulouse-Lautrec had his studio right off the square at 5 av. Frochot. Of course, place Pigalle was the notorious "Pig Alley" of World War II. When Edith Piaf was lonely and hungry, she sang in the alleyways, hoping to earn a few francs for the night.

Walking Tour 2: The Latin Quarter

Start: Place St-Michel (Métro: St-Michel).
Finish: The Panthéon.
Time: 3 hours, not counting stops.
Best Time: Any weekday, Monday to Friday 9am to 4pm.
Worst Time: Sunday morning, when everybody is asleep.

This is the precinct of the Université de Paris (known for its most famous branch, the Sorbonne), where students meet and fall in love over *café crème* and croissants. Rabelais named it the Quartier Latin after the students and the professors who spoke Latin in the classroom and on the streets. The sector teems with belly dancers, exotic restaurants, sidewalk cafes, bookstalls, *caveaux* (basement nightclubs), *clochards* (bums), *chiffonniers* (ragpickers), and gamin boys and girls.

A good starting point for your tour is:

1. **Place St-Michel,** where Balzac used to draw water from the fountain (Davioud's 1860 sculpture of St. Michel slaying the dragon) when he was a youth. This was the scene of frequent skirmishes between the Germans and the Resistance in the summer of 1944, and the names of those who died here are engraved on plaques around the square.

☕ **TAKE A BREAK**　Open 24 hours, **Café le Départ St-Michel,** 1 place St-Michel (☎ **01-43-54-24-55**), lies on the banks of the Seine. The decor is warmly modern, with etched mirrors reflecting the faces of a diversified crowd. If you want to fortify yourself for your walk, opt for one of the warm or cold snacks, including sandwiches.

The quarter centers around:

2. **Boulevard St-Michel** (a.k.a. **Boul'Mich**) to the south. Boul'Mich is virtually the main street of the Latin Quarter as it heads south. This is a major tourist artery and won't give you a great insight into local life. For that, you can branch off onto virtually any of the streets that feed into the boulevard and find cafes, bars, Greek gyro counters, ice cream stands, crêpe stands, and bistros like those pictured in movies set in Paris in the 1950s. The Paris Commune began here in 1871 as did the student uprisings of 1968.

From place St-Michel, with your back to the Seine, turn left down:

3. **Rue de la Huchette,** the setting of Elliot Paul's *The Last Time I Saw Paris* (1942). Paul first wandered into this typical street "on a soft summer evening, and entirely by chance," in 1923 and then moved into no. 28, the **Hôtel Mont-Blanc.** Though much has changed since, some of the buildings are so old they have to be propped up by timbers. Paul captured the spirit of the street more evocatively than anyone, writing of "the delivery wagons, makeshift vehicles propelled by pedaling boys, pushcarts of itinerant vendors, knife-grinders, umbrella menders, a herd of milk goats, and the neighborhood pedestrians." (The local bordello has closed, however.) Today, you'll see lots of Greek restaurants.

Branching off from this street to your left is:

4. **Rue du Chat-qui-Pêche** (Street of the Cat Who Fishes), said to be the shortest, narrowest street in the world, containing not one door and only a handful of windows. It's usually filled with garbage or lovers or both. (Before the quay was built, the Seine sometimes rose above its banks, flooding the cellars of the houses here, and legend has it that an enterprising cat took advantage of its good fortune and went fishing in the confines of the cellars—hence the street's name.)

Walking Tour 2: The Latin Quarter

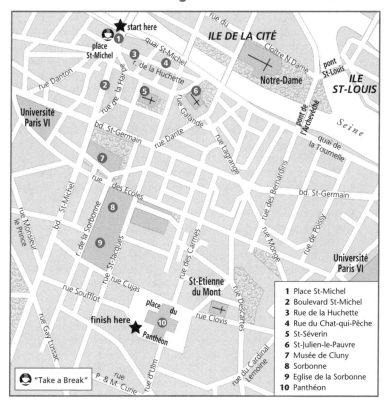

Map legend:

1 Place St-Michel
2 Boulevard St-Michel
3 Rue de la Huchette
4 Rue du Chat-qui-Pêche
5 St-Séverin
6 St-Julien-le-Pauvre
7 Musée de Cluny
8 Sorbonne
9 Eglise de la Sorbonne
10 Panthéon

Now retrace your steps toward place St-Michel and turn left at the intersection with rue de la Harpe, which leads to rue St-Séverin. At the intersection, take a left to see:

5. St-Séverin, a flamboyant Gothic church named for a 6th-century recluse. It was built from 1210 to 1230 and reconstructed in 1458, over the years adopting many of the features of Notre-Dame, across the river. The tower was completed in 1487 and the chapels from 1498 to 1520; Hardouin-Mansart designed the Chapelle de la Communion in 1673 when he was 27 years old, and it contains some beautiful Rouault etchings from the 1920s. Before entering, walk around the church to examine the gargoyles, birds of prey, and reptilian monsters projecting from its roof. To the right, facing the church, is the 15th-century "garden of ossuaries." The stained glass inside St-Séverin, behind the altar, is a stunning adornment using great swaths of color to depict the Seven Sacraments.

After visiting the church, go back to rue St-Séverin and follow it to rue Galande, then continue on until you reach:

6. St-Julien-le-Pauvre, on the south side of lovely **square René-Viviani.** First stand at the gateway and look at the beginning of rue Galande, especially the old houses with the steeples of St-Séverin rising across the way—one of the most frequently painted scenes on the Left Bank. Enter the courtyard and you'll be in medieval Paris. The garden to the left of the entrance offers the best view of Notre-Dame. Everyone from Rabelais to Thomas Aquinas has passed through the doors of this church. Before the 6th century, a chapel stood on this spot. The present church goes back to the Longpont monks, who began work on it in 1170 (making it the oldest existing church in Paris). In 1655, it was given to the Hôtel Dieu and in time became a small warehouse for salt. In 1889, it was presented to the followers of the Melchite Greek rite, a branch of the Byzantine church.

Return to rue Galande and turn left at the intersection with rue St-Séverin. Continue on until you reach rue St-Jacques, turn left, and turn right when you reach boulevard St-Germain. Follow this boulevard to rue de Cluny, turn left, and head toward the entrance to the:

7. Musée de Cluny (see "The Major Museums," in chapter 6). Even if you're rushed, take time out to see *The Lady and the Unicorn* tapestry and the remains of the Roman baths.

After your visit to the Cluny, exit onto boulevard St-Michel, but instead of heading back to place St-Michel, turn left and walk to place de la Sorbonne and the:

8. Sorbonne, one of the most famous academic institutions in the world. It was founded in the 13th century by Robert de Sorbon, St. Louis's confessor, for poor students who wished to pursue theological studies, and by the next century it had become the most prestigious university in the West, attracting such professors as Thomas Aquinas and Roger Bacon and such students as Dante, Calvin, and Longfellow. Napoléon reorganized it in 1806. The courtyard and galleries are open to the public when the university is in session, and in the Cour d'Honneur are statues of Hugo and Pasteur.

At first glance from place de la Sorbonne, the Sorbonne seems architecturally undistinguished. In truth, it was rather indiscriminately reconstructed in the early 1900s. A better fate lay in store for the:

9. Eglise de la Sorbonne, built in 1635 by Le Mercier. The church contains the marble tomb of Cardinal Richelieu, a work by Girardon based on a design by Le Brun. At his feet is the remarkable statue *Learning in Tears.*

From the church, go south on rue Victor-Cousin and turn left at rue Soufflot. At street's end lies place du Panthéon and the:

10. Panthéon (see "Architectural & Historic Highlights," in chapter 6). Sitting atop Mont Ste-Geneviève, this nonreligious temple is the final resting place of such distinguished figures as Hugo, Zola, Rousseau, Voltaire, and Curie.

Walking Tour 3: The Marais

Start: Place de la Bastille (Métro: Bastille).
Finish: Place de la Bastille.
Time: 4¹/₂ hours, with only cursory stops en route. The distance is about 2³/₄ miles.
Best Time: Monday to Saturday, when more buildings and shops are open. If interiors are open, often you can walk into courtyards.
Worst Time: Toward dusk, when shops and museums are closed, and it's too dark to admire the architectural details.

When Paris began to overflow the confines of Ile de la Cité in the 13th century, the citizenry began to settle in Le Marais, a marsh that used to be flooded regularly by the high-rising Seine. By the 17th century, the Marais had become the center of aristocratic Paris and some of its great mansions (*hôtels particuliers*), many now restored or still being spruced up, were built by the finest craftsmen in France. In the 18th and 19th centuries, fashion deserted the Marais for the expanding Faubourg St-Germain and Faubourg St-Honoré. Industry soon took over, and once-elegant *hôtels* deteriorated

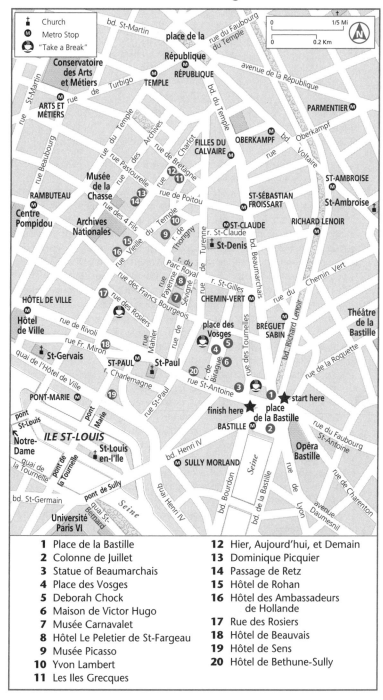

1 Place de la Bastille
2 Colonne de Juillet
3 Statue of Beaumarchais
4 Place des Vosges
5 Deborah Chock
6 Maison de Victor Hugo
7 Musée Carnavalet
8 Hôtel Le Peletier de St-Fargeau
9 Musée Picasso
10 Yvon Lambert
11 Les Iles Grecques
12 Hier, Aujourd'hui, et Demain
13 Dominique Picquier
14 Passage de Retz
15 Hôtel de Rohan
16 Hôtel des Ambassadeurs
   de Hollande
17 Rue des Rosiers
18 Hôtel de Beauvais
19 Hôtel de Sens
20 Hôtel de Bethune-Sully

into tenements. There was talk of demolishing the blighted neighborhood, but in 1962 an alarmed community group banded together and saved the historic district.

Today, the 17th-century mansions are fashionable once again. The *International Herald Tribune* called this area the latest refuge for the Paris artisan fleeing the tourist-trampled St-Germain-des-Prés. (However, that doesn't mean the area doesn't get its share of tourist traffic—quite the contrary.) The "marsh" sprawls across the 3rd and 4th arrondissements bounded by the Grands Boulevards, rue du Temple, place des Vosges, and the Seine. It has become Paris's center of gay/lesbian life, particularly on rues St-Croix-de-la-Bretonnerie, des Archives, and Vieille-du-Temple, and is a great place for window-shopping in trendy boutiques, up-and-coming galleries, and more.

Begin your tour at the site that spawned one of the most celebrated and abhorred revolutions in human history:

1. **Place de la Bastille.** On July 14, 1789, a mob attacked the Bastille prison located here, igniting the French Revolution. Now nothing of this symbol of despotism remains. Built in 1369, its eight 100-foot towers once loomed over Paris. Within them, many prisoners, some sentenced by Louis XIV for "witchcraft," were kept, the best known being the "Man in the Iron Mask." And yet when the revolutionary mob stormed the fortress, only seven prisoners were discovered. (The Marquis de Sade had been shipped to the madhouse 10 days earlier.) The authorities had discussed razing it anyway, so the attack really meant little. But what it symbolized and what it unleashed will never be undone, and each July 14 the entire country celebrates Bastille Day with great festivity. Since the late 1980s, what had been scorned as a dull and grimy-looking traffic circle has become an artistic focal point, thanks to the construction of the Opéra Bastille on its eastern edge (see "The Performing Arts," in chapter 9).

It was probably easier to storm the Bastille in 1789 than it is now to cross over to the center of the square for a close-up view of the:

2. **Colonne de Juillet.** The July Column doesn't commemorate the Revolution but honors the victims of the July Revolution of 1830, which put Louis-Philippe on the throne after the heady but wrenching victories and defeats of Napoléon Bonaparte. The tower is crowned by the winged *God of Liberty,* whose forehead bears an emerging star.

From place de la Bastille, walk west along rue St-Antoine for about a block. Turn right and walk north along rue des Tournelles, noting the:

3. **Statue of Beaumarchais.** Erected in 1895, it honors the 18th-century author of *The Barber of Seville* and *The Marriage of Figaro,* which Rossini and Mozart brilliantly set to music.

Continue north for a long block along rue des Tournelles, then turn left at medieval-looking rue Pas-de-la-Mule (Footsteps of the Mule), which will open suddenly onto the northeastern corner of enchanting:

4. **Place des Vosges,** Paris's oldest square and once its most fashionable, boasting 36 brick-and-stone pavilions rising from covered arcades that allowed people to shop at all times no matter what the weather. The buildings were constructed according to a strict plan—the height of the facades is equal to their width and the height of the triangular roofs is half the height of the facades. It was begun on Henri IV's orders and called place Royal; the king intended the square to be the scene of businesses and social festivities and even planned to live there, but Ravaillac had other plans and assassinated Henri 2 years before its completion. In 1559, Henri II was killed while jousting on the square, in the shadow of the

Hôtel des Tournelles; his widow, Catherine de Médicis, had the place torn down. By the 17th century, the square was the home of many aristocrats. During the Revolution, it was renamed place de l'Invisibilité, and its statue of Louis XIII was stolen (probably melted down). A replacement statue now stands in its place.

In 1800, the square was renamed place des Vosges because the Vosges *département* was the first in France to pay its taxes to Napoléon. The addition of chestnut trees sparked a controversy—critics say they spoil the perspective. Even though its fortunes waned when the Marais went out of fashion, place des Vosges is now back big time. Over the years, the famous often took up residence: Descartes, Pascal, Cardinal Richelieu, courtesan Marion Delorme, Gautier, Daudet, and Mme de Sévigné all lived here. But its best-known occupant was Victor Hugo (his home, now a museum, is the only house you can visit without a private invitation—see below).

Place des Vosges is the centerpiece of many unusual, charming, and/or funky shops. One of the best of these is:

5. **Deborah Chock,** 24 place des Vosges (☎ **01-48-04-86-86**), which sells a constantly changing roster of avant-garde and contemporary paintings. Use it as a debut before you explore the many other art galleries in the neighborhood. The staff is English-speaking and well versed in the currents of the Paris art scene.

☕ **TAKE A BREAK**   Two cafes hold court from opposite sides of place des Vosges, both serving *café au lait,* glasses of wine and *eaux de vie,* sandwiches, pastries, and afternoon tea: **Ma Bourgogne** at no. 19 (☎ **01-42-78-44-64**), on the western edge, and **La Chope des Vosges** at no. 22 (☎ **01-42-72-64-04**).

Near the square's southeastern corner, commemorating the life and times of a writer whose works were read with passion in the 19th century, is the:

6. **Maison de Victor Hugo,** 6 place des Vosges (☎ **01-42-72-10-16**), now a museum and literary shrine you can visit (see "Literary Landmarks," in chapter 6). Hugo lived there from 1832 to 1848, when he went into voluntary exile on the Channel Islands after the rise of the despotic Napoléon III.

Exit from place des Vosges from its northwestern corner (directly opposite the Maison de Victor Hugo) and walk west along rue des Francs-Bourgeois until you reach the intersection with rue de Sévigné, then make a right. At no. 23 is the:

7. **Musée Carnavalet** (☎ **01-42-72-21-13**), a 16th-century mansion that's now a museum devoted to the history of Paris and the French Revolution (see "The Major Museums," in chapter 6).

Continue to a point near the northern terminus of rue de Sévigné, noting no. 29 (now part of the Carnavalet). This is the:

8. **Hôtel le Peletier de St-Fargeau,** bearing the name of its former occupant, who was considered responsible for the death sentence of Louis XVI. It's used as offices and can't be visited.

At the end of the street, make a left onto lovely rue du Parc-Royal, lined with 17th-century mansions. It leads to place de Thorigny, where you'll find the:

9. **Musée Picasso** no. 5. It occupies the Hôtel Salé, built by a salt-tax collector (see "The Major Museums," in chapter 6). You can visit the museum either now or come back at the end of the tour.

Walk northeast along rue Thorigny and turn left onto rue Debelleyme. After a block, near the corner of rue Vieille-du-Temple, is a worthwhile art gallery among the dozens in this neighborhood:

10. Yvon Lambert, 108 rue Vieille-du-Temple (☎ **01-42-71-09-33**), specializing in contemporary and sometimes radically avant-garde art from international artists. The art is displayed in a cavernous main showroom, spilling over into an "annex" room. An excellent primer for the local arts scene, it makes a nice contrast to the 17th-century trappings all around you.

Continue north for 2 short blocks along rue Debelleyme until you reach rue de Bretagne. Anyone who appreciates a really good deli will want to stop at:

11. Les Iles Grecques, 14 rue de Bretagne (☎ **01-42-71-00-56**). This is the most popular of the area's ethnic takeout restaurants, a perfect place to gather picnic supplies before heading to nearby square du Temple (up rue de Bretagne) or place des Vosges. You'll find flavorful Greek cuisine like moussaka, stuffed eggplant, stuffed vine leaves, olives, tarama (a savory paste made from fish roe), and both meatballs and vegetarian balls. It's open Monday 3:30 to 8pm and Tuesday to Sunday 10am to 2pm and 3:30 to 8pm.

After you fill up on great food, note that at the same address is:

12. Hier, Aujourd'hui, et Demain (☎ **01-42-77-69-02**), where you can appreciate France's love affair with 1930s art deco. Michel, the shop's owner, provides a tempting array of bibelots and art objects, with one of the widest arrays of colored glass in town. Works by late-19th-century glassmakers like Daum, Gallé, and Legras are avidly collected. Some items require special packing and great care in transport; others (many amusing) can be carted home as a souvenir.

Now walk southeast along rue Charlot to the corner of rue Pastourelle, where you'll be tempted by the fabrics of:

13. Dominique Picquier, 10 rue Charlot (☎ **01-42-72-39-14**). Looking to redo your favorite settee? This stylish shop sells a wide roster of fabric (50% cotton, 50% linen) that stands up to rugged use. Most patterns are based on some botanical inspiration, like ginko leaves, vanilla pods and vines, and magnolia branches. Everything costs 390F ($62.40) per meter or 346F ($55.35) per yard—proof that the good life has returned to the Marais.

Nearby, adjacent to the corner of rue Charlot and rue du Perche, is the Marais's largest and most experimental art gallery, the:

14. Passage de Retz, 9 rue Charlot (☎ **01-48-04-37-99**). Opened in 1994, this avant-garde gallery has about 2,100 square feet of space to show off its highly amusing exhibits. It has shown Japanese textiles, American abstract expressionist paintings, modern Venetian glass, contemporary Haitian paintings, and selections from affiliated art galleries in Québec.

Walk 1 block farther along rue Charlot, turn left for a block onto rue des 4 Fils, then go right on rue Vieille-du-Temple, where you'll come across Delamair's:

15. Hôtel de Rohan, 87 rue Vieille-du-Temple. It was once occupied by the fourth Cardinal Rohan, the larcenous cardinal of the "diamond necklace scandal" that led to a flood of destructive publicity for Marie Antoinette. The first occupant of the hotel was reputed to be the son of Louis XVI. The interior is usually closed to the public, except during an occasional exhibit—if it's open, check out the amusing Salon des Singes (Monkey Room). Sometimes you can visit the courtyard, which boasts one of the finest sculptures of 18th-century France, *The Watering of the Horses of the Sun,* with a nude Apollo and four horses against a background of exploding sunbursts. (If you want to see another Delamair work, detour to 60 rue des Francs-Bourgeois to see the extraordinary **Hôtel de Soubise,** now housing the Musée de l'Histoire de France—see "Specialty Museums," in chapter 6.)

Along the same street at no. 47 is the:

16. **Hôtel des Ambassadeurs de Hollande,** where Beaumarchais wrote *The Marriage of Figaro.* It's one of the most splendid mansions in the Marais and despite its name was never actually occupied by the Dutch embassy.

    Continue walking south along rue Vieille-du-Temple until you reach:

17. **Rue des Rosiers** (Street of the Rosebushes) and turn left. It's one of the most colorful and typical streets remaining from Paris's old Jewish quarter, and you'll find an intriguing blend of living memorials to Ashkenazi and Sephardic traditions. The Star of David shines from some of the shop windows; Hebrew letters appear, sometimes in neon; couscous is sold from shops run by Moroccan, Tunisian, or Algerian Jews; restaurants serve strictly kosher food; and signs appeal for Jewish liberation. You'll come across many delicacies you might've read about but never seen, such as savory sausage stuffed in a gooseneck, roots of black horseradish, and pickled lemons.

    ☕ **TAKE A BREAK** The street offers a cornucopia of ethnic eateries that remain steadfast to their central European, Ashkenazi origins. **Chez Jo Goldenberg,** 7 rue des Rosiers (☎ **01-48-87-20-16**), has plenty of room to sit down and eat (see chapter 5 for more details).

    Head down rue des Rosiers to rue Pavée, which gets its name from the fact that it was the first street in Paris, sometime during the 1300s, to have cobblestones placed over what had been an open sewer. At this "Paved Street," turn right and walk south until you reach the St-Paul Métro stop. Make a right along rue François-Miron to see the 17th-century:

18. **Hôtel de Beauvais,** 68 rue François-Miron. Though the facade was badly damaged in the Revolution, it remains one of Paris's most charming *hôtels.* A plaque announces that Mozart lived there in 1763 and played at the court of Versailles. (He was all of 7 at the time.) Louis XIV presented the mansion to Catherine Bellier, wife of Pierre de Beauvais and lady-in-waiting to Anne of Austria; she reportedly had the honor of introducing Louis, then 16, to the facts of life. To visit the interior, apply any afternoon to the **Association du Paris Historique** on the ground floor.

    Continue your walk along rue François-Miron until you come to a crossroads, where you take a sharp left along rue de Jouy, cross rue Fourcy, and turn onto rue du Figuier. There you'll see the:

19. **Hôtel de Sens,** 1 rue de Figuier, built between the 1470s and 1519 for the archbishops of Sens. Along with the Cluny on the Left Bank, it's the only domestic architecture remaining from the 15th century. Long after the archbishops had departed in 1605, it was occupied by scandalous Queen Margot, wife of Henri IV. Her new lover, "younger and more virile," slew the discarded one as she looked on in great amusement. Today, the *hôtel* houses the **Bibliothèque Forney** (☎ **01-42-78-14-60**). Leaded windows and turrets characterize the facade; you can go into the courtyard to see more of the ornate stone decoration—the gate is open Tuesday to Friday 1:30 to 8:30pm and Saturday 10am to 8:30pm.

    Retrace your steps to rue de Fourcy, turn right, and walk up the street until you reach the St-Paul Métro stop again. Turn right onto rue St-Antoine and continue until you reach the:

20. **Hôtel de Bethune-Sully,** 62 rue St-Antoine. Work began on this mansion in 1625, on the order of Jean Androuet de Cerceau. In 1634, it was acquired by the duc de Sully, once Henri IV's minister of finance. After a straitlaced life as the "accountant of France," Sully broke loose in his declining years, adorning

himself with diamonds and garish rings and a young bride, who's said to have had a thing for very young men. The *hôtel* was acquired by the government just after World War II and is now the seat of the National Office of Historical Monuments and Sites, with an info center and a bookshop inside. Recently restored, the relief-studded facade is especially appealing. You can visit the interior with a guide on Saturday or Sunday at 3pm and can visit the courtyard and the garden any day; chamber music concerts are frequently staged here.

Shopping 8

Shopping is a favorite pastime of Parisians; some would even say it reflects the City of Light's soul. This is one of the rare places in the world where you don't have to go to any special area to shop—shopping opportunities surround you wherever you may be. Each walk you take will immerse you in uniquely French styles. The windows, stores, and people (even their dogs) brim with energy, creativity, and a sense of visual expression found in few other cities.

You don't have to buy anything to appreciate shopping in Paris—just soak up the art form the French have made of rampant consumerism. Peer in the *vitrines* (display windows), absorb cutting-edge ideas, witness new trends, and take home with you a whole new education in style.

1 The Shopping Scene

BEST BUYS

PERFUMES, MAKEUP & BEAUTY TREATMENTS   A discount of 20% to 30% makes these items a great buy; qualify for a VAT refund (see below) and you'll save 40% to 45% off the Paris retail price, allowing you to bring home goods at half the U.S. price. Duty-free shops abound in Paris and are always less expensive than the ones at the airports.

For bargain cosmetics, try out French dime store and drugstore brands like **Bourjois** (made in the Chanel factories), **Lierac,** and **Galenic. Vichy,** famous for its water, has a complete skin care and makeup line. The newest retail trend in Paris is the *parapharmacie,* a type of discount drugstore loaded with inexpensive brands, health cures, beauty regimes, and diet plans. These usually offer a 20% discount.

FOODSTUFFS   Nothing makes a better souvenir than a product of France brought home to savor later. Supermarkets are located in prime tourist neighborhoods; stock up on coffee, designer chocolates, mustards (try Maille or Meaux brand), and perhaps American products in French packages for the kids. However, to be sure you don't try to bring home a foodstuff that's prohibited, see "Entry Requirements & Customs Regulations," in chapter 2.

FUN FASHION   Sure you can spend and spend on couture or *prêt-à-porter,* but French teens and trendsetters have their own stores where

When you walk into a French store, it's traditional to greet the owner or sales clerk with a direct address, not a fey smile or even a weak *bonjour.* Only a clear and pleasant *"Bonjour, madame/monsieur"* will do.

And if you plan to enter the rarefied atmospheres of the top designer boutiques (to check out the pricey merchandise if not to buy anything), be sure to dress the part. You don't need to wear couture, but do leave the sneakers and sweatsuit back at your hotel. The sales staff will be much more accommodating if you look as if you belong there.

the latest looks are affordable. Even the dime stores in Paris sell designer copies and hotshot styles. In the stalls in front of the department stores on boulevard Haussmann, you'll find some of the latest accessories, guaranteed for a week's worth of small talk once you get home.

GETTING A VAT REFUND

In April 2000, the French **value-added tax** (**VAT—TVA** in French) came down from 20.6% to 19.6%, but you can get most of that back if you spend 1,200F ($192) or more in any store that participates in the VAT refund program. Most stores participate.

Once you meet your required minimum purchase amount, you qualify for a tax refund. The amount of the refund varies with the way the refund is handled and the fee some stores charge you for processing it. So the refund at a department store may be 13%, whereas at a small shop it'll be 15% or even 18%.

You'll receive **VAT refund papers** in the shop; some stores, like Hermès, have their own; others provide a government form. Fill in the forms before you arrive at the airport and expect to stand in line at the Customs desk for as long as half an hour. You're required by law to show the goods at the airport, so have them on you or visit the Customs office before you check your luggage. Once the papers have been mailed to the authorities, a credit will appear, often months later, on your credit-card bill. All refunds are processed at the final point of departure from the **European Union (EU),** so if you're going to another EU country, don't apply for the refund in France.

Be sure to mark the paperwork to request that your refund be applied to your credit card so you aren't stuck with a check in francs that's hard to cash. This also ensures the best rate of exchange. In some airports you're offered the opportunity to get your refund back in cash, which is tempting. But if you accept cash in any currency other than francs, you'll be losing money on the conversion rate.

DUTY-FREE BOUTIQUES

The advantage of duty-free shops is that you never have to pay the VAT, so you avoid the red tape of getting a refund. Both Charles de Gaulle and Orly airports have shopping galore (de Gaulle has a virtual shopping mall with crystal, cutlery, chocolates, luggage, wine, pipes and lighters, lingerie, silk scarves, perfume, knitwear, jewelry, cameras and equipment, cheeses, and even antiques), but prices are often equal or better in the city. You'll find lots of duty-free shops on the avenues branching out from the Opéra Garnier, in the 1st arrondissement.

BUSINESS HOURS

Usual shop hours are Monday to Saturday 10am to 7pm, but the hours vary greatly, and Monday mornings in Paris don't run at full throttle. Small shops sometimes close for a 2-hour lunch break and may not even open until after lunch on Monday. Thursday is the best day for late-night shopping, with stores open to 9 or 10pm.

Sunday shopping is currently limited to tourist areas and flea markets, though there's growing demand for full-scale Sunday hours. The big department stores are now open on the five Sundays before Christmas. The **Carrousel du Louvre,** a mall adjacent to the Louvre, is open and hopping on Sunday but closed on Monday. The tourist shops lining rue de Rivoli across from the Louvre are all open on Sunday, as are the antiques villages, assorted flea markets, and specialty events. There are several good food markets in the streets on Sunday. The **Virgin Megastore** on the Champs-Elysées, a big teen hangout, pays a fine to stay open on Sunday.

SHIPPING IT HOME

Shipping charges will possibly double your cost on goods, and you may have to pay duties on the items (see above). The good news: The VAT refund is automatically applied to all shipped items, so there's no need to worry about the 1,200F ($192) minimum. Some stores do have a $100 minimum for shipping, though. You can also walk into any post office and mail home a jiffy bag or small box of goodies. French do-it-yourself boxes can't be reopened once closed, so pack carefully. The clerk at the post office will help you assemble the box (it's tricky), seal it, and send it off.

GREAT SHOPPING NEIGHBORHOODS

Paris neighborhoods are designated by **arrondissement** (see "City Layout," in chapter 3). When you're planning a day of combined sightseeing and shopping, check a map to see how the arrondissements connect so you can maximize your efforts. Though Paris is made up of 20 arrondissements, only a handful are prime real estate for shopping. Here are the best of the shopping arrondissements:

1ST & 8TH ARRONDISSEMENTS   These two *quartiers* adjoin each other (invisibly) and form the heart of Paris's best Right Bank shopping strip—they're one big hunting ground. This area includes the famed **rue du faubourg St-Honoré,** where the big designer houses are, and the **Champs-Elysées,** where the mass market and teen scene are hot. At one end of the 1st is the **Palais Royal,** one of the best shopping secrets in Paris, where an arcade of boutiques flanks each side of the garden of the former palace.

Also here is **avenue Montaigne,** Paris's most glamorous shopping street, boasting 2 blocks of ultrafancy shops, where you simply float from big name to big name and in a few hours can see everything from Dior to Caron. Avenue Montaigne is also the address of **Joseph,** a British design firm, and **Porthault,** makers of the poshest sheets in the world.

2ND ARRONDISSEMENT   Right behind the Palais Royal is the **Garment District** (Sentier), as well as a few sophisticated shopping secrets, such as **place des Victoires.** This area also hosts a few old-fashioned passageways, alleys filled with tiny stores like **Galerie Vivienne,** on rue Vivienne.

3RD & 4TH ARRONDISSEMENTS   The border between these two arrondissements gets fuzzy, especially around **place des Vosges,** center stage of the Marais. No matter. The districts offer several dramatically different shopping experiences.

On the surface, the shopping includes the "real people stretch" (where all the non-millionaires shop) of **rue de Rivoli** and **rue St-Antoine,** featuring everything from GAP and a branch of Marks & Spencer, to local discount stores and mass merchants. Two "real people" department stores are in this area, **Samaritaine** and **BHV;** there's also **Les Halles** and the **Beaubourg** neighborhood, which is anchored by the Centre Pompidou.

Meanwhile, hidden in the Marais is a medieval warren of tiny twisting streets chockablock with cutting-edge designers and up-to-the-minute fashions and trends. Start by walking around place des Vosges for art galleries, designer shops, and special little finds, then dive in and lose yourself in the area leading to the Musée Picasso.

Finally, the 4th is also the home of the **Bastille,** an up-and-coming area for artists and galleries where you'll find the newest entry on the retail scene, the **Viaduc des Arts** (which actually stretches into the 12th). It's a collection of about 30 stores occupying a series of narrow vaulted niches under what used to be railroad tracks. They run parallel to avenue Daumesnil, centered around boulevard Diderot.

6TH & 7TH ARRONDISSEMENTS   Though the 6th is one of the most famous shopping districts in Paris—it's the soul of the Left Bank—a lot of the really good stuff is hidden in the zone that turns into the wealthy residential district of the 7th. **Rue du Bac,** stretching from the 6th to the 7th in a few blocks, stands for all that wealth and glamour can buy.

9TH ARRONDISSEMENT   To add to the fun of shopping the Right Bank, the 9th sneaks in behind the 1st, so if you choose not to walk toward the Champs-Elysées and the 8th, you can head to the city's big department stores, all built in a row along **boulevard Haussmann** in the 9th. Department stores include not only the two big French icons, **Au Printemps** and **Galeries Lafayette,** but also a large branch of Britain's **Marks & Spencer** and a branch of the Dutch answer to Kmart, low-priced **C&A.**

2 Shopping A to Z

ANTIQUES

Le Louvre des Antiquaires. 2 place du Palais-Royal, 1er. ☎ **01-42-97-00-14.** Tues–Sun 11am–7pm. Closed Sun in July–Aug. Métro: Palais Royal.

Across from the Louvre, Le Louvre des Antiquaires offers three levels of fancy knickknacks and 250 vendors. It's just the place if you're looking for 30 matching Baccarat crystal champagne flutes from the 1930s, a Sèvres tea service dated 1773, or a small signed Jean Fouquet gold-and-diamond pin. Too stuffy? No problem. There's always the 1940 Rolex with the aubergine crocodile strap. Prices can be high, but a few reasonable items are hidden here. What's more, the Sunday scene is fabulous, and there's a cafe with a variety of lunch menus beginning around 100F ($16). Pick up a free map and brochure of the premises from the information desk.

Mlinaric, Henry, and Zervudachi. 54 Galerie de Montpensier, Palais-Royal, 1er. ☎ **01-42-96-08-62.** Mon–Fri 9:30am–1pm and 2–6:30pm (Fri to 5:30pm). Métro: Palais Royal.

David Mlinaric is the British interior designer who redecorated Spencer House (the late Princess Diana's ancestral home in London) as well as all of Lord Rothschild's private residences. Tino Zervudachi is one of the hot young turks of Paris design. Hugh Henry, like Mlinaric, is English. Together, these three musketeers are the chicest antiques dealers on the Right Bank, specializing in museum-quality 18th-century items.

Village St-Paul. 23–27 rue St-Paul, 4e. No phone. Thurs–Mon 11am–7pm. Métro: St-Paul.

This isn't an antiques center but a cluster of dealers in their own hole-in-the-wall hideout. It really hops on Sunday. Bring your camera, because inside the courtyards and alleys is a dream vision of hidden Paris: dealers in a courtyard selling furniture and other decorative items in French country and formal styles. The rest of the street, stretching from the river to the Marais, is also lined with dealers.

ART

✪ **Galerie Adrien Maeght.** 42 rue du Bac, 7e. ☎ **01-45-48-45-15.** Mon 10am–6pm, Tues–Sat 9:30am–7pm. Métro: Rue du Bac.

This art house is among the most famous names in galleries, selling contemporary art on a very fancy Left Bank street that's far more chic and fashionable than the bohemian Left Bank Picasso knew.

Galerie 27. 27 rue de Seine, 6e. ☎ **01-43-54-78-54.** Tues–Sat 10am–1pm and 2:30–7pm. Métro: St-Germain-des-Prés or Odéon.

This tiny closet of a store sells lithographs by some of the most famous artists of the early 20th century, including Picasso, Coll, Miró, and Léger.

Librarie Elbe. 213 bis bd. St-Germain, 7e. ☎ **01-45-48-77-97.** Tues–Sat 10am–1pm and 2–6:30pm. Closed Aug. Métro: Rue du Bac.

The souvenir stands are filled with copies of Toulouse-Lautrec posters, but if you want something original, this shop sells early-1900s advertising and railroad posters, as well as etchings and cartoons, at very reasonable prices.

Viaduc des Arts. 9–147 av. Daumesnil, 12e. ☎ **01-44-75-80-66.** Mon–Sat 11am–7pm. Métro: Bastille, Ledru-Rollin, Reuilly-Diderot, or Gare de Lyon.

This renovated place occupies a long 2-block stretch from the Opéra Bastille to Gare de Lyon and features art galleries and artisans in individual boutiques created within the arches of an old train viaduct. It's nothing spectacular but makes for interesting shopping.

BOOKS

See also the **Marché aux Livres** under "Markets" and **FNAC** and the **Virgin Megastore** under "Music."

Brentano's. 37 av. de l'Opéra, 2e. ☎ **01-42-61-52-50.** Mon–Sat 10am–7:30pm. Métro: Opéra or Pyramide.

A block from the Opéra Garnier, Brentano's is a large English-language bookstore selling guides, maps, novels, and nonfiction as well as greeting cards, postcards, holiday items, and gifts.

Galignani. 224 rue de Rivoli, 1er. ☎ **01-42-60-76-07.** Mon–Sat 10am–7pm. Métro: Tuileries.

Sprawling over a large street level and supplemented by a mezzanine, this venerable wood-paneled bookstore has thrived here since it opened in 1810. Enormous numbers of books are available in both French and English, with a special emphasis on French classics, modern fiction, sociology, and fine arts. Looking for English-language translations of works by Balzac, Flaubert, Zola, or Colette? Most of them are here; if not, they can be ordered.

Les Mots à la Bouche. 6 rue Ste-Croix-la-Bretonnerie, 4e. ☎ **01-42-78-88-30.** Mon–Sat 11am–11pm, Sun 3–8pm. Métro: Hôtel de Ville.

This is Paris's largest and best-stocked gay bookstore, where you can find French- and English-language books as well as gay info magazines like *Illico*, *e.m@le*, and *Lesbia*. You'll also find lots of free pamphlets advertising gay/lesbian venues and events.

Librairie la Bail-Weissert. 5 rue Lagrange, 5e. ☎ **01-43-29-72-59.** Mon–Fri 10am–12:30pm and 2–7pm. Sat only by appointment. Métro: Maubert-Mutualité or St-Michel.

Paris is filled with rare bookshops, but this one has the best collection of atlases, rare maps, and engravings from the 15th to the 19th century. The shop sells original topographical maps of European and world cities, along with various regions of Europe. There's also a superb collection of architectural engravings.

Shakespeare and Company. 37 rue de la Bûcherie, 5e. No phone. Daily 11am–midnight. Métro: St-Michel.

The most famous bookstore on the Left Bank was Shakespeare and Company, on rue de l'Odéon, home to the legendary Sylvia Beach, "mother confessor to the Lost Generation." Hemingway, Fitzgerald, and Stein were frequent patrons, as was Anaïs Nin, the diarist noted for her description of struggling American artists in 1930s Paris. Nin helped her companion, Henry Miller, publish *Tropic of Cancer,* a book so notorious in its day that returning Americans trying to slip copies through Customs often had them confiscated as pornography. (When times were hard, Nin herself wrote pornography for a dollar a page.) Long ago, the shop moved to rue de la Bûcherie, a musty old place where expatriates still swap books and literary gossip and foreign students work in exchange for modest lodgings. Check out the lending library upstairs.

Tea and Tattered Pages. 24 rue Mayet, 6e. ☎ **01-40-65-94-35.** Daily 10am–10pm. Métro: Duroc.

At this largely English-language paperback bookshop, you can take a break from browsing to have tea at a little table. Though it's slightly out of the way, an extra dose of charm makes it worth the trip.

Village Voice Bookshop. 6 rue Princesse, 6e. ☎ **01-46-33-36-47.** Mon 2–8pm, Tues–Sat 10am–8pm, Sun 2–7pm. Métro: Mabillon.

This favorite of expatriate Yankees is on a side street in the heart of the best Left Bank shopping district, near some of the gathering places described in Gertrude Stein's *The Autobiography of Alice B. Toklas.* Opened in 1981, the shop is a hangout for the literati. Its name has nothing to do with the counterculture New York newspaper.

W. H. Smith. 248 rue de Rivoli, 1er. ☎ **01-44-77-88-99.** Mon–Sat 9am–7:30pm, Sun 1–7:30pm. Métro: Concorde.

This store provides books, magazines, and newspapers published in English (most titles are from Britain). You can get the *Times* of London, of course, and the Sunday *New York Times* is available every Monday. There's a fine selection of maps and travel guides, plus a special children's section that includes comics.

CERAMICS, CHINA & PORCELAIN

La Maison Ivre. 38 rue Jacob, 6e. ☎ **01-42-60-01-85.** Mon 2–7pm, Tues–Sat 10:30am–7pm. Métro: St-Germain-des-Prés.

This charming shop is perfect for country-style ceramics that add authenticity to French-country decor. It carries an excellent selection of handmade pottery from all over France, with an emphasis on Provençal and southern French ceramics, including ovenware, bowls, platters, plates, pitchers, mugs, and vases.

✪ **Limoges-Unic/Madronet.** 34 and 58 rue de Paradis, 10e. ☎ **01-47-70-54-49** or 01-47-70-61-49. Mon–Sat 10am–6:30pm. Métro: Gare de l'Est.

Housed in two shops of more or less equal size on the same street, this store is crammed with Limoges china brands like Daum, Baccarat, Lalique, Christofle, Haviland, and Bernardaud. You'll also find other table items: glass and crystal, silver, whatever your heart desires. They'll ship your purchases, and English is widely spoken.

Manufacture Nationale de Sèvres. 4 place André-Malraux, 1er. ☎ **01-47-03-40-20.** Mon–Fri 11am–6pm. Métro: Palais Royal.

This is one of only two official outlets in Paris for the limited production of Sèvres porcelain. The other is in the western suburb of Sèvres, near the Musée National de Céramique de Sèvres (see chapter 6). Since only about 5,000 pieces of the stuff are made every year, the porcelain is prized as one of the most celebrated names in French industry.

CHILDREN: FASHION & TOYS

Au Nain Bleu. 406 rue St-Honoré, 8e. ☎ **01-42-60-39-01.** Mon–Sat 9:45am–6:30pm. Métro: Concorde.

This is the largest, oldest, and most centrally located toy store in Paris. More important, it's probably the fanciest toy store in the world. But don't panic—in addition to the elaborate and expensive stuff, you'll find rows of cheaper items (like penny candy) in jars on the first floor.

Bonpoint. 15 rue Royale, 8e. ☎ **01-47-42-52-63.** Mon–Sat 10am–7pm. Métro: Concorde.

Grandparent alert! Bonpoint is part of a well-known almost-haute-couture chain specializing in clothing for children and adolescents ages 1 week to 16 years. The clothing is well tailored, traditional—and extremely expensive. Drool over formal party and confirmation dresses and the long baptismal robes, embroidered in France and edged in lace.

Dipaki. 18 rue Vignon, 9e. ☎ **01-42-66-24-74.** Mon–Sat 10am–7pm. Métro: Madeleine.

If you prefer clothes that have hip, hot style and color but are wearable, washable, and affordable, forget Bonpoint and try this small shop—it's a representative of a truly sensational French line of clothes for toddlers. And it's only a block from place de la Madeleine.

Natalys. 92 av. des Champs-Elysées, 8e. ☎ **01-43-59-17-65.** Mon–Sat 10am–7:30pm. Métro: F. D. Roosevelt.

Part of a French chain with a dozen stores in Paris and many elsewhere, Natalys sells upscale versions of children's (6 and under) and maternity wear. It has just enough French panache without going over the top in design or price.

CRYSTAL

✪ **Baccarat.** (1) 11 place de la Madeleine, 8e. ☎ **01-42-65-36-26.** Tues–Fri 10am–7pm, Mon and Sat 10am–6:30pm. Métro: Madeleine. (2) 30 bis rue de Paradis, 10e. ☎ **01-47-70-64-30.** Mon–Fri 9am–6:30pm, Sat 10am–noon and 2–5:30pm. Métro: Gare de l'Est.

Opened in 1764, Baccarat is one of Europe's leading purveyors of full-lead crystal. You won't be able to comparison-shop Baccarat crystal at its various branches—a central organization sets rigid prices. But if you're hunting for bargains, head for the rue de Paradis outlet and check out special sales or promotions on discontinued items. These sales are the biggest during 2 weeks in mid-January. Baccarat's more prestigious outlet is on place de la Madeleine, but the rue de Paradis one is larger and contains the **Musée de Baccarat** (see chapter 6).

Lalique. 11 rue Royale, 8e. ☎ **01-53-05-12-12.** Mon 10am–6:30pm, Tues–Fri 9:30am–6:30pm, Sat 9:30am–7pm. Métro: Concorde or Madeleine.

Lalique is known around the world for its smoky frosted glass sculpture, art deco crystal, and unique perfume bottles. The shop sells a wide range of merchandise, including leather belts with Lalique buckles and top-quality silk scarves at about 1,000F ($160), designed to compete directly with those sold by Hermès.

DEPARTMENT STORES

In addition to the stores below, **La Samaritaine,** 19 rue de la Monnaie, 1er (☎ 01-40-41-20-20; Métro: Pont Neuf or Châtelet–Les Halles), and **BHV,** 52 rue de Rivoli, 1er (☎ 01-42-74-90-00; Métro: Hôtel de Ville), offer the department store experience at slightly lower prices. La Samaritaine has a fine inexpensive restaurant with a wonderful view on the fifth floor.

Au Bon Marché. 22 rue de Sèvres, 7e. ☎ **01-44-39-80-00.** Mon–Fri 9:30am–7pm, Sat 9:30am–8pm. Métro: Sèvres-Babylone.

Don't be fooled by the name ("low-budget" or "cheap") of this two-part Left Bank department store—for about 20 years, it has worked hard to position itself in the luxury market, selling fashion for men, women, and children; furniture; upscale gifts; and housewares. There's also a gourmet grocery store. Some visitors compare it to Bloomingdale's with a French accent.

✪ **Au Printemps.** 64 bd. Haussmann, 9e. ☎ **01-42-82-50-00.** Mon–Wed and Fri–Sat 9:35am–7pm, Thurs 9:35am–10pm. Métro: Havre-Caumartin. RER: Auber or Haussmann St-Lazare.

Take a look at the facade of this megastore for a reminder of the gilded age. Inside, the merchandise is divided into housewares (**Printemps Maison**), women's fashion (**Printemps de la Mode**), and men's clothes (**Brummel**). Check out the magnificent stained-glass dome, through which turquoise light cascades into the sixth-floor **Café Flo,** where you can have a coffee or a full meal. Interpreters at the Welcome Service in Printemps de la Mode will help you find what you're looking for, claim your VAT refund, and so on. Au Printemps also has a tourist discount card, offering a flat 10% discount. Behind the store is a branch of the discount clothing/grocery store **Monoprix.**

Colette. 213 rue St-Honoré, 1er. ☎ **01-55-35-33-90.** Mon–Sat 10:30am–7:30pm. Métro: Tuileries or Pyramide.

Named after the still controversial great French writer, Colette is Paris's store of the moment, a swank citadel for *à la mode* fashion. It buzzes with excitement, displaying fashions by some of the city's most promising young talents, including Marni and Lucien Pellat-Finet. Not to be overlooked are home furnishings by designers like Tom Dixon and even zany Japanese accessories. Even if you don't plan to buy anything from the department store, patronize the tea salon, with its fresh quiches, salads, and cakes, plus three dozen brands of bottled water.

Galeries Lafayette. 40 bd. Haussmann, 9e. ☎ **01-42-82-34-56.** Mon–Wed and Fri–Sat 9:30am–6:45pm, Thurs 9:30am–9pm. Métro: Chaussée d'Antin. RER: Auber.

Opened in 1896, with a lobby capped by an early-1900s stained glass cupola classified a historic monument, Galeries Lafayette is Europe's largest department store. It concentrates on an upscale roster of everything you'd need to furnish and maintain a home; thousands of racks of clothing for men, women, and children; and a staggering array of cosmetics, makeup products, and perfumes. Menswear is concentrated in a section called **Lafayette Hommes;** also in the complex is **Lafayette Gourmet,** one of the fanciest grocery stores in Paris, selling culinary exotica at prices usually lower than those at Fauchon (see "Food"). A floor above street level is a concentration of high-end semi-independent boutiques, including Cartier, Vuitton, and Prada Sport. A fashion show is held at least once daily, usually in the grand **Salon Opéra.** At the street-level **Welcome Desk,** you can be told in many languages where you can find this or that in the store, where you can get a taxi back to your hotel, and so on.

FASHION
CUTTING-EDGE CHIC

Azzadine Alaia. 7 rue de Moussy, 4e. ☎ **01-42-72-19-19.** Mon–Sat 10am–7pm. Métro: Hôtel de Ville.

Alaia, who became the darling of French fashion in the 1970s, is the man who put body consciousness back into Paris chic. If you can't afford the current collection, try the **stock shop** around the corner at 18 rue de Verrerie (☎ **01-40-27-85-58**), where last year's leftovers are sold at serious discounts. Both outlets sell leather trench coats, knit dresses, pleated skirts, cigarette pants, belts, purses, and fashion accessories.

Courrèges. 40 rue François-Ier, 8e. ☎ **01-53-67-30-00.** Mon–Sat 10am–7pm. Métro: F. D. Roosevelt.

Don't look now: André Courrèges is hot again. Even those little white vinyl go-go boots and disco purses in silver metallic cloth are back. Courrèges's brings a humorous touch to 1970s retro, with bold color, plastic, and fun. There's another branch of his store in the **Carrousel du Louvre** mall (☎ **01-40-15-05-85**).

Hervé Leger. 29 rue du faubourg St-Honoré, 8e. ☎ **01-44-51-62-36.** Mon–Sat 10am–7pm. Métro: Concorde or Madeleine.

This creator of the Band Aid Dress (*La Robe à bandes*), a tightly wrapped concoction of stretch materials and color, has opened his own shop for those with curves to flaunt and cash to burn.

Jean-Charles de Castelbajac. 26 rue Madame, 6e. ☎ **01-45-48-40-55.** Mon–Sat 10am–7pm. Métro: St-Sulpice.

Castelbajac is the bad boy of French fashion, known for flamboyant and amusing gear in primary colors, often with cryptic but evocative inscriptions. Examples are excerpts from novels and poems by Proust and Mallarmé and autobiographical snippets ("in 1968, I created my first overcoat, using a fabric similar to this one you see here"). His store is in a cluster of designer shops that's great for gawking.

Jean Paul Gaultier. 6 rue Vivienne, 2e. ☎ **01-42-86-05-05.** Mon–Fri 10am–7pm, Sat 11am–7pm. Métro: Bourse.

Tucked in one of Paris's most famous passageways, this large boutique features the typical fare of this master punk turned tailor: street fashion made high fashion for men and women. A slightly newer branch of the store, featuring exactly the same inventory, is at 30 rue du faubourg St-Antoine, 12e (☎ **01-44-68-84-84;** Métro: Bastille).

Lolita Lempicka. 14 rue du faubourg St-Honoré, 8e. ☎ **01-49-24-94-01.** Mon–Sat 10:30am–7pm. Métro: Concorde or Madeleine.

Lolita, formerly of the hidden Marais and the underground fashion scene, has gone mainstream with her own shop, tiny but quite visible, on this street of streets. The women's clothes continue to be inventive and creative and usually very sexy.

DESIGNER BOUTIQUES & FASHION FLAGSHIPS

There are two primary fields of dreams in Paris when it comes to showcasing the international big names: rue du faubourg St-Honoré and avenue Montaigne. Though the Left Bank is gaining in designer status with recent additions like Dior, Armani, and Vuitton, the heart of the international designer parade is on the Right Bank.

Rue du faubourg St-Honoré is so famously fancy it's simply known as "the Faubourg." It was the traditional miracle mile until recent years, when the really exclusive shops shunned it for the wider and even more deluxe avenue Montaigne at the other end of the arrondissement. (It's a long but pleasant walk from one fashion strip to the other.) **Avenue Montaigne** is filled with almost unspeakably fancy shops, but a few of them have affordable cafes (try Joseph at no. 14) and all have sales help that's almost always cordial to the well dressed.

The mix is quite international—from British (**Joseph**), to German (**Jil Sander**), to Italian (**Krizia**). **Chanel, Lacroix, Porthault, Ricci, Dior,** and **Ungaro** are a few of the French big names. Also check out some of the lesser-known creative powers that be. And don't miss a visit to **Caron.** Most of the designer shops sell men's and women's clothing. The Faubourg hosts other traditional favorites: **Hermès, Lanvin, Jaeger, Rykiel,** and the upstart **Façonnable,** which sells preppy men's clothing in the United States through a business deal with Nordstroms. Note that Lanvin has its own men's shop (**Lanvin Homme**), which has a café that's perfect for a light (and affordable) lunch.

Alain Figaret. 21 rue de la Paix, 2e. ☎ **01-42-65-04-99.** Mon–Sat 10am–7:30pm. Métro: Opéra.

Alain Figaret is one of France's foremost designers of men's shirts and women's blouses. Though this store has a broad range of fabrics, 100% cotton is its specialty. Also check out the silk neckties in distinctively designed prints and the silk scarves for women. If you're comparison shopping, Figaret and Charvet (below) are half a block apart.

✪ **Chanel.** 31 rue Cambon, 1er. ☎ **01-42-86-28-00.** Mon–Sat 10am–7pm. Métro: Concorde or Madeleine.

If you can't have the sun, the moon, and the stars, at least buy something with Coco Chanel's initials on it, either a serious fashion statement (drop-dead chic) or something fun and playful (tongue in chic). Karl Lagerfeld's designs come in all different flavors and have added a subtle twist to Chanel's classicism. This store is adjacent to the Chanel couture house and behind the Ritz, where Mlle Chanel once lived. Check out the beautiful staircase of the maison before you shop the two-floor boutique—it's well worth a peek.

Charvet. 28 place Vendôme, 8e. ☎ **01-42-60-30-70.** Mon–Sat 9:45am–6:30pm. Métro: Opéra.

The duke of Windsor made Charvet famous, but Frenchmen of distinction have been buying their shirts here for years. The store offers ties, pocket squares, underwear, and pajamas as well, plus women's shirts, all custom-tailored or straight off the peg.

Christian Dior. 30–32 av. Montaigne, 8e. ☎ **01-40-73-54-44.** Mon–Sat 10am–7pm. Métro: F. D. Roosevelt.

This fashion house is set up like a small department store, selling men's, women's, and children's clothing, as well as affordable gift items, makeup, and perfume on the street level. For several years, cutting-edge Brit designer John Galliano has been in charge of the collections. Unlike some of the other big-name fashion houses, Dior is very approachable.

Favourbrook. Le Village Royal, 25 rue Royale, 8e. ☎ **01-40-17-06-72.** Mon–Sat 10am–7pm. Métro: Concorde or Madeleine.

English taste and conservative style are the hallmarks of this upscale woodsy-looking store resembling a men's club. You'll find vests, dinner jackets, ascots, neckties, shirts, cummerbunds, and the kind of items that make super wedding gifts. Fashion accessories for women are available at its sibling store, **Violet,** also in Le Village Royal.

Givenchy. (1) 3 av. George V, 8e. ☎ **01-44-31-50-00.** Mon–Sat 10am–7pm (all branches). Métro: Alma-Marceau. (2) 28 rue du faubourg St-Honoré, 8e. ☎ **01-42-65-54-54.** Métro: F. D. Roosevelt. (3) 6 rue du Cherche-Midi, 6e. ☎ **01-42-65-03-37.**

Opened in 1962 and noted for high-profile good taste often mentioned in annual lists of best-dressed women (particularly the late Audrey Hepburn), Givenchy still maintains a shop that makes couture clothes to order, and if that's what you're looking for, head a floor above street level. Otherwise, look for ready-to-wear clothing and accessories for men and women on the street level.

✪ **Hermès.** 24 rue du faubourg St-Honoré, 8e. ☎ **01-40-17-47-17.** Tues–Sat 10am–6:30pm, Mon 10am–1pm and 2:30–6:30pm. Métro: Concorde.

France's single most important status item is a scarf or tie from Hermès. Patterns on these illustrious scarves, retailing for about 1,500F ($240), have recently included the galaxies, Africa, the sea, the sun, and horse racing and breeding. But the choices don't stop there—this large flagship store has beach towels and accessories, dinner plates, clothing for men and women, a large collection of Hermès fragrances, and even a saddle shop; a package of postcards is the least expensive item sold. Ask to see the private museum upstairs. Outside, note the horseman on the roof with his scarf-flag flying.

✪ **Louis Vuitton.** (1) 101 av. des Champs-Elysées, 8e. ☎ **01-57-24-00.** Mon–Sat 10am–7pm. Métro: Georges V. (2) 6 place St-Germain-des-Prés, 6e. ☎ **01-45-49-62-32.** Mon–Sat 10am–7pm. Métro: St-Germain-des-Prés.

This Left Bank store is so gorgeous, the famed merchandise becomes secondary. Not content to cover the world's luggage with his initials, Vuitton has branched into assorted colored leather goods, writing instruments, travel products, and even publishing. Look for the traditional collection of leather, including Vuitton's monogrammed brown-on-brown bags in printed canvas, on the street level. The mezzanine showcases upscale pens, writing supplies, and stationery. And the top floor carries the company's newest line of goods—women's shoes and bags.

Yves Saint Laurent Rive Gauche. (1) 38 rue du faubourg St-Honoré, 8e. ☎ **01-42-65-74-59.** Métro: Concorde. (2) 6 place St-Sulpice, 6e. ☎ **01-43-29-43-00.** Métro: St-Sulpice. (3) 19–21 av. Victor-Hugo, 16e. ☎ **01-45-00-64-64.** Métro: Etoile or Victor Hugo.

The rue du faubourg St-Honoré branch sells the most upscale of the women's ready-to-wear clothing by the folk at Saint Laurent. Every season, the entire line is available for viewing here, and sales tend to be brisk. The two other outlets are somewhat smaller but still stocked with choice merchandise. If you're looking for menswear, head to **Yves Saint Laurent Rive Gauche Hommes,** 9 place St-Sulpice, 6e (☎ **01-43-46-84-40;** Métro: St-Sulpice). **Yves St-Laurent Haute Couture** is at 5 av. Marceau, 16e (tel. **01-44-31-64-00;** Métro: Alma-Marceau).

DISCOUNT & RESALE

Anna Lowe. 104 rue du faubourg St-Honoré, 8e. ☎ **01-42-66-11-32.** Mon–Sat 10am–7pm. Métro: Miromesnil.

This is one of the premier boutiques for the discriminating woman who wishes to purchase a little Chanel or Versace at a discount. Many clothes are runway samples; some have been gently worn.

Mendès. 5 rue d'Uzés, 2e. ☎ **01-42-36-83-32.** Mon–Sat 10am–6pm. Métro: Grands Boulevards.

In the center of the French garment district, this store mainly sells Saint-Laurent, Lacroix, and Montana. Prices, though discounted, can be quite steep and you have to get lucky to find anything worth sighing over.

Réciproque. 88–123 rue de la Pompe, 16e. ☎ **01-47-04-30-28.** Tues–Fri 11am–7:30pm, Sat 10:30am–7:30pm. Métro: Rue de la Pompe.

Forget about serious bargains here but celebrate what could be your only opportunity to own designer clothing of this caliber—every major big name is carried along with shoes, accessories, menswear, and wedding gifts. Everything has been worn but some items only on fashion runways or during photo shoots.

FOOD: CHOCOLATE, HONEY, PÂTÉS & MORE

Albert Ménès. 41 bd. Malesherbes, 8e. ☎ **01-42-66-95-63.** Mon 2–7pm, Tues–Sat 10am–7pm. Métro: St-Augustin or Madeleine.

One of Paris's most prestigious small-scale purveyors of foodstuffs prides itself on selling only goods that have been picked, processed, and packaged by hand. The 45 producers represented supply sugared almonds, sardines, exotic honeys, terrines and pâtés, baked goods, and more. It's all esoteric, even by French standards. Ménès prides itself, strangely enough, on being the first food store in France to import both Heinz Ketchup and Kellogg's Corn Flakes, both of which appeared on shelves for the first time here in the 1920s.

Christian Constant. 37 rue d'Assas, 6e. ☎ **01-53-63-15-15.** Mon–Fri 8:30am–9pm, Sat–Sun 8am–8:30pm. Métro: St-Placide or Rennes.

Opened in 1970, Christian Constant sells some of Paris's most delectable chocolates at 490F ($78.40) per kilo. Each is a blend of raw ingredients from Ecuador, Colombia, or Venezuela, usually mingled with scents of spices and flowers like orange blossoms, jasmine, the Asian blossom ylang, and vetiver and verveine (herbs usually made to brew tea).

⊙ **Fauchon.** 26–30 place de la Madeleine, 8e. ☎ **01-47-42-60-11.** Mon–Sat 9:30am–7pm. Métro: Madeleine or Auber.

At place de la Madeleine stands one of the city's most popular sights—not the church, but Fauchon, now a three-part shop crammed with gastronomical goodies perfect for picnics in your hotel room or *en plein air.* One shop sells dry goods; one sells candy, pastry, and bread; and one sells fresh fruits and veggies. A cafeteria and a coffee bar called Brasserie Fauchon are in the basement of one shop, and a full restaurant, Le 30, is located above (see chapter 5). Even though the prices are steep, it's easier than ever to pay for your goods: You're given an electronic card when you enter, and the value of each purchase is electronically encoded on it. When you finish shopping, head for the *caisse* (register), surrender the card, and pay the tally, then return to the counters to pick up your groceries.

Food Markets

Outdoor food markets are plentiful in Paris. Some of the better-known ones are the **Marché Buci** (see "Markets"); the **rue Mouffetard market,** open Tuesday to Saturday 9:30am to 1pm and 4 to 7pm and Sunday 9:30am to 1pm (6e; Métro: Monge or Censier-Daubenton); and the **rue Montorgueil market,** just behind the St-Eustache church, open Monday to Saturday 9am to 7pm (1e; Métro: Les Halles).

Hédiard. 21 place de la Madeleine, 8e. ☎ **01-43-12-88-77.** Mon–Sat 9am–11pm. Métro: Madeleine or Auber.

This 1850 temple of *haute gastronomie* has recently been completely renovated, perhaps to woo tourists away from nearby Fauchon. The decor is now a series of salons filled with almost Disneyesque displays meant to give the store the look of an early-1900s spice emporium. Upstairs, you can eat at the Restaurant de l'Epicerie.

Jadis et Gourmande. 27 rue Boissy d'Anglas, 8e. ☎ **01-42-65-23-23.** Mon 1–7pm, Tues–Fri 9:30am–7pm, Sat 10:30am–7pm. Métro: Madeleine.

This small chain of Parisian chocolatiers has a less lofty rep than Christian Constant and much more reasonable prices. They're best known for their alphabetical chocolate blocks, which allow you to spell out any message you want (well . . . almost), in any language. "*Merci*" comes prepackaged.

Maison de la Truffe. 19 place de la Madeleine, 8e. ☎ **01-42-65-53-22.** Tues–Sat 9am–9pm, Mon 9am–8pm. Métro: Madeleine or Auber.

This tiny shop resembles a New York deli more than a Parisian boutique. It's your source for not only truffles but also foie gras, caviar, and other gourmet foodstuffs. Gift food baskets are a house specialty. There are also a few tables and chairs so you can grab a quick bite.

Maison du Chocolat. (1) 225 rue du faubourg St-Honoré, 8e. ☎ **01-42-27-39-44.** May–Sept Mon–Sat 10am–7pm; Oct–Apr Mon–Sat 9:30am–7:30pm (all branches). Métro: Ternes. (2) 52 rue François-Ier, 8e. ☎ **01-47-23-38-25.** Métro Alma-Marceau. (3) 8 bd. de la Madeleine, 8e. ☎ **01-47-42-86-52.** Métro: Madeleine. (4) 19 rue de Sèvres, 6e. ☎ **01-45-44-20-40.** Métro: Rue de Sèvres. (5) 89 av. Raymond-Poincaré, 16e. ☎ **01-40-67-77-83.** Métro: Victor Hugo.

At its five Paris locations, this shop offers racks and racks of marvelous chocolates priced individually or by the kilo, at near or over 500F ($80) per kilo. These stores offer a variety of chocolate-based products, including chocolate pastries, usually more affordable than the candy, and even chocolate milk!

Maison du Miel. 24 rue Vignon, 9e. ☎ **01-47-42-26-70.** Tues–Sat 10am–7pm. Métro: Madeleine.

"The House of Honey" has been a family tradition since before World War I. The entire store is devoted to products made from honey: honey oil, honey soap, and various honeys to eat, including one made from heather. This store owes a tremendous debt to the busy bee.

Marks & Spencer. (1) 35 bd. Haussmann, 9e. ☎ **01-47-42-42-91.** Mon, Wed, Fri–Sat 9am–8pm; Tues 9:30am–8pm; Thurs 9am–9pm. Métro: Chausée d'Antin. (2) 88 rue de Rivoli, 4e. ☎ **01-44-61-08-00.** Mon–Sat 10am–8pm. Métro: Hôtel de Ville.

Okay, so it's a British department store specializing in clothing for men, women, and children. But the entire ground floor is a giant supermarket devoted to the St. Michael's brand of English foodstuff and includes prepared foods for picnics.

Poilâne. (1) 8 rue du Cherche-Midi, 6e. ☎ **01-45-48-42-59.** Mon–Sat 7:15am–8:15pm. Métro: St-Sulpice. (2) 49 bd. de Grenelle, 15e. ☎ **01-45-79-11-49.** Tues–Sun 7:15am–8:15pm. Métro: Dupleix.

One of Paris's best-loved bakeries, Poilâne hasn't changed much since it opened in 1932. Come here to taste and admire the beautiful loaves of bread decorated with simple designs of leaves and flowers that'll make you yearn for an all-but-disappeared Paris. Specialties include apple tarts, butter cookies, and a chewy sourdough loaf cooked in a wood-burning oven. Breads can be specially wrapped to stay fresh during your journey home. Cash only.

JEWELRY

Bijoux Burma. 50 rue François-Ier, 8e. ☎ **01-47-23-70-93.** Mon–Sat 10am–6:30pm. Métro: F. D. Roosevelt.

If you're feeling crestfallen because you can't afford any of the spectacular and spectacularly expensive bijoux at the city's world-famous jewelers, come here to console yourself with some of the best fakes anywhere. This quality costume jewelry is the secret weapon of many a Parisian woman.

Cartier. 7 place Vendôme, 1er. ☎ **01-44-55-32-50.** Mon–Sat 10:30am–7pm. Métro: Opéra or Tuileries.

One of the most famous jewelers in the world, Cartier has prohibitive prices to match its glamorous image. Go to gawk, and if your pockets are deep enough, pick up an expensive trinket.

✪ **Van Cleef & Arpels.** 22 place Vendôme, 1er. ☎ **01-53-45-45-45.** Mon–Sat 10am–6:30pm. Métro: Opéra or Tuileries.

Years ago Van Cleef's designers came up with an intricate technique that remains a vital part of its allure—the invisible setting, wherein a band of sparkling gemstones, each cut to interlock with its neighbor, creates an uninterrupted flash of brilliance. Come browse with the rich and famous.

KITCHENWARE

A. Simon. 36 rue Etienne-Marcel, 2e. ☎ **01-42-33-71-65.** Mon–Sat 8:30am–6:30pm. Métro: Les Halles.

This large kitchenware shop near the Forum des Halles mall supplies restaurants and professional kitchens. But it will also cover your table with everything from menu cards and wine tags to knives, copper pots, and pans—not to mention white paper doilies and those funny little paper things they put on top of the tablecloth at bistros.

Dehillerin. 18 rue Coquillière, 1er. ☎ **01-42-36-53-13.** Tues–Sat 8am–6pm, Mon 8am–12:30pm and 2–6pm. Métro: Les Halles.

Dehillerin is Paris's most famous cookware shop, located in the "kitchen corridor," alongside A. Simon (above) and several other kitchenware stores. The shop has more of a professional feel to it than beginner-friendly A. Simon, but don't be intimidated. Equipped with the right tools from Dehillerin, you too can learn to cook like a master chef.

LEATHER GOODS

Lamarthe. 219 rue St-Honoré, 1er. ☎ **01-42-96-09-90.** Mon–Sat 10am–7pm. Métro: Tuileries.

A cult hero in France yet virtually unknown elsewhere, this designer is famous for his handbags and small leather goods in funky fashion shades like melon and mint. Sure, he does more conservative colors like navy and black, but if you want the world to know you've been to Paris and you're totally *branché* (plugged in), spring for a risqué shade.

Longchamp. 404 rue St-Honoré, 1er. ☎ **01-43-16-00-12.** Mon–Sat 10am–7pm. Métro: Concorde or Madeleine.

Longchamp is a French brand known for high-quality leather and strong everyday durables that come in basic as well as fashion shades. Check out its pale-pink or steel-colored patent leather for a touch of Paris. The best bet is a series of nylon handbags attached to leather handles that fold for storage or travel and unfold for shopping. Items are priced according to size but begin at around $70.

Morabito. 55 rue François-Ier, 8e. ☎ **01-53-23-90-40.** Mon–Sat 10am–7pm. Métro: F. D. Roosevelt or George V.

While Hermès has the international rep, Morabito is the secret insider's source for chicer-than-thou handbags that begin at a bare minimum of 2,000F ($320) and quickly climb to 35,000F ($5,600) and more.

LINGERIE

Cadolle. 14 rue Cambon, 1er. ☎ **01-42-60-94-94.** Mon–Sat 9:30am–1pm and 2–6:30pm. Métro: Concorde.

Herminie Cadolle invented the brassiere in 1889. Today, the store she founded is managed by her family, and they still make the specialty brassieres for the Crazy Horse Saloon. This is the place to go if you want made-to-order items or are hard to fit.

Marie-Claude Fremau. (1) 16 rue de la Paix, 2e. ☎ **01-42-61-61-91.** Mon–Sat 10am–7pm. Métro: Opéra. (2) 104 rue de Rennes, 6e. ☎ **01-45-48-82-76.** Mon–Fri 10am–7pm, Sat 10:30am–7:30pm. Métro: Rennes.

The French are big on shops that sell towels and bathrobes as well as underwear. Naturally, French bathroom wear has flair and style—we're talking about a yellow silk bathrobe with a ruffled collar for about $300.

Sabbia Rosa. 73 rue des Sts-Pères, 6e. ☎ **01-45-48-88-37.** Mon–Sat 10am–7pm. Métro: Sèvres-Babylone or St-Germain.

Everything here is filmy, flimsy, silky, and sexy. Look for undergarments (slips, brassieres, panties) and the kind of négligées that might've been favored by Brigitte Bardot in *And God Created Woman*. Madonna has been spotted here shopping for panties that can go as high as $400.

MALLS

Carrousel du Louvre. 99 rue de Rivoli, 1er. No phone. Tues–Sun 10am–8pm. Métro: Palais Royal or Musée du Louvre.

If you want to combine an accessible location, a fun food court, handy boutiques, and plenty of museum gift shops with a touch of culture, don't miss the Carrousel. Always mobbed, this is one of the few venues allowed to open on Sunday. There's a Virgin Megastore, a branch of The Body Shop, and several other emporiums for conspicuous consumption. Check out Diane Claire for the fanciest souvenirs of Paris you've ever seen.

Forum des Halles. 1–7 rue Pierre-Lescot, 1er. No phone. Mon–Sat 10am–7:30pm. Métro: Etienne-Marcel or Châtelet–Les Halles.

Once the site of Paris's great produce market, Les Halles is now a vast crater of modern metal with layers of boutiques built around a courtyard. There's one of everything here, but the feel is very sterile, without a hint of the famous French *joie de vivre*.

Les Trois Quartiers. 23 bd. de la Madeleine, 1er. ☎ **01-42-97-80-06.** Mon–Sat 10am–7pm. Métro: Madeleine.

Named after the junction of the three neighborhoods (Madeleine, Opéra, and Concorde) where it sits, this is a mall of at least 15 upscale boutiques specializing in clothing, perfume, and cosmetics for men and women. The largest is Madelios, a menswear store that stocks Yves Saint Laurent, Ralph Lauren, and Hugo Boss, among others.

Marché St-Germain. 14 rue Lobineau, 6e. No phone. Mon–Sat 11am–7pm. Métro: Odéon.

The Marché St-Germain used to be an open-air food market until it was transformed into a modern shopping mall. Now only a few food and vegetable stalls remain in one corner—the rest of the market is dominated by low ceilings, neon lights, and mostly American and British chain stores like Kitchen Bazaar and Kenzo.

Montparnasse Shopping Centre. Between rue de l'Arrivée and 22 rue du Départ, 14e. No phone. Mon–Sat 8:30am–10pm. Métro: Montparnasse-Bienvenue.

This shopping center is sort of a quick fix mini-mall in a business center and hotel (Le Meredien) complex, with a small branch of Galeries Lafayette and some inexpensive boutiques. Visiting it is really worthwhile only if you also take a trip across the street to Inno, with its deluxe supermarket in the basement.

Palais des Congrès de Paris Boutiques. 2 place de la Porte-Maillot, 17e. No phone. Mon–Sat 10am–7pm. Métro: Porte Maillot.

A shopping center for convention-goers inside the Palais des Congrès, this mall offers some 50 shops, including branch stores of many French big names. You'll also find a Japanese department store and hairdresser. Its anonymity and distance from most of touristy Paris has taken its toll on some of the shops, but if you happen to be in the neighborhood, it might be useful.

MARKETS

Marché aux Fleurs. Place Louis-Lépine, Ile de la Cité, 4e. No phone. Daily 8:30am–4pm. Métro: Cité.

Artists and photographers love to capture the Flower Market on canvas or film. The stalls are ablaze with color, and each is a showcase of flowers, most of which escaped the perfume factories of Grasse on the French Riviera. The Flower Market is along the Seine, behind the Tribunal de Commerce. On Sunday it becomes the **Marché aux Oiseaux** (Bird Market).

Marché aux Livres. Square Georges-Brancion, 15e. No phone. Sat–Sun 10am–4pm in winter, 10am–6pm in summer. Métro: Porte de Vanves.

This charming two-building market for used books, old books, rare books, and some ephemera is slightly in the middle of nowhere but nonetheless thronged by serious collectors. The market is covered but open and doesn't close on a rainy day—the really valuable texts are draped in plastic. And don't forget the *bouquinistes* along the left bank of the Seine, on quai de Montebello.

✪ **Marché aux Puces St-Ouen de Clignancourt.** Av. de la Porte de Clignancourt, 18e. No phone. Sat–Mon 9am–7pm. Métro: Porte de Clignancourt (turn left and cross bd. Ney, then walk north on av. de la Porte Montmartre). Bus: 56, 85, 155, or 166.

Paris's most famous flea market is actually a grouping of more than a dozen flea markets—a complex of 2,500 to 3,000 open stalls and shops on the northern fringe of the city, selling everything from antiques to junk, from new to vintage clothing. The market begins with stalls of cheap clothing along avenue de la Porte de Clignancourt. As you proceed, various streets will tempt you. Hold on until you get to rue des Rosiers, then turn left. Vendors start bringing out their offerings around 9am and start taking them in around 6pm. Hours are a tad flexible depending on weather and crowds. Monday is traditionally the best day for bargain seekers, since the market is more sparsely attended, and the merchants are more eager to sell.

First-timers always want to know two things: "Will I get any real bargains?" and "Will I get fleeced?" Actually, it's all relative. Obviously, the best buys have been skimmed by dealers (who often have a prearrangement to have items held for them).

And it's true that the same merchandise displayed here will sell for less in the provinces. But from the point of view of the visitor who has only a few days to spend in Paris—and only half a day for shopping—the flea market is worth the experience. Vintage French postcards, old buttons, and bistro ware are quite affordable; each market has its own personality and an aura of Parisian glamour you can't find elsewhere.

Dress casually and show your knowledge if you're a collector. Most dealers are serious and get into the spirit of things only if you speak French or make it clear you know what you're doing. The longer you stay, the more you chat, the more you show your respect for the goods, the more room you'll have for negotiating the price. Most of the markets have rest-room facilities; some have central offices to arrange shipping. Cafes, pizza joints, and even a few real restaurants are scattered around. Beware of pickpockets and teenage troublemakers.

Marché aux Puces de la Porte de Vanves. Av. Georges-Lafenestre, 14e. No phone. Sat–Mon 6:30am–4:30pm. Métro: Porte de Vanves.

This weekend event sprawls along two streets and is actually the best flea market in Paris—dealers swear by it. There's little in terms of formal antiques and few large pieces of furniture. You'll do better if you collect old linens, used Hermès scarves, toys, ephemera, costume jewelry, perfume bottles, and bad art. Asking prices tend to be high, as dealers prefer to sell to nontourists. On Sunday, there's a food market one street over.

Marché aux Timbres. Av. Matignon, off the Champs-Elysées at Rond-Point, 8e. No phone. Generally Thurs–Sun 10am–7pm. Métro: F. D. Roosevelt or Champs-Elysées–Clemenceau.

This is where Audrey Hepburn figured it out in *Charade*, remember? At this stamp collector's paradise, nearly two dozen stalls are set up on a permanent basis under shady trees on the eastern edge of the Rond-Point. The variety of stamps is almost unlimited—some common, some quite rare.

Marché Buci. Rue de Buci, 6e. No phone. Daily 9am–7pm. Métro: St-Germain-des-Prés.

This traditional French food market is held at the intersection of two streets and is only a block long, but what a block it is! Seasonal fruits and vegetables dance across tabletops as chickens spin on the rotisserie. One stall is entirely devoted to big bouquets of fresh flowers. Monday mornings are light.

MUSEUM SHOPS

La Boutique de la Comédie Française. 2 rue de Richelieu, 1er. ☎ **01-44-58-14-30.** Daily 11am–8:30pm. Métro: Palais Royal.

This is the official gift/souvenir shop of France's most historic and prestigious theater. The plays commemorated inside have elicited in the French as much emotion and loyalty as Shakespeare has in the British. Look for plates and cups depicting 18th-century misers, maidens, and faithful servants, as well as scarves, pens, drinking glasses, and napkins honoring the French theater. You might appreciate the beer mugs (*les chopes*) emblazoned with the frontispiece of Molière's original folio for *Le Bourgeois Gentilhomme*. The gift shop remains open in August, when the theater is closed.

La Boutique du Musée de la Monnaie. 11 quai de Conti (entrance at 2 rue Guénégaud), 6e. ☎ **01-40-46-55-35.** Tues–Fri 11am–5:30pm, Sat noon–5:30pm. Métro: Pont Neuf or Odéon.

Jewelry made from coins and/or semiprecious stones, reproductions of antique coins, and medallions of every imaginable sort are sold here. If your tastes and interests involve small, cunning, and valuable objects, this might be the place for you.

La Boutique du Musée des Arts Décoratifs. In the Palais du Louvre, 105 rue de Rivoli, 1er. ☎ **01-42-61-04-02.** Thurs–Tues 10am–7pm, Wed 10am–9pm. Métro: Palais Royal or Tuileries.

This two-part boutique is divided by the entryway to the museum. On the right is a fabulous bookstore. On the left is a boutique selling reproductions of museum items: gifts, knickknacks, and even a custom-made Hermès scarf.

Musée et Compagnie. 49 rue Etienne-Marcel, 1er. ☎ **01-40-13-49-13.** Mon–Sat 10am–6:30pm. Métro: Etienne-Marcel.

This shop contains a selection of reproductions of originals contained in France's 20 *Musées Nationaux,* including the Louvre, the Musée d'Orsay, the Grand Palais, and the Musée Picasso. Prices range from 100F ($16) for a pair of ear clips to as much as 3,000F ($480) for a reproduction of an object from Greek, Assyrian, or Roman antiquity. It's useful to check out the larger inventories of roughly equivalent merchandise at the sibling shop, the **Musée Halles,** Forum des Halles, Porte-Berger Niveau-2, 2e (☎ **01-40-39-92-21;** Métro: Halles), open Monday to Saturday 10:30am to 7:30pm.

Printemps Design. In the Centre Pompidou, 19 rue Beaubourg, 4e. ☎ **01-44-78-12-33.** Wed–Mon 11am–10pm. Métro: Hôtel de Ville.

This shop's designers liken its merchandise to what's in the MoMA gift shop in New York City. Loosely associated with Le Printemps department store (but without the clothing), it features a frequently changing roster of stylish art objects and gift items. Many of the pieces are the work of well-known masters of their craft, like Phillippe Starck, Ron Arad, and the four-woman French design team known as Tse-Tse.

MUSIC

FNAC Montparnasse. 136 rue de Rennes, 6e. ☎ **01-49-54-30-00.** Mon–Sat 10am–7:30pm. Métro: St-Placide.

This is one of the busiest members of a large chain of music and bookstores known for its wide selection and discounted prices. There are eight other branches in Paris, including **FNAC St-Lazare,** 109 rue St-Lazare, 9e (☎ **01-55-31-20-00;** Métro: St-Lazare), with the same hours as above; **FNAC Champs-Elysées,** 74 av. des Champs-Elysées, 8e (☎ **01-53-53-64-64;** Métro: F. D. Roosevelt), open daily noon to midnight; and **FNAC Forum des Halles,** 1–7 rue Pierre-Lescot, 1er (☎ **01-40-41-40-00;** Métro: Châtelet–Les Halles), open Monday to Saturday 10am to 7:30pm.

Virgin Megastore. (1) 52–60 av. des Champs-Elysées, 8e. ☎ **01-49-53-50-00.** Mon–Sat 10am–midnight, Sun noon–midnight. Métro: F. D. Roosevelt. (2) Carrousel du Louvre, 99 rue de Rivoli, 1er. No phone. Tues–Sun 10am–8pm. Métro: Palais Royal or Musée du Louvre. (3) Gare Montparnasse, Level A, bd. de la Montparnasse, 6e. ☎ **01-45-38-06-06.** Mon–Thurs 7am–8:30pm, Fri 7am–9pm, Sat 7am–8pm. Métro: Montparnasse.

There are three branches of Europe's biggest and most widely publicized tape, CD, and record store. In a landmark building, the Champs-Elysées branch is Paris's largest music store and helped rejuvenate the avenue; there are a bookstore and a cafe downstairs. Besides the branches above, you'll find a Virgin Megastore at each airport.

PERFUME & MAKEUP (DISCOUNT)

Catherine. 7 rue Castiglione, 1er. ☎ **01-42-61-02-89.** Mon–Sat 9:30am–7pm. Métro: Concorde or Tuileries.

This family-owned shop sells an impressive stock of all the big-name perfumes and cosmetics at discounts of 20% to 25%. In addition, its paperwork is usually extremely well organized, allowing refunds of the value-added tax (VAT) to be cleared quickly through Customs. Many of the staff speak English.

Freddy of Paris. 3 rue Scribe, 9e. ☎ **01-47-42-63-41.** Mon–Fri 9am–7pm, Sat 9:30am–6pm. Métro: Opéra.

The discounts here are fabulous: up to 40% on perfumes, handbags, cosmetics, silk scarves, and neckties. Freddy of Paris is near American Express and the Opéra.

Parfumerie du Havre. 9 place de la Madeleine, 8e. ☎ **01-42-66-52-20.** Mon–Sat 10:30am–7:30pm. Métro: Madeleine.

This shop offers good discounts, depending on the brand (10% on Chanel, 30% on Sisley). There are tons of fragrances and a few designer accessories in this bright, modern, chic shop. Discounts are included in the prices as marked.

SOUVENIRS & GIFTS

Au Nom de la Rose. 46 rue du Bac, 7e. ☎ **01-42-22-22-12.** Mon–Sat 10am–7:30pm. Métro: Rue du Bac.

Everything sold here is coming up roses. Inventories include home accessories, fashion accessories, perfumes, scented candles and soaps, and gift items that re-create the spirit of Valentine's Day year-round. Attached to the shop is a florist open Monday to Saturday 9am to 9pm and Sunday 9am to 2pm.

Axis. (1) 14 rue Lobineau, Marché St-Germain, 6e. ☎ **01-43-29-66-23.** Mon–Sat 10am–8pm. Métro: Mabillon. (2) 11 rue de Charonne, 11e. ☎ **01-48-06-79-10.** Tues–Sat noon–8pm. Métro: Bastille.

If you're looking for a set of dinner plates imprinted with the cartoon character TinTin or a Philippe Starck chrome spider lemon press, head here to check out the wonderfully offbeat assortment of contemporary gifts. The stock is generally both cheap and very original.

Galerie Architecture Miniature Gault. 206 rue de Rivoli, 1er. ☎ **01-42-60-51-17.** Mon–Sat 10am–7pm, Sun 11am–7pm. Métro: Tuileries.

This store features Lilliputian town models complete with houses, stores, and fountains—miniature versions of French country villages and Parisian neighborhoods, all built to scale. A hand-painted ceramic depiction of a house or French national monument ranges from 65F to 4,000F ($10.40 to $640), depending on its size and intricacy.

La Boutique de l'Hôtel de Crillon. 10 place de la Concorde, 8e. ☎ **01-49-24-00-52.** Mon–Sat 9am–9pm, Sun 10am–9pm. Métro: Concorde.

To the left of the entrance to Paris's most famous hotel, this is an upscale boutique that trades on its association with prestige and glamour. It sells porcelain dishes, Baccarat crystal, ashtrays, napkin rings, linens, bathrobes and nightgowns, umbrellas, leather gloves, and tasseled silk napkins. About half of the merchandise bears the Crillon's logo.

La Tuile à Loup. 35 rue Daubenton, 5e. ☎ **01-47-07-28-90.** Mon 1–7pm, Tues–Sat 10:30am–7:30pm. Métro: Censier-Daubenton.

This emporium has been selling authentic examples of all-French handcrafts since around 1975, making a name for itself through its concentration of authentic hand-produced woven baskets, cutlery, and wood carvings. Especially appealing are the hand-painted crockery and charming stoneware from traditional manufacturers like Quimper and Lunéville and from small-scale producers in the Savoie Alps and Alsace.

STATIONERY

✪ **Cassegrain.** (1) 422 rue St-Honoré, 8e. ☎ **01-42-60-20-08.** Mon–Sat 10am–7pm (both branches). Métro: Concorde. (2) 81 rue des Sts-Pères, 6e. ☎ **01-42-22-04-76.** Closes daily 1:30–2:30pm. Métro: Sèvres-Babylone.

The Scent of a Parisian

If there's one thing international shoppers come to Paris for, it's cosmetics—after all, the City of Light is the world capital of fragrances and beauty supplies. These are a few of our favorite perfume and makeup shops:

While you can buy **Parfums Caron** scents in any duty-free or discount *parfumerie,* it's worth visiting the source of some of the world's most famous perfumes. The tiny shop is at 34 av. Montaigne, 8e (☎ **01-47-23-40-82;** Métro: F. D. Roosevelt), boasting old-fashioned glass beakers filled with fragrances and a hint of yesteryear. Fleur de Rocaille, a Caron scent, was the featured perfume in the movie *Scent of a Woman.* Store hours are Monday to Saturday 10am to 6:30pm.

While there are other branches and you can test Goutal bathroom amenities at many upscale hotels, the sidewalk mosaic tile and the unique scents make the **Annick Goutal** at 14 rue Castiglione, 1e (☎ **01-42-60-52-82;** Métro: Concorde), worth stopping by. Try Eau d'Hadrien for a unisex splash of citrus and summer. Store hours are Monday to Saturday 10am to 7pm.

Off a small courtyard halfway between place de la Madeleine and the Champs-Elysées, **Makeup Forever,** 5 rue de la Boetie, 8e (☎ **01-42-66-01-60;** Métro: St-Augustin), is where French models and actors go for their makeup. They also have fashion sunglasses at reasonable prices. The outlet was created by French stylist/entrepreneur Dany Sanz in 1984 and now maintains branches in New York and throughout the world. Check out the accessories, like suitcases, purses, and small travel kits ranging from 100F to 3,000F ($16 to $480). Store hours are Monday to Saturday 10am to 7pm.

If you think you've heard of every perfume and aromatherapy gimmick out there, this one will still impress you: At the very new-age **Octée,** 18 rue des Quatre-Vents, 6e (☎ **01-46-33-18-77;** Métro: Odéon), the collection of fragrances is color coded to match your personality, skin type, and mood. There are perfume, sprays, soaps, and body lotion, and you test everything on colored ribbons. Store hours are Tuesday to Saturday 11am to 7pm.

Shiseido, the world's fourth-largest maker of cosmetics and skin-care goods, has become more prominent thanks to the merchandising efforts of the beautiful **Salons du Palais Royal Shiseido,** 142 Galerie de Valois, Palais Royal, 1er (☎ **01-49-27-09-09;** Métro: Palais Royal). In addition to an awesome array of skin-care products and makeup, it stocks over two dozen exclusive fragrances created by the company's artistic director, Serge Lutens. Don't be afraid to wander in and ask for some scent strips.

Nothing says elegance more than thick French stationery and note cards. Cassegrain offers beautifully engraved stationery, most often in traditional patterns, and business cards engraved to order. Several other items for the desk, many suitable for gifts, are for sale as well; there are even affordable pencils and small desktop accessories.

TABLEWARE

Conran Shop. (1) 117 rue du Bac, 7e. ☎ **01-42-84-10-01.** Mon–Fri 10am–7pm, Sat 10am–8pm. Métro: Sèvres-Babylone. (2) 30 bd. des Capucines, 9e. ☎ **01-53-43-29-00.** Mon–Sat 10am–7:30pm. Métro: Madeleine.

This shop might remind you of an outpost of the British Empire, valiantly imposing Brit aesthetics and standards on the French-speaking world. Inside, you'll find articles for the kitchen and dining room, glass and crystal vases, fountain pens and stationery, reading material and postcards, and even a selection of chocolates, teas, and coffees to help warm up a foggy English day.

Geneviève Lethu. (1) 95 rue de Rennes, 6e. ☎ **01-45-44-40-35.** Mon–Sat 10am–7pm. Métro: St-Sulpice. (2) 317 rue de Vaugirard, 15e. ☎ **01-45-31-77-84.** Mon–Sat 10:15am–7pm. Métro: Convention.

This Provençal designer has shops all over France, with 19 others in and around Paris, all selling her clever and colorful Pottery Barn–meets–French Mediterranean tableware. The rue de Rennes branch is the largest, with the rue de Vaugirard branch runner-up. Newer designs stress influences from India, South America, and Africa as well. Energy, style, and verve are rampant here. The prices are moderate.

WINES

Les Caves Taillevent. 199 rue du faubourg St-Honoré, 8e. ☎ **01-45-61-14-09.** Mon 2–8pm, Tues–Fri 9am–8pm, Sat 9am–7:30pm. Métro: Charles de Gaulle–Etoile or Ternes.

This is a temple to the art of making fine French wine. Associated with one of Paris's grandest restaurants, nearby Taillevent, it occupies the street level and cellar of an antique building. Stored here are more than half a million bottles of wine, ranging from 26F ($4.15) to exceptionally rare vintages like a 1995 Romani-Conti Burgundy (Côtes de Nuit) at 22,000F ($3,520).

Nicholas. 31 place de la Madeleine, 8e. ☎ **01-42-68-00-16.** Métro: Madeleine.

The flagship store of this boutique chain, with more than 110 branches in and around Paris, offers very fair prices for bottles you might not be able to find in the States. Aside from the usual Bordeaux and Burgundies, look at some of the rarer regional wines, like Gewürztraminer from Alsace, Collioure from Languedoc-Rousillon, and the pricey but sublime Côte Rotie from the Côtes du Rhône outside Lyon.

9

Paris After Dark

When darkness falls, the City of Light certainly lives up to its name—all the monuments and bridges are illuminated, and the glow of old-fashioned and modern street lamps, the blaze of sidewalk cafe windows, and the glare of huge neon signs flood the avenues and boulevards. Parisians start the serious part of their evenings just as Anglos stretch, yawn, and announce it's time for bed. Once a Paris workday is over, most people go straight to a cafe to meet with friends over a drink and perhaps a meal (see "The Top Cafes," in chapter 5); then they may head home or proceed to a restaurant or the theater; and much later they may grace a nightclub, a bar, or a disco.

In this chapter, we describe Paris's many after-dark diversions— from attending a Molière play at the Comédie-Française to catching a cancan show at the Moulin Rouge to sipping a sidecar at Harry's New York Bar to partying at Le Queen with all the boys.

1 The Performing Arts

Announcements of shows, concerts, and operas are plastered on kiosks all over town. You'll find listings in the weekly *Pariscope,* an entertainment guide with a section in English, or the English-language bimonthly *Boulevard.* Performances start later in Paris than in London or New York—from 8 to 9pm—and Parisians tend to dine after the theater. You may not want to do the same, since many of the less-expensive restaurants close as early as 9pm.

DISCOUNTS There are many ticket agencies in Paris, most of them near the Right Bank hotels. *Avoid them if possible.* You can buy the cheapest tickets at the box office of the theater itself or at discount ticket agencies that sell tickets for cultural events and plays at discounts of up to 50%. One is the **Kiosque Théâtre,** 15 place de la Madeleine, 8e (no phone; Métro: Madeleine), offering leftover tickets for about half price on the performance day. Tickets for evening shows are sold Tuesday to Friday 12:30 to 8pm and Saturday 2 to 8pm. Tickets for matinees are sold Saturday 12:30 to 2pm and Sunday 12:30 to 4pm. Other branches are in the basement of the Châtelet–Les Halles Métro station and in front of Gare Montparnasse.

Students with ID can often get last-minute tickets by applying at the box office an hour before curtain time.

For easy availability of tickets for festivals, concerts, and the theater, try one of these locations of the **FNAC** record store chain: 136 rue de

Rennes, 6e (☎ **01-49-54-30-00;** Métro: Montparnasse-Bienvenue), or in the Forum des Halles, 1–7 rue Pierre-Lescot, 1er (☎ **01-40-41-40-00;** Métro: Châtelet–Les Halles).

THEATER

Comédie-Française. 2 rue de Richelieu, 1er. ☎ **01-44-58-15-15.** Tickets 70–190F ($11.20–$30.40). Métro: Palais Royal or Musée du Louvre.

Those with even a modest understanding of French can still delight in a sparkling production of Molière at this national theater, established to keep the classics alive and promote the most important contemporary authors. Nowhere else will you see the works of Molière and Racine so beautifully staged. The box office is open daily 11am to 6pm, but the hall is dark mid-July to early September. In 1993, a Left Bank annex was launched, the **Comédie Française–Théâtre du Vieux-Colombier,** 21 rue du Vieux-Colombier, 4e (☎ **01-44-39-87-00**). Though its repertoire varies, it's known for presenting some of the most serious French dramas in town. Tickets are 160F ($25.60) or 65F ($10.40) age 26 and under. Discounts are available if you reserve in advance.

OPERA, DANCE & CLASSICAL CONCERTS

Cité de la Musique. 221 av. Jean-Jaurès, 19e. ☎ **01-44-84-45-00,** or 01-44-84-44-84 for tickets. Tickets 80–200F ($12.80–$32) for 4:30 and 8pm concerts.

This testimony to the power of music has been the most widely applauded, the least criticized, and the most innovative of late François Mitterrand's half-dozen *grands projets.* At the city's northeastern edge in what used to be a run-down and depressing neighborhood, this $120-million stone-and-glass structure incorporates a network of concert halls, a library and research center for the study of all kinds of music, and a museum (see "Specialty Museums" in chapter 6). The complex hosts a rich variety of concerts, ranging from Renaissance music through 19th- and 20th-century works, including jazz and traditional music from nations around the world.

Maison de Radio France. 116 av. Président-Kennedy, 16e. ☎ **01-42-30-15-16.** Tickets 50–100F ($8–$16). Métro: Passy-Ranelagh.

This is the site of many of the performances of the **Orchestre Philharmonique de Radio France** and the somewhat more conservative **Orchestre National de France.** The concert hall's box office is open Monday to Saturday 11am to 6pm.

✪ **Opéra Bastille.** Place de la Bastille, 120 rue de Lyon. ☎ **01-43-43-96-96.** Tickets 60–670F ($9.60–$107.20) opera, 60–660F ($9.60–$105.60) dance. Métro: Bastille.

This controversial building—it has been called a "beached whale"—was designed by Canadian architect Carlos Ott, with curtains by Japanese designer Issey Miyake. Since the house's grand opening in July 1989 for the French Revolution's bicentennial, the Opera National de Paris has presented works like Mozart's *Marriage of Figaro* and Tchaikovsky's *Queen of Spades*. The main hall is the largest of any French opera house, with 2,700 seats, but music critics have lambasted the acoustics. The building contains two other concert halls, including an intimate 250-seat room that usually hosts chamber music. Both traditional opera performances and symphony concerts are presented here, as well as both classical and modern dance. Several concerts are given for free in honor of certain French holidays. Write ahead for tickets.

Opéra Comique. 5 rue Favart, 2e. ☎ **01-42-44-45-45.** Tickets 50–610F ($8–$97.60). Métro: Richelieu-Drouot.

This is a particularly charming venue for light opera, on a smaller scale than Paris's major opera houses. Built in the late 1890s in an ornate style that might remind you of the Opéra Garnier, it's the site of small productions of operas like *Carmen, Don Giovanni, Tosca,* and *Palleas & Melisande.* There are no performances mid-July to late August. The box office, however, is open year-round Monday to Saturday 11am to 7pm.

✪ **Opéra Garnier.** Place de l'Opéra, 9e. ☎ **01-40-01-17-89.** Tickets 60–670F ($9.60–$107.20) opera, 30–420F ($4.80–$67.20) dance. Métro: Opéra.

The Opéra Garnier, once the haunt of the ill-fated Phantom, is the premier stage for dance and once again for opera. This rococo wonder was designed as a contest entry by architect Charles Garnier during the heyday of the French Empire; the facade is adorned with marble and sculpture, including *The Dance* by Carpeaux. For a while after the opening of the Opéra Bastille, the Garnier was reserved for dance only, but then it closed for months of painstaking restoration—the boxes and walls were relined with red and blue damask, the gilt was polished, the famous Chagall ceiling was cleaned, and air-conditioning was added. When it reopened in mid-1995, opera made a grand return with Mozart's *Cosí fan tutte.* Because of the competition from the Bastille, the Garnier has made great efforts to present more up-to-date dance works, like choreography by Jerome Robbins, Twyla Tharp, Agnes de Mille, and George Balanchine. The box office is open Monday to Saturday 11am to 6:30pm.

Théâtre des Champs-Elysées. 15 av. Montaigne, 8e. ☎ **01-49-52-50-50** or 01-49-52-07-41 for box office. Tickets 60–750F ($9.60–$120). Métro: Alma-Marceau.

This art deco theater, attracting the haute couture crowd, hosts both national and international orchestras (perhaps the Vienna Philharmonic) as well as opera and ballet. The box office is open Monday to Saturday 11am to 7pm. There are no performances in August.

Théâtre National de Chaillot. 1 place du Trocadéro, 16e. ☎ **01-53-65-30-00.** Tickets 160F ($25.60) adults, 120F ($19.20) over 60, 80F ($12.80) under age 25. Métro: Trocadéro.

Part of the architectural complex facing the Eiffel Tower, this is one of the city's largest concert halls, hosting a variety of cultural events that are announced on billboards in front. Sometimes (rarely) dance is staged here, or you might see a brilliantly performed play by Marguerite Duras. The box office is open Monday to Saturday 11am to 7pm and Sunday 11am to 5pm.

2 The Club & Music Scene

Paris is still a late-night mecca, though some of the once-unique attractions now glut the market. The fame of Parisian nights was established in those distant days when the British and Americans still gasped at the sight of a bare bosom in a chorus line.

The fact is that contemporary Paris boasts less vice than London, Hamburg, or San Francisco.

Nevertheless, both the quantity and the variety of Paris nightlife still exceed that of other cities. Nowhere else will you find such a huge and mixed array of nightclubs, bars, dance clubs, cabarets, jazz dives, music halls, and honky-tonks.

A MUSIC HALL

Olympia. 28 bd. des Capucines, 9e. ☎ **01-47-42-25-49.** Tickets 150–300F ($24–$48). Métro: Opéra or Madeleine.

Charles Aznavour and other big names frequently appear in this cavernous hall. The late Yves Montand appeared once, and the performance was sold out 4 months in advance (nowadays he performs at Père-Lachaise cemetery). Today you're more likely to catch Gloria Estefan. A typical lineup might include an English rock group, showy Italian acrobats, a well-known French singer, a dance troupe, juggling American comedians (doing much of their work in English), and the featured star. A witty MC and an on-stage band provide a smooth transition. Performances usually begin at 8:30pm Tuesday to Sunday, with Saturday matinees at 5pm.

CHANSONNIERS

Chansonniers (literally "songwriters") provide a bombastic musical satire of the day's events. This combination of parody and burlesque is a time-honored Gallic amusement and a Parisian institution. Songs are often created on the spot, inspired by the "disaster of the day."

Au Caveau de la Bolée. 25 rue de l'Hirondelle, 6e. ☎ **01-43-54-62-20.** Fixed-price dinner 260F ($41.60) Mon–Fri, 300F ($48) Sat. Cover 150F ($24) Mon–Sat if you don't order dinner. Dinner Mon–Sat 8:30pm; cabaret 10:30pm. Métro: St-Michel.

To enter this bawdy *boîte,* you descend into the catacombs of the early14th-century Abbaye de St-André, once a famous cafe that attracted Verlaine and Oscar Wilde, who slowly snuffed out his life in absinthe here. The singing is loud and smutty, just the way the predominantly student audience likes it. Occasionally, the audience sings along. You'll enjoy this place a lot more if you can follow the thread of the French-language jokes and satire, but even if you don't, there are enough visuals (magic acts and performances by singers) to amuse. The fixed-price dinner is followed by a series of at least four entertainers, usually comedians. In lieu of paying admission for the cabaret, you can order dinner. If you've already had dinner, you can order just a drink.

✪ **Au Lapin Agile.** 22 rue des Saules, 18e. ☎ **01-46-06-85-87.** Cover (including 1st drink) 130F ($20.80). Tues–Sun 9:15pm–2am. Métro: Lamarck.

Picasso and Utrillo patronized this little cottage near the top of Montmartre, then known as the Cabaret des Assassins, and it has been painted by many artists, including Utrillo. You'll sit at carved wooden tables in a dimly lit room with walls covered by bohemian memorabilia and listen to French folk tunes, love ballads, army songs, sea chanteys, and music-hall ditties. You're encouraged to sing along, even if it's only the "*oui, oui, oui—non, non, non*" refrain of "Les Chevaliers de la Table Ronde." The best sing-alongs are on weeknights after tourist season ends.

Théâtre des Deux Anes. 100 bd. de Clichy, 18e. ☎ **01-46-06-10-26.** Tickets 205–225F ($32.80–$36). Performances Tues–Sat at 9pm, Sun matinee 3:30pm. Closed July–Sept. Métro: Blanche.

Since around 1920, this theater has staged humorous satires of the foibles, excesses, and stupidities of various French governments. Favorite targets are President Jacques

Chirac and other mandarins and kingmakers of the *héxagone française*. Cultural icons, French and foreign, receive a grilling that's very funny and sometimes harshly caustic. The place considers itself more of a theater than a cabaret and doesn't serve drinks or refreshments. The $2^1/2$-hour show is conducted entirely in rapid-fire French slang, so if your syntax isn't up to par, you won't appreciate its charms.

NIGHTCLUBS & CABARETS

Decidedly expensive, these places give you your money's worth by providing some of the most lavishly spectacular floor shows anywhere.

Café Concert Ailleurs. 13 rue Jean-de-Beausire, 4e. ☎ **01-44-59-82-82.** Cover 30F ($4.80), 50F ($8), or 80F ($12.80). Dinner nightly at 8pm. Metro: Bastille.

The young Juliette Greco or Simone de Beauvoir of today gravitates to this cafe/cabaret operated by a collective of artists. Some of the latest and most experimental music is performed here nightly over dinner. You can also show up for the 9pm show if you don't plan on dining here. Surprisingly, the cover charge is what you tell them you can pay (see above).

Chez Michou. 80 rue des Martyrs, 18e. ☎ **01-46-06-16-04.** Cover (including dinner, aperitif, wine, coffee, and show) 590F ($94.40). Dinner nightly at 8:30pm (reservations required); show begins nightly at 10:30pm. Métro: Pigalle.

The setting is blue, the MC wears blue, and the spotlights bathe performers in yet another shade of blue. The creative force behind the color coordination and a hearty dollop of cross-genderism is Michou, veteran impresario whose 20-odd cross-dressing belles bear names like Hortensia and DuDuche; they lip-synch in costumes from haute couture to haute concierge, paying tribute to Americans like Whitney Houston, Diana Ross, and Tina Turner and French stars like Mireille Mathieu, Sylvie Vartan, "Dorothée," and Brigitte Bardot. If you don't want dinner, you'll have to stand at the bar, paying a compulsory 220F ($35.20) for the first drink.

✪ **Crazy Horse Saloon.** 12 av. George V, 8e. ☎ **01-47-23-32-32.** Reservations recommended. Cover 450–560F ($72–$89.60) including 2 drinks at a table; 290F ($46.40) including 2 drinks at the bar; dinner spectacle 660F ($105.60). Shows Sun–Fri 8:30 and 11pm; Sat 7:30, 9:45, and 11:50pm. Métro: George V or Alma-Marceau.

Since it opened in 1951, this sophisticated strip joint has thrived thanks to good choreography and a sly, coquettish celebration of the female form. The theme binding each of the 5-minute numbers (featuring gorgeous dancers in erotic costumes) is La Femme in her various emotional states: temperamental, sad, dancing/bouncy, or joyful. Dance numbers that endure season after season include "The Itch" and "The Erotic Lesson." Dinner is a tasteful event served at Chez Francis, a restaurant under separate management a few steps from the cabaret. Shows last just under 2 hours.

✪ **Folies-Bergère.** 32 rue Richer, 9e. ☎ **01-44-79-98-98.** Cover 150–350F ($24–$56); dinner and show 370–550F ($59.20–$88). Tues–Sat at 9pm, Sun at 3pm. Métro: Rue Montmartre or Cadet.

The Folies-Bergère has been an institution for foreigners since 1886. Josephine Baker, the African-American singer who danced in a banana skirt and threw bananas into the audience, became "the toast of Paris" here. According to legend, the first GI to reach Paris at the 1944 Liberation asked for directions to the club. Don't expect the naughty and slyly permissive skin-and-glitter revues of the past. In 1993, all that ended with a radical restoration and reopening under new management. Today, it's a conventional 1,600-seat theater featuring musical revues with a sense of nostalgia for old Paris.

You're likely to see an intriguing, often charming, but not exactly erotic repertoire of mostly French songs, interspersed with the banter of an MC. A restaurant serves set-price dinners in an anteroom.

L'Ane Rouge. 3 rue Laugier, 17e. ☎ **01-47-64-45-77.** Reservations recommended. Dinner and show 300–500F ($48–$80). Dinner at 8pm; show at 10pm–midnight. Métro: Ternes.

This red-and-black mini-theater has been a showcase for French satire and humor since it opened shortly after World War II. You'll enjoy a well-flavored dinner of conservative French specialties, followed by a 2-hour medley of French-language standup comedy, ribald stories, and politicized jokes. If your knowledge of French is zero, you won't enjoy this place, and if you hate being singled out by a comedian in front of a crowd, stay away.

Le Canotier du Pied de la Butte. 62 bd. Rochechouart, 18e. ☎ **01-46-06-02-86.** Reservations required. Cover 210F ($33.60) including 1st drink. Performances daily 7:30–10:30pm. Métro: Anvers.

The worst thing you can say about this place is that it's touristy, but the visitors who show up share a genuine appreciation of the nuances, lyricism, and poetry of popular French songs. Each performance includes appearances by two men and two women, who interact with their own versions of the hits made famous by Piaf, Montand, Brel, and Chevalier. The byword is nostalgia, unleashed by the bucketful in a cozy red, black, and white theater with room for no more than 70.

Le Paradis Latin. 28 rue Cardinal-Lemoine, 5e. ☎ **01-43-25-28-28.** Cover 465F ($74.40) including half bottle of champagne; dinner and show 680–1,250F ($108.80–$200). Dinner Wed–Mon 8pm, revue at 9:30pm. Métro: Jussieu or Cardinal Lemoine.

Built in 1889 by Alexandre-Gustave Eiffel, with the same metallic skeleton as the famous tower, Le Paradis Latin represents the architect's only venture into theater design. The place is credited with introducing vaudeville and musical theater to Paris. In 1903, the building was a warehouse, but in the 1970s it was transformed into a successful cabaret whose singers, dancers, and special effects extol the fun, frivolity, and permissiveness of the City of Light. The MC speaks in French and English.

۞ Lido de Paris. 116 bis av. des Champs-Elysées, 8e. ☎ **800/227-4884** or 01-40-76-56-10. Cover for 10pm or midnight show 460–560F ($73.60–$89.60) including half bottle of champagne; 8pm dinner dance, including half bottle of champagne, and 10pm show 815–1,015F ($130.40–$162.40). Métro: George V.

The Lido's $15-million current production, *C'est Magique,* is a dramatic reworking of the classic Parisian cabaret show, with eye-popping special effects and bold new themes, both nostalgic and contemporary, including aerial and aquatic ballets using more than 60,000 gallons of water per minute. The show, the most expensive ever produced in Europe, uses 80 performers, $4 million in costumes, and a $2-million lighting design with lasers. There's even an ice rink and a pool that magically appear and disappear. The legendary Bluebell Girls are still here, however. Now that celebrated chef Paul Bocuse is a consultant, the cuisine is better than ever.

Moulin Rouge. Place Blanche, 18e. ☎ **01-53-09-82-82.** Cover 500–560F ($80–$89.60) including champagne; dinner and show from 790F ($126.40). Seats at the bar, cover 370F ($59.20) includes 2 drinks. Dinner nightly at 7pm; shows nightly at 9 and 11pm. Métro: Blanche.

Toulouse-Lautrec immortalized the Moulin Rouge and its habitués in his works, but he'd probably have a hard time recognizing it today. Colette created a scandal here by giving an on-stage kiss to Mme de Morny, but it's harder to shock today's audiences.

Try to get a table, as the view is much better on the main floor than from the bar. The emphasis on the strip routines and saucy sexiness of the belle époque and of promiscuous Paris between the world wars keeps drawing the crowds. Handsome men and women, virtually all topless, contribute to the appeal. The finale usually includes two dozen of the belles ripping loose with a topless cancan in a style that might've been appreciated by Gigi herself.

Villa d'Este. 4 rue Arsène-Houssaye, 8e. ☎ **01-42-56-14-65.** Cover 190F ($30.40) including 1st drink; dinner (including wine) and show 340–750F ($54.40–$120). Daily, doors open at 8pm, the orchestra plays from 8:30pm, the show begins at 9:45pm, and dancing after the show lasts until 2am. Métro: Charles de Gaulle–Etoile.

In the past, this club booked Amalia Rodrigues, Portugal's leading *fadista,* and French chanteuse Juliette Greco. Today you're more likely to hear French singer François de Guelte or other top talent from Europe and America. Villa d'Este has been around for a long time, and the quality of its offerings remains high. You'll probably hear some of the greatest hits of beloved French performers like Piaf, Aznavour, Brassens, and Brel.

JAZZ, SALSA, ROCK & MORE

The great jazz revival that long ago swept America is still going strong here, with Dixieland or Chicago rhythms being pounded out in dozens of jazz cellars, mostly called *caveaux.* Most clubs are between rue Bonaparte and rue St-Jacques on the Left Bank.

Au Duc des Lombards. 42 rue des Lombards, 1er. ☎ **01-42-33-22-88.** Cover 80–120F ($12.80–$19.20). Daily 9pm–3am. Métro: Châtelet.

Comfortable and appealing, this jazz club replaced an earlier club 9 years ago and has thrived in a low-key way ever since. Artists begin playing at 9pm and continue (with breaks) for 5 hours, touching on everything from "free jazz" to more traditional forms like "hard bop." Unlike at many of its competitors, tables can be reserved here and will usually be held until 10:30pm.

Baiser Salé. 58 rue des Lombards, 1er. ☎ **01-42-33-37-71.** Cover 50–100F ($8–$16) Wed–Sun. Daily 6pm–6am, music daily 10pm–3am. Métro: Châtelet.

This musically varied cellar club is lined with jazz-related paintings and has a large central bar and an ongoing roster of videos showing great jazz moments from the past. There's no food or even any particular glamour—everything is very mellow and laid-back. Genres featured include Afro-Caribbean, Afro-Latino, salsa, merengue, R&B, and sometimes fusion.

Bus Palladium. 6 rue Fontaine, 9e. ☎ **01-53-21-07-33.** Cover 100F ($16) for men, 100F ($16) for women Fri–Sat. Tues–Sat 11pm–6am. Métro: Blanche or Pigalle.

In a single room with a very long bar, this rock temple has varnished hardwoods and fabric-covered walls that barely absorb the reverberations of nonstop recorded music. You won't find techno, punk rock, jazz, blues, or soul. It's rock for hard-core, mostly heterosexual, rock wannabes 25 to 35.

Caveau de la Huchette. 5 rue de la Huchette, 5e. ☎ **01-43-26-65-05.** Cover 60F ($9.60) Sun–Thurs, 75F ($12) Fri–Sat; students 55F ($8.80) Sun–Thurs, 75F ($12) Fri–Sat. Sun–Thurs 9:30pm–2:30am, Fri–Sat and holidays 9:30pm–4am. Métro/RER: St-Michel.

This celebrated jazz *caveaux,* reached by a winding staircase, draws a young crowd, mostly students, who dance to the music of well-known jazz combos. In prejazz days, Robespierre and Marat frequented the place.

La Chapelle des Lombards. 19 rue de Lappe, 11e. ☎ **01-43-57-24-24.** Cover 100–120F ($16–$19.20) including 1st drink. Women free Thurs before midnight. Thurs–Sat 10:30pm–dawn. Métro: Bastille.

The club's proximity to the Opéra Bastille seems incongruous, considering the radically experimental African/Caribbean jazz and Brazilian salsa that's the norm. It's a magnet for South American and African expatriates, and the rhythms and fire of the music propels everyone onto the dance floor.

L'Arbuci. 25–27 rue de Buci, 6e. ☎ **01-44-32-16-00.** No cover. Dinner 200–250F ($32–$40). Tues–Sat dinner services at 7:30 and 10:30pm; live music begins at 10pm. Métro: Mabillon or St-Germain-des-Prés.

The artists who perform here are likely to be lesser-known players, sometimes from Southeast Asia, Madagascar, or the Philippines. The venue is subterranean, smoky, and intimate, and the music and ambience are often more appealing than the entrance suggests. If you don't want dinner, you're charged 60F to 75F ($9.60 to $12) per drink. The bar is open to 3am.

Le Bilboquet/Club St-Germain. 13 rue St-Benoît, 6e. ☎ **01-45-48-81-84.** No cover. Le Bilboquet nightly 8pm–2:45am; jazz music 10:30pm–2:45am. Club St-Germain Tues–Sun 11pm–5am. Métro: St-Germain-des-Prés.

This restaurant/jazz club/piano bar, where the film *Paris Blues* was shot, offers some of the best music in Paris. Jazz is played on the upper level in the restaurant, **Le Bilboquet,** a wood-paneled room with a copper ceiling, brass-trimmed sunken bar, and Victorian candelabra. The menu is limited but classic French, specializing in lamb, fish, and beef. Dinner is 180F to 300F ($28.80 to $48). Under separate management is the downstairs **Club St-Germain** disco, where entrance is free but drinks cost 100F ($16). You can walk from one club to the other but must buy a new drink each time you change venues.

Le Petit Opportun. 15 rue des Lavandières Ste-Opportune, 1er. ☎ **01-42-36-01-36.** Cover 80F ($12.80). Tues–Sat 9pm–5am; live music 10:30pm–2:30am. Métro: Châtelet.

Cramped and convivial, with a lingering sense of the 13th-century masons who built the cellar, this is a jazz club seating no more than 45 patrons, many of whom are regulars. Its specialty is the traditional back-to-basics "hard bop" that avoids the dissonance and irregular rhythms of "free jazz." Artists come from Europe and North America and perform for 3-hour sessions. The rest of the time, the place is an arts-conscious cafe/pub.

Les Etoiles. 61 rue du Château d'Eau, 10e. ☎ **01-47-70-60-56.** Cover 120F ($19.20) including 1st drink. Métro: Château d'Eau.

Since 1856, this red-swabbed music hall has shaken with the sound of performers at work and patrons at play. Its newest incarnation is as a restaurant discothèque where the music is exclusively salsa and the food Cubano. Expect hearty portions of fried fish, shredded pork or beef, white rice, beans, and flan as bands from Venezuela play to a crowd that dances to the rhythms.

Le Sunset. 60 rue des Lombards, 1er. ☎ **01-40-26-46-60.** Cover 50–120F ($8–$19.20). Daily 7:30pm–3am; music 8:30pm–2am. Métro: Châtelet.

Since 1976, this club has flourished in a setting that includes a street-level restaurant, where set menus are 82F ($13.10). In the smoky cellar, gloss-white tiles emulate a workaday Métro station. A roster of Italian, French, and American jazz artists—including names like Roy Haynes, Also Romano, and Richard Galliano—play in sets until 2am.

New Morning. 7–9 rue des Petites-Ecuries, 10e. ☎ **01-45-23-51-41.** Cover 100–180F ($16–$28.80). Call ahead, but hours are generally Mon–Sat 8pm–1:30am. Métro: Château d'Eau.

Jazz maniacs come to drink, talk, and dance at this long-enduring club. It remains on the see-and-be-seen circuit, so you might see Spike Lee or Prince. The high-ceilinged loft was turned into a nightclub in 1981. Many styles of music are played and performed, and the club is especially popular with jazz groups from Central and South Africa. A phone call will let you know what's going on the night you plan to visit. Sometimes it's open on Sunday.

Slow Club. 130 rue de Rivoli, 1er. ☎ **01-42-33-84-30.** Cover 80–100F ($12.80–$16). Tues–Thurs 10pm–3am, Fri–Sat 10pm–4am. Métro: Châtelet.

One of the most famous jazz cellars in Europe, capped with medieval ceiling vaults that have been praised for their acoustic intimacy, this presents a revolving set of artists who tend to focus on New Orleans jazz. Patrons, mostly in their 30s and early 40s, appreciate the music's cross-cultural diversity.

DANCE CLUBS

The nightspots below are among hundreds of places where people go chiefly to dance—distinct from others where the main attraction is the music. The area around the church of **St-Germain-des-Prés** is full of dance clubs, but they come and go so quickly you could arrive to find a hardware store in the place of last year's white-hot disco—but, like all things in nature, the new springs up to take the place of the old. Check in *Time Out: Paris* or *Pariscope* to get a sense of the current trends.

Club Zed. 2 rue des Anglais, 5e. ☎ **01-43-54-93-78.** Cover 50–100F ($8–$16), including 1st drink. Wed–Thurs 10:30pm–3am, Fri–Sat 11pm–5:30am. Métro: Maubert-Mutualité.

This popular nightspot in a former bakery with a vaulted masonry ceiling may surprise you with its mix of musical offerings, including samba, rock, 1960s pop, and jazz.

La Balajo. 9 rue de Lappe, 11e. ☎ **01-47-00-07-87.** Cover 50F ($8) including 1st drink on Sun afternoon, 100F ($16) evenings. Thurs–Sat 11:30pm–5am, Sun 1–11pm. Métro: Bastille.

Opened in 1936, this dance club is best remembered as the venue where Edith Piaf first won the hearts of thousands of Parisians. Today, Le Balajo is hardly as fashionable, though it continues its big-band tradition on Sunday afternoon, when patrons 45 and up dance to swing and bebop. Thursday to Saturday nights, they bring out the disco ball or play reggae, salsa, rock, and rap.

La Coupole. 102 bd. Montparnasse, 14e. ☎ **01-43-20-14-20.** Ballroom cover 100F ($16) for evening sessions, 40–80F ($6.40–$12.80) for Sat and Sun matinees. Tues 9:30pm–4am, Fri–Sat 3–7pm and 9:30pm–4am, Sun 3–9pm. Métro: Vavin.

This landmark cafe has a basement ballroom that's a popular place to waltz and tango to orchestra music as well as bump and grind to "disco retro" (the best tunes of the 1960s, 1970s, and 1980s). The upstairs cafe is covered in chapter 5, "The Top Cafes."

La Flèche d'Or. 102 bis rue de Bagnolet, 20e. ☎ **01-43-72-04-23.** No cover–25F ($4). Tues–Sun 10–2am, Mon 6pm–2am. Metro: Alexandre Dumas.

Part of the chic swing to East Paris, this is a particularly lively counterculture cafe/club. After you've visited Jim Morrison at Père-Lachaise, you can enjoy live concerts here on Friday and Saturday, everything from Jamaican reggae to Celtic rock. Salsa or swing music from a live dance band enlivens Sundays at 5pm. Anything might be happening—art shows, political debates, video nights, whatever.

La Java. 105 rue du faubourg du Temple, 11e. ☎ **01-42-02-20-52.** Cover 80F ($12.80) Thurs, 100F ($16) Fri–Sat, 40F ($6.40) Sun. Thurs–Sat 11pm–5am, Sun 8pm–2am. Métro: Belleville.

A Bar Crawl in Trendy Ménilmontant

If **rue Oberkampf** were any hotter, it would melt off the map. How did it all happen so fast? Longtime residents shake their heads in disbelief and worry that the quirky authenticity of the neighborhood may disappear under the swarms of night crawlers who've migrated north en masse from the Bastille. "Too many *banlieusards* go to the Bastille," the owner of Café Cannibale told us, referring to the well-known reluctance of trendy Parisians to socialize with the suburban crowd.

The success of ultra-hip **Café Charbon,** 109 rue Oberkampf (☎ **01-43-57-55-13**), open daily 9am to 2am, encouraged entrepreneurs to renovate abandoned factories and seedy bars for the artists who were flowing into the neighborhood and for the restless crowd that was already tiring of the Bastille. Some of the new spots are intentionally dilapidated, while others evoke the elegance of 19th-century watering holes. The walls often exhibit the work of local artists, the music is kept fairly low-key, and the drinks are reasonably priced (a glass of mint tea makes a refreshing alternative to alcohol). You can have a salad, snack, or hot *plat du jour,* but the food is secondary to the ambience.

Start from the Ménilmontant Métro stop and head down rue Oberkampf. Your first stop should be the divey **Le Scherkhan** at no. 144 (☎ **01-43-57-29-34**), where you can sink into an easy chair under the fangs of a stuffed tiger, inhale the incense, and dream of equatorial Africa. It's open daily 5pm to 2am. Stop in at the live-music club **Le Cithéa** at no. 114 (☎ **01-40-21-70-95**) if it's open or continue on to **Café Mercerie** at no. 98 (☎ **01-43-38-81-30**), open Monday to Friday 5pm to 2am and Saturday and Sunday 3pm to 2am. At the end of the fashionably grungy bar is a tiny back room lined with long sofas. Across the street at no. 109 is **Café Charbon,** set in an early-1900s dance hall with a stunning art nouveau interior; it makes a relaxed place to hang out during the day and a crowded hotspot at night. Farther down on the same side of the street at no. 99 is the plush **Mecano Bar** (☎ **01-40-21-35-28**), open daily noon to 2am. Mysterious old implements on the wall are left over from its days as a tool factory. The spacious back room has a palm tree, a skylight, and murals of seminude ladies lounging about in fin de siècle naughtiness. Backtrack a few steps and turn left onto rue St-Maur to nos. 111–113, the **Blue Billard** (☎ **01-43-55-87-21**), open daily 11am to 2am. This camera factory turned into an upscale bar/pool hall has 22 blue tables under a mezzanine and skylight. A few steps farther on at no. 117 is a local favorite, **Les Couleurs** (☎ **01-43-57-95-61**), open daily noon to 2am. It's outfitted with tacky posters, chrome-and-plastic chairs, and kitschy rec-room lamps. Live bands regularly play "free jazz," alternative rock, and anything experimental. Turn right at rue Jean-Pierre-Timbaud and at no. 93 you'll find **Café Cannibale** (☎ **01-49-29-95-59**), open daily 8am to 2am. This softly lit beauty shimmers with candles, mirrors, and chandeliers. The menu includes a good-value Sunday brunch for 80F ($12.80).

This dance hall used to be one of the most frequented in Paris, and the great Piaf and Chevalier made their names here. Today, you can still dance the waltz and perhaps even tango on a Sunday afternoon. Brazilian and Latin themes predominate on some nights.

More After-Dark Diversions

On a Paris night, the cheapest entertainment, especially if you're young, is "**the show**" staged at the southeasterly tip of Ile de la Cité, behind Notre-Dame. A sort of Gallic version of the Sundowner Festival in Key West, Florida, it spontaneously attracts just about everyone who ever wanted to try their hand at performance art. The entertainment is strictly spontaneous and usually includes magicians, fire eaters, jugglers, mimes, and music makers from all over, performing against the backdrop of the illuminated cathedral. This is one of the greatest places in Paris to meet other young people in a sometimes moderately euphoric setting.

Also popular is a **stroll along the Seine** after 10pm. Take a graveled pathway down to the river from the Left Bank side of pont de Sully, close to the Institut du Monde Arabe, and walk to the right, away from Notre-Dame. This walk, which comes to an end near place Valhubert, is the best place to see spontaneous Paris in action at night. Joggers and saxophone players come here, and many Parisians show up to take part in impromptu dance parties.

To quench your thirst, wander onto Ile St-Louis and head for the **Café-Brasserie St-Regis,** 6 rue Jean-du-Bellay, 4e, across from pont St-Louis (☎ **01-43-54-59-41;** Métro: Musée du Louvre). If you want to linger inside, you can order a *plat du jour* or a coffee at the bar. But try doing as the Parisians do and order a 13F ($2.10) beer to go (*une bière à emporter*) in a plastic cup and take it with you on a stroll around the island. The little cafe is open daily 7 to 2am.

If you're caught waiting for the Métro to start running again at 5am, try the **Sous-Bock Tavern,** 49 rue St-Honoré, 1er (☎ **01-40-26-46-61;** Métro: Pont Neuf), open daily 11am to 5am. Young drinkers gather here to sample some 400 varieties of beer. If you want a shot of whiskey to accompany your brew, you face a choice of 150 varieties. The dish to order is a platter of mussels—curried, with white wine, or with cream sauce; they go well with the brasserie-style fries.

If you're looking for the most flamboyant drag in Paris, head to **Madame Arthur,** 75 bis rue des Martyrs, 18e (☎ **01-42-54-40-21;** Métro: Abbesses or

Le New Riverside. 7 rue Grégoire-de-Tours, 6e. ☎ **01-43-54-46-33.** Cover for men 90F ($14.40) including 1st drink, but women pay cover only after midnight Fri–Sat. Daily 11pm–6am. Métro: St-Michel or Odéon.

If thoughts of Woodstock fill you with nostalgia and you want to meet Parisians between 25 and 40 who feel the same, this is the place for you. The battered Left Bank cellar club attracts droves of people who appreciate the indestructible premises and nostalgic music. You'll hear a range of 1970s electronic rock and pop, especially The Doors.

Le Saint. 7 rue St-Severin, 5e. ☎ **01-43-25-50-04.** Cover 60–90F ($9.60–$14.40) including 1st drink. Daily 11pm–6am. Métro: St-Michel.

Occupying three medieval cellars deep in Paris's university area, this place lures 20- and 30-somethings who dance and drink and generally feel happy to be in a Left Bank student dive. The music melds New York, Los Angeles, and Europe and often leads to episodes of "Young Love Beside the Seine."

Pigalle). It's the longest-running transvestite show in town, attracting both straights and gays. The creative force behind the affair is Mme Arthur, who's no lady and whose stage name during her shticks as MC is Chantaline. The performances include 9 to 11 artists with names like Vungala, Lady Lune, and Miss Badabou. You can visit just to drink or can dine from a fixed-price menu (reservations required). The club is open daily 9 to 10:30pm for dinner, with the show beginning at 10:30pm. Additional shows, according to demand, are Friday and Saturday at 7pm, with dinner beginning at 6pm. After the last show, around 12:30am, the place becomes a disco. Cover (including the first drink) is 165F ($26.40); dinner and the show is 295F ($47.20) Sunday to Thursday and 395F ($63.20) Friday and Saturday.

If drag shows aren't your cup of tea, how about *The Last Tango in Paris?* At **Le Tango,** 13 rue au Maire, 3e (☎ **01-42-72-17-78;** Métro: Arts et Métiers), memories of Evita and Argentina live on. This dive with a bordello decor features zouk music from the French Caribbean and Africa, as well as house, garage, and virtually every form of high-energy dance music known in New York and Los Angeles. Most patrons are gay and lesbian and in their 20s and 30s. The cover is 40F ($6.40). It's open Friday and Saturday midnight to 5am. Another fun and trendy dance place is **La Guinguette Pirate,** Quai de la Gare, 13e (☎ **01-44-24-89-89;** Métro: Quai de la Gare), a Chinese junk moored off the banks of the Seine. This is the latest version of the fabled *guinguette* (river cafe), offering great jazz, zouk, and live salsa. Cover is 50F ($8).

If you're looking for a sophisticated, laid-back venue without the high-energy exhibitionism of nightclubs, consider a drink at the **Sanz-Sans,** 49 rue du faubourg St-Antoine, 4e (☎ **01-44-75-78-78;** Métro: Bastille). It's a multi-ethnic playground where the children of prominent Parisians mingle, testifying to the unifying power of jazz. In this red-velvet duplex, the most important conversations seem to occur over margaritas on the stairway or the back-room couches. The later it gets, the sexier the scene becomes. There's no cover.

Les Bains. 7 rue du Bourg-l'Abbé, 3e. ☎ **01-48-87-01-80.** Cover 120F ($19.20) including 1st drink. Daily 11:30pm–6am. Métro: Réaumur.

This chic enclave has been pronounced "in" and "out," but lately it's very "in," attracting more model types and gays, especially on Monday night. Everyone dresses more for show than for comfort. The name Les Bains comes from the place's old function as a Turkish bath attracting gays, none more notable than Marcel Proust. It may be hard to get in if the bouncer doesn't like your looks. A restaurant has been added.

Les Coulisses/La Bohème. 5 rue du Mont-Cenis, 18e. ☎ **01-42-62-89-99.** Cover 160F ($25.60) Fri–Sat, but free for patrons of either restaurant. Restaurants daily 8pm–5am; disco 11pm–5am. Métro: Abbesses or Funiculaire.

Its premises combine a cellar-level disco with a street-level restaurant that bears two names. During the day, 7:30am to around 8pm, it's known as La Bohème; 8pm to 5:30am, it becomes a bit more formal and is called Les Coulisses. The food remains the same, with a set-price menu at 160F ($25.60) and platters at 70F to 100F ($11.20

to $16). Most nighttime patrons eventually filter down to the disco, where the decor is a cross between a feudal château and a scene from the Italian *Commedia dell'Arte.* The crowd ranges in age from 20 to around 45.

Rex Club. 5 bd. Poissonière, 2e. ☎ **01-42-36-83-98.** Cover 50–80F ($8–$12.80) including 1st drink. Wed–Sat 11:30pm–6am. Métro: Bonne Nouvelle.

This echoing blue-and-orange space emulates the techno-grunge clubs of London, complete with an international mood-altered crowd enjoying the kind of music only someone 18 to 28 could love. A revolving host of DJs is on hand, including regular appearances from a local techno-circuit celeb, Laurent Garnier.

3 Bars, Pubs & Clubs

WINE BARS

Many Parisians now prefer the wine bar to the traditional cafe or bistro. The food is often better and the ambience more inviting. For cafes, see "The Top Cafes," in chapter 5.

✪ **Au Sauvignon.** 80 rue des Sts-Pères, 7e. ☎ **01-45-48-49-02.** Mon–Sat 8:30am–10:30pm. Métro: Sèvres-Babylone.

This tiny place, with old ceramic tiles and frescoes done by Left Bank artists, has tables overflowing onto a covered terrace where wines range from the cheapest Beaujolais to the most expensive St-Emilion Grand Cru. A glass of wine is 21F to 30F ($3.35 to $4.80), and it costs an extra 2F (30¢) to consume it at a table. To accompany your wine, choose an Auvergne specialty, like goat cheese or a terrine. The fresh Poilâne bread is ideal with ham, pâté, or goat cheese.

Aux Négociants. 27 rue Lambert, 18e. ☎ **01-46-06-15-11.** Mon and Fri noon–8pm, Tues–Thurs noon–10:30pm. Métro: Lamarck-Caulincourt or Château Rouge.

Ten minutes downhill from the north facade of Sacré-Coeur, this *bistro à vins* has flourished since 1980 as an outlet for wines produced in the Loire Valley. Artists, street vendors, and office workers come here, linked only by an appreciation of wine (16F to 28F/$2.55 to $4.50 per glass) and the allure of the hearty *plats du jour* (60F to 70F/$9.60 to $11.20).

Juveniles. 47 rue de Richelieu, 1er. ☎ **01-42-97-46-49.** Bar Mon–Sat noon–1am; restaurant Mon–Sat noon–11pm. Métro: Palais Royal.

This is a British-owned spin-off of one of Paris's most successful wine bars, nearby Willi's. Louder, less formal, less restrained, and (at least to wine lovers) more daring than its older sibling, it prides itself on experimenting with a wide roster of wines from "everywhere." High-quality but lesser-known wines from Spain, France, California, and Australia decant for 17F to 47F ($2.70 to $7.50) per glass. Anything you like, including the "wine of the week," can be hauled away uncorked from the wine boutique here. There's also an assortment of tapas-inspired platters for 34F to 64F ($5.45 to $10.25).

La Tartine. 24 rue de Rivoli, 4e. ☎ **01-42-72-76-85.** Thurs–Mon 8:30am–10pm and Wed noon–10pm. Métro: St-Paul.

Mirrors, brass detail, and frosted-globe chandeliers make La Tartine look like a movie set of old Paris. At least 60 wines are offered at reasonable prices, including 7 kinds of Beaujolais and a large selection of Bordeaux by the glass. Glasses of wine are 9F to 16F ($1.45 to $2.55), and the charcuterie platter is 45F ($7.20). We recommend the light Sancerre wine and goat cheese from the Loire Valley.

Le Sancerre. 22 av. Rapp, 7e. ☎ **01-45-51-75-91.** Mon–Sat 8am–10pm. Métro: Alma-Marceau.

Produced in the Loire Valley in red, rosé, and especially white, Sancerre wine is known for its not-too-dry fruity aroma and legions of fans who believe it should be more celebrated than it is. That's all you'll find here, where the wine comes from several producers in the Sancerre district and is 26F ($4.15) per glass. Simple platters of food cost 43F to 74F ($6.90 to $11.85).

Les Bacchantes. 21 rue Caumartin, 9e. ☎ **01-42-65-25-35.** Mon–Sat noon–midnight. Métro: Opéra or Madeleine.

Les Bacchantes prides itself on offering more wines by the glass (at least 50) than any other wine bar in Paris and also does a hefty restaurant trade serving well-prepared *cuisine bourgeoise*. Amid massive exposed beams, belle-époque posters, and old-fashioned paneling, chalkboards announce a great list of vintages and platters. The wines, at 13F to 30F ($2.10 to $4.80) per glass, are mainly French. Platters of food cost 62F to 98F ($9.90 to $15.70).

✪ **Willi's Wine Bar.** 13 rue des Petits-Champs, 1er. ☎ **01-42-61-05-09.** Mon–Sat noon–11pm. Métro: Bourse, Pyramide, or Palais Royal.

Journalists and stockbrokers patronize this increasingly popular wine bar in the center of the financial district, run by Englishman Mark Williamson. About 250 kinds of wine are offered, including a dozen wine specials you can taste by the glass for 22F to 81F ($3.50 to $12.95). Lunch is the busiest time—on quiet evenings you can better enjoy the warm ambience and 16th-century beams. Daily specials are likely to include lamb brochette with cumin and Lyonnaise sausage in truffled vinaigrette, plus spectacular desserts like chocolate terrine.

BARS & PUBS

These "imported" places try to imitate American cocktail bars or masquerade as British pubs—most strike an alien chord. But that doesn't prevent fashionable Parisians from bar hopping (not to be confused with cafe sitting). In general, bars and pubs are open daily 11am to 1:30am.

Académie de la Bière. 88 bis bd. du Port-Royal, 5e. ☎ **01-43-54-66-65.** Daily 11–2:30am. Métro: Port Royal.

The decor is paneled and rustic, an appropriate foil for an "academy" whose curriculum includes more than 150 kinds of beer from microbreweries. Stella Artois, Belgium's best-selling beer, isn't available, though more than half of the dozen on tap are from small-scale breweries in Belgium that deserve to be better known. Snack-style food is available, including platters of mussels, assorted cheeses, and sausages with mustard.

What's in a Name?

Paris's bar scene is hopping, though bars here aren't as clearly defined as in other cities—they can be cafes, and cafes can be bars, restaurants can be bars, and bars can also be clubs. It can get confusing. The best way to think about it is not to let the name give you any preconceived notions of what the place might be like. (Café Marly, for example, is much more than just a cafe, and Buddha Bar is known more for its food than its cocktails. See chapter 5 for descriptions of these two places.)

The Bar at the Plaza Athénée. In the Hôtel Plaza Athénée, 25 av. Montaigne, 8e. ☎ **01-53-67-66-65.** Daily 5:30pm–1:30am. Métro: Alma-Marceau.

Residents of the surrounding neighborhood have always enjoyed dropping into this hotel for a drink in cosseted, well-upholstered comfort. The drinking venue has now moved from the Bar Anglais, on the lower level, to one of the street-level salons. A pianist and singer usually perform between 10:30pm and 1:30am.

Bar du Crillon. In the Hôtel du Crillon, 10 place de la Concorde, 8e. ☎ **01-44-71-15-00.** Daily 11–2am. Métro: Concorde.

Though some visitors consider the Bar du Crillon too stiff and elegant to ever allow anyone to have a good time, its social and literary history is remarkable. Hemingway set a climactic scene of *The Sun Also Rises* here, and over the years it has attracted practically every upper-level staff member of the nearby American embassy, as well as heiresses, stars, starlets, and wannabes. Under its new owner, the Concorde Group, the bar has been redecorated by designer Sonia Rykiel. Down the hall is the Edwardian **Jardin d'Hiver,** where, amid potted palms and upscale accessories, you can order tea, cocktails, or coffee; it's open daily noon to 9pm.

Bar Hemingway/Bar Vendôme. In the Hôtel Ritz, 15 place Vendôme, 1er. ☎ **01-43-16-30-30.** Bar Hemingway daily 6pm–2am; Bar Vendôme daily 10–2am. Métro: Opéra.

In 1944, during Paris's liberation, Ernest Hemingway and a group of Allied soldiers made history by "freeing" the Ritz from the Nazis and ordering a round of martinis at the bar (see "A Hotel Tale," in chapter 4). The Ritz commemorates this event in the **Bar Hemingway** with bookish memorabilia, rows of newspapers, and stiff drinks served in a woodsy English club setting. Look for its entrance, and homage to other writers, close to the hotel's rue Cambon entrance. If you get thirsty during the daytime, when the bar isn't open, head for the **Bar Vendôme,** near the main (place Vendôme) entrance; it's equally cozy, albeit a bit grander. Between 5:30 and 8:30pm, it's wise to reserve a table.

China Club. 50 rue de Charenton, 12e. ☎ **01-43-43-82-02.** Daily 7pm–2am. Métro: Bastille or Ledru Rollin.

Designed to recall France's 19th-century colonies in Asia or a bordello in 1930s Shanghai (on the ground floor) and England's empire-building zeal in India (upstairs), the China Club will allow you to chitchat or flirt with the singles who crowd into the street-level bar, then escape to calmer, more contemplative climes upstairs. You'll see regulars from the worlds of fashion and the arts, along with a pack of postshow celebrants from the nearby Opéra Bastille. A street-level Chinese restaurant serves dinner daily 7pm to 12:30am, and in the more animated (and occasionally raucous) cellar bar, live music is presented every Friday and Saturday 10pm to 3am.

Le Bar de L'Hôtel. In L'Hôtel, 13 rue des Beaux-Arts, 6e. ☎ **01-44-41-99-00.** Daily 7pm–1am. Métro: St-Germain-des-Prés.

This is the hyper-artsy and theatrically overdecorated bar of a hotel that has wooed film-industry types who want to avoid the more mainstream luxury of Paris's palatial hotels. The rose-filter cheeriness is deceptive: This is the hotel where Oscar Wilde died, disgraced and impoverished. The staff is conscientiously straitlaced, but you'd expect a musical comedy to break out at any moment.

Le Floridita. 19 rue de Presbourg, 16e. ☎ **01-45-00-60-63.** Cafe and cigar service Mon–Sat 10:30–2am; meals Mon–Sat noon–2pm and 8–11:15pm. Métro: Etoile.

The macho brown-and-green decor evokes a private men's club. You can drink Cuba libres, cognac, or coffee or eat platters of food. You can also puff away at any of the cigars stocked for the pleasure of the patrons (regulars sometimes store their cigars in a safe originally designed as a safety-deposit vault).

Le Forum. 4 bd. Malesherbes, 8e. ☎ **01-42-65-37-86.** Daily 2pm–midnight. Métro: Madeleine.

Its patrons, who include frequent business travelers, compare this place to a private club in London. Part of that comes from the carefully polished oak paneling and ornate stucco and part from its store of single-malt whiskeys. You can also try 150 cocktails, including many that haven't been popular since the jazz age. Champagne by the glass is common, as is that high-octane social lubricant, the martini.

Le Fumoir. 6 rue de l'Amiral-Coligny, 1er. ☎ **01-42-92-00-24.** Daily 11–2am. Métro: Louvre-Rivoli.

At Le Fumoir, the well-traveled crowd that lives or works in the district provides a kind of classy raucousness. The decor is a lot like that of an English library, with about 6,000 books providing an aesthetic backdrop to the schmoozing. A Danish chef prepares an international menu featuring meal-size salads (the one with scallops and lobster is great), roasted codfish with zucchini, and roasted beef in red-wine sauce. More popular are the stiff mixed drinks, the wines and beers, and the dozen or so types of cigars for sale.

Le Web Bar. 32 rue de Picardie, 3e. ☎ **01-42-72-66-55.** www.webbar.fr. Mon–Fri 8:30–2am, Sat–Sun 11–2am. Métro: République or Temple.

Occupying a three-story space at the eastern edge of the Marais, Le Web Bar echoes with the sound of people schmoozing with one another and with silent computer partners thousands of miles away. On the street level is a restaurant, on the second floor is a battery of at least 25 computers you can use for free, and on the top floor is an art gallery. To keep things perking, there's daily entertainment beginning around 7pm. Menu items stress comfort food like *boeuf bourguignonne.*

Man Ray. 34 rue Marbeuf, 8e. ☎ **01-56-88-36-36.** Brasserie Mon–Fri noon–2:30pm, daily 6pm–2am; bar Sun–Thurs 6pm–2am, Fri–Sat 7pm–2am. Metro: F. D. Roosevelt.

This chic rendezvous off the Champs-Elysées is dedicated to Man Ray, the famous photographer and American dadaist, who usually felt more comfortable roaming Montparnasse than the 8th. Many of Man Ray's photos decorate the club. The entry is discreet through large wrought-iron doors and virtually no sign. In the basement is a bustling brasserie presided over by two winged Oriental goddesses. The bar upstairs is big and bustling, and jazz is often presented there.

Pub St-Germain-des-Prés. 17 rue de l'Ancienne-Comédie, 6e. ☎ **01-43-29-38-70.** Daily 24 hours. Métro: Odéon.

With 9 rooms and 650 seats, this is France's largest pub, offering 450 brands of beer, 26 on draft. The deliberately tacky decor consists of leather booths, faded gilt-framed mirrors, hanging lamps, and a stuffed parrot in a gilded cage. The atmosphere is usually quiet, relaxed, and posh. Featured beers change frequently but usually include Amstel, various Belgian brews, Whitbread, and Pimm's No. 1. If frat houses turn you on, it gets really fun from 10:30pm to 4am.

4 Gay & Lesbian Bars & Clubs

Gay life is centered around **Les Halles** and **Le Marais,** with the greatest concentration of gay/lesbian clubs, restaurants, bars, and shops between the Hôtel de Ville and Rambuteau Métro stops. Gay dance clubs come and go so fast that even the magazines devoted to them—*e.m@ale* and *Illico,* both distributed free in the gay bars and bookstores—have a hard time keeping up. For lesbians, the guide *Exes Femmes* publishes a free seasonal listing of bars and clubs. Also look for Gai Pied's *Guide Gai* and *Pariscope's* regularly featured English-language section, "A Week of Gay Outings."

For all you need to know about Paris's gay and lesbian scene, buy *Frommer's Gay & Lesbian Europe.*

The neighboring **Open Café,** 17 rue des Archives, 4e (☎ 01-42-72-26-18; Métro: Hôtel de Ville or Rambuteau), and **Café Cox,** 15 rue des Archives, 4e (☎ 01-42-72-08-00), get so busy in the early evening the crowd stands on the sidewalk. These places are where you'll find the most mixed gay crowd in Paris—from hunky American tourists to sexy Parisian men. A new place in Les Halles is **Le Tropic Café,** 66 rue des Lombards, 1er (☎ 01-40-13-92-62; Métro: Châtelet–Les Halles), where the trendy good-looking crowd parties until dawn. On Sundays, gays head to **Blockhaus,** 25 bd. Poissonière, 2e (☎ 01-40-26-60-31; Métro: Bonne Nouvelle), a male-only dance club with a military decor and a hot back room. **Le Gibus,** 18 rue du faubourg du Temple, 11e (☎ 01-47-00-78-88; Métro: République), rocks on Fridays and Saturdays with guest DJs. Some of the most drop-dead gorgeous men in Paris show up here, often to be entertained by drag shows.

A restaurant with a bar fast becoming popular with women is **Okawa,** 40 rue Vieille-du-Temple, 4e (☎ 01-48-04-30-69; Métro: Hôtel de Ville), where trendy lesbians (and some gay boys) sip drinks at happy hour. **Les Scandaleuses,** 26 rue des Ecouffes, 3e (☎ 01-48-87-39-26; Métro: St-Paul), continues to be one of the city's most popular rendezvous spots for lesbians. Acquired by a beautiful young woman, **L'Entr'acte,** 25 bd. Poissonnière, 2e (☎ 01-40-26-01-93; Métro: Montmartre), attracts a crowd much like the owner. More butch, **L'Enfer,** 34 rue du Départ, 14e (☎ 01-42-79-94-94; Métro: Montparnasse), rocks with a crowd of trendy lesbians on Friday and Saturday; Thursday is more mixed, with gay men welcome.

Amnesia Café. 42 rue Vieille-du-Temple, 4e. ☎ **01-42-72-16-94.** Daily 10–2am. Métro: Hôtel de Ville.

The Amnesia's function and crowd may change during the day, but you'll always find a cadre of local gays. This cafe/tearoom/bistro/bar includes two beige bar and dining areas, a mezzanine, and a cellar bar open in the evening. The drinks of choice are beer, cocktails, and *café amnesia,* a specialty coffee with cognac and Chantilly cream. Deep armchairs, soft pillows, and 1930s accents create an ambience conducive to talk and laughter—it's not as sexually charged as nearby bars. *Plats du jour* include favorites like Basque chicken and *boeuf bourguignonne.*

Banana Café. 13 rue de la Ferronnerie, 1er. ☎ **01-42-33-35-31.** Daily 5pm–between 4 and 5am. Métro: Châtelet–Les Halles.

This popular bar is a usual stop for gays visiting or doing business in Paris. Occupying two floors of a 19th-century building, it has walls the color of an overripe banana, dim lighting, and a policy of raising the drink prices after 10pm, when things become really interesting. There's a street-level bar and a cellar dance floor that features a live pianist and recorded music—sometimes with dancing. On many nights, go-go dancers perform from spotlit platforms in the cellar.

La Champmeslé. 4 rue Chabanais, 2e. ☎ **01-42-96-85-20.** Mon–Wed 5pm–2am, Thurs–Sat 5pm–5am. Métro: Pyramides or Bourse.

La Champmeslé—with dim lighting, background music, and comfortable banquettes—is a great cozy meeting place for lesbians (and even for "well-behaved" gay men). It's housed in a 300-year-old building with exposed stone and ceiling beams and 1950s-style furnishings. On Thursdays, one of the premier lesbian events of Paris, a cabaret, begins at 10pm; every month there's a well-attended exhibit of paintings by mostly lesbian artists. The bar honors a celebrated 17th-century actress, La Champmeslé, who was instrumental in interpreting the fledgling dramatic efforts of celebrated playwright Racine.

Le Bar. 5 rue de la Ferronerie, 1er. ☎ **01-40-41-00-10.** Daily 5pm–between 4 and 5am. Métro: Châtelet.

Covering the street level and cellar of a sprawling building in an area long known for an availability of commercial sex, this is the largest gay bar in Paris. You'll find three bars on the premises, a mostly blue decor incorporating lots of sinuous lines, and an ambience that's more sexually charged and explicit in the cellar than on the street level. The average age is early 30s.

Le Central. 33 rue Vieille-du-Temple, 4e. ☎ **01-48-87-99-33.** Daily 3pm–between 4 and 5am. Métro: Hôtel de Ville.

Le Central is one of the oldest bars for men in the Hôtel de Ville area. It's tacky and a bit drab but still gets its share of visitors and regulars. A small hotel is upstairs (see "Gay-Friendly Hotels," in chapter 4). Both the bar and its hotel are in a 300-year-old building in the heart of the Marais.

✪ **Le Pulp.** 25 bd. Poissonnière, 2e. ☎ **01-40-26-01-93.** Cover 50F ($8). Fri–Sat 5pm–4am. Métro: Rue Montmartre.

This is one of the most popular lesbian discos, looking like a burgundy-colored 19th-century French music hall. It's best to show up before midnight. The venue, as the French like to say, is *trés cool,* with cutting-edge music played in a setting that just happens to discourage the presence of men.

✪ **Le Queen.** 102 av. des Champs-Elysées, 8e. ☎ **01-53-89-08-90.** Cover 50F ($8) Sun–Mon, 100F ($16) Fri–Sat, 30F ($4.80) Wed. Daily 11pm–between 4 and 5am. Métro: F. D. Roosevelt.

Should you miss gay life à la New York, follow the flashing purple sign on the "main street" of Paris, near the corner of avenue George V. The place is often mobbed, primarily with gay men and (to a lesser degree) models, actresses, and the like. Look for go-go boys, drag shows, muscle shows, and everything from 1970s-style disco nights (Monday) to Tuesday-night foam parties (only in summer), when cascades of mousse descend onto the dance floor. Go very, very late.

5 Literary Haunts

Closerie des Lilas. 171 bd. du Montparnasse, 6e. ☎ **01-40-51-34-50.** Daily 11–2am. Métro: Port Royal.

Hemingway, Picasso, Gershwin, and Modigliani all loved the Closerie, and ever since Parisians and foreigners, literary or not, have flocked here. Even though the lilacs that gave the place its name bloom only in spring, the management strews bouquets of them throughout the bar all year long. Don't expect a reverent hush—on some nights the place is as energetic as a New York singles bar. Look for the brass nameplate of your favorite Lost Generation artist along the banquettes or at the bar. See chapter 5 for a dining review.

✪ **Harry's New York Bar.** 5 rue Daunou, 2e. ☎ **01-42-61-71-14.** Daily 10:30–4am. Métro: Opéra or Pyramides.

The ads tell you to instruct your cab driver, "Sank roo doe Noo." Opened on Thanksgiving Day in 1911 by a bearded Hemingway precursor by the name of MacElhone, it's sacred to Papa disciples as the spot where members of the ambulance corps drank themselves silly during World War I. White lady and sidecar cocktails were invented here in 1919 and 1931, respectively, and it's the alleged birthplace of the bloody Mary and the headquarters of a fraternity of drinkers known as the International Bar Flies (IBF). Harry's New York Bar has stayed in the family: Duncan, MacElhone's bilingual grandson now owns and runs it. In the street-level bar, daytime crowds draw from the area's insurance, banking, and travel industries; evening crowds include pre- and post-theater groupies and night owls. In the cellar, a pianist plays daily 10pm to 2am.

Rosebud. 11 bis rue Delambre, 14e. ☎ **01-43-35-38-54.** Daily 7pm–2am. Métro: Vavin.

The popularity of this place known for a bemused and indulgent attitude toward anyone looking for a drink and some talk hasn't diminished since the 1950s, when it attained its fame. The name refers to the beloved sled of Orson Welles's great *Citizen Kane*. Around the corner from Montparnasse's famous cafes and thick in associations with Sartre and de Beauvoir, Ionesco, and Duras, Rosebud draws a crowd aged 35 to 65, though the staff has recently remarked on the appearance of students. Drop in at night for a glass of wine, a shot of whiskey, or a hamburger or chili con carne.

Side Trips from Paris 10

Paris, the city that began on an island, is itself the center of a curious landlocked island known as the **Ile de France.** Shaped roughly like a saucer, it's encircled by a thin ribbon of rivers: the **Epte, Aisne, Marne,** and **Yonne.** Fringing these rivers are mighty forests with famous names—**Rambouillet, St-Germain, Compiègne,** and **Fontainebleau.** These forests are said to be responsible for Paris's clear gentle air and the unusual length of its spring and fall. This may be debatable, but there's no argument they provide the capital with a fine series of day trips, all within easy reach.

The forests surrounding Paris once were the domain of royalty and the aristocracy, and they're still sprinkled with the magnificent châteaux of their former masters. Together with ancient villages, glorious cathedrals, and cozy country inns, they make the Ile de France irresistible. In this chapter, we offer only a handful of the possibilities for day jaunts. For a more extensive list, see *Frommer's France 2001.*

1 Versailles: Louis XIV's Pleasure Palace

13 miles SW of Paris, 44 miles NE of Chartres

For centuries, the name of the Parisian suburb of Versailles resounded through the consciousness of every aristocratic family in Europe. The palace here outdazzled every other kingly residence in Europe—it was a horrendously expensive scandal and a symbol to later generations of a regime obsessed with prestige above all else.

Back in the *grand siècle,* all you needed was a sword, a hat, and a bribe for the guard at the gate. Providing you didn't look as if you had smallpox, you'd be admitted to the **Château de Versailles,** where you could stroll through salon after glittering salon—watching the Sun King rise and dress and dine and do even more intimate things while you gossiped, danced, plotted, flirted, and trysted.

Today, Versailles needs the return of Louis XIV and his fat treasury. You wouldn't believe it when looking at the glittering Hall of Mirrors, but Versailles is down-at-the-heels. It suffers from a lack of funds, which translates into a shortage of security forces; this budget crunch was made even worse on Christmas Day in 1999, when a horrendous windstorm wreaked havoc here (see below). You get to see only half its treasures; the rest are closed to the public. Some 3.2 million visitors arrive annually, and on average they spend 2 hours.

The Ile de France

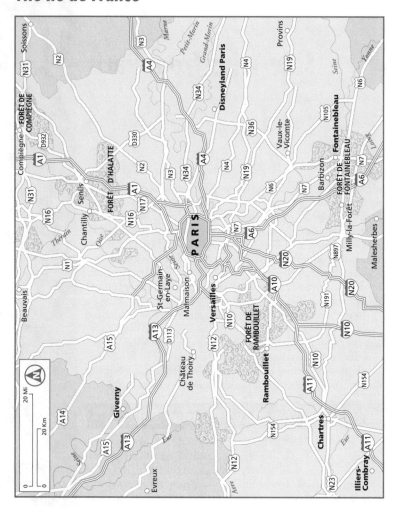

ESSENTIALS

GETTING THERE   To get to Versailles, 13 miles southwest of Paris, catch the **RER** line C at the Gare d'Austerlitz, St-Michel, Musée d'Orsay, Invalides, Ponte de l'Alma, Champ de Mars, or Javel stop and take it to the Versailles Rive Gauche station, from which there's a shuttle bus to the château. The 35F ($5.60) trip takes 35 to 40 minutes; Eurailpass holders travel free on the train but pay 20F ($3.20) for a ride on the shuttle bus. Regular **SNCF trains** make the run from central Paris to Versailles: One train departs from Gare St-Lazare for the Versailles Rive Droite RER station, a 15-minute walk from the château. If you can't or don't want to walk, you can take bus B from Versailles Chantiers to the château for 8F ($1.30) each way.

As a last resort, you can use a combination of **Métro** and **city bus.** Travel to the Pont de Sèvres stop by Métro, then transfer to bus 171 for a westward trek that'll take 20 to 45 minutes, depending on traffic. The bus will cost you three Métro tickets and deposit you near the château gates. If you have a **car,** take N-10, following the signs to Versailles, and then proceed along avenue de Général-Leclerc. Park on place d'Armes in front of the château.

VISITOR INFORMATION Three main avenues radiate from place d'Armes in front of the palace. The **tourist office** is at 7 rue des Réservoirs (☎ **01-39-24-88-88**).

TOURING THE CHÂTEAU & GARDENS

✪ **Château de Versailles.** Place d'Armes. ☎ **01-30-83-78-00.** www.chateauversailles.com. Admission to château 45F ($7.20) adults, 35F ($5.60) ages 18–25, under age 18/over 60 free; Grand Trianon 25F ($4) adults, 15F ($2.40) ages 18–25, under age 18 free; Petit Trianon 15F ($2.40) adults, 10F ($1.60) ages 18–25, under age 18 free; both Trianons 30F ($4.80) adults, 20F ($3.20) ages 18–25, under age 18 free. Reduced rates for adults after 3:30pm. Château, May 2–Sept 30 Tues–Sun 9am–6:30pm (to 5pm the rest of the year); Trianons, same hours as château, but open at 10am; grounds, daily 7am–dusk (between 5:30 and 9:30pm).

THE CHÂTEAU Within 50 years, this residence was transformed from Louis XIII's simple hunting lodge into an extravagant palace. Begun in 1661, the construction of the château involved 32,000 to 45,000 workmen, some of whom had to drain marshes—often at the cost of their lives—and move forests. Louis XIV set out to build a palace that would be the envy of all Europe, and he created a symbol of pomp and opulence that was to be copied, yet never quite duplicated, all over Europe and even in America.

So he could keep an eye on the nobles of France (and with good reason), Louis XIV summoned them to live at his court. Here he amused them with constant entertainment and lavish banquets and balls, and amused himself with a roster of mistresses, the most important of which was Mme de Maintenon (he secretly married her after his queen, Marie-Thérèse of Spain, died). To some he awarded such vital tasks as holding the hem of his ermine-lined robe. While the aristocrats frivolously played away their lives, often in silly intrigues and games, the peasants on the estates, angered by their absentee landlords, sowed the seeds of the Revolution.

When Louis XIV died in 1715, he was succeeded by his great-grandson, Louis XV, who continued the outrageous pomp, though he's said to have predicted the outcome: *"Après mois le déluge"* (After me, the deluge). His wife, Marie Leszcynska of Poland,

A Weekend in London

Of course, Paris offers a seemingly endless list of wonderful things to see and do, but now that transit between the French capital and the British capital is easier than ever, why not take a weekend jaunt to London?

The **Eurostar** train roars through the **Channel Tunnel** (**Chunnel**), reducing the travel time between Paris's Gare du Nord and London's Waterloo Station to a mere 3 hours. One-way fares, with some restrictions, begin at $109 second class and $179 first, with discounts for Eurail or Britrail pass holders, youths under 18, and students. You can get ultra-upscale service, enhanced cuisine, and limousine service to/from Waterloo Station and your hotel for a maximum of $299 each way, tax included. The Eurostar folks can even set up a **rail/hotel package** at a highly discounted rate. For as little as $317 per person, you can buy a package with rail transport, 2 nights (double occupancy) in a hotel, and a city sightseeing tour. From North America, call the **Eurostar** division of RailEurope at ☎ **800/EUROSTAR.** For details about hotel packages, contact **EuroVacations** at ☎ **888/281-EURO.** If you're already in Paris, contact any travel agency or talk to your concierge.

was shocked by the court's blatant immorality. When her husband tired of her, she lived as a nun, and the king's attention turned to Mme de Pompadour, who was accused of running up a debt far beyond that of a full-scale war. Mme de Pompadour handpicked her successor, Mme du Barry, who was just about as foolhardy with the nation's treasury.

Louis XVI found his grandfather's and father's behavior scandalous—in fact, on gaining the throne in 1774 he ordered the "stairway of indiscretion" (secret stairs leading up to the king's bedchamber) be removed. This dull, weak king (who was virtuous and did have good intentions) and his Austrian-born queen, Marie Antoinette, were well liked at first, but the queen's excessive frivolity and wild spending soon led to her downfall. Louis and Marie Antoinette were at Versailles on October 6, 1789, when they were notified that mobs were marching on the palace. As predicted, *le déluge* had arrived.

Napoléon stayed at Versailles but never seemed fond of it. Louis-Philippe prevented the destruction of the palace by converting it into a museum dedicated to the glory of France. To do that, he had to surrender some of his own not-so-hard-earned currency. Many years later, John D. Rockefeller contributed heavily toward the restoration of Versailles and work continues to this day.

The six magnificent **Grands Appartements** are in the Louis XIV style, each named after the allegorical painting on the room's ceiling. The best known and largest is the **Hercules Salon,** with a ceiling painted by François Lemoine, depicting the Apotheosis of Hercules. In the **Mercury Salon** (with a ceiling by Jean-Baptiste Champaigne), the body of Louis XIV was put on display in 1715; his 72-year reign was one of the longest in history.

The most famous room at Versailles is the 236-foot-long **Hall of Mirrors,** built to link the north and south apartments. Begun in 1678 by Mansart in the Louis XIV style, it was decorated by Le Brun and his team with 17 large arched windows matched by corresponding beveled mirrors in simulated arcades, plus amazing chandeliers and gilded lamp bearers. The vaulted ceiling is covered with paintings in classic allegorical style depicting the story of Louis XIV. On June 28, 1919, the treaty ending World War I was signed in this corridor. Ironically, the German Empire was also proclaimed here in 1871.

The royal apartments were for show, but Louis XV and Louis XVI retired to the **Petits Appartements** to escape the demands of court etiquette. Louis XV died in his bedchamber in 1774, a victim of smallpox. In the second-floor **King's Apartments,** which you can visit only with a guide, he stashed away first Mme de Pompadour and then Mme du Barry. Attempts have been made to return the **Queen's Apartments** to their appearance in the days of Marie Antoinette, when she played her harpsichord in front of specially invited guests.

Impressions

When Louis XIV had finished the Grand Trianon, he told [Mme de] Maintenon he had created a paradise for her, and asked if she could think of anything now to wish for. . . . She said she could think of but one thing—it was summer, and it was balmy France—yet she would like well to sleigh ride in the leafy avenues of Versailles! The next morning found miles and miles of grassy avenues spread thick with snowy salt and sugar, and a procession of those quaint sleighs waiting to receive the chief concubine of the gaiest and most unprincipled court that France has ever seen!

—Mark Twain, *The Innocents Abroad* (1869)

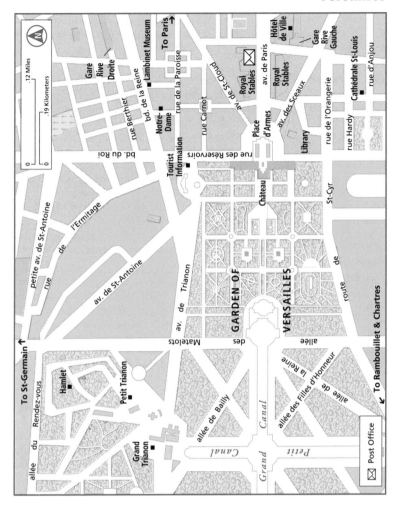

Her king, Louis XVI, had an impressive **Library,** designed by Gabriel, which was sumptuous. Its panels are delicately carved, and the room has been restored and refurnished. The **Clock Room** contains Passement's astronomical clock, encased in gilded bronze. Twenty years in the making, it was completed in 1753 and is supposed to keep time until the year 9999. At the age of 7, Mozart played for the court in this room.

Gabriel designed the **Opéra** for Louis XV in 1748, though it wasn't completed until 1770. In its heyday, it took 3,000 candles to light the place. With gold-and-white harmony, Hardouin-Mansart built the **Royal Chapel** in 1699, dying before its completion. Louis XVI, when still the dauphin (crown prince), married Marie Antoinette here in 1770. At this arranged marriage, both the bride and the groom were teenagers.

THE MUSÉE DE FRANCE   After having been closed for years, the **Musée de France** (☎ **01-39-67-07-73**) has now reopened and is accessible via Porte D (Door D) in the château. The museum traces the history of the parliamentary process in France following the collapse of the monarchy in 1789, with exhibits describing the processes whereby laws and the democratic process are made and enforced. Admission is 20F ($3.20) adults and half-price for children under 18, and rental of a pre-recorded audio guide (English or French) is 25F ($4). It's open Tuesday to Saturday 9am to 5:30pm,

THE GARDENS   Spread across 250 acres, the **Gardens of Versailles** were laid out by the great landscape artist Le Nôtre, who created a Garden of Eden using ornamental lakes and canals, geometrically designed flower beds, and avenues bordered with statuary. At the peak of their glory, 1,400 fountains spewed forth. *The Buffet* is an exceptional one, having been designed by Mansart. One fountain depicts Apollo in his chariot pulled by four horses, surrounded by tritons emerging from the water to light the world. On the mile-long Grand Canal, Louis XV—imagining he was in Venice—used to take gondola rides with his favorite of the moment. On Christmas Day 1999, the most violent windstorm in France's history thundered through Paris, causing extensive damage to parks and gardens in the Ile de France. At Versailles, the wind toppled ten thousand trees and blew out some windows at the magnificent château. The palace has now reopened, but the difficult task of replanting the thousands of trees will take some time, and it'll be years before they return to their lush grandeur.

THE TRIANONS & THE HAMLET   A long walk across the park will take you to the **Grand Trianon,** in pink-and-white marble. Le Vau built a Porcelain Trianon here in 1670, covered with blue and white china tiles, but it was fragile and soon fell into ruin. So in 1687 Louis XIV commissioned Hardouin-Mansart to build the Grand Trianon. Traditionally, it has been a place where France has lodged important guests, though de Gaulle wanted to turn it into a weekend retreat. Nixon once slept here in the room where Mme de Pompadour died. Mme de Maintenon also slept here, as did Napoléon. The original furnishings are gone, of course, with mostly Empire pieces there today.

Gabriel, the designer of place de la Concorde in Paris, built the **Petit Trianon** in 1768 for Louis XV. Louis used it for his trysts with Mme du Barry. When he died, Louis XVI presented it to his wife, and Marie Antoinette adopted it as her favorite residence, a place to escape the rigid life at the main palace. Many of the current furnishings, including a few in her rather modest bedchamber, belonged to the ill-fated queen.

Rousseau's theories about recapturing the natural beauty of life were much in favor in the late 18th century, and they prompted Marie Antoinette to have Mique build her a 12-house **Hamlet** on the banks of the Grand Trianon Lake in 1783. She wanted a chance to experience the simplicity of peasant life—or at least peasant life as seen through the eyes of a frivolous queen. Dressed as a shepherdess, she would come here to watch sheep being tended and cows being milked, men fishing and washerwomen beating their laundry in the lake, and donkey carts bringing corn to be ground at the mill.

SUMMER EVENING SPECTACLES   The **Fêtes de Nuit de Versailles (Rêve de Roi)** is a government-sponsored summer program of evening fireworks and illuminated fountains. These always capture the heightened sense of the glory of France's *ancien régime.* At various dates throughout summer, 200 actors in period costume portray Louis XVI and members of his court. April to June and October shows begin at 10:30pm; 9:30pm in August and September. You sit on bleachers clustered at the château's boulevard de la Reine entrance, adjacent to the Fountain (Bassin) of Neptune. The most desirable seats are 250F ($40), with standing room at 70F ($11.20).

Food Fit for a King

From 1682 to 1789, Versailles housed a royal entourage whose population, except for 8 years during the minority of Louis XV, remained constant at 3,000. To feed them, the sprawling kitchens employed a permanent staff of 2,000. Without benefit of running water or electricity, they labored over banquets that became day-to-day rituals at the most glorious court since the collapse of ancient Rome.

The fruits and vegetables that appeared on the royal tables were produced on-site, in **Les Potagers du Roi** (the King's Kitchen Garden). Surprisingly, the gardens have survived and are a 10-minute walk south of the château's main entrance, at 6 rue du Hardy, behind an industrial-looking gate. Twenty-three acres of fertile earth are arranged into parterres and terraces as formal as the legendary showcases devoted to flowers, fountains, and statuary during the royal tenure.

Meals at Versailles were quite a ritual. The king almost always dined in state, alone at a table visible to hundreds of observers and (in some cases) other diners, who sat in order of rank. Fortunately for gastronomic historians, there are many detailed accounts about what Louis XIV enjoyed and how much he consumed: He was addicted to salads and ate prodigious amounts of basil, purslane, mint, and wood sorrel. He loved melons, figs, pears, and peaches. The real culinary rage at the court, however, was for peas, imported from Genoa for the first time in 1660.

Today, Les Potagers du Roi are maintained by about half a dozen gardeners under the direction of the Ecole Nationale du Paysage. It manages to intersperse the fruits and vegetables once favored by the monarchs with experimental breeds and hundreds of splendidly espaliered fruit trees. You can visit the gardens April to November, Saturday and Sunday 10am to 5pm. Admission is 40F ($6.40) adults and 20F ($3.20) persons under 18. Look for the entrance at 6 rue Hardy (☎ **01-39-24-62-00**), about a quarter-mile south of the château. Free guided tours of the garden, in French, last an hour and depart every hour on the hour. A kiosk sells the fruits and vegetables grown in the gardens.

Gates that admit you into the bleacher area open 90 minutes before show time, and the show itself lasts 90 minutes.

You can buy tickets in advance at the **tourist office** in Versailles—inquire by phone, fax, or mail—or in central Paris at any of the **FNAC** stores (see chapter 8). You can also take your chances and buy tickets an hour prior to the event from a kiosk adjacent to the boulevard de la Reine entrance. Call ☎ **01-30-83-78-88** for general info about any of the nighttime or afternoon spectacles on the grounds.

AFTERNOON PROMENADES IN THE PARK   Every Sunday early April to mid-October and every Saturday early July to late August, between 11am and noon and between 3:30 and 5:30pm, classical music is broadcast throughout the park and every fountain is turned on. The effect of these **Grandes Eaux Musicales** is to duplicate the landscaping vision of the 18th-century architects who designed Versailles. They even allow you to walk freely around the park, enjoying the juxtapositions of grand architecture and lavish waterworks. The cost of admission to the park during these events is 25F ($4) per person.

WHERE TO DINE

Le Potager du Roy. 1 rue du Maréchal-Joffre. ☎ **01-39-50-35-34.** Reservations required. Fixed-price menu 135F ($21.60) at lunch, 179F ($28.65) at dinner. AE, V. Tues–Fri noon–2:30pm and 7–10:30pm, Sat 7–10:30pm. FRENCH.

Philippe Letourneur cooks from the heart, specializing in a simple cuisine with robust flavors. His attractive restaurant occupies an 18th-century building in a neighborhood known during the days of the French monarchs as the Parc des Cerfs ("Stag Park," where courtiers could find paid companionship with B- and C-list courtesans). The skillfully prepared menu is reinvented with the seasons and may include foie gras with vegetable-flavored vinaigrette; roasted duck with a navarin of vegetables; macaroni ragout with a persillade of snails; and roasted codfish with roasted peppers in the style of Provence. For something unusual, order the fondant of pork jowls with a confit of fresh vegetables. Try to save room for the chocolate cake, flavored with orange and served with coconut ice cream.

Le Quai No. 1. 1 av. de St-Cloud. ☎ **01-39-50-42-26.** Reservations required. Main courses 85F ($13.60); fixed-price menu 110F ($17.60) at lunch, 140–185F ($22.40–$29.60) at dinner. MC, V. Tues–Sat noon–2:30pm and 7:30–11pm, Sun noon–2:30pm. FRENCH/SEAFOOD.

This informal bistro occupies an 18th-century building overlooking the château's western facade. Lithographs and wood paneling spangle the dining room, and outside is a terrace. Though the cuisine isn't as opulent or expensive as what's served in chef Gérard Vié's grander Les Trois Marches (below), it's charming and dependable in presentation. The fixed-price menus make Le Quai a bargain. Specialties are seafood sauerkraut, seafood paella, bouillabaisse, home-smoked salmon, and an upscale version of North American surf and turf, with grilled lobster and sizzling sirloin. Care and imagination go into the food, and the service is professional and polite.

۞ Les Trois Marches. In the Hôtel Trianon Palace, 1 bd. de la Reine. ☎ **01-30-84-38-40.** Reservations required far in advance. Fixed-price menu 350F ($56) at lunch Mon–Fri, 625–825F ($100–$132) at lunch Sat–Sun and at dinner. AE, DC, MC, V. Daily noon–2pm and 7:30–10pm. Closed Aug. FRENCH.

The Hôtel Trianon Palace became famous in 1919 when it served as headquarters for signatories to the Treaty of Versailles, and the dining room retains an old-world splendor. Gérard Vié is the most talented and creative chef in town, attracting a discerning crowd that doesn't mind paying the high prices. His *cuisine moderne* is subtle, often daring, and the service is smooth. Begin with the lobster salad with fresh herbs, served with onion soufflé; the galette of potatoes with bacon, chardonnay, and sevruga caviar; or the citrus-flavored scallop bisque. Stars among the main courses are the pigeon roasted and flavored with rosé and accompanied by celeriac and truffles and the celeriac fashioned into ravioli, filled with foie gras, and topped by a thick slice of black truffle. If you arrive in late autumn, you might find penne-like pasta, tossed with morels, mushrooms, and Parmesan and blended in a butter sauce with white Alba truffles. For dessert, opt for the signature assortment.

2 The Forest & Château of Rambouillet

34 miles SW of Paris, 26 miles NE of Chartres

Once known as La Forêt d'Yveline, the **Forest of Rambouillet** is one of the loveliest woods in France. More than 47,000 acres of greenery stretch from the valley of the Eure to the high valley of Chevreuse, the latter rich in medieval and royal abbeys. Lakes, copses of hiding deer, and even wild boar are some of the attractions of this "green lung." Most people, however, come here to see the château, which you can visit when it's not in use as a "Camp David" for French presidents.

ESSENTIALS

GETTING THERE   It takes 2 hours to see the château at Rambouillet. **Trains** depart from Paris's Gare Montparnasse every 30 minutes throughout the day. One-way passage costs 41F ($6.55) for about a 35-minute ride. Information and train schedules can be obtained by contacting **La Gare de Rambouillet,** place Prud'homme (☎ **01-53-90-20-20**). By **car,** take N-10 southwest from Paris, passing Versailles along the way.

VISITOR INFORMATION   The **tourist office** is at the Hôtel de Ville, place de la Libération (☎ **01-34-83-21-21**).

SEEING THE CHÂTEAU

Château de Rambouillet. Parc du Château. ☎ **01-34-83-00-25.** Admission 32F ($5.10) adults, 21F ($3.35) students 12–25; children 11 and under free. Wed–Mon 10–11:30am and 2–4:30pm (to 3:30pm Oct–Mar).

Dating from 1375, the château is surrounded by a park in one of the most famous forests in France. Superb woodwork is used throughout, and the walls are adorned with tapestries, many from the era of Louis XV. Before it became a royal residence, the marquise de Rambouillet kept a house here; it's said she taught Paris's cultured ladies and gentlemen how to talk, introducing them to a long string of poets and painters. François I, the Chevalier king, died of a fever here in 1547 at age 52. When the château was later occupied by the comte de Toulouse, Rambouillet was often visited by Louis XV, who was amused (in more ways than one) by the comte's high-spirited wife. Louis XVI eventually acquired the château, but Marie Antoinette found it boring and called it "the toad." In his surprisingly modest boudoir are four panels representing the continents.

In 1814, Napoléon's second wife, Marie-Louise (daughter of Francis II, emperor of Austria), met at Rambouillet with her father, who convinced her to abandon Napoléon and France itself after her husband's humiliating defeats at Moscow and Leipzig. Afterward, she fled to her original home, the royal court in Vienna, with Napoléon's 3-year-old son, François-Charles-Joseph Bonaparte (also known as l'Aiglon, the young eagle, and, at least in title, the king of Rome). Before his death in Vienna at age 21, his claim on the Napoleonic legacy was rejected by France's enemies, despite the fact that his father had had a special annex to the château at Rambouillet built especially for his use. A year later, before his final exile to the remote island of St. Helena, Napoléon insisted on spending a final night at Rambouillet, where he secluded himself with his meditations and memories.

In 1830, the elderly Charles X, Louis XVI's brother, abdicated the throne at Rambouillet as a Parisian mob marched on the château and his troops began to desert him. From Rambouillet, he embarked for a safe but controversial haven in England. Afterward, Rambouillet fell into private hands. At one time it was a fashionable restaurant attracting Parisians by offering gondola rides. Napoléon III, however, returned it to the Crown. In 1897, it was designated a residence for the presidents of the Republic. And in 1944, Charles de Gaulle lived here briefly before giving the order for what was left of the French army to join the Americans in liberating Paris.

WHERE TO DINE

La Poste. 101 av. du Général-de-Gaulle. ☎ **01-34-83-03-01.** Reservations recommended Sat–Sun. Main courses 119–156F ($19.05–$24.95); fixed-price menu 119–190F ($19.05–$30.40). AE, MC, V. Tues–Sun noon–2pm; Tues–Wed and Fri–Sat 7–10pm. FRENCH.

On a street corner in the town's historic center, this restaurant has been open since the mid-19th century, when it provided meals and shelter for the region's mail carriers. The two dining rooms have rustic beams and old-fashioned accents that complement the flavorful old-fashioned food. Good-tasting menu items include homemade terrines of foie gras and freshly made pastries. A particularly flavorful dish is beef filet served with a Perigueux sauce of Madeira wine and foie gras.

3 The Cathedral at Chartres

60 miles SW of Paris, 47 miles NW of Orléans

Many observers feel the architectural aspirations of the Middle Ages reached their highest expression in the glorious **Cathédrale de Chartres.** Come to see its soaring architecture, highly wrought sculpture, and, above all, its stained glass, which gave the world a new color, Chartres blue.

ESSENTIALS

GETTING THERE It takes a full day to see Chartres. From Paris's Gare Montparnasse, **trains** run directly to Chartres, taking less than an hour and passing through a sea of wheat fields. **By car,** take A10/A11 southwest from the *périphérique* and follow the signs to Le Mans and Chartres (the Chartres exit is clearly marked).

VISITOR INFORMATION The **tourist office** is on place de la Cathédrale (☎ 02-37-18-26-26).

SEEING THE CATHEDRAL

✪ **Cathédrale Notre-Dame de Chartres.** 16 Cloître Notre-Dame. ☎ **02-37-21-56-33.** Admission free. Mon–Sat 7:30am–7pm, Sun 8:30am–7pm.

Reportedly, Rodin once sat for hours on the edge of the sidewalk, admiring this cathedral's Romanesque sculpture. His opinion: Chartres is the French Acropolis. When it began to rain, a kind soul offered him an umbrella, which he declined, so transfixed was he by the magic of this place.

The cathedral's origins are uncertain; some have suggested it grew up over an ancient Druid site that had later become a Roman temple. It is known that as early as the 4th century there was a Christian basilica here. An 1194 fire destroyed most of what had then become a Romanesque cathedral but spared the western facade and crypt. The cathedral you see today dates principally from the 13th century, when it was rebuilt with the efforts and contributions of kings, princes, churchmen, and pilgrims from all over Europe. One of the world's greatest high Gothic cathedrals, it was the first to use flying buttresses to support the soaring dimensions within.

French sculpture in the 12th century broke into full bloom when the **Royal Portal** was added. A landmark in Romanesque art, the sculptured bodies are elongated, often stylized, in their long flowing robes. But the faces are amazingly (for the time) lifelike, occasionally winking or smiling. In the central tympanum, Christ is shown at the Second Coming, with his descent depicted on the right, his ascent on the left. Before entering, walk around to both the **North Portal** and the **South Portal,** each from the 13th century. They depict such biblical scenes as the expulsion of Adam and Eve from the Garden of Eden.

Inside is a celebrated **choir screen;** work on it began in the 16th century and lasted until 1714. The niches, 40 in all, contain statues illustrating scenes from the life of the Madonna and Christ—everything from the *Massacre of the Innocents* to the *Coronation of the Virgin.*

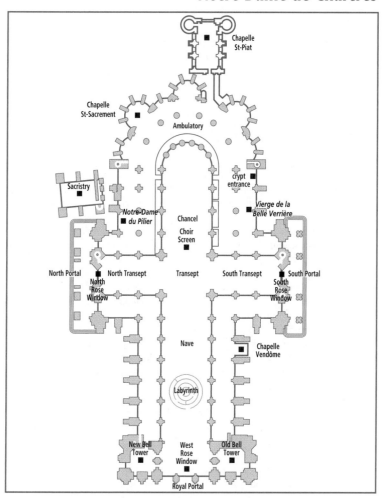

But few rushed visitors ever notice the screen: They're too transfixed by the light from the **stained glass.** Covering an expanse of more than 3,000 square yards, the glass is truly mystical, unlike anything else in the world. The stained glass, most of which dates from the 12th and 13th centuries, was spared in both world wars by painstakingly removing it piece by piece. See the windows in the morning, at noon, in the afternoon, at sunset—as often as you can. Like the petals of a kaleidoscope, they constantly change. It's difficult to single out one panel or window above the others, but an exceptional one is the 12th-century *Vierge de la belle verrière* (**Our Lady of the Beautiful Window**) on the south side. Of course, there are three fiery rose windows, but you couldn't miss those if you tried.

The **nave,** the widest in France, still contains its ancient floor labyrinth, which formed a mobile channel of contemplation for monks. The wooden *Notre-Dame du piller* (**Virgin of the Pillar**), to the left of the choir, dates from the 14th century. The

To Taste a Madeleine

And suddenly the memory returns. The taste was that of the little crumb of madeleine, which on Sunday mornings at Combray (because on those mornings I did not go out before church-time), when I went to say good day to her in her bedroom, my aunt Léonie used to give me, dipping it first in her own cup of real or of lime-flower tea.
                                                    —Marcel Proust, *Remembrance of Things Past*

Illiers-Combray, a small town 54 miles southwest of Paris and 15 miles southwest of Chartres, was once known simply as Illiers. Then Proust groupies started to come and signs were posted: ILLIERS, LE COMBRAY DE MARCEL PROUST. Illiers was and is a real town, but Marcel Proust in his masterpiece, *A la recherche du temps perdu (Remembrance of Things Past),* made it so famous as Combray that life acknowledged fiction, and the town officially changed its name to Illiers-Combray.

It was the taste of a luscious little madeleine that launched Proust on his immortal recollection. To this day, hundreds of his readers from all over the world flock to the pastry shops in Illiers-Combray to eat a madeleine or two dipped in lime-flower tea. Following the Proustian labyrinth, you can explore the gardens, streets, and houses he frequented until he was 13 and wrote about so richly later on. The town is centered around the **Eglise St-Jacques,** where Proust as a boy placed hawthorn on the altar.

Some members of Proust's family have lived in Illiers for centuries. His grandfather, François, was born here on rue du Cheval-Blanc. At **11 place du Marché,** just opposite the church, he ran a small candle shop. His daughter, Elisabeth, married Jules Amiot, who ran a shop a few doors away. Down from Paris, young Marcel would visit his aunt at 4 rue du St-Esprit, which has been renamed **rue du Docteur-Proust** in honor of Marcel's grandfather.

The **Musée Marcel Proust/Maison de Tante Léonie,** rue du Docteur-Proust (☎ 02-37-24-30-97), contains the world's most concentrated dose of memorabilia associated with the novelist, including objects that famously helped spark his creative vision. In his novels, this was Aunt Léonie's home, filled with antimacassars and antiques, all the day's typical bourgeois comforts. Upstairs you can see the bedrooms where the young Marcel and his aunt slept. Today, they contain souvenirs of key episodes in his novels. There's also a meticulously crafted re-creation of the Salon Rouge, which Proust maintained in his second-to-last residence, a site at 102 bd. Haussmann in Paris, filled with furniture owned by his parents and grandparents. Late January to early December, French-language guided tours are given at 2:30 and 4pm every Tuesday to Sunday for 30F ($4.80) adults and 20F ($3.20) students (children under 12 free).

In the center of town, a sign will guide you to further Proustian sights, each of which is open 24 hours without charge. They include the **Eglise St-Hilaire** and the **Pré-Catalan,** the garden maintained by Proust's Uncle Amiot.

crypt was built over 2 centuries, beginning in the 9th. Enshrined within is *Our Lady of the Crypt,* a 1976 Madonna that replaced one destroyed during the Revolution.

Try to take a tour conducted by **Malcolm Miller** (☎ 02-37-28-15-58; fax 02-37-28-33-03), an Englishman who has spent 3 decades studying the cathedral and giving tours in English with a rare blend of scholarship, enthusiasm, and humor. He

Music of the Spheres

If you're visiting Chartres on a Sunday afternoon, the cathedral features a free 1-hour organ concert beginning at 4:45pm, when the filtered light of the Ile de France sunset makes the western windows come thrillingly alive.

usually conducts 75-minute tours at noon and 2:45pm Monday to Saturday for 40F ($6.40). Tours are canceled in the event of pilgrimages, religious celebrations, and large funerals. French-language tours at 35F ($5.60) are conducted by other guides Easter to late October at 10:30am and 3pm and the rest of the year at 2:30pm.

If you feel fit enough, don't miss the opportunity, especially in summer, to climb to the top of the **New Bell Tower.** Open the same hours as the cathedral, except for a closing between noon and 2pm, it costs 25F ($4) adults and 15F ($2.40) students. The **crypt,** gloomy and somber but rich with a sense of medieval history, can be visited only as part of a French-speaking tour conducted whenever there's enough demand. The cost is 11F ($1.75).

After your visit, stroll through the **Episcopal Gardens** and enjoy yet another view of this remarkable cathedral.

EXPLORING THE OLD TOWN

If time remains, you may want to explore the medieval cobbled streets of the **Vieux Quartier** (Old Town). At the foot of the cathedral are lanes containing gabled houses and humped bridges spanning the Eure River. From the pont de Bouju, you can see the lofty spires in the background. Try to find **rue Chantault,** which boasts houses with colorful facades, one 8 centuries old.

A highlight of your visit will be **Musée des Beaux-Arts de Chartres,** 29 Cloître Notre-Dame (☎ **02-37-36-41-39**), next door to the cathedral. A former episcopal palace, the building at times competes with its exhibitions—one part dates from the 15th century and encompasses a courtyard. This museum of fine arts boasts a permanent painting collection covering the 16th to the 20th century, including the work of masters like Zurbarán, Watteau, and Brosamer. Of particular interest is David Ténier's *Le Concert.* Special exhibits are often mounted. October 31 to May 2, it's open Wednesday to Monday 10am to noon and 2 to 5pm; the rest of the year, hours are Wednesday to Monday 10am to noon and 2 to 6pm. Admission is 15F ($2.40) adults and 7.50F ($1.20) children.

WHERE TO STAY

Hôtel Châtelet. 6–8 av. Jehan-de-Beauce, 28000 Chartres. ☎ **02-37-21-78-00.** Fax 02-37-36-23-01. 48 units. TV TEL. 370–510F ($59.20–$81.60) double. 3rd person 60F ($9.60) extra. AE, DC, MC, V.

This relatively modern hotel has many traditional touches. The rustic guest rooms are inviting, with reproductions of Louis XV and Louis XVI furniture. The larger, more expensive rooms face a garden and avoid street noise. Many windows along the front (street) side of the hotel open onto a view of the cathedral. The baths are boxy, without a lot of shelf space. In chilly weather, there's a log-burning fire in one of the salons. Breakfast is the only meal served, but there are numerous restaurants close by.

Le Grand Monarque Best Western. 22 place des Epars, 28005 Chartres. ☎ **800/ 528-1234** in the U.S., or 02-37-21-00-72. Fax 02-37-36-34-18. www.bw-grand-monarque.com. E-mail: info@bw-grand-monarque.com. 54 units. MINIBAR TV TEL. 615–740F ($98.40–$118.40) double; 1,120–1,350F ($179.20–$216) suite. AE, DC, MC, V. Parking 50F ($8).

Chartres's leading hotel occupies a mid-19th-century building enclosing a courtyard. It attracts people who enjoy its old-world charm, with its art nouveau stained glass and Louis XV chairs in the dining room. The guest rooms are decorated with reproductions of antiques, and most have sitting areas. The baths are motel standard. The hotel also has an anachronistic restaurant (a local critic found the kitchen trapped in an "ancien régime time warp").

WHERE TO DINE

Le Buisson Ardent. 10 rue au Lait. ☎ **02-37-34-04-66.** Reservations recommended. Main courses 88–135F ($14.10–$21.60); fixed-price menu 138–250F ($22.10–$40). MC, V. Thurs–Tues noon–2pm and 7:30–9:30pm. FRENCH.

Housed in a charming 300-year-old house in the most historic section of town, this restaurant is one floor above street level in the shadow of the cathedral. The composition of the set-price menus changes with the seasons. Everything is made with fresh meats, produce, and fish. The most popular dishes are escalope of warm foie gras with apples and Calvados and émincée of roasted pigeon with sweetbreads and honey sauce. Other dishes are simpler, the kind you might've noticed in bistros, like codfish flavored with coriander and served with parsley flan. A dessert specialty is crispy hot pineapples with orange and passion fruit salad.

4 Giverny: In the Footsteps of Claude Monet

50 miles NW of Paris

On the border between Normandy and the Ile de France, **Giverny** is home to the Claude Monet Foundation, in the house where the impressionist painter lived for 43 years. The restored house and its gardens are open to the public.

ESSENTIALS

GETTING THERE   It takes a full morning to get to Giverny and to see its sights. Take the Paris-Rouen **train** from Paris's Gare St-Lazare to the Vernon station, where a taxi can take you the 3 miles to Giverny. Perhaps the easiest way to enjoy Giverny is on a full-day **bus tour** whose focal point is Monet's house and garden. In summer you can arrange this through **Cityrama,** 2 rue des Pyramides, 1er (☎ **01-44-55-61-00;** Métro: Palais Royal), or year-round by contacting **American Express,** 11 rue Scribe, 9e (☎ **01-42-27-58-80;** Métro: Opéra).

By **car,** take the Autoroute de l'Ouest (Port de St-Cloud) toward Rouen. Leave the autoroute at Bonnières, then cross the Seine on the pont de Bonnières. From here, a direct road with signs will bring you to Giverny. Expect about an hour of driving; try to avoid weekends. Another way to get to Giverny is to leave the highway at the Bonnières exit and go toward Vernon. Once in Vernon, cross the bridge over the Seine and follow the signs to Giverny or Gasny (Giverny is before Gasny). This is easier than going through Bonnières, where there aren't many signs.

SEEING MONET'S HOUSE & GARDEN

✪ **Claude Monet Foundation.** Rue Claude-Monet Parc Gasny. ☎ **02-32-51-28-21.** Advance reservations required. Admission 35F ($5.60) adults, 20F ($3.20) children ages 7–18; under 7 free. Apr–Oct Tues–Sun 10am–6pm.

French painter Claude Monet was a spiritualist of light, brilliantly translating its effects at different times of the day. In fact, some critics claim he "invented light." His series of paintings of the Rouen Cathedral and of the water lilies, which one critic called "vertical interpretations of horizontal lines," are just a few of his masterpieces.

Monet came to Giverny in 1883, at age 43. While taking a small railway linking Vetheuil to Vernon, he discovered the village at a point where the Epte stream joined the Seine. Many of his friends used to visit him here at Le Pressoir, including Clemenceau, Cézanne, Rodin, Renoir, Degas, and Sisley. When Monet died in 1926, his son, Michel, inherited the house but left it abandoned until it decayed into ruins. The gardens became almost a jungle, inhabited by river rats. In 1966, Michel died and left the house to the Académie des Beaux-Arts. It wasn't until 1977 that Gerald van der Kemp, who restored Versailles, decided to work on Giverny. A large part of it was restored with gifts from American benefactors, especially the late Lila Acheson Wallace, former head of *Reader's Digest*.

You can stroll through the garden and view the thousands of flowers, including the famous *nymphéas* (water lilies). The Japanese bridge, hung with wisteria, leads to a dreamy setting of weeping willows and rhododendrons. Monet's studio barge was installed on the pond.

WHERE TO DINE

Auberge du Vieux Moulin. 21 rue de la Falaise. ☎ **02-32-51-46-15.** Main courses 72–95F ($11.50–$15.20); fixed-price menu 128–148F ($20.50–$23.70). MC, V. Tues–Sun noon–3pm and 7:30–10pm. Closed Jan. FRENCH.

This stone-sided restaurant is a convenient lunch stop where the Boudeau family maintains a series of cozy dining rooms filled with original impressionist paintings. Since you can walk here from the museum in about 5 minutes, leave your car in the museum lot. Specialties include appetizers like snails in puff pastry with garlic-flavored butter sauce, guinea fowl braised in cider, chicken with shrimp, and escalope of salmon with sorrel sauce. Dessert might be a *tarte Normande* prepared with apple slices and Calvados. The kitchen doesn't pretend the food is any more than it is: hearty country fare with panache. The charm of the staff helps a lot, too.

5 Disneyland Paris: Come Meet Monsieur Mickey

20 miles E of Paris

After provoking some of the most controversial reactions in recent French history, the multimillion-dollar **Euro Disney Resort** opened in 1992 as one of the world's most lavish theme parks, situated on a 5,000-acre site (about one-fifth the size of Paris) in the suburb of Marne-la-Vallée. In 1994, it unofficially changed its name to Disneyland Paris. The early days of this megascale project weren't particularly happy: European journalists delighted in belittling it and accusing it of everything from cultural imperialism to the death knell of French culture. But after financial jitters and goodly amounts of public relations and financial juggling, the resort is on track.

In fact, it's now the number-one attraction in France, with 50 million annual visitors. MONSIEUR MICKEY TRIUMPHS! the French press headlined. Disney surpasses the Eiffel Tower and the Louvre in numbers of visitors and accounts for 4% of the tourism industry's foreign currency sales. Disneyland Paris looks, tastes, and feels like its parents in California and Florida—except for the European flair (the use of pastel colors rather than primary colors) and the $10 cheeseburgers *"avec pommes frites."* Allow a full day to see the park.

ESSENTIALS

GETTING THERE   The resort is linked to the **RER** commuter express rail network (Line A), which maintains a stop within walking distance of the park. Board the RER at such Paris stops as Charles de Gaulle–Etoile, Châtelet–Les Halles, or Nation. Get

Disneyland Paris

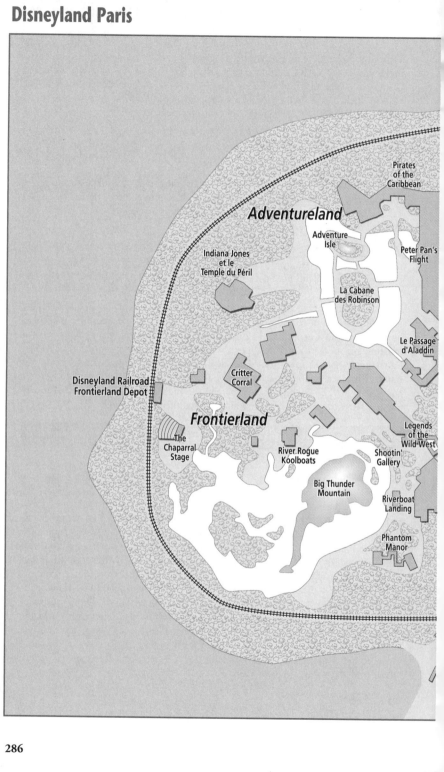

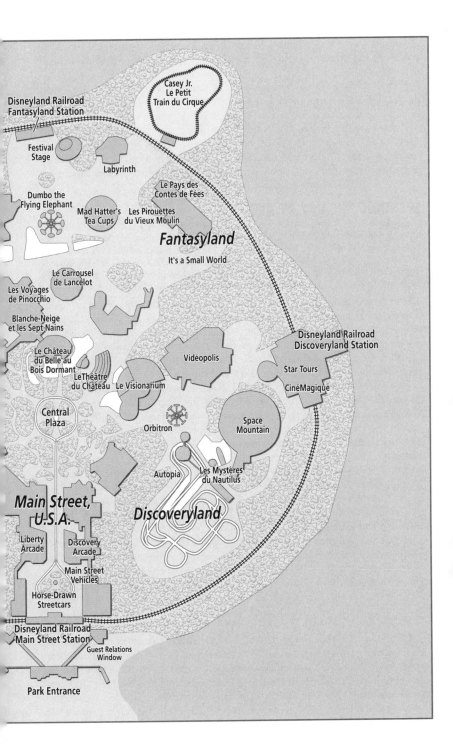

Disneyland Railroad
Fantasyland Station

Casey Jr.
Le Petit
Train du Cirque

Festival
Stage

Labyrinth

Le Pays des
Contes de Fées

Dumbo the
Flying Elephant

Mad Hatter's
Tea Cups

Les Pirouettes
du Vieux Moulin

Fantasyland

It's a Small World

Le Carrousel
de Lancèlot

Les Voyages
de Pinocchio

Blanche-Neige
et les Sept Nains

Disneyland Railroad
Discoveryland Station

Le Château
du Belle au
Bois Dormant

Vidéopolis

Star Tours

CinéMagique

LeThéâtre
du Château

Le Visionarium

Central
Plaza

Orbitron

Space
Mountain

Autopia

Les Mystères
du Nautilus

Main Street,
U.S.A.

Discoveryland

Liberty
Arcade

Discovery
Arcade

Main Street
Vehicles

Horse-Drawn
Streetcars

Disneyland Railroad
Main Street Station

Guest Relations
Window

Park Entrance

287

off at Line A's last stop, Marne-la-Vallée/Chessy, 45 minutes from central Paris. The round-trip fare from central Paris is 80F ($12.80). Trains run every 10 to 20 minutes, depending on the time of day.

Each of the hotels in the resort connects by **shuttle bus** to both Orly and Charles de Gaulle. Buses depart from both airports at intervals of 45 minutes. One-way transportation to the park from either airport costs 85F ($13.60).

If you're coming by **car,** take A-4 east from Paris, getting off at exit 14, marked PARC EURO DISNEYLAND. Guest parking at any of the thousands of parking spaces is 40F ($6.40) per day. An interconnected series of moving sidewalks speeds up pedestrian transit from the parking areas to the theme park's entrance. Parking for guests at any of the resort's hotels is free.

SPENDING THE DAY AT DISNEY

Disneyland Paris. Marne-la-Vallée. ☎ **01-60-30-60-53** (Disneyland Paris Guest Relations office, in City Hall on Main Street, U.S.A.). www.disneylandparis.com. Admission to park for 1 day, depending on season, 165–220F ($26.40–$35.20) adults, 135–170F ($21.60–$27.20) children 3–12; for 2 days 320–420F ($51.20–$67.20) adults, 260–330F ($41.60–$52.80) children 3–12. Children 2 and under always admitted free. July–Aug daily 9am–11pm; Sept–June Mon–Fri 10am–6pm, Sat–Sun 9am–8pm. Hours vary with the weather and the season.

The resort was designed as a total vacation package: Included within one enormous unit are the Disneyland Park with its five entertainment "lands," six large hotels, a campground, an entertainment center (Village Disney), a 27-hole golf course, and dozens of restaurants, shows, and shops. Peak season is mid-June to mid-September, as well as Christmas and Easter weeks. Entrance to Village Disney is free, though there's usually a cover charge for the dance clubs.

One of the attractions, **Main Street, U.S.A.,** features horse-drawn carriages and street-corner barbershop quartets. From the "Main Street Station," steam-powered railway cars leave for a trip through a Grand Canyon Diorama to **Frontierland,** with paddle-wheel steamers reminiscent of the Mississippi Valley described by Mark Twain. The park's steam trains chug past **Adventureland**—with swashbuckling 18th-century pirates, the tree house of the Swiss Family Robinson, and reenacted legends from the Arabian Nights—to **Fantasyland.** Here you can see the symbol of the theme park, the Sleeping Beauty Castle (*Le Château de la belle au bois dormant*), whose soaring pinnacles and turrets are a spectacular idealized interpretation of the châteaux of France.

Visions of the future are displayed at **Discoveryland,** whose tributes to human invention and imagination are drawn from the works of Leonardo da Vinci, Jules Verne, H. G. Wells, the modern masters of science fiction, and the *Star Wars* series. Discoveryland has proven among the most popular of all the areas and is one of the few that was enlarged (in 1995) after the park's inauguration. As Disney continues to churn out animated blockbusters, look for its newest stars to appear in the theme park. The fact that the characters from such films as *Aladdin, The Lion King,* and *Pocahontas* are actually made of celluloid hasn't kept them out of the Ice Capades, and it certainly won't keep them out of Disneyland Paris.

Disney also maintains an entertainment center, **Village Disney,** whose indoor/outdoor layout is a cross between a California mall and the Coney Island boardwalk. Scattered on either side of a pedestrian walkway, illuminated by overhead spotlights, it's just outside the boundaries of the fenced-in acreage containing the bulk of Disneyland's attractions. The complex accommodates dance clubs, snack bars, restaurants, souvenir shops, and bars for adults who want to escape from the children for a while. Unlike the rest of the park, admission to **Village Disney** is free, so it attracts night owls from Paris and its suburbs who wouldn't otherwise be particularly interested in the park itself.

Guided 3¹/₂-hour tours for 20 or more people can be arranged for 50F ($8) adults and 35F ($5.60) children 3 to 11. In view of the well-marked paths leading through the park and the availability of ample printed information in any language, the guided tours aren't really necessary. You can rent coin-operated lockers for 10F ($1.60) and can store larger bags for 15F ($2.40) per day. Children's strollers and wheelchairs rent for 30F ($4.80) per day, with a 20F ($3.20) deposit. Baby-sitting is available at any of the hotels if 24-hour advance notice is given.

WHERE TO STAY

The resort's six theme hotels share a reservation service. In North America, call ☎ 407/W-DISNEY. In France, contact the **Central Reservations Office,** Euro Disney Resort, S.C.A., B.P. 105, F-77777 Marne-la-Vallée Cedex 4 (☎ 01-60-30-60-30).

Disneyland Hotel. Disneyland Paris, B.P. 105, F-77777 Marne-la-Vallée Cedex 4. ☎ **01-60-45-65-00.** Fax 01-60-45-65-33. www.disneylandparis.com. 496 units. A/C MINIBAR TV TEL. 2,260–3,320F ($361.60–$531.20) double; from 4,950F ($792) suite. Rates include 2-day pass and breakfast. AE, DC, DISC, MC, V.

At the park entrance, this flagship hotel is Victorian, with red-tile turrets and jutting balconies. The spacious guest rooms are plushly furnished but evoke the image of Disney, with cartoon depictions and a candy-stripe decor. The beds are king, double, or twin; in some rooms armchairs convert to day beds. Paneled closets, large mirrors, and safes are found in some units. The luxurious baths have hair dryers, marble vanities, and twin basins. On the Castle Club floor, you get free newspapers, all-day beverages, and access to a well-equipped private lounge.

Dining/Diversions: There are three restaurants (The California Grill is recommended under "Where to Dine") and two bars.

Amenities: Concierge, 24-hour room service, laundry, baby-sitting, health club with indoor/outdoor pool, whirlpool, sauna, private dining and banqueting rooms.

Hotel Cheyenne/Hotel Santa Fe. Disneyland Paris, B.P. 115, F-77777 Marne-la-Vallée Cedex 4. ☎ **01-60-45-62-00** (Cheyenne) or 01-60-45-78-00 (Santa Fe). Fax 01-60-45-62-33 (Cheyenne) or 01-60-45-78-33 (Santa Fe). 2,000 units. TV TEL. Hotel Cheyenne 1,200–1,850F ($192–$296) double; Hotel Santa Fe 1,100–1,760F ($176–$281.60) double. Rates include 2-day pass and breakfast. AE, DC, DISC, MC, V.

Next door to each other near a re-creation of Texas's Rio Grande and evoking the Old West, these are the resort's least expensive hotels. The Cheyenne accommodates visitors in 14 two-story buildings along Desperado Street; the Santa Fe, sporting a desert theme, encompasses four "nature trails" winding among 42 adobe-style pueblos. The only disadvantage, according to some parents with children, is the absence of a pool. Tex-Mex specialties are offered at La Cantina (Santa Fe), and barbecue and smokehouse specialties predominate at the Chuck Wagon Cafe (Cheyenne).

Hotel New York. Disneyland Paris, B.P. 100, F-77777 Marne-la-Vallée Cedex 4. ☎ **01-60-45-73-00.** Fax 01-60-45-73-33. www.disneylandparis.com. 563 units. A/C MINIBAR TV TEL. 1,650–2,420F ($264–$387.20) double; from 3,350F ($536) suite. Rates include 2-day pass and breakfast. AE, DC, DISC, MC, V.

Inspired by the Big Apple, this hotel was designed around a nine-story central "skyscraper" flanked by the Gramercy Park Wing and the Brownstones Wing. (The exteriors of both wings resemble row houses.) The guest rooms are comfortable, with art deco accessories, New York–inspired memorabilia, safes, and roomzy baths with hair dryers and twin basins. Some rooms are set aside for nonsmokers and others are wheelchair accessible.

Dining/Diversions: The hotel has a diner, a restaurant, a cocktail and wine bar, and an art deco bar.

Amenities: Concierge, 24-hour room service, laundry, baby-sitting, indoor/outdoor pool, two outdoor tennis courts, health club.

Newport Bay Club. Disneyland Paris, B.P. 105, F-77777 Marne-la-Vallée Cedex 4. ☎ **01-60-45-55-00.** Fax 01-60-45-55-33. www.disneylandparis.com. 1,098 units. A/C MINIBAR TV TEL. 1,520–2,160F ($243.20–$345.60) double; from 2,970F ($475.20) suite. Rates include 2-day pass and breakfast. AE, DC, DISC, MC, V.

This hotel was designed with a central cupola, jutting balconies, and a blue-and-cream color scheme, reminiscent of a harbor-front New England hotel circa 1900. The layout is irregular, with nautically decorated guest rooms in various shapes and sizes, all with safes. The most spacious rooms are the corner units. Some rooms are reserved for nonsmokers, and others are equipped for those with disabilities. The baths are roomy, with deluxe toiletries. The upscale Yacht Club and the less formal Cape Cod are the dining choices. Facilities include a lakeside promenade, a glassed-in pool pavilion, an outdoor pool, and a health club.

Sequoia Lodge. Disneyland Paris, B.P. 114, F-77777 Marne-la-Vallée Cedex 4. ☎ **01-60-45-51-00.** Fax 01-60-45-51-33. www.disneylandparis.com. 1,011 units. A/C MINIBAR TV TEL. 1,410–2,060F ($225.60–$329.60) double; from 2,630F ($420.80) suite. Rates include 2-day pass and breakfast. AE, DC, DISC, MC, V.

Built of gray stone and roughly textured planking and capped by a gently sloping green copper roof, this hotel resembles a lodge in a remote section of the Rockies. It consists of a large central building with five chalets nearby, each housing 100 rooms. The guest rooms are comfortably rustic, with tiled baths (hair dryers are available on request). The Hunter's Grill serves spit-roasted meats carved on your plate. Less formal is the Beaver Creek Tavern. Facilities include an indoor pool and a health club.

WHERE TO DINE

Within the resort are at least 45 restaurants and snack bars, each trying hard to please millions of European and North American palates. Here are a few recommendations:

Auberge de Cendrillon. In Fantasyland. ☎ **01-64-74-24-02.** Reservations recommended. Main courses 105–140F ($16.80–$22.40); fixed-price menu 175F ($28). AE, DC, DISC, MC, V. Daily 11:30am–90 min. before park closing. FRENCH.

This is a fairy-tale version of Cinderella's sumptuous country inn, with a glass couch in the center. A master of ceremonies, in a plumed tricorne hat, wearing an embroidered tunic and lace ruffles, welcomes you. For an appetizer, try the warm goat-cheese salad with lardons or the smoked-salmon platter. If you don't choose one of the fixed-price meals, you can order from the limited but excellent à la carte menu. Perhaps you'll try the poultry in puff pastry, loin of lamb roasted with mustard, or sautéed veal medallions. Since the restaurant follows the park's seasonal schedules, lunches are usually easier to arrange than dinners.

California Grill. In the Disneyland Hotel. ☎ **01-60-45-65-00.** Reservations required. Main courses 55–205F ($8.80–$32.80); children's menu 85F ($13.60). AE, DC, MC, V. Sun–Fri 7–11pm, Sat 6–11pm. CALIFORNIAN/FRENCH.

Focusing on the lighter specialties for which the Golden State is famous, with many concessions to French palates, this elegant restaurant manages to accommodate both adults and children gracefully. It features specialties like oysters with leeks and salmon, foie gras with roasted red peppers, roasted pigeon with braised Chinese cabbage and black-rice vinegar, and salmon roasted over beechwood, served with walnut oil, sage sauce, asparagus, and a fricassée of mushrooms. Many items, like "Mickie's pizzas," spaghetti Bolognese, and grilled ham with fries, are specifically for children. If you're looking for a quiet, mostly adult venue, go here as late as your hunger pangs will allow.

6 Fontainebleau: House of the Centuries

37 miles S of Paris, 46 miles NE of Orléans

Within the vestiges of a forest that bears its name (the Forêt de Fontainebleau), this suburb of Paris has offered refuge to French monarchs throughout the country's history. Kings from the Renaissance valued it because of its nearness to rich hunting grounds and its distance from the slums and smells of the city. Napoléon referred to the **Palais de Fontainebleau,** which he reembellished with his distinctive monogram and decorative style, as "the house of the centuries." Many pivotal and decisive events have occurred inside, perhaps none more memorable than when Napoléon stood on the horseshoe-shaped exterior stairway and bade farewell to his shattered army before departing for Elba.

ESSENTIALS

GETTING THERE   If you stay for lunch, a trip to Fontainebleau should last a half day. **Trains** depart from Paris's Gare de Lyon. The trip takes between 45 and 60 minutes each way and costs 94F ($15.05) round-trip. Fontainebleau's rail station is 3 miles from the château, in the suburb of Avon. A local bus (it's marked simply *château*) makes the trip to the château at 15-minute intervals every Monday to Saturday, and at 30-minute intervals every Sunday, for 10F ($1.60) each way. By **car,** take A-6 south from Paris, exit onto N-191, and follow the signs.

VISITOR INFORMATION   The main squares are place du Général-de-Gaulle and place d'Armes. The **tourist office** is at 4 rue Royale (☎ **01-60-74-99-99**).

SEEING THE PALACE

✪ **Palais de Fontainebleau.** In the Forêt de Fontainebleau. ☎ **01-60-71-50-70.** Combination ticket for *grands appartements* 35F ($5.60) adults, 23F ($3.70) students 18–25; under age 18 free. Ticket to *petits appartements* and Napoleonic Rooms 16F ($2.55) adults, 12F ($1.90) students 18–25; under age 18 free. Sept–June Wed–Mon 9:30am–12:30pm and 2–5pm; July–Aug Wed–Mon 9:30am–6pm.

Napoléon's affection for this palace was understandable. He was following the pattern of a succession of French kings in the pre-Versailles days who used Fontainebleau as a resort and hunted in its magnificent forests. François I, who tried to turn the hunting lodge into a royal palace in the Italian Renaissance style, brought along several artists, including Benvenuto Cellini, to work for him. Under this patronage, the School of Fontainebleau gained prestige, led by painters Rosso Fiorentino and Primaticcio. The artists adorned the 210-foot-long **Gallery of François I,** where stucco-framed panels depict such scenes as *The Rape of Europa* and the monarch holding a pomegranate, a symbol of unity. The salamander, the symbol of the Chevalier king, is everywhere.

Sometimes called the Gallery of Henri II, the **Ballroom** displays the interlaced initials "H&D," referring to Henri and his mistress, Diane de Poitiers. Competing with this illicit tandem are the initials "H&C," symbolizing Henri and his ho-hum wife, Catherine de Médicis. At one end of the room is a monumental fireplace supported by two bronze satyrs, made in 1966 (the originals were melted down during the Revolution). At the other side is the balcony of the musicians, with sculptured garlands. The ceiling displays octagonal coffering adorned with rosettes. Above the wainscoting is a series of frescoes, painted between 1550 and 1558, which depict mythological

Fontainebleau

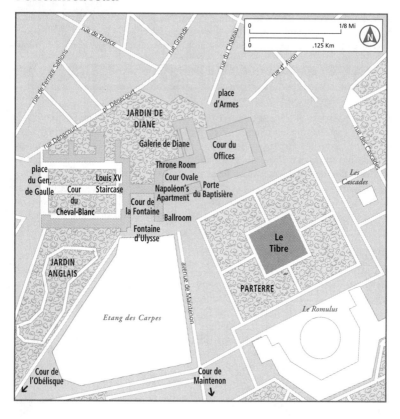

subjects like *The Feast of Bacchus*. An architectural curiosity is the richly adorned **Louis XV Staircase.** The room above it was originally decorated by Primaticcio for the bedroom of the duchesse d'Etampes, but when an architect was designing the stairway, he simply ripped out her floor. Of the Italian frescoes that were preserved, one depicts the queen of the Amazons climbing into Alexander the Great's bed.

When Louis XIV ascended to the throne, he neglected Fontainebleau because of his preoccupation with Versailles. However, he wasn't opposed to using the palace for houseguests, specifically such unwanted ones as Queen Christina, who had abdicated the throne of Sweden in a fit of religious fervor. Under the assumption that she still had "divine right," she ordered the brutal murder of her companion Monaldeschi, who had ceased to please her. Though Louis XV and then Marie Antoinette took an interest in Fontainebleau, the château found its renewed glory under Napoléon. You can wander around much of the palace on your own, visiting sites evoking the Corsican's 19th-century imperial heyday. They include the **throne room** where he abdicated his rulership of France, his **offices,** his monumental **bedroom,** and his **bathroom.** Some of the smaller Napoleonic Rooms contain his personal mementos and artifacts.

After your long trek through the palace, visit the **gardens** and, especially, the **carp pond;** the gardens, however, are only a prelude to the Forest of Fontainebleau.

WHERE TO STAY

Hôtel de l'Aigle-Noir (The Black Eagle). 27 place Napoléon-Bonaparte, 77300 Fontainebleau. ☎ **01-60-74-60-00.** Fax 01-60-74-60-01. 56 units. A/C MINIBAR TV TEL. 1,210–1,380F ($193.60–$220.80) double; from 2,400F ($384) suite. AE, DC, MC, V. Parking 55F ($8.80).

Once the home of Cardinal de Retz, this mansion opposite the château was built with a formal courtyard entrance, using a high iron grille and pillars crowned by black eagles. It was converted into a hotel in 1720 and has recently been remodeled, making it the finest lodgings in town. The guest rooms are decorated with Louis XVI, Empire, or Restoration antiques or reproductions with plush mattresses and elegant bathroom amenities. Have a drink in the Napoléon III–style piano bar before dinner. Later, you can dine on an elegant French cuisine with formalized service in the grand dining room of the hotel, Le Beauharnais. Facilities include an indoor pool, a gymnasium, a sauna, and an underground garage.

WHERE TO DINE

Le Caveau des Ducs. 24 rue de Ferrare. ☎ **01-64-22-05-05.** Reservations recommended. Main courses 85–130F ($13.60–$20.80); fixed-price menu 125–250F ($20–$40). AE, MC, V. Daily noon–2pm and 7–10pm. FRENCH.

Beneath a series of 17th-century stone vaults, this restaurant occupies what was once a storage cellar for the château. Wood and flickering candles preserve the illusion. In terms of grandeur, it's not in the same league as Le Beauharnais, the dining room of the Hôtel de l'Aigle Noir, but it offers simpler food in dramatic antique setting. Each dish could stand in a museum of 1950s French food: snails in garlic butter, roast leg of lamb with garlic-and-rosemary sauce, and virtually everything that can be done with a duck. The rump steak filet is quite tasty, served in Brie sauce, as is the platter of sole, crayfish tails, and salmon served on a bed of pasta.

Le François-Ier. 3 rue Royale. ☎ **01-64-22-24-68.** Reservations required. Main courses 75–125F ($12–$20); fixed-price menus 160–250F ($25.60–$40). AE, DC, MC, V. Mon–Sat noon–2:30pm and 7:30–10pm, Sun noon–2:30pm. FRENCH.

The premier dining choice has a Louis XIII decor, winemaking memorabilia, and walls the owners think are about 200 years old. If weather permits, sit on the terrace overlooking the château and the Cour des Adieux. In game season, the menu includes hare, roebuck, duck liver, and partridge. Other choices may be cold salmon with *cèpes* (flap mushrooms), *rognon de veau* (veal kidneys) with mustard sauce, and a salad of baby scallops with crayfish. The cuisine is meticulous, with an undeniable flair. The *magrêt de canard* (duck) flavored with cassis is delicious.

Appendix A:
Paris in Depth

1 History 101

Dateline

- **2000 B.C.** Ancient Lutétia (Paris) thrives along a strategic crossing of the Seine, the fortified headquarters of the Parisii tribe.
- **52 B.C.** Julius Caesar conquers Lutétia during the Gallic Wars.
- **A.D. 150** Lutétia flourishes as a Roman colony, expanding to the Left Bank.
- **200** Barbarian Gauls force the Romans to retreat to the fortifications on Ile de la Cité.
- **300** Lutétita is officially renamed Paris; Roman power weakens in northern France.
- **350** Paris's Christianization begins.
- **400s** The Franks invade Paris, with social transformation from the Roman to the Gallo-Roman culture.
- **466** Clovis, founder of the Merovingian dynasty and first non-Roman ruler of Paris since the Parisii, is born.
- **800** Charlemagne, founder of the Carolingian dynasty and first Holy Roman Emperor, is coronated and rules from Aachen in modern Germany.
- **987** Hugh Capet, founder of France's foremost early

continues

IN THE BEGINNING

Paris emerged at the crossroads of three major traffic arteries on the muddy island in the Seine that today is known as Ile de la Cité.

By around 2000 B.C., the island served as the fortified headquarters of the Parisii tribe, who called it Lutétia. The two crude wooden bridges connecting the island to the river's left and right banks were among the region's most strategically important, and the settlement attracted the attention of the Roman Empire. In his *Commentaries,* Julius Caesar described his conquest of Lutétia, recounting how its bridges were burned during the Gallic War of 52 B.C. and how the town on the island was pillaged, sacked, and transformed into a Roman-controlled stronghold.

Within a century, Lutétia became a full-fledged Roman town, and some of the inhabitants abandoned the frequently flooded island in favor of higher ground on what is today the Left Bank. By A.D. 200, barbarian invasions increasingly threatened the stability of Roman Gaul, and the populace from the surrounding hills flocked to the island's fortified safety. Over the next 50 years, a Christian community gained a tenuous foothold there. According to legend, St. Denis served as the city's first bishop (beginning around 250). Though by this time the Roman Empire's political power had begun to wane in the region, the cultural and religious attachment of the community to the Christian bishops of Rome grew even stronger.

During the 400s, with the great decline of the Roman armies, Germanic tribes from the east (the Salian Franks) were able to invade the island successfully, founding a Frankish dynasty and prompting a Frankish-Latin cultural fusion in the burgeoning town. The first of these Frankish kings, Clovis (466–511), founder of the Merovingian dynasty, embraced Christianity as his tribe's official religion and spearheaded an explicit rejection of Roman cultural imperialism by encouraging the adoption of Parisii place names like "Paris," which came into common usage during this time.

The Merovingians were replaced by the Carolingians, whose heyday began with Charlemagne's coronation in 800. The Carolingian Empire sprawled over western Germany and eastern France, but Paris was never its capital. The city remained a commercial and religious center, sacred to the memory of St. Geneviève, who reputedly protected Paris when it was attacked again and again by the Huns in the final days of the Roman Empire. The Carolingians came to an end in 987, when the empire fragmented because of the growing regional, political, and linguistic divisions between what would become modern France and modern Germany. Paris became the seat of a new dynasty, the Capetians, whose kings ruled France throughout the Middle Ages. Hugh Capet (c. 938–996), the first of this line, ruled as comte de Paris and duc de France from 987 to 996.

THE MIDDLE AGES

Around 1100, Paris began to emerge as a great city, boasting on its Left Bank a university that attracted scholars from all over Europe. Meanwhile, kings and bishops began building the towering Gothic cathedrals of France, one of the greatest of which became Paris's Notre-Dame, a monument rising from the beating heart of the city. Paris's population increased greatly, as did the city's mercantile activity. During the 1200s, a frenzy of building transformed the skyline with convents and churches (including the jewel-like Sainte-Chapelle, completed in 1249 after just 2 years). During the next century, the increasingly powerful French kings added dozens of monuments of their own.

As time passed, Paris's fortunes became closely linked to the power struggles between the French

medieval dynasty, rises to power; he and his heirs rule from Paris.

- **1100** The Université de Paris attracts scholars from throughout Europe.

- **1200s** Paris's population and power grow, though the city is frequently unsettled by plagues and feudal battles.

- **1422** England invades Paris during the Hundred Years' War.

- **1429** Joan of Arc tries unsuccessfully to regain Paris for the French; the Burgundians later capture and sell her to the English, who burn her at the stake in Rouen.

- **1500s** François I, first of the French Renaissance kings, embellishes Paris but chooses to maintain his court in the Loire Valley.

- **1549** Henri II rules France from Paris; the construction of public and private residences begins, many in the Marais.

- **1564** Construction begins on Catherine de Médicis's Palais des Tuileries; building facades in Paris move from half-timbered to more durable chiseled stonework.

- **1572** The Wars of Religion reach their climax with the massacre of Protestants on St. Bartholomew's Day.

- **1598** Henri IV, the most eccentric and enlightened monarch of his era, endorses the Edict of Nantes, granting tolerance to Protestants; because of this, a crazed monk fatally stabs him 12 years later.

- **1615** Construction begins on the Palais du Luxembourg for Henri IV's widow, Marie de Médicis.

- **1636** The Palais Royal is launched by Cardinal Richelieu; soon thereafter, two marshy islands in the Seine are interconnected and filled in to create Ile St-Louis.

continues

- **1643** Louis XIV, the "Sun King" and the most powerful ruler since the Caesars, rises to power; he moves his court to the newly built Versailles.
- **1776** The American Declaration of Independence strikes a revolutionary chord in France.
- **1789** The French Revolution breaks out.
- **1793** Louis XVI and his Austrian-born queen, Marie Antoinette, are publicly guillotined.
- **1799** Napoléon Bonaparte crowns himself Master of France and embellishes Paris further with neoclassical splendor.
- **1803** Napoléon abandons French overseas expansion and sells Louisiana to America.
- **1812** Napoléon is defeated in the Russian winter campaign.
- **1814** Aided by a military coalition of France's enemies, especially England, the Bourbon monarchy under Louis XVIII is restored.
- **1821** Napoléon Bonaparte dies.
- **1824** Louis XVIII dies and Charles X accedes.
- **1830** Charles X is deposed and the more liberal Louis-Philippe is elected king; Paris prospers as it industrializes.
- **1848** A violent working-class revolution deposes Louis-Philippe, who's replaced by autocratic Napoléon III.
- **1853–70** On Napoléon III's orders, Baron Haussmann forcibly redesigns Paris's landscapes and creates the grands boulevards.
- **1860s** The impressionist style emerges.
- **1870** The Franco-Prussian War ends in the defeat of

continues

monarchs in Paris and the various highly competitive feudal lords of the provinces. Because of this tug-of-war, Paris was dogged by civil unrest, takeovers by one warring faction after another, and a dangerous alliance between the English and the powerful rulers of Burgundy during the Hundred Years' War. Around the same time, the city suffered a series of plagues, including the Black Death. To the humiliation of the French monarchs, the city was invaded by the English army in 1422. Joan of Arc (ca. 1412–31) tried unsuccessfully to reconquer Paris in 1429, and 2 years later the English, supported by a tribunal of French ecclesiastics, burned her at the stake in Rouen. Paris was reduced to poverty and economic stagnation, and its embittered and greatly reduced population turned to banditry and street crime to survive.

Despite Joan's ignominious end, the revolution she inspired continued in protracted form until Paris was finally taken from the English armies in 1436. During the several following decades, the English retreated to the port of Calais, abandoning their once-mighty French territories. France, under the leadership of Louis XI (1423–83), witnessed an accelerating rate of change that included the transformation of a feudal and medieval social system into the nascent beginnings of a modern state.

THE RENAISSANCE & THE REFORMATION

The first of the Renaissance monarchs, François I (1494–1547), began an extensive enlargement of Paris's Louvre (which had begun as a warehouse storing the archives of Philippe Auguste before being transformed into a Gothic fortress by Louis IX in the 1100s) to make it suitable as a royal residence. Despite the building's embellishment and the continued designation of Paris as the French capital, he spent much of his time at other châteaux amid the fertile hunting grounds of the Loire Valley. Many later monarchs came to share his opinion that Paris's narrow streets and teeming commercialism were unhealthy and upsetting, and chose to reside elsewhere.

In 1549, however, Henri II (1519–59) triumphantly established his court in Paris and successfully ruled France from within its borders, solidifying the city's role as the nation's undisputed capital. Following their ruler's lead, fashionable aristocrats quickly began to build private residences (*hôtels particuliers*) on the Right Bank, in a marshy low-lying area known as Le Marais (the swamp).

It was during this period that Paris, as the world knows it today, came into existence. The expansion of the Louvre continued, and Catherine de Médicis (1518–89) began building her Palais des Tuileries in 1564. From the shelter of dozens of elegant urban residences, France's aristocracy imbued Paris with its sense of architectural and social style, as well as the Renaissance's mores and manners. Stone quays were added to the Seine's banks, defining their limits and preventing future flood damage, and royal decrees established a series of building codes. To an increasing degree, Paris adopted the planned perspectives and visual grace worthy of the residence of a monarch.

During the late 1500s and 1600s, Protestants were brutally persecuted by the French kings. The bloodletting reached a high point under Henri III (1551–89) during the St. Bartholomew's Day massacre of 1572. Henri III's tragic and eccentric successor, Henri IV (1553–1610), ended the Wars of Religion in 1598 by endorsing the Edict of Nantes, offering religious freedom to the Protestants of France. Henry IV also laid out the lines for one of Paris's memorable squares: place des Vosges. As a reward for his leniency, he was stabbed in 1610 by a deranged monk infuriated by the king's support of religious tolerance.

After Henri IV's death, his second wife, Marie de Médicis (1573–1642), acting as regent, planned the Palais du Luxembourg (1615), whose gardens have functioned ever since as a rendezvous for Parisians. In 1636, Cardinal Richelieu (1585–1642), who virtually ruled France during the minority of Louis XIII (the period in which the boy king was still too young to rule), built the sprawling premises of the Palais Royal. Under Louis XIII (1601–43), two uninhabited islands in the Seine were joined together with landfill, connected to Ile de la Cité and to the mainland with bridges, and renamed Ile St-Louis. Also laid out were the Jardin des Plantes, whose flowers and medicinal herbs were arranged according to their scientific and medical category.

France; Paris is threatened with bombardment by Prussian cannons placed on the outskirts; a revolution in the aftermath of this defeat destroys the Palais des Tuileries and overthrows the government; the Third Republic rises with its elected president, Marshal MacMahon.

- **1878–1937** A series of international expositions adds many enduring monuments to the Paris skyline, including the Tour Eiffel and Sacré-Coeur.

- **1914–18** World War I rips apart Europe.

- **1940** German troops invade Paris; the official French government, under Marshal Pétain, evacuates to Vichy, while the French Resistance under Gen. Charles de Gaulle maintains symbolic headquarters in London.

- **1944** U.S. troops liberate Paris; de Gaulle returns from London in triumph.

- **1948** The revolt in the French colony of Madagascar costs 80,000 French lives; France's empire continues to collapse in Southeast Asia and equatorial Africa.

- **1954–62** War begins in Algeria and is eventually lost; refugees flood Paris and the nation becomes bitterly divided over its North African policies.

- **1958** France's Fourth Republic collapses; General de Gaulle is called out of retirement to head the Fifth Republic.

- **1968** Paris's students and factory workers engage in a general revolt; the French government is overhauled in the aftermath.

- **1981** François Mitterrand is elected France's first socialist president since the 1940s; he's reelected in 1988.

continues

- **1989** Paris celebrates the bicentennial of the French Revolution.
- **1992** Euro Disney opens on the outskirts of Paris.
- **1994** François Mitterrand and Queen Elizabeth II take a ride together under the English Channel in the new Chunnel.
- **1995** Mitterrand dies and Jacques Chirac is elected; Paris is crippled by a general strike; terrorists bomb the subway.
- **1997** Authorities enforce strict immigration laws, causing strife for African and Arab immigrants and dividing the country; French voters rebuff Chirac, electing Socialist Lionel Jospin as his new prime minister.
- **1998** Socialists triumph in local elections across France.
- **1999** The euro is introduced; on Christmas Day a violent storm assaults Paris and the Ile de France, damaging several buildings and toppling thousands of trees.
- **2000** Paris welcomes the new millennium.

THE SUN KING & THE FRENCH REVOLUTION

Louis XIV (1638–1715) was crowned king of France when he was only 9 years old. Cardinal Mazarin (1602–61), Louis's Sicilian-born chief minister, dominated the government in Paris during the Sun King's minority. This era marked the emergence of the French kings as absolute monarchs. As if to concretize their power, they embellished Paris with many of the monuments that still serve as symbols of the city. These included new alterations to the Louvre and the construction of the pont Royal, quai Peletier, place des Victoires, place Vendôme, Champs-Elysées, and Hôtel des Invalides. Meanwhile, Louis XIV absented himself from the city, constructing, at a staggering expense, the Château de Versailles, 13 miles southwest. Today, the palace stands as the single most visible monument to the most flamboyant era of French history.

Meanwhile, the rising power of England, particularly its navy, represented a serious threat to France, which was otherwise the world's most powerful nation. One of the many theaters of the Anglo-French conflict was the American Revolution, during which the French kings supported the Americans in their struggle against the Crown. Ironically, within 15 years the fervor the monarchs had nurtured crossed the Atlantic and destroyed them. The spark that kindled the fire came from Paris itself. For years before the outbreak of hostilities between the Americans and the British, the Enlightenment and its philosophers had fostered a new generation of thinkers who opposed absolutism, religious fanaticism, and superstition. Revolution had been brewing for almost 50 years, and after the French Revolution's explosive events, Europe was completely changed.

Though it began with moderate aims, the Revolution had soon turned the radical Jacobins into overlords, led by Robespierre (1758–94). On August 10, 1792, troops from Marseilles, aided by a Parisian mob, threw Louis XVI (1754–93) and his Austrian-born queen, Marie Antoinette (1755–93), into prison. Several months later, after countless humiliations and a bogus trial, they were guillotined at place de la Révolution (later renamed place de la Concorde) on January 21, 1793. The Reign of Terror continued for another 18 months, with Parisians of all political persuasions fearing for their lives.

THE RISE OF NAPOLÉON

It required the militaristic fervor of Napoléon Bonaparte (1769–1821) to unite France once again. Considered then and today a strategic genius with almost limitless ambition, he restored to Paris and to France a national pride that had been diminished during the Revolution's horror. After many impressive political and military victories, he entered Paris in 1799, at the age of 30, and crowned himself "First Consul and Master of France."

A brilliant politician, Napoléon moderated the atheistic rigidity of the early adherents of the Revolution by establishing peace with the Vatican. Soon thereafter, the legendary love of Parisians for their amusements began to revive; boulevard des Italiens became the rendezvous point of the fashionable, while boulevard du Temple, which housed many of the capital's vaudeville and cabaret theaters, became the favorite watering hole of the working class. In his self-appointed role as a French Caesar, Napoléon continued to alter Paris's face with the construction of the neoclassical arcades of rue de Rivoli (1801), the triumphal arches of the Arc du Carrousel and Arc du Triomphe, and the neoclassical grandeur of La Madeleine. On a less grandiose scale, the city's slaughterhouses and cemeteries were sanitized and moved away from the center of town, and new industries began to crowd workers from the countryside into the cramped slums of a newly industrialized Paris.

Napoléon's victories had made him the envy of Europe, but his infamous retreat from Moscow during the winter of 1812 reduced his formerly invincible army to tatters as 400,000 Frenchmen lost their lives. After a complicated series of events that included his return from exile, Napoléon was defeated at Waterloo by the armies of the English, the Dutch, and the Prussians. Exiled to the British-held island of St. Helena in the remote South Atlantic, he died in 1821, possibly the victim of an unknown poisoner. Some time later, his body was returned to Paris and interred in a massive porphyry sarcophagus in the Hôtel des Invalides, Louis XIV's monument to the ailing and fallen warriors of France.

In the power vacuum that followed Napoléon's expulsion and death, Paris became the scene of intense lobbying over the future fate of France. The Bourbon monarchy was soon reestablished, but with reduced powers. In 1830, the regime was overthrown. Louis-Philippe (1773–1850), duc d'Orléans and the son of a duke who had voted in 1793 for the death of Louis XVI, was elected king under a liberalized constitution. His prosperous reign lasted for 18 years, during which England and France more or less collaborated on matters of foreign policy.

Paris reveled in its new prosperity, grateful for the money and glamour that had elevated it to one of the world's top cultural and commercial centers. Moving into the modern age, Paris received its first railway line in 1837 (running from the center of town to a suburb near St-Germain) and its first gas-fed streetlights shortly thereafter. It was a time of wealth, grace, culture, and expansion for some people, though the industrialization of certain working-class districts of Paris produced horrible poverty. The era also witnessed the development of French cuisine to the high form that still prevails, while a newly empowered bourgeoisie reveled in its attempts to create the good life.

THE SECOND EMPIRE

In 1848, a series of revolutions spread from one European capital to the next. The violent upheaval in Paris revealed the increasing dissatisfaction of many members of the working class. Fueled by a financial crash and scandals in the government, the revolt forced Louis-Philippe out of office. That year, on the dawn of the Second Republic, Emperor Napoléon's nephew, Napoléon III (1808–73), was elected president by moderate and conservative elements. Appealing to the property-owning instinct of a nation that hadn't forgotten the violent revolution of less than a century before, he established a right-wing government and assumed complete power as emperor in 1851.

In 1853, Napoléon III undertook Europe's largest urban redevelopment project by commissioning Baron Eugène-Georges Haussmann (1809–91) to redesign Paris. Haussmann created a vast network of boulevards interconnected with a series of squares that cut across old neighborhoods. While this reorganization gave the capital the look for which it's now famous, screams of outrage sounded throughout the neighborhoods the construction split apart. By 1866, the entrepreneurs of an increasingly industrialized Paris began to regard the Second Empire as a hindrance. In 1870, during the Franco-Prussian War, the Prussians defeated Napoléon III at Sedan and held him prisoner along with 100,000 of his soldiers. Paris was threatened with bombardments from German cannons, by far the most advanced of their age, set up on the city's eastern periphery.

Although agitated diplomacy encouraged a Prussian withdrawal, international humiliation and perceived military incompetence sparked a revolt in Paris. One of the immediate effects of the revolt was the burning of one of Paris's historic landmarks, the Palais des Tuileries. Today, only the sprawling gardens of this once-great palace remain. The tumultuous events of 1870 ushered in the Third Republic and its elected president, Marshal Marie Edme Patrice Maurice de MacMahon (1808–93), in 1873.

Under the Third Republic, peace and prosperity gradually returned, and Paris regained its glamour. Universal Expositions held in 1878, 1889, 1900, and 1937 were the catalyst for the construction of such enduring Paris monuments as the Trocadéro, the Palais de Chaillot, the Tour Eiffel, the Grand Palais and the Petit Palais, and the neo-Byzantine Sacré-Coeur. Simultaneously, the *réseau métropolitain* (the Métro) was constructed, providing a model for subsequent subway systems throughout Europe.

WORLD WAR I

International rivalries and conflicting alliances led to World War I, which, after decisive German victories for 2 years, degenerated into the mud-slogged horror of trench warfare. Industrialization during and after the war transformed Paris and its environs into a vast interconnected whole, by now one of the largest metropolitan areas in Europe and undisputed ever since as the center of France's intellectual and commercial life.

Immediately after the Allied victory, grave economic problems, coupled with a populace demoralized from years of fighting, encouraged the rise of Socialism and the formation of a Communist party, both movements centered in Paris. Also from Paris, the French government, led by the vindictive Georges Clemenceau (1841–1929), occupied Germany's Ruhr Valley, then and now one of that country's most profitable and industrialized regions, and demanded every centime of reparations it could wring from its humiliated neighbor, a policy that contributed to the outbreak of World War II.

THE 1920S—AMERICANS IN PARIS

The so-called Lost Generation, led by American expatriates Gertrude Stein and Alice B. Toklas, led the list of celebrities who "occupied" Paris after World War I, ushering in one of its most glamorous eras. The living was cheap in Paris. Two people could manage for about a year on a $1,000 scholarship,

Impressions

The French will only be united under the threat of danger. Nobody can simply bring together a country that has 265 kinds of cheese.

—Charles de Gaulle

providing they could scrape up another $500 or so in extra earnings. Paris attracted the littérateur, bon viveur, and drifter, and writers like Henry Miller, Ernest Hemingway, and F. Scott Fitzgerald all lived here. Even Cole Porter came, living first at the Ritz, then at 13 rue de Monsieur. James Joyce, half blind and led around by Ezra Pound, arrived in Paris and went to the salon of Natalie Barney, a leading exponent of Amazon Love. She became famous for pulling off stunts like inviting Mata Hari to perform a Javanese dance, completely nude, at one of her parties, labeled "for women only, a lesbian orgy." Colette was barred, though she begged her husband to let her go.

With the collapse of Wall Street, many Americans returned home, except hard-core artists like Henry Miller, who wandered around smoking Gauloise cigarettes and generating several pages a day of *Tropic of Cancer,* which was banned in America for decades. "I have no money, no resources, no hopes. I am the happiest man alive," Miller said. Eventually, he met the narcissistic diary writer, Anaïs Nin, and they began to live a life that gave both of them material for their prose. But even such diehards as Miller and Nin eventually realized 1930s Paris was collapsing as war clouds loomed. Gertrude and Alice remained in France, as other American expats fled to safer shores.

THE WINDS OF WAR

Thanks to an array of alliances, when Germany invaded Poland in 1939, France had no choice but to declare war. Within only a few months, on June 14, 1940, Nazi armies marched arrogantly down the Champs-Elysées and passed beneath the Arc de Triomphe. Newsreel cameras recorded the French openly weeping at the sight. The city suffered little from the war materially, but for 4 years it survived in a kind of half life, cold, dull, and drab, fostering scattered pockets of fighters who resisted sometimes passively and sometimes with active sabotage.

During the Nazi occupation of Paris, the French government, under Marshal Henri Pétain (1856–1951), moved to the quiet and isolated resort of Vichy and cooperated (or actually collaborated, depending on your point of view) with the Nazis. Tremendous internal dissension, the memory of which still simmers today, pitted many factions against one another. The Free French Resistance fled for its own safety to London, where it was headed by Charles de Gaulle (1880–1970), who became president of France's Fourth Republic after the war.

POSTWAR PARIS

Despite its gains in prestige and prosperity after the end of World War II, Paris was rocked many times by internal dissent as domestic and international events embroiled the government in dozens of controversies. In 1951, Paris forgot its cares by celebrating the 2,000th anniversary of the city's founding and poured much of its energy into rebuilding its image as a center of fashion, lifestyle, and glamour. Paris became internationally recognized as both a staple in the travel diets of many North Americans and as a beacon for art and artists.

The War of Algerian Independence (1954–58), in which Algeria sought to go from being a French *département* (an integral extension of the French nation) to an independent country, was an anguishing event, more devastating than the earlier loss of France's colonies. The population of France (Paris in particular) ballooned immediately as French citizens fled Algeria and returned home with few possessions and much bitterness. In 1958, as a result of the enormous loss of lives, money, and prestige in the Algerian affair, France's

Fourth Republic collapsed, and de Gaulle was called out of retirement to form a new government: the Fifth Republic. In 1962, the Algerian war ended with victory for Algeria, as France's colonies in central and equatorial Africa became independent one by one. The sun had finally set on the French Empire.

In 1968, a general revolt by Parisian students, whose activism mirrored that of their counterparts in the United States, turned the capital into an armed camp, causing a near-collapse of the national government and the very real possibility of total civil war. Though the crisis was averted, for several weeks it seemed as if French society was on the brink of anarchy.

CONTEMPORARY PARIS

In 1981, François Mitterrand (1916–96) was elected the first Socialist president of France since World War II by a very close vote of 51%. Massive amounts of capital were taken out of the country, and though the drain slowed somewhat after initial jitters, many wealthy Parisians still prefer to invest their money elsewhere.

Paris today still struggles with social unrest in Corsica and from Muslim fundamentalists both inside and outside of France. In the mid-1990s, racial tensions continued to nag at France, as the debate over immigration raged. Many right-wing political parties have created a racial backlash against North Africans and against "corruptive foreign influences" in general.

On his third try, Jacques Chirac (b. 1932), survivor of many terms as mayor of Paris, won the presidency of France in 1995 with 52% of the vote. Mitterrand turned over the reigns on May 17 and died shortly thereafter. France embarked on a new era, but Chirac's popularity soon faded in the wake of unrest caused by an 11.5% unemployment rate. In the spring of 1998, France ousted its Conservative parties in a powerful endorsement of Prime Minister Lionel Jospin (b. 1937) and his Socialist-led government. The triumph of Jospin and his Communist and Green Party allies represented a fresh disavowal of the center-right Conservatives. This was a stunning blow to Chirac's Neo-Gaullists and the center-right parties led by François Leotard, and certainly to Jean-Marie Le Pen's often fanatical National Front.

By putting the Left back in charge, the French had voted against all the new ideas proposed to them for pushing their country into competitiveness and out of its economic doldrums. In spite of this resistance to change, Jospin is still ever so gently moving France into the new millennium. Without breaking the budget or losing public favor, the prime minister has picked his way through the minefields of French politics—militant unions, a public wedded to generous benefits, and widespread resistance to change. Jospin refers to his path as "leftist realism."

In 1999, France joined with 10 other European Union countries in adopting the Euro as its standard of currency, though the French franc will still be in circulation until 2002. The new currency will accelerate the creation of a single economy, comprising nearly 300 million Europeans, with a combined gross national product approaching, by some estimates, $9 trillion, larger than that of the United States.

On Christmas night in 1999, one of the worst storms in recorded history ravaged the north of France. Wind gusts of 100 miles per hour caused massive damage to buildings, homes, monuments, and gardens. One of the hardest hit was the Château de Versailles, which lost 10,000 trees planted during the 18th and 19th centuries; the loss included two juniper trees planted for Marie Antoinette. Even though it will take quite a long time for the replacement trees to mature, most of the damage to buildings was quickly repaired and all sights should be open when you arrive.

Paris has moved into the new millennium with a new currency and a brighter city that has dusted off monuments and beautified streets to greet another century.

2 City of the Arts

Paris is arguably Europe's premier artistic capital. For centuries, the city has produced and been home to countless artists and artistic movements, and it's still a hotbed of creativity and an important center of the international art world.

Paris's true artistic flowering began around 1150, when the city's active trade, growing population, and struggles for political and ecclesiastic power added dozens of new buildings to the skyline, including Paris's everlasting architectural symbol, the Cathédrale de Notre-Dame, and (to the north of the city) the Cathédrale de St-Denis. In these and other Gothic buildings, the medieval sculptures on the facades and inside depended less on the structures they adorned and became more fully developed as freer artistic expressions of their anonymous creators. Secondary crafts, such as the manufacture and installation of stained glass (as represented by the windows in Paris's Sainte-Chapelle), became art forms in their own right, and French glass of this age attained an intensity of blues and reds that has never been duplicated.

Gothic painters became adept at the miniaturization of religious and secular scenes art lovers could richly appreciate close at hand. The most famous of these, *Les Très riches heures du duc de Berri* by **Pol de Limbourg** (c. 1385–c. 1416) and *Les Heures d'Etienne Chevalier* by **Jean Fouquet** (c. 1420–c. 1480), showed occasional scenes of medieval Paris in a charmingly idealized celebration of the changing of the seasons. Around 1360, Paris provided the setting for the painting of what is usually credited by art historians as the first (known) portrait, of Jean le Bon (artist unknown), and the weaving of one of the most famous tapestries in history, the *Angers Apocalypse.*

A FRENCH RENAISSANCE

The evolution of French art slowed during the 1400s. By the 1500s, however, Paris enjoyed a great artistic rebirth, thanks to a military campaign into Italy and a consequent fascination with all things Italian. Two of that era's main sculptors embellished the facades and fountains of Paris: **Jean Goujon** (1510–85), whose inspirations melded ancient Greek forms and Renaissance themes, and **Germain Pilon** (1535–90), whose carvings of the French kings at St-Denis kept to mostly religious, rather than neoclassical, themes. By the late 1500s, under the auspices of Renaissance king François I, the royal château at Fontainebleau became a caldron of the arts, eventually producing a style of painting known later as the school of Fontainebleau.

The arts in and around Paris during the 1600s so permeated French culture that the century is known as the *Grand Siècle* (grand century). France's monarchy by now was entrenched and its society sufficiently stable and centralized that the arts were able to flourish, and Paris was embellished with hundreds of aristocratic mansions in Le Marais. Important painters included **Philippe de Champaigne** (1602–74), famous for his severe portraits; **Charles Le Brun** (1619–90), who painted the Galerie d'Apollon at the Louvre; and his rival **Pierre Mignard** (1610–95), painter of the interior of the cupola in

Val-de-Grâce. Simultaneously, the art of tapestry weaving was given a tremendous boost thanks to the establishment and royal patronage of the Manufacture Royale des Gobelins.

THE SUN KING RISES

During the early 1700s, the taste for the grandiose was profoundly influenced by the personality of the Sun King, Louis XIV. His construction and furnishing of Versailles called for mind-boggling quantities of art and decoration, affording lavish commissions for sculptors and craftsmen of every kind. In furnishing the palace's thousands of salons and apartments, the techniques of fine cabinetry reached their apogee under cabinetmakers like **André Charles Boulle** (1642–1732). Boulle's writing tables, secretaries, and *bombé*-fronted chests—ebonized or inlaid with tortoiseshell, mother-of-pearl, and gilded bronze ornaments (ormolu)—are today among the finest pieces of cabinetry in European history and command stratospheric prices. Boulle was supplanted by **Charles Crescent** (1685–1768) and **Jean-François Oeben** (ca. 1715–63), under Louis XV, who were themselves replaced by neoclassically inspired master **Adam Weisweiler** (1744–1820) during the reign of Louis XVI.

Painters from the era of Louis XIV and XV include **Nicolas de Largilière** (1656–1746) and **Hyacinthe Rigaud** (1659–1743) and the skilled portraitists **Maurice La Tour** (1704–66) and **Jean-Baptiste Perronneau** (1715–88), whose coloring techniques have been likened to those used by the impressionists more than a century later. Also noteworthy, both as an artist and as a sociological phenomenon, was **Elisabeth Vigée-Lebrun** (1755–1842), whose lavish but natural style won her a position as Marie Antoinette's preferred painter. Especially famous paintings from this era are those of **Honoré Fragonard** (1732–1806) and **Antoine Boucher** (1703–70), whose canvases captured the sweetness and whimsy of aristocratic life during the *ancien régime*.

In sculpture, painting, and furniture, the 18th century in Paris began with an allegiance to the baroque curve and a robustly sensual kind of voluptuousness and ended with a return to the straight line and the more rigid motifs of the classical age. Especially indicative of this return to sobriety was **Jean Antoine Houdon** (1741–1828), who's remembered for his extraordinarily lifelike portrait busts like that of Voltaire.

A DEFT POLITICAL ART

The French Revolution, whose first violence had erupted in 1789, brought a new politicization to the arts. Noteworthy was **Jacques Louis David** (1748–1825), whose painting *Oath of the Horatii* has been credited as a real revolutionary catalyst. To reward his zeal, David was appointed Director of the Arts of the Revolution, surely incentive for such richly idealized paintings as *The Murder of Marat*. Always in control of his own political destiny, David was later appointed court painter to Napoléon.

Meanwhile, as France grew wealthy from the fruits of the Industrial Revolution and the expansion of its Colonial Empire, Paris blossomed with the paintings of **Jean Auguste Dominique Ingres** (1780–1867) and his bitter rival, **Eugène Delacroix** (1798–1863). Primary among their academic disputes were allegiances to the beauty of line (Ingres) versus the subtleties of color (Delacroix).

THE BIRTH OF IMPRESSIONISM

The subtle colorings of landscape artist **Jean Baptiste Camille Corot** (1796–1875) were probably the first hints of what later become known as impressionism. The movement is commonly thought to have been born at the 1863 Salon des Refusés, where works of painters rejected by the mainstream art establishment, like **Claude Monet** (1840–1926) and **Edouard Manet** (1832–83), were shown. Monet's *Impression: Sunrise* was the impetus for the name. One of the most memorable paintings displayed was Manet's then-scandalous *Déjeuner sur l'herbe* (*Picnic on the Grass*). Soon after, such artists as **Alfred Sisley** (1839–99), **Camille Pissarro** (1830–1903)**, Edgar Degas** (1834–1917)**, Pierre Auguste Renoir** (1841–1919), and the immortal Monet painted in the open air, often evoking the everyday life and cityscapes of Paris and its surroundings.

Later, the best scenes ever painted of Paris would be credited to **Maurice Utrillo** (1883–1955) and, to a lesser degree, **Albert Marquet** (1875–1947). Utrillo in particular concentrated on the unpretentious, often working-class neighborhoods (especially Montmartre) rather than the city's more famous monumental zones. Marquet, whose work helped define the fauve school, often executed his stylized and brightly colored works from the balcony of his Paris apartment.

Though many of them never made a career out of painting Paris itself, other 20th-century painters who made Paris their home were **Maurice de Vlaminck** (1876–1958), **André Derain** (1880–1954), **Edouard Vuillard** (1886–1940), **Pierre Bonnard** (1867–1947), **Georges Braque** (1882–1963), **Pablo Picasso** (1881–1973)**, Raoul Dufy** (1877–1953), and **Henri Matisse** (1869–1954). Many of these artists used their canvases as rebellions against the restrictions of "official" art as defined at the time by the aesthetic hierarchies of the Academy. Several movements that emerged from this artistic rebellion have, since their origins, been classified among the most potent schools of art in the world. Included among them were **fauvism,** employing vivid and arbitrary use of color in a manner that paved the way for the nonfigurative movements that were to follow. **Cubism,** the favorite style of early Picasso and Braque, developed as a means of breaking the subject matter into a stylized version of its basic geometric forms. **Dadaism,** an elaboration of the avant-garde movements that developed out of cubism and fauvism, managed to permeate painting with some of the absurdist moral and political philosophies then pervasive in Paris. Most stylized of all was **surrealism,** carrying realism to boundaries never before explored, twisting everyday objects into bizarre, sometimes terrifying permutations that only a slightly mad genius, such as Salvador Dalí, could have conceived of.

Among sculptors, Paris's greatest contribution to the art of the late 19th century was **Auguste Rodin** (1840–1917), whose figures added new dimensions to the human form. Especially famous was the raw power emanating from his rough-surfaced sculptures *The Thinker* and *The Kiss.*

FRENCH ART TODAY

French artists today struggle in the shadow of the great modernists who transformed the world's artistic perceptions during the early 20th century. Though the oeuvre of these contemporary artists will doubtless not surpass the fame, notoriety, and market value of, say, Matisse, Braque, or Monet, they're enjoying popularity and even energetic biddings whenever their works are presented. **Oliver DeBré** (b. 1920), whose early studies in architecture and literature influenced his role as the most important abstract artist in France today, has garnered a significant reputation through a retrospective of his work at the Jeu de Paume. And there are many others. **Gérard Garouste** (b. 1926), who does much of his painting in a studio in the Normandy countryside, is one of Europe's contemporary masters of the postmodern still life.

Ernest Pignon-Ernest (b. 1942), on the other hand, has succeeded in taking contemporary art to the streets. Inspired by the canvases of 17th-century Italian master Caravaggio, Pignon-Ernest executes "neo-Renaissance" serigraphs, produced cheaply and abundantly, which he then plasters over hundreds of buildings as an artistic statement. Although based in Paris throughout most of the year, his "decoration" of the walls of Naples was widely publicized and brought a new appreciation of Caravaggio even to Italy. Detractors of **Pierre Soulages** (b. 1919) compare him to a Gallic version of Mark Rothko; his fans praise his all-black canvases as "sumptuous" and claim he can imbue shades of black with more meaning and subtlety than most artists can evoke with a full palette. He's the most controversial of France's contemporary artists and possibly the most depressing.

Whatever the personal stylistic idiosyncrasies of this new generation of artists, all are part of an artistic tradition that has endured in the City of Light for centuries. Art is, and has been, a vital and integral part of Parisian society since its humble beginnings, and Paris's current artistic sophistication is the product of centuries of development. The city's current art scene pays tribute to the legacy of all who came before and is as diverse and volatile as ever.

3 Architecture Through the Ages

Not only is Paris a world art capital, but also the city itself is art, an organic collection of beautifully designed and constructed buildings representing diverse architectural styles and periods. Walking through Paris can be like excavating layers of sediment at an archaeological dig: Each edifice bears the characteristic signatures of the period in which it was constructed. Paris's buildings are certainly (for the most part) ornate and elegant, but they also tell the tale of the city's long and impressive architectural history.

Despite its role as an outpost of ancient Rome, the development of Paris into a bustling community of traders, merchants, and clerics didn't really come to pass until the 1100s. Historians cite the abandonment of Romanesque building techniques in the Ile de France at around 1150. Because of that, the city has surprisingly few Romanesque buildings, good examples of which are more common in French provinces like Burgundy. Identified by their thick walls, barrel and groined vaults, small windows, and minimal carvings, the city's most important Romanesque buildings are the churches of St-Germain-des-Prés, St-Pierre de Montmartre, St-Martin des Champs, and (in the suburbs) Morienval.

THE GENIUS OF THE GOTHIC AGE

The genius of Paris's architects, however, arrived during the Gothic age, signaled early in the 1200s with the construction of the cathedrals of St-Denis, in Paris's eastern suburbs; Notre-Dame de Chartres, 60 miles southwest; and Notre-Dame de Paris, on Ile de la Cité. By the mid–15th century, Gothic architecture transformed Paris's skyline as dozens of new churches, chapels, and secular buildings outdid their neighbors in lavishness, beauty, and intricacy of design.

Though Gothic architecture was firmly rooted in Romanesque principles, it differs from its predecessor in its penchant for complicated patterns of vaulting and columns and walls that become increasingly thinner as the weight of ceilings and roofs were transferred onto newly developed systems of abutment piers (flying buttresses). Because of the thinner walls, larger openings became architecturally feasible. Churches became filled with light filtered through stained glass, and enormous rose windows awed observers with the delicate tracery.

A CLASSICAL RESURGENCE

During the Renaissance, beginning around 1500, influences from Italy rendered the Gothic style obsolete. In its place arose the yearning for a return to the aesthetics of ancient Greece and Rome. Massive arcades, often decorated with bas-relief sculpture of symbols of triumph, as well as Corinthian, Doric, and Ionic pediments, added grandeur to the Paris of the Renaissance kings. All links of royal residences to feudal fortresses vanished as the aristocrats competed with one another to construct elegant town houses (*hôtels particuliers*) filled with sunlight, tapestries, paintings, music, and fine furniture.

During the early 17th century, many of Paris's distinctive Italianate baroque domes were created. Louis XIV employed such Italian-inspired architects as Le Vau, Perrault, both Mansarts, and Bruand for their buildings and Le Nôtre for the rigidly intelligent layouts of his gardens. Paris and its environs flourished with the construction of the lavish château of Vaux-le-Vicomte and the even more elaborate royal residence of Versailles. Meanwhile, wealthy entrepreneurs encouraged the development of new expressions of artistic and architectural beauty from the many salons sprouting up throughout the city.

By the early 19th century, a newly militaristic Paris, flushed with the titanic changes of the Revolution and the subsequent victories of Napoléon, returned to a restrained and dignified form of classicism. Modeling their urban landscape on an idealized interpretation of imperial Rome, buildings like La Madeleine evoked the militaristic rigidity and grandeur of the age.

ART NOUVEAU & ART DECO

By 1850, enjoying a cosmopolitan kind of prosperity, Paris grew bored with things Greek and Roman. After a brief flirtation with Egyptology (inspired by Napoléon's campaign in the Egyptian desert and the unraveling of the Rosetta stone's secrets), a new school of eclecticism added controversial but often elegant touches to the city. Among them were the voluptuous lines of the art nouveau movement, inspired by the surging curves of the botanical world. Stone, cast iron, glass, and wood were carved or molded into forms resembling orchids, vines, laurel branches, and tree trunks, each richly lyrical and based on new building techniques made possible by the Industrial Age. Art nouveau entrances were built for the Métro stations—only a couple remain, such as the one at Porte Dauphine. Creative architects began to specialize in the use of iron as the support of bridges, viaducts, and buildings, such as the Bibliothèque National (1860). These techniques opened the way for Gustave Eiffel to design and erect the most slandered building of its day, the Tour Eiffel, for the 1889 Universal Exposition.

During the 1920s and 1930s, art deco, a streamlined modernist style incorporating the new materials and decorative techniques of the machine age, captured sophisticated sensibilities around the world. After Braque defined cubism, the angular simplicity of the new artistic movement influenced architectural styles as well. Le Corbusier, a Swiss-born architect who settled in Paris in 1917, developed his jutting, gently curved planes of concrete, opening the doors for a new, but often less talented, school of modern French architects.

ARCHITECTURE TODAY

Since the 1970s, Paris's architectural additions have tended to be controversial and monumental, most of them the *grands projets* of the late François Mitterrand. In 1977, the opening of Richard Rogers and Renzo Piano's Centre Pompidou, with its exoskeletal design and brightly painted pipes and ducts crisscrossing the transparent facade, provoked heated criticism. In the 1980s, an obsolete rail station beside the Seine was transformed into the exciting Musée d'Orsay, boasting an arching glass-and-iron roof, and an expanse of dreary 19th-century slaughterhouses was refigured into the Parc de La Villette, now the city's largest park, boasting a hypermodern science museum.

In 1989, screams of outrage could be heard when I. M. Pei's 71-foot glass pyramid was revealed as the postmodern centerpiece of the Louvre's 17th-century Cour Napoléon, and on July 14 François Mitterrand inaugurated the Grande Arche de La Défense, a 35-story steel-and-masonry office complex shaped like a hollow cube in the suburb of La Défense (it's estimated that Notre-Dame could fit into its hollow core). In the same year, Carlos Ott's Opéra Bastille brought new life to the decaying eastern edge of the Marais but sparked a controversy over its iconoclastic design. The latest additions have been Christian de Portzamparc's Cité de la Musique (1995), a complex of interconnected post-cubist shapes, and the Bibliothèque National de France (1996), a complex of four futuristic buildings resembling open books.

Although the buildings of the Mitterrand presidency were "designed for eternity," flaws have become apparent in his $5.8-billion "chance for immortality." Many of these buildings are suffering defects and mishaps, including ducts rusting at the Centre Pompidou (which reopened in 2000 after a major renovation), stone slabs falling from the Opéra Bastille, fragments of the Grand Arche flaking off into a net, and rain gushing into the Cité de la Musique's orchestra pit. The Bibliothèque National was about to open when the builders realized the light bathing the building was going to destroy the fragile paper of the rare books inside; after much tinkering with tinted glass, the flaws were corrected. The pyramid at the Louvre remains trouble-free—so far.

Because of budgetary constraints, President Jacques Chirac will probably not be able to match his predecessor's cultural monuments (or be plagued with the fallout from such projects, like falling slabs of marble). He has announced an expansion of the somewhat dusty Musée de l'Homme, presently in the Passy Wing of the Palais de Chaillot; construction of a large-scale aquarium to be built somewhere on the Right Bank; and the inception of the not clearly defined Projet du Musée du Quai Branly, probably devoted to exhibits of primitive art and tentatively located on the Right Bank opposite the Eiffel Tower.

Appendix B:
Useful Terms & Phrases

1 Glossary of French-Language Terms

A well-known character is the American or lapsed Canadian who returns from a trip to Paris and denounces the ever-so-rude French. "I asked for directions, and he glowered at me, muttered inaudibly, and turned his back." "She threw her baguette at me!" While Parisians often seem to carry upon their backs a burden of misery that they famously dole out to immigrants and foreigners, it's often amazing how a word or two of halting French will change their dispositions, and if not bring out the sun, at least put an end to the Gallic thunder and rain. At the very least, try to learn a few numbers, basic greetings, and—above all—the life-raft, "*Parlez-vous anglais?*" As it turns out, many Parisians do speak passable English and will use it liberally if you demonstrate the basic courtesy of greeting them in their language. Go out, try our glossary on, and don't be bashful. *Bonne chance!*

BASICS

English	French	Pronunciation
Yes/No	**Oui/Non**	wee/nohn
Okay	**D'accord**	dah-*core*
Please	**S'il vous plaît**	seel voo *play*
Thank you	**Merci**	mair-*see*
You're welcome	**De rien**	duh ree-*ehn*
Hello (during daylight hours)	**Bonjour**	bohn-*jhoor*
Good evening	**Bonsoir**	bohn-*swahr*
Good-bye	**Au revoir**	o ruh-*vwahr*
What's your name?	**Comment vous appellez-vous?**	ko-mahn-voo-za-pell-ay-*voo*?
My name is . . .	**Je m'appelle** . . .	jhuh ma-*pell* . . .
Happy to meet you	**Enchanté(e)**	ohn-shahn-tay
Miss	**Mademoiselle**	mad mwa-*zel*
Mr.	**Monsieur**	muh-*syuh*
Mrs.	**Madame**	ma-*dam*
How are you?	**Comment allez-vous?**	kuh-mahn-tahl-ay-*voo*?
Fine, thank you, and you?	**Très bien, merci, et vous?**	tray bee-ehn, mare-ci, ay *voo*?
Very well, thank you	**Très bien, merci**	tray bee-ehn, mair-*see*
So-so	**Comme ci, comme ça**	kum-*see,* kum-*sah*

English	French	Pronunciation
I'm sorry/excuse me	**pardon**	pahr-*dohn*
I'm so very sorry	**désolé(e)**	day-zoh-*lay*
That's all right	**il n'y a pas de quoi**	eel nee ah pah duh kwah

GETTING AROUND/STREET SMARTS

English	French	Pronunciation
Do you speak English?	**Parlez-vous anglais?**	par-lay-voo-ahn-*glay*?
I don't speak French	**Je ne parle pas français**	jhuh ne parl pah frahn-*say*
I don't understand	**Je ne comprends pas**	jhuh ne kohm-*prahn* pas
Could you speak more loudly/more slowly?	**Pouvez-vous parler un peu plus fort/ plus lentement?**	Poo-vay voo par-lay un puh ploo for/ ploo lan-te-*ment*?
Could you repeat that?	**Répetez, s'il vous plait**	ray-pay-*tay*, seel voo *play*
What is it?	**Qu'est-ce que c'est?**	kess-kuh-*say*?
What time is it?	**Qu'elle heure est-il?**	kel uhr eh-*teel*?
What?	**Quoi?**	kwah?
How? or What did you say?	**Comment?**	ko-*mahn*?
When?	**Quand?**	kahn?
Where is . . . ?	**Où est . . . ?**	ooh-eh . . . ?
Who?	**Qui?**	kee?
Why?	**Pourquoi?**	poor-*kwah*?
Here/there	**ici/là**	ee-*see*/lah
Left/right	**à gauche/à droite**	a goash/a drwaht
Straight ahead	**tout droit**	too-drwah
I'm American/ Canadian/British	**Je suis américain(e)/ canadien(e)/ anglais(e)**	jhe sweez a-may-ree-*kehn*/can-ah-dee-*en*/ ahn-glay (*glaise*)
Fill the tank (of a car), please	**Le plein, s'il vous plaît**	luh plan, seel-voo-*play*
I'm going to . . .	**Je vais à . . .**	jhe vay ah . . .
I want to get off at . . .	**Je voudrais descendre à . . .**	jhe voo-*dray* day-son drah-ah
I'm sick	**Je suis malade**	jhuh swee mal-*ahd*
airport	**l'aéroport**	lair-o-*por*
bank	**la banque**	lah bahnk
bridge	**pont**	pohn
bus station	**la gare routière**	lah gar roo-tee-*air*
bus stop	**l'arrêt de bus**	lah-*ray* duh boohss
by means of a bicycle	**en vélo/par bicyclette**	uh *vay*-low, par bee-see-*clet*
by means of a car	**en voiture**	ahn vwa-*toor*
cashier	**la caisse**	lah *kess*
cathedral	**cathédral**	ka-tay-*dral*
church	**église**	ay-*gleez*
dead end	**une impasse**	ewn am-*pass*
driver's license	**permis de conduire**	per-mee duh con-*dweer*
elevator	**l'ascenseur**	lah sahn *seuhr*
entrance (to a building or a city)	**une porte**	ewn port
exit (from a building or a freeway)	**une sortie**	ewn sor-*tee*
fortified castle or palace	**château**	sha-*tow*

English	French	Pronunciation
garden	**jardin**	jhar-dehn
gasoline	**du pétrol/de l'essence**	duh pay-*troll* de lay-*sahns*
ground floor	**rez-de-chausée**	ray-de-show-*say*
highway to . . .	**la route pour**	la root por
hospital	**l'hôpital**	low-pee-*tahl*
insurance	**les assurances**	lez ah-sur-*ahns*
luggage storage	**consigne**	kohn-*seen*-yuh
museum	**le musée**	luh mew-*zay*
no entry	**sens interdit**	sehns ahn-ter-*dee*
no smoking	**défense de fumer**	day-*fahns* de fu-may
on foot	**à pied**	ah pee-*ay*
one-day pass	**ticket journalier**	tee-kay jhoor-nall-ee-*ay*
one-way ticket	**aller simple**	ah-*lay* sam-pluh
police	**la police**	lah po-*lees*
rented car	**voiture de location**	vwa-*toor* de low-ka-see-on
round-trip ticket	**aller-retour**	ah-*lay* re-*toor*
second floor	**premier étage**	prem-ee-*ehr* ay-*taj*
slow down	**ralentir**	rah-lahn-*teer*
store	**le magazin**	luh ma-ga-*zehn*
street	**rue**	roo
suburb	**banlieu, environs**	bahn-*lieu*, en-veer-*ohns*
subway	**le Métro**	le may-tro
telephone	**le téléphone**	luh tay-lay-*phone*
ticket	**un billet**	uh *bee*-yay
ticket office	**vente de billets**	vahnt duh bee-*yay*
toilets	**les toilettes/les WC**	lay twa-*lets*/les vay-*say*
tower	**tour**	toor

NECESSITIES

English	French	Pronunciation
I'd like . . .	**Je voudrais . . .**	jhe voo-*dray* . . .
a room	**une chambre**	ewn *shahm*-bruh
the key	**la clé (la clef)**	la clay
I'd like to buy . . .	**Je voudrais acheter . . .**	jhe voo-dray ahsh-*tay* . . .
aspirin	**des aspirines/des aspros**	deyz ahs-peer-*eens*/deyz ahs-*prohs*
cigarettes	**des cigarettes**	day see-ga-*ret*
condoms	**des préservatifs**	day pray-ser-va-*teefs*
dictionary	**un dictionnaire**	uh deek-see-oh-*nare*
dress	**une robe**	ewn robe
envelopes	**des envelopes**	days ahn-veh-*lope*
gift (for someone)	**un cadeau**	uh kah-*doe*
handbag	**un sac**	uh sahk
hat	**un chapeau**	uh shah-*poh*
magazine	**une revue**	ewn reh-*vu*
map of the city	**un plan de ville**	unh plahn de *veel*
matches	**des allumettes**	dayz a-loo-*met*
necktie	**une cravate**	uh cra-*vaht*
newspaper	**un journal**	uh zhoor-*nahl*
phone card	**une carte téléphonique**	uh cart tay-lay-fone-*eek*
postcard	**une carte postale**	ewn carte pos-*tahl*
road map	**une carte routière**	ewn cart roo-tee-*air*

English	French	Pronunciation
shirt	**une chemise**	ewn che-*meez*
shoes	**des chaussures**	day show-*suhr*
skirt	**une jupe**	ewn jhoop
soap	**du savon**	dew sah-*vohn*
socks	**des chaussettes**	day show-*set*
stamp	**un timbre**	uh *tam*-bruh
trousers	**un pantalon**	uh pan-tah-*lohn*
writing paper	**du papier à lettres**	dew pap-pee-*ay a let*-ruh
How much does it cost?	**C'est combien?/ ça coûte combien?**	say comb-bee-*ehn*?/sah coot comb-bee-*ehn*?
That's expensive	**C'est cher/chère**	say share
That's inexpensive	**C'est raisonnable/ C'est bon marché**	say ray-son-*ahb*-bluh/ssay bohn mar-*shay*
Do you take credit cards?	**Est-ce que vous acceptez les cartes de credit?**	es-kuh voo zaksep-*tay* lay kart duh creh-*dee*?

IN YOUR HOTEL

English	French	Pronunciation
Are taxes included?	**Est-ce que les taxes sont comprises?**	ess-keh lay taks son com-*preez*?
balcony	**un balcon**	uh bahl-cohn
bathtub	**une baignoire**	ewn bayn-*nwar*
bedroom	**une chambre**	ewn *shawm*-bruh
for two occupants	**pour deux personnes**	poor duh pair-sunn
hot and cold water	**l'eau chaude et froide**	low showed ay fwad
Is breakfast included?	**Petit déjeuner inclus?**	peh-*tee* day-jheun-*ay* ehn-*klu*?
room	**une chambre**	ewn *shawm*-bruh
shower	**une douche**	ewn dooch
sink	**un lavabo**	uh la-va-*bow*
suite	**une suite**	ewn sweet
We're staying for . . . days with	**On reste pour . . . jours avec**	ohn rest poor . . . jhoor ah-*vek*
with air-conditioning	**avec climatisation**	ah-*vek* clee-mah-tee-zah-sion
without	**sans**	sahn
youth hostel	**une auberge de jeunesse**	oon oh-bayrge-duh-jhe-ness

IN THE RESTAURANT

English	French	Pronunciation
I would like . . .	**Je voudrais**	jhe voo-*dray*
to eat	**manger**	mahn-*jhay*
to order	**commander**	ko-mahn-*day*
Please give me . . .	**Donnez-moi, s'il vous plaît . . .**	doe-nay-*mwah*, seel voo play . . .
a bottle of . . .	**une bouteille de . . .**	ewn boo-*tay* duh . .
a cup of . . .	**une tasse de . . .**	ewn tass duh . . .
a glass of . . .	**un verre de . . .**	uh vair duh . .
a plate of . . .	**une assiette de . . .**	ewn ass-ee-*et* duh . . .
an ashtray	**un cendrier**	uh sahn-dree-*ay*
bread	**du pain**	dew pan

English	French	Pronunciation
breakfast	**le petit déjeuner**	luh puh-*tee* day-zhuh-*nay*
butter	**du beurre**	dew burr
check/bill	**l'addition/ la note**	la-dee-see-*ohn*/la noat
Cheers!	**à votre santé**	ah vo-truh sahn-tay
Can I buy you a drink?	**Puis-je vous payer un verre?**	*pwee*-jhe voo pay-ay uh *vaihr*?
cocktail	**un apéritif**	uh ah-pay-ree-*teef*
coffee	**du café**	dew ka-fay
coffee—black	**un café noir**	uh ka-*fay* nwahr
coffee—with cream	**un café crème**	uh ka-*fay* krem
coffee—with milk	**un café au lait**	uh ka-*fay* o *lay*
coffee—decaf	**un café décaféiné**	uh ka-*fay* day-kah-fay-*nay*
coffee—espresso	**un café express**	uh ka-fay ek-*sprehss*
dinner	**le dîner**	luh dee-*nay*
fixed-price menu	**un menu**	uh may-new
fork	**une fourchette**	ewn four-*shet*
Is the tip/ service included?	**Est-ce que le service est compris?**	ess-ke luh ser-vees eh com-*pree*?
knife	**un couteau**	uh koo-*toe*
napkin	**une serviette**	ewn sair-vee-*et*
pepper	**du poivre**	dew *pwah*-vruh
platter of the day	**un plat du jour**	uh plah dew jhoor
salt	**du sel**	dew sell
soup	**une soupe/un potage**	ewn soop/uh poh-*tahj*
spoon	**une cuillère**	ewn kwee-*air*
sugar	**du sucre**	dew *sook*-ruh
tea	**un thé**	uh tay
tea—with lemon	**un thé au citron**	uh tay o see-*tron*
tea—herbal	**une tisane**	ewn tee-*zahn*
Waiter!/ Waitress!	**Monsieur!/ Mademoiselle!**	mun-*syuh*/ mad-mwa-*zel*
wine list	**une carte des vins**	ewn cart day *van*
appetizer	**une entrée**	ewn en-*tray*
main course	**un plat principal**	uh plah pran-see-*pahl*
tip included	**service compris**	sehr-*vees* cohm-*preez*
wide-range sample of the chef's best efforts	**menu dégustation**	may-new day-gus-ta-see-on
drinks not included	**boissons non comprises**	bwa-*sons* no com-*preez*
cheese tray	**plâteau de fromage**	plah-*tow* duh fro-*mahj*

SHOPPING

English	French	Pronunciation
antiques store	**un magasin d'antiquités**	uh maga-*zan* d'on-tee kee-*tay*
bakery	**une boulangerie**	ewn boo-lon-zhur-*ree*
bank	**une banque**	ewn bonk
bookstore	**une librairie**	ewn lee-brehr-*ree*
butcher	**une boucherie**	ewn boo-shehr-*ree*
cheese shop	**une fromagerie**	ewn fro-mazh-*ree*
dairy shop	**une crémerie**	ewn krem-*ree*
delicatessen	**une charcuterie**	ewn shar-koot-*ree*

English	French	Pronunciation
department store	**un grand magasin**	uh grah maga-*zan*
drugstore	**une pharmacie**	ewn far-mah-*see*
fishmonger shop	**une poissonerie**	ewn pwas-son-*ree*
gift shop	**un magasin** **de cadeaux**	uh maga-*zan* duh ka-*doh*
greengrocer	**un marchand** **de légumes**	uh mar-*shon* duh lay-*goom*
hairdresser	**un coiffeur**	uh kwa-*fuhr*
market	**un marché**	uh mar-*shay*
pastry shop	**une pâtisserie**	ewn pa-tee-*sree*
supermarket	**un supermarché**	uh soo-pehr-mar-*shay*
tobacconist	**un tabac**	uh ta-*bah*
travel agency	**une agence de voyages**	ewn azh-ahns duh vwa *yazh*

COLORS, SHAPES, SIZES, ATTRIBUTES

English	French	Pronunciation
black	**noir**	nwahr
blue	**bleu**	bleuh
brown	**marron/brun**	mar-*rohn*/bruhn
green	**vert**	vaihr
orange	**orange**	o-*rahnj*
pink	**rose**	rose
purple	**violet**	vee-o-*lay*
red	**rouge**	rooj
white	**blanc**	blahnk
yellow	**jaune**	jhone
bad	**mauvais(e)**	moh-*veh*
big	**grand(e)**	gron/gronde
closed	**fermé(e)**	fer-*meh*
down	**en bas**	on *bah*
early	**de bonne heure**	duh bon *urr*
enough	**assez**	as-*say*
far	**loin**	lwan
free, unoccupied	**libre**	*lee*-bruh
free, without charge	**gratuit(e)**	grah-*twee*/grah-*tweet*
good	**bon/bonne**	boa/bun
hot	**chaud(e)**	show/shoad
near	**près**	preh
open (as in "museum")	**ouvert(e)**	oo-*ver*
small	**petit(e)**	puh-*tee*/puh-*teet*
up	**en haut**	on *oh*
well	**bien**	byehn

NUMBERS & ORDINALS

English	French	Pronunciation
zero	**zéro**	zare-*oh*
one	**un**	uh
two	**deux**	duh
three	**trois**	twah
four	**quatre**	*kaht*-ruh

English	French	Pronunciation
five	**cinq**	sank
six	**six**	seess
seven	**sept**	set
eight	**huit**	wheat
nine	**neuf**	nuf
ten	**dix**	deess
eleven	**onze**	ohnz
twelve	**douze**	dooz
thirteen	**treize**	trehz
fourteen	**quatorze**	kah-*torz*
fifteen	**quinze**	kanz
sixteen	**seize**	sez
seventeen	**dix-sept**	deez-*set*
eighteen	**dix-huit**	deez-*wheat*
nineteen	**dix-neuf**	deez-*nuf*
twenty	**vingt**	vehn
twenty-one	**vingt-et-un**	vehnt-ay-*uh*
twenty-two	**vingt-deux**	vehnt-*duh*
thirty	**trente**	trahnt
forty	**quarante**	ka-*rahnt*
fifty	**cinquante**	sang-*kahnt*
sixty	**soixante**	swa-*sahnt*
sixty-one	**soixante-et-un**	swa-*sahnt*-et-*uh*
seventy	**soixante-dix**	swa-sahnt-*deess*
seventy-one	**soixante-et-onze**	swa-sahnt-et-*ohnze*
eighty	**quatre-vingts**	kaht-ruh-*vehn*
eighty-one	**quatre-vingt-un**	kaht-ruh-vehn-*uh*
ninety	**quatre-vingt-dix**	kaht-ruh-venh-*deess*
ninety-one	**quatre-vingt-onze**	kaht-ruh-venh-*ohnze*
one hundred	**cent**	sahn
one thousand	**mille**	meel
one hundred thousand	**cent mille**	sahn meel
first	**premier**	*preh*-mee-ay
second	**deuxième**	*duhz*-zee-em
third	**troisième**	*twa*-zee-em
fourth	**quatrième**	kaht-ree-em
fifth	**cinquième**	*sank*-ee-em
sixth	**sixième**	*sees*-ee-em
seventh	**septième**	*set*-ee-em
eighth	**huitième**	*wheat*-ee-em
ninth	**neuvième**	*neuv*-ee-em
tenth	**dixième**	*dees*-ee-em
eleventh	**onzième**	*ohnz*-ee-em
twelfth	**douzième**	*dooz*-ee-em
thirteenth	**treizième**	*trehz*-ee-em
fourteenth	**quatorzième**	kah-*torz*-ee-em
twentieth	**vingtième**	*vehnt*-ee-em
thirtieth	**trentième**	*trahnt*-ee-em
one-hundredth	**centième**	*sant*-ee-em

Useful Terms & Phrases

THE CALENDAR

English	French	Pronunciation
January	**janvier**	*jhan*-vee-ay
February	**février**	*feh*-vree-ay
March	**mars**	marce
April	**avril**	a-*vreel*
May	**mai**	meh
June	**juin**	jhwehn
July	**juillet**	*jhwee*-ay
August	**août**	oot
September	**septembre**	sep-*tahm*-bruh
October	**octobre**	ok-*to*-bruh
November	**novembre**	no-*vahm*-bruh
December	**decembre**	day-*sahm*-bruh
Sunday	**dimanche**	dee-*mahnsh*
Monday	**lundi**	*luhn*-dee
Tuesday	**mardi**	*mahr*-dee
Wednesday	**mercredi**	*mair*-kruh-dee
Thursday	**jeudi**	*jheu*-dee
Friday	**vendredi**	*vawn*-druh-dee
Saturday	**samedi**	*sahm*-dee
yesterday	**hier**	ee-*air*
today	**aujourd'hui**	o-jhord-*dwee*
this morning /this afternoon	**ce matin/ cet après-midi**	suh ma-*tan*/ set ah-preh mee-*dee*
tonight	**ce soir**	suh *swahr*
tomorrow	**demain**	de-*man*

2 Glossary of Basic Menu Terms

Note: To order any of these items from a waiter, simply preface the French-language name with the phrase "Je voudrais" (jhe voo-*dray*), which means, "I would like . . ." Also see the **"In the Restaurant"** entries above. *Bon appétit!*

MEATS

English	French	Pronunciation
beef stew	**du pot au feu**	dew poht o *fhe*
marinated beef braised with red wine and served with vegetables	**du boeuf à la mode**	dew bewf ah lah *mhowd*
brains	**de la cervelle**	duh lah ser-*vel*
chicken	**du poulet**	*dew poo*-lay
rolls of pounded and baked chicken, veal, or fish, often pike, usually served warm	**des quenelles**	day ke-*nelle*
chicken, stewed with mushrooms and wine	**du coq au vin**	dew cock o vhaihn
chicken wings	**des ailes de poulet**	dayz ehl duh poo-lay
frogs' legs	**des cuisses de grenouilles**	day cweess duh gre *noo* yuh

English	French	Pronunciation
ham	**du jambon**	dew jham-bohn
haunch or leg of an animal, especially that of a lamb or sheep	**du gigot**	dew *jhi*-goh
kidneys	**des rognons**	day *row*-nyon
lamb	**de l'agneau**	duh l'ahn-*nyo*
lamb chop	**une cotelette d'agneau**	ewn koh-te-lette duh l'ahn-*nyo*
rabbit	**du lapin**	dew lah-pan
sirloin	**de l'aloyau**	duh l'ahl-why-*yo*
steak	**du bifteck**	dew beef-*tek*
filet steak, embedded with fresh green or black peppercorns, flambéed and served with a cognac sauce	**un steak au poivre**	uh stake o *pwah*-vruh
double tenderloin, a long muscle from which filet steaks are cut	**du chateaubriand**	dew sha-tow-bree-ahn
stewed meat with white sauce, enriched with cream and eggs	**de la blanquette**	duh lah blon-*kette*
sweetbreads	**des ris de veau**	day *ree* duh voh
veal	**du veau**	dew *voh*

FISH

English	French	Pronunciation
fish (freshwater)	**du poisson de rivière,** or **du poisson d'eau douce/**	dew pwah-sson duh ree-vee-*aire,* dew pwah-sson d'o *dooss/*
fish (saltwater)	**du poisson de mer**	dew pwah-sson duh *mehr*
mediterranean fish soup or stew made with tomatoes, garlic, saffron, and olive oil	**de la bouillabaisse**	duh lah booh-ya-*besse*
eel	**de l'anguille**	duh l'ahn-*ghee*-uh
herring	**du hareng**	dew ahr-*rahn*
lobster	**du homard**	dew oh-*mahr*
mussels	**des moules**	day *moohl*
mussels in herb-flavored white wine with shallots	**des moules marinières**	day moohl mar-ee-nee-*air*
oysters	**des huîtres**	dayz hoo-*ee*-truhs
pike	**du brochet**	dew broh-*chay*
shrimp	**des crevettes**	day kreh-*vette*
smoked salmon	**du saumon fumé**	dew sow-mohn *fu-may*
tuna	**du thon**	dew tohn
trout	**de la truite**	duh lah tru-*eet*

wolffish, a Mediterranean sea bass	**du loup de mer**	dew loo-duh-*mehr*

SIDES/APPETIZERS

English	French	Pronunciation
butter	**du beurre**	dew bhuhr
bread	**du pain**	dew pan
goose liver	**du foie gras**	dew fwah grah
liver	**du foie**	dew fwah
potted and minced pork and pork by-products, prepared as a roughly hopped pâté	**des rillettes**	day ree-*yett*
rice	**du riz**	dew ree
snails	**des escargots**	dayz ess-car-*goh*

FRUITS/VEGETABLES

English	French	Pronunciation
cabbage	**du choux**	dew *shoe*
eggplant	**de l'aubergine**	duh l'oh-ber-*jheen*
grapefruit	**un pamplemousse**	uh pahm-pluh-moose
grapes	**du raisin**	dew ray-*zhan*
green beans	**des haricots verts**	day ahr-ee-coh *vaire*
green peas	**des petits pois**	day puh-tee-*pwah*
lemon/lime	**du citron/ du citron vert**	dew cee-*tron*/ dew cee-tron *vaire*
orange	**une orange**	ewn or-*ahn*-jhe
pineapple	**de l'ananas**	duh l'ah-na-*nas*
potatoes	**des pommes de terre**	day puhm duh *tehr*
potatoes au gratin	**des pommes de terre dauphinois**	day puhm duh tehr doh-feen-wah
french fried potatoes	**des pommes frites**	day puhm *freet*
spinach	**des épinards**	dayz ay-pin-*ards*
strawberries	**des fraises**	day *frez*

SOUPS/SALADS

English	French	Pronunciation
cucumber salad	**une salade de concombres**	ewn sah-lahd duh con-*con*-bruh
fruit salad	**une salade de fruit/ une macédoine de fruits**	ewn sah-lahd duh *fweel* ewn mah-say-doine duh fwee
green salad	**une salade verte**	ewn sah-lahd *vairt*
lettuce salad	**une salade de laitue**	ewn sah-lahd duh lay-tew
onion soup	**de la soupe à l'oignon**	duh lah soop ah low-*ñon*

salad, native to Nice, composed of lettuce, tuna, anchovies, capers, tomatoes, olives, olive oil, wine vinegar, and herbs	**une salade niçoise**	ewn sah-lahd nee-*swaz*
sauerkraut	**de la choucroute**	duh lah chew-*kroot*
vegetable soup with basil	**soupe au pistou**	duh lah soop oh pees-tou

BEVERAGES

English	French	Pronunciation
beer	**de la bière**	duh lah bee-*aire*
milk	**du lait**	dew *lay*
orange juice	**du jus d'orange**	dew joo d'or-*ahn*-jhe
water	**de l'eau**	duh lo
red wine	**du vin rouge**	dew vhin *rooj*
white wine	**du vin blanc**	dew vhin *blahn*
coffee	**un café**	uh ka-*fay*
coffee (black)	**un café noir**	uh ka-fay *nwahr*
coffee (with cream)	**un café crème**	uh ka-fay *krem*
coffee (with milk)	**un café au lait**	uh ka-fay o *lay*
coffee (decaf)	**un café décaféiné** (slang: **un déca**)	un ka-fay day-kah-fay-*nay* (uh *day*-kah)
coffee (espresso)	**un espresso** *(un express)*	un ka-fay ek-*sprehss-o* (uh ek-*sprehss*)
tea	**du thé**	dew *tay*
herbal tea	**une tisane**	ewn tee-*zahn*
drinks not included	**boissons non compris**	bwa-sons nohn com-*pree*

DESSERTS

English	French	Pronunciation
cake	**du gâteau**	dew gha-tow
cheese	**du fromage**	dew fro *mahj*
thick custard dessert with a caramelized topping	**de la crème brûlée**	duh lah krem bruh-*lay*
caramelized upside-down apple pie	**une tarte tatin**	ewn tart tah-*tihn*
tart	**une tarte**	ewn tart
vanilla ice cream	**de la glace à la vanille**	duh lah glass a lah vah-*nee*-yuh
fruit, especially cherries, cooked in batter	**du clafoutis**	dew kla-foo-*tee*

SPICES/CONDIMENTS

English	French	Pronunciation
mustard	**de la moutarde**	duh lah moo-*tard*-uh
pepper	**du poivre**	dew *pwah*-vruh
salt	**du sel**	dew *sel*
sour heavy cream	**de la crème fraîche**	duh lah krem *fresh*
sugar	**du sucre**	dew *sooh*-kruh

COOKING METHODS

English	French	Pronunciation
cooked in parchment paper	en papillotte	ehn pah-pee-*yott*
cooked over a wood fire minced and potted meat, seasoned and molded into a crock	cuit au feu de bois une terrine	kwee oh fhe duh *bwoi* ewn tair-*een*
puff pastry shell	vol-au-vent	vhol-o-*vhen*
a method of food preparation native to Lyon and its region that usually includes wine sauce accented with shredded and sautéed onions	à la lyonnaise	ah lah lee-ohn-*nehz*
in the style of Burgundy, usually with red wine, mushrooms, bacon, and onions	bourgignon/ à la bourguignonne	boor-geehn-*nyon*/ a lah boor-geeh-ny-*uhn*
method of cooking whereby anything (including fish, meat, fruits, or vegetables) is simmered in a reduction of its own fat or juices	un confit	uh khon-*feeh*

MISCELLANEOUS

English	French	Pronunciation
I'm a vegetarian	Je suis végétarien/ Je suis végétarienne	Jhe swee vay-jhay-tar-e-en/ Jhe swee vay-jhay-tar-e-*enne*
a fixed-price, precomposed meal, usually offering a limited choice of the specific dishes that comprise it	le menu/le prix fixe/ la formule/ la table d'hôte	le meh-noo/le pree-feex/ lah for-*muhl*/ lah tah-bluh *doht*
tasting menu	le menu gastro-nomique/ le menu dégustation	le meh-noo gah-stroh-noh-meek/ le meh-noo day-goo-stah-sion

Index

See also Accommodations and Restaurant indexes, below.

GENERAL INDEX

Accommodations
airport, 97
bathrooms, 72
family-friendly, 75
gay & lesbian travelers, 97
government ratings, 65
Left Bank, 88, 89
Right Bank, 64–65, 68–82
Addresses, 52
Airlines, 25, 27–28, 38
Airports, 26, 28–29, 97
American Cathedral of the
Holy Trinity, 183
American Church in Paris, 4
American Expatriates, 300
American Express, 15, 59
Amusement parks
Disneyland Paris, 285,
288–89, 304, 307–309
Foire du Trône, 16
Jardin d'Acclimatation, 213
Antiques, 19, 234
Arc de Triomphe, 154–55, 167
Architecture, 306–08
Arènes de Lutèce, 186
Armistice Day, 19
Arrondissements, 49, 52–56
shopping, 233–34
Art, 303–06. See also Galleries;
Museums; and individual
artists and works of art
Asian cuisine, 99
Atelier Brancusi, 178
ATMs (automated teller
machines), 14, 41
Au Lapin Agile, 221
Away.com, 37

Baccarat, 201, 237
ballet, 2
Banks, 59
Bars, 3, 119, 155, 261,
265–67, 270
gay & lesbian friendly,
267–69
literary connections, 269
wine bars, 100, 264–65
Basilique du Sacré-Coeur, 167

Basilique St-Denis, 183
Bastille, 226
Bastille Day, 18
Bateau-Lavoir (Boat Ware-
house), 194, 218
Beaujolais Nouveau, 20
Beaumarchais statue, 226
Bibliothèque Information
Publique, 178
Bibliothèque Nationale de
France, Site Tolbiac/François
Mitterand, 187
Bicycling, 18, 59
Bid for Travel, 39
Biennale des Antiquaires, 19
Bike tours, 217. See also
Bicycling
Bistros, 100. See also Restaurant
Index
Boat travel, 59
Books, 235–36
Boulevard, 252
Boulevard de Clichy, 221
Boulevard St-Michel, 222
Boutiques, 232
Brasseries, 100. See also
Restaurant Index
Bus tours, 216
Bus travel, 30, 57
Business hours, 59
museums, 178, 199
shopping, 232

Cabaret des Assassins, 221
Cabarets, 256–58
Cafes, 2, 100, 148–53. See also
Restaurant Index
Calendar of events, 16–20
California Grill, 290
Car rental, 58
Cartier jewelry, 244
Catacombs, 215
Cathédral de Notre-Dame de
Chartres, 280, 282–84
Cathédrale de Notre-Dame,
154, 168–70, 191
CDC, 41
Cemeteries, 4, 189, 207,
210–211, 221, 224

Center for Nature Discovery,
Garden in Memory of Diana,
Princes of Wales, 177
Centre de Création Industriel,
178
Centre Pompidou, 155, 177
Ceramics, shopping, 236
Champs-Elysées, 49, 154
Chanel, 240
Channel Tunnel (Chunnel), 31,
272
Chansonniers, 255
Charvet, 240
Château de Rambouillet, 279
Château de Versailles, 271–72,
274–78
Cheap Tickets, 39
Children, 5, 38, 211
amusement parks, 16, 213,
285, 288–89, 304,
307–309
family-friendly accommo-
dations, 75
family-friendly restaurants,
129
museums, 211–13
shopping for, 237
China, shopping, 236
Chock, Deborah, 227
Chunnel. See Channel Tunnel
Churches and Cathedrals
American Cathedral of the
Holy Trinity, 183
Basilique du Sacré-Coeur,
167
Basilique St-Denis, 183
Cathédrale de Notre-Dame
(Paris), 154, 168–70,
191
Cathédrale Notre Dame de
Chartres, 280, 282–84
Eglise de la Sorbonne, 224
Eglise du Dôme, 171
La Madeleine, 184
Mosquée de Paris, 184
Panthéon, 224
Sacré-Coeur, 155, 194, 220
Sainte Chapelle, 175, 176
St-Etienne du Mont, 185

Churches and Cathedrals *(cont.)*
St-Eustache, 186
St-Germain l'Auxerrois, 186
St-Germain-des-Prés, 184, 196
St-Louis-en-l'Ile, 192
St-Pierre, 220
St-Séverin, 223
St-Sulpice, 185
Val de Grâce, 186
Cimetière de Montmartre, 211, 221
Cimetière de Passy, 210
Cimetière du Montparnasse, 210
Cimetière du Père Lachaise, 207, 210
Cimetière St-Vincent, 210
Cité de la Musique, 253
Cité des Sciences et de l'Industrie, 211–12
City code, telephone calls, 62
City layout, 48–49, 52–56
Classical music, 253–54
Claude Monet Foundation, 284
Climate, 15
Club and Music scene, 254–69
Colonne de Juillet, 226
Comédie-Française, 253
Comédie-Française–Théâtre du Vieux Colombier, 253
Conciergerie, 155, 187–188
Consulates, 60. *See also* Embassies
Cooking classes, 109
Country code, telephone calls, 62
Couture fashion, 231
Credit cards, 14
Crime, 62
Cruises, 216
Crystal, shopping, 237
Currency, 13, 14, 42, 59
Customs, 11–12, 42
Cybercafé Latino, 61

Dalí, Salvadore, 194
Espace Montmartre Dalí, 194, 220
Dance, 253–54
Festival du Marais, 18
Dance clubs, 260–64
Degas, Edgar, 305
Dental services, 60
Department stores, 238–39
Diana, Princess of Wales, 177
Dining. *See also* Restaurant Index
Asian cuisine, 99
bistros, 100
brasseries, 100
cafes, 100, 148–53
cheese, 122

cooking classes, 109
dress code, 101
Ducasse, Alain, 99, 104, 120
family-friendly, 129
gay friendly, 153
ice cream, 111
pastry, 146–47
picnics, 117
reservations, 105
Rostang, Michel, 132
street vendors, 137
tourists and, 133
Web guides, 47
wine bars, 100
Dior, Christian, 240
Disneyland Paris, 285, 288–89, 304, 307–309
Driving, 30, 58
Drugstores, 60
Ducasse, Alain, 99, 104, 120
Duty-free shopping, 232

E-mail, Internet cafes, 43
Eglise de la Sorbonne, 224
Eglise du Dôme, 171
Eiffel Tower, 154, 176–77
Electricity, 60
Embassies, 11, 60
Emergencies, 60
Espace Montmartre Dalí, 194, 220
Euro currency, 14
Euro Disney Resort. *See* Disneyland Paris
Exchange rate, currency, 13–14, 42

Fashion, 239–41. *See also individual designers*
children's, 237
couture, 231
International Ready-to-Wear Fashion Shows, 16, 19
Faubourg St-Honoré, 2
Favourbrook, 240
Ferries from England, 30–31
Fêstival d'Automne (Autumn Festival), 19
Festival du Marais, 18
Fête de St-Denis, 17
Fête Chopin, 17
Fête d'Art Sacré, 19
Fête de Jazz de Paris, 19
Fête de la Musique, 18
Fête de St-Sylvestre, 20
Fête Musique en l'Ile, 19
Figaret, Alain, 240
Foire du Trône amusement park, 16
Folies-Bergère, 3, 155, 256
Food shopping, 231, 242–44

Forest of Rambouillet, 278–80
French Government Tourist Office, 10
French Open Tennis Championship, 17
French Revolution, 298
Frommer's Gay & Lesbian Europe, 22
Frommer's Budget Travel Online, 35, 41
Frommer's Daily Newsletter , 35

Galerie Nationale du Jeu de Paume, 178
Galleries, 235
Gardens. *See* Parks and Gardens
Gardens of Versailles, 276
Gay & Lesbian interest
accommodations, 97
bars, 268–269
dining, 153
Gay Pride Parade, 18
Out & About, 23
traveling, 22–23
Gift shopping, 249–50
Givenchy, 241
Giverny, 284–85
Go4less, 39
GORP.com, 38
Grand Steeplechase de Paris, 17

Hamlet, The (Versailles), 276
Harry's New York Bar, 269
Hemingway, Ernest, 70, 155, 269
Hermès, 241
Hier, Aujourd'hui, et Demain, 228
History of Paris, 294–08
Holidays, 15
Horse racing, 3, 17, 19, 217
Hospitals, 61
Hugo, Victor, 214, 227

iExplore, 37
Ile de la Cité, 49, 191
Ile St-Louis, 49, 191–92
InnSite, 38
Institut de France, 188
Institut de Recherche et de Coordination Acoustique Musique, 178
Institut du Monde Arabe, 202
Insurance, 20–21
International Association for Medical Assistance to Travelers, 20
International Gay & Lesbian Travel Association, 22
International Marathon of Paris, 16

International Ready-to-Wear Fashion Shows, 16, 19
Internet access, 61
Internet cafes, 42, 43

Jardin de Tuileries, 155
Jewelry, shopping, 244

Kiki de Montparnasse, 197

La Course des Garçons de Café, 18
La Grande Arche de La Défense, 188
La Madeleine, 155, 184
La Villette Jazz Festival, 18
Lalique, 237
Language, 41
LastMinuteTravel.com, 40
Latin Quarter, 222–24
Layout of city, 48–49, 52–56
Le Cordon Bleu cooking school, 109
Le Pass Musée et Monuments, 177
Le Petit Train de Montmartre, 220
Le Rendez-vous Toyota, 61
Left Bank, 64, 83–92, 94–97, 196, 198
Les Catacombs, 215
Les Egouts, 215–16
Les Grandes Eaux Musicales, 17
Les Trois Marches, 278
Liquor laws, 61
Literary landmarks, 213–15
Longchamp, 3
Lost Generation, 300

Magazines, 61
Mail, 61
Maison de Balzac, 214
Maison de Radio France, 253
Maison de Victor Hugo, 214, 227
Makeup, shopping, 231, 248
Mall shopping, 245–46
Manet, Edouard, 305
Manufacture Nationale des Gobelins, 201
Mapquest, 41
Marais, The (walking tour), 224, 226–30
Marché aux Fleurs, 3
Markets, 3, 4, 242, 246–47
Medical travel insurance, 20
Moment's Notice, 40
Mona Lisa, 172
Monet, Claude, 155, 180, 284–85, 305
Money, 13–14, 59

Montmartre, 3, 194
Le Petit Train de Montmartre, 220
walking tour, 218, 220–21
Monuments and Memorials
Arc de Triomphe, 154–55
Le Pass Musée et Monuments, 177
Tour Eiffel, 154
Mosquée de Paris, 184
Moulin de la Galette, 221
Moulin Rouge, 221, 257
Musées. *See* Museums
Museums, 178, 181, 198–03, 214–15, 247–48
Centre Pompidou, 177
Cité des Sciences et de l'Industrie, 211–12
Espace Montmartre Dalí, 194
Galerie Nationale du Jeu de Paume, 178
Institut du Monde Arabe, 202
Le Pass Musée et Monuments, 177
Maison de Balzac, 214
Maison de Victor Hugo, 214
Manufacture Nationale des Gobelins, 201
Musée Bourdelle, 198
Musée Carnavalet, 155, 179, 191, 227
Musée Cernuschi, 198
Musée Cognacq Jay, 198
Musée d'Art et d'Histoire du Judaïsm, 202
Musée d'Art Moderne de la Ville de Paris & Musée des Enfants, 199
Musée d'Orsay, 154, 174–75
Musée de Baccarat, 201
Musée de Cluny, 224
Musée de France (Versailles), 275
Musée de l'Armée, 170
Musée de l'Erotisme, 203
Musée de l'Histoire de France, 202
Musée de l'Orangerie, 180
Musée de la Chasse, 203
Musée de la Marine, 212
Musée de la Musique, 199
Musée de Vieux Montmartre, 194, 221
Musée des Arts d'Afrique et d'Océanie, 199
Musée des Arts Décoratifs, 199

Musée des Beaux-Arts de Chartres, 283
Musée des Plans-Reliefs, 171
Musée du Louvre, 154–55, 172–74
Musée du Parfum, 204
Musée du Vin, 204
Musée Edith Piaf, 200
Musée Grévin, 212
Musée Jacquemart André, 179
Musée Marcel Proust/Maison de Tante Léonie, 282
Musée Marmottan–Claude Monet, 155, 180
Musée National d'Art Moderne, 178
Musée National d'Histoire Naturelle, 213
Musée National de Céramique de Sèvres, 201
Musée National des Arts Asiatiques–Guimet, 200
Musée National du Moyen Age/Thermes de Cluny (Musée de Cluny), 180
Musée National Eugène Delacroix, 181, 196
Musée Nissim de Camondo, 200
Musée Picasso, 155, 181, 227
Musée Rodin, 155, 182
Musée Zadkine, 200
Panthéon Bouddhique, 201
Paristoric, 203
Petit Palais, 183
Music, 17–19, 176, 184, 186, 258–60
chansonniers, 255
classical, 253–54
free concerts, 4
museums, 198–01
opera, 2, 253–54
shopping, 248
tickets, 253

Napoléon, 170–71, 298–99
Neighborhoods, 190
Ile de la Cité, 191
Ile St-Louis, 154, 191–92
Latin Quarter, 155
Left bank, 196, 198
Les Halles, 192, 194
Marais, 155
Montmartre, 155, 194
Montparnasse, 155, 196
place de la Concorde, 154
place des Vosges, 155
place St-Michel, 154
place Vendôme, 155

Neighborhoods *(cont.)*
    Right bank, 192, 194, 196
    St-Germain-des-Prés, 154,
        196
    St-Germain-en-Laye, 4
Net Cafe Guide, 42
Neumont, Maurice (Place du
    Calvaire), 220
New Year's Eve, 20
Newport Bay Club, 290
Newspapers, 61
Nightclubs, 155, 256–58
Notre-Dame. *See* Cathédrale de
    Notre-Dame (Paris)

Office de Tourisme de Paris, 48
Olympia, 255
1travel.com, 39
Online booking, 34–36, 38–41
Opera, 2, 253–54
Opéra Bastille, 2, 253
Opéra Comique, 254
Opéra Garnier, 2
Opéra Garnier, 254
Out & About, 23

Package tours, 32–33
Packing, 42
Palais Bourbon/Assemblée
    Nationale, 155, 189
Palais de Fontainebleau, 291–93
Panthéon, 189, 224
Panthéon Bouddhique, 201
Parc Zoologique de Paris, 213
Paris Air Show, 17
Paris Auto Show, 19
Paris Boat Show, 20
Paris Turf, 3
Paris Visite pass, 57
Pariscope, 252
Paristoric, 203
Parks and Gardens, 204–07, 276
Passage de Retz, 228
Passports, 11
Père-Lachaise, 4, 207, 210
Performing arts, 2, 252–54, 276
Perfumes, 204, 231, 248
Petit Palais, 183
Pets, traveling with, 61
Pharmacies, 60
Picasso, Pablo, 155, 181, 305
    Bateau-Lavoir, 218
    Musée Picasso, 227
Picquier, Dominique, 228
Place de l'Alma, 177
Place de la Bastille, 226
Place des Vosges, 226
Place du Calvaire, 220
Place du Tertre, 220
Place Pigalle, 221
Place St-Michel, 222

Police, 61
Political art, 304
Pont Neuf, 191
Porcelain, shopping, 236
Post offices, 61
Priceline.com, 40
Prix de l'Arc de Triomphe, 19
Prix Diane-Hermès, 17
Prix du Jockey Club, 17
Proust, Marcel, 282
Public transportation, 56–57
Pubs, 265–67
Puppet shows, 211

Reformation, 297
Renaissance, 296–97, 303
Renoir, Pierre Auguste, 305
    Musée de Vieux Mont-
        martre, 221
Rest rooms, 62
Revolution, French, 298
Right Bank, 192, 194, 196
    dining, 104–05, 108–18,
        120–33
    hotels, 64–65, 68–82
Ritz-Escoffier Ecole de Gas-
    tronomie Française cooking
    classes, 109
Rodin, 155, 182
Rostang, Michel, 132
Rue de la Huchette, 222
Rue de Rosiers, 229
Rue du Chat-qui-Pêche, 222

Sacré-Coeur, 155, 194, 220
Sainte-Chapelle, 4, 155, 175–76
Second Republic, 299–300
Senior travelers, 23, 24
Sequoia Lodge, 290
Sewers, 215–16
Shopping, 231–51
Siene, 2
SkyAuction, 40
Smarter Living, 40
Sorbonne, 224
Souvenir shopping, 249–50
Sports16–18
St-Etienne du Mont, 185
St-Eustache, 186
St-Germain-des-Prés, 184, 196
St-Germain-en-Laye, 4
St-Germain l'Auxerrois, 186
St-Julien-le-Pauvre, 223
St-Louis-en-l'Ile, 192
St-Pierre, 220
St-Séverin, 223
St-Sulpice, 185
Statue of Beaumarchais, 226
Stein, Gertrude, 197
Student travelers, 24
Sun King (Louis XIV), 298, 304

Taxes (VAT), 232
Taxis, 58
Tea, 2
Telephones, 62
Theater, 253
Théâtre des Champs Elysées, 254
Théâtre National de Chaillot,
    254
Time zone, 62
Tipping, 63
Toulouse-Lautrec, 221
Tour de France, 18
Tour Eiffel, 154, 176–77
Tourism Offices, 10, 42
Toys, shopping, 237
Train travel, 29–30, 272
Transportation, 47
Travel planning Web sites,
    34–36, 38–42
Traveler's checks, 15
Travelers' Tales, 42
Travelzoo.com, 40
Trianons, The (Versailles),
    276
Trip-cancellation insurance, 20

Val de Grâce, 186
Van Cleef & Arpels jewelry, 244
VAT (value-added tax), 232
VE day, 17
Venus de Milo, 172
Versailles, 17, 271–72,
    274–78
Visas, 11
Vuitton, Louis, 241

Walking tours
    Latin Quarter, 222–24
    Marais, the, 224, 226–30
    Montmartre, 218, 220–21
Warnings, 42
Water, drinking, 63
Weather, 15, 41
Web sites, 10, 34–36, 38–42,
    44–47
WebFlyer, 41
Wine, 251
    Beaujolais Nouveau, 20
    Musée du Vin, 204
Wine bars, 100, 264–65
Winged Victory, 172
World War I, 300
World War II, 301–02

Yves Saint Laurent Rive
    Gauche, 241
Yvon Lambert, 228

Zoos, Parc Zoologique de
    Paris, 213

ACCOMMODATIONS

Au Palais de Chaillot Hôtel, 80
Best Western Hôtel Derby Eiffel, 94
Delhy's Hôtel, 91
Des Deux Continents, 90
Disneyland Hotel, 289
Familia Hôtel, 86
Galileo Hôtel, 77
Grand Hôtel de l'Univers, 89
Grand Hôtel L'Eveque, 95
Grand Hôtel St-Michel, 83
Hilton Paris Orly Airport, 97
Hotel Châtelet, 283
Hotel Cheyenne/Hotel Santa Fe, 289
Hotel de l'Aigle Noir (The Black Eagle), 292
Hôtel Abbatial St-Germain, 83
Hôtel Agora St-Germain, 83
Hôtel Aviatic, 89
Hôtel Balzac, 4, 74
Hôtel Bristol, 75
Hôtel Britannique, 70
Hôtel Burgundy, 71
Hôtel Caron de Beaumarchais, 74
Hôtel Central, 98
Hôtel Clément, 91
Hôtel Concorde St-Lazare, 76
Hôtel Costes, 6, 65, 68
Hôtel de Beaune, 95
Hôtel de Beauvais, 229
Hôtel de Bethune-Sully, 229
Hôtel de Crillon, 5, 76
Hôtel de Fleurie, 5, 87
Hôtel de l'Abbaye St-Germain, 88
Hôtel de l'Académie, 94
Hôtel de l'Empereur, 95
Hôtel de l'Université, 94
Hôtel de la Tour d'Auvergne, 79
Hôtel de Lauzun, 192
Hôtel de Lutèce, 5, 74
Hôtel de Nevers, 95
Hôtel de Rohan, 228
Hôtel de Sens, 229
Hôtel de Vendôme, 4, 68
Hôtel Delavigne, 92
Hôtel des Ambassadeurs de Hollande, 229
Hôtel des Arènes, 83
Hôtel des Chevaliers, 73
Hôtel des Deux Iles, 74
Hôtel des Grandes Ecoles, 86
Hôtel des Grands Hommes, 84
Hôtel des Invalides (Napoléon's Tomb), 170, 171
Hôtel des Jardins du Luxembourg, 84–85
Hôtel des Ste-Pères, 90
Hôtel des Tuileries, 70
Hôtel du Champ de Mars, 96
Hôtel du Globe, 92
Hôtel du Louvre, 5, 68
Hôtel du Lys, 92
Hôtel du Ministère, 78
Hôtel du Palais Bourbon, 96
Hôtel du Parc Montsouris, 96
Hôtel du Pas de Calais, 90
Hôtel du Quai-Voltaire, 5, 94–95
Hôtel du Vert Galant, 97
Hôtel Eber, 81
Hôtel Ermitage, 82
Hôtel Flaubert, 81
Hôtel Henri IV, 71
Hôtel Jardin Le Bréa, 90
Hôtel Lambert, 192
Hôtel Le Clos Médicis, 90
Hôtel Le Home Latin, 87
Hôtel Le Peletier de St-Fargeau, 227
Hôtel Lenox, 95
Hôtel Les Haute de Passy, 81
Hôtel Lindbergh, 96
Hôtel Louis II, 91
Hôtel Masart, 71
Hôtel Meurice, 68–69
Hôtel Moderne St-Germain, 86
Hôtel Montalembert, 92
Hôtel New York, 289
Hôtel Observatoire Luxembourg, 86
Hôtel Opal, 78
Hôtel Pavvillon Bastille, 79
Hôtel Pierre, 98
Hôtel Plaza Athénée, 6, 76
Hôtel Queen Mary, 78
Hôtel Regent's Garden, 81
Hôtel Regina, 69
Hôtel Résidence St-Christophe, 86
Hôtel Ritz, 5, 69–70
Hôtel Saint Dominique, 96
Hôtel Saint-James Paris, 80
Hôtel Sofitel Paris Aéroport CDG, 97
Hôtel St-Germain des Prés, 91
Hôtel St-Louis, 74
Hôtel Victoires Opéra, 72
Hôtel William Du Pré, 79
L'Hôtel, 6, 88
La Villa, 88
Le Duc de St-Simon, 94
Le Grand Monarque Best Western, 284
Le Stendhal, 72
Les Trois Couronnes, 82
Libertel Croix de Malte, 79
Libertel Quartier Latin, 91
Marmotel Etoile, 82
Nouvel Hôtel, 80
Odéon-Hôtel, 5, 89
Pavillon de la Reine, 5, 73
Relais Christine, 87
Relais du Louvre, 71
Relais St-Germain, 89
Résidence Alhambra, 80
Résidence Lord Byron, 5, 78
Terrass Hôtel, 5, 82
Timhôtel Jardin des Plantes, 87
Timhôtel Louvre, 72
Tulip Inn de Noailles, 73

RESTAURANTS

Al Dar, 136
Alain Ducasse, 6, 128
Alcazar Bar & Restaurant, 138
Allard, 6, 138
Androuët, 8, 122
Angélina, 8, 108
Aquarius, 8, 115
Astier, 127
Au Clair de Lune, 112
Au Gourmet de l'Ile, 115
Au Petit Riche, 124
Au Pied de Cochon, 8, 105
Au Pied de Fouet, 144
Au Trou Gascon, 126
Auberge de Cendrillon, 290
Auberge du Vieux Moulin, 285
Auberge Etchegorry, 144
Aux Charpentiers, 139
Aux Lyonnais, 7, 112
Babylone, 112
Berthillon, 111
Bistro de la Grille, 140
Blue Elephant, 127
Bofinger, 114
Brasserie Balzar, 7, 136
Brasserie de l'Ile St-Louis, 115
Brasserie Flo, 125
Brasserie Lipp, 149
Buddha Bar, 7, 119
Café Beaubourg, 149
Café Cosmos, 149

Café de Flore, 149
Café de l'Industrie, 150
Café de la Musique, 149
Café de la Paix, 150
Café des Hauteurs, 150
Café Indochine, 122
Café la Parisienne, 115
Café le Départ St-Michel, 222
Café Marly, 150, 174
Café/Restaurant/Salon de Thé Bernardaud, 151
Café de la Paix, 9
Campagne et Provence, 136
Carré des Feuillants, 104
Charles Baudelaire, 71
Chartier, 125
Château de Rambouillet, 280
Chez André, 121
Chez Diane, 140
Chez Edgard, 121
Chez Georges, 111, 132
Chez Gramond, 139
Chez l'Ami Jean, 144
Chez Janou, 113
Chez Jean, 123
Chez Jo Goldenberg, 8, 116, 229
Chez Lulu (L'Assiette), 145
Chez Michel, 126
Chez Pauline, 105
Chez René, 136
Chez Vong, 108
Chicago Pizza Pie Factory, 8, 122
China Club, 127
Closerie des Lilas, 138
Closerie-des-Lilas, 9
Copenhague/Flora Danica, 8, 120
Crémerie Restaurant Polidor, 7, 140
Dalloyau, 147
Dame Tartine, 116
Eclache & Cie, 153
Fauchon, 9
Faugeron, 6, 130
Fouquet's, 151
Goumard, 7, 104
Guy Savoy, 131
Hard Rock Cafe, 123
Il Cortile, 108

Isama, 114
Jacques Cagna, 137
Jamin, 130
Joe Allen, 8, 109
Julien, 126
Kambodia, 130
Keryado, 145
L'Amazonial, 153
L'Ambassade d'Auvergne, 113
L'Ambrosie, 113
L'Ami Louis, 113
L'Arpège, 141
L'Astor, 6, 117
L'Ebauchior, 128
La Bastide Odéon, 140
La Butte Chaillot, 131
La Cagouille, 145
La Chope des Vosges, 227
La Clementine, 112
La Coupole, 151
La Crémaillère, 220
La Fermette du Sud Ouest, 110
La Fontaine de Mars, 144
La Grille, 125
La Petite Chaise, 142
La Petite Hostellerie, 137
La Poste, 280
La Poule au Pot, 110
La Régalade, 146
La Rose de France, 110
La Rotonde, 151
La Rôtisserie d'Armaillé, 7, 132
La Rôtisserie d'en Face, 139
La Tour d'Argent, 7, 134
La Tour de Monthléry (Chez Denise), 110
Ladurée Royale, 147
Lasserre, 8, 117
Laudurée, 121
Le Bambouche, 142
Le Berry's, 123
Le Bistro d'à Côté Flaubert, 132
Le Bistro de l'Etoile, 131
Le Buisson Ardent, 284
Le Café du Commerce, 147
Le Café Zephyr, 152
Le Canton, 141
Le Caveau des Ducs, 292

Le François-ler, 293
Le Fumoir, 108
Le Grain de Folie, 133
Le Grand Véfour, 7, 105
Le Grand Zinc, 125
Le Gutenberg, 152
Le Manguier, 128
Le Potager du Roy, 278
Le Procope, 152
Le Quai No. 1, 278
Le Rouquet, 152
Le 30 (Chez Fauchon), 120
Le Train Bleu, 7, 127
Le Vaudeville, 111
Le Vieux Bistro, 114
Le Violon d'Ingres, 141
Leccure, 111
Lerch, 147
Les Ambassadeurs, 8
Les Deux Magots, 152
Les Gourmets des Ternes, 123
Les Iles Grecques, 228
Lucas Carton (Alain Senderens), 117
Ma Bourgogne, 227
Mansouria, 128
Marc Annibal de Coconnas, 114
Marie Louise, 133
Maxim's, 7, 118
Michel Rostang, 132
Paris Dakar, 126
Paul Minchelli, 142
Perraudin, 7, 137
Pierre Gagnaire, 118
Restaurant Bleu, 148
Restaurant des Beaux-Arts, 141
Restaurant du Marché, 146
Restaurant Opéra, 124
Shing Jung, 123
Shozan, 120
Spoon, Food & Wine, 99, 120
Stohrer, 146
Taillevent, 6, 118
Trumilou, 116
Versailles, 277–78
Wally Le Saharien, 124
Willi's Wine Bar, 8
Yugaraj, 139

FROMMER'S® NATIONAL PARK GUIDES

Family Vacations in the
National Parks
Grand Canyon

National Parks of the
American West
Rocky Mountain

Yellowstone & Grand Teton
Yosemite & Sequoia/
Kings Canyon
Zion & Bryce Canyon

FROMMER'S® MEMORABLE WALKS

Chicago
London

New York
Paris

San Francisco
Washington D.C.

FROMMER'S® GREAT OUTDOOR GUIDES

New England
Northern California

Southern California & Baja
Southern New England

Washington & Oregon

FROMMER'S® BORN TO SHOP GUIDES

Born to Shop: China
Born to Shop: France

Born to Shop: Italy
Born to Shop: London

Born to Shop: New York
Born to Shop: Paris

FROMMER'S® IRREVERENT GUIDES

Amsterdam
Boston
Chicago
Las Vegas

London
Los Angeles
Manhattan
New Orleans

Paris
San Francisco
Seattle & Portland
Vancouver

Walt Disney World
Washington, D.C.

FROMMER'S® BEST-LOVED DRIVING TOURS

America
Britain
California

Florida
France
Germany

Ireland
Italy
New England

Scotland
Spain
Western Europe

THE UNOFFICIAL GUIDES®

Bed & Breakfasts in
California
Bed & Breakfasts in
New England
Bed & Breakfasts in
the Northwest
Beyond Disney
Branson, Missouri
California with Kids
Chicago

Cruises
Disneyland
Florida with Kids
Golf Vacations in the
Eastern U.S.
The Great Smoky &
Blue Ridge
Mountains
Inside Disney

Hawaii
Las Vegas
London
Miami & the Keys
Mini Las Vegas
Mini-Mickey
New Orleans
New York City
Paris

Safaris
San Francisco
Skiing in the West
Walt Disney World
Walt Disney World
for Grown-ups
Walt Disney World
for Kids
Washington, D.C.

SPECIAL-INTEREST TITLES

Frommer's Britain's Best Bed & Breakfasts and
Country Inns
Frommer's Britain's Best Bike Rides
The Civil War Trust's Official Guide
to the Civil War Discovery Trail
Frommer's Caribbean Hideaways
Frommer's Food Lover's Companion to France
Frommer's Food Lover's Companion to Italy
Frommer's Gay & Lesbian Europe
Frommer's Exploring America by RV
Hanging Out in Europe
Israel Past & Present

Mad Monks' Guide to California
Mad Monks' Guide to New York City
Frommer's The Moon
Frommer's New York City with Kids
The New York Times' Unforgettable
Weekends
Places Rated Almanac
Retirement Places Rated
Frommer's Road Atlas Britain
Frommer's Road Atlas Europe
Frommer's Washington, D.C., with Kids
Frommer's What the Airlines Never Tell You